Helicopter Aerodynamics

Ray W. Prouty

H-555

Ray Prouty's Rotor and Wing columns 1979 - 1992

Eagle Eye Solutions

The text contained in this book was originally published in three separate volumes:
Helicopter Aerodynamics, ©1985 by Phillips Business Information, Inc.
More Helicopter Aerodynamics, ©1988 by Phillips Business Information, Inc.
Even More Helicopter Aerodynamics, ©1993 by Phillips Business Information, Inc.
Original figures and drawings by Luu Trong Mai, Jeffrey J. Stoecker, Lisa A. Craig and David Bennett

This compilation is ©2007 by Access Intelligence LLC., with additional material not contained in the original volumes ©2007 by Eagle Eye Solutions, LLC

ISBN
0-9792638-1-6

Published under license from Phillips Business Information, Inc.by:
Eagle Eye Solutions LLC
P.O. Box 46885
Cincinnati, OH, 54246
Email: matt@helicopterseminars.com
www.helicopterseminars.com

Printed and Bound by 360 Digital, Books, Kalamazoo, MI

Publishers Cataloging in Publication Data
Prouty, Ray W
Helicopter Aerodynamics
Second Edition
Biblography: p.
I. Books - United States - Aviation1. Prouty, Ray
II. Title - Helicopter Aerodynamics, 2007
III. Title - Helicopter Aerodynamics

1	*Answering Questions About Helicopters*	*1*
2	*Progress In Helicopter Aerodynamics**	*9*
3	*Hover Power*	*13*
4	*Hover Figure of Merit & Forward Flight Ratios*	*19*
5	*Ground Effect in Hover*	*25*
6	*Aerodynamic Environment at the Rotor Blade*	*29*
7	*Is The Rotor A Gyro?*	*37*
8	*The Rotor Wake*	*39*
9	*Vortex-Ring State*	*43*
10	*Downwash Patterns*	*49*
11	*Rotor Upwash*	*57*
12	*Blade Flapping and Feathering*	*63*
13	*Effects of Rotor Flapping*	*71*
14	*Blade Stall*	*79*
15	*The Search For A Stable Helicopter*	*83*
16	*Static Stability*	*87*
17	*Dynamic Stability*	*97*
18	*Maximum Load Factor*	*105*
19	*Forward Flight Performance*	*109*
20	*Vertical Climbs and Descents*	*117*
21	*Crosscoupling*	*123*
22	*Field-Of-View, Field-Of-Fire*	*127*
23	*Emergency Maneuvering*	*131*
24	*Flying Qualities*	*137*
25	*High Performance Takeoffs*	*143*
26	*Translational Lift and Transverse Flow*	*147*
27	*Low Speed Flight*	*151*
28	*Turns, Pullups and Pushovers*	*161*
29	*Sideslip And Bank*	*165*
30	*Maneuverability and Aerobatics*	*169*
31	*Flying in Steady Winds*	*179*
32	*Flight In Turbulent Air*	*183*
33	*Angle Limitations*	*185*
34	*Coping with a Power Failure*	*187*
35	*Low Speed Power Failures*	*193*
36	*Stretching the Glide*	*197*
37	*Autorotation And Low Load Factors*	*201*
38	*Instrument Flight*	*205*
39	*External Loads*	*209*

40	Blade Tracking	213
41	Tying The Helicopter Down	217
42	Accidents Waiting to Happen	219
43	Helicopter-Ship Operations	225
44	Preliminary Design	231
45	Axes Systems And Trim Considerations	235
46	Main Rotor Design	243
47	Tail Rotor Design	261
48	Airfoils For Rotor Blades	269
49	The Lead-Lag Hinge	285
50	Pitch-Link Loads	289
51	Considerations Of Blade/Hub Geometry	293
52	Blade Anhedral	297
53	Blade Strikes	301
54	Designing For Maneuverability	305
55	Designing For High Speed	311
56	Dynamic Inflow	315
57	Mysteries About Inflow And Power	319
58	Control Systems	323
59	Directional Stability & Autorotation Control Problems	329
60	Stability Augmentation Systems	333
61	Fly-By-Wire	337
62	Smart Control Systems	341
63	New Criteria for Flying Qualities	347
64	Parameter Identification	353
65	Computational Fluid Dynamics	357
66	Aerodynamic Modifications	361
67	Wind Tunnel Testing and Simulation	365
68	Horizontal and Vertical Stabilizers	375
69	Tail-Boom Strakes	383
70	Landing Gear Choices	387
71	Structural Loads and Component Lives	391
72	Designing Reliable Helicopter Structural	401
73	Airspeed Systems	407
74	Icing and Deicing	411
75	The Turbine Engine and the Helicopter	417
76	Modern Turboshaft Speed Governing	421
77	Engine Snow Protection	425
78	Helicopter Noise	429

79	Helicopter Noise Research	433
80	Helicopter Vibration	437
81	Vibration Sources	443
82	Vibration Criteria	449
83	Higher Harmonic Control	453
84	Spiral Dives And Dutch Rolls	457
85	Crashworthiness And Escape	463
86	Tip-Driven Rotors	467
87	Which Do You Tilt: Wing Or Rotor?	473
88	Tandem Rotor Helicopters	479
89	Coaxials and Synchropters	483
90	Antitorque Schemes For Compound Helicopters	489
91	Stopping a Rotor in Flight	491
92	A New Look At The Autogyro	495
93	Attempts To Revive The Autogyro	499
94	Low Observables	505
95	Windmills	511
96	Helicopter Development: The First 50 Years	515
97	The Hughes XH-17 Flying Crane	523
98	The Lockheed Experience	531
99	Attack Helicopters*	549
100	The Mil Mi-28 Havoc	557
101	Evolution Of Sikorsky Tails	561
102	Which Way Should The Rotor Turn?	565
102	And Where Should The Pilot Sit?	565
103	One-Man Helicopters*	573
104	Convertiplanes	581

1 Answering Questions About Helicopters

One of my neighbors keeps abreast of the technical world by reading such magazines as *Popular Mechanics*. When we get together, he asks some good questions about helicopters. I suspect that you also have relatives, friends, or neighbors who have similar questions. Perhaps this chapter will help answer them.

Hover performance

The first question we'll address is: Why do helicopters have such big rotors, especially since aircraft like the Harrier hover so well without any rotor at all?

For high efficiency, according to one principle of aeronautics, it is important to work with as much air as possible. This is why jet transports, which are expected to go a long distance on their fuel loads, have such long wings.

The principle also applies to sailplanes, man-powered aircraft, and helicopters. A big rotor handles a large amount of air. Thus it needs to exert less energy than a smaller rotor to develop the required thrust.

Figure 1-1 graphically illustrates this principle, showing the relationship between power loading (the amount of rotor thrust that one horsepower can generate) to disc loading (the rotor thrust divided by the disc area). The lower the disc loading – or the bigger the rotor for the same gross weight –the more thrust can be developed by one horsepower.

Figure of merit

The three lines in Figure 1-1 represent different values of hover efficiency, or "figure of merit." A value of 1.0 applies to a rotor with no skin drag or other losses; all of the power goes into developing thrust. It is as good as a rotor can be without violating the basic laws of physics.

Of course, no rotor has a figure of merit of 1.0 since there will always be some skin drag. The best rotor designers can attain is a value of about 0.8 or a little more. In such a rotor, about 20% of the power delivered to the rotor shaft is being used to overcome skin drag while the other 80% is producing thrust.

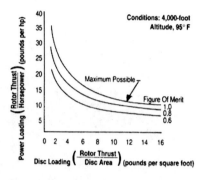

Figure 1-1 Main-Rotor Hover Performance

Figure 1-2 Robinson R22

Many rotors operate at figures of merit well below 0.8. This doesn't mean these designs are bad. Rather it indicates that the rotors are meant for helicopters that must fly fast. Designing rotors for high speed compromises the ability to design for good hovering efficiency.

The range of disc loadings in Figure 1-1 is typical of modern helicopters. The Robinson R22 (Figure 1-2) uses a low disc loading of 2.5 pounds per square foot (12.2 kg per m^2) in order to hover on the relatively low power of its Lycoming piston engine.

On the other end of the scale is the fully loaded Sikorsky CH-53E (Figure 1-3) with a disc loading of 14 pounds per square foot (68.3 kg per m^2). In this aircraft, the designers took advantage of the tremendous power available from its three General Electric T64 turbines to make a relatively compact helicopter for its gross weight. The CH-53E has a rotor diameter of 79 feet (24 m). If the disc loading had been as low as on the R22, the diameter would have been 190 feet (58 m)—a real problem for shipboard operation.

Figure 1-3 Sikorsky CH-53E

On the other hand, it would have required less than half as much power to hover. Thus higher disc loading allows the designers to minimize the helicopter's overall size at the expense of requiring more power. One of the helicopter designer's main jobs is to make "tradeoff" studies of such conflicts.

The extremes

The range of disc loadings in Figure 1-1 can be extended to cover other aircraft. For instance, at very low disc loadings, we would find man-powered helicopters. Assuming a gross weight of 250 pounds (113 kg) and a ½-horsepower rating for the pilot/engine, the required power loading is 500 pounds per horsepower (170 kg per kW).

To get to this value, the curves in Figure 1-1 must be extended far up the vertical axis, and the allowable disc loading would be measured in ounces per square foot. This is why the man-powered helicopter that was designed by the student team at California Polytechnic Institute at San Luis Obispo has a rotor diameter of more than 100 feet (30.5 m).

Meanwhile, the right side of Figure 1-1's graph could be extended to depict the performance of aircraft that depend on propellers or jet engines for hover. Some of the propeller-supported hovering aircraft of the 1960s had disc loadings of 40 to 80 pounds per square foot (200 to 400 kg per m^2) and consequently required very powerful engines to hover.

Figure 1-4 McDonnell Douglas/ BAe Harrier

At the extreme right of such a plot would be the McDonnell Douglas/ BAe Harrier Figure 1-4). Its equivalent disc loading is measured in thousands of pounds per square foot. Although its power is not measured in horsepower, we can relate the performance to fuel flow.

The Harrier has a fuel line as big as a fire hose, and can hover for only a few minutes before it sucks the fuel tanks dry. Thus it is not a good aircraft for long-time hovering, but that is not its role.

Flying fast

Another question often asked is: Why don't helicopters fly faster than they do?

The basic problem in flying a rotor edgewise through the air is illustrated in Figure 1-5. I am sure that anyone looking at that diagram 100 years ago would have pronounced the system to be impossible, because of the extreme asymmetry of flow conditions over the advancing and retreating sides.

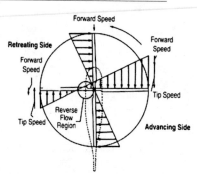

Figure 1-5 Velocity Distribution In Forward Flight

We now know that because of some inspired engineering by autogyro and helicopter developers, it is actually possible to fly a rotor edgewise through the air—but not too fast. The lack of airflow symmetry still represents the basic problem.

To keep the rotor balanced, the lift on the advancing and retreating sides must be about the same. Lift is proportional to the angle of attack multiplied by the square of the local velocity. Thus on the retreating side, where the local velocity is low, the angle of attack is high. But on the advancing side, the angle of attack must be low to maintain balance.

As the helicopter flies faster and faster, the difference in the local velocities increases, thus forcing an even greater difference in the angle of attack. At some forward speed, the angle of attack on the retreating side becomes large enough to exceed the stalling limit of the airfoil. Beyond that speed it is no longer possible to balance the aerodynamics; we have encountered retreating blade stall. Symptoms include an increase in blade drag and a nosedown twisting moment which produces high loads in the blades and control system—and thus, high vibration.

On the other side

While the advancing blade has no angle-of-attack problem, it may run into trouble of a different kind—compressibility. This occurs because the designer, to minimize the troubles on the retreating tip, chooses a relatively high tip speed (the speed of the tip in hover). When this is added to the forward speed on the advancing tip, the result may be a speed which is approaching the speed of sound-or Mach 1.

For most airfoils, when the speed reaches about Mach 0.9, shock waves appear, the drag rapidly increases, and a nosedown pitching moment is generated, creating high structural loads. Vibration and noise also increase.

Thus we have conditions on both the retreating and advancing sides that limit the helicopter's allowable forward flight speed.

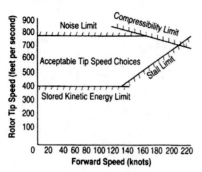

Figure 1-6 Constraints On Tip Speed Choices

Figure 1-6 shows how these limits affect the rotor's speed capability in terms of the designer's choice of allowable tip speeds. For rotors of "pure helicopters" as we know them today, the stall and compressibility limits come together at a forward speed of about 200 knots. By doing some special things with its Lynx, Westland exceeded this apparent limit and in 1986 set a speed record at 216 knots.

Figure 1-6 also shows two more limits. The upper one is based on experience of the past 20 years that indicates that rotors with tip speeds above about 760 feet per second (fps) are unacceptably noisy. The lower boundary is simply a reminder that the rotor's kinetic energy is very useful for safely getting into autorotation when an engine fails.

Bypassing the limit

How would you get even more forward speed out of an aircraft that relies on a rotor for its hovering performance? One proposal is to use two counter-rotating rotors and forget about the requirement to balance the lift on the retreating and advancing sides. This is done with very stiff rotors on the Sikorsky S-69 (Figure 1-7).

Figure 1-7 Sikorsky S-69

Sikorsky S-69 ABC Demonstrator

The S-69 uses the Advancing Blade Concept (ABC) in which the resulting unbalance of one rotor is simply compensated for by the equal and opposite unbalance of the other. This allows the retreating blade on each rotor to be operated at well below its stall angle, while the advancing blades develop the main share of the thrust. The maximum speed capability of this configuration would be expected to be above 230 knots. Adding a propeller or a jet engine for forward propulsion might raise its capability to the 300-knot range.

Figure 1-8 Lockheed AH-56 Cheyenne

Another way to overcome the speed limits of a rotor is to add a wing to support the aircraft and some form of forward propulsion device to relieve the rotor of this duty. One such configuration is the compound helicopter, as embodied in the Lockheed AH-56 Cheyenne (Figure 1-8).

In this aircraft, a separate propeller was used to provide forward propulsion at high speed. The rotor was essentially relieved of both its lifting and propulsion tasks but was still used for pitch and roll control. By slowing the rotor down to avoid compressibility problems, the potential high speed of this configuration should be around 350 knots.

Figure 1-9 Bell V-22 Osprey

Another high-speed configuration is the tiltrotor, illustrated by the Bell/Boeing V-22 Osprey (Figure 1-9). In this scheme, in forward flight the rotors become propellers that have no stall limits and greatly relieved compressibility limits. The potential speed capability of this configuration is about 450 knots.

Even higher speeds are envisioned by some designers who think they have the answer for getting rid of the rotor limitations altogether. They would do this by converting the rotor into a wing as in the X-wing design or by stopping and storing the rotors of a tiltrotor aircraft, as in the trailing rotor design. In either case, the forward propulsion would come from some form of a jet engine, and presumably, supersonic speeds are feasible.

It may be seen that to go faster than the roughly 200-knot limit of pure helicopters, alternative aircraft become more complicated. As the speed goal is raised, designers must be prepared to accept more and more cost and weight penalties that affect the hover performance.

High load factors

Another frequently asked question is: Why can't helicopters develop high load factors like airplanes can? The answer to that question is that helicopters could be designed to develop high load factors if there were a requirement. But such a requirement would penalize hover performance.

Understanding this hover/load-factor relationship starts with a look at how a wing works. If in flight the wing lift suddenly becomes greater than the weight of the aircraft—as it might be when flying through a vertical gust—the airplane would start accelerating upward. This simply follows the laws of dynamics first deduced by Isaac Newton.

This vertical acceleration is measured in "Gs," starting at 1 G in level flight. If the wing lift were equal to twice the airplane weight, we would say that the airplane wing is developing 2 Gs. It would be accelerating the airplane up at the same rate that a dropped rock would be accelerating down under the force of the Earth's gravity. The accelerating force would act on everything in the airplane, including the crew and passengers, who would suddenly feel twice as heavy as normal.

The lift on a wing is proportional to the product of three terms: a nondimensional number (known as a lift coefficient, C_L, the wing area, and the dynamic pressure. The dynamic pressure, in turn, is proportional to the density of the air and to the square of the forward speed.

At a given forward speed and altitude, the amount of lift a wing generates is limited by the maximum lift coefficient that it can reach before it stalls. For a plain wing, this limit is about 1.5, which it would typically reach at an angle of attack of about 20°. By using flaps on the trailing edge and slats on the leading edge, a maximum lift coefficient of over three can be reached.

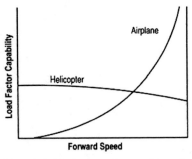

Figure 1-10 Comparison of Load Factor Capabilities

In maneuvering flight the airplane pilot increases the wing's angle of attack by using the elevator to produce a noseup motion. In so doing, he causes the wing to generate a load factor. At low speeds, the ability to do this will be limited. But at high speeds, it is almost unlimited—so much so that the aerodynamic capability might be more than the pilot or the wing structure could stand.

Rotors are different

This phenomenon on the helicopter rotor is not quite the same. In this case, the ability to generate high thrust during a pullup is not increased by going faster.

Although it is true that the advancing main rotor blade sees velocities equal to the sum of the hover rotational speed (which would seem to increase its capabilities), the retreating blade sees the difference between the two velocities, and thus has less capability before stalling.

The requirement to balance the aerodynamic loads on opposite sides of the main rotor means that the advancing blade cannot make use of its increased capability without destroying the balance. Meanwhile, the blades over the nose and the tail are operating in essentially the same velocity environment that they had in hover, and therefore, have no different lifting capability.

For these reasons, the ability of the rotor to develop high load factors in a maneuver before stalling is actually at a maximum in hover and decreases as it goes into forward flight (Figure 1-10).

Maximum rotor load factor

The maximum load factor that a helicopter can develop, just like a wing, depends on how close to stall it was in the first place.

The airplane aerodynamicist works with the wing lift coefficient to determine this. For level flight, the value of the required lift coefficient is proportional to the weight of the airplane. But it is inversely proportional to wing area and the square of the airspeed. Thus, the lift coefficient's value decreases as the airplane flies faster and the margin between the level-flight lift coefficient and its stall value becomes greater and greater.

The helicopter aerodynamicist makes his analysis using a similar nondimensional thrust/solidity coefficient known as "Cee-Tee over Sigma," C_T/σ. In level flight, it is directly proportional to the weight of the helicopter and inversely proportional to blade area and tip speed squared (rather than to wing area and forward speed squared).

Since the tip speed stays constant, the value of this coefficient is essentially the same in level forward flight as it is in hover. As a rule of thumb, it is equal to about one-sixth of the average lift coefficient at each airfoil section. This means that if the airfoil used on the rotor stalls at a maximum lift coefficient of 1.2, the maximum value of the thrust/

solidity coefficient will be about 0.2. The results of wind tunnel and flight tests verify that this is a reasonable upper limit for the type of helicopter rotors that we know today.

What can the designer do?

By choosing a low value of the thrust/solidity coefficient for level flight, the designer can provide a rotor that can develop high maneuvering load factors before stalling.

For example, if the rotor had to be able to pull a load factor of 5 Gs in a pullup, the designer would start out with a value of the coefficient of 0.04 by choosing the right combination of blade area and tip speed for his rotor. Usually his freedom to vary tip speed is limited because of the constraints discussed earlier, so the designer's primary option for enhancing the rotor's load factor capability is to add blade area. This can be done either by increasing blade chord or by adding more blades of the same chord.

The designer would, however, be aware that in selecting a low value for the coefficient, he would be compromising the hover performance. This is because the hover figure of merit is also related to the thrust/solidity coefficient.

Figure 1-11 shows that for most rotors, the figure of merit is maximum at a thrust/solidity value of C_T/σ of about 0.10 and that it may be less than half its maximum value at a value of 0.04. This is because with either high blade area or high tip speed, the blades are operating at low angles of attack where their lift-to-drag ratios are also low. A helicopter designed on this basis would take more than twice as much power to hover as it would have if it had been designed with hover performance as the highest priority. Most present day helicopters are designed to operate at an initial blade loading coefficient of about 0.06 at the design gross weight at sea level so that their aerodynamic load factor capability is in the neighborhood of three-higher at lower gross weights and lower at higher altitudes.

Even if maneuvering is not a prime consideration in the rotor design, the designer will usually choose not to use a higher initial value of the thrust/solidity coefficient to improve the hover performance because that would limit the maximum forward speed capability of the helicopter.

This is shown in Figure 1-12, which plots the maximum allowable trim value of C_T/σ as a function of the tip speed ratio, μ. This indicates that the value of the coefficient must be limited at high speeds to avoid stalling the retreating tip. The horizontal scale also shows the speed in knots that corresponds to a typical helicopter's tip speed ratio. The current speed record for helicopters was set at a tip speed ratio of about 0.5.

Without some way of eliminating blade stall—or at least decreasing its penalties—the designer faces choices leading to conflicting trends with

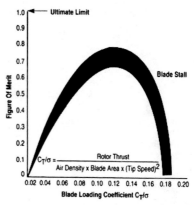

Figure 1-11 Hover Figure of Merit

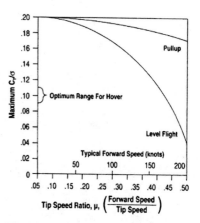

Figure 1-12 Maximum Rotor Capacity In Forward Flight

regard to the rotor parameters that define the thrust/solidity coefficient. At this time, the most logical way of increasing the load factor capability of a conventional helicopter, such as the McDonnell Douglas Apache, would be to add more or wider blades and then to accept the decrease in hover performance.

Other options

That is not to say that there are no other ways of doing it. Higher pullup load factors at high speeds could be achieved by including a wing in the design. This, however, brings along its own penalties. The wing's download and weight decreases the hover performance, and its drag decreases level-flight performance.

Another possibility is to redesign the rotor, such as on the Sikorsky ABC aircraft discussed earlier. Each ABC rotor was individually out of balance, but the total system was in balance. With this concept, the advancing blade's increased capabilities— due to their higher velocity environment—could be used to develop high rotor load factors without being limited by retreating blade stall. This program might be worth looking at again.

Other designers have toyed with the idea of installing flaps, slats, or boundary-layer control systems on the blades to increase their maximum lift coefficients, as is done with wings. So far, the mechanical complexity of these schemes as applied to rotating blades have prevented them from being practical. There is still an opportunity for a clever solution to the helicopter load-factor dilemma.

2 Progress In Helicopter Aerodynamics*

*This chapter was written for the 25th anniversary issue of *Rotor & Wing*, May 1991.

The laws of physics that govern aerodynamics do not change. The complicated aerodynamics that applied to helicopters in 1967, when *Rotor & Wing* began publication, still apply. Our understanding of them is somewhat improved—but not yet perfect.

Three fields of endeavor have helped make us smarter since then. The first, a fairly new one, is computational fluid dynamics (CFD). The second is wind tunnel testing, and the third, that old standby, flight-testing.

CFD

Today's computer power has given the theoretical aerodynamicist the tool he'd long dreamed of to use on problems that previously were too complicated to even contemplate. He can now program the very basic equations governing fluid dynamics almost down to the molecular level. He can also quickly solve the equations without making many of the assumptions that had previously been needed to make the old computational methods practical.

Currently this capability is used to design new rotor-blade airfoil sections that can go to high angles of attack before stalling and to high Mach numbers before suffering from compressibility effects. High-speed computers allow the designer to account for the complicated interactions between shock waves and boundary layers that affect these characteristics.

The computer has also found a place in studying one of the helicopter aerodynamicist's biggest challenges: determining the velocity distribution in and around a rotor. This information is needed to calculate the local blade element angle of attack vis-à-vis the element's position along the blade and around the azimuth. By knowing the local angle of attack, we can estimate blade loads, and the rotor's performance at high forward speeds and/or when developing high load factors.

This information is also essential to make good noise estimates from a rotor in given flight conditions. Additionally, it helps in estimating pressures on the portions of the fuselage and the tail surfaces in the rotor wake. And it helps to determine how the wake may affect the flight path of a missile that is launched from hover or low-speed flight.

This field was just in its adolescence in 1967. Several theoretical approaches had been proposed that varied from fairly simple to quite complicated, but since the computer power to work the latter methods was not yet available, it was the fairly simple methods that were receiving the attention.

Today with the use of high-speed computers, the simplifying assumptions can be relaxed, and the confidence level in the calculations is increased— but not yet to 100%. This is because it is very difficult to experimentally measure the velocity field in and around a rotor' in order to get data with which the computer results can be correlated. Some progress along these lines has recently been made in wind tunnels through the use of a piece of sophisticated measuring equipment known as a laser velocimeter.

At this time, the equipment is so bulky that it must be mounted at the side of the wind tunnel to probe the fluctuating velocity field at points just above or just below the rotor disc. In the future we should expect that it can be mounted on the rotating hub and focused at a spot just in front of the blade element to measure its true angle of attack— not only on wind-tunnel models but also on full-scale helicopters in flight.

Wind-tunnel testing

Helicopter engineers are sometimes accused of not taking as much advantage of the wind tunnel as their fixed-wing brethren. But the fixed-wing folk commonly use such testing to make their aircraft fly as helicopters do-at low speed. They place their airplane models in the wind tunnel in their landing and takeoff configurations, with an emphasis on developing flaps and control surfaces to ensure safe airport operation. For this type of testing, only a part of the wind tunnel time is spent testing for cruise or maximum speed.

Figure 2-1 McDonnell Douglas AH-64 in Wind Tunnel

Much wind tunnel testing for helicopters is done with rotorless models to get a first, crude, estimate of the airframe's drag and stability characteristics (Figure 2-1). Helicopter models with powered rotors are rare, and to my knowledge, have not yet played a significant role in any production helicopter's development. For the V-22 Osprey tiltrotor, however, the wind tunnel has been important because the ship's dynamic/aerodynamic couplings had to be thoroughly understood before building the aircraft.

These couplings are also of concern on hingeless rotors. Thus each team that competed in the Light Helicopter Experimental (LHX) program (now Boeing Sikorsky RAH-66 Comanche) in the early 1990s tested models of its rotors in wind tunnels.

Although wind tunnel testing of rotors has not yet been essential in the development of a specific design, it has been valuable in the research of a rotor's performance, stability, and noise in conditions difficult to achieve in flight tests.

An area that's not yet fully understood and therefore appropriate for future wind-tunnel research is the complicated aerodynamic reactions between the main rotor, the tail rotor, and the fuselage in sideward flight.

Another wind-tunnel function in the helicopter industry has been in developing new rotor-blade airfoil sections. In 1966, aerodynamicists were just starting to look at airfoils different from the symmetrical NACA 0012 and 0015 (12% and 15% thick, respectively), which had been accepted as the norm.

Since then, we've used wind tunnel testing toward the conflicting goals of more lift and less drag by developing two new generations of airfoils for rotor blades. The first, based on the NACA "six-series" contours that were originally developed for high-speed fighter airplanes, is now flying on the Sikorsky Black Hawk, Boeing Chinook, and McDonnell Douglas Apache.

The next generation of airfoils, which are more slab-sided, is flying on prototypes like the EH Industries EH-101 and the Boeing 360 technology demonstrator. They've been developed using both CFD programs and wind-tunnel tests.

Still another reason to test airfoil sections in a wind tunnel is to investigate "dynamic stall" which should really be called "stall delay." The stalling characteristics of an airfoil that is rapidly changing its angle of attack are not the same as they are in a wind tunnel where the angle of attack is held fixed long enough for the boundary layer and the shock waves to settle down.

Thus special tests are done with airfoil models that can be rapidly oscillated in both pitch and plunge to simulate what actually happens on a rotor in forward flight. The information, in turn, helps compute the thrust and power for an entire rotor.

The wind tunnel's cousin is the whirl tower, used to investigate the rotor's hover performance. Remarkably, after all these years, precisely calculating a rotor's hover performance remains difficult. Whirl towers do, therefore, help the engineers gain confidence in their design, as well as make changes before building the full-scale aircraft.

Flight testing

No matter how high the confidence level in a completed design, flight-testing almost always produces some surprises. Over the past 25 years, such surprises have provided much knowledge of helicopter aerodynamics.

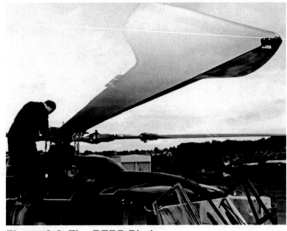

Figure 2-2 The BERP Blade

For example, the excessive trim change through transition with a large, fixed, horizontal stabilizer was discovered in flight testing; first on the YUH-60 Black Hawk and then on the YAH-64 Apache. This anomaly probably could not have been discovered any earlier by either CFD, wind tunnel testing, or even simulation.

Both aircraft had to be fitted with a movable stabilator to avoid excessive pitch up during low-speed flight. (It should be pointed out, however, that Boeing did have a stabilator on its YUH-61, the YUH-60's competitor, from the beginning.)

Similarly, flight testing unearthed another surprise: too little clearances between the rotor and the top of the fuselage on the YUH-60, YUH-61, and YAH-64. Rotor masts were subsequently extended.

In England, the British Experimental Rotor Program (BERP) also delivered a surprise during flight test. For these tests, a conventional, constant-chord blade was modified to enhance its advancing tip characteristics by sweeping the leading edge of the tip first forward and then aft by simply attaching a leading edge "glove." To maintain the proper balance between aerodynamic and dynamic effects, an even bigger glove was attached to the trailing edge (Figure 2-2).

Testing revealed the design's benefits on the rotor's advancing side as predicted. But unexpectedly, the benefits applied to the retreating side as well; the tip could be flown to a higher angle of attack before stalling than could the original, unmodified blade. In 1986, Westland Helicopters Ltd. went on to set the world's helicopter speed record this blade design on a Lynx.

The results of other surprises from flight testing can be seen on helicopters in the forms of spoilers, slats, ventral fins, tip plates, and stabilizer trailing-edge modifications, which were not in the original design. In my opinion, neither CFD nor wind tunnel tests could have predicted the potential problems or helped very much in the solutions.

Conclusion

So the tools to study helicopter aerodynamics have greatly improved over the years. But they are not a cure-all, and good helicopters can still be designed without extensive use of wind tunnels and large computers for CFD. Perhaps the best example is the helicopter with the current highest production rate, the Robinson R22. It was developed with neither.

3 Hover Power

"As the Red Queen said to Alice, 'Now here, you see, it takes all the running you can do to keep in the same place.'"

Lewis Carroll - *Through the Looking Glass*

Helicopter aerodynamicists have two ways of explaining the effort required for a helicopter to "run in place." The first is called Momentum Theory and the second, Blade Element Theory. They really are two parts of the same explanation—although they start from different points.

Momentum Theory

The Momentum Theory is based on Newton's observation that for every action there is an equal and opposite reaction. For the hovering helicopter, the action is the production of an upward rotor thrust and the reaction is found in the downward velocity imparted to the air in the rotor wake.

Newton also said that a body will accelerate at a rate proportional to the force applied, divided by the mass of the body. This applies directly to a cannonball being pushed out a gun barrel; however, to apply it to a rotor requires that we turn Newton's relationship around by saying that a force is equal to acceleration times mass. In the case of a helicopter in a steady hover, the force is the rotor thrust; the acceleration is the change in air velocity from far above the rotor (where it is zero, of course) to a steady value below the rotor; and the mass is the mass flow of the air being pumped through the rotor disc every second.

The mass flow is the product of the mass in a cubic foot of air, the disc area, and the induced velocity at the rotor disc. Since both the mass flow and the acceleration terms depend on the induced velocity, the rotor thrust is proportional to the square of the induced velocity times the rotor disc area.

For this reason, a small rotor must induce a higher velocity than a large rotor to produce the same thrust. There is a power penalty associated with this higher velocity that must be considered when choosing the rotor diameter for a new helicopter design. Years ago, the available reciprocating engines were relatively heavy for the power they produced and so it was necessary to use large rotors — or low disc loadings in terms of gross weight divided by disc area — in order to lift the aircraft by using as small an engine as possible. Disc loadings as low as three pounds per square foot meant that one hp delivered to the main rotor could be used to lift 12 to 15 pounds of airframe weight

The development of the turbine engine with its much higher power-to-weight ratio has permitted designers to increase the disc loading and to develop helicopters with smaller rotors that have shorter and more compact fuselages, which save on weight, cost, and drag. These helicopters are also easier to hangar and safer to maneuver around trees and cliffs. Many modern helicopters have rotors with disc loadings as high as seven to 10 pounds per square foot and can lift eight to 11 pounds per main rotor horsepower. Of course, based on the total engine output the pounds per horsepower is 20% to 30% less, since such things as tail rotors, gearboxes, generators, and hydraulic pumps are also absorbing power in hover.

Design Tradeoff

As a simple illustration of the designer's choices, let us look at the Hughes Model 500D with characteristics as shown in Figure 3-1. This helicopter has 350 shp available for continuous use from its Allison Model 250-C2OB turboshaft engine. Suppose Hughes decided to reduce the cost by replacing the $43,000 Allison with the 190-hp $15,000 Lycoming HIO-360-D1A used in the Model 300C —while keeping the 500D's gross weight and hover performance. The resulting "500X" would have to look something like the second aircraft in Figure 3-1. Because of its larger rotor, longer fuselage, and heavier engine, the empty weight would go up and the useful load would go down.

Maximum Disc Loading

Despite the trend for higher and higher disc loadings in the past 20 years, there does seem to be a practical upper limit. Values of more than about 10 pounds per square foot generate such high induced velocities under the rotor that it is difficult to operate from unprepared sites without filling the air full of flying sticks and stones to break one's bones. It also becomes increasingly difficult to obtain safe autorotational characteristics as disc loadings go up. These are two reasons why VTOL aircraft that depend on heavily loaded propellers for hovering have not yet become operational.

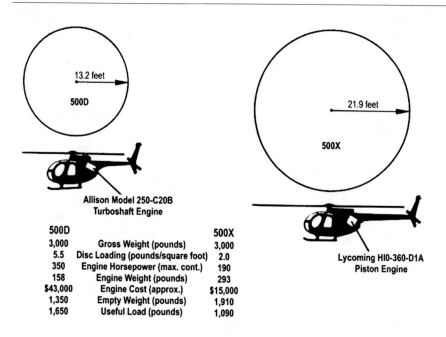

Figure 3-1 Design Tradeoffs: Turbine vs. Piston Engines

500D		500X
3,000	Gross Weight (pounds)	3,000
5.5	Disc Loading (pounds/square foot)	2.0
350	Engine Horsepower (max. cont.)	190
158	Engine Weight (pounds)	293
$43,000	Engine Cost (approx.)	$15,000
1,350	Empty Weight (pounds)	1,910
1,650	Useful Load (pounds)	1,090

Vertical Drag

The strength of the airflow in the wake is measured by its dynamic pressure, which turns out to equal to the disc loading. Besides blowing loose objects around, the rotor wake also produces a download — or vertical drag force. While vertical rag on the fuselage may be substantial, it is usually of no importance to the operator since it was there when the helicopter was certificated.

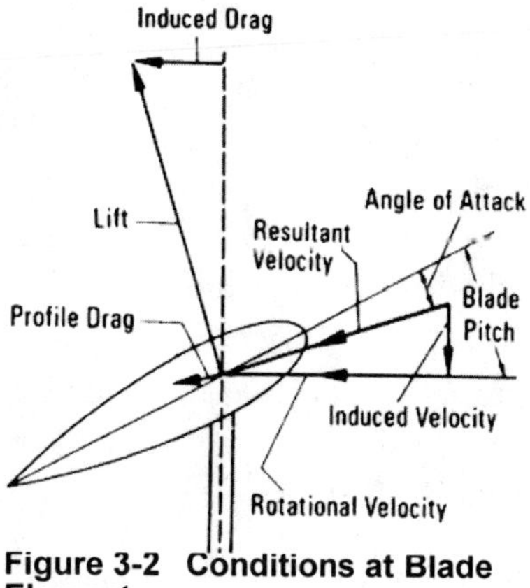

Figure 3-2 Conditions at Blade Element

It should be recognized, however, that external loads either fastened to the side of the fuselage or carried below, as a slingload will be subjected to vertical drag—which is effectively like standing on your shoelaces. The resulting hover-performance penalty may be critical in some cases. You an estimate the additional download by multiplying the rotor disc loading by the area of the external load that is broadside to the flow in the rotor wake.

Blade Element Theory

Although the Momentum Theory provides a good general explanation of hover power, it fails to deal with the nitty-gritty of what is actually happening at the blade. For this we need the Blade Element Theory. Figure 3-2 shows the conditions a typical blade element. The blade sees air coming toward it both due to rotor rotation and to downward induced velocity. These two velocities combine to form a resultant velocity vector that is pointed slightly down. Since by definition lift is perpendicular to the local vector velocity, it is moved slightly back. The rearward component of lift is known as induced drag.

We multiply this induced drag by the distance from the shaft to the blade element, we get its contribution to the torque in the shaft — and if we ~n sum up all such contributions, we get the to-induced torque. Multiplying this sum by rotor speed and dividing by the proper factors from freshman physics gives the induced horsepower required by the rotor— which value would be exactly the same had we based our calculations on Momentum Theory.

Figure of Merit

A glance at Figure 3-3 will show, however, that something is missing. The little arrow labeled "profile drag" has not yet been accounted for. This is the result of air friction acting on the de element. For a hovering rotor, the profile drag typically accounts for about one-quarter of total power. The other three-quarters is induced power. This ratio—0.75 in this case—is called the figure of merit.

Designers have some control over the figure of merit by selecting optimum blade area, optimum blade twist, and a low-drag airfoil. The optimum blade area for hovering is a low one that forces the blade elements to operate at high angles of attack and just below stall. This condition gives the highest ratio of lift to profile drag as well as the lowest blade structural weight. Unfortunately, for most helicopter designs, this desirable approach cannot be fully used because high-speed maneuver requirements will dictate more blade area than is optimum for hover.

Blade twist is used to even out the induced flow across the rotor disc. A rotor without blade twist tends to produce higher induced velocities in the outer portion of the disc than in the inner portion. The optimum condition, however, is with uniform induced velocity over the entire disc. This situation is approached by twisting the blades to a lower pitch at their tips than at their roots. Here again, the application is usually modified by high-speed considerations. Experience has shown that the large amount of blade twist optimum for hover performance (as much as 30°) will generate high oscillating blade loads and vibration at high speeds. The usual design compromise is to use moderate values of 6° to 12°, which provide most of the benefits of ideal twist in hover while avoiding most of its disadvantages in forward flight.

Interference Effects

A phenomenon that affects hover performance was discovered several years ago from motion pictures of a rotor on a whirl tower on a damp day. It was observed that the tip vortex from one blade — made visible by condensation — stayed approximately in the plane of the rotor until the next blade came along, as shown in Figure 3-3. The proximity of the vortex to the second blade produces a distorted local induced velocity pattern over a small region of the tip, which can

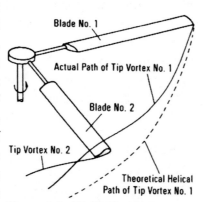

Figure 3-3 Blade Tip Vortex Interference Effect In Hover

cause some very high angles of attack, sometimes exceeding the stall angle of the airfoil. Sikorsky has made an attempt to overcome this problem on its Black Hawk by providing a high nose-down twist just inboard of the tip where the high angles of attack occur.

Yet another interference effect that adversely affects hover performance has been recently discovered. It is due to the proximity of the main and tail rotors and the ability of the tail rotor to locally distort the induced velocity pattern of the main rotor away from the uniform distribution that is optimum for minimum hover power. There is some indication that this unfavorable interference effect is decreased by a vertical rate of climb.

Engine Power

Of course for successful hovering, the engine power available must be equal to the power required. Aircraft engines have a rating at which they can deliver power continuously, and usually one or more higher ratings for brief durations. The nomenclature has not been completely standardized but it is common to have a 30-minute rating called "intermediate" or "military" or simply "30-minute power," and a two- to five-minute rating designated as "takeoff" or "emergency." Typically, the 30-minute rating is 20% above the continuous rating and the short-time rating another 10% above that.

Hovering either on continuous rating or on the 30-minute rating is usually no problem on a cool day near sea level, but might become impossible for more extreme conditions. Reciprocating engines without superchargers typically lose 25% of their power capability when going from sea level to 10,000 feet because of the thinness of the air. On the other hand, the power required by the rotor remains relatively constant. At altitude, the rotor's profile power is down because of the decreased air density — but the induced power is up because the thinner air must be given a higher induced velocity to produce the same thrust.

Turbine engines also lose power capability with altitude. Power loss due to increased outside temperatures, however, is sometimes an even more important factor. Since the basic operational limit for these engines is the maximum temperature the turbine blades can stand, an increase in outside temperature limits the amount of fuel that can be burned before reaching these temperatures. Whereas a typical reciprocating engine might lose 10% of its power between 600°F and 120°F, a typical turbine engine might lose as much as 30%.

Engine Derating

One way of coping with these power losses is to match the engine with the helicopter airframe to provide good hover performance at some combination of altitude and temperature at which it may have to operate. The difficulty with this approach is that different operators are interested in different environments. For example, the Army has settled on 4,000 feet and 95°F, whereas the Navy uses sea level and 112°F. Since the customer is always right, it is relatively straightforward to design for such specific conditions, but how do we design for a nonmilitary helicopter we would like to sell to commercial operators all over the world?

If we design to a high altitude and temperature combination, the engine will be bigger than would be required for more modest conditions. Nevertheless, this is often done and a power limit is established to avoid using more torque than the transmission has been designed for. This practice of derating the engine has a good effect on engine life, since the powerplant is seldom operated at its maximum output. But what if our competitor uses the same engine *but without a limit* so that his 'helicopter can lift heavier loads at sea level, but because of a heavier transmission somewhat less at our high-design conditions? Will he run away with the market? As my old economics professor used to say, "That's a good question. Does anyone else have a question?"

4 Hover Figure of Merit & Forward Flight Ratios

There is a difference between efficiency and effectiveness.

An efficient engineering department would keep a small number of people busy on a steady basis to support the company's long-range objectives. This small but efficient department, however, might not be adequately staffed to be effective in responding to short-term crises that occasionally arise in even the best of organizations. (The difference is even more striking when applied to a fire department.)

A similar analogy can be made for an aircraft design. It should be efficient in doing its routine missions-but not at the expense of inadequacy in occasional high-need circumstances. Some categories of aircraft - such as fixed-wing transports - can be designed with the balance tilted toward the side of efficiency but most helicopters are still designed by effectiveness considerations.

For this reason, the two measures of rotor efficiency: figure of merit in hover and lift-to-drag ratio in forward flight, are not of prime importance to the rotor designer-but if his rotor happens to come out better in these areas than his competitor's, he will certainly take the credit. Although not overwhelming design drivers, these two terms come up often enough to warrant some discussion.

Figure of merit

It may come as a shock but, as the word is used in physics, a hovering helicopter is not doing any "work." Thus its efficiency, as measured by its work output divided by its energy consumption, is zero. This, of course, is not fair to the hovering helicopter; so another way of quantifying its efficiency was invented. This is the figure of merit, which tells us how a rotor is actually doing, compared to how it might be doing if no skin friction or pressure drag due to boundary-layer separation acted on its blades-and the power required was only that induced by the rearward tilt of the lift vectors at each blade element (Figure 4-1).

This "induced" power can be related to a fictitious amount of work being done every second as the product of rotor thrust times the induced velocity at the rotor disc. The magnitude of the induced velocity depends on the disc loading (the rotor thrust divided by the disc area).

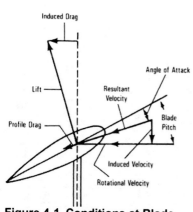

Figure 4-1 Conditions at Blade Element

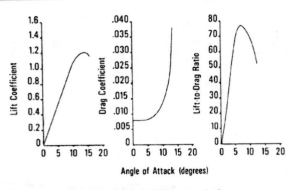

Figure 4-2 Typical Airfoil Characteristics

Modern helicopters have fairly low disc loadings (from about four to as much as 16 pounds per square foot). This range induces relatively gentle downwash velocities from 17 to 34 knots at the disc. For the same rotor thrust, the induced power is proportional to the induced velocity. Thus, if the rotor size is reduced but its thrust requirement isn't, the power required will increase.

During the '50s and '60s, a number of propeller supported vertical takeoff and landing (VTOL) prototypes were designed and tested. These had disc loadings of 35 to 75 pounds per square foot, induced hurricane-type downwash velocities, and took lots and lots of power. None of them got into production but an even more extreme concept did.

The jet-supported British Harrier and its Soviet Yak-36 counterpart have "disc loadings" measured in thousands of pounds per square foot and fuel must be pumped through lines as big as fire hoses at such a rate that allowable hover time is limited to just a few minutes. The trends of induced power as a function of disc loading are independent of how much skin friction is acting on the blades and theoretically a rotor with no friction and an uniform induced velocity distribution has a figure of merit of one. Adding friction and accounting for the other real effects reduces the figure of merit at least 15% and, in some cases, even more. How much more depends on a number of factors.

Hover vs. forward flight

The most important factor is the average angle of attack on the blades, which governs the lift-to-drag ratio of each blade element. Figure 4-2 shows how an airfoil's lift, drag, and the resulting lift-to-drag ratio change as the angle of attack is increased. Note that not much dramatic happens to drag until just before the onset of stall.

The designer could chose the amount of blade surface area to force the blade elements to operate at the angle of attack corresponding to the maximum lift-to-drag ratio. This would also result in the maximum figure of merit (Figure 4-3).

In the real world, however, this option is of only academic interest unless one is designing a helicopter to do nothing but hover. If it is also expected to fly forward, the designer must back off from the peak and choose more blade area than is optimum for hover.

In forward flight, the blades on the retreating side, operating at low velocities, must have high angles of attack that would push them into stall if they were already close to it. Other considerations leading to even more blade area (and lower hover efficiency) are requirements to fly at high altitudes and/or to develop substantial rotor-load factors during maneuvers.

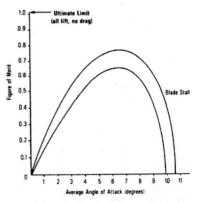

Figure 4-3 Hover Figure of Merit

More complications

Even though increasing the disc loading steps up the power required to hover, the increase is not as high as might be expected because the figure of merit also rises slightly. The reason is illustrated in Figure 4-4, which shows the velocities and forces acting at a typical blade element of two rotors developing the same thrust.

The second rotor has half the diameter, resulting in four times the disc loading—which doubles the induced velocity and thus the induced drag. The figure of merit is proportional to the induced drag vector divided by the total of the induced and profile drag vectors. At the higher disc loading, this ratio is closer to one because the profile drag, assuming that the lift-to-drag ratio is the same, remains constant and is therefore a smaller portion of the total.

This illustrates why designers of very high disc loading aircraft can claim higher figures of merit than those of us working with helicopters. Their advantage, however, is not quite as much as it might seem from this simple demonstration. They are subject to higher "swirl" losses.

Figure 4-5 shows the blade tip and root vortices are both oriented in such a way as to induce a horizontal velocity in the wake which tends to spin it in the same direction the rotor is turning. This rotational velocity represents an energy loss that accounts for an increase in induced power of 2% or 3% for conventional main rotors, up to 5% on tail rotors - which usually have higher disc loadings - and 10% for lifting propellers. This loss can be eliminated by using coaxial, counter rotating rotors, or propellers in which the lower unit cancels out the swirl induced by the upper.

Another potential way to increase the figure of merit is to reduce the rotor tip speed. This does the same thing to the vector diagram as increasing the disc loading (Figure 4-4). In this case, with half the rotor tip speed, the lift vector is tilted further aft, leading to twice as much induced drag. However, since the induced power is proportional to the product of the induced drag and the velocity, it is not changed as it was in the case of the increased disc loading. Decreasing the tip speed is seldom a viable option because it increases the weight of the main-rotor blades, the transmission, and the tail rotor and may prematurely limit the forward speed capability by making the rotor susceptible to retreating blade stall.

Improving the situation Theory shows the highest figure of merit will be obtained when the induced velocity is uniform across the rotor disc. If the blades had no twist, both the lift and the induced velocity would rapidly increase toward the tips, as shown in Figure 4-6. Twisting the blades down as they go outboard tends to make the lift distribution triangular and the induced flow more uniform, resulting in a few percent increase in the figure of merit.

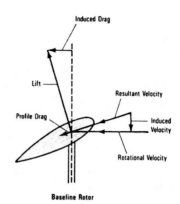

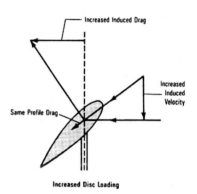

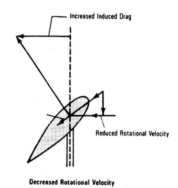

Figure 4-4 Effect of Changing Conditions

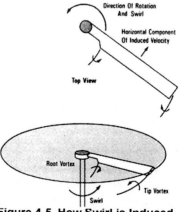

Figure 4-5 How Swirl is Induced by Tip and Root Vorticies

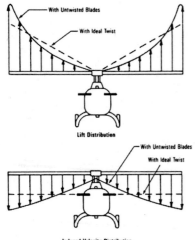

Figure 4-6 Hover Lift and Induced Velocities as Affected by Twist

Tapering the blade by reducing the chord toward the tip can also be used for this purpose - and the optimum blade would be both twisted and tapered. Most helicopters use twist but no taper; but you may see more tapered blades in the future as advantage is taken of the ease with which composite materials can be formed into odd shapes compared to sheet metal.

There are limits, however, to the amount of both twist and taper that can realistically be used. Theoretically, a twist distribution that reduces the pitch 20° to 30° between the tip and the root is desired for the best hover figure of merit. Unfortunately, experience has proven that vibration and oscillatory loads in forward flight are increased by twist, and so a reasonable compromise has been reached in the neighborhood of about 10°.

The desire to taper the blade also runs up against practical constraints. Although you can't see it, almost every rotor blade has a concentrated tip weight made up of a chunk of dense material such as brass, tungsten, or even depleted uranium. It is there for two reasons: to modify the blades' dynamic characteristics to reduce vibration and oscillatory loads; and to increase rotor inertia to help keep the rotor speed up during those critical seconds following a power failure.

If the designer decides tapering to a very small chord at the tip is a good idea from an aerodynamic standpoint, he may find there is not enough volume to install the required tip weight. For small helicopters, he might also find that if the tip chord goes below about five inches (13 cm), the rotor starts losing its good aerodynamic characteristics even at normal helicopter tip speeds because of low Reynolds numbers.

Another possible use of taper has recently been demonstrated during model tests of rotors originally designed with very high tip speeds and therefore significant compressibility losses at the tips even in hover. Tapering reduced the chord at the tip and thus the compressibility losses. (I suspect in this case the same improvement could have been achieved by reducing the blade length a few inches with a hacksaw and never telling the data-reduction computer what had been done.)

Distortions

Anything that distorts the induced flow from its theoretical optimum uniform distribution over the disc will reduce the hover efficiency. One source of distortion is the proximity of the tail rotor, which is doing its own thing and moving air near the aft edge of the main-rotor disc.

Recent model tests show this effect can reduce the main-rotor figure of merit by as much as 2.5%. The same tests show that moving the tail rotor aft by three-fourths of its radius reduces the penalty to less than 1%.

Another distortion occurs near each blade tip because it is close to the tip vortex generated by the previous blade, as illustrated by Figure 4-7.

This can induce a very high angle of attack near the tip which might produce a locally stalled region.

This is especially likely on rotors with many blades since the tip vortex does not have much time to get out of the way. Some blade designers have attempted to circumvent this penalty by including a sudden nosedown twist where the vortex interference effect is the greatest.

Although not a distortion in the sense of the two effects discussed above, "tip losses" do reduce the rotor efficiency from the theoretical value. Because the lift must fall off to zero at the tip and requires a finite length to do so, a portion of the blade area is producing drag but little useful thrust.

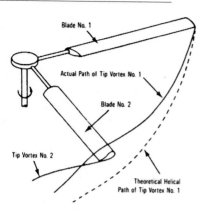

Figure 4-7 Blade tip Vortex Interference Effect in Hover

If the blades are long and skinny, the tip-loss area is small; but if the blades are short and wide, the losses can be substantial. Here we have another dilemma for the designer. Spreading the required blade area among a large number of blades is good. from a tip-loss standpoint but bad from an interference-by-the-proceeding-tip-vortex standpoint.

Slicker or skinnier blades

Another factor that affects the figure of merit is the skin friction of the blades. Some airfoils have lower skin friction than others as a result of maintaining low-drag laminar flow as far back from the leading edge as possible. These "laminar-flow" airfoils tend to have gently ramped leading edges with the maximum thickness well back. They are used on a number of rotors.

The current design trend in airfoils, however, seems to be in a direction to throw this hovering advantage away in favor of obtaining better forward- flight characteristics with airfoils that are more slab-sided and consequently have earlier transitions from laminar to turbulent boundary layers.

This might not be as shortsighted as it sounds. If a new airfoil has a higher maximum-lift coefficient, the same rotor performance in forward flight can be obtained with less blade area. The corresponding decrease in blade surface will directly reduce profile power in all flight conditions-including hover- thus making up for the loss of laminar flow (maybe).

Rotor lift-to-drag ratio

For many airplane missions, it is important to achieve the highest lift-to-drag ratio possible to fly as far as possible per gallon of fuel. Considering only the wing, the way to maximize this ratio is to reduce either the induced or profile drag.

The airplane designer has some well-established guidelines for doing this. Induced drag can be minimized by designing a very long wing. This is based on the same laws of aerodynamics that make the helicopter designer want to use a low disc loading. Further optimization is achieved by selecting wing taper and twist to make the lift distribution elliptically shaped. This produces a uniform induced velocity across the wing, just as the rotor designer uses the same parameters to do the same thing in hover.

The wing designer can also minimize profile drag by choosing the wing area that makes every wing element operate at the angle of attack for the maximum airfoil lift-to-drag ratio at the design cruise condition. If that wing area is not enough to make safe landings and takeoffs, he simply adds flaps and slats.

The lift-to-drag ratio is easy to calculate for a wing. It has a definite drag overcome by a separate compulsive device such as a propeller or a jet engine. A rotor, however, has a definite shaft power instead of drag and is acting both as a lilting and as a propulsive device.

This presents a problem in bookkeeping. The accepted procedure is to calculate an equivalent drag as the main-rotor power divided by the forward speed and then to subtract the parasite drag of the rest of the helicopter.

In doing this calculation, the rotor-hub drag should not be subtracted as part of the rest of the helicopter. This forces the rotor designer to consider the entire rotor and not just the blades when comparing his design with another.

Any hub mechanism is difficult to streamline and thus for low drag, the hub should be as small as possible. As an aerodynamicist, I have been disappointed with the recent crop of bearingless, composite hub designs which, with few exceptions, appear to be significantly bulkier and therefore draggier than the old-fashioned hubs.

Facts of life

A rotor in forward flight will never be as efficient as a comparable wing. Besides the built-in penalty of the hub, the different aerodynamics on the advancing and retreating sides demand that the induced-velocity distribution cannot be uniform nor can each blade element be operating at the most optimum angle of attack.

Whereas an airplane wing may have a lift-to-drag ratio of 30 or more, a good helicopter rotor has 10 or less. Design studies have shown, however, that for a given helicopter forward-flight condition, small improvements can be achieved by selecting twist and taper distributions which minimize the effects of local high-drag regions on the advancing or retreating sides, or even over the nose or tail.

These distributions may be somewhat different than would be chosen for hover or for some other forward flight condition and may be quite different from the distributions that would be chosen to guarantee the highest effectiveness for a high load factor maneuver at high speed.

5 Ground Effect in Hover

Every pilot has noticed that a helicopter hovering close to the ground requires considerably less power than when it is hovering high in the air. This is due to ground effect, a benefit that can be used to provide significant operational advantages when an aircraft is loaded to the point where the power available for hovering is marginal.

The source of the benefit may be visualized by picturing a mirror-image helicopter flying upside down at the same distance below the ground as the actual rotor is above it, but with no velocity across the ground boundary as shown in Figure 5-1. The image wake is composed of a series of spiral-vortex filaments generated at the blade tips and carried upward by the image rotor's wake.

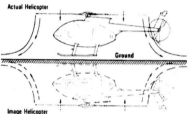

Figure 5-1 Simulation of Ground Effect with Image Helicopter

Aerodynamicists use this concept to calculate the upward velocity "induced" at the actual rotor by the image rotor's vortex field. Subtracting this upward velocity from the actual rotor's out-of-ground-effect induced downward velocity, produces the in-ground-effect induced velocity distribution.

(That the ground's presence can influence the flow conditions at the rotor can be demonstrated at the breakfast table. The characteristics of a syrup stream leaving the lip of the pitcher will depend upon the pancake's proximity as shown in Figure 5-2.)

Figure 5-3 illustrates the local effect of the ground-modified velocity at the blade element and shows that when the rotor is operating in ground effect, the local velocity approaching the blade element has less downward slope than when operating out of ground effect. Most of the power required to hover is due to the lift vector's rearward tilt, which is perpendicular to the local-velocity vector.

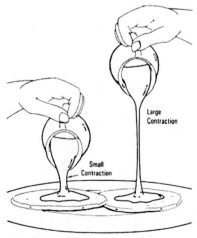

Figure 5-2 Changes in Flow Characteristics

The smaller the slope, the smaller is the rearward tilt of "induced drag." The "profile drag," due to skin friction, accounts for only about a third of the power and is relatively unaffected by ground proximity.

Testing

Much of what is known about ground effect has been obtained by testing model rotors on balance systems that measure both thrust and torque in the presence of a ground plane that can be positioned at various

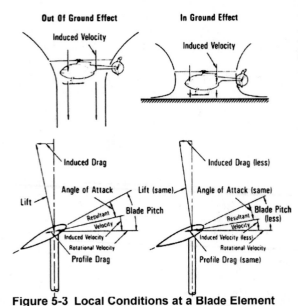

Figure 5-3 **Local Conditions at a Blade Element**

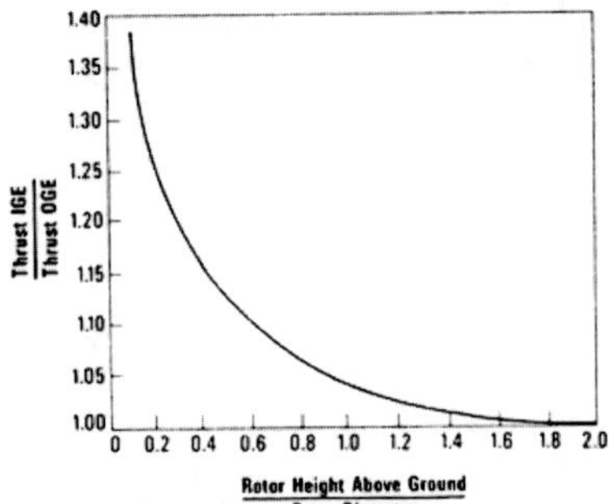

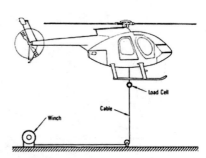

Figure 5-4 **Thrust Capability for Same Power**

distances from the rotor. The results are generally presented as a ratio of thrust that can be generated in ground effect to the thrust out of ground effect at constant power, plotted against the ratio of rotor height above the ground to the rotor diameter as shown in Figure 5-4.

Besides model testing, engineers can measure ground effect in hover during actual helicopter flight. The first such tests relied on the pilot to hold a precise hover height while reading the power from his engine instruments. Changing height then produced another test point and gave the change of power for a given thrust. Repeating the procedure at several gross weights gave enough data to cross plot and determine the effect of ground proximity on the thrust capability at constant power.

An improvement in the test procedure has been the development of the "tethered hover," shown in Figure 5-5 where a cable between the helicopter and a winch on the ground is used to precisely fix the height. The cable's tension is measured with a load cell so that several values of rotor thrust corresponding to gross weight plus cable tension can be quickly obtained at each height.

Velocity ratios

The ratio of thrust in and out of ground effect as a function of rotor-height-to-diameter ratio is useful in determining how much a helicopter can be overloaded and still get off the ground. However, a more-basic presentation for the aerodynamicist is that of the ratio of induced velocities at the rotor disc, since this information can be used for a wider variety of calculations by correcting the induced-power portion of the performance equations.

It is used, for example, in determining the effect of ground proximity on hover ceilings. By working backward from the test data, this velocity ratio can be deduced.

Figure 5-6 shows the ratio based on model and full-scale test data. Down in the corner is a single point at a very low rotor height obtained from model tests directed by Professor Bill Patterson at California Polytechnic State University (Cal Poly) at San Luis Obispo. This point indicates that close to the ground, the induced velocity-and thus the induced power- is nearly zero.

This has encouraged the Cal Poly people to design the man-powered helicopter, shown in Figure 5-7. Their calculations say that a light but muscular cyclist pedaling half a horsepower can hover this helicopter for the minute required to win the American Helicopter Society's prize.

Figure 5-5 **Test Setup for Tethered Hover**

More mundane designs cannot count on an almost total elimination of induced power—but can benefit from a 20% to 30% reduction.

The Cal Poly ground-effect test set-up has also been used to investigate the influence of ground surface. Some pilots have reported that hovering over long grass or water provides less ground effect than over a solid surface like a concrete slab. Mike Baker and Jonathon Scarcello made ground-effect measurements over Astroturf and over water. The Astroturf results tend to refute the pilots' observations. The ground effect at half a rotor diameter was roughly 30% stronger than over the smooth solid surface. Over water, however, there was little measurable difference.

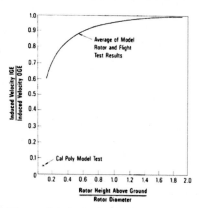

Figure 5-6 Induced Velocity Ratios

Secondary effects

The ground's proximity provides another benefit that can be explained after observing the details of flow through the rotor disc made visible by smoke or dust. Since rotor blades are made with an arm at the root to connect the lifting surface to the hub, the lifting shape of the blades does not come to the center of rotation.

This means that a hole is left in the disc's middle through which air can escape upward. Although one is tempted to think of this as flow from a high- to low-pressure region, a more scientifically correct description is to attribute it to the induction effects of the root vortices. These must exist to balance the tip vortices at the blades' other end, as shown on Figure 5-8.

Figure 5-7 The Designers of this Man-powered Helicopter are Counting on a Large Ground Effect (David Monroe photo)

This upflow region can be observed even when the rotor is far from the ground but when it is close, the upflow is augmented by the flow's "fountain effect" generated by the disc's inboard portion being deflected in and up after it impinges on the ground (Figure 8-3 on page 40).

Tests on both models and full-scale aircraft show that the increased upflow can eliminate the penalty of the aerodynamic download on the airframe. This penalty normally amounts to an increase in the effective gross weight of an out-of-ground-effect hovering aircraft by 3% to 10%. Root vortices are more difficult to make visible than tip vortices, since they are smeared out by the hub hardware, but their effect can be felt as large-scale turbulence by an observer standing near a hovering helicopter.

Pilots occasionally report that when hovering in ground effect, they experience random yaw disturbances. This is probably due to the effect of the combined root vortex as it writhes near the tail rotor. A report on some model tests described random disturbances at the vertical stabilizer with the main rotor one-quarter diameter above the ground plane.

Raising the rotor to half a diameter made the disturbances vanish.

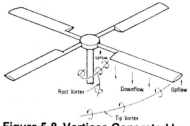

Figure 5-8 Vortices Generated by One Blade

6

Aerodynamic Environment at the Rotor Blade

Because of the unsymmetrical velocity pattern in forward flight discussed in Chapter 4, the angles of attack of the blade elements on the retreating side must be higher than on the advancing side. While several flight conditions and geometric parameters influence the angle-of-attack distribution, in the final analysis, it is the pilot with his collective and cyclic controls who determines the correct distribution for the flight condition he wants.

Angle-of-Attack Distribution

Figure 6-1 shows calculated contours of the local angle of attack for a typical helicopter at a tip-speed ratio of 0.30, trimmed at three different steady-flight conditions: level flight, climb, and autorotation. It may be seen that the flight condition primarily affects the distribution of angle of attack on the retreating side. In level flight, the main region of maximum angles is at about the 80%-radius station. In climb, the angles peak further outboard where they may cause tip stall, and in autorotation there are regions of very high angles that, however, are so far inboard they seldom are troublesome.

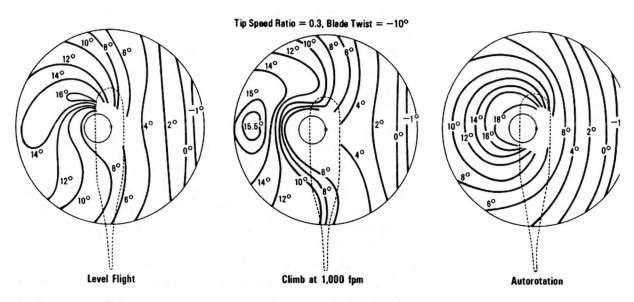

Tip Speed Ratio = 0.3, Blade Twist = −10°

Level Flight   Climb at 1,000 fpm   Autorotation

Figure 6-1 Angle of Attack Distribution in Forward Flight

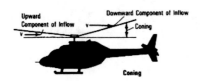

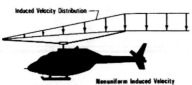

Figure 6-2 Two Fore and Aft Inflow Effects

The fore-and-aft asymmetry of the patterns in Figure 6-1 can be traced to two effects—coning and non-uniform induced velocity. Both are illustrated in Figure 6-2. Coning causes a component of forward speed to be more up with respect to the blade over the nose than at the blade over the tail, thus changing the relative angles of attack. The other effect—the non-uniform induced velocity (sometimes called transverse flow)—is due to the fact that the vorticity in the wake extending behind the rotor can create more downward induced velocity at the trailing edge of the rotor disc than it can at the leading edge. As a matter of fact, smoke studies made in a wind tunnel indicate that a good approximation to the induced velocity distribution is zero at the leading edge, increasing to the average momentum value halfway back, and to double that value at the trailing edge. The effect on angle of attack distribution is similar to the effect of coning.

The contours of Figure 6-1 are the result of calculations based on fairly simple assumptions. Calculations that use more complicated ideas of what the induced velocity looks like, how the nose of the fuselage changes the flow, and what blade bending and twisting can do result in even more distortions to the contours. So far, formidable instrumentation problems have prevented any experimenter from satisfactorily measuring the instantaneous angles of attack at a rotor blade.

The lift on the retreating blade is low because the local velocities are low. The lift on the advancing blade is low because it must not overbalance the lift on the retreating blade. The result is that in forward flight the primary burden of keeping the helicopter in the air must be borne by the blades over the nose and tail.

Download on the Advancing Tip

Figure 6-1 shows what may seem to be a surprising feature: the angle of attack on the advancing tip is actually negative! This is primarily due to twist being built into the blade. Blades are twisted so their pitch is less at the tip than at the root for two reasons: to improve hover performance by making the induced velocity more uniform; and to reduce the angle of attack on the retreating tip to delay blade stall at high speed. Figure 6-1 shows that -10° of twist has achieved this second objective for the example helicopter in level flight, since the angle of attack on the tip of the retreating blade is slightly less than it is just inboard.

The same map for an untwisted blade would show the angle of attack increasing all the way to the tip. Twist that helps on the retreating tip hurts on the advancing tip by reducing the angle of attack and thus the lift carried on that portion of the disc. For this reason, and because high blade twist has sometimes resulted in severe vibrations at high speeds, rotor designers use it sparingly. Instead of the -20° or -30° optimum for good performance in hover and minimizing retreating blade stall at high speeds, the designers tend to use -6° to -12° as a compromise.

The download region on the advancing side is especially wasteful from an energy standpoint. These blade elements are absorbing significant power while helping less than nothing to keep the helicopter flying. It is also one of the reasons why the equivalent lift-to-drag ratio of a rotor is always less than a comparable wing where all of the elements are cooperating toward the common good.

Reverse-Flow Region

Inside the reverse-flow region, the air is striking the trailing edge of the blade. In auto-rotation, it is usually impinging on the bottom of the trailing edge and so is producing positive lift. In level flight and climb, however, where the rotor disc is tilted down in front, the flow strikes the top of the trailing edge and produces a download. This is not much consequence at low speeds because the area of the reverse-flow region is small but at high speeds this download can cause a significant performance penalty.

For this reason, some designers have considered building the rotor blades with the actual airfoil section starting well outboard; that is, with a large root cutout. This desire, however, is counterbalanced by the need to streamline the inboard portion of the blade when it is on the advancing side. Thus the rotor should have a large root cutout when the blade is retreating and a small root cutout when it is advancing—another dilemma for the helicopter designer.

Collective and Cyclic Pitch

The average angle of attack over the disc determines the rotor thrust; while the unsymmetrical distribution balances the rolling and pitching moments. The average value is controlled by the collective pitch, which also must be high enough to compensate for the inflow velocity through the disc. At hover, the inflow is only the induced velocity, but in level forward flight a component of the forward velocity perpendicular to the disc is also coming through the rotor—due to its forward tilt. Because the induced velocity is falling off as speed increases while at the same time the forward flight component perpendicular to the disc is increasing, the collective pitch needed to overcome inflow is changing in a way similar to the power required curve.

Figure 6-3 shows the collective pitch as it varies in level flight, and also in climb and autorotation. Also shown are the values of longitudinal and lateral cyclic pitch required to keep the rotor in trim. Longitudinal cyclic pitch controls the difference between the pitch on the advancing and retreating blades in order to compensate for the difference in velocity. It is varied by fore-and-aft displacement of the pilot's control stick.

Lateral cyclic pitch controls the difference between the pitch on the blades over the nose and the tail in order to compensate for the effects of coning and non-uniform induced velocity. It is varied by side-to-side stick displacements. Both components of cyclic pitch are increasing with

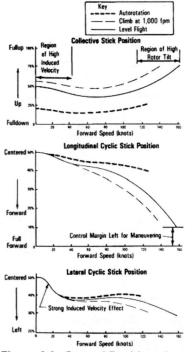

Figure 6-3   Control Positions in Foward Flight

31

speed, and the corresponding stick motion is forward and to the left. The sharp increase in lateral cyclic pitch at low speed is entirely due to the strong effect of the non-uniform induced velocity in this flight regime.

In making Figure 6-3, it has been assumed that no rotor flapping is required to balance external moments due to an offset CG position or to airframe aerodynamics. Any nose-up rotor flapping that might be required for balancing (for example, because of a forward CG position) will reduce the forward stick displacement, and any required flapping up to the left will decrease the left stick.

Maneuvers

Going from steady to maneuvering flight introduces some changes in the angle-of-attack distribution. Of special interest are those maneuvers that require more rotor thrust than needed in steady flight and can therefore invite blade stall; more specifically, pullups and turns.

In a symmetrical pullup done only by pulling back on the cyclic stick, the increase in thrust is produced by the rearward tilt of the rotor disc just as if it were a wing. In this situation, there are two compensating effects: the upward flow increases the average angle of attack at the blade elements, but it also changes the distribution to look more like the autorotation case of Figure 6-1. The highest angles are near the root of the retreating blade where they are relatively harmless.

In a steady turn, on the other hand, the increased rotor thrust necessary to balance both the weight of the helicopter and its centrifugal force must be obtained by increasing collective pitch. This not only raises the average angle of attack, but also drives the region of highest angles outboard along the retreating blade—similar to the climb condition of Figure 6-1. Thus, the possibility of retreating-blade stall is more likely during a 2 G steady turn that during a 2 G cyclic pullup at the same speed.

Stall and Compressibility

Helicopters are different from airplanes. In most respects, the differences are obvious but the way a helicopter reacts to stall and compressibility conditions—as compared to how an airplane behaves—requires some explanation.

When the wing of an airplane stalls, the important effect is the loss of lift (especially if one wing stalls before the other). The accompanying nosedown pitching moment is only a minor effect. On the other hand, when a rotor blade stalls the important effect is the nosedown pitching moment.

Similarly, when the wing of an airplane flies at a high enough Mach number to compress the air ahead of it, the important effect is the rapid increase in drag. The accompanying nosedown pitching moment is only a minor effect. On the other hand, when a rotor blade experiences

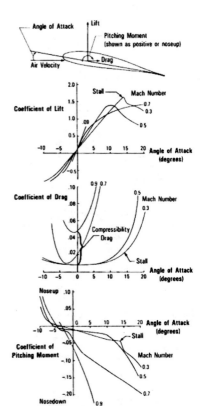

Figure 6-4 Aerodnamic Characteristics of a Modern Rotor Airfoil Section

compressibility, the important effect is, again, the nosedown pitching moment.

The primary reason for the importance of pitching moments in the case of the helicopter is the torsional flexibility of the long, skinny rotor blades and the ease with which they can be twisted into odd shapes. The aerodynamic characteristics of an airfoil for a rotor blade can be measured in a high-speed wind tunnel. Figure 6-4 shows the two-dimensional lift, drag, and pitching-moment coefficients of a typical airfoil at several Mach numbers ("two-dimensional" because the airfoil model spans the tunnel from wall to wall, eliminating any wing-tip effects). Notice that at low angles of attack and low Mach numbers, the data forms either straight lines or gentle curves. At high angles of attack as the airfoil stalls, it loses lift, its drag rises rapidly, and it develops a sharp nosedown pitching moment. At high Mach numbers, the airfoil suffers from compressibility effects: drag increases rapidly, and a large change in pitching moment again develops.

Most helicopters are designed so that their blades do not normally operate in conditions in which a significant pitching moment is generated —either by stall on the retreating blade or by compressibility on the advancing blade. Effective design practices dictate, however, that at high speeds the blade tips should be operating just under these limits.

It is always possible, therefore, for a pilot to penetrate into the troublesome regions during turns that can put the retreating blade into stall or dives that can put the advancing tip beyond its compressibility Mach-number limit. Since in either case only a small portion of the disc is being subjected to high pitching moments, each blade sees them for only a portion of a revolution. The resulting twisting and untwisting pattern can do two things: it can act like cyclic pitch, causing unexpected flapping that forces the pilot to move his stick in order to keep the helicopter in trim; or it can generate high oscillating loads at the rotor hub and in the control system—which produces vibrations throughout the entire aircraft. Or it can do both.

Dynamic Stall—Lift

Although stall might be expected to cause a loss of rotor lift as the local angles of attack on the retreating side exceed the stall angles shown in Figure 6-4, this usually does not occur. Early wind-tunnel tests of model rotors surprised the engineers who ran them. Test conditions that should have placed large portions of the rotor into stall instead produced thrust measurements that continued to rise with no sign of peaking. These unexpected results (one of the few times when test results exceeded theoretical limits) cried for an explanation.

That explanation was discovered in the know-how acquired by airplane aerodynamicists 20 years before, when they found that during a quick pullup, a wing could momentarily develop more lift than could be measured in conventional wind-tunnel tests. This is because the

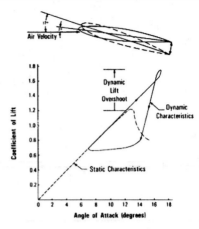

Figure 6-5   LIft Characteristics of an Oscillating Airfoil

separation of the boundary layer from the top surface of the airfoil requires a little time to become. complete and when separation does occur, a vortex is shed from the leading edge that sweeps back across the airfoil—momentarily increasing lift even further.

If the increase in angle of attack is rapid enough, the maximum lift can be significantly increased. For airplanes, this can amount to about a 20% increase during a pullup but on a rotor blade, which is rapidly changing its angle of attack every revolution, the overshoot can be as much as 100%. Figure 6-5 shows the results of a wind-tunnel test in which the airfoil model was rapidly oscillated through an angle-of-attack range from 7° to 17°. Compared to the static tests, there is a large overshoot in lift.

In addition, the airplane people had found that the stall angle of a swept wing was higher than that of a straight wing. Since a rotor blade is swept either fore or aft with respect to the flight path for most of each revolution, it also takes advantage of this effect. The result is that rotors in flight do not lose thrust because of lift stall.

Dynamic Stall—Drag and Moment

The same argument does not apply to the increase in drag or the nosedown break in pitching moment, however. For a rapid increase in angle of attack, these effects are delayed only slightly above the static stall angle until the boundary layer separates. When the leading-edge vortex is shed, the drag goes up and a large nosedown pitching moment is produced.

If the blade is flexible enough, the aerodynamic moment will twist the blade nose down to an angle of attack below stall. This can reduce the nosedown moment enough to allow the blade to spring back into a stall condition. In addition to this rather straight-forward effect, there may be another outcome caused by the lag in the pitching moment. In some cases, this effect will produce a nosedown moment while the blade is twisting down and a noseup moment while it is twisting up. This results in "negative damping" and means the oscillating system is being fed by energy taken out of the passing air—a potentially dangerous condition that in other situations causes wings to flutter and suspension bridges to gallop. For the rotor blade on the retreating side, the negative damping can cause the blade to oscillate rapidly for several cycles with ever-increasing amplitude until it passes over the tail boom and out of the thigh angle-of-attack region of the rotor disc. This is sometimes called "stall flutter."

Effect of Stiffness

The reaction of a rotor to moment stall depends primarily on the stiffness of the blade and the control system in resisting twisting moments. Model rotors designed for wind tunnels can be built so stiff that they are virtually "stall proof." This degree of stiffness is usually not built into actual helicopter rotors because of the extra weight required. Blades on most multi-bladed rotors will go through two to four oscillations while traversing the troublesome region. The blades on most two-bladed rotors are relatively soft (when the entire system including the controls is considered) and only go through one excursion of twisting motion when stalled. This does not produce oscillations but does cause some uncommanded flapping.

Most helicopters will pitch up during blade stall—but some may tend to roll right whereas others will roll left. Instinctive pilot reaction with the cyclic in an attempt to maintain attitude will always aggravate the condition. Proper corrective action is to gently lower collective and then slow down. Blade stall is such a variable phenomenon that two adjacent blades will not see quite the same aerodynamic environment and will twist and flap differently every revolution. Because of this, stall will almost always cause some erratic, out-of-track tip-path plane condition.

Compressibility

Penetration of the advancing blade tip into the compressibility regime also produces aerodynamic pitching moments. Depending upon the local angle of attack, the airfoil, and the shape of the tip, these moments may be either noseup or nosedown. In any case, rotor blades that twist under stall conditions will also twist due to compressibility.

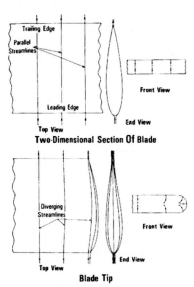

Figure 6-6 Illustration of Tip Relief

Just as the static two-dimensional wind-tunnel airfoil data is misleading with respect to stall, it is also somewhat misleading with respect to compressibility. The reason here is an effect commonly called "tip relief," which enables a blade tip to go to a higher Mach number before being subjected to compressibility effects than the airfoil can in a two-dimensional wind-tunnel test.

Figure 6-6 illustrates the source of tip relief by showing the streamline patterns over a two-dimensional blade segment and a blade tip of the same thickness ratio. The streamlines over the blade segment are constrained to be parallel but the streamlines over the tip have room to spread out. This decreases the local airspeed and Mach number—and thus delays compressibility effects. For this reason, a tip will be able to go to a higher Mach number than a two-dimensional wind-tunnel model before experiencing significant drag rise or a pitching moment break. The difference in the critical Mach number is a measure of the tip relief.

Since twisting the blade does not get it out of compressibility as it does out of stall, there are no sustained oscillations but only one twisting response as the tip passes through the high-Mach-number region. This response can cause blade flapping and a resultant trim shift for which the pilot must correct. The sudden change in pitching moment may also produce a sharp spike in control loads and a high vibration level at a frequency corresponding to the passage of each blade.

Pilot Cues

Besides the possible trim shifts already discussed, the pilot will generally sense stall or compressibility as an increase in vibration levels. The magnitude of the increase, however, will vary from one helicopter design to another—depending on the structural and dynamic characteristics of the blades, the control system, the transmission support, and the fuselage between the rotor and the cockpit. For this reason, different pilots report different symptoms for stall and/or compressibility for different helicopters. It is true, however, that by flying within the flight-manual limitations, the pilot will seldom encounter severe effects of either stall or compressibility.

Swept Tips

You may have noticed that some modern helicopter rotors have swept-back blade tips. One of the reasons for this is to give the download on the advancing tip a chance to relieve itself by twisting the blade nose up. At the same time, the upload on the retreating tip is twisting the blade nose down to decrease the local angle of attack in that region. A rotor that uses airloads to dynamically twist and untwist the blade each revolution is called an "aeroelastically conformable rotor." The sweep also fools the tip into thinking it is at a lower Mach number, thus delaying compressibility effects.

7 Is The Rotor A Gyro?

You might remember your first experience with a toy gyroscope (like the one shown in Figure 7-1) and the amazing things it did in apparent disregard for the obvious laws of nature.

It displayed remarkable stability. If it was set spinning horizontally, it wanted to stay horizontal no matter how you moved the support, but if you were determined to move the axis by brute force, the gyro moved in a strange way—at right angles to the applied moment. Even if you were later exposed to the gyroscopic equations and acquired a confidence in your ability to manipulate them, you were probably still vaguely disturbed by this device's strange behavior (I know I was).

The disc of a spinning helicopter rotor certainly looks much like a toy gyroscope. So does it act like one? Yes and no. The reason for the "no" is the existence of very large aerodynamic forces on the rotor blades. As a matter of fact, if you remove the aerodynamics by running a rotor in a vacuum, it will demonstrate gyroscopic stability.

A rotor with blades hinged at the center of rotation (such as a teetering rotor) is shown in the top part of Figure 7-2. In a vacuum, there are no aerodynamic forces, only centrifugal forces acting in the plane of rotation, and these can produce no moments about the flapping hinges. If the shaft is tilted, no changes in moments will be produced and the rotor disc will remain in its original position as if it were a gyroscope. (Of course, if the rotor had had offset flapping hinges, as in the bottom part of Figure 7-2, the centrifugal forces would have produced moments that would have aligned the blades perpendicular to the shaft.

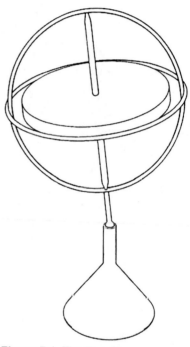

Figure 7-1 The Toy Gyroscope

A rotor in air

In air, the aerodynamic forces will cause any rotor to align itself perpendicular to the shaft. The sequence of events is shown on Figure 7-3.

First, there is the tilt of the shaft alone as the rotor disc acts as a gyroscope and remains in its original plane. However, since the blade feathering is referenced to the shaft, the angle of attack of the right-hand blade is increased and that of the left-hand blade decreased by the same amount.

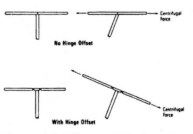

Figure 7-2 Effects of Shaft Tilt in a Vacuum

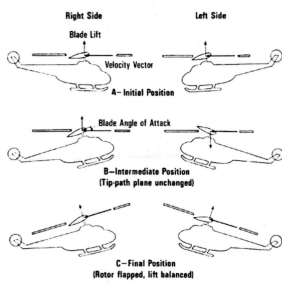

Figure 7-3 Shaft Tilted in Hover

This causes the rotor to flap until it is perpendicular to the shaft, where it will again be in equilibrium with a constant angle of attack around the azimuth and the moments will be balanced. This alignment is very rapid, usually taking less than one revolution following a sudden tilt. Because of this, the flapping motion in hover has practically no effect on the stability of the helicopter in terms of holding a given attitude.

This was not recognized by many people in the early days of helicopters. They spoke of the rotor as a gigantic stabilization device similar to those used on ships of the day.

A rotor as a gyro

So, if a rotor does not act like a gyro trying to retain its position in space, when does it act like a gyro? This answer has to do with how the rotor moves if you put an unbalanced aerodynamic lift on the disc. It will respond by moving at right angles to the unbalance just as the toy gyro does, and it does so in exact compliance with the gyroscopic laws that say the angular rate of motion-the "precession rate" —will be proportional to the applied moment.

This is in apparent contrast to Newton's Law that states that an angular acceleration should be the result of an applied moment. (The rotor/gyro is actually obeying Newton's Law but its high rate of rotation is producing this overwhelming side effect.)

The unbalanced lift distribution can come either from external sources such as a gust or from control inputs using cyclic pitch. For example, right stick will lower the angle of attack of the blade over the tail and raise it on the blade over the nose. This noseup unbalance on the disc will cause it to precess down to the right and the rest of the helicopter will soon follow. For a given helicopter, the resulting right roll rate will be directly proportional to the change of cyclic pitch from trim. Not all helicopters, however, will roll at the same rate for the same cyclic pitch. In response to the gyroscopic laws, the rate will be higher for those helicopters whose rotors are lighter or turning faster.

Thus, it may be seen that the rotor is like the mysterious toy gyro as it responds to applied moments but it has practically none of the toy's inherent stability. If required, this last drawback can be compensated. Early Bell helicopters used a stabilizer bar that acted like a gyro and controlled cyclic pitch in a way that transferred some of the gyro stability to the rotor. The Lockheed rotor and gyro system did the same thing. Nowadays, the designer can use a hidden black box containing a small, rapidly turning gyro with appropriate connections to the control system to make the helicopter achieve as much stability as desired.

8 The Rotor Wake

Any aircraft flies by pushing air down in most situations, this downwash causes only minor effects but in the case of a helicopter flying slow and low, the downwash may find dramatic ways to call attention to itself.

One effect is to produce a disturbance at the ground, the magnitude of which depends both on the disk loading (which governs the downwash velocity) and on the gross weight (which governs how much air is being moved). When the rotor is hovering more than about its diameter above the ground, the down-wash velocity starts at one value at the rotor disc and then doubles as the wake contracts about a quarter of a diameter downstream (Figure 8-1).

The higher the disc loading, the higher the initial and the fully developed downwash velocities. Figure 8-2 shows this relationship for some familiar helicopters. As you can see, any helicopter is an effective wind machine and with the modern trend to higher disc loadings, they have become more effective.

Tests have shown that even when the helicopter is hovering with the rotor two diameters high, the wake reaches the ground with very little loss of energy. With the rotor closer to the ground, the wake does not contract so the velocities are reduced Gross Weight (Pounds) but the total energy is about the same.

Whether hovering high or low, the wake can do significant "placer mining" of an unprepared surface. Snow, dust, and newspapers are easily moved by any helicopter. Those with disc loadings of 10 pounds per square foot (50 kg/m^2) or more can also dislodge gravel- and high disc loadings of 30 to 60 pounds per square foot (150 kg/m^2 to 300 kg/m^2) associated with the propeller-supported VTOLs of the 1960s could blow the rose bushes right out of your garden.

As the wake reaches the ground (Figure 8-3), it spreads into an outflowing layer whose thickness starts out at about 10% to 15% of the rotor diameter and then gradually gets thinner and slower, until several diameters out it turns up to recirculate back into the rotor. The

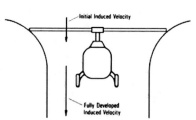

Figure 8-1 Wake of Hovering Helicopter

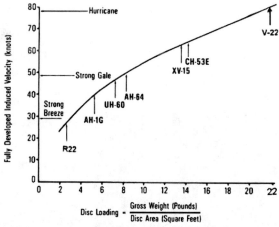

Figure 8-2 Wind Generating Capabilities

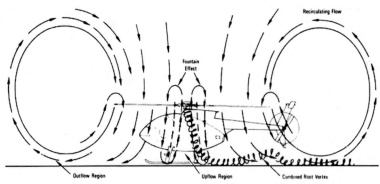

Figure 8-3 Flow Pattern Around Helicopter Hovering Close to the Ground

thickness of the flow has an effect on operations near the hovering helicopter.

For example, tests with a Sikorsky CH-53E which has a rotor diameter of 79 feet (24 m) and a disc loading of 14.2 pounds per square foot (69 kg/m^2) showed that not even a strong ground crewman could stand close to the rotor, since he was completely immersed in the flow and strong random gusts made it difficult to brace himself. This is in contrast to the Bell XV-15 tilt-rotor with nearly the same disc loading but only 25-foot (7.6-m) rotors. The high-velocity ground layer produced by this aircraft is only waist high and thus not nearly so upsetting.

A possible source of the gusty flow is the action of the blade-root vortices. Vortices generated by blade tips have always gotten a lot of attention but root vortices also exist. It is conjectured that the root vortices from each blade get together to form one big vortex that goes down, strikes the ground, and then wanders around in an unpredictable manner to influence the flow throughout the wake.

And up through the center

The top of the rotor disc is a region of low pressure and its bottom one of high pressure. Since on most helicopters, the blades do not extend all the way to the rotor shaft, air will leak upward through this hole in its desire to equalize the pressure. This is especially evident when hovering near the ground.

Many investigators have reported this upflow pattern (Figure 8-3), which is characterized as a "good news-bad news" situation. The good news is that the upflow reduces the normal download on the fuselage caused by the rotor wake - thus increasing the ability to take off heavily loaded. The bad news is that the upflow may bring dust, sand, and other such environmentally undesirable materials up to the engine intakes.

A lesser, but real, problem can exist when similar debris is stirred up by the outflow along the ground and then rises to eventually be recirculated back down through the rotor. This is the primary source of blade erosion damage.

The ABC shuffle

Another unexpected effect of the rotor wake has been observed on several helicopters, most recently with the Sikorsky Advancing Blade Concept (ABC) test bed aircraft, which when hovering close to the ground is subjected to random side forces. This aircraft has a nicely rounded fuselage bottom that presents no logical point where the downwash can separate (Figure 8-4). This wandering separation point produces erratic side forces the pilot has trouble anticipating.

Figure 8-4 Sikorsky's ABC Test Bed

Flying with the cockpit doors open improves the situation by breaking up the aerodynamic shape of the fuselage. A possible fix is the installation of lower fuselage strakes to force the separation at a definite point and eliminate the changing side force.

Tip vortices

Although it is convenient to draw the rotor wake (as in Figure 8-1) as a continuous downflow of air, it is a little more discretely organized than that. At each blade tip, the air, going from the high-pressure bottom to the low-pressure top, generates a tip vortex that, acting like a small whirlpool, induces rotational velocities in the nearby air.

Figure 8-5 Blade Tip Vorticies of a Bell 214B

Figure 8-5 shows the pattern that tip vortices reveal as they are made visible by moisture condensation. This vortex organization at the edge of the wake is usually of no consequence but an exception arises with armed helicopters when it is necessary to fire unguided rockets from hover or low speed with some degree of accuracy.

A rocket passing just over a tip vortex will be subjected to a different aerodynamic nudge than one passing just under a vortex and will thus be launched into a different flight path and will hit in a different part of the landscape. Since the instantaneous positions of the vortices change with gross weight, proximity to the ground, relative wind, and control inputs, there appears to be no feasible way to satisfactorily time the firing so that each rocket passes through the same point of the vortex pattern.

9 Vortex-Ring State

A rotor can get itself into the darndest state! At the beginning of the vertical flight era, it was thought that helicopters would operate from such confined sites as Rockefeller Plaza where vertical climbs and descents of a thousand feet or so would be standard operating practice. Going straight up was no problem once helicopters with adequate power became available, but going straight down proved to be surprisingly difficult because of the large and unpredictable control and power changes required to maintain steady descent.

Much flight and wind-tunnel testing went into investigating this condition, which became known as the "vortex-ring state" because of its resemblance to a smoke ring's flow. As helicopter operations matured, however, it was found that in actual practice, very few landings required prolonged vertical descent and as a consequence, the problem became a low-priority item in both pilot training and in scientific investigations.

Resurrecting the question

In recent years, military tactics have required that helicopters be able to hover over a spot on the ground with the wind coming from any direction. And, lo and behold, the vortex-ring state has again raised its head, not on the main rotor this time but on the tail rotor.

Most tail rotors will have trouble maintaining steady thrust when hovering in a left sidewind (with American rotation of the main rotor) of between 15 and 30 knots. The reason is that the air velocity induced toward the left is approximately equal to the wind coming from the left and so the air is not sure what it is supposed to be doing. As a consequence, the thrust varies in a random fashion and the pilot must be very active on his pedals to hold heading.

On each side of this confused situation, the flow is better behaved and can be represented by simple equations based on the balance of momentum in the air stream. For a descending main rotor (or a tail rotor in left sideward flight), Figure 9-1 shows the velocity induced by the rotor while producing steady thrust plotted against the rate of descent.

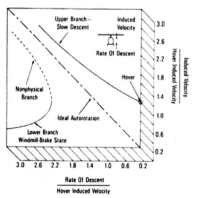

Figure 9-1 Velocity Rates in Vertical Descent

Windmill in the air

Both velocities have been non-dimensionalized by dividing the induced velocity in hover. As the rotor slowly descends from the hover point, the descent velocity decreases the mass flow by opposing the downward induced velocity which must therefore be increased since thrust is proportional to the product of mass flow and induced velocity. This is represented by the upper branch on the plot.

At the speed regime's other end, when the rotor is descending very fast, it is acting as a windmill taking energy out of the passing airstream; and the thrust-induced velocity only slightly slows the upward flow. In this situation, the faster the descent, the higher the mass flow and thus the smaller the induced velocity has to be to keep the thrust constant. This is represented by the lower branch on the plot which corresponds to the "windmill- brake state."

Another branch which comes out of the momentum equations, but which has no physical significance, is plotted as short dashes. Also shown is a 45° line labeled "Ideal Autorotation." Besides being a limit for two of the theoretical branches, this line defines a condition where the induced velocity is equal to the rate of descent.

Under this condition, there is theoretically no net flow across the disc and so there would be neither aft nor forward tilt of the lift vectors. Here the ideal rotor-without blade profile drag-would be in vertical autorotation. Autorotation of an actual rotor, of course, takes place somewhat below this line as the rotor is jumping the gap between the upper branch and the lower one and near where the non dimensionalized rate of descent is equal to two.

Vortex-ring characteristics

Even before jumping from the upper to the lower branch, the rotor starts getting "nervous," as the in-flow through the disc begins to be affected by the two contradictory velocity influences. For instance, as a filament of the upward flow impinges on a portion of the disc, the thrust increases, which, in turn, increases the downward induced velocity, which then deflects the upcoming airstream and puts the rotor back to its original condition - ready for another impingement of the upward flow, probably on another portion of the disc.

Theoretically, the vortex-ring state exists from hover until the rate of descent is high enough to put the rotor onto the lower windmill-brake branch. But from a practical standpoint, the extreme flow variations do not start until the rate of descent is about half the hover induced velocity and they taper off before vertical autorotation is reached.

Blade-twist effects

Both wind-tunnel and flight tests show that different rotors behave differently in the vortex-ring state. During wind-tunnel tests made at Georgia Tech in the 1950s, a rotor with untwisted blades and one with a-12° twist were tested. Figure 9-2 shows that the rotor with -12° of twist climbed higher on the upper branch before falling to the lower branch than did the rotor with no twist.

It is interesting to see on Figure 9-2 that this difference is also reflected in the power required to maintain constant thrust. The fact that the -12° rotor eventually required more power to descend than to hover is a verification of pilots' observations of "power settling," a phenomenon where power management in vertical descent does not seem to be responding to logical laws of physics.

The extended dwell on the upper branch for the -12° twist rotor apparently is the source of the following Georgia Tech observation: "The fluctuations in the forces and moments on the rotor with twisted blades were very much larger at the higher rates of power-on descent than for the rotor with untwisted blades."

This observation was backed up thirty years later during flight tests of the Hughes YAH-64 (predecessor to McDonnell Douglas' AH-64 Apache). Left sideward flight in the 20-to-40 knot region - which put the tail rotor into its vortex-ring state - was difficult because of large-scale thrust fluctuations that required large pedal inputs as shown on Figure 9-4.

During these flight tests, a Bell AH-1G "Huey Cobra," was on the test site for use as a chase aircraft. A Hughes pilot, also current in the Cobra, flew it-as part of the investigation-in the same sideward flight test sequence that had been giving him so much trouble in the YAH-64.

He found that the AH-1G had excellent flying qualities through the tail-rotor vortex-ring state even with the stability augmentation system (SAS) turned off! It appears that the basic parameter difference was that the AH-lG had no twist in the tail rotor blades, whereas the YAH-64 had a twist of -8°.

What's the difference?

From an aerodynamics standpoint, the difference between an untwisted and a twisted rotor blade is that the untwisted blade, being more heavily loaded outboard, produces a stronger tip vortex. The stronger tip vortex must somehow stabilize the flow and contribute to an earlier and more gentle departure from the upper branch.

Just why this is so, is not clear. It is also not clear why raising the tail rotor three feet during the change from the YAH-64 with a T-tail to the AH-64 with a stabilator reduced the unsteadiness.

Is twist always bad? Apparently not. The Sikorsky CH-53E and UH-60 have tail-rotor blades with -8 ° and-17° of twist, respectively. Sikorsky engineers say that neither aircraft has a vortex-ring problem in left sideward flight and they attribute this to the 20° cant (tilt) built into each tail rotor. This conclusion is backed up by the observation that vortex-

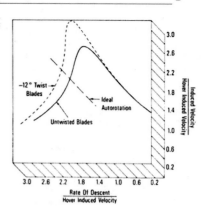

Figure 9-2 Effect of Twist in Descent

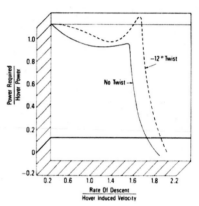

Figure 9-3 Power Required

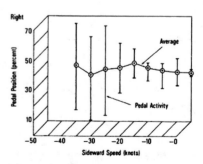

Figure 9-4 Hughes YAH-64 Pedal Required in Left Sideward Flight

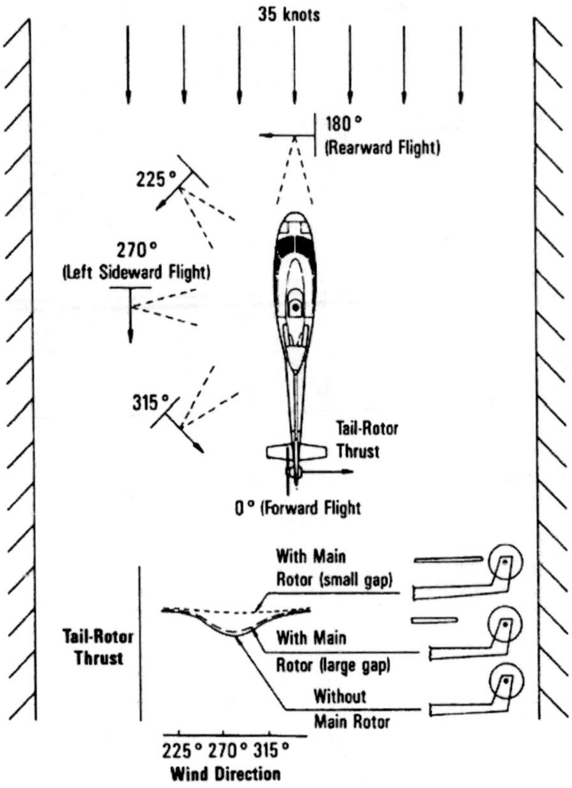

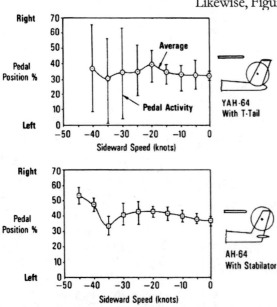

Figure 9-5 Effects of Main Rotor on Tail Rotor Thrust (In Wind Tunnel)

ring characteristics exist on the CH-53A/D, which have conventional upright tail rotors.

Also, the cant and the left bank in left sideward flight means that the tail rotor is not moving directly into its own downwash. It is known from wind tunnel tests, however, that a rotor not quite moving into its own wake by 20° to 30° is actually more susceptible to the vortex-ring state than when it is moving directly into its downwash. From this, it can be concluded that cant can't suppress the vortex-ring state - as Sikorsky contends. (But I don't have a better explanation.)

Main rotor-tail rotor interference

Wind-tunnel tests have been made of various main and tail rotors to determine their mutual interference. Contrary to what one might expect, the main rotor reduces the tail rotor's vortex-ring-state effects as compared to when the tail rotor is tested alone.

This is shown in Figure 9-5 where the tail rotor is held at a constant pitch as the model revolves slowly on a yaw table in the wind tunnel. When the tail rotor is alone, its thrust falls off in the region of left sideward flight-as expected. The result isn't much different when the main rotor is included, as long as the gap between the rotors is large. However, when the gap is small, the tail rotor loses practically no thrust as it goes through the left sidewind region.

The reason for this remains a mystery to me.

Likewise, Figure 9-6 shows another indication that main-rotor proximity is important. It reveals an improvement in steadiness when the AH-64A Apache tail rotor was moved closer to the main rotor to accommodate the stabilator.

I accept this but admittedly don't understand it.

Direction of tail-rotor rotation

This benefit of main-rotor proximity apparently applies only to tail rotors that rotate with the blade closest to the main rotor swinging up. This was discovered the hard way by many design teams. Helicopters that started with tail rotors going the BA(d) way (bottom aft) included the Kaman UH-2K (predecessor to the SH-2 Seasprite), Bell UH-1 and AH-1, Lockheed AH-56A Cheyenne, Mil Mi-24 Hind, Westland WG-30, MBB BO-105, and the Aerospatiale Gazelle (with fenestron). Each had poor directional-control characteristics that were much

Figure 9-6 Effect of Rotor Proximity on the Apache's Left Sideward Flight Characteristics

improved when the direction of tail-rotor rotation was reversed.

Some helicopters, such as the McDonnell Douglas 500, have been successful despite tail rotors that go the "wrong" direction. Sikorsky consistently used the correct rotation except on the S-56, which was relatively unsuccessful, although probably not because of directional control.

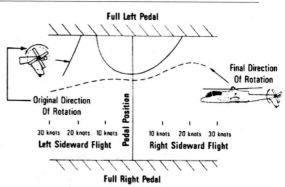

Figure 9-7 Effect of Tail Rotor Direction of Rotation on Sideward Flight Characteristics of Lockheed Cheyenne

Evidence shows that while the main rotor's proximity can benefit a bottom-blade-forward tail rotor in the vortex-ring state, it is detrimental to a bottom-blade-aft-rotor. This is dramatically illustrated in Figure 9-7 which plots pedal position vs. sideward-flight speed for the Cheyenne with the two directions of tail-rotor rotation.

The original bottom-aft direction was chosen to avoid batting gravel forward into the missile pods on the Cheyenne's wings during ground operation. But pilots found the pedal displacement going left-ward from hover was both unstable and excessive. So the direction was reversed and the bad control characteristics were eliminated.

This problem was not unique to the Cheyenne. It also affected early versions of Bell's UH-1 Huey and AH-1 Cobra. Bell subsequently reversed the rotation's direction by simply swinging the tail rotor to the vertical stabilizer's other side. It thus changed from a pusher to a tractor installation, greatly improving the flying characteristics of those two helicopters. Since there was no blade twist, Bell could use the same tail-rotor blades.

Apparently the Mil design office in the Soviet Union experienced similar problems since it, too, moved the tail rotor on the Mi-24 Hind, during the production run of the "A" version.

Right sideward flight

Figure 9-7 also shows that reversing the tail rotor's rotation on the Cheyenne even improved right side-ward flight. In this case, the tail rotor was mounted on the horizontal stabilizer's left end so that it led the main rotor in left sideward flight but followed it in right sideward flight.

It seems possible, at least in right sideward flight, that the main rotor's tip vortices were being sucked into the tail rotor. With the original rotation, these vortices produced a swirl that subtracted from the dynamic pressure at the tail-rotor blades. But when the direction was reversed, the swirl added to the pressure.

Experience with helicopters that had trouble in a right-quartering wind reinforce this observation, as shown in Figure 9-8. Here the main-rotor tip vortices start to roll up and aim directly at the tail rotor.

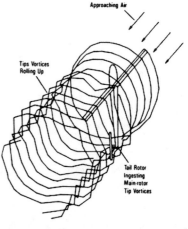

Figure 9-8 Conditions in Right Quartering Flight

In this case, flight was made easier when the tail-rotor blade closest to the main rotor goes up.

The effect is even evident in hover-at least close to the ground. Figure 3-9 reveals the results from tie-down tests of the Cheyenne. At this low height, the main-rotor wake was spreading and undoubtedly covered much of the tail rotor. The curves show that the main rotor decreased the thrust at a given tail-rotor pitch angle when the tail rotor rotates with the bottom blade going aft, but increased thrust when the tail rotor's rotation is reversed. Since the flow field was the same in both cases, the change must have been due to difference in effective dynamic pressure caused by the vorticity in the main rotor's wake.

Effects of tail-rotor rotation appear consistent but are still a puzzle. Coming up with equations that correlate theory with test data remains a challenge to aerodynamicists.

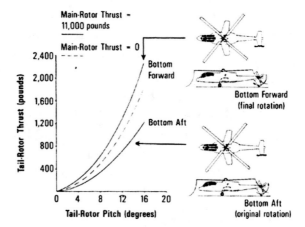

Figure 9-9 Effect of Main Rotor Thrust and Direction of Tail Rotor Rotation for Tied Down Cheyenne

10 Downwash Patterns

If we could see air, we would all be a lot smarter. This is especially true for the helicopter engineer who has to wonder about the mysterious things that happen to his aircraft whether it be in the fields of performance, flying qualities, loads, vibration, or noise. Some of these mysterious happenings can be traced to the rotor wake and to the presence in it of tip vortices.

They come and they go

Vortices are formed at the blade tips as the air tries to go from a high-pressure region to a low-pressure region (bottom to top). This sets the air to spinning, leaving long whirlpools where each blade tip has passed. Airplane wing tips do the same thing.

Wing-tip vortices trailing behind an airplane tend to retain their energy and their relative position for several minutes. Their primary mutual interference on each other slowly forces them downward, corresponding to the wake's induced velocity.

Smaller vortices or even vortex sheets are also generated wherever or whenever lift changes, but they are never as influential as those generated at the wing's tip or the rotor blade's tip. Since theoretically a vortex cannot have an end, each blade-tip vortex must be accompanied by a corresponding blade-root vortex. These have a less-direct—but still significant—effect than tip vortices.

Rotors are different

Tip vortices from rotor blades are not as long lasting as those behind wings. But because they "loiter in the neighborhood," they have more effect. In hover, they generate the induced velocity and go down with it, but stay close enough together to interact and entwine in knots.

This happens even during model tests in a quiet room where under the best of conditions only three or four healthy vortices can be traced down into the wake. As they mutually destroy each other, they induce local fluctuations in the entire wake, even at the rotor disc itself.

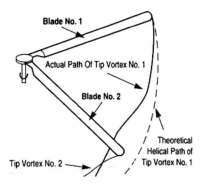

Figure 10-1 Blade-Tip Vortex Interference Effect In Hover

Additionally in many cases, the vortex shed by one blade stays near the rotor's plane until the next blade comes along (Figure 10-1). When this happens, that blade's aerodynamics will be affected.

Specifically, the local angle of attack will change depending on the strength and proximity of the vortex. Since both positive and negative changes are possible, a portion of the blade may find itself either being stalled or producing less than normal lift, thus changing its aerodynamic characteristics from what would be expected.

Observations indicate that this is a fluctuating phenomenon that seems to affect only a part of the rotor at any one time, probably as a function of the unevenness in the induced flow field at the rotor disc. As evidence of this, rotor tests made on whirl towers produce time histories of thrust and torque that vary in a random manner.

A nearly ideal test

One of the most carefully controlled whirl-tower tests that I know of was done with a six-foot-diameter rotor at the NASA Ames Research Center. Ray Piziali and Fort Felkner reported on that test.

As part of a study of rotor-wake recirculation effect, the rotor was tested on an outside whirl tower nearly 30 feet above the ground. It was installed upside-down so that its wake went up instead of down to minimize the recirculation due to the ground. Testing was done at night during periods of dead calm.

Even with all of these precautions, time histories of thrust and torque varied randomly (Figure 10-2). The variation in these two parameters was almost 1% from their mean over a time period of almost a minute, and it is not clear that, even with this long time slice, the maximum variations were captured.

Because of the randomness in thrust and torque, the Figure of Merit, which represents hover efficiency, varied almost 1.5%. This magnitude is often used to distinguish between a good rotor and a bad one, and so depending on the instant the performance was recorded, this rotor could have been either.

Is it any wonder that hover performance measured under less-ideal circumstances on a whirl tower produces "scatter of the datter," as illustrated for the Boeing YUH-61A rotor in Figure 10-3?

Calculating hover performance

Besides the difficulty in accurately measuring rotor performance, the not-so-well-understood positioning of the tip vortices and their effect on the induced flow field at the rotor disc also make it difficult to accurately predict hover performance. Even if the flow were rock-steady, its distribution would depend heavily on the actual location of the first several tip-vortex spirals down in the wake.

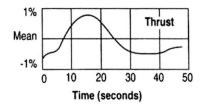

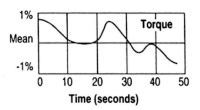

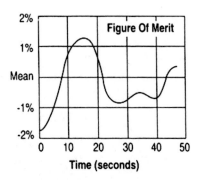

Figure 10-2 Results Of Whirl Tower Hover Test

Trying to calculate these positions has been the subject of much research in the past 20 years. One approach is to use flow-visualization techniques with model and full scale rotors to measure the radial contraction and vertical position of the vortices as a function of thrust, twist, and number of blades.

Then this knowledge is generalized into a method for generating a "prescribed wake." This can be used to analytically produce the induced flow field for performance calculations using the equation known as the Biot-Savart Law.

A more-sophisticated method is that of the "free wake," in which the effect of each vortex in forcing all the others into the final pattern is accounted for theoretically without need of previous knowledge about vortex spacing.

Despite all of the effort in this work since 1960, it has not noticeably increased the accuracy of hover calculations for conventional rotors over those calculations made with the old-fashioned empirical methods developed at the beginning of the helicopter era. This is shown by the correlation of both simple and sophisticated calculating methods with Boeing whirl-tower data of a CH-47B rotor (Figure 10-4).

The main argument for the sophisticated methods is that they do a better job with heavily loaded rotors, such as tail rotors, tiltrotors, and unconventional rotors that have sudden changes in twist, taper, or sweep.

Forward flight, the difference

In hover, the mutual destruction of the tip vortices under the rotor disc is important in that it produces a gusty inflow. That is not the case in forward flight. Here the rotor quickly moves away from the vortices it has produced so that their tangling behind in the "far wake" has little effect on the induced flow at the rotor.

However, the fact that a blade passes close to healthy tip vortices that were just laid down is important. It means that the blade sees local changes of angle of attack regularly, instead of randomly as in hover.

In forward flight, the blade tip traces out a figure called a "cycloid" as the result of both translation and rotation. Figure 10-5 shows the track of the vortices laid down in still air and not distorted by their mutual interference—an effect we will get to later.

The number of possible close encounters of a blade with a tip vortex from another blade, or even one deposited by itself on a previous revolution, depends on the number of blades and the ratio of forward speed to tip speed or the "tip-speed ratio".

With data from a specially instrumented helicopter, the influence of vortex proximity can be seen in the measured lift distribution. Figure 8-6 shows this for a station 85% of the radius out toward the tip for one

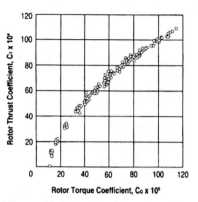

Figure 10-3 Typical Whirl Tower Data Scatter ForBoeingYUH-61ARotor

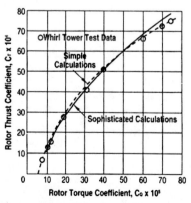

Figure 10-4 Correlation Of Calculating Methods With Whirl Tower Test Data

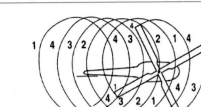

a. Tip Speed Ratio = 0.2–Moderate Speed

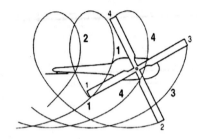

b. Tip Speed Ratio = 0.4–High Speed

Figure 10-5 Vortex Trails In Forward Flight

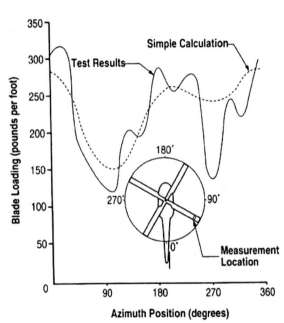

Figure 10-6 Test And Calculated Blade Loading

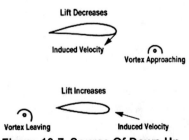

Figure 10-7 Source Of Down-Up Pulse

blade of a four-bladed Sikorsky H-34 (S-58) rotor at a tip-speed ratio of 0.2 (about 77 knots).

Also shown is the lift, calculated using a simple method that ignores the presence of discrete tip vortices. It may be seen that for this case, there are important variations on both the advancing and retreating sides. This would be expected looking at the density of the vortices in these regions (Figure 10-5a). In particular, on the advancing side there is a distinct down-up characteristic. Figure 10-7 shows the relative positions of the blade and the vortex that explains this.

Despite this wide variation in blade loading, the average is the same. Most rotor aerodynamicists will accept that the simple method is satisfactory for computing overall rotor performance, even though it does not do a good job on the local distribution of airloads.

Changes at high speed

At higher speeds, the helicopter tends to outrun the vortices laid down on the retreating side as illustrated by the vortex pattern for the tip-speed ratio of 0.4 in Figure 10-5b. Thus the effect on the retreating side diminishes, but not so much on the advancing side where the density is still high.

In addition, another strange thing has been seen from high-speed data. On the advancing side near the tip, instead of the pulse being down-up, it is up-down. This is explained by the fact that in high speed flight, rotors carry a download on their advancing tips and leave a tip vortex that rotates opposite to the normal one.

The influence of a vortex on a blade is most pronounced where they lie nearly parallel to each other. Here the entire blade is influenced at once, instead of being subjected to the relatively local influence when it and the vortex are more perpendicular to each other.

Whether they are parallel or perpendicular can be seen by replotting Figure 10-5 in a different format. This involves looking at the pattern as it would be seen by an observer standing on the hub and sighting along blade No. 1. Figure 10-8 shows the location on the blade that would be directly above each of the tip vortices generated by blades of a four-bladed rotor.

It may be seen that at about a 60° azimuth angle, which is on the advancing side in the right-rear quadrant, there is a tendency for the blade's outer portion to line up parallel with a series of vortices. Here the interference is significant because a large part of the blade is affected rather than just a local segment.

Wake distortions

Calculations that attempt to account for the effect of the nearby tip vortices must also account for their actual position at the time the blade passes. This is done with a "free-wake" analysis that uses vortex theory in the form of the Biot-Savart Law to calculate the wake's distortion as influenced by all of the vortices in it.

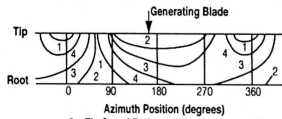

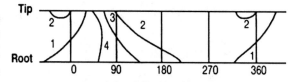

Figure 10-8 Location Of Vortices For Blade No. 1

A comparison of non-distorted and distorted wakes at a fairly low forward speed is given in Figure 8-9. Doing the free-wake analysis by computer takes too long to be used routinely in the blade-load calculation, so various schemes to specify a "prescribed wake" have been developed using the results of a few free-wake computations as guides.

Even with the most sophisticated of these procedures, those working in the field are not satisfied with their ability to match test data. But perhaps it is not too critical. The argument for developing advanced methods for calculating blade loadings is that if these were known very accurately, the designers could use the knowledge to either design lighter blades or blades with longer fatigue lives.

In real life, however, it is not the loads in straight and level flight that cause most of the fatigue damage, but loads during maneuvers when the rotor is being used to pitch or roll the helicopter or to make it go up or down. These loads would be relatively easy to estimate if you had a good crystal ball to predict the pilot's control actions. Since we hear of few in-flight blade failures, I conclude that the designers are doing OK even if they do not exactly know what the vortex-caused loadings are.

Blade slap and rocky road

In most forward-flight conditions, the blades do not actually strike the vortices. But when they do, this produces very large and rapid changes in pressure just like you do in slapping a table with your hand instead of pressing on it.

This is one source of the type of impulse noise commonly called "blade slap" or, as noise experts call it, "blade-vortex interaction" (BVI). It is most often heard when rolling into a turn or during low-power descents, which give the blades the chance to pass through the vortices in the wake.

Even if a helicopter has a smooth ride in other flight conditions, it will probably be rough in at least one: the landing flare. This is because at some point, the blades will actually strike tip vortices left, by previous blade passages. Figure 10-10 shows how the relative positions of the rotor and its wake change during the landing maneuver. Descending at low power, the air is approaching the rotor from below and carrying the wake up and above the tip-path plane.

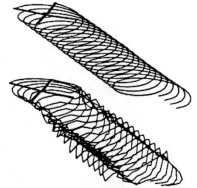

Figure 10-9 Undistorted And Free-Wake Distorted Vortex Patterns At Low Speed

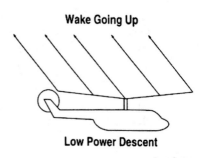

Wake Going Up

Low Power Descent

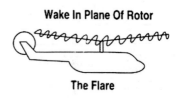

Wake In Plane Of Rotor

The Flare

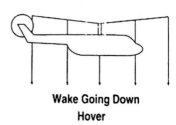

Wake Going Down
Hover

Figure 10-10 Changes In Flow Conditions During Landing

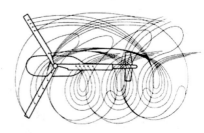

Figure 10-11 The Vortex Wake Of A Three-Bladed Rotor

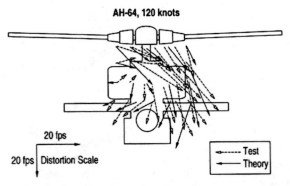

AH-64, 120 knots

20 fps

20 fps | Distortion Scale

- - - - Test
—— Theory

Figure 10-12 Rotor-Induced Velocities At Aft End Of Fuselage—Theory Vs. Test

As the helicopter comes to a hover, the wake must be directed down below the rotor. It follows, therefore, that at some point between these two flight conditions, the wake is right in the rotor's plane. And because of the low forward speed, there are many vortices to run into. For these reasons, it is not unreasonable to expect that tip vortices will be responsible for high levels of vibration in the landing flare.

Theory and practice

Since the Renaissance, one feature of science has been a continual leapfrogging of theory and practice. Sometimes one leads the way and then the other.

The steam engine, for example, had been a practical source of power long before the theory of thermodynamics explaining how it worked was developed. On the other hand, Einstein came up with his Theory of Relativity years before the physicists had a way of experimentally confirming its validity. So it is with some aspects of helicopter aerodynamics.

Regardless of whether theory or practice comes first, it is eventually backed up by the other. This backup is called "correlation" and it is necessary to raising the confidence in either the theory or the test results, so they can be used in the design of a new helicopter.

Two examples of the correlation process as applied to the flow field induced by a helicopter rotor were presented at the 1988 American Helicopter Society forum.

One case in which practice led theory concerned the effect of the main-rotor's wake on the flow field at the helicopter's tail rotor and stabilizing surfaces. When this became important during the AH-64 Apache's development, a wind-tunnel test of a model with a powered rotor indicated that the flow is quite chaotic at this location.

It was my feeling then, after plotting the data, that no computational procedure would ever be able to duplicate the test results. I am happy to say that a recent study has given evidence that I may have been too pessimistic.

As discussed above, blade-tip vortices are important in defining the flow field at the rotor blades. But those generated by the blade's inboard portions are important in their effect on the flow behind the main rotor's center portion, where the stabilizers and the tail rotor are located (Figure 10-11).

By accounting for all the vorticity in the rotor wake, rather than just that due to the tip vortices, a new program has been developed by Todd Quackenbush and Don Bliss for computing the flow characteristics in the wake behind the rotor.

Shown in the comparison of theory and practice in Figure 10-12, their program captures most of the characteristics of the chaos. These include the lack of downwash behind the rotor's reverse-flow region on the left side, and the start of the wake's rollup on the right.

However, even with such a complete wake representation, the program must still use a number of simplifying assumptions and approximations to represent this very complicated situation. And the investigators admit that there are still some areas of inexact correlation. But you will have to agree that they have made a good start.

Measuring the almost unseen

The first investigators of autogyro aerodynamics realized that theoretically the induced flow into the rotor disc should be non-uniform. So, like Einstein, they developed equations to represent this non-uniformity even though they had no real experimental evidence that it existed.

Since then, experimenters have used both flight test and wind tunnels to measure the rotor-wake characteristics with various degrees of accuracy, and the theoreticians have refined their equations to more nearly represent what the experiments show.

Recently several test facilities have made great strides in accuracy by using "laser velocimeters" to measure flow velocities. The scheme is about as close as you can get to painting a molecule of air red and then following it where it goes.

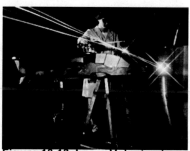

Figure 10-13 Laser Velocimeter At NASA Langley

At one of these facilities, the Army Aerostructures Directorate at the NASA Langley Research Center, the laser equipment is mounted in a traversing rig just outside the open test section of the 14-by-22-foot Subsonic Wind Tunnel (Figure 10-13).

The equipment generates four narrow beams that intersect each other where the velocities are to be measured. The volume of air where the beams intersect is about a centimeter long and 0.2 millimeters in diameter (smaller than a pencil lead and about a ⅜ inch long).

The laser light in this volume is reflected from tiny plastic particles, which have been introduced into the tunnel upstream of the test section, as a very fine powder. The reflected light is captured by the receiving optics package, which uses a sophisticated electro-optical device to compute the local vertical and streamwise velocities.

Compared to other ways of measuring velocity, such as using various probes, the laser velocimeter has the advantage. It does not affect the velocities by its presence and—especially for rotors and other moving equipment—it will not cause damage if it gets too close.

The ultimate in this technology is still sometime in the future. In such an application, the laser would be mounted on the rotor hub and turn with it. Thus it would survey the instantaneous flow just in front of one blade

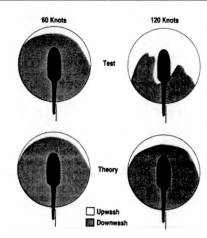

Figure 10-14 Rotor Upwash/ Downwash Boundaries Theory Vs. Test

to measure the true induced-velocity environment that is encountered in flight.

Danny Hoad, Susan Althoff, and Joe Elliott have used the present NASA wind-tunnel equipment to measure the instantaneous induced-velocity field just above the disc of model rotor with a six-foot (1.8-m) diameter. They have compared the averages of these velocities with those calculated using several well-accepted theoretical methods.

Their analyses shows that at a moderate forward speed (tip-speed ratio of 0.15 corresponding to about 60 knots for a typical helicopter), the induced-velocity pattern is similar to those predicted by almost all the theoretical methods, in that just the forward edge of the disc is subject to upwash with the rest having downwash.

At twice that speed, however, the measured upwash extends over almost all of the front half of the disc; much further back than any of the existing computational theories would indicate. The comparisons (Figure 10-14) are now giving the theoreticians something to think about.

11 Rotor Upwash

The term "rotor downwash" is so widely used by helicopter aerodynamicists that it might come as a surprise to find that the rotor also produces upwash. In certain cases, this has an important influence on performance and flying-qualities characteristics.

One place the rotor produces upwash is along the leading edge of the disc in forward flight. This can be seen in wind-tunnel tests by using smoke to make the airflow visible. The source of this region of upflow can be related to a similar phenomenon on a wing.

Figure 11-1 shows a wing that theoretically can be replaced by three vortices: One being the "bound vortex" placed at the quarter-chord of the wing and the other two being the "trailing vortices" shed at each wing tip. Because of its shape, this system is sometimes called a "horseshoe vortex system".

The strength of the bound and trailing vortices is known as "circulation," and its value is proportional to the lift of the wing divided by the forward speed.

Thus for a given lift, the slower the airplane flies, the stronger the circulation must be to generate that lift. Each vortex acts like a little cyclone and induces velocities in the air all the way around it.

Behind the wing, the effects of the bound and trailing vortices combine to induce a downwash, but in front of the wing, the bound vortex induces an upwash.

A rotor too

Using this analogy, a rotor can be roughly thought of as a wing with a horseshoe vortex pattern that induces downwash in the rear portion of the disc and behind the rotor, but produces upwash not only ahead of the rotor but also in some portion of the forward part of the disc. Figure 11-2 shows this pattern as measured in a wind tunnel by a laser velocimeter at two different forward speeds.

Rotor aerodynamicists have long recognized the existence of this fore-and-aft non-uniformity of the induced velocity and have generally made allowance for it in their analyses. For simple computations, a form of

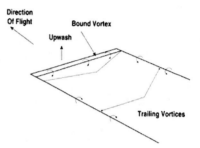

Figure 11-1 A Wing And Its Horseshoe Vortex System

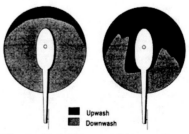

Figure 11-2 Measured Upwash And Downwash Regions

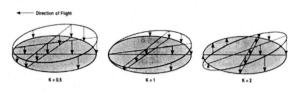

Figure 11-3 Induced Velocities Used In Analysis

induced velocity such as shown in Figure 11-3 has been used.

This was first suggested by H. Glauert, a noted British aerodynamicist working with autogyros in the 1920s. With this scheme, at the center of the rotor, the induced velocity is equal to that computed from "momentum theory" which can be related to the circulation of an airplane wing. The slower the helicopter flies, the higher this quantity is. From this value, the induced velocity is sloped linearly so that it is less at the leading edge of the disc and more at the rear.

However, the exact slope constant (K) has never been completely agreed upon. Many rotor aerodynamicists (including me) have used a slope constant of 1; this places the induced velocity at the extreme forward portion of the disc at zero for all forward speeds. The large region of upwash shown in Figure 11-2 probably should make us increase the value we use for the slope constant.

Getting more complicated

Other, more sophisticated methods for computing the distribution of induced velocity are now available, but they require long computer times to use them. Thus, the simple "Glauert distribution" is still used for most performance and stability analyses, where it generally gives good correlation with test results.

The more complicated systems are used in predicting blade loads and noise, but even these are perhaps not on solid ground. A study using several of them showed that they could correlate with the measured induced-velocity patterns for the low-speed case of Figure 11-2, but did not predict the extent of the upwash region for the higher speed.

One result of this non-uniform induced-velocity pattern is that it affects the lateral cyclic pitch required to control the rotor's flapping. Since the downward induced velocity in the front part of the rotor disc is less than it is at the rear, the local angles of attack on the blade passing through the front would normally be increased. This would produce high lift, which would make the blade want to flap up 90° later on the retreating side (the left side for American helicopters). Pilots sometimes explain this lateral flapping as due to "transverse flow" since the flapping trend is similar to that which would be caused by a side wind.

To trim for level flight, the pilot must use left stick to keep the helicopter from rolling to the right. This is especially true at low forward speeds where the average induced velocity is high, making large differences between the fore and aft portions of the disc.

Figure 11-4 shows the lateral stick displacement required to achieve lateral trim for a typical helicopter. The low-speed portion is almost entirely due to the non-uniform induced-velocity pattern. But at high speeds, the effect of rotor coning takes over.

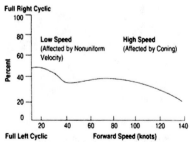

Figure 11-4 Lateral Cyclic Stick Position Required For Level Flight

The lateral-trim phenomenon is not much of a problem on conventional helicopters, but it did become a "show-stopper" on two experimental helicopters.

One of these was the coaxial Sikorsky Advancing Blade Concept (ABC) aircraft. As first designed, it did not have enough cyclic-control power to compensate for the induced-velocity variation; as a result, an accident occurred. Analysis of the flight-test data revealed that the non-uniformity reached a peak at about 60 knots. At this speed, the upwash at the front of the disc was equal to the momentum value, and the downwash at the rear was three times the momentum value, corresponding to a slope constant (K) of 2.

The control system had to be modified by doubling the cyclic-pitch travel before the program could continue.

The second experimental program that ran into this problem was with a circulation-control rotor installed on a Kaman UH-2. Here again, the aircraft ran out of control power at low speeds, and never could make the transition to high speed.

Vibration

Another effect that can be traced to upwash is the vibration felt when starting into forward flight from hover. While going through the so-called "transition regime," the upwash over the front of the disc sends the blade-tip vortices that are generated in this region up rather than down (Figure 11-5). Further back, they fall under the influence of the downwash over the rear of the rotor, where they come down and pass through the rotor disc.

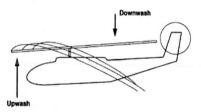

Figure 11-5 Path Of Forward Rotor-Tip Vortices In Transition

When the following blades strike these little whirlpools of air, they are subjected to large transient changes in local angle of attack. This in turn produces sudden changes in air loading, leading to "transition vibration."

Of course, transition vibration is worse when decelerating from forward flight to hover. For a considerable period of this maneuver, the flow up through the rearward-tilted rotor disc cancels out the normal downwash over the rear of the disc, and many tip vortices stay around long enough to be struck by the following blades. Hence, the "rocky road" description of this vibration problem.

At speeds above the transition speed, the vibration is less. The upwash is lower and the rotor plane is tilted forward with respect to the flight path, so that the vortices tend to go below the rotor.

And on the advancing tip

Although the vortex-interference problem due to upwash tends to go away as the helicopter flies faster than its transition speed, it may come back later at high speeds due to another consideration.

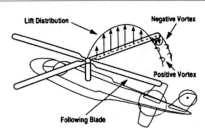

Figure 11-6 Double Tip Vortex At High Forward Speed

For good hover performance, most rotor blades are twisted so the tip has a lower pitch than the root. However, this is usually detrimental to high speed performance, where the advancing tip may actually be working at negative angles of attack and producing negative lift (Figure 11-6).

As the lift goes from some positive value to zero inboard of the tip, a conventional trailing vortex is generated. Further out, at the very tip, a secondary vortex with the opposite—or negative—rotation is produced, inducing upwash inboard of itself. This, thus, tends to keep the main vortex from sinking out of the way of the following blades.

Aerodynamicists at Boeing Helicopters have identified the resulting blade-vortex interaction produced by this double vortex system as a major source of high-blade loads and resulting rotor vibration. This is because large local changes in angles of attack are produced on the following blades. And this provides just one more illustration of the helicopter law: "Whatever helps hover hurts high speed, and whatever helps high speed hurts hover."

Another upwash

In forward flight, most of the rotor is producing positive lift and a resulting downwash. However, the portion known as the "reverse-flow region" on the retreating side is actually "lifting" down and is therefore generating an upwash.

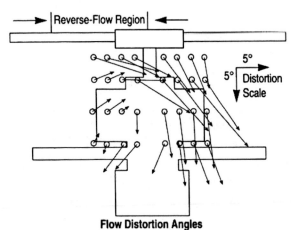

Figure 11-7 Flow Pattern At Tail Of Apache

At very high forward speeds, the performance penalty due to the negative lift and to the drag produced—because the backward-facing airfoil may be stalled—is significant. Even at lower speeds, the upwash left behind the reverse-flow region may affect the trim conditions.

As far as I know, this was first observed on the McDonnell Douglas Apache. As the pilot trimmed the aircraft at various sideslip angles, he found that the requirement for longitudinal stick displacement was not symmetrical. The reason for this was that the rotor downwash at the horizontal stabilizer was weaker behind the retreating—left— side than behind the advancing side. The wake survey made at the empennage location on a powered wind-tunnel model of the Apache illustrates this phenomenon (Figure 11-7).

The effect in flight is shown in Figure 11-8. When the helicopter is sideslipped to the left (wind coming in the pilot's left ear in an open cockpit), more of the stabilizer is in the region of weak downwash behind the reverse-flow region. As a result, the stabilizer download is less than in non-slipping flight. This produces a nosedown

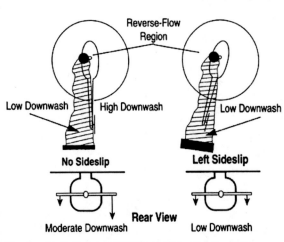

Figure 11-8 Source Of Pitch-Sideslip Coupling

moment that the pilot must compensate for with aft stick. Conversely, for a right sideslip, the pilot must hold forward stick.

Another aspect of the upwash behind the reverse-flow region helps explain several accidents. In these, some light object, such as a jacket, fell out of the passenger compartment and instead of going down—as might be expected—was buoyed up by the main-rotor wash until it was entangled in the tail rotor, with disastrous results.

12 Blade Flapping and Feathering

Compared to hover, the big difference in forward flight is obviously the variation in the local velocity that a blade sees as it goes round and round. Figure 12-1 shows the local velocity distributions at four blade positions for a rotor turning counterclockwise. The right-hand position is for the blade going in the direction of flight and so is the advancing blade, while the left-hand position is the retreating blade.

(The direction of rotor rotation has been established purely on ideological grounds. American rotors advance to the *right* but Russian rotors advance to the *left*. European rotors are uncommitted and may advance in either direction.)

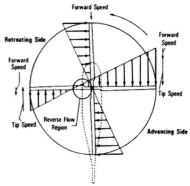

Figure 12-1 Velocity Distribution in Forward Flight

Velocity Distributions

A parameter that uniquely describes the velocity distribution is the tip-speed ratio. This is the ratio of forward speed to the tip speed in hover. It is, of course, zero at hover — but for modern helicopters may be as high as 0.45 at top speed. Figure 12-1 represents a rotor with a tip-speed ratio of 0.30, which is a typical cruise condition (110-to-140 knots, depending on rotor tip speed). The blades over the nose and over the tail have the same velocity distributions as in hover, but the retreating tip is going 30% slower and the advancing tip 30% faster.

Note that some of the blade elements near the hub actually traverse a region on the retreating side where the flow impinges on their trailing edges. This portion of the disc, quite naturally, is known as the reverse-flow region. It is a circle that extends out the retreating side a fraction of the rotor radius equal to the tip-speed ratio. At low speeds, it is hidden in the hub and blade attachment hardware —but at maximum speed it may extend as much as 45% of the way out to the tip.

Flapping Blades

The asymmetry of the velocity distribution is a dominant factor in the forward flight of helicopters and accounts for most of the differences between helicopters and airplanes.

Compared to the wing of an airplane, the rotor of a helicopter appears to be, at best, only loosely attached to its aircraft. While this is a key feature of the rotorcraft's success, it is also the source of some unique stability and control characteristics.

This idea of flexibly attaching rotor blades to the hub was developed in the 1920's as an engineering fix. The inventor was the Spanish designer of autogyros, Juan de la Cierva.

Cierva learned early the meaning of the cliché, "back to the drawing board," when his first attempted takeoff resulted in the autogyro rolling over and thrashing its blades into toothpicks. He hadn't even reached takeoff speed. Hence, the Spaniard rebuilt his craft, but the second try was no better than the first. (At this point, Cierva had not added much to rotary-wing technology but he had advanced the art of Spanish windmills. Don Quixote had mounted a horse to tilt with windmills but Cierva had one that tilted all by itself.) The rolling-over effect was a mystery to Cierva, since he had successfully flown a rubber-band powered model that exhibited absolutely no tendency to roll.

Finally, while watching an opera, Cierva had a flash of inspiration. Suddenly, the difference between his full-scale autogyro and the model was apparent -- it was the difference between rigidity and flexibility.

On the aircraft, he had obtained structural integrity by rigidly bracing the blades with struts and wires —just as airplane wings were braced in those days. On the other hand, the model had been built with flexible rattan spars, since in model size this type of construction was adequate.

As the rigidly braced autogyro taxied forward, the airspeed seen by one blade changed during each revolution. On the advancing side, the airspeed was higher than on the retreating side. This unbalance is shown in Figure 12-2.

Since each blade had the same pitch setting and, therefore, angle of attack, the difference in velocity produced more lift on the advancing side than on the other—thus generating an unbalanced rolling moment. But on the model, the flexible rattan spars could bend up and down. Thus the advancing blade, which had high lift, began to flap upward. As it did, it was also being rotated toward the nose, where the local velocity was reduced to its mean value. The retreating blade was undergoing a similar experience, except that it was flapping downward as it rotated to a position over the tail. This flapping produced a climbing condition on the advancing side, decreasing its angle of attack and the opposite effect on the retreating side.

Flapping equilibrium came when the model's rotor had an angle of attack just sufficient to compensate for the airspeed at each point in the revolution. In this

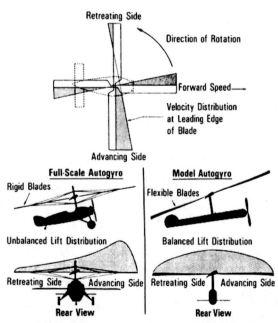

Figure 12-2 Comparison of Cierva's Full-Scale and Model Autogyros

equilibrium condition, the model rotor was tilted fore and aft and the lift distribution was balanced.

When the opera was over (was it *The Flying Dutchman?*), Cierva knew what he had to do— add flexibility to his full-scale rotor. The simplest solution, he decided, would be mechanical hinges allowing the blades to flap—just as they had on the model In flight, the blades were kept extended by centrifugal forces and coned slightly upward by the lift.

With this technological breakthrough, Cierva was able to fly his autogyro and begin a long line of development that resulted in most present-day helicopters having mechanical flapping hinges.

Lead and Lag

The invention of flapping hinges, however, did not cure all of Cierva's rotor riddles. In his early blades, he was plagued with high stresses and structural failures resulting from drag and inertia loads on each blade revolution.

He figured that if one hinge in a blade was good, two would be better, so he incorporated a vertical hinge such that the blades could move back and forth in the rotor-disc plane without generating stresses in the roots. These are now known as lead-lag hinges and, in conjunction with the flapping hinges, produce the fully articulated rotor systems used today.

For dynamic reasons, two-bladed rotor systems generally do not have lead-lag hinges. These rotors are designed with enough structure in the blade root and hub so that the stresses can be kept to safe levels. On most of these rotors, the flapping hinges are in the form of a single teetering hinge that allows the two blades to flap as a unit.

Recently, some rotor designers have developed hingeless rotors in which the actual mechanical hinges are replaced by flexible portions of the hub or blade. These flexible, hingeless rotors flap almost as much as if they had hinges—just as Cierva's model did — and can be treated as if hinged. There is a temptation to refer to such systems as rigid rotors, a term that falls trippingly off the tongue, but, in light of their actual flapping characteristics, it is misleading.

The fact that the blade flaps up over the nose after experiencing high velocity on the advancing side is a consequence of its being a dynamic system in resonance. By definition, a system in resonance is one that receives a periodic exciting force at the same frequency as the system's natural frequency. A child being pushed in a swing is a good example.

The natural flapping-motion frequency of the blade hinged at the rotor-hub center is exactly equal to its speed of rotation. This means that no matter what the rotor speed, a blade hinged at the center of rotation will always be in resonance. As a consequence, it will have its maximum response 90° after its maximum periodic excitation.

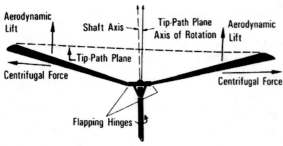

Figure 12-3   Balance of Forces on the Rotor

Once the rotor—is established in an equilibrium position, there are no accelerating forces causing it to flap with respect to the axis system referenced to the tip-path plane as shown in Figure 12-3. (To justify use of this axis system instead of one referenced to the shaft, think of the blade hinges as a universal joint. The shaft, then, is simply a means of keeping the rotor disc turning and the angle it happens to make with the disc is immaterial to the dynamics of the disc itself.) Any change in flight conditions that causes a lift imbalance will result in the rotor flapping to a new equilibrium position.

Lateral lapping

Besides the fore-and-aft, or longitudinal, flapping caused by the unequal velocity distribution of forward flight, the rotor also has a tendency to flap laterally. Lateral flapping, like longitudinal flapping, is initiated by asymmetric airloads. In this case, the asymmetry is on the blades over the nose and the tail. It is due to coning. Figure 12-4 shows that in forward flight, the coning causes the blade over the nose to be affected by an upward component of forward velocity.

This initial asymmetry of vertical velocity produces a corresponding asymmetry of angle of attack and airload distribution that causes a maximum response 90° later and, thus, a lateral-flapping displacement that is maximum upward on the retreating side.

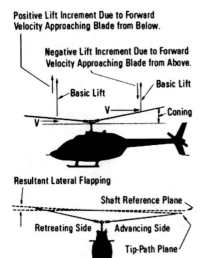

Figure 12-4   The Source of Lateral Flapping

Ride Quality

One additional note on blade flapping: This characteristic is also responsible for a helicopter behaving better in gusty air than an airplane. The fact is, the rotor blades flap individually in response to the gusts — allowing the rest of the helicopter to have a relatively smooth ride, whereas an airplane's wing transmits its unsteady loading directly into the fuselage. This gust-alleviation feature has been demonstrated by flying same-sized helicopters and airplanes in formation through gusty air. Recording instrumentation showed that the helicopter had the smoother ride. The difference can be compared to that of an automobile with independent wheel suspension compared to one with wheels rigidly attached to the frame.

Rotor Control

On the early autogyros, the rotor was simply a lifting device and was allowed to flap in order to balance the lifting forces on the advancing and retreating sides. Roll control was obtained with ailerons on stub wings and pitch control by a conventional elevator. Neither method, however, was very effective at low speed.

Following his early successes, Cierva developed a means of obtaining direct control by tilting the entire rotor on a gimbal with respect to the shaft. With this scheme, pitch and roll control were generated by tilting

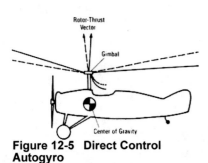

Figure 12-5   Direct Control Autogyro

the rotor-thrust vector as shown in Figure 12-5 to provide a moment with respect to the aircraft's center of gravity.

Cyclic Pitch

Direct control was satisfactory for small auto-gyros (and is still in use today on some), but as the machines became larger, the force required to tilt the rotor became so high that control was difficult. At this stage, a means of rotor control called cyclic pitch was developed.

In this system, practiced almost universally today, the pilot cyclically changes the pitch of the blades about the feathering axes by tilting a mechanism known as a swashplate. This system is shown in Figure 12-6. In operation, if the swashplate is perpendicular to the rotor shaft, the blade angle is constant; but if the swashplate is tilted, the blade pitch will go through one complete feathering cycle during each revolution.

If the pilot pushes the stick forward, the swashplate is tilted forward. Since the pitch arm from the blade is attached to the swashplate 90° ahead, the blade has its pitch reduced when it is on the right-hand (advancing) side and increased when it is on the left-hand (retreating) side. When the blade is over the nose or the tail, the forward tilt of the swashplate has no effect on the blade pitch. Cyclic pitch can be used for two purposes: to trim the tip-path plane with respect to the shaft, and/ or to produce control moments for maneuvering. In the first case, the pilot can mechanically change the angle of attack of the blades by the same amount as the flapping motion would have, thus eliminating the flapping. This adjustment can be used to eliminate all of the flapping, or to leave just enough to balance pitching and rolling moments on the aircraft—such as those due to an offset center of gravity.

In the second case, the pilot deliberately introduces an unbalanced lift distribution to tilt the rotor for maneuvering. For example, if the helicopter is hovering and the pilot wishes to tilt the nose down to go into forward flight, he pushes the stick forward, causing the swashplate to tilt down in front. The pitch of the blade on the right side is decreased as the left side is increased. The resultant lift unbalance accelerates the right-hand blade down as it moves toward the nose and the left-hand blade up on its way to the tail. The rotor flaps down over the nose and up over the tail— tilting the rotor-thrust vector forward to produce a nose-down pitching moment about the aircraft's center of gravity as shown in Figure 12-6. The procedure is similar if the pilot wishes to pitch the nose up or to roll in either direction.

Cockpit Controls

With the cyclic stick held in his right hand, the pilot tilts the swashplate. The rigging is arranged so that the swashplate's axis follows the tilt of the stick. With his left hand, the pilot operates the collective stick, which changes the pitch on all of the blades simultaneously by raising and lowering the entire swashplate.

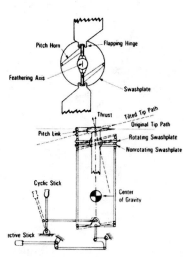

Figure 12-6 Functional Drawing of Cyclic and Collective Control System

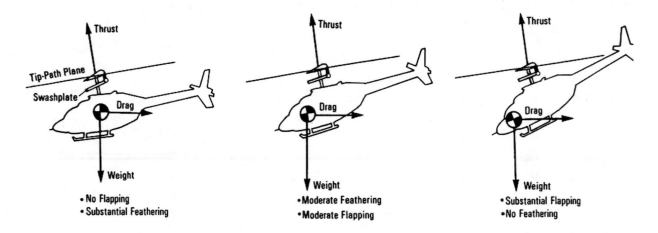

Figure 12-7 Illustration of Equivalence between Flapping and Feathering

Operation of the collective with the left hand was established in the early single-seat helicopters and followed the usage on most single-seat airplanes, where the stick is held in the right hand and the engine controls are operated with the left.

The pilot also has foot pedals that control the collective pitch of the tail rotor. Tail rotor thrust is used to balance the torque of the main rotor and to make changes in heading. Tail rotors are either built with flapping hinges, or as flexible hingeless rotors.

Helicopter designers did not break with airplane tradition on the direction of rudder-pedal motion. The pedals move in the same anti-sled manner adopted by the Wright Brothers—push the right pedal to turn to the right. This despite the fact that Igor Sikorsky had successfully tested the other rigging on one of his early airplanes and later wrote in his autobiography, "I still believe it would be a better method of arranging the directional control of a plane, in spite of the fact that the generally accepted way is the opposite."

Equivalence of Flapping and Feathering

An important concept in rotor analysis is the equivalence of feathering and flapping. As far as the blade is concerned, its angle of attack with respect to the tip-path plane is the only thing of importance. Figure 12-7 shows a helicopter in forward flight at a constant speed, but with three different trim conditions as might be achieved with three different CG positions—or with an adjustable horizontal stabilizer. Assuming that the fuselage lift and drag are the same in each case, the rotor-thrust vector and hence the tip-path plane attitude will be the same. The angle of attack of a blade element on the retreating side is shown for illustration.

In the first case, the tip-path plane is perpendicular to the shaft — so there is no flapping, but feathering is used to obtain the correct blade angles of attack. In the last case, there is no feathering but nose-up flapping is used to achieve the same result.

The middle case is in between, where both feathering and flapping are being used to trim the helicopter. The blade sees a 1° change in nose-up flapping as giving the same angle-of-attack change as 1° of feathering achieved with a nose-down swashplate tilt, thus illustrating the equivalence of feathering and flapping.

Although we have been looking at only the retreating blade, the same argument can be made for the blade at any point of rotation.

The use of cyclic pitch makes it possible to eliminate the flapping hinges in a hingeless-rotor system. If a rotor with hinged blades is trimmed with cyclic pitch so that the tip-path plane is perpendicular to the shaft—as in the first case in Figure 12-7—then it's possible to freeze the flapping hinges with no change to rotor conditions, since there was no hinge motion in the first place. This and eliminating the lead-lag hinges by using sufficient structural material will convert a fully articulated rotor into a hingeless rotor.

13 Effects of Rotor Flapping

The way a helicopter rotor flaps is the most important factor in both stability and control. Stability is the tendency for a system to *remain as is* — and differences in the level of stability are illustrated by the increasing skill required to master a tricycle, a bicycle, and a unicycle. Control, on the other hand, is primarily a *measure of the accelerations a system can generate*. For example, imagine the increasing difficulty in docking a rowboat, a cabin cruiser, and an aircraft carrier.

When considered in the light of these definitions, blade flapping can contribute to both the stability and the control of a helicopter. If flapping occurs as a result of changes in flight conditions while the pilot holds his controls fixed, then it is a stability characteristic. But, if it results from pilot action, then it is a control characteristic. In both cases, the effect is primarily felt as a moment about the aircraft's center of gravity.

The two factors that contribute to this moment are shown in Figure 13-1. They are the tilt of the thrust vector — normally perpendicular to the tip-path plane — and the hub moment due to flapping-hinge offset. Rotors without a flapping-hinge offset obtain all of the effect of flapping from the tilt of the thrust vector. These rotors are generally placed high above the CG to maximize this effect for control purposes.

Hub moment from offset flapping hinges can be visualized (as in the illustration) as a couple generated by centrifugal forces on the blades on opposite sides of the rotor. The hinge offset allows the rotor to be located close to the fuselage. These rotors also have the advantage of being able to produce control moments even at very low values of rotor thrust— such as in zero-G maneuvers.

They have a disadvantage, however, in that any adverse stability characteristic due to flapping is magnified. For very large offsets, care must be taken to avoid tipping over on the ground with inadvertent control motions.

Stability characteristics due to flapping are those associated with changes in shaft attitude with respect to the initial flight path, rates of pitch or roll, and changes in velocities. Flapping characteristics can be explained on the basis that at the flapping hinges (or at the effective

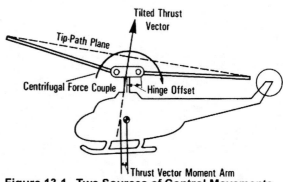

Figure 13-1 Two Sources of Control Movements

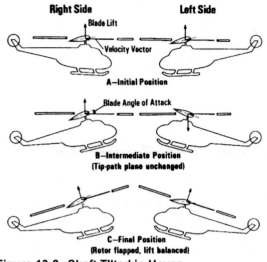

Figure 13-2 Shaft Tilted in Hover

hinge in the case of a hingeless rotor), the summation of moments produced by aerodynamic, inertial, and centrifugal forces must be zero.

Both stability and control characteristics are essential to the pilot's perception of the overall handling qualities of his helicopter, so we will now look at how these factors affect the machine under various conditions.

Shaft Tilted in Hover

If the rotor shaft is tilted while the aircraft is in hover, aerodynamic forces will be generated forcing the tip-path plane to align itself perpendicular to the shaft. The sequence of steps leading to this is shown in Figure 13-2.

First, there is the tilt of the shaft alone as the rotor disc acts as a gyroscope and remains in its original plane. However, since blade feathering is referenced to the shaft, the angle of attack of the right-hand blade is increased and that of the left-hand blade decreased by the same amount.

This causes the rotor to flap until it is perpendicular to the shaft, where it will again be in equilibrium with a constant angle of attack around the azimuth and the moments will be balanced. This alignment is very rapid, usually taking less than one revolution following a sudden tilt. Because of this, the flapping motion in hover has practically no effect on the stability of the helicopter in terms of holding a given attitude.

Shaft Tilted in Forward Flight

If the shaft is tilted laterally (rolled) in forward flight, the effect is the same as it is in hover— the tip-path follows the shaft and the flapping with respect to the shaft remains unchanged. However, if the shaft is tilted longitudinally (pitched), the non-uniformity of velocity distribution produces a different situation.

Figure 13-3 illustrates this with a rotor that, for simplicity's sake, starts from a condition of zero lift on the advancing and retreating blades. Following a, sudden nose-up tilt, the immediate result is the same as in hovering: the advancing blade receives an increase in angle of attack and the retreating blade receives a decrease —producing an unbalanced lift that causes the tip-path plane to flap nose up. In forward flight, however, when the blade flaps up until it is perpendicular with the shaft, the forces are not yet balanced.

This unbalance is due to the forward-flight velocity vector. The airflow coming at the machine as a result of its forward motion modifies both the local velocity and

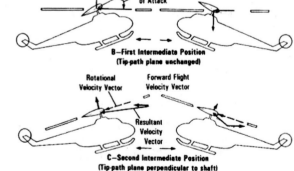

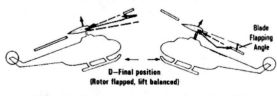

Advancing Blade   Retreating Blade

Figure 13-3 Shaft Tilted in Forward Flight

the local angle of attack on the advancing and retreating blades. Both blades have positive angles of attack, with the angle on the retreating blade actually being greater than on the advancing side, as you see in Figure 13-3C. The aerodynamic lift on the retreating blade is less than on the advancing blade, because the lift of a blade is proportional to the product of the angle of attack and the square of the resultant velocity.

This causes the rotor to flap past the perpendicular to the shaft to a more nose-up position where the forces are in balance, as shown in Figure 13-3D. The magnitude of the excessive flapping is approximately proportional to the square of the forward speed. The result is negative rotor angle-of-attack stability, since the aft flapping generates a nose-up pitching moment about the CG that tends to cause a further increase in the shaft's angle of attack.

Horizontal Stabilizer

To compensate for this undesirable characteristic, the helicopter designer follows the airplane designer and adds a horizontal stabilizer. Since the effectiveness of the stabilizer is proportional to the square of the forward speed, it will correct for the rotor instability at all speeds, once it is sized for a given flight condition.

A stabilizer is not an absolute necessity, however, and most pilots can cope with an unstable aircraft—just as they can learn to ride a unicycle. Many helicopters designed before 1960 had inadequate or no stabilizers but they were considered successful. Actually, they were following a trail blazed by the Wright Flyer— an unstable but controllable aircraft.

Pilots, of course, prefer their aircraft to be both stable and controllable but given the choice between high stability and high controllability they will choose the latter, since it allows them to escape tight situations that even a stable aircraft occasionally encounters.

Another effect of a longitudinal shaft tilt in forward flight is an increase in lateral flapping along with the change in rotor coning. For the nose-up tilt just described, the rotor thrust increases and with it the coning and the lateral flapping. This change in lateral flapping is also proportional to the square of the forward speed but is somewhat less than the change in longitudinal flapping. The resultant rolling moment is a source of cross-coupling, where a change in pitch results in a roll. This particular cross-coupling effect doesn't work both ways, since a change in roll angle will not result in pitch. Airplanes are largely free from this problem, with the exception of some high-powered propeller-driven models.

Shaft with angular velocity

If the helicopter is pitching or rolling due to a wind gust or a pilot's control pulse, the rotor will flap such as to reduce the rate of pitch or roll. That is, it will act as a damper. This damping is very helpful to the pilot in mollifying the effects of gusts or overenthusiastic control motions.

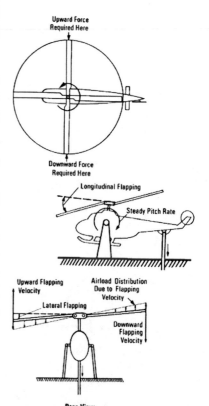

Figure 13-4 Flapping Due to a Steady Pitch Rate

The damping is produced because the tilt of the tip-path plane lags behind the motion of the shaft by an amount proportional to the rate of pitch or roll. Figure 13-4 illustrates this effect by using a helicopter mounted on a trunnion. If we force the model to pitch up at a steady rate, the rotor disc will follow the shaft — since it has an equilibrium position to achieve once the pitching motion stops.

The flapping angle by which the rotor lags the shaft produces flapping velocities on the left and right sides. These, in turn, generate unbalanced aerodynamic moments that precess the rotor disc as a gyroscope. (That is, they have their maximum effect 90° later.) The faster the rate of pitch, the more the rotor must lag to produce a sufficient precessional moment. Similarly, a rotor with a high inertia will lag more than one with a low inertia. The resulting blade flapping produces a nose-down pitching moment on the helicopter that resists the forced pitching motion and is, therefore, a damping moment. The flapping that produces the damping effect is also accompanied by some flapping cross-coupling in the other axis. For example, during a nose-up pitching motion, the blades over the nose and over the tail initially have different angles of attack caused by the vertical velocity associated with the pitch rate. This difference in angle of attack is automatically compensated for by the blade flapping down on the left side and up on the right side enough to produce flapping velocities at these two blade positions equal and opposite the velocities due to the pitch rate.

The production of both a lateral and a longitudinal flapping by a pure pitch rate is another source of cross-coupling. This effect is a two-way street, since either pitch or roll rates will produce flapping in the other axis. For most rotors, the cross-coupling flapping is approximately half the primary damping flapping.

Change in Forward Speed

The flapping caused by a change in forward speed was explained in our discussion of de la Cierva's rattan-sparred autogyro model. The amount of this flapping is approximately proportional to the product of forward speed and rotor thrust. If the individual blades have no lift to start with, the increase in forward speed will produce no flapping.

The rearward tilt of the rotor produces a nose-up pitching moment with respect to the helicopter's center of gravity as shown in Figure 13-5. This change in pitching moment due to a change in forward speed is known as speed stability or static longitudinal stability and is one of the most important differences between a helicopter and an airplane. The airplane has no corresponding change in pitching moment with respect to speed.

This difference can be illustrated with an airplane model mounted in a low-speed wind tunnel. If an adjustable elevator is used to trim the pitching moment to zero at one tunnel speed and fixed angle of attack, the moment will remain zero for any other tunnel speed. A helicopter

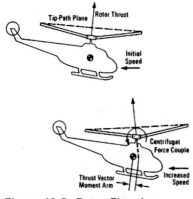

Figure 13-5 Rotor Flapping Caused by Change in Forward Speed

model in a similar test, however, will generate a pitching moment due to rotor flapping as the tunnel speed is changed.

In free flight, the change in longitudinal flapping with increasing speed is stabilizing since it produces a nose-up moment causing the helicopter to pitch up and slow down to its original speed. A manifestation of positive speed stability is the requirement for the pilot to move the cyclic stick forward to keep the helicopter trimmed as he increases speed.

In some cases, the effect of a horizontal stabilizer carrying positive lift (or the interference effects of the front rotor on the rear rotor of a tandem helicopter) can overpower the natural speed stability of the rotor and produce negative stability. This happens when an increase in speed with the controls held fixed produces a nose-down pitching moment, causing the helicopter to go into a dive as the speed and nose-down moment increase. With negative speed stability, the pilot will push the stick forward to accelerate to a new speed but when he finally trims at that speed, the stick will be further aft than when he started. This characteristic is undesirable from a flying-qualities standpoint but pilots who can learn to ride unicycles can learn to handle such problems.

Since the flapping due to a change in speed is actually generated by a change in the asymmetry of the velocity distribution at the blades, the effect can also be produced by holding forward speed constant and changing rotor speed.

Normally, helicopters fly with almost constant rotor speed but in case of a sudden engine failure, the rotor speed initially decreases while the forward speed remains about the same. The result is an increase in the asymmetry of the velocity distribution with corresponding nose-up flapping. This helps the pilot make the safe transition to an autorotative condition where air must be coming up from below the rotor disc rather than from above as in normal flight.

Change in sideslip angle

In addition to the flapping effects due to changes in forward speed, the rotor also responds to changes in sideslip angle, since blade flapping is produced by conditions referenced to the flight path rather than to whatever orientation the fuselage might have at the time.

Imagine a helicopter in forward flight with no sideslip and the rotor trimmed so that the tip-path plane is perpendicular to the shaft. If the flight direction is suddenly changed (Figure 13-6) so that the helicopter is flying directly to the right without changing the fuselage heading or control settings, the blade over the tail becomes the advancing blade and the one over the nose the retreating blade. Since the cyclic pitch no longer corresponds to trim conditions, the rotor will flap down on the helicopter's left side because of the asymmetrical velocity distribution — thus producing a rolling moment to the left.

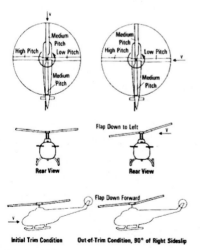

Figure 13-6   Effect of Sideslip on Rotor Flapping

In practice, sideslip angles are less than the 90° used for illustration, but the trend is the same — the helicopter tends to roll away from the sideward velocity. This is the same characteristic found on airplanes with dihedral (both wings slanted up) and is known as the positive dihedral effect.

It is a desirable characteristic that helps the pilot. With negative dihedral, a sideslip would tend to roll the aircraft into an ever-tightening spiral dive. Positive dihedral manifests itself during flight as a lateral stick displacement required in the direction of the sideslip to stabilize the aircraft.

The rolling moment due to dihedral is also accompanied by a pitching moment. Again going back to the case of the helicopter flying directly to the right, the blade pointing in the direction of flight was originally the advancing blade and had a low pitch in the zero-sideslip trim condition. It still has a low pitch and thus will cause the rotor to flap down over the nose, producing a nose-down pitching moment.

Similarly, during flight to the left, the blade pointing in the direction of flight has a high pitch and will cause the rotor to flap up over the tail— also producing a nose-down pitching moment. Thus, steady sideslip in either direction requires aft stick displacement, an effect that does not exist on an airplane.

Somewhat surprisingly, if the same analysis is made on a rotor turning clockwise when viewed from above, the pitching moment direction is unchanged — nose-down for sideslip in either direction. This pitching effect is not always observable in flight, since other pitching moments may be generated by changes in airflow conditions on the horizontal stabilizer and tail boom as they move out from behind the fuselage during sideslip.

Cyclic Pitch Change

For a rotor with blades hinged at the center of rotation, a 1° change in cyclic pitch in hover will result in a 1° change in flapping a quarter of a revolution later. This is because the rotor's stable condition is with no cyclic-pitch variations in respect to the tip-path plane without regard to the relative position between the shaft and the tip-path plane. Thus, the rotor flaps just enough to cancel out the initial cyclic input and return, to its initial configuration with respect to the tip-path plane. This is one result of the equivalence between flapping and feathering.

If the rotor has a flapping-hinge offset, the maximum flapping will be at somewhat less than 90°. This phasing means that the helicopter will be subjected to some roll motion during a maneuver when the pilot is calling for only pitching motion by moving his stick straight fore and aft. This is known as acceleration cross-coupling, since it occurs while the pilot is attempting to generate an angular acceleration in either pitch or roll. Because the phasing is constant for a given rotor, it is sometimes compensated for by rotating the control system orientation such that pure stick motions automatically generate the appropriate anti-cross-coupling cyclic-pitch corrections.

For example, a fore-and-aft stick motion would produce maximum cyclic pitch on the right side slightly ahead of the lateral axis so that the flapping would be purely aligned with the longitudinal axis.

Following a change in cyclic pitch from trim, the helicopter soon reaches a steady rate of pitch or roll as the angular acceleration is reduced to zero by the inherent damping of the system. The helicopter rapidly stabilizes at a steady angular rate where the cyclic pitch input is exactly equal and opposite to the flapping that would have occurred if the angular rate had been imposed by an external agency.

Since in this condition, no acceleration and thus no unbalanced moment exists, the tip-path plane is perpendicular to the shaft (ignoring the small damping effects of the airframe). This is yet another illustration of the equivalence of feathering and flapping.

The net result is that cyclic pitch is a rate control. That is, a steady cyclic-pitch change from trim produces a steady rate of pitch or roll. This is the same on airplanes, where a steady aileron deflection from trim produces a steady rate of roll and a steady elevator deflection from trim produces a steady rate of pitch.

The cross-coupling flapping due to a steady externally caused pitch or roll rate discussed earlier manifests itself as a control requirement when the pilot is trying to generate pitch or roll rates with his cyclic. For example, during a steady pitch-up maneuver, the pilot must hold some right stick as well as aft stick to prevent roll to the left.

This rate cross-coupling effect is the same whether the rotor has hinge offset or not, because the rotor disc has no physical flapping with respect to the shaft during a steady angular rate maneuver.

Changes in the helicopter's response to cyclic-pitch changes during forward flight due to the asymmetrical velocity distributions are mixed. From hover to maximum speed, typical changes are a 25% increase in pitch acceleration response to a given cyclic input but a 10% decrease in the maximum pitch rate due to that same cyclic pitch. Roll acceleration response is essentially unchanged but roll rate is increased 10%.

Collective change in forward flight

Blade flapping is induced if the collective pitch is changed in forward flight. For example, if the collective pitch is increased, both the advancing and retreating blades receive the same increase in angle of attack, but the advancing blade—having higher velocities —develops more additional lift than the retreating blade and nose-up flapping results.

Normally, the collective is changed gradually during flight and the pilot corrects the out-of-trim flapping with almost subconscious movements of cyclic. One of the results is a modification of the cyclic trim position as a function of forward speed.

From hover to approximately the speed for minimum power, the collective pitch required for trim decreases, thus causing the tip-path plane to want to tilt forward and to require an aft-cycle motion to keep the helicopter in trim. This effect may be larger than the aft flapping caused by the increase in forward speed and, as a consequence, the trimmed stick position may initially move aft or have an unstable gradient. At high speeds, where collective pitch is increasing, the gradient will almost always be stable.

The collective pitch is not always moved gradually. Following a power failure, the pilot will usually quickly lower the collective to minimize the initial loss of rotor speed. In forward flight, this results in a nose-down flapping and pitching that must be compensated for by aft-cyclic movement.

At high forward speeds, the aft-cyclic motion required becomes large and some pilots have found that it is preferable not to lower the collective initially, but instead to perform a rapid nose-up cyclic flare, putting the rotor into an autorotative condition with the air approaching from below. Because of the energy that can be extracted from the air-stream at high speeds, this maneuver can be done without losing excessive rotor speed.

The resulting high-speed cyclic flare slows the helicopter down while letting it gain some altitude. When it slows to a normal autorotative forward speed, the collective is lowered and a standard autorotative landing is made.

14 Blade Stall

If you ask airplane pilots what happens when a wing stalls, you get a fairly consistent response. They describe the dropping of the nose, loss of aileron control, and the subsequent falling off to one side or the other.

If, however, you ask helicopter pilots what happens when a rotor stalls, you get more varied and less confident answers. Rotor stall is not as straightforward a phenomenon as wing stall.

Even from wind-tunnel tests, where rotors can be carefully observed and measured, a complete understanding has yet to be produced. Small wonder then that when Frank Harris—once with Vertol but later at Bell Helicopter Textron—published a classic study on the subject he entitled it: "Blade Stall—Half Truth, Half Fiction."

Why do blades stall?

Let's start at the beginning. A rotor going through the air edgewise has both an advancing and a retreating blade, so while one blade travels fast through the air, the other travels slow. For the slow, or retreating, blade to generate its share of the rotor thrust, it must operate at high angles of attack.

Logically, as the rotor flies faster or is asked to develop more and more thrust in a maneuver, the required blade angles on a portion of the retreating blade will come up to and then exceed the airfoil's stall angle.

If this condition is duplicated in a wind-tunnel test of a blade section, the results will agree with thousands of other wind-tunnel tests: as the angle of attack is increased beyond its stall value, the lift will stop rising, drag will increase, and a nosedown pitching moment will develop. This all results from the boundary layer's separation from the airfoil's top surface.

Does this really happen on a helicopter's retreating blade? Well, yes and no.

A surprising conclusion reached when researchers first compared test results with theory was that the rotor seemed to be more tolerant of stall than expected. The rotor continued to gracefully produce thrust in test

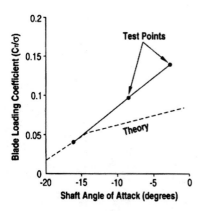

Figure 14-1 Static Stall Characteristics

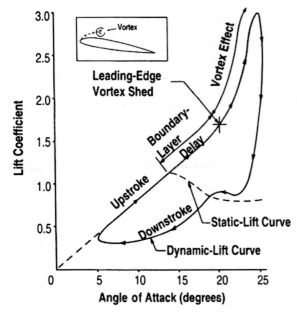

Figure 14-2 Overshoot Of Lift Due To Rapid Increase In Angle Of Attack

conditions where the theory said it should be in deep trouble (Figure 14-1).

Part of the explanation involves what is now known as "dynamic stall." In most wind-tunnel tests of airfoil sections, the angle of attack is increased slowly enough to give flow conditions plenty of time to adjust

On a blade in flight, however, the angle of attack may be changing very rapidly. The blade is going quickly from low angles of attack to high as it goes around the azimuth, and it is being affected locally by discrete tip vortices left by preceding blades.

Special wind-tunnel tests in which the angle of attack is quickly changed, either as a "ramp" or as an oscillation, have given some insight into what must happen on a rotor blade.

First, the boundary layer on the top surface takes a little time to react to the high angle of attack, and delays the stall until a higher angle is reached. Then, when the boundary layer does separate, it does so in the form of a vortex that sheds at the leading edge, and rolls back across the blade. This temporarily causes a low pressure that produces even more lift (Figure 14-2).

Thus for a short time, the "stalled" airfoil can generate up to twice as much lift as would be expected based on the results of a conventional airfoil wind-tunnel test. This short time may be about as much as is required for the blade to pass through the retreating side and reach a less-demanding environment over the tail.

Oh, those other effects!

The rotor may not exhibit much lift stall, but it does suffer from those other effects—high drag and high nosedown pitching moments.

High drag creates a requirement for increased power to maintain the flight condition. This may be a problem if the engine is already putting out nearly all it can.

Usually a bigger effect is the nosedown pitching moment acting on a long, limber rotor blade. At first, this effect might be considered beneficial—the nosedown twisting relieves the angle of attack, and thus might force it down below the stall limit.

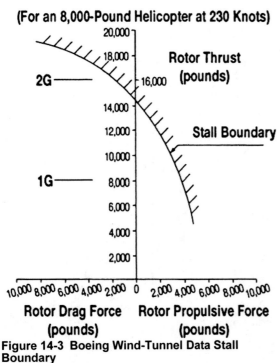

Figure 14-3 Boeing Wind-Tunnel Data Stall Boundary

But there's a catch: not every blade on the rotor will act in exactly the same way. This is because blade structure varies, and one blade is influenced by the turbulent wake left by another. Therefore, each blade starts doing its own thing, and the rotor goes out of track, with a high vibration being felt throughout the helicopter.

This is especially evident if the blade and control-system stiffness is high enough so that, following the initial nosedown twisting, each blade springs back up into the high angle of attack condition, where it again stalls, leading to a recurring cycle before leaving the retreating side.

This is often called "stall flutter." When it causes an out-of-track condition while pushing out the forward-speed envelope, the pilot will report that he has reached the maximum speed based on "roughness."

Other responses

Not all helicopters exhibit stall flutter. On most two-bladed Bell helicopters, for example, the control system is flexible enough so that only part of the flutter cycle occurs before the blade safely exits the high angle-of-attack region on the retreating side.

On these helicopters, the nosedown blade twisting simply produces an equivalent aft cyclic-pitch input. The rotor responds by pitching up without a significant out-of-track condition.

Thus, instead of losing lift in a stall, as a wing would do, these rotors actually gain lift. The blades over the nose and tail boom are put into a condition that produces sufficient additional lift to balance any lift lost on the retreating side.

Since a stall affects only a small portion of the rotor, the pilot should be able to control pitch and roll with his cyclic stick. This is true even in deep stall, and whether or not the helicopter exhibits an oscillating stall flutter. Wind-tunnel tests confirm this. They show that a model rotor can be trimmed out and controlled at speeds well above the current helicopter speed record even at thrust values representing 2 Gs or more.

Figure 14-3 shows the limits of one test in the Boeing wind tunnel reported in the 1970s. I converted the nondimensional test results into full-scale dimensional quantities for illustration.

As shown, the limit on thrust depends on whether the rotor is pulling the helicopter along, as in forward flight, or whether the helicopter is pulling the rotor along, as in autorotation.

In autorotation, the air comes from the bottom and the angle-of-attack distribution over the rotor disc is much more benign than in high-speed level flight. Also, any stall on the retreating side is confined to the blade's inboard portion. There, it can do less damage than nearer the blade tip, as in level flight. The angle-of-attack patterns in Figure 14-4 illustrate this difference.

This condition of high-angle inboard doesn't just apply to autorotation, however. It is also attributed to a pitch up maneuver in which cyclic pitch is used to tilt the rotor noseup to provide high load factors. In this condition, of course, the requirement for additional thrust and higher

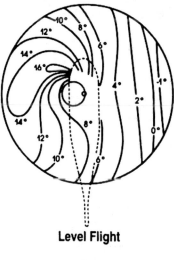

Level Flight

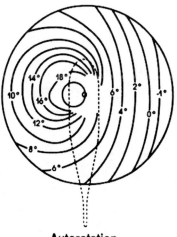

Autorotation

Figure 14-4 Angle-Of-Attack Distribution

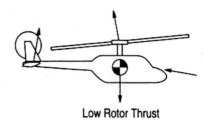

Low Rotor Thrust

More Nose-Up Pitching Moment

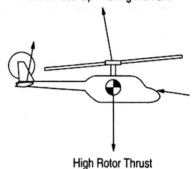

High Rotor Thrust

Figure 14-5 Effect Of Rotor Thrust In Reaction To Up-Gust

angles of attack all over the rotor may nullify the beneficial effects of moving the stall region from outboard to inboard.

Another pitch up source

A rotor that reacts to blade stall primarily by fluttering may not pitch up greatly because of stall. But under certain conditions it may pitch up because of another factor.

As illustrated in Figure 14-5, a pitch up "imitation" can occur. Here's what happens: When subjected to an up-gust, the rotor will flap back about the same amount, no matter how much thrust it develops. With high thrust, however, the destabilizing noseup moment developed around the center of gravity will be greater than at low thrust. The horizontal stabilizer, on the other hand, will always produce the same amount of stabilizing nosedown moment.

Thus, at high load factors, the tail's stabilizing influence may be overpowered by the rotor's destabilizing influence. And if subjected to an up-gust, the helicopter will pitch up or "dig in" all by itself. This can fool a pilot who believes he pitched up due to blade stall.

One can demonstrate this effect in flight by executing turns at higher and higher bank angles at the same airspeed. (The helicopter may have to descend if it doesn't have enough power to hold altitude.)

For moderate bank angles—and the associated load factors—the pilot must hold aft stick to keep the nose up. Airplane pilots call this "stick-force per G" or "maneuvering stability." Reportedly, acrobatic and fighter airplanes pilots don't mind low or even negative maneuvering stability since it makes their aircraft maneuver more easily. On airplanes, this is usually the result of a far-aft center-of-gravity position.

Back to the helicopter high-bank-angle-turn test:

Because the rotor's stability characteristics change as rotor thrust is increased by tightening up the turn, the pilot will find that he needs less and less aft stick to increase the load factor.

Figure 14-6 shows typical test data. The critical condition is when the curve on the graph goes flat and starts to bend over. Up to that point, the helicopter has positive maneuvering stability. But after it, the helicopter wants to pitch up by itself, and the pilot will have to counteract it with forward stick.

Incidentally, if you noticed words indicating uncertainty such as "may," "probably," and "usually" in the above discussions, it is because blade stall is still not well understood. There are still questions to be answered.

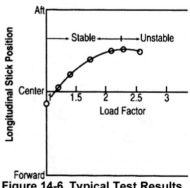

Figure 14-6 Typical Test Results For Wind-Up Turn

15 The Search For A Stable Helicopter

Hovering a helicopter over a spot is more difficult than almost any other vehicle-guidance task. That's why inventors have sought means to give pilots a more-stable platform.

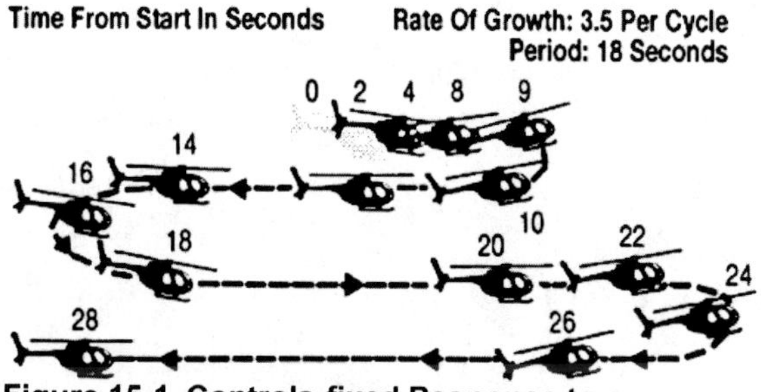

What makes hovering so difficult? One reason is that more integration—in a mathematical sense— is required. In most vehicles, the operator is primarily interested in governing speed, which he does by generating accelerations and then integrating them once to obtain the desired velocity.

Moving a helicopter to a precise position, however, requires one more level of integration to convert velocities into displacements. As car drivers, we do a similarly demanding task only occasionally; for instance, when we must parallel-park in a spot that is just barely long enough. Hovering a helicopter precisely over a spot is like doing parallel parking continuously.

The helicopter task, though, is even harder. Unlike a car, the helicopter has six degrees of freedom, instead of only two, and the hovering helicopter is unstable. It wants to start an ever-increasing oscillation, as shown in Figure 15-1. The pilot must suppress this if he is to do a good job.

Because of the relatively long natural period, and the time lag associated with the double integration to get position from acceleration, the pilot must anticipate the response to his control inputs by several seconds. For the new pilot learning to hover, this is one of the primary sources of difficulty.

The inventors tried

Not much can be done to relieve the degree-of-freedom complication, but a number of inventors have attempted to solve the instability problem. Three of these systems are shown in Figure 15-2.

Arthur Young, the developer of the original Bell helicopter, used models as research tools. After much experimentation, he came up with the idea of the stabilizer bar, which tended to remember where the horizon was

Time From Start In Seconds   Rate Of Growth: 3.5 Per Cycle
Period: 18 Seconds

Figure 15-1 Controls-fixed Response to a Disturbance in Hover

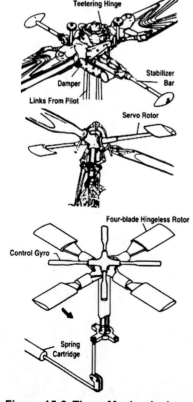

Figure 15-2 Three Mechanical Means For Obtaining Stability

Figure 15-3 Art Young And His Stable Helicopter

and controlled cyclic pitch to keep the rotor tip-path plane fixed in space.

His electrically powered model (Figure 15-3) was very stable and easy to fly, with a solenoid-operated control system responding to signals from the operator. When he actually scaled the model up to full-scale, however, he found that the aircraft responded sluggishly to the pilot's commands; that is, it was too stable! Young had found the dilemma that has faced many aircraft designers—the necessity to tradeoff between stability and control.

(The Wright brothers had succeeded by making their very unstable Flier very controllable whereas other designers, such as Langley, had unsuccessfully tried to fly inherently stable but nearly uncontrollable aircraft.)

Young had to add dampers to his stabilizer bar to make it pay more attention to the helicopter's attitude and less to the horizon before the Bell Model 30 was considered acceptable.

Stanley Hiller used a variation of the stabilizer bar on his designs. The difference was that the damping was achieved aerodynamically with paddles instead of with mechanical dampers. The paddles also provided the means to easily control rotor position by applying cyclic pitch to the rotor blades instead of the entire rotor.

Here again the tradeoff between stability and controllability was demonstrated. By adding weights to the paddles to make them into very effective gyros, stability was greatly improved; non-pilots could get in and hover with just a few minutes of instruction. But, until the weights were removed, no one could do much in the way of snappy maneuvering.

The Lockheed rotor system, shown on the prototype Model 475 (Figure 15-4) was an improvement on both the Bell and Hiller systems (see Chapter 39). In this concept, the marriage of a gyro to a rotor with high effective hinge offset simultaneously provided very good levels of both stability and controllability.

Non-helicopter pilots had little trouble mastering hovering in this aircraft. This prompted one military helicopter pilot to respond, "If you have a bird that any private or general can fly, who needs me?"

Another development was the Kellett Stable Mable. This was a research testbed powered at the tips with hydrogen-peroxide rockets. Gyros much like the ones used at Lockheed provided sufficient stability for hands-off hovering.

Quite surprisingly, the hovering instability illustrated by Figure 15-1 can be traced to the fact that the rotor is above the center of gravity. It follows, therefore, that if the rotor were below, the aircraft would be stable. One application of this was the DeLackner "stand-on" helicopter (Figure 15-5). True, it was stable in a hover, but its obvious operational

Figure 15-4 The Stable Lockheed Prototype

drawbacks limited the machine to the status of an interesting dead-end project.

It's not necessarily so

Even when a helicopter's devices or the geometric arrangement promise stability, there is a little problem. The flying-qualities engineer investigates the stability characteristics by solving for the roots of the "characteristic equation" of the helicopter (a mathematical description of the flying qualities).

If all of the roots are negative, he can say that the machine is stable and could be flown hands-off. If there is at least one positive root, he knows that it is unstable.

Figure 15-5 The Stable DeLackner Helicopter

In the process of solving for the roots, he will find that several are zero, denoting neither stability nor instability so he ignores them. The truth is, however, that these roots are only zero because he cannot write the equations accurately enough.

In the actual flying situation, one or more of these roots may really be slightly positive. This will cause the helicopter to slowly drift away from the initial trim condition. Even those helicopters with good stabilizing systems cannot be hovered over a spot hands-off for more than a few seconds, unless the system includes some sort of a ground reference.

Why don't we see any of these stability-improving systems on today's helicopters? I believe there are two reasons.

First, although learning to hover takes some time, once it is done, pilots thereafter seem to have little trouble with it. You might say it is like learning to ride a bicycle (or if you insist—an unicycle).

Secondly, where very good hover stability is a definite requirement, it can be bought—at a price— by the inclusion of electronic black boxes in the control system. These can range from simple gyros that increase damping in pitch and roll to very sophisticated "hover-hold" systems using radar to accurately fix altitude and position over the ground.

In the 1950s, the development of the inherently stable helicopter was thought to be the first step leading toward using rotary-wing aircraft as a supplement to the family automobile. These helicopters—it was hoped—could be flown by anyone who could drive a car and without the extensive training required to become a helicopter pilot. That market did not develop then but who knows? Maybe it will come with the 21st Century and the quest for the stable helicopter will not have been in vain.

16 Static Stability

If an aircraft has static stability, it will tend to return toward its trim flight condition following any external disturbance. Although this characteristic is necessary for good flying qualities, pilots can learn to fly even unstable aircraft by concentrating on the task. Sometimes a helicopter will have static stability but be unstable dynamically. In this case, it will oscillate back and forth about the trim condition with ever-increasing amplitude. We'll take up dynamic instability in the next chapter.

Speed Stability

During the discussion in the last chapter of what makes a rotor flap, we noted that an increase in speed causes the rotor to flap back, thus producing a nose-up pitching moment. At the same time, the horizontal stabilizer may also be producing either a nose-up or a nose-down moment. The combined effect determines the level of the characteristic known as "speed stability" or, in a less-descriptive term, "static longitudinal stability". If an unintended increase in speed produces a net nose-up pitching moment, the stability is said to be positive -- since, if left alone, the helicopter would pitch up and slow down to its original trim speed.

The degree to which a helicopter possesses speed stability can be determined by a rather simple two-step flight-test technique. First, establish a trimmed steady flight condition and note the position of the cyclic stick. Then, while holding collective pitch constant, dive to a speed 10 knots faster and note the new control position. If the stick is farther forward than it was at the initial trim point, the helicopter is *stable*, since the increase in speed would have caused a nose-up response if the pilot had not held the new speed with forward stick.

The aircraft is *neutrally stable* if the stick is the same distance forward at the final speed and *unstable* if the stick actually ends up behind its initial position. Figure 16-1 shows the possibilities. Note that the proof of the pudding is with collective pitch fixed because this simulates what happens with an inadvertent speed change in normal flight. Going from one level-flight trim speed to another while adjusting collective pitch to

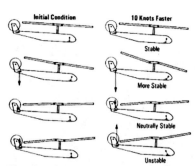

Figure 16-1 Examples of Speed Stability

maintain altitude may show an apparent stability by stick position that does not really exist.

This flight-test technique for measuring speed stability is somewhat different than one employed in a wind tunnel, since in flight the aircraft's angle of attack must be changed during the test to maintain 1 G flight. Thus angle-of-attack stability also has an influence on the results. Had the aircraft been an airplane, the angle of attack would have decreased as the speed went up—but a helicopter may not follow this pattern. At low speeds, it has the same trend as an airplane but at high speeds, the growth of the reverse-flow region with its download requires that the rotor angle of attack be slightly increased to maintain 1G flight.

Although the rotor plays a major role in speed stability, the horizontal stabilizer can be used to increase or decrease the stability level of the helicopter as a whole. Setting the stabilizer incidence to a negative value (nose-down) so that it carries a download will improve the speed stability since an increase in speed will increase the download, thus producing a stabilizing nose-up pitching moment. Note that, for this effect to work, the stabilizer must start out with some download—even though it might hurt performance.

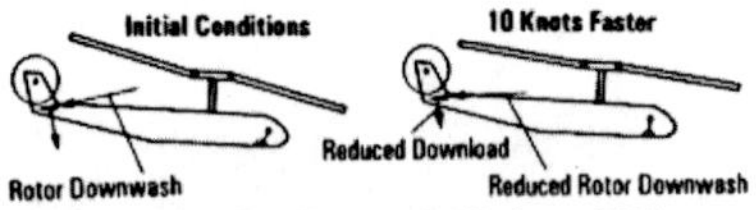

On some helicopters, a significant destabilizing effect is generated by an aerodynamic interference between the wake of the main rotor and the horizontal stabilizer (or the aft rotor on a tandem-rotor helicopter) as illustrated on Figure 16-2. As speed is increased, the downwash behind the main rotor decreases. This causes the angle of attack at the stabilizer to increase (or become less if it starts out negative), thus increasing its lift and producing a destabilizing effect that may be bigger than the stabilizing effect coming from rotor flapping.

Figure 16-2 Destabilizing Effect of Reduced Rotor Downwash

This interference phenomenon has become more acute as both rotor disc loadings and stabilizer areas have been increased over the past 10 *years*. In some cases, the effect has required the help of electronic black boxes to sense changes in airspeed and actuate cyclic pitch or stabilizer incidence changes in the right direction, independent of the pilot's actions.

As a general rule, pilots prefer a level of speed stability that is just slightly positive. Too much stability could result in running out of forward stick travel—or at least putting the stick into an uncomfortable far-forward position at high speeds.

A moderately unstable helicopter is flyable but it has a tendency to wander off its trim speed if not constantly corrected. This may not be much of a problem in normal flight but is generally considered unacceptable during instrument flight when the pilot has other things to think about. It should be pointed out that the change in pitching moment with speed is unique to rotary-wing aircraft and does not normally exist on fixed-wings.

For airplanes, any change in control position while changing speed is due only to the resulting change in angle of attack and not to the change in speed itself. (Except for high-speed airplanes, for which compressibility effects might be significant.)

Angle-of-Attack Stability

Although the helicopter does not share its characteristic of speed-induced pitching moments with the airplane, it does react similarly to changes in the angle of attack. The angle-of-attack stability can be measured directly in a wind tunnel but in flight it shows up indirectly as maneuver stability.

Unlike the stabilizing nose-up rotor flapping due to an increase in speed, the nose-up flapping due to an increase in angle of attack is destabilizing, since it causes a nose-up pitching moment that increases the angle of attack even more. Just as on airplanes, a horizontal stabilizer is used to give positive stability by producing a nose-down moment as the angle of attack increases. The net stability characteristic shows up in flight as the level of maneuver stability, measured by the amount of longitudinal stick motion required to do pull-ups and pushovers or to hold the nose up in a turn.

The degree of maneuver stability can be determined in flight by trimming on a level flight point and then, with collective held fixed, going into a steady turn at the same speed. In this maneuver, the helicopter will be descending and the extra rotor thrust required to hold more than 1G flight will come from the increase in angle of attack. If the stick position after stabilizing is more aft during the turn than at the original trim point, the helicopter has positive maneuver stability. Figure 16-3 shows the possibilities. Had the increased angle of attack come from a gust, the aircraft would have automatically pitched nose-down to return toward its original trim condition.

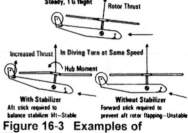

Figure 16-3 Examples of Maneuvering Stability

Balancing Act

A helicopter with negative maneuver stability would require a forward stick displacement to balance the nose-up pitching moment in the descending turn. It would also tend to pitch up or down by itself when flying through gusty air. Flying such an aircraft can be done but it is like riding a unicycle— a full-time job. Too much maneuver stability, on the other hand, will require excessive control motions to do ordinary maneuvering. For this reason, pilots prefer a level that is just slightly stable.

Just as the flight-test procedure used to determine speed stability is affected by angle-of-attack stability, the procedure for determining angle-of-attack stability is somewhat influenced by the beneficial damping effects of the rotor and the horizontal stabilizer as they are subjected to a steady nose-up pitch rate during the turn. These effects result in a slightly aft stick movement that increases the apparent

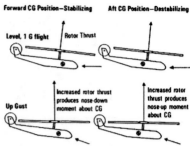

Figure 16-4 Effect of CG Position

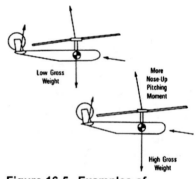

Figure 16-5 Examples of Maneuvering Stability

maneuvering stability of a stable helicopter or, at least, decreases the instability of an unstable helicopter.

The destabilizing effect of the aft rotor flapping is approximately proportional to the square of the forward speed—and since the stabilizing effect of the horizontal tail is approximately proportional to the same factor, the area of the stabilizer selected to provide stability at one speed will be generally suitable for other speeds.

Another significant effect on maneuvering stability is the position of the center of gravity (CG). If it is forward of the rotor, *any* increase in rotor thrust will produce a stabilizing nose-down pitching moment about the CG, as shown in Figure 16-4. On the other hand, with an aft CG position, an increase in rotor thrust will produce an unstable nose-up moment. This is the reason a maximum-allowable aft CG position is specified in the operator's manual. (The forward limit is usually established by the manufacturer either to prevent high oscillatory rotor loads or to provide adequate, aft stick margin for a landing flare or rearward flight.)

The destabilizing effect of aft rotor flapping is made even more destabilizing by raising the gross weight or by maneuvering at above 10 in a steady turn or a pull-up. As shown in Figure 16-5, for the same change in angle of attack, the stabilizer produces the same nose-down stabilizing moment but the tilt of the higher rotor thrust vector produces a more destabilizing nose-up moment about the center of gravity. This can lead to a pitch-up or "dig-in" situation where the helicopter has positive maneuvering stability during gentle maneuvers but goes unstable at some higher load factor.

Bob Weight

Even if the helicopter is not provided with enough inherent angle-of-attack stability to produce positive maneuver stability, some pilots will be satisfied if the stick force, if not the stick position, is aft during the descending turn or during a pull-up—as it is on fixed-wing aircraft. This can be accomplished by mounting a "bob weight" on the stick or on some other appropriate place in the longitudinal control system so that when the load factor is above one, the weight tries to pull the Stick forward against the pilot's hand. If he gives a little, the cyclic input is in the right direction to be stabilizing. The force needed by the pilot to balance the bob weight is measured by "stick force per G". Some recent Army requirements have specified a level of six pounds per G, but many helicopter pilots find this effect to be uncomfortable in maneuvers.

The opinions on this matter appear to be highly influenced by whether the pilot is used to flying fixed-wing aircraft that normally have this characteristic. On a fixed-wing, the increase in stick force is used to warn the pilot not to overload the wings in a pull-up; helicopters develop other clues—such as vibration—that give the same kind of intelligence.

Down Into the Black Hole

Another feature used to describe the level of maneuver stability is the time history of the load factor following a small rearward pull-and-hold motion of the control stick. If the helicopter has negative maneuvering stability, the load factor will continue to rise at an ever-increasing rate. That is, the load-factor time history will be concave upward, indicating that, if held long enough, the helicopter would do a series of ever-tightening loops (until it disappears into a black hole—presumably).

Although a stable helicopter might show an initial concave-upward characteristic, it would soon change to concave downward in anticipation of eventually peaking and starting down. One well-known criterion designed to separate bad helicopters from good helicopters specifies that the load-factor time history must become concave downward no more than two seconds after a pull-and-hold control displacement (as shown in Figure 16-6).

If an airplane lacks angle-of-attack stability, it will not hold a trim condition by itself in gusty air. A helicopter, on the other hand, can fly steadily even if it has a moderate amount of angle-of-attack instability, providing it has some positive speed stability to compensate.

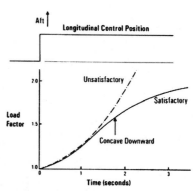

Figure 16-6 Load Factor Time Histories Following an Aft Control Step

Trim Changes

A large horizontal stabilizer that provides a desirable positive angle-of-attack stability can also have an undesirable effect. For example, as shown in Figure 16-7, in a full-power climb the stabilizer has a large negative angle of attack and carries a download but in autorotation the angle of attack is positive and the stabilizer is lifting up. Thus, in climb, the pilot has the stick forward to keep the nose down but, in autorotation, it is aft. A too-large stick displacement between the two flight conditions is considered undesirable.

The problem is especially acute on helicopters with relatively low control power, since a large amount of stick motion is required to balance the pitching moment caused by the change in stabilizer load. Bell designers have used several methods to decrease the stabilizer upload in autorotation. One is to promote early stall by using an upside-down cambered airfoil, sometimes in conjunction with a spoiler. (Once the surface is stalled, of course, it loses most of its effectiveness as a stabilizing device.)

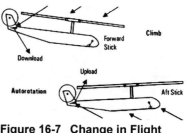

Figure 16-7 Change in Flight Condition

Another solution to the problem is to use a variable-incidence stabilizer with changes commanded by control position. On many of the Bell helicopters the stabilizer is coupled to the cyclic stick but on the Sikorsky Black Hawk and the Hughes Apache, the stabilator is coupled with the collective control so that incidence is decreased as the collective stick is lowered to decrease the upload in autorotation.

Directional stability

Just as an arrow must have directional stability to go where it is aimed, so must an aircraft. Since the tail rotor is an effective device for directional stability, helicopter designs that include one start off with a significant advantage over those tailrotorless designs with tandem, side-by-side, synchropter, coaxial, or tip-driven rotor systems. Even helicopters with tail rotors differ significantly in directional stability characteristics, thus influencing a pilot's opinion of their relative flying qualities.

Slipping Around

Flying with sideslip, like flying rearward, is not a normal flight condition but it can occur during crosswind landings and other maneuvers. The best way to investigate the effect of inadvertent side-slips is to do them deliberately. Of course, it would require an engineering flight test program to accurately evaluate sideslip angle, bank angle, and control positions, but a pilot can still feel the effects of a sideslip, even in an uninstrumented helicopter.

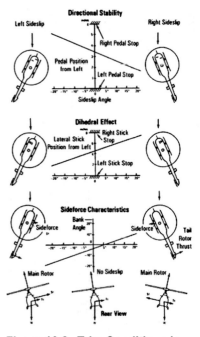

Figure 16-8 Trim Conditions in Steady Sideslips

Figure 16-8 shows the trim conditions in side-slips. The amount of pedal position required to hold a sideslip angle indicates the magnitude of directional stability and tail-rotor control power. While a helicopter may resist flying with sideslip because of high directional stability, only a little pedal displacement may be needed to hold a sideslip if large changes in tail-rotor thrust can be obtained with small pedal movements.

The change in tail-rotor thrust per inch of pedal displacement is usually established by factors that have nothing to do with holding sideslips in forward flight. The maximum thrust capability of the tail rotor is chosen to produce the required antitorque force during a full powered vertical climb with some margin left for maneuvering. The pitch range is dictated on the high end by the right side-ward flight condition and on the low end by the requirement to be able to do right turns in autorotation. Finally, the pedal travel is usually set at about six inches, stop to stop, to make it compatible with how far the pilot can comfortably move his feet.

Dihedral Effect

Besides the change in pedal position during steady sideslips, the change in lateral cyclic control position and roll attitude influences pilot opinion. This change in lateral control position to hold a sideslip angle is an indication of the dihedral effect – an effect both positive and stable if the stick has to be moved to the right when flying in a right sideslip (wind coming in the pilot's right ear in an open cockpit). Positive dihedral results in a roll to the left when the helicopter inadvertently slips to the right—just as with an airplane with both wings tilted up.

On most helicopters, the rotor is producing positive dihedral while the rest of the airframe usually has a negative effect. The result, however, has always been positive on single-rotor helicopters, as far as I know; and a positive dihedral effect is desirable, for it insures dynamic lateral-directional stability. A negative effect will generally result in a divergent spiral dive.

Sideforce Characteristics

The change in roll attitude, or bank angle, to hold a given sideslip is an indication of the sideforce characteristics of the helicopter. As discussed in Chapter 9, tail-rotor thrust to the right requires the main rotor be tilted to the left. The tilt can be made zero in forward flight by side slipping to the right. This develops a sideforce on the fuselage equal and opposite to the tail-rotor thrust. In this condition, the main rotor and the fuselage do not have to be tilted. The more right sideslip required to level up the fuselage, the smaller the sideforce characteristic. A Bell 47 has weak sideforce characteristics— since the fuselage consists of a ball followed by a skinny tail boom, but a Sikorsky S-58 with its big, slab-sided fuselage has strong sideforce characteristics.

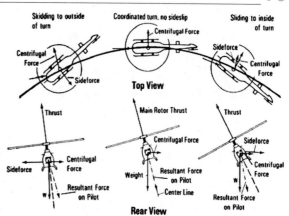

Figure 16-9 Coordinated and Uncoordinated Turns

Strong sideforce characteristics help the pilot make coordinated turns in which, by definition, the sideslip is zero (Figure 16-9). A feature of a coordinated turn is that the aircraft is banked so that the pilot feels the seat of his pants pressing directly down in his seat (except for the slight tilt due to the tail-rotor thrust). As an analogy, this is the same as would be felt by the driver of a car taking a banked highway turn at the speed for which the turn was designed.

A pilot flying a helicopter with strong sideforce characteristics that is slipping in the turn will feel himself forced to the side of his seat—since the bank angle will not balance out his weight and centrifugal force. The bank angle will be too small if be is skidding to the outside of the turn and too large if he is sliding toward the inside.

In response to the resulting lateral force cues, the pilot can use pedal to eliminate the sideslip and Coordinate his turn. This is where the expression, "flying by the seat of your pants" comes from. (A flying-wing airplane has little or no sideforce generated with sideslip and is therefore difficult to fly in coordinated turns by feel alone.)

Single Control Turns

Most helicopters give the pilot the option of making a turn using only pedals or only lateral stick motion. For example, in the first case, right pedal produces an initial sideslip to the left. Dihedral effect will generate a roll moment to the right and the helicopter will enter a right turn. Once the turn is established, the bank angle can be held with pedal alone— although some sideslip will exist (the larger the sideforce and dihedral effects, the smaller the sideslip angle).

The other option is to make a pedal-fixed turn using only lateral stick. When the stick is displaced, the helicopter rolls and starts sliding toward

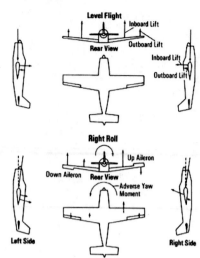

Figure 16-10   Change in Flight Condition

the low side. Directional stability then makes it weathervane into the direction of flight. After the desired bank angle is achieved, the stick is returned to the initial trim position—or nearly so—since to hold it would result in a continuous roll rate. In this case, the sideslip is minimized by strong sideforce and directional stability characteristics. Thus, one consequence of strong sideforce characteristics is that they help coordinate single-control turns.

To hold a steady coordinated turn requires both pedal and lateral stick displacements. In almost all helicopters, the stick must be held *against* the turn and the pedal *with* the turn. (On many airplanes, pedal must be held against the turn because the down aileron on the inside of the turn has more drag than the up aileron.)

During the initial roll into the turn, the yaw may first be in the wrong direction—a condition known as adverse yaw and its source is perhaps easier to see on a wing than on a rotor. Figure 16-10 shows that, compared to level flight, the change in flow direction during a right roll tilts the lift on the left wing aft and lift on the right wing forward to produce a yawing moment to the left.

The same effect also works on the advancing and retreating blades of a rotor, trying to speed it up for right roll rates and slow it down for roll to the left. For a helicopter with a governed engine, the fuel control will respond to these potential speed changes by increasing engine torque in left rolls and decreasing it in right rolls (for American rotation, of course).

Pitch-Roll Coupling

Another nonsymmetrical result of rolling into a turn can be noticed in the pitch-down when rolling left and the pitch-up when rolling right. This difference is caused by the way the rotor flaps when it is being asked to roll the ship.

Let's take a left roll, for instance. To roll, the blade pitch is reduced over the nose and increased over the tail boom with lateral stick. This unbalances the lift forces and the rotor flaps down on the left side, causing the fuselage to follow it. For a given amount of stick displacement, the helicopter reaches a certain steady rate of roll, which occurs when the lift of the fore and aft blades come back into balance because of the change in angle of attack. This change is just equal and opposite to the cyclic pitch the pilot is holding.

For example, when the blade is over the nose, it is on its way down from its high point on the right side to its low point on the left side. In this position, it has its maximum downward velocity with respect to the air. This increases the angle of attack and lift until it matches that of the blade over the tail, which is doing the opposite. At this point, the rate of roll will hold steady and the lift unbalance shifts to the blades when they are out to the sides. On the right, the blade is coming up through the air because of the rolling velocity and sees a decrease in angle of attack that makes it flap down 90° later over the nose. Thus the rotor wants to flap nose-down unless aft stick is used to balance the effect. Obviously, the opposite effect, called "rate cross-coupling," holds for a right roll. Once a steady turn is established, of course, there is no longer any rolling velocity and this particular effect disappears.

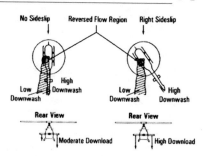

Figure 16-11 Source of Pitch-Sideslip Coupling

Pitch-Sideslip Coupling

An effect noticed on helicopters with big horizontal stabilizers is a tendency to pitch up in a right sideslip and down in a left. This phenomenon can be traced to the asymmetrical distribution of induced downwash in the main-rotor wake.

Wind-tunnel measurements of wake strength have shown that the induced velocity is higher behind the advancing side than behind the retreating side, where the reversed-flow region with its negative lift is decreasing the downwash. Figure 16-11 shows how a sideslip to the right moves the stabilizer into a region of high downwash with a resulting increase in download and a corresponding nose up pitching moment.

Wander

Some helicopters appear to have weak directional stability around trim because the nose is continually "hunting". One widely accepted explanation for this is that the tail rotor and the vertical stabilizer are operating in the turbulent wake of the rotor hub and upper fuselage, but this may not be the whole story. A more likely explanation is that the flow field at the empennage is being affected by the roll-up of the main-rotor tip vortices, as dramatically illustrated in Figure 16-12.

Figure 16-12 Roll-up of Rotor Tip Vortices

The flow near the bottom of the wake, where the tail rotor is usually operating, is directed outwards. Figure 16-13 shows how this effect decreases the stabilizing change in angle of attack (which in this case is sideslip angle) at the tail rotor in a sideslip compared to a no-wake situation. This explanation leads to the conclusion that the tail rotor should be placed as high as possible, putting it in a region where the flow is directed inward by the main-rotor wake. In this situation, the tail rotor should produce more directional stability than in clean air.

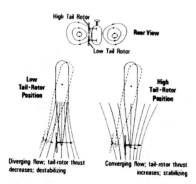

Figure 16-13 Change in Flight Condition

17 Dynamic Stability

A student pilot with a gift for expressive language described his first attempt at hovering "It was like trying to ride a pogo stick over a floor covered with greasy ball bearings."

The primary reason for his difficulty was that the machine he was trying to fly—like most helicopters—was inherently unstable in hover. Other reasons were that the helicopter responded to control motions slower than most vehicles he was familiar with and it produced its own gusty air. Hovering over a spot is a precision maneuver comparable to landing an airplane, and it doesn't come easy.

It would take a mathematical analysis to completely understand the inherent instability of a hovering helicopter, but let's stick with words and drawings.

Step-by-Step

Picture a helicopter hovering in calm air when suddenly a gust makes it nose down slightly. Figure 17-1 shows what would happen each two seconds if the pilot did nothing with his controls. (The apparent loss of altitude is only artistic license to keep the images from interfering with one another. The actual maneuver would be at a nearly constant altitude.)

The sequence would go something like this:

— Two seconds—The helicopter starts to move forward, since its rotor is no longer horizontal;

— Four seconds—The forward speed causes the rotor to flap back;

— Six seconds—The aft flapping produces a nose-up pitching moment and a resultant nose-up attitude;

— Eight seconds—The nose-up attitude causes the rotor to provide a braking force, eventually stopping the forward motion;

— 10 seconds—The rearward tilt starts a rearward motion and the process proceeds in reverse;

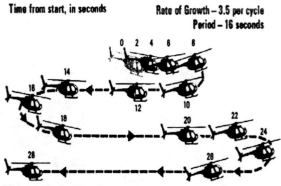

Time from start, in seconds   Rate of Growth – 3.5 per cycle
Period – 16 seconds

Figure 17-1 The Controls-Fixed Response to a Disturbance in Hover

— 12 seconds—Passing over the point on the ground where it started, it has rearward velocity and is pitched nose-up; and

— 14 seconds—The cycle begins to repeat itself but with ever-increasing displacement from the original hover point.

The fact that the helicopter had rearward speed as it passed over the hover point at about 12 seconds means that it gained energy since it was first disturbed, which is the sign of an unstable system. Had it slowed down and returned to a hover, we would call it a stable helicopter.

As it is, a typical helicopter will go back and forth across its starting point with an ever-increasing swinging motion until the pilot (or something else) stops it. The swinging motion has a constant period that is governed by the size and rotor characteristics of the machine, just as the period of a child on a swing is a constant governed only by the length of the ropes.

The period of most helicopters without artificial stability augmentation is between 10 and 20 seconds (slightly less in roll than in pitch). The rate of growth from one cycle to the next—a measure of the degree of instability—is also a function of the physical characteristics. For the machine in Figure 17-1, the period is 16 seconds and the motion at the end of each cycle compared to the previous one is growing by a ratio of about 3.5 to one.

Enter the Pilot

These characteristics mean the pilot must be constantly moving his controls to calm the skittishness of his mount. In developing the ability to do this, he must learn to anticipate the motion and to put in just enough control without overreacting, a job complicated by the helicopter's failure to react instantaneously to his commands. The time lag between a control input and the maximum movement over the ground is about half the period of the natural oscillation—or five to 10 seconds.

This encourages the impatient student to use too much control—with the resulting overshoot and panic correction. That, coupled with the instability and the necessity to control altitude and heading at the same time, soon gets him in trouble.

That this is not an impossible task is illustrated by the fact that most fledglings eventually put it all together and become experienced helicopter pilots.

(Historical note: When Igor Sikorsky was learning to fly his VS-300, he had his cameraman shoot movies in slow motion to minimize his violent control motions. These movies were then shown to the United Aircraft board of directors to show how easy it was to fly a helicopter.)

The Inconstant Air

Another source of trouble for the pilot is the tendency of the rotor to produce its own gusty air —even in a steady hover on a deed calm day. This happens because a lifting surface develops lift by producing a high pressure on the bottom and a low pressure above.

Along most of the blade, the air is kept from going from the high-pressure area to the low-pressure area by the sharp trailing edge. At the tip, however, nothing prevents the air from curling around the tip from the bottom to the top. This air is then dropped off to form the trailing-tip vortex. The vortex has a core spinning as if it were a solid bar but outside the core the velocity falls off with distance. Physically, it is much like the little whirlpool that forms in a draining sink.

We rarely see tip vortices, but sometimes, when conditions are right, the low pressure due to the high velocities in the vortex causes moisture in the air to condense into a miniature cloud. Vapor trails from rotor-blade tips can thus be seen on very humid days. Figure 17-2 shows tip vortices from a hard-working Bell 214B in the jungles of Peru. The moisture has condensed in the region just outside the core.

One thing that can be seen in the photo is some wobbling of the tip vortices as they descend in two more-or-less steady spirals. Observations of model-rotor tip vortices made visible with smoke show that even out of ground effect and in calm air, this wobble is present. Two or three loops down from the rotor the individual vortices get tangled up with each other and produce mutual annihilation —long before they would normally break up due to friction effects in the air. (Airplane tip vortices sometimes persist for several minutes.)

Figure 17-2 Tip Vortices Around a Bell 214B

Since the tip vortices are producing the induced velocity through the rotor, any unsteadiness in their locations will cause unsteadiness in the flow field as seen by the individual blades. For this reason, a hovering rotor produces its own gusty air and keeps the pilot from relaxing on the job.

Besides wobbly tip vortices, there are nervous root vortices. One of the laws of fluid dynamics states that a vortex must be balanced somewhere by one with equal and opposite effect. For a helicopter rotor, the tip vortex must be matched by a root vortex which is seldom seen since it is smeared out by the hardware at the root of the blade. Someone standing near the aircraft, however, can feel erratic gusts due to the root vortices combining into a single vortex that writhes around like a snake pinned at the head—sometimes going up through the rotor and sometimes down.

Its effect may also be noted when hovering close to the ground as sudden heading changes caused by the vortex impinging on the tail rotor. These effects of the root vortex generally disappear when the rotor is more than one radius above the ground.

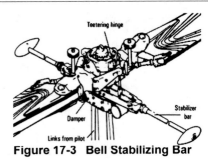

Figure 17-3   Bell Stabilizing Bar

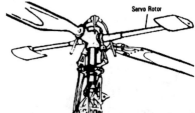

Figure 17-4   Hiller Servo Rotor System

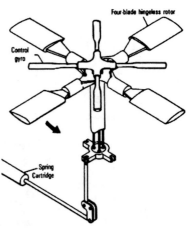

Figure 17-5   Lockheed Rotor System

Trying to Help

In an effort to make the helicopter easier to hover, the designers have come up with a variety of devices. One of the first was Bell's stabilizer bar (Figure 17-3), developed by Arthur Young when he was working with electric-powered models in his Pennsylvania stable in the 1930s. The bar acted as a gyroscope and was installed in the control system so that its motion would produce stabilizing cyclic-pitch inputs if the model Was disturbed.

The first Bell helicopter used a bar scaled up from the model configuration. This bar was not restrained by dampers and resulted in a machine that was very stable—but also very uncontrollable. The addition of dampers restrained the bar to the aircraft slightly and gave, a better balance between stability and controllability.

As the development program advanced, it was found that the dampers had to be stiffened to solve a rotor dynamic problem known as weaving. Because of this, the bar became relatively ineffective in helping the pilot. Later, Bell developed a rotor design free of weaving tendencies and helicopters such as the UH-1 could be equipped with soft dampers— allowing the stabilizer bar to again do the job it was originally designed for.

Another mechanical device developed somewhat later was the Hiller servo rotor (Figure 17-4), which worked much like the bar but used air forces to produce the required damping—as well as to provide forces for changing cyclic pitch. By adding weights to the tips of the servo rotor, a Hiller could be made so stable that it could hover by itself (for short periods, at least). At one stockholders' meeting, a specially set-up aircraft was hovered by a secretary with only a few minutes of instruction. The additional weights were not used on production Hillers, since the high stability was gained at the expense of sluggish response to control inputs. This later proved to be a blessing for radio controlled helicopter enthusiasts, since slowing the response of a model is necessary to permit a human to keep up. Almost all successful model helicopters now use a Hiller servo rotor.

Another development was the Lockheed rotor system (Figure 17-5), which used a gyro coupled by springs to the helicopter and its control system. In this case, fast response to control inputs was obtained by using blades that had no actual flapping hinges but flapped anyway around flexible parts of the hub. The combination of the gyro and the high stiffness of the hingeless blades produced a period of one to two seconds—instead of the 10 to 20 seconds on a comparable conventional helicopter. This degree of stability allowed the Lockheed to hover hands-off for relatively long periods of time.

Phugoid

Dynamic characteristics in forward flight can either be stable or unstable, depending on the configuration of the helicopter.

If a helicopter in forward flight is momentarily upset in pitch by a gust, it will respond in two modes of motion: one occurs during such a short period and is so heavily damped that the pilot may not even notice it. The other, often called porpoising, is an oscillation that takes 10 to 60 seconds and may or may not have positive damping.

It was an English aerodynamic pioneer named Lanchester who first noticed this porpoising motion while experimenting with model gliders about the time of the Wright brothers' first flight. He searched for a name for this oscillation and came up with "phugoid", based on a Greek word that he interpreted to mean "to fly" but actually means "to flee".

Oh well, you can't expect an aerodynamicist to know everything.

To the pilot, phugoid oscillations on both airplanes and helicopters appear much the same, involving an energy exchange between speed and altitude, as shown on Figure 17-6. Technically, however, the two types of aircraft have slightly different ways of phugoiding, since the helicopter has inherently stronger speed stability effects than the airplane.

In addition, with pedals fixed, an airplane will hold heading during the phugoid because it is symmetrical. But a helicopter will wander because tail rotor thrust will vary as forward speed changes and main-rotor torque will be affected by both speed and angle of attack.

Whether the pitch motion is stable or unstable depends primarily on relationships between the angle of attack and speed stability. As shown on a stability map for these two parameters (Figure 17-7), a helicopter without a horizontal stabilizer lies in the unstable region. While adding a stabilizer can place it in the stable region, changing the stabilizer incidence either up or down may, once again, destabilize the aircraft.

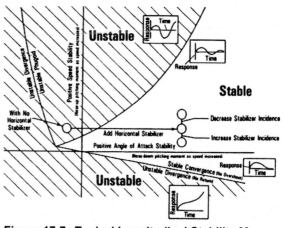

Figure 17-7 Typical Longitudinal Stability Map

Unless the phugoid is extremely unstable, the pilot will have ample time to correct for the instability with instinctive control motions. This situation is acceptable under normal flying conditions but could be marginal during IFR flight, especially if the period of the phugoid is short.

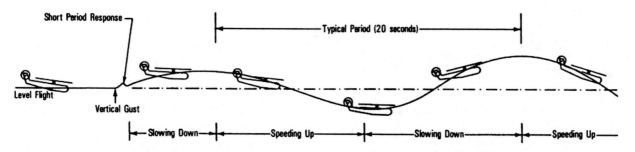

Figure 17-6 Phugoid (Slightly Unstable)

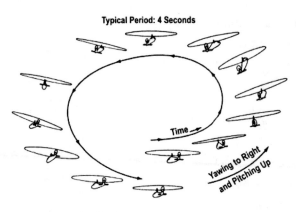

Typical Period: 4 Seconds

Time

Yawing to Right and Pitching Up

Figure 17-8 Dutch Roll Action (Slightly Unstable)

If designers can find no practical way of securing inherent stability in an aircraft, they can add a stability augmentation system (SAS). Such a system can shift both the boundaries and the helicopter point on the stability map, thus giving improved flying qualities.

Dutch Rolls...

A combination of yaw and roll in an oscillating pattern is called "Dutch roll" after the motion that two Dutch ice skaters with linked arms make as they travel down the canal. Although it was first discovered on airplanes, helicopters too have a mode of oscillation that is similar to the Dutch roll. However, in addition to roll and yaw, rotor-craft also exhibit a significant amount of pitch motion, as shown on Figure 17-8. The typical length of time for this type of oscillation is three to eight seconds. (You can see what the jet transport people do about Dutch roll by watching the inboard ailerons going up and down in a fairly regular way about every three or four seconds as the yaw damper does its job.)

Just like the phugoid, there are combinations of physical parameters that govern the stability of lateral-directional motions. Another stability map (Figure 17-9) shows variations in dihedral effect and directional stability, and although both of these characteristics are good, the map indicates too much of a good thing can be bad. Too much directional stability, for example, can produce an unstable spiral dive and too much dihedral effect can produce an unstable Dutch roll.

...and spiral dives

An unstable spiral dive can be detected in flight by trimming for level flight, making a shallow banked turn, and then returning the controls to their trim position. If the helicopter returns to level flight, it is stable, but if the angle of bank increases, it is unstable.

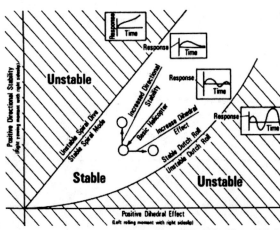

Figure 17-9 Dutch Roll Action (Slightly Unstable)

Moderately unstable Dutch rolls and spiral dives are acceptable in normal flight and indeed may go undetected. I know of experienced test pilots who were surprised to discover unstable Dutch roll characteristics in conditions they had been flying in for many hours. Although these instabilities could be dangerous, the addition of SAS, which artificially increases damping in roll and yaw, will generally make the lateral-directional characteristics satisfactory in all types of flying.

As a rule, helicopters have an SAS-off Dutch roll mode that is stable at low speeds but may become unstable at high speeds. This can happen when the pitching motion affects the main-rotor torque by changing the angle of attack. At low speeds, the torque decreases (that is, the rotor starts to autorotate) as the angle of attack is increased. At high speeds, the effect is reversed.

Figure 17-8 shows that over most of the cycle, when the helicopter is yawing to the right, the angle of attack is increasing. Thus at low speeds, the resulting decrease in torque is in a direction that would oppose the yawing motion, increasing the apparent damping in yaw.

At high speeds, the opposite is true. The apparent negative damping in yaw drives the Dutch roll motion to higher amplitudes.

As shown in Figure 17-9, too much dihedral effect can produce an unstable Dutch roll. As a result, reducing this parameter is sometimes suggested to improve the SAS-off stability.

Most inherent dihedral effect comes from the main rotor, however, vertical stabilizers and tail rotors mounted above the center of gravity also contribute to this roll-with-sideslip coupling. When, for example, Sikorsky engineers were developing the S-76, they reduced the height of the vertical stabilizer 15 inches to improve the Dutch roll characteristics. On another helicopter design, the Dutch roll was stabilized by raising the tail rotor two feet. Apparently there is a complex interaction between the main-rotor wake and components at the rear of the aircraft but, as yet, no one fully understands this effect.

Unstable Pilots

Sometimes it is the pilot, not the aircraft, that is unstable. Because of the time it takes for messages to go from the eye to the brain to the hand, a pilot can find he is doing the wrong thing at the wrong time. Called pilot-induced oscillation (PIO), this situation is sometimes described as "getting behind the motion."

You don't have to be a pilot to experience this phenomenon. Try carrying a very full cup of coffee across the room without sloshing it on the floor. Your performance will be better if you don't look at the cup.

Potential PIO problems are generally associated with precision tasks such as landing a fixed-wing aircraft on a carrier deck or hovering a helicopter on a gusty day. Because PIO doesn't always happen (and cannot be predicted), it is a little-understood phenomenon. The best advice to a pilot facing this situation is: relax for a second and let the ship sort itself out.

18 Maximum Load Factor

To maneuver aggressively, to quickly go up or down, or to maintain a turn, the sum of rotor thrust and airframe lift must vary from what is required to just support the aircraft's gross weight. The ratio of thrust-plus-lift to weight is known as the "load factor."

That factor is 1.0 for steady, level flight. It's higher during turns and pullups but lower for downward acceleration. And it is zero if the aircraft is falling like a rock. Fighter airplanes are designed for load factors from -1.0 (falling faster than a rock or flying upside down) all the way to about eight, which is as much as most pilots can tolerate.

Can we design a helicopter to match that capability? Yes, but it will cost us.

Wing vs. rotor

An airplane wing cannot develop a load factor above 1.0 until it reaches its minimum flying speed. From then on, its load-factor capability increases as the square of the airspeed.

Conversely, a helicopter rotor develops its maximum load factor at zero airspeed but from then on, it is all downhill. To understand that difference, let's start at the beginning.

Jump takeoff

The maximum load factor a rotor can develop at zero airspeed depends on the maximum lift coefficient each blade element can produce before it stalls. To demonstrate this capability, imagine doing a jump takeoff by quickly changing the collective from flat pitch to a value just equal to the stall angle of the airfoil used on the blades.

In actual practice, of course, it is unlikely that all blade elements would simultaneously be at their optimum angles of attack, so actual maximum thrust capability would be something less than the theoretical maximum—perhaps 90%. Airfoils used on rotor blades have stall angles of between about 10° and 14° as measured in two-dimensional wind tunnel tests. These result in maximum lift coefficients of about 1.0 to 1.4.

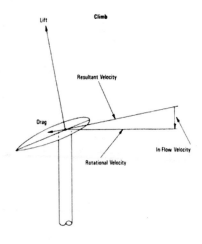

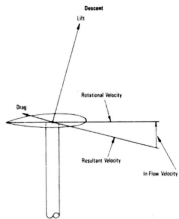

Figure 18-1 Orientation of Local Force Vectors

The helicopter aerodynamicist translates these into another coefficient, the thrust/solidity coefficient, C_T/σ (the Greek letter, sigma, is the rotor solidity or the ratio of blade area to the disc area). Its equation is:

$$C_\tau/\sigma = \frac{Rotor \ \ Thrust}{(Density \ \ of \ \ Air) \times (Blade \ \ Area) \times (Tip \ \ Speed)^2}$$

It turns out that in hover, the maximum value of C_T/σ is one-sixth the average effective maximum lift coefficient. So one should expect a rotor in a jump takeoff situation to produce maximum values of C_T/σ from about .15 to .21.

So what is the maximum load factor? It is simply the maximum value of C_T/σ divided by the value corresponding to hover. As you can see from the equation, the designer who knows the hovering thrust and the density altitude can pick the hover C_T/σ he wants by selecting the right combination of blade area and tip speed.

Until now, designers have settled for values of about .06 at sea level. Thus, a load factor of 2.5 to 3.5 is possible for a maximum-performance jump takeoff at sea level.

At higher altitudes, this capability is degraded until at, say, 30,000 feet, the helicopter is hovering on the verge of stall, with no margin for going any higher.

The other way

There is a special situation in which a rotor can develop even higher load factors. If the airflow is coming up through the rotor as in a descent or flare, the drag on each blade element contributes to the total rotor thrust rather than diminishing it.

Figure 18-1 illustrates this. It shows the local forces at a blade element both with the helicopter going up and coming down.

If the rotor is heavily stalled as in an extreme transient flare, drag can be a major contributor to thrust, and the maximum thrust/solidity coefficient could possibly be doubled. But because the rotor would be slowing down fast, any increased load factor capability in this condition would be very short-lived.

Designer's choice

Short of developing new high-lift airfoils, the designer who wants greater hover load factors has relatively few choices. He can increase tip speed or increase blade area. Increasing tip speed will increase noise and may lead to advancing tip compressibility problems in high-speed forward flight.

Increasing blade area will add to weight and cost, and hurt hover performance-the reason for helicopters.

How does it hurt hover performance? The blade elements will be operating at angles of attack far below the optimum for maximum lift-to-drag ratio.

Figure 4-3 on page 20 shows how the hovering efficiency, or figure of merit, is affected by angle of attack. Lowering below about 7° to enhance the load-factor capability will require more power to hover.

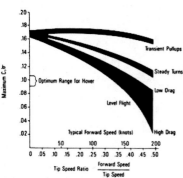

Figure 18-2 Maximum Rotor Thrust Capabilities

Forward flight

A wing increases its load factor capability in forward flight but a rotor does not. Because the retreating blade is actually going slower through the air than in hover, its maximum lifting capability decreases and, to avoid unbalancing the rotor, the lift on the advancing side must be decreased using cyclic pitch.

This means that since only the blades over the nose and the tail retain the same potential in forward flight as in hover, the maximum lifting capability of the entire rotor decreases as speed increases.

The result is verified by both flight and wind tunnel experience, and is plotted as the lower band in Figure 18-2. In this format, forward speed is represented by the nondimensional tip-speed ratio, or forward speed divided by rotor tip speed. The band is painted with a broad brush because several secondary effects influence it.

One important effect is how much the rotor-tip path plane must be tilted to overcome airframe drag. The higher the drag, the more the nose-down tilt and the higher the angle of attack becomes on the retreating side.

The lower band in Figure 18-2 applies only to straight and level flight. It can be used to determine the maximum speed as limited by retreating-blade stall at the operating value of C_T/σ determined by gross weight and air density. It's worth noting that helicopter altitude records are set at very low forward speeds to take advantage of the highest allowable thrust/solidity coefficient.

Turning flight

The middle band in Figure 18-2 represents the limit during a steady turn. It is higher than for level flight because, to maintain the turn, the rotor must be processed noseup as a gyro.

(Imagine the helicopter banked to 90°; it will have a high pitch rate. Even with less bank, it must still have some nose-up pitch.)

To precess the rotor nose-up, the advancing blade is loaded higher than in level flight, and this extra load accounts for the increased rotor-thrust capability in a turn. This general curve or one specifically made for the rotor in question can be used to estimate the load-factor capability in a steady turn. At their cruise speeds, most modern helicopters with level-flight C_T/σ values of about .06 have trouble holding steady-turn load factors much above 2.0 or 2.5 (60° to 66° bank angle before running into retreating blade stall.

The top band

Since nosedown tilt of the rotor-tip-path plane is detrimental, one would assume a noseup tilt would be beneficial. It is. This has been demonstrated by both flight and wind-tunnel tests. It gives us the top curve in Figure 18-2 for rotors tilted far enough back with respect to the flight path to put them into autorotation.

Not only is the angle of attack environment better but, as described earlier, even the drag at the blade element is beneficial. Autogyros in the 1930s took advantage of these effects and routinely operated at tip-speed ratios above 0.5.

This curve can be used to estimate the rotor's load factor capability during a transient pull-up. Again, using a typical rotor design, one can see that transient load factors of about 3.0 represent a practical maximum. With a greatly stalled rotor, the drag effect may increase that maximum even more-but it would be for a very short time.

Add a wing?

Rotor capability might be augmented by adding a wing. The main benefit would be expected in the transient pullup. Here again, the additional load factor gained carries a high price tag in terms of cost, empty weight, download in hover, and drag in forward flight. Usually, given a choice between adding a wing or more blade area, it's best to select more blade area.

19 Forward Flight Performance

Helicopters justify their existence by their ability to hover and fly straight up and down. That is not enough, however. They must also be able to fly from Point A to Point B. In the early days of the development of the Sikorsky VS-300, the machine could hover, climb vertically (barely), and fly backward and sideways. It couldn't, however, fly forward without going out of control.

When asked about it, Igor Sikorsky explained, "This is just a minor engineering problem that we have not yet solved." Fortunately, by relocating the horizontal tail rotors he was then using for control, he soon solved this particular "minor" problem.

Trim Conditions

The balance of forces and moments that must exist to maintain steady, level flight is shown on Figure 19-1. In this view, all vertical forces must balance, all horizontal forces must balance, and all pitching moments about the center of gravity (CG) must balance.

The primary horizontal force is made up of the parasite drag from all of those aircraft components that we aerodynamicists grudgingly permit the designers to attach to our rotor blades: Things like hubs, fuselages, and landing gear. A smaller horizontal force is produced by the unbalanced profile and induced drag of the rotor blades themselves and is known as the *rotor H-force*. To overcome both of these horizontal forces, the rotor must be tilted forward. The amount of tilt required is relatively small, varying from a fraction of a degree at low speed to about 10 degrees at maximum speed.

Since the rotor blades are connected to the shaft through flapping hinges (or flexible structures in the case of hingeless rotors), the rotor disc does not necessarily have to be perpendicular to the shaft. The angle between the rotor disc and a plane perpendicular to the shaft is the longitudinal flapping angle. Its direction and value depend *only* on the requirement to balance pitching moments about the CG. This includes the moments produced by the aerodynamics of the fuselage and the

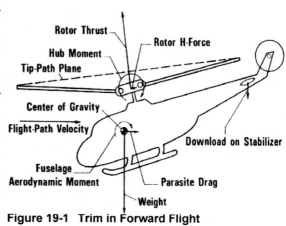

Figure 19-1 Trim in Forward Flight

horizontal tail, and by the misalignment of the rotor shaft with the CG (fore or aft offset CG position). This means that at the same speed, the fuselage may ride either nose up or nose down with respect to the rotor tip-path plane, depending on the net direction of those moments.

The amount of flapping required to balance a given external moment depends upon the stiffness of the rotor. A teetering rotor whose only source of stiffness is the tilt of the thrust vector is "soft," whereas a hingeless rotor is "stiff," and a rotor with offset flapping hinges falls somewhere in between. The stiffer the rotor, the less flapping is required.

For a given flight condition, the pilot finds the correct direction and magnitude of flapping by using his control stick to hold the helicopter steady. Strange as it might seem, what he is actually finding in this process is the correct tilt of the fuselage with respect to the flight path - not the tilt of the rotor disc, since that angle is fixed entirely by the requirement to overcome the parasite drag and rotor H-force. (These forces remain essentially constant for the relatively small changes in fuselage attitude we are considering.)

Once the pilot finds the right trim condition, his ability to hold onto it is greatly helped if the helicopter has an effective horizontal stabilizer that can correct for inadvertent wandering, just as the feathers on an arrow keep it flying straight.

Power Required

Now that we have the helicopter in trim, the next question is how much power does it take? Two types of power were identified for a rotor in hover—*induced* and *profile*. In forward flight, these are joined by yet another—*parasite,* which, as its name implies, is needed to overcome the parasite drag.

Induced Power

Taking these components one at a time, the induced power is that associated with producing rotor thrust and starts out at its hover value - normally 60% to 85% of the total main-rotor power. It rapidly decreases as the helicopter goes into forward flight and the rotor encounters more and more air per second on which to operate.

Determining the amount of the mass flow is simple if you know how, but one can easily take the wrong path by trying to extend the hover situation where the correct mass flow to use is that passing down inside the rotor perimeter. It would seem natural, therefore, to assume the same thing applied to forward flight - even though the disc is flying through the air nearly edgewise and so the air passing inside its perimeter is very small.

This assumption does not give the right answer. Instead, we must go back to what the airplane aerodynamicists learned 50 years ago. When an airplane flies past, the wing theoretically disturbs all the air in the neighborhood from far above to far below and to both sides. Of course, it is the air closest to the flight path that is influenced most, but the generality still holds.

When the mathematics of the problem are worked through, it may be shown that moving all of that air in varying amounts is exactly the same as if every molecule of air in a cylindrical stream tube whose diameter is the wingspan were given the same value of downward velocity. This mathematical fiction is also the correct way to handle a rotor in forward flight and means that by coincidence the rotor disc is the key area to the induced-power calculations both in hover and in forward flight.

As the helicopter goes faster, there is more air going through the stream tube and the rotor has to do less work on it to maintain a constant thrust. For this reason, induced power decreases with speed until at maximum speed it is approximately one-quarter or less of its hover value as in Figure 19-2.

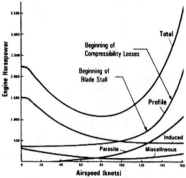

Figure 19-2 Elements of Power Required in Forward Flight

At the same speed and gross weight, the bigger the rotor, the smaller the induced power used because of the increase in mass flow. This reasoning causes designers of high-performance, low-speed airplanes such as sailplanes and man-powered aircraft to use as long a wing as they can.

Profile Power

Profile power is used to overcome friction drag on the blades and accounts for 15% to 40% of the main-rotor power in hover. Figure 19-2 shows it remains at a fairly constant level as the helicopter goes out into forward flight, since increases on the advancing side tend to be compensated for by decreases on the retreating side - until at high speed when blade stall or compressibility, or both, rear their ugly heads. At this point, the profile power increases and usually becomes the dominant component.

H-force

Blade drag also contributes to the rotor H-force in the plane of the rotor disc. Drag on the advancing blade acts aft, but drag on the retreating blade acts forward - like an oar in water - and helps propel the rotor forward. Thus, if the retreating tip were stalled before the advancing tip encountered severe compressible flow, the blade drag could be producing a forward-acting rotor horizontal force. In any case, the rotor H-force, when compared to parasite drag, is usually relatively small, seldom exceeding a few percent of rotor thrust. No matter which way the H-force acts, any increase in blade drag must be overcome with increased engine power.

Parasite Power

The power needed to overcome the drag of all the aircraft components except the rotor blades is parasite power. This is no problem at low speed, but since it increases as forward speed cubed (as shown in

Figure 19-3 Lockheed XH-51A

Figure 19-2), it becomes important at high speeds. This power is proportional to the equivalent flat plate area, which depends upon the size and general cleanliness of the aircraft.

The equivalent flat-plate area is a parameter of convenience that compares the drag characteristics of the helicopter with a fictitious body having a frontal area of one square foot and a drag coefficient of one. (A very good streamlined body has a drag coefficient of 0.04 and a flat plate broadside to the flow has a drag coefficient of about 1.2.) Small, clean helicopters have equivalent flat-plate areas as low as five square feet while large flying cranes have over 100 square feet. Comparable airplanes run from one to 10 square feet.

One of the objectives for the helicopter aerodynamicist during the development of a new design] is to convince the rest of the design team of the importance of minimizing drag. Suggestions ranging from retracting the landing gear to using flush rivets invariably involve weight and cost penalties and are, therefore, sometimes not readily accepted.

In some cases, a chief engineer will help by set ting a design policy: "Make it look fast." This was true for the Lockheed XH-51A shown in Figure 19-3 and for many of today's commercial designs. You can appreciate what a clean helicopter the XH-51A was if you do not let your eyes rise above the top of the fuselage. The draggy main rotor hub on this aircraft is an example of the aerodynamicist's dilemma. The size of the structural elements and their awkward relationships were dictated by loads, required stiffness, and mechanical travel.

Attempts to put fairings on rotor hubs have not yet had much success. Although it may be possible to make a more streamlined shape with a fairing, the increase in frontal area generally eats up most of the gain. When coat, weight, and interference with preflight hub inspections are also considered, it is evident why we do not see helicopters flying around with hub fairings. This is a rather discouraging picture, but it should be pointed out that some hub configurations are inherently small and, thus less drag - as illustrated by the Robinson R22 in Figure 19-4.

During the design process, the aerodynamicist continually updates his estimates of the drag of the new helicopter. These estimates are based on a mixture of theory, published drag studies of other aircraft, and wind tunnel testing with small scale models. Unfortunately, all of these sources are at best only guides, so a certain amount of educated guessing must also be done. (I have never heard of an aerodynamicist being pleasantly surprised by flight-test results showing that the ship had less drag than he had estimated.)

Figure 19-4 Robinson R22

Total Power

The engine has to put out enough power to provide for the induced, profile, and parasite components already discussed - and for some others that we can lump together under a "miscellaneous" heading, including the tail rotor, gearbox losses, hydraulic pumps, electrical generators, etc. When all of the various types of power are added up in Figure 19-2, we get a picture of the total engine power required for steady level flight. One of the most important characteristics of this curve is that, until it is flying very fast, a helicopter takes less power to fly forward than to hover.

Another characteristic is that the curve starts out from hover with a horizontal slope, since the helicopter cannot distinguish between small forward speeds and small rearward speeds.

Effects of Altitude

Going up in density altitude has different effects on the various power components. As the air density decreases, the rotor has to blow harder to produce the same thrust - so the induced power goes up. At the same time, the thinner air reduces parasite drag on the airframe and profile drag on those blade elements that are below stall. Blade stall, however, begins sooner, so at high speed more of the rotor may be deeper into stall and the profile power is up instead of down. The result of all these ups and downs is that the power required near hover and at high speed at altitude is usually higher than at sea level. It may, however, be lower at moderate forward speeds, depending upon the relative disc loading and parasite drag characteristics of the helicopter - for example, if the disc loading is low and the parasite drag high.

Optimum Speeds

Some flight conditions can be done better at one forward speed than another and knowing this can make for better effectiveness and safety. The basic reason for this is the bowl shape of the power-required curve of Figure 19-5. The various optimum speeds determined by this characteristic are those for the best rate of climb, minimum rate of descent in autorotation, maximum glide distance, maximum loiter time, and maximum range.

The best rate of climb is done at the speed where the difference between the power required and the power available is a maximum. The power available from a reciprocating engine is nearly constant with speed, but a turbine picks up a slight increase due to ram recovery as you go faster - as shown on Figure 19-5. The speed for best rate of climb is at the bottom of the bowl or the "bucket" of the curve. The bucket speed depends on the relative values of the disc loading, which controls induced power, and the drag area, which controls parasite power. A draggy ship with a low disc loading will have a lower bucket speed than a clean ship with a high disc loading. Typical bucket speeds range from 40 to 100 knots.

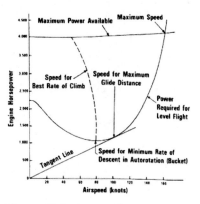

Figure 19-5   Power Required and Available (Gross Weight = 20,000 pounds)

Maximum Climb Rate

The rate of climb in forward flight (as for an elevator) can be estimated from the change in potential energy. This same type of procedure was discussed for vertical climbs, where the increase in mass flow actually reduces the climb power required compared to an elevator. In forward flight, the induced power is already so low that there is little to be gained from the increase in mass flow.

On top of that, the climb condition produces a large negative angle of attack of the fuselage, increasing the drag and the fuselage download at the same time the tail-rotor power is increasing. The result is that more of the excess engine power is used to overcome parasite drag and drive the tail rotor. For this reason, the maximum rate of climb may be as little as 60% of what would be calculated by multiplying the excess horsepower by 33,000 and dividing by the gross weight (the elevator formula).

The increased drag also shifts the bucket to a lower speed. For the helicopter corresponding to Figure 19-5, the maximum rate of climb occurs at 50 knots and is 3,250 fpm - or 67% of that calculated from the elevator analogy.

Minimum Sink Rate

The bucket of the speed-power curve is also the best speed for making the slowest descent in autorotation. At this speed, the power required to satisfy the demands of keeping airborne are at a minimum, so the potential energy corresponding to the gross weight and the height above the ground can be used up as slowly as possible.

The same line of reasoning also can be used to explain a somewhat surprising result of flight tests: At the same rotor rpm, a heavily loaded helicopter will autorotate at a lower steady rate of descent than one that is nearly empty. Let's take as an example a helicopter that when heavily loaded weighs 50% more than when flown light. At a given height above the ground, it will represent 50% more potential energy - but the power required will be less than 50% higher, since only the induced component depends upon the gross weight. The profile and parasite power will be about the same at the heavier weight as the light. Thus, the higher potential energy (which is like money in the bank) will supply the necessary power for a longer time. This does not work, of course, if the rotor is so heavily loaded that it has significant blade stall, and it certainly does not guarantee a more gentle return to earth when the time comes to make the landing flare.

The steady rate of descent in forward flight autorotation can be estimated by using the elevator analogy once more. The fuselage angle of attack is positive but usually not enough to represent a big drag penalty. In this condition, little or no tail-rotor power is required. The result is that the helicopter comes down at 75% to 85% of the rate that would be calculated by multiplying the power required for level flight by

33,000 and dividing by the gross weight. For the helicopter of Figure 19-5, the rate of descent at 80 knots is 1,400 fpm or about 80% of the potential energy value.

Maximum Glide Distance

Coming down at the slowest rate and stretching the autorotation to reach that distant clearing are two different flight conditions. The maximum distance is achieved at a speed where a line from the origin of the plot is tangent to the power-required curve and, thus, is higher than the bucket speed. This condition is the same as gliding an airplane at the speed that gives the highest lift-to-drag ratio.

Figure 19-5 shows the speed along the flight path for our example helicopter is about 100 knots. The autorotative rate of descent based on the power required in level flight, at this speed, is approximately 1,500 fpm. Converting these two rates into the same units and dividing one by the other gives a glide ratio of 7-to-1. That is, for every foot of altitude lost, the helicopter will go forward seven feet. This ratio is also the equivalent lift-to-drag ratio for the helicopter at this speed. It is typical of helicopters but would be considered low for comparable airplanes not burdened with such draggy items as rotor hubs.

One more speed that can be read for our example helicopter from Figure 19-5 is the maximum as limited by the maximum power available where the two power curves cross at 160 knots.

Maximum Loiter Time

Sometimes it may be necessary to remain airborne for the longest possible time while waiting for the weather to change or a landing spot to be cleared. This is a matter of making the fuel last as long as possible. If the fuel flow were exactly proportional to engine power, the loitering should be done at the bucket speed. For helicopters with recips, this is a good rule of thumb, but turbines introduce a new factor.

A turbine engine that can develop 1,000 horsepower at its shaft is actually about a 1,300 horsepower engine, the extra 300 being used internally to spin the compressor. The engine is burning up a corresponding amount of fuel even when developing no shaft power.

For this reason, the fuel flow is higher than a value proportional to output power and to find the optimum speed for any flight condition involving fuel management, a curve of fuel flow vs. speed such as Figure 19-6 is used - rather than the power-required curve we have been working with. Now that we have Figure 19-6, the speed for maximum loiter time - or minimum fuel flow - can be read at this new bucket. For this example, the speed is 85 knots and the helicopter can stay up about seven minutes for each 100 pounds of fuel burned.

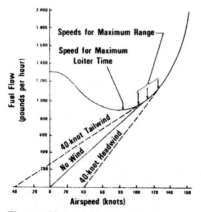

Figure 19-6 Fuel Flow Curve

Maximum Range

The speed for maximum range can be found from the fuel-flow curve, just as the speed for maximum glide distance was found from the power-required curve, by drawing a line tangent to the curve from the origin. The ratio of speed to fuel flow is the "specific range" or nautical miles you can go on a pound of fuel. Note that this parameter is at a maximum when the slope of the line is as shallow as it can be and that this occurs at the point of tangency. From Figure 19-6, we get a specific range of 0.114 nm per pound at 114 knots.

This is the right set of values for a flight without head or tail winds. If there is a headwind, the tangent line should be started at the headwind value so the airspeed for best range is slightly above the calm-air speed but since the slope of the tangent line is higher, the specific range is lower. Conversely, a tailwind is handled by starting the line at a negative speed equal to the tailwind - resulting in a slightly lower optimum airspeed but a significantly better specific range, as might be expected. While 100 pounds of fuel will take this helicopter 11.4 nm with no wind, the same quantity will only take it 7.6 nm with a 40-knot headwind but 15.3 nm with a 40-knot tailwind.

A twin-turbine helicopter with enough power to fly at the speed for best range on one engine can go farther if the other engine is shut down. This eliminates the fuel required to keep one compressor going and, thus, reduces the rate at which the fuel is burned. It is, of course, a desperation move that jeopardizes the twin-engine safety of the aircraft - unless it is absolutely certain that the shut down engine can be immediately restarted. It may, however, give the pilot the option of landing on the beach rather than in the surf at the end of a long over water flight.

Ferry Flight

The maximum power available from both reciprocating and turbine engines decreases with altitude so that maximum speed usually suffers from both power-required and power-available standpoints.

Cruise performance, on the other hand, may benefit from flight at altitude, especially on turbine helicopters whose engines become more efficient at altitude. A typical turbine burns 10% to 15% less fuel at 10,000 feet than at sea level to produce the same power. For this reason, maximum range can usually be achieved at altitude. On most helicopters, this conclusion does depend, however, on gross weight. Loaded heavily for a ferry flight, the best range initially is at sea level - but as fuel is burned off, the optimum altitude increases so that the desired flight profile involves a slow "drift up." By the end of the flight, the optimum altitude may be so high that oxygen is needed.

20 Vertical Climbs and Descents

Compared to other aircraft, the helicopter is unique in its ability to go straight up and down.

Conditions of Flow

For an understanding of these maneuvers, we must distinguish between cases in which flow goes up through a rotor and those in which the flow goes down through it. To illustrate the various possibilities, Figure 20-1 shows a small rotor —developing a constant thrust — installed in a large vertical wind tunnel. The tunnel fan can generate a flow either up or down. (Aerodynamicists like this kind of analogy because they are all firmly convinced that aircraft stand still while the air blows past them.)

For hover, the tunnel fan is turned off and the rotor is inducing flow downward as it would for a normal hover. To represent a vertical climb, the fan is used to suck air down the tunnel, increasing the downflow through the rotor.

Vertical descent is simulated by reversing the pitch of the fan to blow air up the tunnel. For low levels of tunnel upflow (representing a slow descent), the rotor-induced downwash will still dominate the flow in the vicinity of the rotor and, except for a decrease in rotor power, conditions will be similar to hover.

Turning the fan up a notch puts the rotor into the vortex-ring state where the tunnel upflow is approximately the same as the rotor-induced downwash. In this condition, tip vortices cannot move away from the rotor disc and some of the air becomes trapped in a smoke-ring-shaped body enclosing the outer rim of the rotor. For the pilot trying to fly the aircraft under these conditions, the vortex-ring state produces some interesting effects, which we'll get into a little later.

Turning the fan up full blast so that the flow is greater than the rotor-induced velocity makes the net flow *upward* through the rotor. The rotor is now slowing the tunnel flow a little and actually is extracting energy from the passing wind. Naturally this condition is known as the windmill-brake state. It is important to windmills that pump water, grind corn, or generate electricity, but it is somewhat academic in our

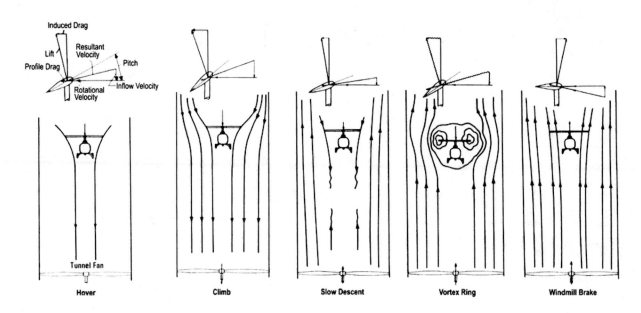

Figure 20-1 Examples of Rotor Flow States in Vertical Wind Tunnel

discussion—since helicopters have no good way to either dissipate or store energy.

Also shown in Figure 20-1 are the conditions at a blade element. Comparing these diagrams, we can see how the net flow through the rotor disc changes the collective pitch required to maintain constant thrust. The flow also causes the lift vector to tilt back in climb — increasing the power required. At low rates of descent and in the windmill-brake state, the flow causes the lift vector to tilt forward — decreasing the power required.

The vortex-ring state is more difficult to characterize, since the inflow pattern is not well defined. We know from experiments, however, that both the collective pitch and the power required to maintain a constant thrust are high and, therefore, the average conditions at the blade element must be similar to those in climb.

Climb and Descent Power

If a climbing helicopter were a rising elevator, the power required above that necessary to hover would be simply the product of the gross weight and the rate of climb in feet per minute (fpm) — all divided by 33,000 to get it into horsepower. (Our horsepower unit comes from old British coal-mining technology. A "standard" horse could lift 100 pounds out of a vertical shaft while walking away at about four mph or 330 fpm.)

A helicopter is not quite like an elevator. The aircraft gets a windfall advantage from the extra flow through the rotor due to the climb velocity. With this increase, the rotor doesn't have to work quite as hard as might be expected — with the result that the extra power required for climb (above that required for hover) is theoretically only half of what it would be if the helicopter were an elevator.

Two other benefits exist in climb that even further reduce the power required; first, the trailing tip vortices are further down when the next blade passes by and, second, the tail rotor is less disturbing to the induced-velocity distribution of the main rotor. Recent Army tests on the Sikorsky Black Hawk have shown that these effects are significant. Although, as on all helicopters, more collective pitch is required to climb than to hover, the power required is actually less for low rates of climb.

For rates of descent low enough to stay away from the vortex-ring state, the same relationship applies — only half the rate of change in potential energy could possibly be realized as a power reduction. Of course, the two benefits that apply in climb are detriments in descent, so the power required is somewhat higher than theory says.

Flight In the Vortex Ring

Because of the non-uniform and unsteady characteristics of the flow through the rotor in the vortex-ring state, the challenge to the theoretician is greater than for the other more straightforward flight conditions and much of our knowledge of this state comes from flight and wind tunnel tests. Based on this experience, we know that unsteadiness starts at about one-quarter, peaks at three-quarters, and disappears at 1¼ times the hover induced velocity.

Depending on their disc loading, various current helicopters enter the state when descending 300 to 600 fpm and have to be going 1,500 to 3,000 fpm to get clear of it. Staying in the vortex ring for any length of time isn't easy. It depends upon maintaining a nearly vertical flight path. There is some evidence, however, that a "glide" slope of about 70° is worse than a true 90° descent. Shallower approaches than about 50°, corresponding) forward speeds of 15 to 30 knots, will introduce enough fresh air into the system to blow the tip vortices away from the rotor and free it from the clutches of the vortex-ring state.

The unsteadiness of the flow has been seen during wind-tunnel tests of model rotors using smoke for flow visualization. Figure 20-2 is a sequence of events based on an interpretation of the smoke movies.

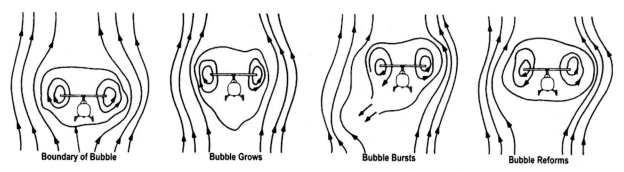

Boundary of Bubble   Bubble Grows   Bubble Bursts   Bubble Reforms

Figure 20-2 Vortex Ring Conditions

According to this concept, the rotor is continuously pumping air into a big bubble under the rotor. This bubble fills up and bursts every second or two, causing large-scale disturbances in the surrounding flow field. The bubble appears to erupt first from one side and then another so that not only does the rotor thrust vary, but the rotor Laps erratically in pitch and roll - requiring prompt pilot action.

Power Settling

Besides the unsteadiness, one of the most unusual characteristics of the vortex-ring is the high power required to maintain rotor thrust. Pilots call it "power settling" based on their observation that in some cases the helicopter keeps coming down even though full engine power is being used. Figure 20-3 shows the power and the collective pitch required to maintain constant rotor thrust in vertical descent for a typical helicopter. Not only does the power required increase in the vortex-ring state, but so does the collective pitch — apparently due to local blade stall during flow fluctuations. The range between 750 and 2,300 fpm for the helicopter shown in Figure 20-3 is the power-setting condition. This situation can become a problem when making a nearly vertical landing approach with a heavily loaded helicopter on a hot day when the power available is low.

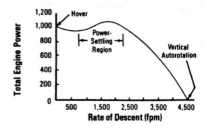

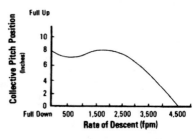

Figure 20-3 Power And Pitch Required in Vertical Descent for Typical Helicopter

Another scary scenario is an engine failure on a multiengine helicopter making a takeoff from a rooftop. In this operation, the prudent takeoff path is vertical — or even slightly backward — so that in case of an engine failure the helicopter can either return to the rooftop or (if high enough) go into forward flight without descending below the level of the roof—according to FAA rules. It is obvious that if the rate of descent back to the roof with one engine inoperative puts it into the vortex-ring state, then the landing may be more traumatic than the pilot might have anticipated.

Power settling has also been experienced during the downwind flare used for a quick stop or during crop-dusting turn. In any case where the helicopter catches up with its own wake, the power required to keep from falling out of the sky will suddenly increase.

The Tail Rotor, Too

The problems of operation in the vortex-ring state were first discovered on main rotors, but tail rotors may get their share in conditions such as right hover turns and left sideward flight (for helicopters with main rotors turning counterclockwise). Not all helicopters experience these troubles, but for those that do, a common symptom is a sudden increase in the turn rate, referred to by some pilots as "falling into a hole." This is due to the collective-pitch characteristics shown on Figure 20-3. A more detailed discussion of this problem will be found in Chapter 9.

Vertical Autorotation

After the helicopter is descending fast enough) pass through the worst of the unsteadiness in the vortex-ring state, it will achieve vertical autorotation. Usually, there is still a little induced downflow through portions of the rotor disc — although most of the flow will be upwards. This fixed-flow condition technically qualifies the rotor to still be classified as in the vortex-ring state.

In those portions of the disc subject to upflow, the lift vectors will be tilted forward. When enough of the vectors are tilted in this fashion, they will overcome the drag of the blades and even provide enough extra power to drive the tail rotor, gearboxes, and accessories, thus requiring no power from the engine.

Vertical autorotation is a stable condition and for one value of collective pitch the helicopter will settle on one rotor speed and one rate of descent. Using collective pitch, the pilot can control the rotor rpm. The lower the pitch, the faster the rotor will turn. The safe rpm range usually varies from about 75% to 110% of the normal power-on speed.

A too-low rotor speed will put the rotor blades into stall where they cannot autorotate and a too-high speed will produce excessive centrifugal loads in the hub and blade roots. Within this safe rotor-speed range, the rate of descent does not change much. It is equal to about twice the hover induced velocity which gives rates of descents — depending on disc loadings — of between 2,500 and 5,000 fpm for modern helicopters. Incidentally, these rates in vertical autorotation are approximately the same as if the rotor had been replaced by a parachute of the same diameter.

21 Crosscoupling

Symmetry—or, better put, the lack of it in helicopters—is something pilots must be aware of when maneuvering. While airplanes are symmetrical, helicopters are not. So helicopter pilots must use somewhat different control strategies than their fixed-wing brethren when maneuvering.

Make a turn

Let's examine what happens in such a simple maneuver as going from straight forward flight into a coordinated turn—one without sideslip. Both airplanes and helicopters turn by banking so that their lift or thrust vectors have a horizontal component.

This horizontal component, known as "centripetal force" in high-school physics, is what pulls the aircraft around, making it turn. This maneuver can be divided up into three distinct phases: rolling acceleration, rolling velocity, and holding a steady bank.

Rolling acceleration

To produce rolling acceleration, the airplane pilot deflects his ailerons with a sideward motion of the stick or wheel. This immediately produces a rolling moment by creating more lift on one wing than on the other.

The helicopter pilot does essentially the same thing in the cockpit, but the rotor, being only loosely connected to the rest of the aircraft, does its thing somewhat differently. It generates the required rolling moment by a sideward flapping of the rotor disc.

This produces the moment in two ways: by tilting of the thrust vector, and by generating a moment at the top of the mast if the rotor has offset flapping hinges—either actual or effective as in the case of the "hingeless" rotor.

The lateral flapping comes from cyclic pitch applied approximately a quarter of a revolution ahead. This effect is in response to the sideward motion of the control stick.

Just how close to a quarter of a revolution depends on the type of rotor hub. If it is a teetering rotor, it is exactly a quarter. But if the rotor has

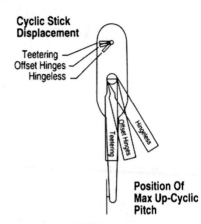

Figure 21-1 Control Displacement: Left Roll Acceleration With Different Rotor Types

hinge offset, the response is quicker. Figure 21-1 shows what the pilot and the control system must do to accelerate directly to the left.

With a teetering rotor, the motion is "pure," responding to the maximum change in up-cyclic pitch being applied right over the tail boom (for rotors turning counterclockwise when viewed from the top). For the rotor with hinge offset and for the hingeless rotor, however, the pilot must use a little aft stick to avoid getting some nosedown pitching moment. This aft motion is a measurement of "acceleration crosscoupling."

Note that the type of rotor also influences the amount of control motion needed. The higher the hinge offset, the more control moment is produced for the same flapping. This flapping is essentially equal to the change in cyclic pitch.

Rolling velocity

To maintain a steady rolling velocity, the airplane pilot simply leaves his ailerons deflected and the wings "screw" themselves into the air after they have accelerated to the rate dictated by the wing design and the aileron deflection.

The rotor, however, is a device of another nature. It acts as a gyroscope and must be "processed" to make it have a steady rate.

For the left roll, the maximum up-cyclic pitch must still be applied somewhere near the tail boom so the stick remains to the left, as it was to accelerate. But now another effect has to be accounted for.

Since the blade on the left side is going down with respect to the air, its angle of attack and therefore its lift is increased compared to the blade on the right side. To avoid up-flapping over the tail and down-flapping over the nose, the pilot must hold some aft stick to compensate for these changes.

The amount of this "rate crosscoupling" does not depend on the type of rotor hub. If we ignore the airframe damping in roll—a reasonable assumption for helicopters without long wings—we can say that, once the rolling velocity is steady, there is no need for a rolling moment from the rotor. It follows then, that there is no need for rotor tilt with respect to the mast, and thus no need for lateral flapping. If there is no flapping, it does not matter how the blades are fastened to the hub.

What does matter, however, is how heavy the blades are. The heavier the blades, the more lateral cyclic pitch is required to precess the rotor at a given rate. The longitudinal cyclic pitch required to balance the aerodynamics, however, will be the same for both light and heavy blades. Figure 21-2 illustrates the overall results when holding a steady left-roll rate with both light and heavy blades.

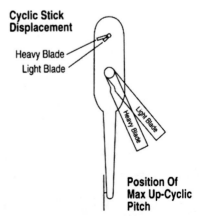

Figure 21-2 Control Displacement: Left Roll Velocity With Heavy And LightBlades

In this case, the distinction between light and heavy blades is one of relativity. The important factor is the ratio between the blade's aerodynamic and inertia characteristics. This ratio, called the Lock number, would be the same if the blades were built to the same design using the same construction materials, no matter what their physical size.

In practice, we find single-engine helicopters, which have to possess good autorotative entry characteristics, have heavier blades than multiengine machines, where it is assumed that all engines will not stop simultaneously. Very heavy blades were a characteristic of helicopters with tip-jet engines that were in vogue during the 1950s.

Holding the bank

Getting to the desired bank angle is only part of the turn maneuver. To maintain the bank, the wing lift or the rotor thrust must be increased over that required just to maintain level flight. That is, the wing or rotor must produce more than 1 G.

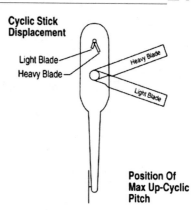

Figure 21-3 Control Displacement: Steady Left Bank With Heavy And LightBlades

The airplane pilot accomplishes this by holding aft stick to increase the wing's angle of attack. The helicopter pilot does it by increasing collective pitch.

Now, instead of having a rolling velocity, the helicopter has a pitching velocity (easy to see if it is in a 90° bank) and the rotor must be processed nose- up, using aft stick.

Since this pitching velocity means the blade over the nose sees more air coming down than the blade over the tail, it might be expected that cyclic pitch, that is, right stick, must be used to prevent a rolling moment to the left. There is another and opposing effect, however, that might be stronger.

Since the thrust is higher than in level flight, coning is also higher. This effect makes the blade over the nose see more air coming up than the one over the tail. If this effect is stronger than the one due to the noseup pitching velocity, the pilot might have to hold left stick instead of right. This coning effect is again a function of blade weight, and is stronger on rotors with light blades. Figure 21-3 illustrates the difference in control positions required to hold a steady bank with both heavy and light blades.

What to do about it

In an actual maneuver, of course, the acceleration, velocity, and steady crosscoupling effects phase in and out, and they may be accompanied by other effects, due to such things as inadvertent sideslip.

While it might be possible to eliminate one of these crosscouplings by biasing the linkages between the cockpit and the swashplate in the right way, it would be difficult to eliminate all of them. So control-system designers usually leave it up to the pilot to use his flying skills to compensate. Perhaps in the future, some sophisticated fly-by-wire systems will make the helicopter respond purely to cockpit control motions with no "Kentucky Windage" corrections required of the pilot.

22 Field-Of-View, Field-Of-Fire

The most important flying cue a helicopter pilot can have is a good view of the ground and of everything around him. From this standpoint, it must be said that Igor Sikorsky, with his original version of the VS-300, did it about right.

Later, he enclosed the pilot seat to provide partial protection from the elements, but at the cost of giving up valuable field-of-view (Figure 22-1). Helicopter designers have always faced this dilemma, and Figure 22-2 illustrates how some have settled it—from the bubble canopies of the early Bells to the airplane-type cockpits of more recent designs.

For low-level flying, and especially during a landing, it is valuable for the pilot to see past his feet. It is particularly helpful if he can see a skid or wheel to help in making a gentle touchdown. In many helicopters, this is provided by "chin" windows, but not in all because that space may be used for equipment, or for structure in the interests of reducing vulnerability or ensuring good crashworthiness.

Figure 22-1   Sikorsky VS-300

It would seem that if helicopter air-to-air combat is to become a fact of life, the pilot should have improved rearward visibility via a mirror or a rear-facing television camera to spot approaching threats. This is especially true for those twin-engine combat helicopters in which the

Figure 22-2 Field-Of-View Options

rearward field-of-view is partially blocked by engines that have been widely-spaced to reduce the vulnerability from a single hostile round.

Dilemmas

In military helicopters, it is not only protection from the elements that is important, but protection from enemy bullets as well. Since it is difficult to make transparency panels bulletproof, helicopter designers try to minimize the areas of transparency and install plate armor below the sill line.

One factor in this regard is the operational concept of slowly flying nap-of-the-earth to take advantage of terrain features to hide from the enemy. This, however, introduces the possibility of flying within point-blank rifle range of an unfriendly who is also taking advantage of the same terrain features to hide from the helicopter.

The Russians in Afghanistan found that continued use of the same mountain canyons ensured small arms ambushes from the surrounding ridges. These scary scenarios have led some to propose a tank-like, fully enclosed and armored cockpit with the pilot using periscopes and television for his only outside view.

Another dilemma is that large areas of transparencies turn the cockpit into a greenhouse on a sunny day and increase the air-conditioning requirements.

Who sits in front?

The designer of an attack helicopter with a two-man crew arranged in tandem must decide who gets the front seat with the best field-of-view: the pilot or the copilot/observer. Both have strong claim to it.

In the past, designers have generally put the pilot in back except for Bell in its YAH-63. One rationale for the usual choice is that the aft position, being closer to the center of gravity gives the pilot a better feel when maneuvering the aircraft. In some attack helicopters, the nose position of the weapon sight is given as the reason to put the gunner there.

Figure 22-3 Bell OH-58D With Mast-Mounted Sight

If the cockpit's view is not the best, or if it is desirable to mask as much of the helicopter as possible, a sight mounted on the cabin roof or above the rotor will be considered. A case where the perceived advantages of a mast-mounted sight outweigh the disadvantages of drag, weight, and cost is the Bell OH-58D (Figure 22-3).

Field-of-fire

What about another field, the field-of-fire for armed helicopters? When installing a gun on a helicopter, the designer has two choices; it can be fixed to the airframe as on fighter airplanes or installed in a turret.

The fixed-gun installation is lighter and easier to align accurately with its sight, but requires the whole aircraft be aimed at the target. The turreted weapon is heavier and less accurate, but can be quickly fired in almost any direction. The 30 mm gun on the Apache gives a good example (Figure 22-4).

It is desirable to maximize the field-of-fire of the turreted gun. Bombers in World War II accomplished this by using as many as six turrets to provide complete spherical protection. Most combat helicopters will probably have only nose or belly-mounted weapons; their fields-of-fire are somewhat limited by the airframe and by the rotor disc.

It is true, of course, that a similar problem was solved in World War I by using an interrupter that allowed machine guns to fire through the propeller. Since a rotor generally has less solidity than a propeller, it seems reasonable that with modem technology, a similar solution could be developed to allow the gun to ignore the rotor disc as a restraint.

Figure 22-4 McDonnell Douglas AH-64A Wwith 30mm Gun

Rockets and missiles

In the case of rockets and missiles, they are usually fired straight forward, but there is a desire to have some flexibility in the elevation of launch. It is especially desirable when firing from a hover position to adjust for the relative height of the target or to obtain the maximum range from unguided rockets.

This is accomplished on the Apache by the use of actuators in the wing-mounted racks that can change their elevation 5° up or down. Studies of the geometry of this helicopter, however, indicated that with the 5° noseup elevation, it would be possible to have a blade strike a missile as it passed through the forward edge of the disc if fired during maneuvers in which the blades were flapping down (as in the start of a pushover maneuver). The Apache's fire-control system was therefore programmed to inhibit firing during low G maneuvers.

23 Emergency Maneuvering

John Q. Pilot is scooting along in his helicopter doing contour flying at high speed. The visibility is not too good. It is only good enough to SUDDENLY SEE THE HIGH-VOLTAGE LINES JUST IN FRONT!

To avoid being responsible for a region wide power failure while producing a shower of sparks that would do neither him nor his machine any good, Johnny must either pull up to go over, push down to go under, or make a sharp U-turn.

Now, TV-fashion, let's freeze-frame Johnny with a startled look on his face. Fortunately, we can make time stand still while we calmly discuss what the designers have or have not done to help him.

The design of any vehicle is an exercise in the art of rational compromise and that is nowhere more evident than in the development of a helicopter. The two primary design influences are the desire to keep the weight down so it can hover and to keep the cost down so it can compete in the marketplace. This last consideration is very important in the Free World where competition exists both in the civil and the military markets.

As a result, the helicopter capabilities Johnny can call on are limited, since they were established during the early stages of design when the engineers were under constant pressure to hold down both weight and cost.

Pullup!

To go over those power lines, Johnny wants to use maximum rotor thrust to pullup. Despite what is generally thought, thrust is not limited by the onset of retreating blade stall. A model rotor in a wind tunnel will go gracefully into deep retreating blade stall, producing higher and higher thrust while maintaining the ability to be trimmed out with cyclic pitch. As far as I know, no one has actually gotten the thrust to peak on a model rotor.

This apparent ignoring of retreating blade stall is because most of the thrust is being generated by the blades over the nose and tail and even after an airfoil stalls, it will still develop a high lift coefficient. The most

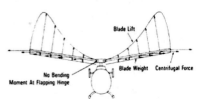

Figure 23-1 Load Distribution on Rotor

thrust will occur on a rotor that has a high nose-up disc angle of attack-and enough collective pitch to make even the blades over the nose and tail stall. In this case, both the lift and the drag acting at a blade element will be oriented upward, adding to the total rotor thrust.

A wind-tunnel rotor in this situation should be able to generate a thrust/solidity coefficient (C_T/σ) of at least 0.3. Since a normal value might be 0.06 for level flight at sea level, this rotor could have the capability to develop a load factor of 5 Gs in flight! But will it?

No, not really. Unlike a wind-tunnel model that is held fixed in space, the helicopter with rotor thrust greater than the gross weight will follow a curved flight path as it climbs and will never reach the high nose-up angle of attack required for the 5-G pullup. Flight tests show that a maximum value of C_T/σ of about 0.2 has been achieved, corresponding to about 3 Gs at sea level and, of course, lower at altitude. The highest values recorded were during flares from autorotation where the disc angle of attack was already nose-up.

If higher load-factor capabilities are required, the designers will have to choose a lower value of C_T/σ in level flight by increasing blade area—or add a wing. Unfortunately, both will hurt the hover performance but that is just one of the compromises that must be considered in the design process.

Nothing breaks

The pilot of an airplane might be concerned with breaking the wings off during a high-G maneuver. The pilot of a helicopter need not worry. As shown in Figure 23-1, as the rotor cones up under load, centrifugal forces try to bend the blades down as much as lift forces try to bend them up. Thus, steady blade bending moments are relatively low. Since most of the rest of the airframe is designed to be stout by other considerations, such as landing loads, nothing breaks unless it has already been weakened by previous fatigue damage-a subject we will come to later.

The statement that "nothing breaks" during a high maneuver might seem at odds with the V-N Diagram (Figure 23-2) used to guide the structural design and which, at least indirectly, implies that it is dangerous to fly outside of it. However, a good indication that the V-N diagram has never been considered a serious operational limit is the fact that only on recent combat helicopters such as the U.S. Army's AH-64A Apache have the designers bothered to give the pilot a G-meter,

Pushover!

Lowering the collective and pushing over is another possible escape maneuver but it generates a control problem. If the pullup maneuver was done with 3 Gs, a mirror-image pushover would require minus 1 G; that is, both require a 2-G change from 1 G, level flight.

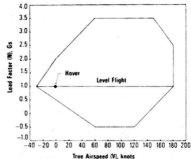

Figure 23-2 A Typical Design V-N Diagram

Depending on the rotor design, pitch and roll control will be lost at some low load factor. For a teetering rotor, the critical point is when it is developing no thrust in zero-G flight—but even an offset flapping-hinge rotor or a hingeless rotor will lose control at some level of negative thrust.

At minus 1 G, a rotor needs a hinge offset—or equivalent hinge offset-of at least 7% of the rotor radius to maintain half the control power it had in level flight. If Johnny's helicopter does not have this much, the pushover may not be such a good idea.

Do a 180!

A sharp U-turn requires a combination of capabilities. First, high roll acceleration and high roll rate are needed to get into the turn—and then high thrust and high power are needed to stay in it.

Maximum roll acceleration and maximum roll rate come from two different design decisions. The type of hub determines the acceleration capability. A stiff, hingeless rotor gives the highest and a teetering rotor the lowest. An articulated rotor with offset hinges is somewhere in between.

When it comes to roll rate, however, the type of rotor does not matter. Maximum roll rate is governed almost entirely by the amount of lateral cyclic-pitch travel the designers have built into the control system, and the rotor's Lock number—which is the ratio of its aerodynamic lifting capability to its inertia.

For the same lateral-cyclic pitch, a light rotor with lots of blade area will roll faster than a heavy rotor with a small blade area. So you can see that Johnny's ability to quickly get into the turn has been determined by early design decisions that probably had nothing to do with the immediate situation.

Once banked over, all these roll considerations become moot. Now the question becomes: "Can the rotor/engine combination produce the thrust/power required to maintain this high-G turn?"

The type of turn for which the answer is most likely to be "No" is one in which the pilot tries to maintain both the initial altitude and speed. For the pullup maneuver, he could get some benefit from increased disc angle of attack to produce rotor thrust but in a constant-speed-and-altitude turn, the disc has to be tilted nosedown to overcome the drag and the increased thrust must come from collective pitch alone. As a rule of thumb, the maximum rotor thrust in this condition would be about 70% of what it would be in a pullup.

Engine and transmission limits

The other limit to this maneuver is the maximum power that can be delivered to the rotor. Most modern turbine engines have an automatic limit to fuel flow when the turbine-inlet temperature reaches a preset value. Thus, on cold days the engine can put out more power than on hot days. In an emergency, the pilot would want to use the engine power up to this "topping" limit but in so doing, he might be violating the transmission limit.

On most modern helicopters, the transmission has not been qualified to accept all of the power the engine(s) can put out on a cold day at sea level. Instead, in the interest of saving weight, the transmission is "derated" by designing it to accept only the power the engine(s) can produce at some high altitude and temperature such as the 4,000-foot, 95° F (35° C) condition used by the U.S. Army.

The engine-torque gauge in a single-engine helicopter is marked at 100% at the transmission limit. On a twin-engine helicopter, 100% on each torque gauge represents half of the transmission limit. This limit has been set after bench tests in which the transmission was run at even higher power levels so there is no immediate danger of the transmission failing if asked to transmit more than 100% torque for short periods of time. However, some progressive damage might occur due to gear-tooth and bearing wear at the high temperatures generated under these extreme conditions.

At any rate, this is only a minor concern in an emergency situation. Of course, both the rotor thrust and the engine/transmission requirements are relieved if the helicopter is permitted to slow up or to descend during the turn.

Sideslip envelope

One way to make the turn faster is to generate a high sideslip-that is, to make an uncoordinated turn. This introduces the possibility of exceeding the designer's sideslip envelope, such as in Figure 23-3, that was used to design the strength of the tail boom and the fastening of side windows and doors that are subject to suction loads during high speed sideslips.

If the designer has done his job right, the sideslip envelope cannot be exceeded in flight. This is not always true but, since the designer does not give the pilot a sideslip indicator (except in flight-test aircraft), it is a limit meant to be ignored.

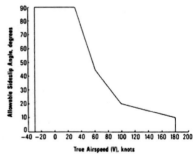

Figure 23-3 A Typical Design Sideslip Envelope

How about fatigue damage?

Even though Johnny won't break anything in his maneuvering, he may be doing some fatigue damage as he develops oscillating loads higher than the "endurance limit" in the rotating components. This has to be a minor consideration in an emergency but it might become a major consideration sometime later if a part were to develop a fatigue crack before its scheduled replacement time.

This problem can be traced back to the original spectrum of flight conditions used in design. As part of the "design criteria," somebody guessed at the time a typical helicopter would spend doing hover, cruise, dash, and other things such as jumping over power lines. This was used by the designers to determine how strong (and heavy) each part must be to last the required operational hours-4,500 for the Apache, for instance.

Let's say someone guessed that an extreme maneuver capable of doing some fatigue damage would occur every three hours, and in actual operations, the aircraft is flown such that this maneuver, or an equivalent one, is done every hour. Then, we shouldn't be surprised that parts develop fatigue cracks before their calculated time. This situation especially applies to aircraft being used to train for emergency procedures.

Recording history

To avoid being surprised by premature failures in the field, aircraft manufacturers may have to adopt a practice already used by the engine manufacturers-a history recorder. For engines, these automatically record the time spent over a certain turbine-inlet temperature. By correlating this with test-cell results, a mechanic can determine when the engine should be pulled for overhaul.

The ultimate procedure for the airframe would be to strain gauge each fatigue-critical component and record each cycle of load above the endurance limit and by how much it was exceeded. This is a method now used during flight test in a "flight-load survey" and allows the structures engineer to predict when each part will suffer enough fatigue damage to warrant its replacement.

This would be quite a complicated solution in operation, so it is logical that some simpler method will be used-such as recording load factor or extreme vibration levels or whatever other parameter is indicative of high fatigue loads.

Epilogue

Did John Q. Pilot avoid running into the transmission lines? Since he was a good pilot and was flying a good helicopter, sure he did-this time.

24 Flying Qualities

The words, "flying qualities" have to do with how the helicopter helps or hinders the pilot, not only in his routine duties but also in coping with emergencies. In the broad sense, some flying qualities are performance characteristics, such as the ability to fly fast enough, high enough, and to turn quickly enough.

Other phases of flying qualities have to do with *task performance*, which is measured by how successfully the pilot can make the aircraft go where he wants, and with *workload* which has to do with how much and how often he must move the controls— and how hard he must concentrate while doing it. Workload in combination with communication, navigation, and other necessary duties contributes to pilot fatigue, which in turn is also affected by ride quality (gust response), vibration, noise, seat comfort, and cockpit climate, to say nothing of those other critical factors reflecting the pilot's physical, mental, and emotional status.

Flying Qualities Criteria

It is the designer's goal to provide a helicopter that can do all it is supposed to without tiring the pilot to the point where he cannot physically or mentally perform his job effectively after a reasonable time in the cockpit. (Although, contrary to logic, some statistics indicate that more accidents occur near the *beginning* of the flight.)

To give the designer some guidelines, both military and the civil authorities have adopted flying-quality criteria in the form of Military Specifications and Federal Aviation Regulations.

There is significant difference between the civil and the military documents. The civil regulations, of which FAR Part 29, "Airworthiness Standards: Transport Category Rotorcraft" is a current example, are primarily concerned with minimum requirements for safety of flight. On the other hand, military requirements such as MIL-H-8501A, "Helicopter Flying and Ground Handling Qualities; General Requirements for," are more mission-oriented.

As an example, with respect to controllability, FAR Part 29 says only: "The rotorcraft must be safely controllable and maneuverable;" leaving the judgment of this to the FAA certification pilot. In MIL-H-8501A,

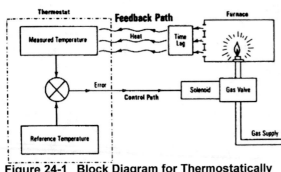

Figure 24-1 Block Diagram for Thermostatically Controlled Furnace

however, specified minimum values of pitch, roll, and yaw displacements are required at the end of one second following a sudden one-inch displacement of the appropriate control.

These differences in rules are not entirely based on different governing philosophies but also reflect the expectation that military helicopters flying nap-of-the-earth and doing violent maneuvers to avoid being shot down will need control characteristics generally not required when just flying from point A to point B.

At this time, the specifications for military helicopters are somewhat less specific than for military airplanes. This seems to be in recognition of the difficulty of achieving good flying qualities in all helicopter flight regimes —especially those in which fixed-wing pilots fear to fly, such as below 60 knots (in all directions) and within touching distance of the ground. As an indication of this, it is generally recognized that three hours of piloting a helicopter is as tiring as four or five in a comparable airplane.

Servo Jargon

There is an increasing trend among flying-quality experts to use a jargon originally developed for describing servomechanisms. To introduce some terms, let's examine a servomechanism system that we're familiar with: the thermostatically controlled home furnace, shown as a block diagram in Figure 24-1.

The desired temperature is set on the thermostat as a reference. When the actual temperature falls below this reference, the thermostat sees this as an *error* and uses the forward *control path* to turn the furnace on. The flow of heat between the furnace outlet and the thermostat serves as a *feedback path* and with the control path makes a *closed loop*. The feedback tells the thermostat the command has been obeyed and gives a quantity (temperature in this case) to measure and compare against the preset goal to trigger turning the furnace off.

A home furnace has a relatively low *gain*. That is, for any temperature error detected by the thermostat, the furnace puts out a moderate amount of heat that gradually warms the room until the measured temperature is equal to the reference temperature. If it were required to very quickly correct either a low or a high error, a very big furnace and also a very big air-conditioner might be used. This would be a *high-gain* system. Because of the distance between the heat/cold outlet and the thermostat, the *time lag* in the feedback path might result in the thermostat getting out-of-step with the furnace and begin oscillating the system to bigger and bigger temperature changes by doing the wrong thing at the wrong time.

This is characteristic of many servomechanisms. By increasing the gain— the ratio of response to error— the system can be made unstable.

We are all exposed to the consequences of this type of instability whenever we hear a public-address system begin to squeal because of feedback. As might be expected, the cure is to turn down the gain of the amplifier or to make the feedback path more difficult by turning the microphone away from the loudspeaker.

Many of our machines are not controlled by automatic devices, but by us. It is possible, however, to think of even these systems in servomechanism terms. For instance, in driving your car on a busy highway, you mentally set minimum and maid-mum goals for the distance from the lane markers and the car ahead. When you detect errors from these goals, you use the steering wheel and the accelerator (or even the brake pedal) to correct them. The feedback is through your eyes, which tell you that your goals are being achieved. Your gain level depends upon how hard you are trying to maintain your goals. The time it takes the brain to process information and send the appropriate messages to the hand and leg muscles (combined with the response time of the car) is the time lag of the system.

During normal flying, the pilot's gain may be either low or high. Flying en route on a cloudless day, he can afford to be relatively relaxed (low gain) since there is no reason to immediately correct small errors. If, on the other hand, his job is to precisely locate a sling-loaded TV transmitter antenna on the top of a skyscraper, his gain will be high as he strives to correct even the smallest position and altitude errors. A high-gain task may lead to pilot-induced oscillation (PIO) where the aircraft does not instantaneously obey the pilot's intentions because of the lags mentioned above— and the whole system goes unstable.

Closing the Loop

As part of a servomechanism system, the pilot has to control not only direction and speed but bank angle and altitude as well. In doing this, he is continuously "closing the loop".

Almost all operational flying is closed-loop but during flight testing almost all of the emphasis is put on determining the open-loop characteristics of the helicopter. This is done by pulsing one of the controls momentarily or by displacing it and then holding it fixed while the helicopter does its thing. Either way, the pilot simply goes along for the ride until he is ready to set up the next test point— or has to regain control to save the situation. This type of testing is aimed at determining the control response characteristics and the inherent stability of the aircraft.

Most of the requirements in the present flying qualities criteria are aimed at determining these open-loop characteristics and, as such, lead to rather simple flight-test programs in terms of getting the test points and then in analyzing them. Many of our flying-quality problems, however, occur in closed-loop flying, that is, in the field of *machine-man matching*, and recently there has been more and more recognition that a flight-test

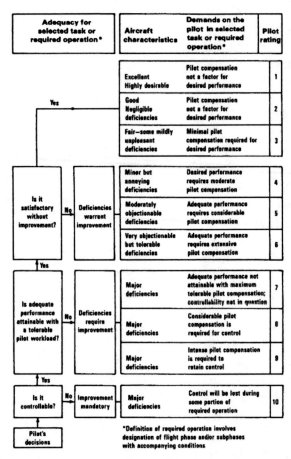

Figure 24-2 Cooper-Harper Pilot Rating Scale

program is incomplete without some rigorous high-gain tasks that test this matching.

An objective of those trying to make helicopter flying-quality specifications reflect the facts of life is to find some way of specifying closed-loop characteristics, so designers can take them into account and/or test pilots can identify problems early in the flight test program. Compared to helicopter people, airplane flying-quality people have more high-gain precision tasks they can study using pilot workload and measurable errors. Included in this category are carrier spot landings, formation flying, instrument landing system approaches, in-flight refueling, and target tracking.

Most helicopter high-gain tasks have to do with operation close to the ground, where the object is to avoid chopping down trees or plowing furrows with the main rotor, tail rotor, or landing gear— which are all out of the pilot's line of sight. The situation is complicated by the fact that the characteristics of an important part of the system — the pilot —vary widely and are not in conformance with any set of standardized specifications.

Cues

To do a good job of *flying,* the pilot uses various cues in closing the loop. By far the most important cue is a clear view of the horizon, not only straight ahead but also to the side out of the corners of the eyes (peripheral vision). Flight in these conditions is under visual flight rules (VFR) or, in the more recent semantics, visual meteorological conditions (VMC). When the view of the horizon disappears, as when flying into a cloud, a pilot without special instrument flight training becomes uneasy at the very least and in some cases develops vertigo, where he literally cannot tell which way is up.

You don't have to be a pilot to experience the effect of the lack of a good cue. The yellow line down the middle of a two-lane highway gives us the confidence to drive within a few feet of opposing traffic but we are much more cautious when driving on a newly blacktopped highway before the road crew has repainted the little yellow line.

An aircraft expected to be flown when the natural horizon is not visible is said to be equipped for instrument flight rules (IFR), or for instrument meteorological conditions (IMC). The cockpit instruments required to do this vary from relatively simple to relatively sophisticated — and as far as the pilot is concerned, vary in performance from very bad all the way up to fair. Thus to use them requires extensive special training. It is also significant that navigation becomes much more difficult in IMC, increasing the mental workload greatly.

Flying on instruments is a more difficult task than flight in VMC so a level of aircraft stability that might be quite acceptable for visual flight is often not good enough for instrument flight. For this reason, almost all helicopters approved for instrument flight also have stability augmentation systems (SAS), which help free the pilot to concentrate on his many other duties. Some recent military helicopters take a different approach by giving the pilot some electronic help in seeing at night. This is especially valuable if he has to fly close to the ground.

Rating Scale

A formalized way of judging whether the aircraft is helping or hindering the pilot is the Handling Qualities Rating Scale, often referred to as the Cooper-Harper scale for its originators. When using this scale (Figure 24-2), the test pilot, pretending to be an "average" pilot, does a specific task, such as a landing, and then assigns a rating from 1, which is perfect, to 10, which is awful (note the difference from the girl rating scale).

A rating of 3½ is the dividing line between a helicopter that is OK and one with shortcomings that *should* be fixed. A rating of 6¼ and above is applied to a helicopter with deficiencies that *must* be fixed.

Besides identifying necessary configuration changes, the test pilot is also using his experience and judgment to predict the amount of fatigue that a given maneuver in a given aircraft will impose on the pilot.

If we knew more about people, we could perhaps predict when a pilot would get so tired that he could no longer function effectively. Structural engineers investigate materials by torturing samples in a laboratory until they break. I will leave to someone else the transference of this technology to the prediction of pilot fatigue limits.

25 High Performance Takeoffs

A takeoff—whether of an airplane or helicopter— is almost always a routine, unexciting event. The exception is when an engine loses power right in the middle of it — a possibility that influences both the aircraft's design and the manner of its operation to assure maximum safety.

When approving helicopters as transports, the FAA has two categories of rules. The main difference is that Category A rules require that the helicopter have a "stay-up" capability (essentially the ability to climb at least 100 fpm in forward flight after failure of one engine) while Category B rules do not. Automatically, this means that only multi-engined helicopters can qualify as Category A and all single-engine ships are Category B.

The advantage of Category A certification is that these helicopters are permitted to make takeoffs and landings from such challenging heliports as center-city rooftops and to fly en route over areas that have no emergency landing sites. Category B transports, on the other hand, are restricted to flying a route/altitude pattern in such a manner that, at any point, an immediate safe landing can be made in case of engine failure.

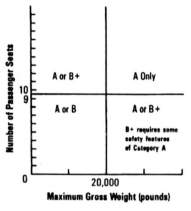

Figure 25-1 Towing Equilibrium Diagram

The Federal Aviation Administration (FAA) has recently modified its rules governing which multi-engine helicopters can be certificated in which categories. Figure 25-1 illustrates the distinctions, based on maximum gross weight and number of passenger seats. Usually, manufacturers consider it a competitive advantage to obtain Category A certification even on the smaller multiengine helicopters — and many recent twin-engine designs have been certificated as Category A at one gross weight and Category B at a higher gross weight.

Safe Takeoffs

The right takeoff procedure for Category A helicopters depends on the type of heliport. Figure 25-2 shows both normal and rejected takeoffs from a relatively large heliport. In this case, the pilot's takeoff objective should be quick acceleration to the speed at which the power demand is low enough that a climb of 100 fpm could be maintained if one engine were to go out. The higher the takeoff weight, altitude, and temperature, the higher the minimum climb speed, which is known as takeoff safety speed or V_{TOSS}. The point along the flight path from which V_{TOSS} can

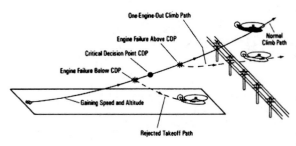

Figure 25-2 Operation from a Large Heliport

be achieved without coming closer to the ground than 35 feet is called the critical decision point (CDP).

Below the CDP, a power failure is handled as a rejected takeoff by flaring and landing straight ahead. The total distance from the original takeoff spot to the final stopping place will depend on where along the flight path the CDP is located. This, in turn, depends on the gross weight of the helicopter and the effects of altitude and temperature on the maximum power that can be obtained from the remaining engine(s).

A heliport large enough to handle a rejected takeoff of a fully loaded helicopter on a cold day may be too small on a hot day. In this case, payload will have to be offloaded to maintain the same degree of safety. This is not unique to transport helicopters. Fixed-wing transports occasionally face the same circumstances.

If the power failure occurs beyond the CDP, the helicopter can fly to another location or return to its takeoff spot in a more-or-less normal flight pattern.

Operation from a very small heliport such as a rooftop is shown in Figure 25-3. This situation requires that a rejected takeoff be terminated back at the original takeoff spot. For this reason, the takeoff flight plan must be vertical — or slightly backing up — to keep the heliport in view so that up to the CDP the pilot can get back down to the same place he just left. If the power failure occurs above the CDP, the pilot can trade altitude for speed and go into forward flight while maintaining a clearance from the roof of 15 feet vertically and 35 feet horizontally.

The vertical climb to the CDP means there must be no unsafe region in the helicopter's height-velocity diagram (or deadman's curve) up to this height. For a given helicopter, this usually means that the allowable gross weight for rooftop operation is less than for operation from large, ground-level areas. This, of course, has a bearing on the economics of the operation if, with the same helicopter, fewer paying customers can be flown from a rooftop.

Since the loss of only one engine has to be provided for, the more engines a helicopter has, the less penalty there will be for rooftop operations.

Oil-rig takeoffs

Another takeoff site similar to a rooftop but at the same time different is the helipad on an oil-drilling platform. This is usually a 100 or more feet above the sea, which generally means that the helicopter is in the "avoid" region of the operating manual's height-velocity curve as soon as it leaves the helipad.

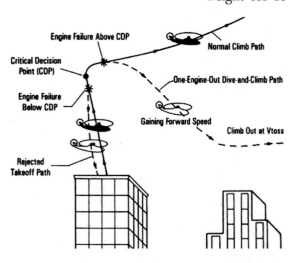

Figure 25-3 Operation from a Rooftop Heliport

If the helicopter is amphibious or equipped with emergency flotation gear adequate to accomplish a safe emergency ditching on open water, the FAA allows momentary flight through the avoid region. Part of the rationale for this waiver is that the height-velocity curve established for emergency touchdowns on solid ground is conservative when applied to a well-equipped helicopter ditching in water. Thus, these helicopters can use a forward flight takeoff such as in Figure 25-2. If, however, the sea was too rough for ditching or the helicopter not approved for water landings, the vertical takeoff of Figure 25-3 should be used.

Figure 25-4 shows the Category A takeoff and landing procedures for the Sikorsky S-61 as used in the North Sea.

Heavy Takeoffs

The fact that it takes less power to fly forward than to hover can be used to get a heavily loaded helicopter into the air. In some circumstances, it can make a running takeoff from a runway or cleared field, just like an airplane. In other places, however, it has to get at least a little way above the ground to avoid stubbing its toe.

The U.S. Army has done extensive testing to find the best way to clear a nearby 50-foot obstacle. In setting up the tests, the Army covered the full range of takeoffs. The baseline case being when a helicopter is light enough to allow it to climb straight up. The other limit is when the machine is so heavy that it can just barely hover in ground effect.

For this latter case, illustrated in Figure 25-5, the Army procedure is as follows:

1—Hover in ground effect and note the pitch angle the fuselage makes with the ground;

2—Tilt the helicopter forward to accelerate it in-to forward flight, using cyclic pitch to keep the ship low to take advantage of ground effect and keeping the power up to its limit with collective pitch until the transitional flight vibration disappears;

3— Rotate back to the hover attitude to initiate the climb;

4—Hold this speed (usually about 30 knots) and attitude until the 50-foot obstacle is cleared; and

5— Increase speed to the best rate of climb.

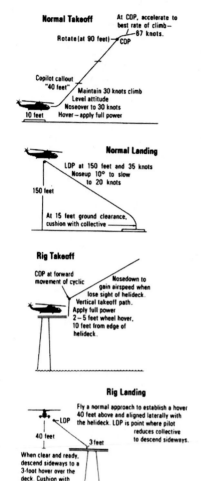

Figure 25-4   S-61 Category A Procedures

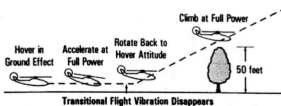

Figure 25-5   Technique for Heavyweight Takeoff

26 Translational Lift and Transverse Flow

Not long after the pilot leaves hover to go into forward flight, he will recognize a need to manipulate the controls if he is to stay on his intended flight path. The reason is found in the rapid change of flow conditions at the rotor disc.

Translational lift

A rotor produces thrust by inducing a downward velocity in the air going past it. The amount of velocity required depends on the "mass flow". When the mass flow is small, the rotor has to work harder and produce a larger downward induced velocity than is required for the same thrust when the mass flow is large.

In hover, the mass flow is small, being made up only of the air flowing downward at the hover-induced velocity. But, in forward flight, the air coming horizontally at the rotor increases the effective mass flow and allows the induced velocity to decrease (Figure 26-1).

Whether in hover or forward flight, a rotor producing a constant thrust will have about the same average angle of attack at its blade elements. In hover, the collective pitch must be high enough to provide this angle of attack while compensating for the high downward velocity. If the collective pitch is left at the hover position as the helicopter goes into forward flight, it will overcompensate for the continually decreasing induced velocity, the average angle of attack will increase, thrust will be more than the gross weight of the aircraft, and the helicopter will begin to climb.

It will increase its rate of climb until the relative velocity coming down due to climb makes up for the decreased downward induced velocity. At this point, the thrust will again be equal to the gross weight (with perhaps some difference caused by increased aerodynamic download on the airframe), and the helicopter will be in a steady climb.

This tendency to automatically go into a climb first becomes noticeable at forward speeds as low as 10 or 20 knots and is known as "translational lift" or sometimes "transitional lift". It can be very helpful in getting heavily loaded helicopters into the air. Translational lift is simply the

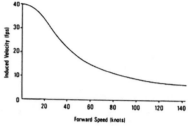

Figure 26-1 Typical Induced Velocity Trend

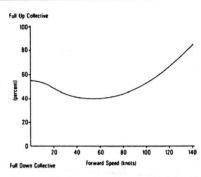

Figure 26-2 Collective Stick Position Required for Level Flight

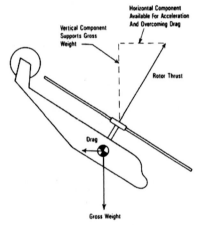

Figure 26-3 Accelerating in Level Flight

result of the collective pitch being in an out-of-trim position for level flight.

If the pilot does not want to climb during the transition to forward flight, he has two options. During a slow acceleration, he can decrease the collective pitch to keep the average angle of attack of the blade elements constant as the induced velocity decreases. Figure 26-2 shows that the decrease will not go on indefinitely. At some speed, the forward tilt of the rotor required to overcome the parasite drag of the helicopter will increase the "inflow velocity" through the rotor, even as the induced velocity continues to decrease. At about the speed for minimum power (50 to 80 knots depending on the helicopter), the required collective pitch for level flight will also be a minimum and will begin to rise as speed is increased.

The second option may be used during a fast acceleration by leaving the collective in the hover position but tilting the helicopter nose down with the cyclic pitch so that the vertical component of the ever-increasing thrust is supporting the gross weight, while the horizontal component accelerates the helicopter along the flight path (Figure 26-3).

This goes on until the collective required is again equal to the hover value. At that speed, the helicopter will stop accelerating and will settle into steady, level flight. To go faster, the pilot will have to increase the collective. In actual operation, a combination of the two options is generally used.

Transverse flow

The other thing the pilot will notice as he goes from hover to forward flight is that the helicopter has an apparent desire to roll down toward its advancing blade (to the right on American helicopters). This is caused not by the change in the average induced velocity but by the change in its distribution over the disc. The induced velocity can be thought of as being generated by the action of the whirlpool-like vortices left by each blade tip. In hover, these tip vortices spiral down, forming a cylinder and inducing an equally distributed downward flow around the rotor.

In forward flight, however, the vortices trail out behind the rotor and are thus much more influential in affecting the flow at the back of the disc than at the front. Wind-tunnel observations have shown that at moderately fast forward speeds, the induced velocity at the front of the disc is essentially zero, whereas at the back it is twice the average value.

If the pilot holds the lateral cyclic pitch at its hover value as he goes into forward flight, the blade over the nose will soon be subjected to the decrease in induced velocity. This will increase its angle of attack (Figure 26-4), its lift will increase, and, because of the quarter-revolution delay in response, it will flap up on the retreating side.

Conversely, the local angle of attack on the blade over the tail will decrease. This will lead to flapping down on the advancing side. The flapping produces a rolling moment similar to what would be caused by a side wind- and so it is called a "transverse-flow" effect, even though its root cause is a longitudinal change in the flow pattern.

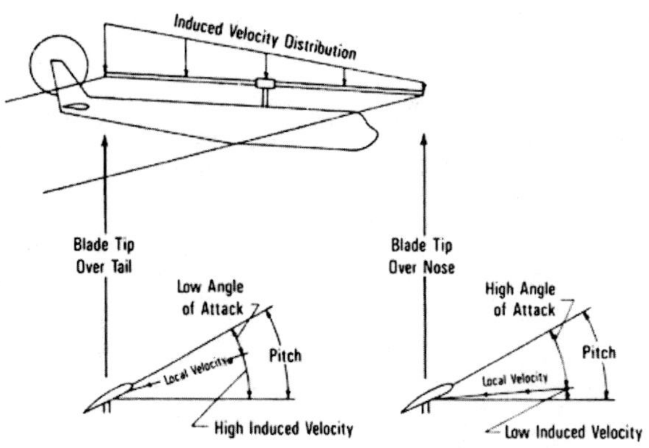

To fly straight and level, the pilot must use left stick (with American rotors) to compensate for the change in the induced velocity distribution to prevent the roll. The lateral stick displacement required (Figure 8-5) is highest at low forward speeds, quickly peaks and then fades almost as quickly. The French have a phrase for the shape of the resulting plot. They call it "bosse du manche" (the hill of the stick).

As speed is increased still further, another effect becomes important; that of coning, which increases the angle of attack on the blade over the nose and decreases it on the blade over the tail. To compensate for this also requires left stick.

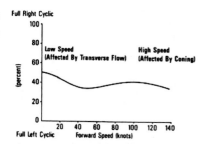

Figure 26-4 Source of Transverse Flow Effect

Figure 26-5 Lateral Cyclic Stick Position Requled for Level Flight

27 Low Speed Flight

Most of the time, a helicopter flight will go from hover to high speed without spending any more time than is necessary in the transition flight regime. Sometimes, however, flying low and slow is required to get the job done and this flight regime has some interesting characteristics.

Sideward Tilt

Almost all single-rotor helicopters with the American rotation hover with the left landing gear low. This is because the rightward thrust of the tail rotor must be balanced by leftward tilt of the main rotor. Besides gross weight and tail-rotor thrust, the degree of fuselage tilt depends on two physical parameters: the amount of hinge offset in the main-rotor hub and the vertical position of the tail rotor with respect to the main rotor and the aircraft's center of gravity (CG).

Figure 27-1 shows rear views of four helicopters. The first depicts a general case with some hinge offset and the tail rotor located between the main rotor and the CG. It has some left fuselage tilt. Also shown are three special cases: one in which the parameters are arranged to produce

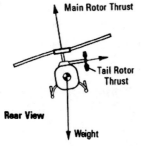

General Case

Type of Main Rotor: With Some Hinge Offset
Height of Tail Rotor: Between CG and Main Rotor
Results: Some Flapping Down to Left
Some Fuselage Left Tilt

	Special Cases		
Type of Main Rotor	**Teetering**	**Any**	**Very High Offset**
Height of Tail Rotor	**As High as Main**	**As Low as CG**	**Any**
Results	Fuselage Level	Fuselage Tilted, No Flapping	Fuselage Tilted, Very Little Flapping

Figure 27-1 Lateral Tilt in Hover

no tilt, and two others in which the fuselage is tilted as much as the rotor tip-path plane.

In forward flight, the aircraft can be leveled up by flying with enough right sideslip so that the fuselage, not the main rotor, develops the required aerodynamic sideforce to balance tail-rotor thrust. This centers the ball of the turn-and-bank indicator but usually requires extra power because the fuselage drag is higher than it would be for zero sideslip.

Few operational helicopters have sideslip indicators. Therefore, in order to obtain maximum performance (if not maximum comfort), the pilot should keep the ball in approximately its hover position. The main rotor shaft on some helicopters is made with a slight tilt to the left so that the fuselage can be more or less level in all flight conditions.

Turning While in Hover

The possibility of putting the tail rotor into the vortex-ring state in certain flight conditions was discussed in Chapter 2. A right (clockwise) hover turn as shown in Figure 27-2 is one of those conditions.

The severity of the problem, from the pilot's standpoint, depends upon the helicopter. In a bad helicopter, a slow right turn can suddenly become a fast right turn without any pilot action because the tail rotor loses thrust in the vortex-ring state. A good helicopter, on the other hand, will allow easy and precise control of the rate of turn in either direction by the amount of pedal used.

The difference between a good and bad design apparently involves the characteristics of the resultant airflow that the tail rotor has to operate with and how the airflow is affected by tip vortices from the main rotor. I will admit that our understanding of this interaction is sketchy. It is known, however, that the tail rotor should rotate with the blade closest to the main rotor going up, and there is some evidence that raising the tail rotor with respect to the main rotor is a step in the right direction.

Overloading the Tail Rotor

Maintaining a right hover turn is one thing but stopping it is quite another. If a helicopter makes a right turn fast enough so that the tail rotor operates beyond its vortex-ring condition, stopping the turn with full opposite pedal can be a traumatic experience for the tail-rotor drive system. During the turn, the main-rotor torque is doing most of the work and the tail rotor is acting like a main rotor in vertical descent with a correspondingly low value of pitch.

When the pilot steps on the left pedal to stop the turn, the tail-rotor blade pitch is rapidly increased by 20° to 30°. Since the induced velocity through the tail rotor cannot change instantaneously, the tail-rotor blades are suddenly forced to operate at large angles of attack —possibly above their stall limits. Thus the tail rotor can absorb much more power than usual during the short time required for the induced velocity to develop.

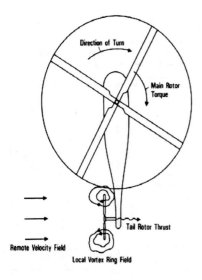

Figure 27-2 Conditions in Right Hover Turn

If the drive system is not designed for such transient overloads, it could mean real trouble. The moral is: make recoveries from fast right hover turns as gentle as the situation allows.

Tandem-rotor helicopters, of course, have none of these tail-rotor problems, but they, too, can encounter an interesting situation during hover turns. A turn made around the CG of the tandem will put both rotors into similar sideward flight conditions, but a hover turn around the cockpit will leave the forward rotor in hover while an appreciable sideward velocity will increase the rear rotor's thrust. There have been cases where all of the aft longitudinal control margin was used up trying to get the ship back into trim during this type of maneuver.

Flight at Low Forward Speeds

There are several main-rotor aerodynamic effects that are unique to flight at low speed. One is the decrease in induced velocity at the rotor. As the induced velocity decreases, the setting of the collective pitch will be too high and, if it is not reduced, the helicopter will begin to climb. Pilots describe this phenomenon as picking up "translational lift."

The reverse is noticed when going from forward flight into hover. If the collective pitch is not increased, translational lift will be lost and the aircraft will begin to settle.

An alleviating factor for this is the ground effect, which decreases the net downward-induced velocity at the rotor disc as the helicopter settles. This decreases the local angles of attack on the blade elements, thus producing a beneficial cushion effect as the helicopter approaches the ground during a landing flare.

Another effect involves the distribution of the induced velocity flow pattern across the rotor. In hover, the pattern is more or less symmetrical but at 15 to 20 knots, the distribution has been skewed enough so that the induced flow at the leading edge of the disc is essentially zero, increasing to twice the momentum value at the rear of the disc. This is sometimes called "transverse flow" and was illustrated in Figure 6-2 on page 30. The change causes the blade over the nose to see an increase in angle of attack, which makes the rotor flap up on the left side.

Wind-tunnel tests of flapping rotors have shown that rotors flap up on the left as much as 3° or 4° at low speeds due to this effect. During accelerations, this can require a sudden left-stick motion to suppress the flapping and trim the rotor.

Where to Place the Stabilizer

Yet another important low-speed phenomenon involves the rotor wake impinging on the horizontal stabilizer. Horizontal stabilizers were small or even nonexistent on old-time helicopters, however, to improve forward-flight flying qualities, horizontal stabilizers became larger. At the same time, main-rotor disc loadings have increased. These trends

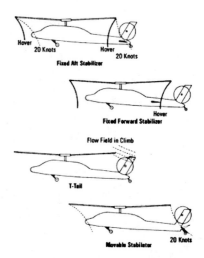

Figure 27-3 Stabilizer Options

have now set up a situation in which the interaction between the stabilizer and the rotor wake becomes very important.

If the stabilizer is mounted at the end of the tail boom, it will be behind the rotor wake in hover. As a result, it will experience a download when the rear of the rotor wake passes over it during the transition to forward flight. This produces a sudden nose-up pitching moment that requires a forward stick motion to trim. At some higher speed, the wake will rise above the stabilizer and much of the download will be relieved. A look at Figure 27-3 will show several possible solutions to this problem.

One is to mount the stabilizer forward on the tail boom, placing it in the rotor wake even in hover. The stabilizer thus has no awkward transient condition — at least until the wake rises above it at a fairly high speed. This option hampers hover performance because of the download and because more tail area is required for stability than if it were mounted farther back.

Another approach is the T-tail configuration in which the stabilizer is mounted high on the vertical stabilizer to put it above the influence of the rotor. It has been found, however, that unless the tail is placed very high, the rotor will still induce a significant downward velocity field at low speeds —especially in climbs. At high speeds, the turbulence in the wake as it impinges on the stabilizer may produce unacceptable oscillatory airloads and vibration.

Yet another modern solution is to mount a variable incidence stabilator at the end of the tail boom. This surface can be aligned with the flow in the wake at low speeds to minimize the airloads. This solves the trim shift problem but results in additional weight, cost, and complexity.

Thus none of the current solutions to the problem are ideal. No one has yet seen fit to accept my suggestion of putting the stabilizer out in front.

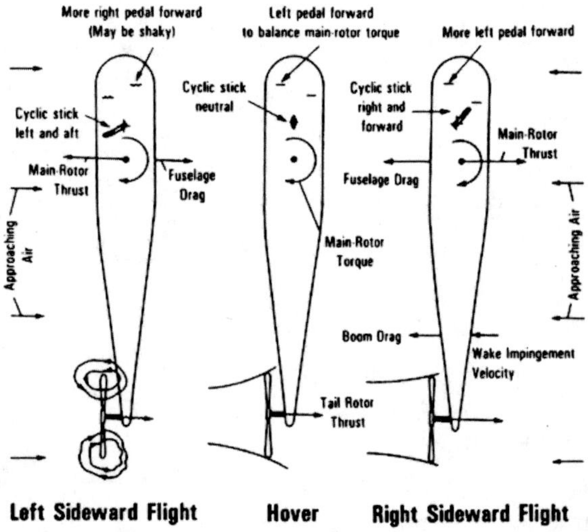

Sideward Flight

Except for showing off, there is seldom reason to fly a helicopter sidewards or rearwards. With respect to the local air mass, however, the pilot may find himself in these flight regimes whenever he hovers, takes off, or lands on a windy day.

As far as the main rotor alone is concerned, there is little difference between flying sideways and flying forward. The induced power decreases from the hover value as in forward flight but the effect of the large fuselage parasite drag begins to make itself felt sooner, so the bucket speed (speed for minimum power) is lower during sideward flight.

A more significant effect is due to the change in the induced velocity distribution that alters the longitudinal

Figure 27-4 Conditions in Sideward Flight

control position in sideward flight. This situation is similar to the change in lateral control position that takes place in low-speed forward flight. As shown in Figure 27-4, flight to the right requires *forward* stick to trim and flight to the left, *aft* stick.

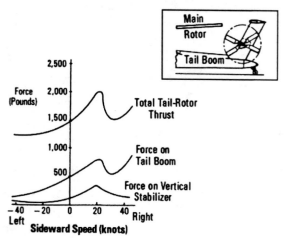

Figure 27-5 **Measured Forces on YAH-64 in Sideward Flight**

Also significant are the effects of sideward flight on the tail rotor. Sideward flight to the left can put the tail rotor into the same vortex-ring situation discussed above for right hover turns. It has similar control—or rather lack of control—characteristics. When these characteristics become bad, the pilot will find it impossible to maintain a steady heading in left sideward flight in the 15- to 30-knot speed regime (or while trying to hover over a spot in a left crosswind).

Sideward flight to the right is generally steady but it can produce a requirement for high tail-rotor thrust and power. From a simple view of trim equilibrium in sideward flight, there is no apparent reason why the tail-rotor thrust required should be much different for flight to the right than for flight to the left. Flight tests on several helicopters have shown, however, that there is an aerodynamic interference effect — apparently involving the impingement of the main-rotor wake on the tail boom. This significantly increases the drag of the boom when flying to the right but not to the left. Because of this, the tail-rotor thrust in right sideward flight is higher than it is for flight to the left, as shown on Figure 27-5 from measurements made on the Hughes YAH-64. This is another interference phenomenon we do not yet fully understand. In addition to the higher thrust requirement, the tail-rotor power is higher for right sideward flight than for left simply because the tail rotor is in a climb situation.

Quartering Winds

Direct sideward flight may not be the most critical condition. Some helicopters have run out of directional control when flying slowly with the wind coming from the right front. In this case, the disturbing factor is the wad of tip vortices coming from the advancing edge of the main rotor and being ingested into the tail rotor as shown in Figure 27-6.

Some helicopters run out of pedal in this condition, which is called "flying in the slot". This was a big problem with Bell UH-ls and AH-ls before the tail rotor was moved from the left side to the right side of the vertical stabilizer. The resulting reversal in the direction of tail rotor rotation (tail-rotor blade closest to the main rotor now going up) significantly improves the controllability in this flight condition.

Tandem-rotor helicopters have a good reason to fly sidewards at low speeds — their performance is better because the larger "wing span" has the opportunity to operate with more air than in forward flight and consequently the induced power is less. Even though the parasite drag is

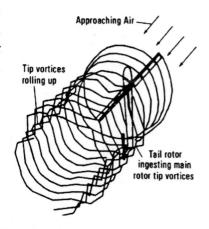

Figure 27-6 **Conditions in Right Quartering Flight**

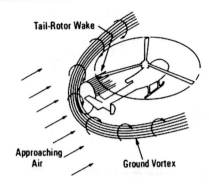

Figure 27-7 Ground Vortex Interference in Rearward Flight

higher, the total benefit is generally enough to justify low-speed flight in this condition.

When the Piasecki HUP tandems were used by the U.S. Navy as plane guards during carrier launches and recoveries, they were flown in left sideslip to improve performance. For the same reason, tandem-helicopter climb performance is usually improved by ascending with sideslip. These benefits are inherent in aircraft with side-by-side rotors such as the Bell XV-15.

Rearward Flight

The primary difference between the aerodynamics of rearward and forward flight is that the empennage and tail rotor, which are stabilizing in forward flight, are destabilizing in rearward flight. (Try shooting an arrow backwards.) In addition, the aerodynamic interactions may be stronger. For example, in low and slow rearward flight, the ground vortex, shown in Figure 27-7, can greatly distort the flow at the rear end, causing a large download on the horizontal stabilizer and large-scale gusts through the tail rotor. Another observed interference effect is that of the tail-rotor wake going into the main rotor and erratically changing its torque and flapping. Add to these the obvious poor visibility while actually flying backward and we have enough good reasons to restrict the rearward flight envelope.

Things aren't always as they seem

The Landgraf H-2 was a cute little side-by-side rotor helicopter developed right after World War II. Due to an unfortunate accident, the project was relatively short-lived. Ten years later, Fred Landgraf was showing movies of early flights of the H-2 at a meeting in Los Angeles. The movies showed the helicopter gracefully doing hover turns, rearward flight, sideward flight, and lazy spirals in all directions. Landgraf's comment: "It is out of control—the pilot is trying to hold it

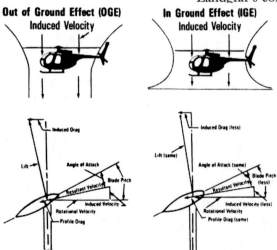

Figure 27-8 Conditions at Rotor

Ground Effect

When any aircraft is flying close to the ground, it requires less power —the result of a favorable aerodynamic phenomenon known as ground effect, a singularly useful bit of physics that also allows helicopters to take off at higher gross weights than can otherwise be hovered.

Under certain conditions, however, ground effect can all but disappear, leaving the pilot with that famous sinking feeling.

To understand how ground effect can fail us, we first must review a bit about just how it works. The reason a helicopter, either in hover or forward flight, requires less power while in ground effect is because of the reduction in power necessary to overcome induced drag.

Figure 27-8 illustrates the conditions that exist around a helicopter's rotor both in and out of ground effect. Out of ground effect (OGE), the velocity of air passing through the rotor begins at zero far above the disc, increases to a value determined by the helicopter's weight and size as it passes through the disc, and then doubles in the wake below the rotor.

The blade sees air coming at it due to both the rotor's speed of rotation and the downflow through the disc (called the induced velocity). These two components combine to form a resultant vector that is pointed slightly down at the blade.

Since, by definition, lift is perpendicular to the resultant vector, it is tilted slightly back. This rearward tilt produces a drag force on the blade known as the induced drag, which must be overcome by the engine.

The other drag component in hover is due to air friction and is known as profile drag. For most helicopters, profile drag in hover accounts for only about one-third of the total.

If the rotor is close to the ground (IGE), the velocity of air passing through the disc must go to zero at the ground and all of the induced velocities are reduced—including those at the rotor itself. This means that the resultant vector is not tilted back quite as much as it was out of ground effect, reducing the induced drag and, thus, the total power required from the engine.

Power Savings

The magnitude of the ground effect depends on the height of the rotor above the ground. When the rotor is hovering at about 20% of its diameter (about as low as rotors on conventional helicopters can get), the induced velocity at the disc is reduced by about 30% and the total power savings amount to about 20%.

The benefit may be actually somewhat larger if a bulky fuselage normally carries a large download in hover. Near the ground, the fuselage may be in a region of local upwash and, thus, experience a degree of buoyancy.

As the helicopter rises, ground effect diminishes rapidly. Tests show that at one rotor diameter, the induced power is reduced only about 3% and at two diameters, no reduction can be measured.

Some pilots report that there is less ground effect when hovering overlong grass or water than over a solid surface but as far as I know, no tests have been done to verify this observation.

Forward Flight

Ground effect applies to a helicopter in forward flight, just as it does in hover since the induced velocity at the rotor disc is still influenced by the conditions in the wake below the rotor. Tests show that the percent

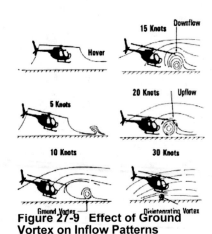

Figure 27-9 Effect of Ground Vortex on Inflow Patterns

reduction in induced velocity as influenced by rotor height is about the same in forward flight as it is in hover.

The reduction in power required, however, is less in forward flight because the induced drag effects are less of the *total* power picture. At hover, the induced drag accounts for approximately two-thirds of the power required, but at cruise speed, the induced drag may account for less than one third of the total — so any reduction in this component has a smaller effect.

Exception to the rule

The preceding explanation sounds OK, but most helicopter pilots would object that it doesn't explain their experiences of suddenly "running off the ground cushion". This is the result of another phenomenon that at low rotor heights and airspeeds can nullify the normal beneficial ground effect — and might actually require an increase in collective pitch and power as the helicopter goes from hover to forward flight. Tests have identified this phenomenon as existing for rotor heights less than about half a diameter and for speeds between about five and 20 knots.

The problem is associated with the development of a ground vortex out ahead of the helicopter that is overrun at some forward speed. Figure 27-9 shows what the velocity patterns look like. Note how the vortex develops and influences the flow conditions at the rotor.

Until the vortex is overrun, its effect is to increase the downwash through the rotor, as if it were in a climb. This causes the power required to increase, rather than to decrease as ground effect would normally indicate. Since the vortex stays close to the ground, its effects are most significant for low rotor heights. For high rotor heights, the vortex is overrun at lower speeds, but its overall effects are less.

Caught in the Vortex

Figure 27-10 shows the power required as a typical helicopter goes into forward flight at three rotor heights. The height of 30% of the diameter is good for hover but does show a rise that the pilot would quickly discover if his available power had been just enough to hover in the first place.

In practice, this type of takeoff is accomplished by doing it as quickly as possible and sacrificing a few feet of altitude. This technique is recognized by the FAA when they establish the maximum gross weight for certification of single-engine helicopters. They require that the helicopter must be capable of hovering IGE at a landing-gear height that permits transition into forward flight at a fixed collective pitch without touching the ground. Most helicopters require a skid height of three to five feet to accomplish this maneuver.

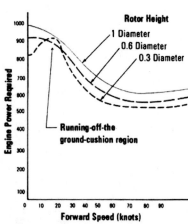

Figure 27-10 Ground Effect in Forward Flight

Stick to the Left

As illustrated in Figure , the change in inflow through the rotor not only affects the power required but the lateral trim as well. Normally, at low speeds the downflow through the front part of the rotor is lower than through the rear part, causing the rotor to want to flap up to the left—unless the pilot holds it down with left stick.

The effect of the ground vortex is to increase the downflow through the front part of the disc, making the flow more uniform and reducing the requirement for left stick. This condition applies only until the vortex gets under the leading edge of the disc, producing a strong upflow and a sudden requirement for substantial left stick that may take the pilot by surprise.

Although Figure 27-9 indicates more-or-less steady flow induced by the vortex, this is mostly artistic license. The flow actually has much random turbulence, especially as the vortex passes under the rotor, so that besides the average effects on power and trim, the pilot must also contend with erratic trim changes.

Since velocities are relative, it does not matter whether the helicopter is moving over the ground on a calm day or hovering over a spot on a windy day, the effect of the ground vortex is the same. This leads to the conjecture that the observed hover performance IGE of a given helicopter may seem worse with a 1O-to-20-knot wind than it is on a calm day. I have never heard a pilot complain of this, but I am listening.

Agility

Two low-speed maneuvers that can be used to measure the agility of a helicopter are the return-to-target maneuver and the crop-dusting turn, both shown in Figure 27-12. The first is based on the scenario that an attack pilot sights a target as he flies over it and must get back into position to fire rockets before the target can defend itself.

Similarly, the crop-dusting turn is done at the edge of the field to get back to work before the finance company can repossess the aircraft. In each case, the maneuver is done by quickly decelerating to almost a hover, turning, and then accelerating as fast as possible.

Although the crop duster can use a zoom to decelerate and a dive to accelerate, the attack pilot may. have to do the entire maneuver at low altitude to avoid exposure. Some flight tests have shown that the deceleration phase can be enhanced by flying at large sideslip angles to increase drag but this might lead to the pilot becoming disoriented and losing the target.

Overload Takeoffs

Takeoffs at high gross weight or at high altitudes (or under any condition where the power available is just barely enough to hover in ground effect) puts the pilot's faith to a test. The U.S. Army has done extensive

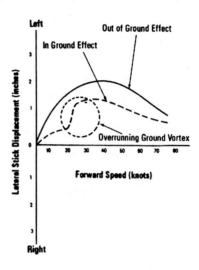

Figure 27-11 Effect of Ground Vortex on Lateral Stick Displacement Required for Trim

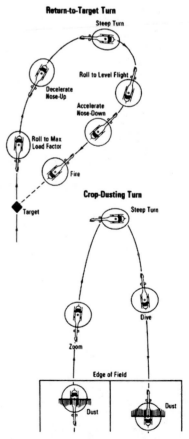

Figure 27-12 Agility Testing Maneuvers

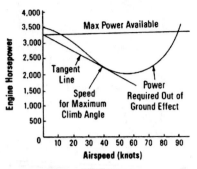

Figure 27-13 Determining Overload-Takeoff Speed for Maximum Climb Angle

experimentation, looking for the shortest distance to clear an obstacle—whether it be a hedge or a mountain. This research has shown that the helicopter should make a full-powered acceleration as close to the ground as possible to take full advantage of ground effect until it gets up to a predetermined rotational speed, at which point the climb is started.

The best rotation speed depends upon the height of the obstacle. If the obstacle is a mountain, the optimum rotation speed is the speed for maximum angle of climb. This can be determined graphically from the plot of power required and available, as shown on Figure 27-13. For lower obstacles, the optimum rotational speed is also lower.

Since a pilot in this situation is unlikely to be able to make this analysis, the Army suggests that he use one rotation speed for all obstacles: for example, 28 knots for the UH-1C. He can get an inkling of whether he will be successful or not by seeing how high he can hover, which depends on the individual helicopter. For instance, Army tests show that if a UH-1C can hover at a 15-foot skid height, it will take 300 feet to clear a 50-foot obstacle but if its maximum hover height is only four feet, at least 600 feet will be required.

Another consideration in overload or high-altitude operation is the possibility of inducing blade stall by sudden over-control of cyclic or collective pitch. An experienced operator has told me, "A pilot who handles the controls smoothly in critical hover conditions will be able to lift considerably more load than a pilot who is rough on the controls."

Towing

Helicopters are occasionally used for towing in special situations such as minesweeping, rescue, or salvage operations. When towing at a fairly flat cable angle, a helicopter can generate a surprisingly high amount of pull.

Figure 27-14 shows the equilibrium diagram for a 20,000-pound gross weight helicopter with enough power to develop 30,000 pounds of rotor thrust. For a towline angle of 10°, it can put 19,000 pounds of tension in the line—plenty for a tug of war.

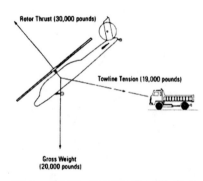

Figure 27-14 Towing Equilibrium Diagram

2 8 Turns, Pullups and Pushovers

So far, our discussions of aerodynamics have dealt primarily with steady flight. There are, however, several conditions that require special consideration --such as turns, pullups, and pushovers.

Turns and Pullups

During both of these maneuvers in forward flight, the rotor thrust will exceed the gross weight of the aircraft. This thrust-to-gross-weight ratio is known as the load factor and is greater than 1 for these operations. Units of measure for the load factor are Gs, or the acceleration constant due to gravity. Straight and level flight is 1 G and fighters engaged in dogfights can pull up to 6 Gs positive and 3 Gs negative. Free fall is zero G. As a general rule, helicopters can do all of their required maneuvers without exceeding a load factor bounded by 2 Gs on the top and ½ G on the bottom.

In a steady level turn, the rotor thrust must balance the vector sum of both the gross weight and the centrifugal force, as shown in Figure 28-1. The power required is higher than in level flight because the rotor thinks the gross weight has suddenly been increased. No matter what the speed, as long as level flight is maintained the load factor is related to the bank angle as illustrated in Figure 28-2.

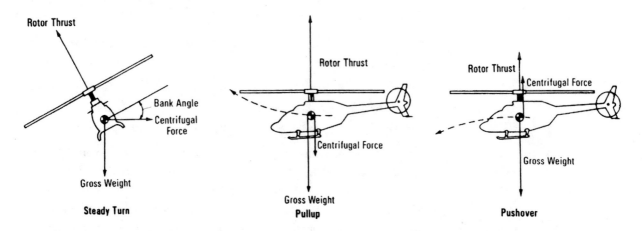

Figure 28-1 Equilibrium Diagrams for Maneuvers

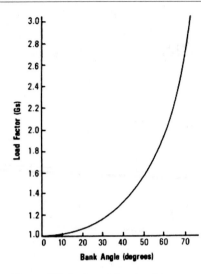

Figure 28-2 Load Factor in Steady Turn

A pullup is similar to the start of a loop and so again the rotor thrust must balance both the gross weight and a downward-pointing centrifugal force. If the pullup is done only with the cyclic control, the additional rotor thrust is obtained by increasing the angle of attack of the main rotor. This slows the helicopter and since the rotor is going toward an autorotative condition, the power required may go down rather than up as in a steady turn.

As a matter of fact, extreme cyclic pullups at moderate speeds can result in the rotor going through autorotation to an overspeed condition. At low forward speeds, there is less danger of over-speeding because there is less airflow to work with. At high speeds, the rotor may have significant regions of stall and compressibility that will also prevent overspeeding. On the other hand, pullups done with collective pitch will almost always require an increase in engine power.

Maximum Load Factor

The maximum load factor that a given helicopter can develop in a turn or in a pullup depends upon what sort of limit is first encountered. In Chapter 5, the statement was made, "Rotors in flight do not lose thrust because of blade stall." They can, however, experience high blade drag and/or blade twisting because of stall.

From the pilot's standpoint, these limits may manifest themselves as reaching maximum engine power (in a steady turn), losing control power, experiencing an unacceptable level of vibration, getting to a frightening nose-up rate or attitude, sensing loads rapidly building up in the blades or control system, hearing ominous noises, or observing sudden out-of-track conditions. Any of these symptoms are enough to stop a prudent pilot —unless he is trying to save his neck in an emergency. Running out of power in a steady turn is relatively easy to analyze but the other limits are more subjective. They largely depend on the pilot's willingness to subject himself to uncomfortable or potentially dangerous flight conditions and on the dynamic and aeroelastic characteristics of the blades, control system, transmission mounting, and structure between the rotor and the seat of his pants.

Both the steady turn and the pullup benefit slightly with respect to retreating-blade angles of attack as long as they have a nose-up pitch rate.

(If you have trouble associating a pitch rate with a steady turn, imagine a turn with a 90° bank angle. Then the turn is just a loop laid on its side. Even a turn with a shallow bank angle involves some pitch rate.)

If the pilot wants a nose-up maneuver, he must make the rotor do it first and the helicopter will follow. Pulling back on the stick increases angles of attack on the advancing side and reduces them on the retreating side. This initially causes nose-up flapping of the rotor disc, which gives a nose-up acceleration to the aircraft. In a short time, the helicopter is pitching up at a constant rate but to maintain this pitch rate, the unbalanced-lift distribution must be maintained to precess the rotor like a gyroscope. Thus, a maneuver involving a nose-up pitch rate decreases the angles of attack on the retreating side and allows the rotor to develop more thrust before stalling than would otherwise be possible.

Pushovers

During nap-of-the-earth flying over rolling terrain, the helicopter does a pullup with a load factor greater than 1 but a load factor of less than 1 is required to descend into the next valley. The critical factor in a pushover is the reduction of control power experienced as rotor thrust is decreased.

For rotors on which control power depends entirely on thrust — such as teetering rotors — the ability to control the helicopter will disappear if the load factor ever gets to zero. Hingeless rotors or rotors with hinge offset hang on to more of their control power when rotor thrust is low but a pilot may notice that it takes more stick motion to return to level flight from a 0.5-G pushover than from a 1.5-G pullup.

Not only is control power jeopardized by trying to maneuver at low rotor thrust, but it sets up the potentially dangerous condition leading to "mast bumping" on teetering rotors or "droop-stop pounding" on hinged rotors. The reason is that the tip path plane responds willingly to cyclic-pitch movements but doesn't do much good in controlling roll and pitch motions. Thus, the pilot tends to use much more stick movement than normal and may produce more teetering or flapping than was allowed for in the design of the rotor.

.

29 Sideslip And Bank

A single-rotor helicopter, unlike an airplane, is not symmetrical and therein lies a possible source of confusion for those who fly both.

When a helicopter with counterclockwise (American) main-rotor rotation is in steady flight, the tail rotor/ vertical stabilizer combination must produce enough sideforce to the right to balance main-rotor torque. This sideforce, in turn, must be balanced by an equal sideforce to the left to keep the helicopter flying straight forward.

Figure 29-1 shows two possible sources of balancing sideforce:

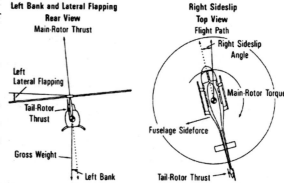

Figure 29-1 Two Methods of Balancing Tail Rotor Thrust

1 - A sideward tilt of the main-rotor thrust vector is obtained by a combination of lateral flapping and banking the entire helicopter to the left.

2 - A left sideforce due to fuselage aerodynamics is obtained by side slipping to the right (available only in forward flight, of course).

Thus, a single-rotor helicopter in steady flight will trim with a left bank, a right sideslip, or some combination of both.

Fixed-wing facts

The symmetrical airplane, on the other hand, needs neither bank nor sideslip to trim in straight flight. The only exception is a twin-engine airplane with a dead engine. The trim situation, in that case, is essentially the same as for the single-rotor helicopter. In normal circumstances, the pilot can trim the airplane by holding the rudder pedals in their neutral position or even by taking his feet off them.

Deliberately holding a sideslip angle with some rudder displacement is possible and, if the airplane is equipped for flight-test work with a sideslip vane and indicator, it can be done very precisely.

In most airplanes, however, the pilot only has an indirect indication of sideslip through his bank angle. For this he has two cues:

1 - The seat of his pants tell him which way is straight down.

2-The turn-and-bank indicator or "turn coordinator" shown in Figure 29-2.

The lower portion of this instrument is an inclinometer consisting of a ball bearing in a curved glass tube. The upper portion is the silhouette of the rear of the airplane whose bank angle is actuated by the precession of a gyroscope, thus indicating the rate of turn. When a wing tip is lined up with one of the marks, the aircraft is in a "standard-rate turn" of 3° per second, requiring two minutes to make a complete circle of 360°.

In non-turning flight, the position of the ball will indicate the bank angle since it responds only to the force of gravity. In turning flight, however, the ball is affected by centrifugal force as well. In a perfectly coordinated turn, the effects of centrifugal force and gravity will be exactly equal and opposite and the ball will remain in the bottom of the tube. The pilot will also feel no tendency to slide to either side of his seat.

If the ball is not centered during the turn, it is showing that the turn is not coordinated. The ball will be displaced to the outside of the turn if the airplane is "skidding" with insufficient bank angle and to the inside if it is slipping into the turn because of too much bank angle.

In both cases, the airplane has sideslip and the displacement of the ball can, therefore, be thought of as indicating sideslip, even though it is actually only showing the error from the ideal bank angle.

Because of this, the instrument is sometimes known as a "turn-and-slip" indicator. Even in non-turning flight, an off-center ball position indicates a sideslip since the tilt of the wing lift must be balanced by a fuselage sideforce that can only be generated by side slipping.

Figure 29-2 Turn-and-Bank Indicator

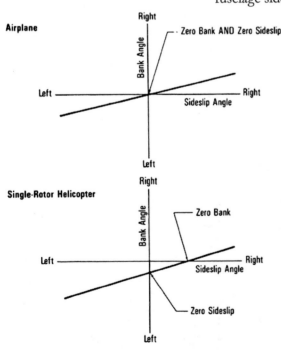

Figure 29-3 Comparison of Airplane and Helicopter Sideforce Characteristics

(I will leave it up to you to figure out what this all means if we were talking about flying-wing airplanes.)

The relationship between bank angle and sideslip at one speed for an airplane in straight flight is shown on the top portion of Figure 29-3. The slope of the line is a measure of its "sideforce characteristics."

Compensating for asymmetry

A single-rotor helicopter is slightly different from an airplane because it is not symmetrical and in steady, straight flight, zero-bank angle and zero sideslip do not coincide. This is shown by the lower line in Figure 29-3.

The bias also affects the ball position during turns. In contrast to an airplane, a centered ball in a helicopter is not a sign of a coordinated turn but of one with some degree of sideslip. For this reason, when installed in a helicopter, it is incorrect to refer to the turn-and-bank indicator as a turn-and-slip indicator.

Knowing all of this, would it be a good idea to install the inclinometer with an initial tilt to nullify the bias so that a centered ball would correspond to zero sideslip in straight flight and coordinated turns? This would make it easier to fly at zero sideslip where the fuselage drag is minimum. A slight complication, of course, is that the required bank angle varies in flight because it is proportional to the tail-rotor thrust needed to balance main-rotor torque-and that changes throughout the flight.

Hughes test pilots recently evaluated the inclinometer tilt and turned it down. They objected to feeling a bank angle in the seat of their pants when the ball was in the traditional no-bank position.

A more fundamental fix is to tilt the rotor mast to the left during preliminary design. This was done on the Sikorsky S-64 Sky Crane to insure nearly simultaneous landing gear liftoff and touchdown.

30 Maneuverability and Aerobatics

A helicopter main rotor is a magnificent device for controlling an aircraft. As part of a team with the powerplant, control system, and tail rotor, it can provide maneuverability and agility characteristics unmatched by any other man-carrying vehicle. But this requires the designers work toward some ambitious goals.

Up-and-Down, Back-and-Forth

The phrase, "maneuverability and agility" describes the ability to quickly and precisely change the speed and the direction of flight (in all six directions: forward, rearward, right, left, up, and down). The need for this ability is often to avoid some undesirable consequence. For example: hopping over those suddenly noticed power lines; making a quick, unexpected 180° turn at the head of a box canyon; taking evasive action or heading for the nearest cover when being shot at; playing cat-and-mouse with an enemy tank; avoiding that Canadian goose who seems intent on joining the pilot in the cockpit; or landing on the deck of a ship in a storm.

Not only is it necessary to have the raw ability to do these things, but in most cases they must be done with considerable precision; that is, the pilot should be able to easily direct the helicopter quickly to where he wants within a few feet—or inches in some cases. In a word, the control characteristics should be "crisp".

Three of the most important parameters that define maneuverability are the margin of power available from the engine, the margin of thrust available from the rotor, and the pitch-and-roll control power.

Power Margin

The power margin is used to climb or to satisfy the increased power requirements of the rotor during~ accelerations or turns. The thrust margin is used to keep the rotor blades from staffing in those maneuvers in which the rotor thrust must be substantially greater than the gross weight. These not only include pullups and turns but all maneuvers in which the rotor is tilted significantly from the horizontal — such as in longitudinal and lateral accelerations from hover.

An adequate power margin usually exists automatically in forward flight at speeds near the speed for minimum-required power or at high speeds where the engine power can be easily supplemented by borrowing some of the kinetic energy from the forward motion; for instance, by losing speed while climbing or making a tight turn. This leaves flight near hover as the critical regime where the power required is high and there is no convenient source of extra energy—except for rotor-speed decay after the engine "tops out". (On most helicopters without extremely heavy blades, this energy is relatively small and must be used very carefully to avoid blade stall.)

The accepted way to provide adequate maneuverability near hover is to install an engine that can produce significantly more power than required to hover. But how much more? An excessive requirement will place design penalties on the engine and transmission, while an insufficient requirement will jeopardize the usefulness of the helicopter.

The U.S. Army, in the specifications for both the Sikorsky UH-60 Black Hawk transport helicopter and for the Hughes AH-64 Apache attack helicopter, required a minimum vertical rate of climb of 450 fpm under a specific set of conditions: mission takeoff gross weight, altitude of 4,000 feet, temperature of 95°F, and at 95% of the 30-minute power rating under these conditions. (Note: the military refers to the 30-minute rating as the "intermediate rated power" or IRP.) The use of 95% of IRP was specified in anticipation of some engine deterioration in service. The altitude and temperature were specified since increasing either will decrease the power the engine can deliver. These extremes were expected to cover almost all worldwide conditions in which these helicopters would be operated.

For the occasional more-adverse combination, the Black Hawk and the Apache will have to be flown at less than their design gross weight or suffer a loss in vertical-climb performance and maneuverability at low speeds. Although it might seem that a transport helicopter could have less performance than an attack helicopter, the Army apparently feels all of its helicopters that might get shot at should have the same high maneuverability.

Proof of the Pudding

The vertical rate-of-climb requirement puts a burden on the flight-test organizations that must verify it. Test pilots normally have very sparse cues to keep them from acquiring some translational airspeed while trying to climb straight up.

This has led to some clever techniques, such as climbing beside the smoke column from a burning tire or the string of a tethered balloon in the dawn's early light, or using special, auxiliary low-speed airspeed systems. Even with these techniques, the best of these tests have substantial "scatter of the datter" as shown in Figure 30-1.

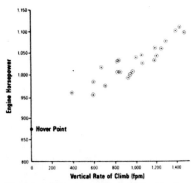

Figure 30-1   Results of Vertical Climb Tests on Bell AH-1G

(Even on a good whirl tower, a five-knot breeze is enough to give non-repeatable hover data. The basic reason is that the trailing vortex from one blade tip significantly affects the angle-of-attack distribution at the following blade. Even a shift of a few inches in the vortex location can have a large effect on lift and drag near the blade tip.)

A modest proposal

I have a proposal for simplifying the vertical climb test technique. Since a typical turbine engine loses about 30% of its power capability going from standard sea-level conditions to 4,000 feet, 950 F and since a vertical climb rate of 450 fpm requires about 10% more power than to hover, I propose that the requirement be changed to state that the helicopter must be capable of hovering out of ground effect on 55% of its 30-minute rating on a standard sea-level day (59° F). This should then result in the same performance as the just-as arbitrary but harder-to-verify 450 fpm climb on 95% of the 30-minute rating at 4,000 feet and 95° F.

Difference between Rule Makers

The Army's definition of mission takeoff gross weight is the one at which the helicopter can do the prescribed vertical climb but the FAA's definition of maximum takeoff gross weight is the one at which the helicopter can hover in ground effect (IGE) at 2,500 feet, 90° F. For the same helicopter this results in the allowable FAA gross weight being about 10% higher than the allowable Army gross weight.

This difference reflects the divergence in philosophy between the two types of specifications — the FAA is primarily interested only in safety of flight but the military organizations are also concerned with performance.

Thrust Margin

The requirement for a thrust margin before the rotor stalls is one that drives the design decision concerning total blade area. Here again, the U.S. Army has imposed the same requirement on both its new transport and attack helicopters. This is the so-called UTTAS maneuver (UTTAS stands for Utility Tactical Transport Aircraft System, which the Sikorsky Black Hawk is). It is a longitudinal roller-coaster maneuver done at an air density corresponding to 4,000 feet, 95°F (81% of sea-level density) involving a pullup at 150 knots to 1.75 Gs, sustained for three seconds (a 30-knot speed loss is allowed) followed by a pushover to 0 Gs or less, sustained for two seconds.

Figure 30-2 illustrates the phases of the maneuver, which might be used to do contour flying over hilly terrain. Designing to this criteria gives a rotor-thrust margin over level flight of 75% at the test condition and even larger margins at lower altitudes and speeds. (The Hughes Apache has demonstrated load factors above three in transient maneuvers.)

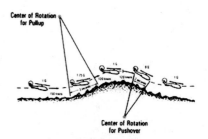

Figure 30-2 UTTAS Maneuver

A load-factor capability of 1.75 might seem small compared to fixed-wing fighters and dive bombers designed for load factors of five or more but consider the difference in the normal speed range. A helicopter in a 1.75 G turn at 150 knots can reverse its direction in 17 seconds. An airplane flying at 400 knots requires a load factor of four to make its turn in the same time.

The requirement to demonstrate at least two seconds of 0 G flight during the UTTAS maneuver means that the helicopter must be controllable in this condition. Teetering rotors lose all pitch-and-roll control power in 0 G flight, since they depend on tilting the rotor thrust to produce a moment about the center of gravity. Thus they cannot safely demonstrate the maneuver — unless they have hub springs, like the Bell 222.

Flight-test programs including the most violent maneuvers that might be experienced in combat have shown that a helicopter with the capability of developing load factors of more than 2.5 seldom uses more than two. At least one reason for this —especially at low speeds — is that the helicopter pilot is not limited to coordinated turning but can use large sideslip angles to achieve his goals.

Another justification for the lower requirement on the attack helicopter than on the airplane is the use of fixed guns on the airplane but a flexible gun (or a very agile guided missile) on the helicopter. This allows the helicopter's weapon to do much of the maneuvering.

Tilting

Changing the flight path at constant altitude requires tilting the rotor tip-path plane to provide a horizontal force in the desired direction. Initially, this tilting is done with cyclic pitch— but as the fuselage quickly follows the rotor, most of the cyclic pitch must be taken out to avoid going too far— unless, of course, the object is a barrel roll or a loop. The cyclic pitch must be taken out because it is a "rate control", meaning a change from trim produces a steady rate of pitch or roll — similar to what happens on an airplane where deflecting the ailerons and holding them there achieves a constant roll rate.

Once the helicopter achieves its steady rate and no acceleration exists (Figure 30-3), the rotor is simply precessing itself as a gyroscope and no moments from flapping are needed — except for relatively small ones required to overcome the aerodynamic damping of the airframe components.

(This explanation is very good for pitch and roll in hover and also for roll in forward flight. For pitch in forward flight, it gets more complicated since changes in the angle of attack on both the rotor and horizontal stabilizer muddy the water.)

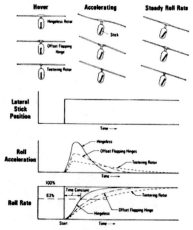

Figure 30-3 Control Characteristics in Roll

If excess moments were being produced by rotor flapping, the angular motion would be accelerating and not holding a steady rate. Because of this absence of significant flapping, the type of rotor does not greatly influence the achievable pitch and roll rate. A teetering rotor can reach the same maximum rate as can a stiff hingeless rotor. It will just take longer to get to that rate— a consideration we'll discuss a bit later.

Designing for Response

Two design parameters that do affect the steady rates are rotor rpm and the Lock number of the rotor blade. The higher the rpm, the more the rate per degree of cyclic pitch. Since tip speeds are nearly the same for all sizes of helicopters (600 to 800 fps), a helicopter with a small rotor will have a higher rpm and thus be more sensitive, in terms of the angular rate generated per degree of cyclic pitch, than a large helicopter.

As a consequence, small one-man machines are often difficult to fly and radio-controlled models are usually impossible without some special control device — such as the Huller servo control rotor which most of them use.

The Lock number is named for a British rotor aerodynamicist and is a non-dimensional ratio of a combination of blade aerodynamic parameters to the blade's inertia. Heavy blades or blades with large tip weights, such as jet engines, have low Lock numbers and reduced sensitivities.

Of course, the pilot is only aware of how much he must move the stick to get a given rate, not how much the swashplate is tilting to put in cyclic pitch. Thus, the designer has the capability of tailoring the control sensitivity by selecting the best gearing between the stick and swashplate. If the sensitivity in terms of rate per inch of stick motion is too low, the pilot will complain of sluggishness —but if the sensitivity is too high, the pilot will have a hard time holding the helicopter steady, since even very small inadvertent control movements will produce motion. Too high sensitivity can even lead to pilot-induced oscillations (PIO) as the pilot tries to chase the aircraft motions with his controls without being able to precisely compensate for his inherent reaction time.

Many studies have been made to determine the limits of control sensitivity. It is a fairly general consensus that the roll-rate sensitivity should be greater than 8° but less than 20° per second per inch of stick and that the corresponding limits for pitch rate should be between 50 and 12°.

Not only is the rate important, but so is the time to achieve the final rate—or, more technically, 63% of the final rate. This is the so-called time constant of the system. If it is too long, the pilot may become impatient and be tempted to over control

This is where the differences in rotors come in. A short time constant is inherent in a rotor with a high acceleration capability. A hingeless rotor with a high flapping stiffness can accelerate the helicopter faster than an articulated or teetering rotor, as shown in Figure 30-3.

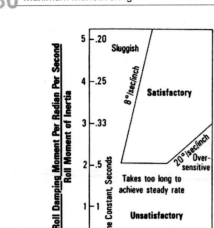

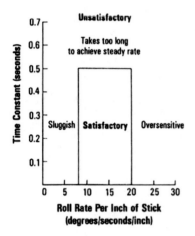

Figure 30-4 Two Ways of Presenting Requirements for Roll Control

The same studies that have guided the choice of desirable levels of control sensitivity have also led to the conclusion that the time constant should be no longer than half a second in roll and one second in pitch — with shorter times desired. Time constants are proportional to the corresponding moments of inertia and since inertia is almost always lower in roll than in pitch, the physics of the situation are fortunately compatible with the pilot's desires.

There has been some speculation that if the time constant were too short, the resulting high accelerations would provide a jerky ride but, as far as I know, no helicopter has ever approached this situation. The requirements on roll time constant and rate of roll per inch of stick are shown in Figure 30-4 in two forms. The first is in the format best known to stability and control specialists. I believe the second format provides the same information in a more straightforward manner.

On most modern helicopters, an electronic stability and control augmentation system (SCAS) is used. One of the functions of such a device is control shaping— modifying the control signal between the cockpit and the swashplate to either speed up or slow down the response.

Maximum Maneuvering

Control sensitivity and the time constant have big effects on the precision of control but the overall level of maneuverability is determined by the maximum rates reachable with full control motion. Based on flight tests and simulation studies, the maximum rate of roll used to start a fast turn in forward flight is between 70° and 100° per second. (Maneuverable World War II fighters such as the British Spitfire could roll dizzily at about 150° per second.) The desired maximum pitch rates are only 20° to 30° per second, considerably less than the roll rates. Part of this difference is in consideration of the pilot's feelings should he quickly find himself in a 45° nose-up or nose-down attitude compared to a much less scary 45° bank.

In combination with the control sensitivity, the maximum rate requirement tells the designer what cockpit control motion is required. For instance, if a maximum roll rate of 100° per second in each direction and a control sensitivity of 20° per second per inch is selected, the lateral stick motion must be five inches in each direction from the center. In practice, this is about as far as the stick can move without running into the pilot's thighs.

The corresponding longitudinal stick motion for a 30° per second maximum rate and a control sensitivity of 6° per second per inch of stick results in the same travel. In forward flight, the stick must be held forward to trim the helicopter, reducing the ability to achieve a high nose-down pitch maneuvering rate. This is not a serious problem since this type of maneuver — starting an outside loop at high speed—is seldom required. A control margin of 10% of full travel will usually assure adequate control in gusty air.

Yaw Maneuvers

The desirable maximum rate, control sensitivity, and time constant in yaw are primarily set by the use of the helicopter at low speeds. For example, an armed helicopter that must be able to turn quickly and bring its weapons to bear on a target should have a maximum rate of at least 100° per second in either direction. Corresponding control sensitivity recommendations obtained from flight-test investigations are 30° to 50° per second per inch of pedal travel with a time constant of a quarter of a second or less. A helicopter that does not have a firing task is usually satisfactory with half the control sensitivity and twice the time constant.

A special factor for the tail-rotor design is the requirement to provide a margin of turn maneuverability even under the worst of conditions, usually sideward flight to the right (for a helicopter with the American main-rotor configuration). The critical factor here is giving the pilot enough tail-rotor pitch travel to compensate for the high in-flow velocity through the tail-rotor plus the margin needed for initiating a turn to the left.

Pilot Limitations

A flight task frequently cited as a design condition for maneuverability and agility is nap-of-the-earth (NOE) flight; something combat helicopters do to escape detection. Ideally, the design goal should be to give the pilot the capability to fly as low and as fast as possible through an unfamiliar obstacle course consisting of trees, hills, power-lines, winding stream beds, and live firing.

In practice, even if the helicopter had a very high capability, the aircraft would be limited by how fast the pilot could use the information rushing at him from the outside world and how fast he could move the controls in the right direction. His primary difficulty is judging how close he can bring his main-rotor blade tips and his tail rotor to obstacles. I believe that most helicopters designed in the last decade already have such high levels of maneuverability and agility that pilot capability is almost always the limiting factor on fast NOE flight.

Equality for All?

Airplanes have different maneuverability requirements according to their missions. For example, we would not expect a Boeing 767 to be as maneuverable as an F-16. For helicopters, however, the situation is different. First, because the natural habitat of the helicopter is close to the ground, almost every one of them will sooner or later face an expected situation where high maneuverability could prevent disaster.

Second, the airplane designer is forced to use heavy wing structures to achieve high load factors — whereas the helicopter designer must only

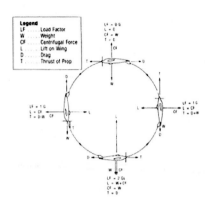

Figure 30-5 An Ideal Loop

add blade area, which need not make the main rotor heavier (if, for instance, a given amount of rotor inertia is required to provide good autorotative characteristics).

Further, once the power margin and the rotor-thrust margin are specified and designed for, there is little weight or cost penalty associated with designing a control system to provide the high pitch, roll, and yaw rates and the low time constants that make the helicopter maneuverable, agile, and safe. For these reasons, all helicopters should be created equal.

Aerobatics

Can helicopters do loops and rolls?

Of course they can and many have — some on purpose. (I hope that publishing this fact does not earn the same results as telling a three-year-old, "Don't put a bean in your ear"~ Remember, no current helicopter is officially approved for aerobatics and some attempts have been spectacularly unsuccessful.)

A well-done loop does not put excessive loads on any of the aircraft components. Figure 30-5 shows a loop being done by an airplane which, having separate propulsion and lift systems—i.e., propeller and wing, is easier to visualize through the maneuver than a helicopter.

The loop shown is idealized in that a constant speed is being maintained and the flight path is a perfect circle. The highest load factor is at the bottom of the loop where it is only 2 Gs. No airplane or helicopter can do such a perfect loop but, still, this can be considered a relatively mild maneuver as far as loads go.

There is a problem with respect to control, however. At the top of the loop, where the rotor thrust is zero or at least very low, all helicopters have reduced control power in pitch and roll, and some —those with teetering rotors — may have none at all.

If the pilot wants to make a cyclic correction in this situation, he might be surprised by how far he has to move the stick to get a response. This is the classic set-up for mast bumping on teetering rotors and for droop-stop pounding on fully articulated rotors.

Several Sikorsky helicopters, including the tiny S-52 in 1949 and the giant CH-53A in 1968, have done documented loops. One aircraft which did them routinely at air shows was the original Sikorsky S-67 Blackhawk (Firgure 12-6), an attack version of the S-61 built on speculation during the Vietnam War as an alternative to the Lockheed AH-56A Cheyenne.

In a paper written for the American Helicopter Society (AHS), the Sikorsky flight-test engineer explains how the maneuver was done:

"The loop is initiated from a slight dive at approximately 175 knots. The cyclic is pulled aft and collective lowered slightly to limit control loads. As the aircraft passes the 90° point (going straight up), collective is added to maintain positive G. Airspeed at the inverted point in the maneuver

Figure 30-6 Sikorsky S-67 Blackhawk

averages 50 knots. The average time to execute a loop is 21 seconds. The load-factor range for the maneuver runs from 2.5 plus G at the entry to 0.7 G inverted to 2.5 plus G during the recovery."

Another successful looper was the Lockheed Model 286, which had a "rigid rotor" that produced good control power at all levels of rotor thrust. In the early '60s, this helicopter demonstrated its aerobatics ability at air shows in the United States and abroad. Figure 30-7 shows a practice session over some Southern California orange groves. Also included in the "looper" category are the Piasecki HUP and the Messerschmitt-Boelkow-Blohin (MBB) BO-105 (Figure 30-8).

Rolling Around

A roll is similar to a loop, as shown in Figure 30-9. Most aerobatics airplanes rely on substantial fuselage sideforce to support them when the wings are straight up and down. The Sikorsky description of the rolling maneuver in the original S-67 Blackhawk goes as follows:

"The roll maneuver is conducted only to the right to eliminate the problem of interference between the collective stick, the pilot's leg, and the cyclic stick. Generally, the maneuver is started from 150 knots in level flight. The aircraft is pulled to 20° noseup and the pitch rate is reduced to a minimum. As the airspeed reaches 130 knots, full right and a slight amount of aft cyclic are introduced.

"As the aircraft reaches the 270° point (three fourths of the way through the roll), lateral cyclic is returned to neutral and additional aft cyclic is introduced to counteract the nose tucking which initiates at approximately the 270° point. The aircraft generally exits the roll at level attitude. The roll takes an average of six seconds to complete and the load factor ranges from 0.8 G to 1.7 G for the maneuver."

Splitting the S

The split S turn consists of the first half of a roll to get inverted and then a recovery like the second half of a loop. Here is the Sikorsky description:

"The entry is made at approximately 70 knots. Higher speeds were investigated but were found unacceptable due to excessive speed build-up when the nose is pointed straight down. The maneuver is initiated by introducing full right cyclic stick.

"When the aircraft is inverted, the roll is stopped, a slight increase in collective is introduced to maintain positive G, and the cyclic is brought aft. The recovery is a standard symmetrical pullout using cyclic only. The collective is held fixed or lowered slightly depending on the load factor

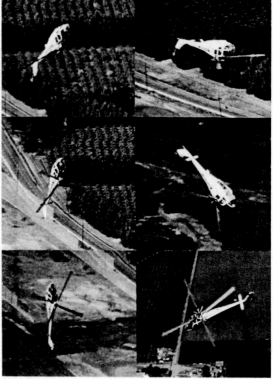

Figure 30-7   Lockheed Model 286 Practicing a Loop

Figure 30-8   MBB BO-105 Going Over the Top

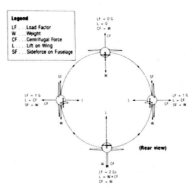

Figure 30-9   An Ideal Roll

demanded. The load-factor range for the total maneuver can run from 0.5 Gin the inverted position to 2.5 plus G in the recovery."

Flat on Your Back

Can a helicopter do steady inverted flight?

Theoretically, yes; practically, no.

A rotor could produce enough negative thrust to support the helicopter's weight inverted if it were designed with enough negative collective pitch range. Some radio-controlled helicopter models have illustrated this possibility.

No actual helicopters are rigged in this manner for two reasons:

1—It would require a collective-control system with twice the normal travel and thus would require more space and weight than a normal system; and

2—It would lose the important safety feature of having the down-collective stop approximately corresponding to the right position for autorotation.

Yes, helicopters can do aerobatics and, given enough motivation, designers and pilots could develop impressive capability in this field. But, perhaps at this time, it is more important to maintain our image as a safe-and-sane industry.

31 Flying in Steady Winds

If the earthly atmosphere would just stand still, some of flight's complications would not exist. But it won't.

It's all relative

When people who are familiar with land vehicles first start to fly, they almost always have difficulty in understanding the concept of relative airspeed as it applies to their aircraft. In one form, the question might be: "In cruise flight with the aircraft in trim, does the wind blow against the aircraft? For example, an aircraft is traveling west at 100 knots but there is a wind from the west at 20 knots. Will the aircraft feel the air striking against its front proportional to 120 knots? Or will it not because it is moving backwards 20 knots with the wind?"

The answer is that almost everything is relative. In this case, once an aircraft leaves the ground, the forces on it depend only on its relative speed with the surrounding air-that is, its airspeed. Its only connection with the ground is through the force of gravity acting toward the center of the earth. It might become clearer if you imagine yourself flying above a cloud layer that is moving along with the wind. Up there, you could circle a cloud top just as easily as you could circle a mountain top on a calm day no matter how fast the earth is turning under this peaceful scene.

It is the same with a fly buzzing around in the cockpit; he doesn't care how fast you are flying. You can even take this one step further by imagining the fly buzzing around in a model airplane flying up or down the aisle of a jet transport. He will do the same thing no matter how fast the jet is flying, nor how fast the earth is turning below, nor how fast the earth is going around the sun, nor how fast our galaxy is rotating. He only cares about the speed of his wings through that little bit of air that's his.

Crosswinds

When the wind is crosswise to the flight path, it gives rise to a navigational problem not unique to aircraft. Seafarers have been faced with crosswinds, in addition to ever-changing ocean currents, for centuries.

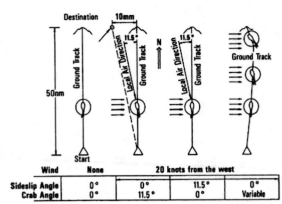

Wind	None	20 knots from the west		
Sideslip Angle	0°	0°	11.5°	0°
Crab Angle	0°	11.5°	0°	Variable

Figure 31-1 Fjour Ways of Reaching the Mountain

To illustrate the crosswind problem for helicopters, let's follow a pilot delivering cargo to the summit of a mountain peak some 50 nm north. Figure 31-1 illustrates the scenario. The pilot plans to cruise at 100 knots, so the flight will take 30 minutes. On a calm day, he would set, and hold, a course directly to the peak. The navigation task is easy.

But let's impose a 20-knot crosswind from the west. Now if he holds his initial, direct heading, he will wind up 10 nm east of the summit. Since this is obviously unacceptable, he must select from several possible corrective measures.

An obvious solution is to set an initial course toward a point 10 nm west of the peak (11.5° west of true north) and then hold. He is assuming, of course, that the 20-knot wind will be constant throughout the flight. His ground track will be straight north but, both from the air and ground, the helicopter will appear going slightly sideways to the right, "crabbing" even though there is no sideslip with respect to the air mass. In fact, if the flight were above clouds moving with the wind and the pilot could not see the ground, no crabbing would be detected.

Another way of reaching the peak is to hold the aircraft's nose on the peak while continually side slipping 11.5° to the left. Again the ground track is straight north and a ground observer would say "right on." But the sideslip would cause higher drag, requiring more fuel for the mission.

A third possibility is to initially head due north with no sideslip and then "chase" the peak by changing heading toward the west whenever a correction appears required. The result is a fishhook-shaped ground course. It's a likely solution for a pilot unaware of the crosswind.

Turning in wind

Almost since the Wright Brothers, airplane pilots have been aware of the danger of downwind turns in which airspeed is lost. Unlike Wilbur, Orville, and the rest of the fixed-wing crowd, helicopter pilots fly machines that are much less dependent on airspeed for lift and control. Nevertheless, several helicopter accidents have been attributed to such situations. These incidents occur largely because the pilot, flying low enough to perceive cues from the ground, tries to maintain constant groundspeed instead of constant airspeed.

For airplane pilots, stall and loss of control can be fatal. For their rotary-wing brethren, the main trouble occurs when they find themselves behind the curves of power and collective-pitch requirement. Thus, without increased collective, a pilot may run out of power and fly into the ground.

The downwind-turn problem diminishes as the helicopter pilot gains altitude. He loses immediate cues of ground motion and turns his attention to the airspeed indicator, where it should have been all along.

Making lazy circles

Tracing perfect circles around a spot on the ground on a calm day is simple; it only requires constant airspeed and bank angle. It's that simple even on a windy day, provided the center of the circle is a cloud or free balloon. This despite the fact that the ground track appears like a spiral or, more precisely, a cycloid, the same pattern traced by a rotor blade tip in forward flight.

When circling a free-floating cloud or balloon, the aircraft is only concerned with its relationship to air mass. It carries its inertial frame of reference with it and thus feels no varying inertial forces, even though its ground track is continually changing from upwind to downwind.

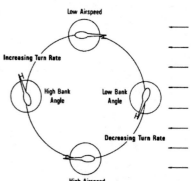

Figure 31-2 Changing Conditions WHile Tracing a Perfect Ground Circle in a Wind

The situation is different, of course, when flying perfect circles at a constant ground velocity about a spot on the ground on a windy day. Now both airspeed and bank angle must be constantly adjusted. Figure 31-2 shows the varying conditions that complicate the task.

By observing the helicopter's motion with respect to the ground instead of the air, a pilot might be convinced that the turn is uncoordinated, since the rate of turn changes. Such misreading has caused accidents during a turning approach to land because the pilot tried to compensate to make the aircraft fly like his eyes told him it should.

32 Flight In Turbulent Air

Does a helicopter behave any differently than an airplane when flying through turbulence? Yes and no.

From the standpoint of ride quality, a helicopter flying through turbulence has an advantage over an airplane because of the looser attachment of the rotor to the fuselage compared to a wing. This allows the inertia of the blades to absorb some of the gust-induced variations in thrust before they are transmitted down to the airframe.

A classic demonstration of this difference was made many years ago by the NACA (NASA's predecessor), which flew two aircraft of the same size, a Sikorsky S-51 and a Cessna airplane, in formation through rough air. Each aircraft carried an instrumentation package that recorded the cockpit's vertical acceleration in Gs. The data analysis showed that the airplane's ride was nearly twice as bouncy as the helicopter's.

Wind shear

While making a landing approach, an airplane is particularly vulnerable to horizontal wind shear (Figure 32-1), especially if the headwind that it was depending on for airspeed suddenly quits or even momentarily becomes a tailwind.

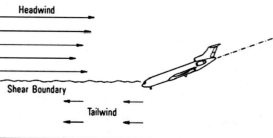

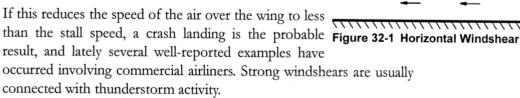

Figure 32-1 Horizontal Windshear

If this reduces the speed of the air over the wing to less than the stall speed, a crash landing is the probable result, and lately several well-reported examples have occurred involving commercial airliners. Strong windshears are usually connected with thunderstorm activity.

For a helicopter, the existence of a horizontal windshear is inherently less dangerous. However, if the horizontal shear were also accompanied by a strong downflow, the helicopter might be driven into the ground before the pilot could react. I have heard of at least one accident where this might have been the case.

Wind shift

The same local meteorological phenomena that produce a change in wind with altitude can also cause a change with time so that a wind reported to be out of the north a few minutes ago may now be out of the south and if the direction is important in making piloting decisions, the pilot may be now making the wrong one.

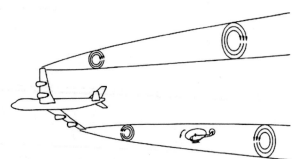

Figure 32-2 Wingtip Vorticies from a Large Airplane can Roll a Smaller Aircraft

Wingtip vortices

Flying into a vortex left by the wingtip of a large airplane can upset a helicopter just as easily as an airplane. One of these invisible whirlpools (Figure 32-2) can persist for several minutes before becoming unstable and self-destructing. Up until then, it is strong enough to roll any small- or medium-sized helicopter or airplane unfortunate enough to try and fly down the center-or even close to it.

Some people have said that a helicopter rotor will destroy the vortex by chopping it up. Don't you believe it! Even if it were true, the destruction would come too late.

The vortex pattern left by helicopters has, on occasion, been blamed for upsetting small aircraft. However, the more-likely culprit was the downwash in the immediate vicinity of the rotor. Inherently much less stable, the complex pattern of rotor-tip vortices contains the seeds of its own rapid conversion into unorganized turbulence that quickly dissipates.

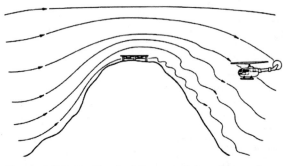

Figure 32-3 An Upwind Approach to a Pinnacle Landing Site

Mountain flying

Wind blowing over mountain ridges and peaks generates flow patterns that can surprise an inexperienced helicopter pilot. For instance, approaching a landing site by flying upwind is usually good advice—but if that site is on the top of a mountain ridge, the approach is through air that is tumbling down into the valley below so the helicopter has to climb just to maintain altitude (Figure 32-3).

If the power available is marginal, as it often is in hot-and-high conditions, the landing might be in jeopardy. Experienced mountain fliers cautiously approach such spots along a crosswind path over the upwind side of the ridge, turning into the wind just at touchdown.

On a smaller scale, the same type of flow disturbances are present near the ground whenever a building, wall, or tree line presents an obstruction to the wind.

33 Angle Limitations

In movies, we've recently seen various helicopters performing such airshow maneuvers as full rolls and Immelmann turns. This may seem surprising, considering that flight restrictions imposed on most helicopters limit the allowable bank and sideslip angles.

Listed in the pilot's handbook, these restrictions are there to ensure flight safety, structural integrity, and generally to keep the pilot out of some potentially dangerous conditions.

Bank angle

The bank-angle restriction warns the pilot that while his helicopter may have the control capability to roll steeply, it has only enough power and/or thrust to maintain a turn up to a certain limit of tightness. A number of helicopter (and airplane) accidents have been attributed to losing altitude while trying to exceed this limit too close to the ground.

The load factor in a turn is related to the bank angle (Figure 33-1). For instance, a bank angle of 60° corresponds to a load factor of 2.

To hold this bank angle in a turn, the rotor has to develop twice as much thrust as in straight and level flight. For the helicopter not to lose altitude or speed during the maneuver, the engine must have enough reserve power to satisfy the requirements of this suddenly doubled effective weight. Very few helicopters can rise to this challenge.

The result: the engine limit is reached and the rotor slows down—leading to rotor stall and loss of thrust just when it's needed most. Making use of the kinetic energy of forward flight by slowing down in the turn may supply some of the extra power required.

Calculations for a typical helicopter indicate that slowing down from 115 knots to 100 knots while going halfway around a 2-G turn can increase the available power by an increment equal to about 70% of that required to fly level. But that still might not be enough.

Similarly, some potential energy can be converted into power by losing altitude (if there is altitude that can be lost). Calculations for the same typical helicopter show that a loss of 100 feet during the 180° turn at 2

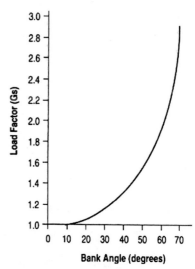

Figure 33-1 Load Factor In Steady Turn

185

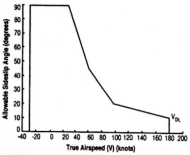

Figure 33-2 A Typical Design Sideslip Envelope

Gs could provide an effective boost of power equal to about 50% of the level-flight power.

Sideslip angles

Many helicopter pilot's manuals contain allowable sideslip envelopes such as that shown in Figure 33-2. The sideslip angle is restricted at high speed to avoid excessive loads on the tail boom and excessive flapping of the tail rotor.

The limits were set after the helicopter's builder studied the results of his "flight-strain survey." This survey involves using a prototype with a full set of instrumentation, including strain gauges, flapping sensors, and a sideslip indicator.

The fallacy of presenting the limit in the pilot's manual for the production helicopter is that the pilot has no sideslip indicator in the cockpit! And it is perhaps just as well, since a pilot who got himself either deliberately or inadvertently into a maneuver that involved high sideslip angles would probably not have time to look at the indicator anyway.

The possibility of overstressing the helicopter, however, does exist. The air-to-air trials at the Navy's Patuxent River flight facility resulted in at least one tail boom suffering some permanent damage. And I know of at least one case where excessive tail-rotor flapping due to a high sideslip angle at high speed led to a fatal crash.

The designers' challenge is to make sure that their helicopters can stand up to whatever a pilot might do to them. One of my test-pilot friends wants to be able to spin completely around during a dogfight to bring his guns to bear on someone chasing him.

Pitch angles

There are usually no restrictions on pitch angles. Pulling the nose up during a quick stop might interfere with the field-of-view, but it does not require extra power or put excessive loads onto any components. A nosedown attitude is used to accelerate, but the pilot can prevent the helicopter from losing altitude during this maneuver even if the power limit is reached by simply backing off. Thus it's up to the pilot as to how much pitch attitude change he can tolerate.

34 Coping with a Power Failure

The fact that a single-engine helicopter has a much better chance to make a safe landing following a power failure than a single-engine airplane probably comes up in more general discussions of rotor-craft than any other talking point. Despite some glowing descriptions, however, the maneuver does not occur automatically but requires some clever management of energy on the pilot's part to bring it off without doing damage to man or machine.

Entry into Autorotation

Failure to make a good entry into autorotation after the engine stops is one of the primary causes of helicopter accidents. The key to making a good entry is to keep the rotor speed up. If the rpm is allowed to decay too much, the rotor may stall and come to a fatal stop when asked to support the full weight of the helicopter. Even before reaching this point of no return, other bad things—like generators dropping off the line and hydraulic pressure going below minimums —may occur.

The reason for the rpm decay is that when the engine suddenly quits providing power, the rotor will begin to feed on its own energy by slowing down to make up for the power loss. If the rotor has high inertia because of heavy blades or tip weights, the rpm will fall off slower than if it were a lightweight rotor. The flight condition at the time of engine failure will also affect the rate of decay: a failure in a high-powered climb will result in a faster decay than had it happened in a descent.

The accepted way to stop the decay is to quickly reduce the power demands on the rotor by lowering the collective stick. This results in an initial loss of thrust but does get the helicopter going down through the air — the first prerequisite for autorotation. The upcoming air through the rotor will soon increase the thrust, even at low collective pitch. If the rotor speed has not dropped too far in the meantime, the pilot can maneuver the ship into steady autorotation with the thrust equal to the gross weight and the rotor speed controllable by small changes in collective —lowering the stick for increased speed and raising it to prevent overspeed. This procedure is associated with a substantial loss in altitude as potential energy is sacrificed to put kinetic energy back into the rotor.

There is an alternate procedure, however, that can work if the power failure has occurred at a moderately high forward speed. In this situation, the pilot can take advantage of the kinetic energy associated with forward speed by doing a mild cyclic flare before lowering the collective pitch. This puts the rotor into a nose-up attitude that reduces the decelerating torque and maintains thrust and altitude until the forward speed is decreased to the best autorotational speed. At that point, the collective pitch is reduced for entry into autorotation.

I know of one test pilot who developed this technique on a UH-1 to the point where he could delay dropping the collective for nine seconds after the power chop. (I also know of one test pilot who takes exception to this alternative procedure. Bob Ferry of Hughes says, "Always lower the collective pitch the very first thing! I know of several dead pilots who didn't.")

Steady Autorotation

During steady autorotation, the energy balance is achieved by the continuous rate of loss of potential energy due to the aircraft's descent. This steady airflow produces enough power to satisfy the helicopter's flight requirements at that speed. The minimum rate of descent occurs at the speed for minimum power on the level-flight power-required curve. It is prudent, however, to autorotate at five to 10 knots faster than the bucket speed for the extra margin of kinetic energy available for increasing rotor speed in the landing flare.

Most helicopters have recommended rotor speeds selected for high-speed power-on flight and are therefore not as efficient as they might be in other flight conditions. Specifically, the glide can usually be stretched by reducing the rotor speed somewhat below the normal power-on rpm. This, however, must be done carefully, since at some lower rotor speed, the rate of descent will increase rather than decrease. The higher the gross weight, the higher will be the optimum rpm. These effects were discussed in Chapter 13.

Even with the lowest possible rate of descent in steady autorotation, the helicopter is carrying far too much energy along its flight path for the landing gear to absorb at the moment of truth. Once again, it is up to the pilot to cleverly manage his various energy resources to insure the touchdown will be within the capabilities of the landing gear.

In short, the problem becomes one of reducing the kinetic energy along the flight path to near zero at the same time that ground contact is made —while continually absorbing enough power from the passing air and from stored rotor kinetic energy to supply the power requirements of flight — all without letting the rotor rpm droop to a stalling condition!

The solution is a maneuver starting with a well-timed cyclic nose-up flare that simultaneously increases rotor thrust due to the increased angle of attack while tilting the thrust vector aft, thus braking both the forward and the vertical velocities. It can also be used to store energy in the rotor in the form of an rpm overspeed —up to the rotor-speed redline. The extra rotor energy is not important for itself but for the time cushion it gives the pilot to correct for non-optimum control motions in the final critical seconds. (An Army report on the subject beautifully understates the situation when it says, "Pilot apprehension is a factor because of ground proximity and rate of closure.") Army tests on a UH-1C indicated that, at most, only 15% of the energy associated with loss of altitude and forward speed could be converted into rotor energy in the flare. During the cyclic flare, a low-inertia rotor can be rapidly brought up to a state of high kinetic energy, making it comparable to a high-inertia rotor whose speed cannot be so rapidly increased.

The cyclic flare should continue until the helicopter slows down to 30 or 40 knots, where most of the available forward-flight kinetic energy has been used up. Now is the time to use the rotational energy stored in the rotor by pulling up on the collective to maintain thrust as the rotor slows down. The Army tests on the UH-1C indicate the rotor energy can be used for slowing the helicopter with about a 25% efficiency. A final forward push on the cyclic stick should level the helicopter just before the landing gear touches down. Figure 34-1 summarizes the steps in a successful autorotation event.

It is evident that the success of the landing flare depends on precise timing of the various pilot actions. This comes from practicing with the engine declutched but running—so that it is available to immediately add power in case the timing is a little off. Unfortunately, even this precaution is not foolproof and a number of helicopters are damaged every year while practicing landings from autorotation.

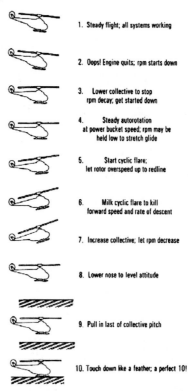

1. Steady flight; all systems working

2. Oops! Engine quits; rpm starts down

3. Lower collective to stop rpm decay; get started down

4. Steady autorotation at power bucket speed; rpm may be held low to stretch glide

5. Start cyclic flare; let rotor overspeed up to redline

6. Milk cyclic flare to kill forward speed and rate of descent

7. Increase collective; let rpm decrease

8. Lower nose to level attitude

9. Pull in last of collective pitch

10. Touch down like a feather; a perfect 10!

Figure 34-1   Conditions in Right Hover Turn

Deadman's Curve

No matter how clever the pilot is in juggling the energy in both the entry into and the flare from autorotation, there remain some combinations of initial altitudes and speeds from which he will surely crash.

The diagram that illustrates this awful truth is the Deadman's Curve or, more politely, the height-velocity diagram—illustrated by Figure 34-2.

Along the boundary of the curve, a pilot should be able to do the right thing at the right time to safely set the helicopter down (providing that there is a decent landing spot down there somewhere) but from inside the curve, various degrees of damage will occur. Taking a closer look, we see that several definite points define the curve, the first being the low hover height. Up to this height, a pilot can handle a power failure in hover by coming straight down and using collective pitch to cushion the landing as the rotor slows down. Above that point, the rotor will either slow down and stall if the pilot does not reduce collective pitch —or the helicopter will hit too hard if he does.

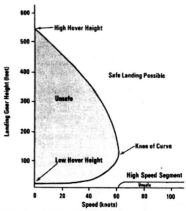

Figure 34-2 Height-Velocity Curve for Single Engine Helicopter

We can raise the low hover height by any of the following changes: decrease the power required to hover; increase the rotor inertia increase the blade area so that a lower rotor speed is required to stall; and, finally, increase the capability of the landing gear to absorb more energy without damage.

The dangerous hover altitude runs up from the low hover height to the high hover height. At this second point, there is enough altitude to make a diving transition into forward flight autorotation and execute a normal power-off flare.

A power failure in forward flight is also perilous —but not quite so much as in hover, since it is easier to get into forward flight autorotation. At speeds greater than the knee of the curve, a power failure should be survivable at any altitude —except possibly right on the deck.

The height-velocity curve shown in the operator's manual for each type of helicopter has been established by skilled test pilots who tried to make their reactions simulate those of average pilots. This was done, in part, by specifying a definite delay time following the power chop before moving the controls. This delay time depends on who is writing the rules.

When certificating a helicopter for the FAA, the bottom of the curve is established in a full-power climb with "normal" pilot reaction time between power chop and collective reduction. This accounts for the degree of alertness that should exist close to the ground. The top of the curve is established for level-flight power and a delay of normal pilot reaction time plus one second. The military, on the other hand, assumes that their pilots may be distracted during an engine failure and will not react in less than two seconds in any flight condition.

Whether the specified delay should be applied to the pedals and cyclic stick as well as the collective stick is another subject of debate. Conservatively, it should. But realistically, it can be assumed that the pilot will almost instantaneously react to sudden yaw, pitch, and roll motions from an engine failure just as he would if these motions were caused by turbulent air.

The size of the Deadman's Curve depends on several factors. For a given helicopter, increasing gross weight and density altitude both expand the unsafe region. As a rough rule of thumb, a curve established at sea level can be considered to expand like a balloon directly as the gross weight goes up and inversely as the air density decreases. For example, simultaneously increasing gross weight by 20% and going to 10,000 feet where the air is only 74% as dense as at sea level would give an expansion factor of 1.6. On Figure 34-2, the high-hover point would go from 540 to 900 feet, the knee of the curve would increase from 60 to 100 knots, and the low-hover height would drop from 15 to 9 feet. For different helicopters, the greater the disc loading, the higher the hover point—up to 1,000 feet on some modern designs.

If the helicopter is already descending, such as on a landing approach, the collective pitch is already low and the unsafe region on the Deadman's Curve is reduced.

Of course, the main effect on the curve is the number of engines —if we assume that only one will fail at a time. (Simultaneous fuel starvation can usually be avoided by having separate fuel tanks supply each engine and by using fuel lines of unequal length.) Single-engine power in most twin-engine helicopters is not sufficient to completely eliminate the unsafe region but it can shrink it considerably and produce another boundary — one outside of which the helicopter does not have to land but can fly away on the remaining power, as in Figure 34-3.

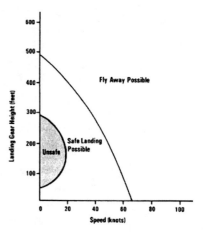

Figure 34-3   OEI Height-Velocity Curve for Multiengine Helicopter

We should recognize, however, that the Dead-man's Curve applies to more than loss of power — it also accounts for tail-rotor loss. In that case, the pilot would remove all power from the main rotor, no matter how many engines he had.

A separate way to reduce the size of the curve is by using a very high inertia rotor. This came naturally with such tip-jet powered helicopters as the Dutch Kolibrie and the French Djinn. (I have been told that the Djinn could make a power-off landing —and *then take off* fly 100 yards, and make another landing, all before the rotor wound down.) Bell Helicopter Textron recently demonstrated the elimination of the Deadman's Curve on a Model 206L by adding enough tip weights to more than double the normal rotor inertia. Other current suggestions include standby tip rockets or a high-speed flywheel to furnish that little bit of energy just when it is needed the most.

High-speed segment

The high-speed portion of the Deadman's Curve merely warns you of the obvious —it is dangerous to fly low and fast, and a power failure is just one circumstance that could lead to an accident in this regime. Over the years, the top of this part of the curve has been lowered and a survey of operators' manuals shows the following interesting trend:

Helicopter	Year Certificated	Height of High-Speed Boundary (feet)
Bell 47J-2	1959	50
Bell OH-4A	1963	15
Hughes 500	1964	5

As a matter of fact, the rotor has a flapping characteristic that benefits the unfortunate pilot who has an engine failure at high speed. As the rotor slows down, its tip-speed ratio increases and it flaps back. This produces a nose-up pitching moment that will automatically start the ship into a climb. This automatic climb may not last very long and the nose-up attitude might cause the tail to strike the ground—but you must agree that it beats an automatic dive.

With sufficient speed during a power failure, the climb can be deliberately prolonged to result in an appreciable gain in altitude as speed is bled off. This zoom maneuver can greatly widen the area available for a safe touchdown. A standard demonstration on the OH-6A entailed chopping the power while flying at a five-foot altitude at maximum speed and then climbing high enough to make two 360° turns before landing in autorotation.

35 Low Speed Power Failures

All good helicopter pilots-especially those who fly single-engine helicopters-are aware of the serious consequences of an engine failure while flying low and slow. Manufacturers put their best recommendation of the low-and-slow region to avoid in operator's manuals as height-velocity diagrams -or the Deadman's Curve. A sample curve (for the Hughes 500D) is shown in Figure 35-1.

There are some situations, however, when the pilot must ignore these recommendations and enter the warning area if he is to do the kind of job that only helicopters can do. In those rare instances when a power failure occurs inside the Deadman's Curve, a crash is to be expected. How much damage is done depends on how well the pilot has managed his meager energy reserves.

Saving rpm

The objective of energy management in this situation is to keep the rotor speed up as long as possible so it can be used to develop thrust to cushion the crash.

For the purpose of illustration, rotor rpm can be compared to the water level in the leaky bucket of Figure 35-2. The size of the leak corresponds to the power required.

Normally, the loss of water leaking out is exactly balanced by the water being pumped in by the engine but when this source fails, there are two reserves that can be called on. The first is the potential energy corresponding to the height above the ground and the second is the kinetic energy corresponding to forward speed.

Neither reserve comes automatically to the rescue. Each requires quick pilot reaction to bring it on line before the rotor speed drops below a minimum value where the rotor would stall if asked to produce thrust equal to the weight of the helicopter.

Power failure at high hover

In hover, of course, the forward-flight kinetic energy reserve tank is empty, so the pilot must initially do whatever he can with his potential energy.

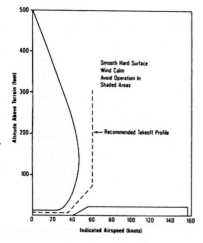

Figure 35-1 Height-Velocity Diagram for Hughes 500D

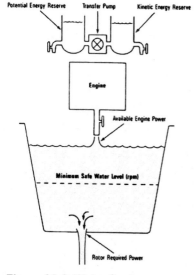

Figure 35-2 Water System Analogy for Helicopter Power Balance

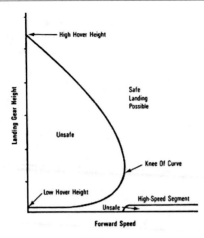

Figure 35-3 Height-Velocity Curve for Single-Engine Helicopter

For guidance, let us look at the techniques that assure successful landings from the point marked "High Hover Height" on Figure 35-3. From this point, the management of energy has two objectives. The first is achieved by rapidly dropping collective pitch. This does two things. It reduces the power extracted from the rotor, thus saving precious rotor speed, and it gets the helicopter going down through the air toward an autorotative condition.

The second objective is to build up some forward speed. Even though the transfer of energy from the potential reserve to the kinetic reserve is not 100% efficient, it has an overall benefit in reducing the power required. Even in autorotation, the rotor requires about as much power as in level flight. However, instead of coming from the engine, the power is supplied by using up the potential energy or altitude. For most helicopters, a speed of about 60 knots is the speed for minimum power and thus also the speed for minimum rate of descent.

Upon reduction of collective pitch, the rotor will flap down and forward. While one might think this a powerful means of pitching the helicopter nose-down and accelerating it forward, the rotor thrust will initially be low and both the ability to pitch the helicopter forward and to accelerate it forward will be degraded.

The low control power will be especially noticeable on helicopters with teetering rotors. These rotors will happily flap in response to cyclic-pitch commands but little pitching moment will be applied to the fuselage until rotor thrust builds up as the helicopter approaches autorotation. Helicopters with offset flapping hinges will not suffer as much loss of control power but their ability to accelerate forward initially will be no better.

The final flare

Even before getting into autorotation or to the speed for minimum sink rate, the pilot should be able to make a cyclic flare to take advantage of his newly acquired forward-flight kinetic energy to develop a rotor thrust higher than the gross weight. This thrust, tilted back in the cyclic flare, will kill off both the forward speed and the vertical speed to the point where the landing gear can cope with both.

During the first part of the flare, a slight rotor overspeed might be obtained, which will help develop the rotor thrust required to cushion the touchdown. The "High Hover Height" is the minimum altitude at which the pilot can accomplish all of this without bending anything.

A bit of speed helps

For a power failure with some forward speed along the upper boundary, the pilot has a head start toward achieving the desired flight conditions and so can go through the process faster. Thus, he requires less altitude—as reflected in the shape of the Dead-man's Curve. If his speed is beyond the nose of the curve, he should be able to make a satisfactory touchdown from any altitude more than a few feet above the ground.

At low altitude, the pilot's reactions are also influenced by how much speed he has. A successful landing from the "Low Hover Height-which is usually with the landing gear only 10 or 15 feet off the ground-can be made by maintaining a level altitude and letting the helicopter settle, using the collective only to soften the final impact. With forward speed, the use of a cyclic flare to keep the rotor speed up is possible. This explains why the boundary goes up with speed.

High-speed segment

The high-speed segment of the height-velocity diagram simply calls attention to the fact that when flying low and fast, it is no time for anything to go wrong. Combat pilots flying nap-of-the-earth might have to fly in this region but most others can easily avoid it.

The rotor has an automatic reaction characteristic that is both good and bad in this situation. As it loses rpm following the engine failure, it will flap nose-up. This pitches the helicopter up and gets it started into a climb-but it might also slam the tail into the dirt if the ground clearance were too small to start with.

The crash situation

So far we have discussed making successful landings from outside the Deadman's Curve but the question we started with was "What should the pilot do if the power failure occurs inside the manufacturer's height-velocity diagram?"

His primary objective should be to hit in a level attitude to take the maximum advantage of the energy-absorbing characteristics of the landing gear and fuselage belly. To accomplish this, he should try to do-as nearly as possible-what he would do if he were just outside the boundary at that speed. That is, from the upper portion of the diagram, drop collective, try to gain some forward speed, and then make a cyclic flare followed by a leveling maneuver just before touching down.

If the rotor thrust is still low after the collective reduction and the pushover to pick up speed, the ability to do the final cyclic flare will be degraded because of the low control power. And, the impact might be more on the nose than on the landing gear.

For this reason, the descent from low heights and low speeds within the Deadman's Curve should avoid extreme nosedown attitudes. From this low corner of the curve, let it settle in; only using collective at the last moment to get as much thrust as the rotor can develop before stalling.

Obviously, these recommendations are full of "ifs" and "buts" depending on the exact situation and in the final analysis, I can only say "Good Luck".

36 Stretching the Glide

An engine will seldom pick the most convenient time and place to quit. For this reason, it is sometimes valuable to know how to milk the last drop out of the autorotative procedure — to either provide the most time for restarting the engine or to stretch the glide to that distant landing spot. The pilot has two parameters to work with: indicated forward speed and rotor speed.

The "Right" Forward Speed

For a given helicopter, the best forward speed can be determined from the curves of power required to maintain level flight. To illustrate this, let's look at the results of some calculations made for a typical — but hypothetical —helicopter. Figure 36-1 shows the power required at several gross weights in level flight.

The power required for autorotation is almost the same as in level flight (a little less because the tail rotor is not working quite so hard and because autorotation gives a slightly more efficient distribution of local angles of attack) but instead of coming from the engine, the power must come from the rate of decrease in potential energy as the helicopter loses altitude. The approximate rate of descent in feet per minute required to provide this power can be found by multiplying the horsepower for level flight by 33,000 and then dividing the result by the gross weight. Figure 36-2 shows the results of the calculation as the maximum glide time available per thousand feet of height above the terrain before the terrain comes up to meet the helicopter. Curves are plotted for sea level and two higher altitudes.

It is sometimes said that gross weight and altitude have no effect on the rate of descent. This is approximately true for the example helicopter in the weight range between 15,000 and 18,000 pounds at sea level and at 5,000 feet but the generality breaks down for other conditions. The sea-level curve from 15,000 to 17,000 pounds illustrates a trend that has been verified in flight-test programs of several helicopters: within a certain range, the autorotative performance is improved as the weight is increased because the potential energy goes up faster than the power increases. At higher gross weights, however, because the induced power is proportional to the square of the weight, the trend reverses — so the

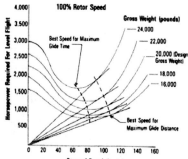

Figure 36-1 Power Required for Typical Helicopter

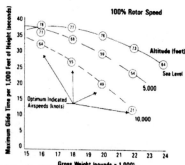

Figure 36-2 Maximum Time Available to Restart Engine

197

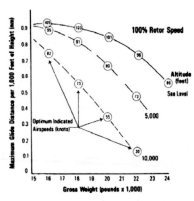

Figure 36-3 Maximum Distance Glide can be Stretched

maximum glide time starts to go down again. At altitude, the rate of descent at low gross weights is about the same as it is at sea level—but at higher weights, this equality no longer holds. Figure 36-2 shows that the optimum indicated airspeeds decrease drastically as both altitude and gross weight are increased.

Stretching the Glide

The speed for maximum glide distance is higher than for the maximum glide time as shown on Figure 36-1. It is where the ratio of forward speed to power is a maximum and where a line from the origin is tangent to the power-required curve. This best-distance speed also defines the conditions for the maximum lift-to-drag ratio (which airplane aerodynamicists are always interested in) and is approximately the optimum cruise speed for both helicopters and airplanes.

The maximum glide distance in terms of nautical miles per thousand feet of altitude can be determined from the parameters of Figure 36-1 by dividing the product of gross weight and optimum speed by 1,980 times the horsepower. Figure 36-3 shows the results of this process for sea level and for two higher altitudes. For each point, the optimum indicated airspeed is noted.

The results of Figure 36-2 and 36-3 are somewhat low because the calculations have been based on the power required in level flight rather than the lower power required in autorotation. A check using measured flight-test data on a Bell AH-1G indicates that this approximation has introduced an error of about 20%. This is a conservative error and if the pilot relies on the approximate calculations, he has a little margin to do the wrong thing during this exciting period in his career.

The "Right" RPM

Besides the optimum indicated forward airspeed, there is also an optimum autorotative rotor speed that can be used to stretch the glide. This is the speed resulting in the most blade elements working at the best angles of attack for producing maximum local lift-to-drag ratios. As an average on a typical rotor in autorotation, this is about 5°. Many helicopters are designed to operate at lower angles under normal conditions so that they have adequate capability to go to abnormal conditions such as high weights, high speeds, high altitudes, and high maneuvering load factors. This means that in gentle flight conditions such as steady autorotation, especially at low gross weight and altitude, the rotor efficiency can be increased somewhat by lowering the rpm until the rotor is operating at the desired 5° of average blade element angle of attack.

As discussed in Chapter 19, the average angle of attack is related to the nondimensional blade-loading coefficient, C_T/σ just as the average angle of attack on an airplane wing is related to the lift coefficient, C_L.

For both the airplane and the helicopter aerodynamicist, their coefficient tells them how close the wing or rotor is to stall. A wing without flaps or slats can usually be counted on up to a lift coefficient of about 1.3 and a rotor in forward flight can operate comfortably up to a blade-loading coefficient of about 0.1. In each case, the optimum coefficient for best performance is 15% to 25% lower than these values. To be specific, most rotors are at the peak of their efficiency in forward flight when C_T/σ is about .08. If the normal value is less than this, slowing the rotor will give better autorotative performance and if the coefficient is already above the optimum, the rotor speed should be increased.

Figure 36-4 shows the trend for this example helicopter. Note that decreasing rotor speed too much can reverse the trend by inviting blade stall and a violent end to autorotation.

At altitude, the lower air density makes the helicopter seem heavier. For instance, at 5,000 feet, the example helicopter at its design gross weight of 20,000 pounds would act like it was loaded to 23,000 pounds at sea level.

Whether to increase or decrease rotor speed to stretch the glide depends upon the initial value of that parameter, C_T/σ. Figure 36-5 shows the recommended action based on rotor blade area, radius, normal rpm, gross weight, and density ratio. If a pilot has chosen a low rotor speed to stretch the glide, he will probably want to get rpm back up as he nears the ground to enhance his ability to carry out a good flare.

In principle, each power-on flight condition also has a unique optimum rotor speed but designers are reluctant to give the pilot too much choice in the matter, primarily because of the trouble they have taken to insure an absence of resonance conditions in blades and other components at the design rpm. Continued operation outside the range specified in the operator's handbook could lead to high vibration and shortened component fatigue byes. Autorotation is such a brief and infrequent flight condition, however, that some relaxation can be allowed if it would mean the difference between a vibrating landing in that distant clearing or a jet smooth ride into the trees.

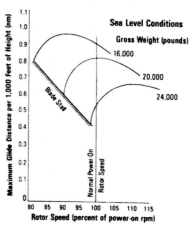

Figure 36-4   Effect of Rotor Speed on Stretching the Glide

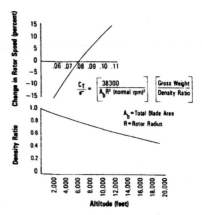

Figure 36-5   Recommended Rotor Speed Change to Stretch Glide

37 Autorotation And Low Load Factors

A term that is confusing to pilots, flight schools, and certificating authorities is "hovering autorotation." Should it be applied to an engine-off landing from a hover at low altitude? In this maneuver, the rotor is kept rotating and producing lift as it slows down by feeding on its own kinetic energy.

It has been reported that some licensing agencies, such as the New Zealand CAA, will disqualify an applicant for a rotary-wing rating who uses "hovering autorotation" to describe this emergency maneuver. Yet other authorities accept the use.

If I had my way, the word "autorotation" would only apply to power-off situations in which the rotor rpm stays constant due to airflow up through the disc. Thus, I would be on the side of the New Zealand CAA.

On the other hand, the English language changes when many people mutually agree on the meaning of a word or phrase. The dictionary writers cite usage, and when they get a sufficient number of citings, they put the word in the next edition. Thus, I can say that "hovering autorotation" was used in Guy Maher's pilot report on the Brantly B-2B (December 1991 issue of *Rotor and Wing*). This and other citings may be enough to make the term legitimate.

Some autogyro answers

Many builder/fliers of small autogyros eventually become interested in the aerodynamic characteristics of their vehicles. Several questions to me have prompted the following discussions.

• Rotor-speed considerations—Autogyros have a fixed collective pitch (except for jump takeoffs), which means that the pilot has no direct control over rpm in flight. For most flight conditions, however, the rotor speed will stay nearly constant.

Calculations that I have made for level flight indicate that a rotor with no twist—like most autogyros—and a collective pitch of about 3° will hold a rotor speed within ±15% over a speed range between 25 knots and 130 knots.

In some maneuvers, such as the initial portion of a landing flare, the rpm may go higher than this.

But the designers had to stress the rotor for at least 25% over the highest operational rotor speed to get the autogyro certificated.

For simple autogyros, the highest rotor speed is what it would encounter in flight. For autogyros with jump-takeoff capability, the rotor might be sped up on the ground to as much as 150% of the flight rpm, and the designer has to include at least a 25% margin on top of that. A helicopter designer must also do this to take care of centrifugal loading and flutter margins.

• Tip-speed limits—To get a quiet main rotor for either a helicopter or an autogyro, the design tip speed should be kept below some 650 feet per second. For helicopters, this low tip speed may cause a problem with retreating blade stall at high speeds. On an autogyro, this should be less of a problem, since the retreating tip is not operating at high angles of attack and is therefore not near stall.

• Autogyro disc loading—Disc loading on both helicopters and autogyros govern low-speed performance characteristics. Low disc loading on a helicopter ensures good hover performance. Low disc loading on an autogyro produces a low minimum speed.

A low disc loading is also important if the autogyro is to be capable of jump takeoffs. The lower the disc loading, the higher it can jump.

• Rotor inertia—On an autogyro, it is not as important to worry about the stored kinetic energy from a safety standpoint as on a helicopter. This is so because there is no sudden transition to autorotation after the engine quits. But stored kinetic energy is important in achieving good jump-takeoff performance. Thus, there maybe a tradeoff consideration between high tip speeds and total rotor inertia.

Flight near zero Gs

For flight at zero Gs, the rotor thrust must be zero. This is a function both of the tip-path plane's angle of attack and of the collective-pitch setting— much like the zero-lift condition on an airplane would depend on the flap setting.

In a maneuver such as flying over the crest of a hill pointed at the bottom of the next valley, the pilot—for a short time—may put the rotor into a zero-thrust condition with the right combination of collective pitch and rotor-disc angle of attack.

If he is flying a rotorcraft with a teetering rotor, the absence of rotor thrust will also mean an absence of pitch and roll control. Helicopters with offset flapping hinges or hingeless rotors will not lose control altogether, but will suffer some decrease.

To regain control, pulling aft on the cyclic stick will make the rotor flap back, increasing its angle of attack and thrust. This is the normal—and recommended—recovery maneuver from flight at a low-load factor. Even a helicopter or autogyro with a teetering rotor should pull out safely if the pilot is patient.

If he is impatient, however, he might pull all the way back before the rotor has had a chance to start producing a significant recovery. The subsequent full-aft flapping may result in a tail-boom strike if the designers had not accounted for this situation.

The recovery can also be done with collective pitch, which immediately produces thrust and also makes the rotor flap back some to increase its angle of attack. A collective recovery is not recommended by some military organizations because of the possibility of over-torquing the transmission as the engine tries to maintain rpm.

Lateral cyclic

Using lateral cyclic at zero Gs will only make the rotor flap sideways without changing the thrust. This is apparently the usual case for mast bumping on helicopters with teetering rotors. In this instance, the pilot gets no rolling response and in frustration puts in full lateral cyclic, getting full lateral flapping that is more than the designers allowed for.

38 Instrument Flight

A clear view of the earth below, the sky above, and everything in between is the best flying cue a pilot can have. When the good view goes away and "blind flying" is required, the pilot is immediately faced with three questions: "Which way is up?" "Where am I?", and "How the Hell do I get down?" For a price, the aircraft can be equipped and the pilot trained to answer all of these questions satisfactorily.

There are two types of terms that describe the prevailing visual environment. One type is general and is used primarily by the military. If the view is good, the term "visual meteorological conditions" (VMC) is used. A poor, or nonexistent, view is referred to as "instrument meteorological conditions" (IMC), meaning simply that the pilot must rely on his cockpit instruments to complete the mission.

The Federal Aviation Administration also sometimes uses these terms, but more often you hear more specific words - visual flight rules (VFR) and instrument flight rules (IFR). Here the emphasis is on rules.

For VFR, the primary rule is "see and be seen." For IFR, the rules are more restrictive, reflecting the tradeoffs between inherent stability, artificial stability, cockpit aids, pilot number and proficiency, positive separation from other aircraft, and minimum visibility conditions at landing sites.

One of the main differences between a helicopter equipped for IFR compared to one equipped for VFR is the number of dials, knobs, and switches in the cockpit. For VFR, it would conceivably be possible to fly with no instruments at all but all helicopters come with at least an airspeed indicator, an altimeter, an engine/rotor tachometer, and engine- and fuel-status indicators.

For IFR operation, add at least a turn-and-bank indicator, an artificial horizon (two for redundancy), and a vertical speed indicator. Also add whatever communication and navigation equipment is appropriate for the ground facilities being used.

Defining workload

Besides the additional equipment to answer the questions: "Which way is up?" "Where am I?", and "How do I get down?"; the FAA also requires that the workload-just to fly on instruments while doing navigation and communication duties—be low enough so the crew can safely handle both routine and emergency situations. Workload can be physical, mental, and/or emotional. For example, consider tuning your car radio to a distant station while driving on a winding mountain road on a dark, rainy night while the kids are fighting in the back seat. Now, that's workload!

For a helicopter in IFR flight, the situation might be similar—and so in most helicopters, two pilots are needed to split the duties, although both do not necessarily have to be human. The use of suitable black boxes to handle the stability and control problems can make it so easy to fly that the FAA will certificate the aircraft for IFR operation by a single human pilot. As matter of fact, a helicopter with very good basic inherent flying qualities can obtain the coveted certification without any black boxes.

Bell has done this on the 222B and its sister ship, the 222UT, even though the earlier 222A needed an autopilot. The required improvement in basic flying qualities was apparently achieved by improving directional stability with a vertical stabilizer tip-extension and trailing-edge strips, and decreasing the dihedral effect with small vertical surfaces on the bottoms of the sponsons (Figure 38-1). This is a typical fix for an unstable Dutch roll (combined roll and yaw) oscillation.

Figure 38-1 Bell 222U Certificated for Single-Pilot IFR Without Autopilot

Terminal operations

Some airplanes with very-sophisticated avionics equipment have been approved for making takeoffs and landings in dense fog at suitably equipped airports. This type of operation is known as "Category III." Similarly, some helicopters, such as those used for antisubmarine warfare (ASW) by the U.S. Navy, can operate to the surface of a fog-shrouded sea. Most airplanes and helicopters, however, are more limited in their terminal operations.

Typically, an aircraft without special equipment cannot legally make a landing approach if the cloud ceiling is less than 600 feet above the ground and the visibility is less than two miles. A pilot who planned to land at a site that has just gone below minimums is expected to wait for a break in the weather or go to a previously selected alternate field.

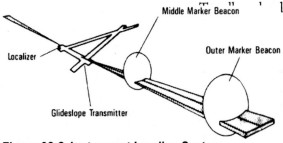

Figure 38-2 Instrument Landing System

lings with reduced minimums, many airports are now equipped with an instrument landing system (ILS), shown in Figure 38-2. This projects an electronic beam into the clouds that can be followed down by a suitably equipped aircraft. In most ILS installations, the slope of the beam is only 3°, so the approach path is relatively flat. The pilot follows the beam down, but if, at the allowable minimum height above the ground (usually no less than 200 feet), he has not established visual contact with the runway lights, he must abort the landing.

Riding the waves

A helicopter equipped with an ILS receiver can land at an ILS-equipped airport—but being limited to airports in bad weather is a source of frustration to the helicopter operator. Up until now, there have been only a handful of experimental installations at heliports allowing for true IFR-helicopter operations.

Someday this all might be different. Systems known as MLS-microwave landing systems-are being developed. Figure 38-3 shows that these provide a more-flexible approach path than ILS. The descent slope will probably be steeper than the 3° used by the airport ILS but a practical limit appears to be about 9°, to avoid putting the helicopter into autorotation at its most comfortable approach speed of 50 to 70 knots. Even though steeper approaches could be made at lower speeds, the flying qualities deteriorate and the measurement of airspeed becomes more questionable; both effects make the pilot's job harder.

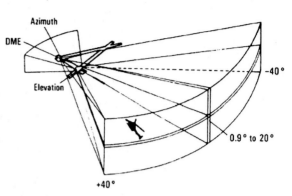

Figure 38-3 Microwave Landing System

Initially, even MLS systems will have some operational minimum ceiling and visual range, so the pilot can make his final deceleration and touchdown within sight of the ground. At the very least, the pilot should be able to tell whether the previous helicopter has moved off the landing pad before he settles right down on top of it.

Eventually, special lighting and fog-dispersal equipment might be developed for as close to zero-zero heliport operation as anyone would want. Of course, all this costs money and since any heliport will be socked in only occasionally, an intense lobbying effort by helicopter users will undoubtedly be required to justify these expenditures.

Look at all those dials!

A look into the cockpit of a modern IFR-equipped helicopter will show some familiar instruments and some not so familiar and if you ask the pilot, you might only get parts of the alphabet. This is because instruments that started out simple have gotten more-and-more complicated and have acquired longer and longer names.

Figure 38-4 shows a typical instrument panel which helps the pilot in answering those three critical questions: "Which way is up?" "Where am I?," and "How the Hell do I get down?," when all he can see on the other side of the windshield is cloud.

Which way is up?

Besides a ball in the turn-and-bank indicator, the IFR helicopter will have another indication of attitude. This is the artificial horizon which is driven from a rapidly spinning horizontal gyro that, once "erected," remembers where straight up is — and is therefore able to show not only the bank angle but the pitch attitude as well. The same instrument is often expanded to help the pilot get down-but more of that in a minute.

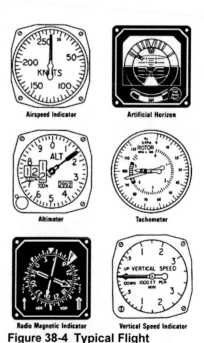

Figure 38-4 Typical Flight Instruments for IFR-equipped Helicopters

Where am I?

The answer to this question can be supplied by various types of devices giving various levels of information. A compass shows the direction the nose is pointing but its usefulness is multiplied by adding another needle that points to a known radio source on the ground.

The source can be a radio station, in which case the instrument is working in its ADF (automatic direction finding) mode, or it can be a VOR (very high frequency omnidirectional radio range) beacon especially maintained for aerial navigation. The combined instrument may be known as a radio magnetic indicator (RMI). In some installations, the compass component is a vertical gyro or directional gyro (DG), erected at the beginning of the flight to point toward true north.

The RMI can be further upgraded by incorporating distance measuring equipment (DME), which shows the distance to the selected VOR beacon. In this case, the instrument is often referred to as a horizontal situation indicator (HSI). If incorporated onto a cathode ray tube display-as is the current trend, it is called an electronic horizontal situation indicator (EHSI) and can be upgraded to display other goodies such as the radar picture of upcoming weather, ground features, and even a moving map.

How the Hell do I get down?

Dorothy got to the Emerald City of Oz by following the yellow brick road. The yellow brick road in the sky for pilots, however, can only be sensed by electronic devices. The most common beam (or road) is that projected by the instrument landing system (ILS) at an airport. Even after we get MLS, the instruments in the cockpit will all probably be similar to those used for ILS-each will have a pair of needles to guide the pilot in altitude and azimuth to follow the beam.

The next step up is the attitude direction-or director—indicator (ADI) incorporated in the artificial horizon instrument with needles that show the pilot how to use his cyclic and collective sticks to stay on the beam. In advanced systems, pedal commands are also given.

When this electro-mechanical device is replaced by a cathode ray tube, it is called an electronic attitude direction indicator (EADI). The EADI usually also shows the approach path so that if a pilot fails to see runway lights on reaching the predetermined decision height (DH), he can call off the landing attempt and go around. On a really full-up system, the autopilot is coupled to the approach system and the pilot simply sits there while the black boxes take him down the glideslope to a point where he can take over for the final touchdown.

39 External Loads

Carrying loads outside the helicopter is often convenient and sometimes necessary. It does, however, introduce some potential safety-of-flight problems that pilots, operators, and engineers should be aware of.

The most common way of carrying an external load is on a single cable. With this system, it is relatively easy to attach and detach the load, and, if necessary, to jettison it in flight. Many types of cargoes, though, ride along on a single line like an untamed mustang. This can lead to spectacular accidents. Listen as a couple of pilots describe how things can go wrong.

Horrible example No. 1

(From a letter to me.)

"I attempted to sling a small helicopter from a larger helicopter and found myself in such a pickle that I had to drop the load to avoid it looping over us.

"For some reason, at about 70 knots, the small helicopter turned its nose away from the relative wind and began to travel laterally from our flight path, reaching a point where it would turn and accelerate back the other way with increasing speed and force. After about a minute of this, the situation had deteriorated so badly that I had to release it.

"My employer and I are being sued for damages due to 'said' negligence on our part. While I feel partly responsible, a good share of the blame should rest on the parties who rigged the load."

Horrible example No. 2

(From the book Chickenhawk by Robert Mason.)

"I saw the maintenance ship take off carrying a damaged rotor blade attached to the sling hook, to carry it out to sea and drop it.

"As the ship took off, it became obvious that carrying a rotor blade dangling vertically beneath the ship was not going to work. It swung wildly under the ship as it gained speed.

"I saw the blade whipping around under the ship at 300 feet. Apparently, the pilot could not tell that the blade was gyrating under him. Before he reached the beach, the blade slashed up behind the ship, knocking off a section of the tail rotor. He flared back, trying to slow the ship, but it was no use. As he flared, the blade knifed forward under the ship and swept up and hit the main rotor. The damaged main rotor flew off. Time seemed to stop, and I saw the ship nose down, invert, and then disappear behind some tents and smash onto the beach."

Safe at any speed?

Some external loads will behave themselves up to any reasonable speed on a single line. These include heavy spheres and cubes and loads with good weathervane stability such as an airplane fuselage with the empennage (tail section) still attached. Most other loads, however, will stay put only up to a certain speed and then begin to oscillate as the aerodynamic forces increase. The oscillation is often unstable, building up to such amplitude that the pilot feels he must jettison the load as in the first example.

Wind-tunnel tests show that a rectangular or oblong load on a single line will first orient itself broadside to the wind as in Figure 39-1 and then will go into a steady oscillation with combined yawing and side-to-side motion. The faster the tunnel speed, the higher the amplitude of oscillation.

I have been told by one experienced pilot that he can interrupt the swinging of a load by suddenly lowering the collective pitch. This apparently decreases the tension on the line and temporarily changes the dynamics of the system enough to break the vicious cycle. In some cases, by jury-rigging a vertical stabilizer or attaching a drogue chute, enough stability may be obtained to make the load straighten up and fly right.

Figure 39-1 Oblong Loads on a Single Line Tend to Orient Broadside to the Flight Path

Even after the load has been delivered, a potential problem exists in that, at high speed, an unloaded cable can fly up and wind itself around the tail rotor.

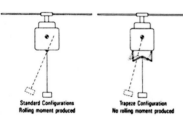

Figure 39-2 Rolling Moment Caused by Load Displacement

On most helicopters, the strong point for cable attachment is some distance below the center of gravity (CG), so that a swinging load will produce a pitching or rolling moment on the aircraft as shown in Figure 39-2. This makes the helicopter seem to fly differently than when not carrying a load and the pilot must adapt his flying techniques for each loading condition.

Locating the attachment point near the CG alleviates this additional complication. This is done on the Sikorsky Skycrane by mounting the strong point to the bottom of the transmission (Figure 39-3). On the Skycrane's younger—and stronger-brother, the Sikorsky CH-53E, the same effect is achieved by bringing the cable up through a hatch in the floor to a special fixture that can be swung into place when needed for longline operation. How a special trapeze arrangement can also be used to aim the cable toward the center of gravity is shown in Figure 39-2.

Figure 39-3 Cable Attachment Point (Near CG) of Sikorsky Skycrane

Multiline

Supporting the load on two or more lines is one way to improve stability. It does, however, introduce the potential problem of a non-simultaneous release in case jettisoning becomes necessary.

Some schemes have been tested involving attaching the cable to the lower ends of "active arms" which, controlled by a special black box, move in such a way as to oppose the motion of the load. An even surer way to control the load is to snub it up tight against the bottom of the helicopter. This is the most practical when the helicopter has been designed with this feature in mind. For instance, the long landing gear on the Sikorsky Skycrane can straddle a load on the ground while it is being attached. Helicopters without this type of landing gear might be able to snub their load but it would have to be done from the hover.

Vertical bouncing

Another possible problem when using a flexible cable is a "pogo" mode where the load starts bouncing up and down, and shakes the helicopter enough that the pilot cannot help moving his collective control in a way that reinforces the plunging motion. This situation requires that the natural frequency of the load on the line be between two and four cycles per second.

In this frequency range, the time lag in the pilot's reflex action is such that no matter how hard he tries to stop the motion, he will do the wrong thing at the wrong time and increase it. Many sling loads have been jettisoned as the amplitude of the plunge increased to a frightening level.

A less-drastic cure is to lock the collective with friction and then leave it alone. A possible way of skirting the problem is to install a soft spring in the line so the natural frequency is below two cycles per second, slow enough that the pilot can control the system with normal actions.

Shaky wings

Attack helicopters usually carry expendable stores or ferry tanks on their stubby wings, which can get into special dynamic problems because of the changing natural frequency of the wing in bending as stores are released or fuel used. Figure 39-4 shows some of the things that can be mounted on the wing of the Agusta A129.

A fully loaded wing will have a natural frequency considerably lower than when the store stations are empty. If, in the process of going from full to empty, the wing natural frequency coincides with one of the frequencies caused by rotor rotation, the wing will be in resonance and may bend up and down or twist at large amplitudes. These critical frequencies can correspond to once per revolution of an unbalanced main rotor-or to higher frequencies corresponding to the number of blades per revolution, to twice the number of blades, to the number of blades minus one, and to the number of blades plus one.

Figure 39-4 Wing Stores That Can Be Carried by the Agusta A129

211

Because of the large combination of wing store loadings possible, it may not be practical to forewarn the pilot of when he might expect resonance but a fairly straightforward way of getting out of it is to release yet one more store or to transfer fuel from one tank to another.

Multi-helicopter lifting

What does the operator do when he is asked to lift a one-piece load just beyond the capability of his helicopter? If he wants the business, he can try and find a bigger helicopter.

The alternative is to harness two of his machines together so that they can do the job. Figure 39-5 and Figure 39-6 show how this has been done in the past. This bi-helicopter lifting capability has not become a standard operating procedure because close pilot coordination is a difficult job. With the development of helicopters with extensive electronic help for control, it now becomes feasible for one pilot to fly two (or more) helicopters in formation while the other pilot(s) simply monitor the safety aspects.

It appears to me that this is a better way to occasionally lift a very big load such as an army tank than using one gigantic helicopter, since between heavy lifts the individual machines could transport smaller loads in several directions.

Figure 39-5 Two Bell 206Bs Carrying a Utility Pole Neither Could Lift Alone

Figure 39-6 Two Sikorsky CH-54Bs Team to Transport a 35,000-pound Cargo

4 0 Blade Tracking

The wheels of a railroad train follow each other - almost always. The blades of a helicopter rotor should follow each other but often do not. Of course, when the train wheels fail to track, a wreck is in the making. Out-of-track rotor blades, on the other hand, produce only an irritating vibration - but this is enough motivation to interest pilots, passengers, and mechanics in getting the system back in track.

Why blades mistrack

If every blade on a rotor was identical in contour, twist, weight distribution, stiffness distribution, and installation on the hub, then in steady flight each would fly in the path of the blade before it. In practice, however, not every blade is identical in these respects and mistracking can almost always be traced to effects classified as aerodynamic, dynamic, or a combination of the two known as aeroelasticity.

Figure 40-1 Inflight Tracking Device on Bell 214ST

The most obvious reason for mistracking - and the easiest to fix - is when otherwise identical blades are not attached to the hub at the same pitch angle and therefore have different lifts. Because this can easily happen, all helicopters have pitch links whose length can be adjusted in small increments between the rotating swashplate and the blades.

Usually these adjustments are made by a mechanic with a wrench butFigure 40-1 shows an installation on the Bell 214ST that allows in-flight tracking using an electrically driven actuator controlled by a button in the cockpit. Kaman uses a similar system in some versions of the H-2.

Another common source of mistracking is when blades are attached to the hub at the same pitch angle but produce different lifts because they are not identical. Pitchlink adjustment may bring the blade in track - or it may not.

If the differences are in airfoil contour or twist distribution, the adjustments are made at the trailing edge of the blade by slightly bending a tracking tab or the entire trailing edge, or in some cases by gluing a small wedge of suitable material to the trailing edge. These changes have two effects: they change the airfoil's angle of zero lift and they produce a local pitching moment in flight that tends to twist the blade to a different twist distribution than was built into it during manufacture.

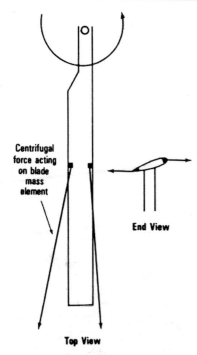

Figure 40-2 Twisting Moment Due to Centrifugal Forces

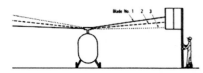

Figure 40-3 Using a Tracking Flag

Figure 40-4 Tracking Target Installed on Westland Sea King Blade Tip

Mistrack can sometimes be traced to a difference in chordwise balance between otherwise identical blades. Figure 40-2 shows how the centrifugal forces operating on mass elements near the leading and trailing edges produce a nosedown pitching moment couple that tries to force the blade to flat pitch. If this effect is stronger on one blade than another because of different weight distribution, that blade will twist down more and so carry less lift in flight.

The nosedown pitching moment due to the chord-wise weight distribution is sometimes called the tennis-racket effect from the twist you feel in your wrist with almost every swing. It is a problem on helicopters without power controls since the effect resists the pilot when he tries to increase collective pitch.

Some helicopters without power controls use "helper springs" to hold collective pitch and some use a weight attached to the blade on a vertical stalk. Centrifugal forces acting on the weight try to increase pitch noseup just opposite of the effect of the horizontal leading- and trailing-edge weight distribution. The axis of the stalk of the vertical weight is located *crosswise* to the blade chord line. This led somebody in the 1930s to refer to it as a "Chinese weight" based on some old sailors' tales concerning Oriental women. For better or for worse, that name has stuck.

Scoping the Problem

To make meaningful tracking adjustments, the amount the blades are out of track must be determined. In the olden days, autogyro blades had to be tracked in forward flight since the aircraft could not hover. At Kellet Aircraft Corp. during the '30s, the process was done by a mechanic in the rear cockpit who touched the lowest blade with a primed paintbrush tied to a stick. Since it was difficult to carry a long enough stick in the cockpit, the mechanic had to stand up to do his job!

Early helicopters were tracked on the ground with a tracking flag (Figure 40-3). Each blade tip had been previously smeared with a different colored paint or chalk, so the color order on the flag showed the relative positions. A roll of masking tape was kept handy to renew the flag after each run.

Modern technology has a crewmember using a stroboscopic light that "stops" all the blades at the same place on the tip path. Targets of different colors or different patterns mounted under each tip reflect the light back to the cockpit where the relative positions are noted. Figure 40-4 shows a tracking target installed on the blade of a Westland Sea King.

Cures

The method for curing an out-of-track rotor depends on what is causing the problem and thus no one method will work in every situation. In addition, different helicopter companies have developed different philosophies.

The procedure used by Hughes Helicopters Inc. for both flight test and field tracking is typical enough to be used as an illustration. This starts with a ground run at flat pitch and approximately 70% of the full rpm. If the blades are out of track at this condition, pitch-link adjustments are made to change the pitch of the individual blades until the track is satisfactory.

The next step is to again run the rotor at flat pitch but this time at 100% rpm. Now, out-of-track conditions are corrected by bending the trailing edge tab in the outboard portion of the blade. To lower a blade, the tab is bent down. This produces an up force at the trailing edge that twists the entire blade nosedown, thus decreasing its lift.

The next step is to track in forward flight, where successively more inboard bending is used as the forward speed increases.

The procedure used for Sikorsky helicopters is quite different. New-production blades are mounted on a tracking tower, along with a "master blade". The new blades are made to track with the master at various combinations of rotor speed and thrust by bending the trailing edges. From then on, for the life of the blade, no bending is done; all tracking corrections are made with the adjustable pitch links.

Sometimes It Doesn't Work

Despite these well-accepted methods, occasionally a blade is installed which, for no apparent reason, refuses to march with its mates no matter what the engineers and mechanics do to it. Scrapping these blades is very expensive and all the companies are looking for ways to identify these mavericks in the production process so they can be eliminated early. So far, we are not completely successful; so there are still good opportunities for bright people to make significant contributions to the art of making blades track with a minimum of fuss.

41 Tying The Helicopter Down

Helicopters are designed to fly, and they don't like to be tied down except for their own safety. For those times when helicopter and rope come together, operators should know how to handle the helicopter properly.

Learning to fly

The early helicopter pioneers relied on a tiedown for various reasons. For one, they had to learn to fly by themselves. As a matter of prudence, they generally fastened the helicopter down with a short tether so that if it did go up, it wouldn't be very high. One obvious tiedown point was the bottom of the fuselage just under the rotor.

Figure 41-1 Igor Sikorsky And The VS-300

Figure 41-1 shows how Igor Sikorsky used this method on his prototype VS-300 with four cables going down from the framework to a large weight. Art Young in developing the Bell Model 30 did it slightly differently (Figure 41-2). His restraint cable went up to a trapeze arrangement that was fastened to outriggers near the fuel tank—that is above the aircraft's center of gravity (CG)—and then down to a pulley fastened in the ground, then to a solid anchor.

The system on the VS-300, with the attachment below the CG, may have caused a turnover accident that was recorded on film. Figure 41-3 illustrates what happens if a helicopter that is tied down below the CG drifts and the tiedown cable tightens up.

Figure 41-2 The Bell Model 30

The bottom of the fuselage stops, but the CG keeps going. The resultant sideward component of the cable tension makes the helicopter roll away from the anchor in an unstable way, resulting in a crash as the rotor tilts enough to strike the ground.

On the other hand, if the attachment is above the CG, as on the Bell arrangement, drifting to the limit of the cable is stabilizing as the helicopter is rolled to bring it back over the anchor in the ground.

The same geometry applies to the helicopter that becomes attached to the ground because a sling load has snagged something immovable. Except for helicopters like the Sikorsky Skycrane—shown in Figure 41-4—

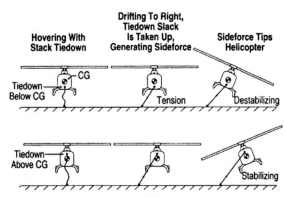

Figure 41-3 Tiedown Position's Affect On Stability

217

Figure 41-4 Sikorsky Skycrane Cable-Attachment Point

which was designed especially for sling work, most helicopters have the attachment for external loads well below the CG. These aircraft can be inadvertently driven into the ground if the pilot tries to free the load by doing anything but pulling vertically.

The wind-tunnel dilemma

Tying the helicopter down to the balance system of a wind tunnel also creates a dangerous situation. When being subjected to different test conditions such as changes in speed or shaft angle of attack, a rotor produces moments about the CG by flapping.

In flight, the pilot either cancels the flapping out with his control system or uses the moments to maneuver by accelerating the fuselage in the direction he wants. During maneuvering, the fuselage keeps out of the way of the rotor blades (if it doesn't, we have a tail-boom or canopy strike).

If flapping occurs in a wind tunnel, however, the moments cannot accelerate the fuselage because it is solidly tied down. As a result, moments caused by flapping are not relieved unless the tunnel operator can uses cyclic pitch just as the pilot would.

The trouble is that, whereas the pilot is well-trained to use the good clues from the motion of the horizon, the tunnel operator usually has much weaker clues and less training for doing the right thing at the right time. Many model and full-scale rotors have been damaged or even destroyed during wind-tunnel tests in conditions that would have been perfectly safe in flight.

When to tie it down

Connecting the helicopter to a solid foundation when the rotor is turning must be considered carefully, but tying it down when the rotor is not turning is usually a very good idea. Because the helicopter generally has a minimum landing gear tread, it is a candidate for being blown over by a strong wind coming either from natural sources or from another helicopter air-taxiing by.

Non-rotating blades are especially susceptible since they are long, limber structures without the stiffening effects of centrifugal force. Given a good wind, they will try to fly—sometimes with damaging results.

42 Accidents Waiting to Happen

Looking back over the history of our industry, we should all be grateful that the early pioneers persisted in making progress, despite the number of unexpected problems they encountered. (Perhaps we should be even more grateful that they did not have high-quality crystal balls.)

However, even after the dedicated work of those pioneers, some of the original problems are still with us. Two types of mishaps that have destroyed many helicopters before the vehicle has even lifted off are ground resonance and dynamic rollover.

Ground Resonance

A destructive oscillation may be encountered if for some reason the blades move on their lead-lag hinges, thus placing their combined center of gravity (CG) toward one side of the rotor disc. In most flight conditions, such an unbalance will rapidly right itself as the individual blades sort themselves out. In this sorting-out process, each blade leads and lags in such a way as to spiral the combined CG in toward the shaft where it belongs.

The potential problem exists if the aircraft is not airborne. A gust of wind, a sudden control motion, or a hard landing can displace the blades. The resultant whirling motion due to the offset centrifugal force may be at just the right frequency to rock the airframe on its landing gear.

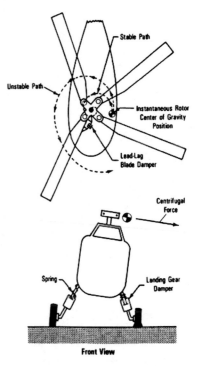

Figure 42-1 Conditions Affecting Ground Resonance

Figure 42-1 illustrates the situation. Once that happens, the two motions get in step and instead of the CG spiraling gently inward, it spirals violently outward—producing a rotating force at the rotor hub that can shake the aircraft to pieces almost instantaneously.

Despite this dire possibility, ground resonance does not happen every time it has an opportunity —just often enough to scare everyone concerned. The first recorded ground resonance accident was in the 1930s, when a Kellett autogyro apparently hit a rock while taxiing. This accident attracted the attention of scientists, who eventually produced a mathematical and physical understanding of the, phenomenon. They found ground resonance can be prevented with damping but that the damping must be both in the rotor around the lead-lag hinges and in the landing gear. Thus the most critical condition is just before the ship becomes airborne — since the landing gear is extended and can provide little damping — although there is still a little stiffness to the rocking motion.

As far as the pilot is concerned, prevention consists of making sure that all dampers are operational during the preflight inspection. If, despite this, the beginning of oscillation is detected, the safest action is to either shut down or (if up to flying rpm) immediately take off. When composure is regained, the pilot should make the gentlest landing possible to a high-friction surface. This will produce damping in case the gear begins a scuffing action.

Rotors with high in-plane stiffness and no lead-lag hinges are not susceptible to ground resonance and therefore do not need damping in their rotors or landing gear. Other hingeless rotors may or may not need dampers — depending on how high their in-plane stiffness is.

In some rare cases, the equivalent of ground resonance can occur in the air with a sling load. Operation in compliance with the operator's manual should allow the pilot to avoid this situation but jettisoning the load is a sure —if drastic —cure.

Dynamic Rollover

In flight, high bank angles are of no great concern because control around the roll axis is usually where the helicopter is at its best. On the ground, however, even a moderate bank angle can be disastrous if it is enough to tip the machine over.

The primary helicopter upsetting moments are due to rotor flapping, with the resultant tilted rotor thrust and hub moments as shown in Figure 42-2. Sometimes tail-rotor thrust and wind on the fuselage also contribute. The moment that keeps the helicopter from tipping over comes from the weight acting between the two wheels or skids. If the helicopter rolls on its landing gear, this stabilizing moment diminishes - it goes to zero if the ship ever rises on one wheel far enough to put the CG right over that wheel. If the helicopter is sitting on a slope, it already has a reduced restoring moment and a lateral CG position (perhaps caused by fuel sloshing). A narrow landing-gear tread or a rolling deck compounds the problem.

A rollover can happen in calm air if the stick is being held off-center enough during takeoff, but a crosswind can make it even more likely. Even in a strong crosswind, there is little or no main-rotor flapping due to nonsymmetrical aerodynamics until the collective is raised for takeoff, then the non-symmetrical aerodynamics produce flapping— sometimes referred to as "blowback". In addition, as the shaft is tilted against the springiness of the landing gear, the increased angle of attack generates even more flapping. Thus, if the pilot is not compensating for the disc tilt with cyclic pitch, he will find the upsetting effects increasing at the same time that the restoring effects are decreasing.

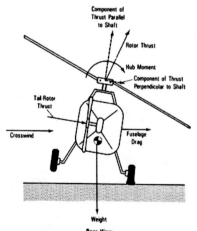

Figure 42-2 Start of a Possible Rollover

In a normal takeoff of most single-rotor helicopters, one landing gear comes off the ground first but, since this happens just as the aircraft becomes airborne, this action is not associated with a rollover. If, however, one landing gear comes off the ground with only' partial thrust on the rotor, a rollover may be starting. In this situation, the pilot might try to hurry the takeoff by raising the collective. This is usually a mistake since the increased thrust in the same direction results in an increase of the upsetting moment.

Another choice is to apply lateral control to put the gear back on the ground — but this action may be too late, especially if the initial motion came as a surprise. If an appreciable rolling velocity has developed, it will take a second or two to stop the motion and by this time the helicopter may have tilted irrevocably beyond its critical tip over angle.

A reduction of collective pitch to get both gears firmly on the ground is the accepted cure for a dynamic rollover but this should be done gently. If the helicopter is dropped too fast it might bounce on the gear that was in the air and start rolling in the other direction.

Although pilot distraction or inattention is usually required to set up the conditions for a dynamitic rollover, some accidents have occurred when the liftoff was attempted with one landing gear still stuck to the ground by mud, ice, or a tiedown.

The ability of the pilot to roll a helicopter over on the ground is enhanced by very stiff hingeless rotors, since even at flat pitch a little out-of-trim cyclic pitch can produce a high, upsetting hub moment. In the Lockheed AH-56 Cheyenne, to discourage the pilot from holding the stick off-center, a device was installed that stiffened up the control centering springs whenever the aircraft had its full weight on the landing gear. The device was deactivated on takeoff as "squat switches" sensed the partial extension of both landing gear oleos.

Mast Bumping/Droop-Stop Pounding

Juan de la Cierva's invention of the flapping hinge led to the successful development of rotary-winged aircraft — but it also opened the door to a problem. The mechanical design and the geometry of the total aircraft dictate that the downward flapping—or teetering—must have some physical limit.

The designer tries to allow for normal motions, plus some margin for abnormal motions, but, as per Murphy, "If anything can go wrong, it will." Thus we continue to have cases — depending on the type of rotor — where the teetering limits are exceeded, leading to mast bumping, or the flapping limits are exceeded, leading to droop-stop pounding.

Most of these cases are caused by trying to maneuver during low rotor load conditions. Since most teetering rotors obtain pitch and roll control by tilting the rotor-thrust vector (exceptions are helicopters with hub

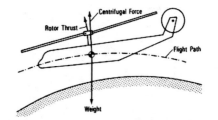

Figure 42-3 Low Rotor Thrust Available for Maneuvering During a Pushover

springs, such as the Bell 222), control power depends entirely on maintaining load on the rotor.

When, as in Figure 42-3, a pilot tries to maneuver with cyclic pitch during a pushover when the rotor load is low, he will find himself having to tilt the rotor disc much more to produce the desired control response than he would have had to do in level flight. Even at zero thrust, the rotor tip-path plane will happily respond to cyclic pitch inputs by tilting. As a matter of fact, it will override any mechanical teetering or flapping stop by simply bending the blades, since the aerodynamic effects are much stronger than structural stiffness — at least in conventional rotors. A similar dangerous low thrust condition can exist following the reduction of collective pitch during an entry into autorotation.

If the tilt being requested is more than the designers had in mind, mast bumping will result. A similar argument applies to rotors with flapping blades, although with offset hinges, they maintain a somewhat higher level of control power as rotor thrust is decreased. Thus, the pilot will not be tempted to use quite as much rotor tilt to perform the same maneuvers. At low thrust, a rotor with hinged blades does, however, have a factor penalizing it, since the coning will be low and the blades will be closer to their droop stops than in normal straight-and-level flight. At any rate, both mast bumping and droop-stop pounding are dangerous because they generate high oscillatory stresses —sometimes high enough to break things—in the parts of the rotor that are banging together.

The steepness of a hillside suitable for landings and takeoffs may be limited by mast bumping or droop-stop pounding characteristics — or simply by the amount of cyclic pitch allowed by the design. This is especially true during the cautious planting of the downhill landing gear while trying to prevent the aircraft from sliding down the hill. The sequence is shown in Figure 42-4. Takeoffs from a slope, on the other hand, can usually be done with less flapping by making a "hop-takeoff" at a right angle to the slope. This will rapidly clear the landing gear.

Blade Strikes

Designers should always design rotors with the flapping freedom required for maneuvers (including those concerned with escaping from unexpected dangerous situations) while ensuring the blades will never hit any part of the aircraft structure. Designers *should,* but they have not always. Their most common error has been to underestimate the amount of blade flapping the pilot will ask for, which has led to predicting adequate clearance where subsequent flight test has shown otherwise.

The discrepancy has forced configuration changes in at least two helicopters. The Sikorsky S-55, or H-19, originally had a straight tail boom. Following a series of tail-boom strikes, the tail boom was angled down 30 to provide additional clearance. On a more recent project, it was found that snappy pushovers put the forward blades too close to the canopy, forcing a redesign that raised the main rotor.

One of the most common tail-boom strike conditions is a hard landing. Figure 42-5 illustrates two scenarios for this type of accident. In the first, the landing gear sets down firmly and stops the downward motion of the fuselage — but the rotor blades keep coming down. Low rotor speed and a quick reduction of collective pitch contribute to the downward flapping and bending of the blades.

The other type of tail-boom strike is likely to occur during a run-on landing when the flare angle is high and the aft part of the landing gear hits first. This tends to bounce the rear part of the helicopter back up while the front part and the rotor continue to descend. Also, the sudden nose-down pitching motion makes the pilot instinctively pull his control stick back, causing the rotor to tilt even closer to the tail boom. Designing the landing gear to have a long energy-absorbing stroke alleviates these landing problems.

Other tail-boom strike incidents have occurred on some helicopters during the entry into autorotation. The rapid reduction of collective pitch makes the rotor flap down in front and produces a sudden pitch-down condition. If the pilot overreacts with aft cyclic stick, the combination of low coning and aft flapping may be enough to reduce the clearance to zero.

When the rotor is up to speed, the centrifugal forces stiffen the blades and limit their possible bending deflections — but at very low rotor speeds during startups and shutdowns, the centrifugal stiffening effect is low and gusty conditions can cause erratic, high-amplitude flapping and bending. For this reason, many rotors with flapping hinges have centrifugally operated droop stops. At low rotor speeds, these stops limit the down movement of the blades. However, once the rotor is up to speed, the droop stops move out of the way to allow more flapping for the now-stiffened blades.

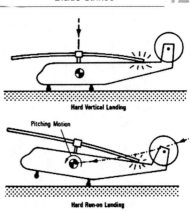

Figure 42-4 Hard Landings Inviting Tail Boom Strikes

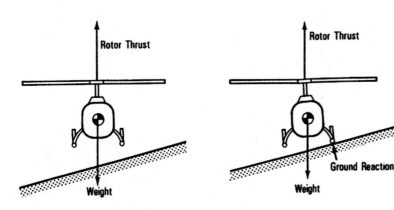
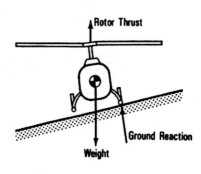

Figure 42-5 Slope Landing Sequence

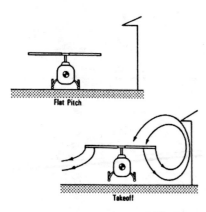

Figure 42-6 Wake Recirculation

A special case of droop-stop pounding once occurred on a parked Sikorsky S-56 when another S-56 landed beside it. The rotor wash from the landing aircraft lifted one blade of the parked helicopter high into the air, and then withdrew its support, letting the blade slam down on its droop stop. The result was a badly bent rotor blade, demonstrating why blades should be tied down.

Operation Near Obstructions

A white-water boatman can see the currents and rough stuff that might upset him but a helicopter pilot very seldom gets such clues. It is bad enough that the ambient wind gets distorted by nearby obstructions — producing unseen currents and rough air, but the helicopter, being a wind machine, can add to the confusion with the recirculation of its own rotor wake.

Figure 42-6 shows one of the most noticeable effects that can occur when taking off near an obstacle. The recirculating wake produces an increasingly non-uniform inflow pattern at the rotor disc as thrust is increased to lift off. This will require a nonstandard hover cyclic stick position that might come as a surprise to the unsuspecting pilot.

For example, if, because of recirculation, the downflow is stronger on the left side, the helicopter will tend to move backwards because of the 90° lag in flapping. Not only is the cyclic pitch affected but the increased downflow looks like a climb condition which requires more power to the main rotor and therefore to the tail rotor also. This represents a decrease in ground effect and might keep a heavily loaded helicopter grounded.

Distortions of the inflow distribution also occur whenever the helicopter is maneuvered into a region of disturbed wind — such as around a rooftop landing pad, mountain ridge, drilling platform, or ship's deck. In these cases, inflow changes might be either up or down but will generally come on suddenly during a takeoff or landing. To minimize the surprise when landing, some pilots recommend a slow crosswind approach, which gives the best chance of reversing the decision if things get too rough.

Finally, care should be taken around airports where large fixed-wing aircraft are laying down strong but invisible wingtip vortices that can persist for several minutes. Crossing through one of these can be very upsetting, even for large helicopters.

43 Helicopter-Ship Operations

Precisely operating a helicopter to and from a small piece of land on a calm, sunny day is challenging enough. Imagine flying that same helicopter to and from a small spot on the deck of a small ship— in a storm and at night. This is the task naval helicopter pilots worldwide must do.

The approach

Compared to flying over land, low-level flight over the sea is more difficult. It is much harder to judge altitude and "groundspeed" by looking at moving waves instead of at stationary trees and houses. At night, of course, the situation is worse, and the pilot must rely on instruments until he is close enough to the ship to use its lights as a visual-reference system.

It has been standard practice to make approaches on a 30° or 40° angle to the ship, to stay out of the ship's turbulence as long as possible. For this type of approach, the pilot must solve some tricky navigation problems in his head to keep up with the ship and to account for winds.

If, for instance, the ship is traveling at 15 knots into a 20-knot Wind, the helicopter must maintain a 35-knot component of airspeed along the ship's path just to keep up (Figure 43-1). Considering the closure rate needed to catch up, the pilot must hold an airspeed of about 45 to 50 knots during the final phases of the approach.

At this low airspeed, the helicopter is flying on the "backside of the power-curve." Here, power management is difficult because it takes more power and collective pitch to fly slower instead of faster as in normal forward flight.

The objective is to solve all these navigational and piloting problems so the helicopter can be brought to a hover just over the landing spot on the stern. More than once, pilots thinking they were doing a good job have found themselves hovering 100 feet behind the ship. This situation is especially likely when visibility is poor, so electronic devices such as TACAN and radar are routinely used to provide range and closure rates.

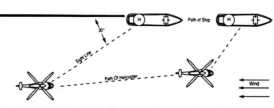

Figure 43-1 Landing Approach

If the pilot is having trouble with all of this, he may require more than one time-consuming attempt to get the helicopter safely on board. For this reason, simpler straight-in, over-the-stern approaches have been recently recommended to speed up the operation, despite the complication of spending more time in the turbulence generated by the ship's superstructure.

A Soviet pilot writing advice to new helicopter pilots points out that paying too much initial attention to the deck may lead one into trouble. There have been instances in the Soviet navy in which the pilot was continually chasing the moving deck, i.e. he was using the deck as a fixed reference as if it were a spot on land. If, for instance, he tried to maintain a descent angle of 6° with respect to the deck and the ship pitched up 7°, the pilot's intended flight path would take him 1° under the water's surface!

The ship prepares

There is also action aboard the ship prior to the arrival of the helicopter. About 15 minutes before, the ship will set "Flight Quarters." All antennas, guns, and railings that could interfere with the helicopter are stowed or lowered, and a crash and fire team is set up. As the helicopter approaches, the captain will—if possible—turn the ship into the wind to provide wind over the deck, and he will also try to pick a course that provides the smoothest ship motion through the waves.

Landing is the greatest challenge. There are two big problems: the effect of the ship's superstructure on the wind patterns at the helideck, and the timing of the touchdown (considering the motion of the deck).

The helicopter platform's usual location is at the rear of the ship, on the fantail. There wind flow is most affected by how it has negotiated its way around the forward part of the ship. If the ship is going fast or heading into the wind, the structure produces a following wake of relatively low-speed air, just as does a truck on the highway. Flying the helicopter into this wake will result in "drafting," sucking the helicopter forward toward the hangar. This changes the helicopter's relative airspeed and the control positions for steady flight.

As you can imagine, landing safely on a pitching and rolling deck takes great piloting skill. After getting the signal that it is safe to land, the pilot will attempt to line up with a stripe painted on the deck, positioning the helicopter's nose over another mark. He tries to anticipate an instant when the motion of the ship is relatively quiet. When that moment comes, he plants the landing gear firmly on the deck with full down-collective pitch, while the deck crew installs chocks and tiedown chains.

RAST and SAMAHE

At some "sea state" (a measure of the wave and wind conditions), the ship's motion and the gustiness will be so extreme that no amount of pilot skill is sufficient to make this type of landing nor to ensure that the helicopter will not slide off the deck before the ship's crew can secure it.

Not to worry! To help the pilot in such situations are systems that actually attach the helicopter to the ship while it is still in the air. The one used by the U.S. Navy is known as RAST (Recovery Assist, Secure, and Traverse), which was first developed in Canada. Its basic function is to attach a cable to the hovering helicopter and then firmly—but gently—winch it down.

As the helicopter hovers at an altitude of about 15 feet, it lowers a light cable down to two crewmen on the deck. They attach this "messenger" cable to a much heavier "haul-down" cable. The heavier cable is then drawn up and locked to the RAST probe, which is permanently attached to a strongpoint under the helicopter's center of gravity. Figure 13-2 shows a Canadian Forces Sikorsky Sea King attached to the RAST system.

Figure 43-2 Sea King Using RAST

At this point, the Landing Safety Officer (LSO) takes command from his vantage point in a bunker, with his eyes at deck level. For a helicopter the size of the Sikorsky SH-60 Seahawk, he applies approximately 2,000 pounds (900 kg) of tension to the cable to stabilize the aircraft. By using a constant-tension winch, the system maintains this force as the helicopter lowers to about four feet above the deck, in preparation for touchdown.

During this operation, not only is the required rotor thrust increased by 2,000 pounds, but the cable also tends to put some rolling and pitching moments on the helicopter. These are somewhat different from what the pilot is used to in free flight (see Chapter 12).

The LSO waits for the pilot to get ready and for the ship to be more-or-less steady. At that moment, he applies 4,000 pounds (1,800 kg) to the cable to pull the helicopter down.

At all times, the pilot can release the haul-down cable and abort the landing, or by pulling more than 4,000 pounds, he can pull all 200 feet (61 m) of cable out of the winch and fly away with it (something frowned upon by the ship's crew.)

Providing it is a good landing and the helicopter is pulled firmly down to the deck, the jaws of the "bear-trap" (the rectangular device shown in Figure 13-2 properly called a Rapid Securing Device) closes on the EAST probe thus locking the helicopter to the deck.

The British and French navies use a device whose purpose is similar to RAST but which differs in operation. The SAMAHE (System de Manutention pour Helicopteres) consists of a grid into which the hovering helicopter shoots a harpoon attached to a cable from a winch in the helicopter. The winch is then used to pull the aircraft down to the deck.

Stopping and folding rotors

Once the helicopter is down and secured, the next step is to stop the rotor. Much of the resistance to flapping on a rotating rotor comes from the centrifugal forces acting on the blades. Slowing the rotor down eliminates this stiffness and allows the blades to respond to gusty wind conditions.

For this reason, devices known as "droop stops" are incorporated in the rotor hub. These are spring-loaded devices which, at normal rotor speeds, are kept out of play by centrifugal forces.

As the rotor slows down and the centrifugal forces become less than the spring forces, the droop stops engage and limit the amount of down-flapping that the blades can do. This prevents them from striking the tail boom or the top of the cockpit, and gives clearance for persons working under the rotor while it is turning slowly. For instance, the droop stops on the Seahawk are designed to not let the blade tips come lower than seven feet above the deck. On some helicopters, the amount of up-flapping is also restricted.

As the main rotor slows down, a vulnerable time comes just before the droop stops are actuated. A sudden down-gust coming over the hangar can cause the tip-path plane to come dangerously close to the helicopter structure or to anyone standing under it. A similar situation can exist even after the stops have come into place, since they can only restrain the flexible blades at their roots.

Once the rotor is stopped, the blades must be folded to get the helicopter into the hangar. This can be done manually on small helicopters, but large helicopters use electric and/or hydraulic actuators that extract one pin from the blade-hub joint and then pivot each blade about the other one.

Once the blades are folded and fastened down, the helicopter is moved into the hangar, either by hand or by the hydraulically powered RAST or the cable-actuated SAMAHE trolley.

At night

Understandably, approach and landing operations to a ship deck are especially challenging at night. On a dark night, the pilot can't discern the horizon to steady his orientation; all he can see are lights on the ship, and these may be heeling over while it pitches and rolls.

Some newer ships are equipped with a "light bar"—known officially as the HRS or Horizon Reference System—installed over the hangar door. The HRS is gyrostabilized to remain horizontal and take the place of the lost horizon. Pilots who have flown this system say that while it helps, it does not completely take the place of an actual horizon.

Nighttime takeoffs are also more challenging than daytime ones. This is primarily due to the sudden departure from the well-lit shipboard environment into the complete and utter darkness, and the urgent need to transfer from flying with external cues to flying on instruments.

Defining limits

In some conditions, operation from a ship will be too dangerous to try. The limiting conditions will depend on a combination of the characteristics regarding the ship, the helicopter, the visibility, and the weather.

For this reason, the Navy conducts shipboard-compatibility trials in which a given helicopter is flown on and off a given ship both in daylight and at night. These are done in sea and wind conditions that are progressively worse, until the experienced test pilot can say that he would not ask an average pilot to go any further into deteriorating conditions.

The safe combinations of the velocity and direction of the wind over the deck with limits on the allowable amount of roll motion of the ship are then published and adhered to for that particular helicopter-ship combination.

Figure 43-3 illustrates such a combination for launch and recovery of the Sikorsky SH-60H operating from a U.S. Navy frigate during the day. The entire envelope can be used for both launches or recoveries with RAST; but without RAST, the recoveries are only permitted when the wind conditions are in the hatched areas. Note that the patterns are not symmetrical. This is apparently due to the way the wind at the fantail is affected by the ship's configuration.

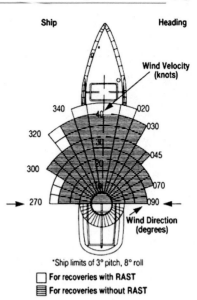

Figure 43-3 SH-60H Day Launch And Recovery Wind Limits* On U.S. Navy Frigate

44 Preliminary Design

The January 1981 issue of *Rotor and Wing International* contained an article about a brainstorming session to develop the requirements for a "dream machine for public service." The first paragraph read: "Aw, c'mon, you guys. A helicopter that turns up 200 knots all the time, 300 knots for 30 minutes, and with four hours' endurance? One that will hover out of ground effect at 10,000 feet on one engine and 20,000 on both? With a max gross weight of 10,000 pounds and a 20-foot rotor? You've gotta be kidding."

Well, kidding or not, this ambitious wish list can be used as the basis for a mini-exercise in the art of back-of-the-envelope preliminary design.

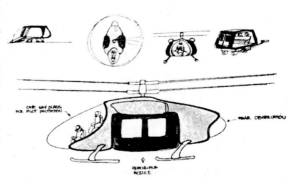

Figure 44-1 Typical Starting Cartoon for a New Design

A designer will start his preliminary effort by drawing "cartoons" much like those in Figure 44-1 – but he can't go very far without also doing some calculations in the fields of aerodynamics, powerplants, and weights. With a few state-of-the-art charts, however, he can make ballpark estimates of most critical design parameters in a surprisingly short time.

Start at the Beginning

The gross weight is usually not known at first, so most design efforts start with a guess that gets refined as the calculations go on. In this case, a gross of 10,000 pounds (4,500 kg) has been specified and so will be used as a firm requirement. The initial round of calculations are aimed at determining how much of this 10,000 pounds is available for structural weight. The first step is to get a handle on the useful load—which in this case will be defined as people plus special equipment required for "public service" plus fuel. Assuming a crew of two and six passengers, at 180 pounds each, gives a people weight of 1,440 pounds. The weight of the special equipment over a plain vanilla helicopter is assumed to be 1,000 pounds. That's the easy part. To determine the fuel required, we have to estimate the size of the powerplant. This will be dictated either by the high-speed requirement or by the hover requirement.

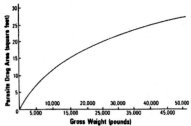

Figure 44-2 Estimated Drag Area for Streamlined Helicopters

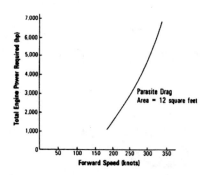

Figure 44-3 Power Required at High Speed

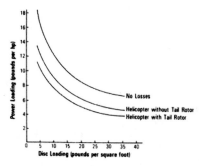

Figure 44-4 Power Loading at Sea Level

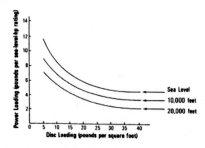

Figure 44-5 Effect of Altitude on Power Loading for Helicopter Without Tail Rotor

At this stage, it is hard to tell which flight condition requires the most power, so both have to be examined.

Power Required at High Speed

Leaving the challenge of actually designing a 300-knot rotor for later, we can make a rough estimate of how much power is required by assuming that at very high speeds, 70% of the installed power is needed to overcome parasite drag. Drag is a function of speed and the aircraft's drag area. 44-2 shows a curve of parasite drag area vs. gross weight for reasonably streamlined helicopters based on past experience. Using this curve for our purposes, our 10,000-pound helicopter will have a parasite drag area of 12 square feet.

Figure 44-3 gives the installed power to push 12 square feet of drag area through the air at sea level. To do the 30-minute dash at 300 knots, our helicopter needs 4,830 hp. For cruise at 200 knots, the required power is only 1,430 hp.

Power Required to Hover

At a given altitude, the number of pounds of airframe weight that can be hovered by one horsepower is primarily governed by induced power—which is a function of the disc loading. Such factors as rotor profile power, tail-rotor power, transmission losses, and download characteristics affect the power required only in secondary ways and so assumptions made about these losses do not have to be extremely accurate to be useful for our immediate purposes.

Figure 44-4 shows the installed power loading at sea level as a function of disc loading. The top curve is for no losses and represents only induced power. This is an absolute maximum above which the laws of physics would be violated. The second curve is for helicopters without tail rotors where all the losses have been assumed to be 30% of induced power. The third curve is for helicopters with tail rotors where an additional 10% power penalty has been applied.

At altitude, the induced power goes up because the rotor must work harder on the thinner air. At the same time, the ability of the engine to put out power goes down. At 10,000 feet, a typical turbine engine can generate only about 75% of what it could at sea level. The effect of these two trends on the power loading is shown on Figure 44-5 for the tail-rotorless configuration as defined by the number of pounds that can be lifted by each horsepower of the sea level power rating.

Our helicopter design with a gross weight of 10,000 pounds and a rotor diameter of 20 feet has a disc loading of 31.8 pounds per square foot (which creates a problem in itself in terms of downwash velocity and autorotational capability). Hovering at 10,000 feet with one engine out requires a sea level rating of 2,940 hp or a total of 5,880 if this is to be a twin-engine helicopter. Hovering at 20,000 feet with all engines operating is a little less demanding, requiring only 4,170 horsepower.

Since the power required to fly 300 knots was 4,830, hover at 10,000 feet on one engine is the critical condition for choosing the powerplant.

Fuel Required

The mission statement implied a leg of 3½ hours at 200 knots and 30 minutes at 300 knots. The fuel flow per horsepower hour (or specific fuel consumption) at full power and at partial power are the critical parameters to determine the fuel required. Figure 44-6 shows the trend for specific fuel consumption (SFC) at their 30-minute ratings for turbine engines for the past several decades with an extrapolation into the future. Figure 44-7 shows the partial power ratio that applies to to-day's turbines and can be assumed to apply to to-morrow's engines. From Figure 44-6, we find that in 1990 the specific fuel consumption at the 30-minute rating of 5,880 hp should be down to .43 pounds per horsepower hour. At the power required for 300 knots (4,830 hp), the SFC is 3% higher, which gives a fuel flow of 2,140 pounds per hour and thus 1,070 pounds will be burned off during the high-speed dash portion of the mission. The power required at 200 knots is 1,430 hp and from Figure 44-7, the SFC at this partial power is 1.65 times the full power value— or .71 pounds per horsepower hour. Thus, for the 3-hour leg at 200 knots, the fuel required is 3,550 pounds.

The useful load of fuel plus people plus special equipment is 7,060 pounds or 71% of the 10,000-pound gross weight specified in the wish list. This indicates a problem, especially in light of the extrapolation of industry experience indicated by Figure 44-8 showing that we should only expect to achieve a ratio of 61% by 1990. (Unless we can fabricate the structure out of "unobtainium".)

Time to Rethink

It appears that if a feasible design is to be achieved, something has to give in the requirements. Since the curves are quite general, they can be used to do tradeoff studies on the primary specification items of dash speed, cruise speed, endurance, hover ceilings, gross weight, and rotor diameter.

One of the obvious tradeoffs is suggested by the fact that the installed power is dictated by the requirement to hover on one engine at 10,000 feet and is larger than what is required for the 300-knot dash speed. A better balance could be achieved by increasing the diameter of the rotor from 20 to 25 feet so that the power required to hover would come down to the power required to dash. This would then reduce the size of the engines and of the fuel load by decreasing the partial power SFC. Calculations summarized in Figure 44-9 indicate that at 300 knots, this will only bring the weight fraction down to 66% but if we can also get the customer to relax on the dash speed, we can make the design work. Figure 44-9 shows the reduction in the weight ratio achieved by decreasing the dash speed while holding everything constant except the rotor diameter, which is allowed to grow to maintain the power balance between hover and dash. The curve shows that reducing the dash-speed

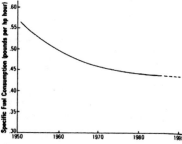

Figure 44-6 Historic Trend of Specific Fuel Consumption at 30-Minute Rating

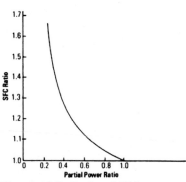

Figure 44-7   Ratio of SFC at Partial Power to SFC at 30-Minute Rating

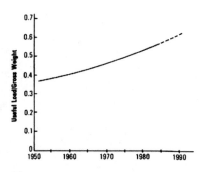

Figure 44-8 Historic Trend of Ratio of Useful Load to Gross Weight

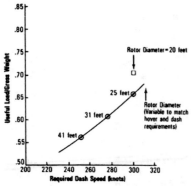

Figure 44-9   Ratio of SFC at Partial Power to SFC at 30-Minute Rating

requirement from 300 to 275 knots while letting the rotor diameter grow from 20 to 31 feet will produce a feasible design.

If the customer insists on sticking with the small rotor, there is another possibility —use more than two engines so that the loss of one in hover will not be so traumatic. The 275-knot speed requires 3,720 hp but the hover requirement with the 20-foot rotor only requires 2,940 of remaining horsepower. Five 750-hp engines would therefore satisfy both requirements by giving 3,750 hp for dash and 3,000 for hovering with one out. This would bring the design into balance but would introduce two major problems: how do you install five engines and where do you find a 750-hp engine?

(Or, for that matter, one of any specific rating? Since engines take longer to develop than aircraft, the designer is limited to choosing engines that are already in production or at least are running in a test cell.)

Either approach might be unacceptable to the customer. He might prefer to give up on some of his other wishes. If he were inflexible, we would probably "no-bid" on this project as being too far from the state-of-the-art as we know it, but if the customer agrees with a modification of the requirements, we have generated a couple of more-or-less feasible starting points with about a half hour of work.

It is only a starting point, of course. From now on, a team of specialists in the fields of design, aerodynamics, stress, weights, powerplants, and others will put in several months of detail work that will eventually result in adjustments to the generalized curves of Figures 18-2 to 18-8 to make them reflect the actual design as the team zeroes in on it.

45 Axes Systems And Trim Considerations

Engineers who do stability and control analyses must keep careful books to get the right answer. Keeping track of which terms are positive and which are negative is a big part of the job. In order to do this, standard conventions have been nearly universally adapted.

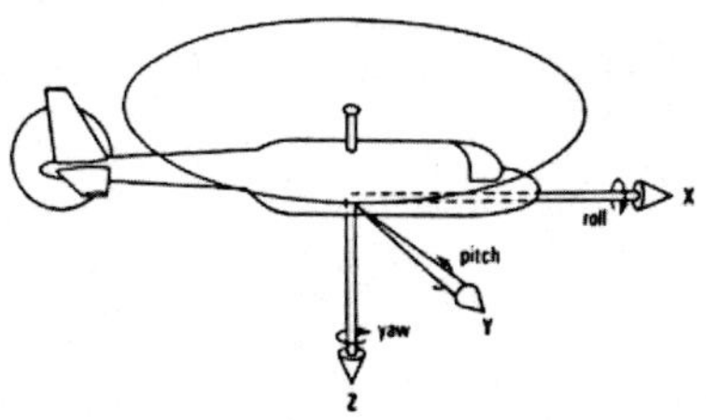

Axes systems

Figure 45-1 shows the axes systems used by most of us. The motion of any aircraft can be defined by combinations of three linear displacements along three mutually perpendicular axes and three angular rotations about those same axes. The direction of positive motion is defined by two "right-hand rules".

The first defines positive linear displacements. Using your right hand, point the thumb in the direction of flight, this becomes the X-axis. The index finger extended to the right is the Y-axis and the second finger pointing down is the Z-axis, with each digit pointing in the direction of positive displacement. Thus positive motion is that which is forward, to the right, and down. Forces acting in these directions are also considered to be positive.

Angular motions about each axis are defined as positive using the other right-hand rule. Point your right thumb in the positive direction of an axis. Your curled fingers will be pointing in a positive direction for pitch, roll, and yaw motion about the appropriate axis. Positive angular motions are roll down to right, pitch up, and yaw nose right. Moments producing these motions are also positive.

A point of confusion sometimes arises when distinguishing between a positive yaw angle and positive sideslip angle. Positive yaw motion involves turning the nose of the aircraft to the right of the flight path. This, however, produces left or negative sideslip. Right or positive sideslip is present when the wind comes in the pilot's right ear in an open cockpit.

Wind, stability, or body?

Once the sign convention is accepted, the engineer has a choice of how these axes are referenced to an aircraft. The first system used was one we now refer to as "wind axes", in which the longitudinal, or X-axis, always

Figure 45-1 Helicopter Axes System

235

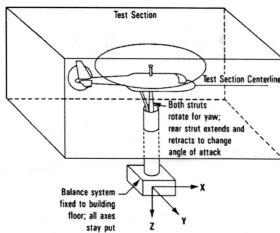

Figure 45-2 WInd Tunnel System Measuring in Wind Axes

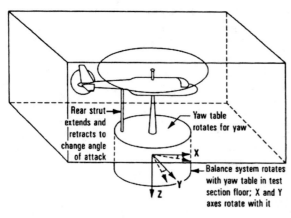

Figure 45-3 Wind Tunnel Balance System Measuring in Stability Axes

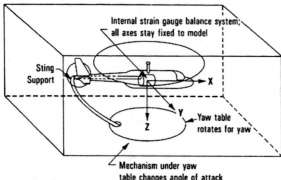

Figure 45-4 Wind Tunnel Balance System Measuring in Body Axes

points along the line of flight no matter what the pitch or yaw attitude of the aircraft.

Fixed-wing aerodynamicists usually prefer the "stability" axes system. This is like the wind axes system except that in the top view, the X-axis is aligned with the aircraft fuselage, while pointing along the flight path in the side view.

The third option is known as the "body" axes system. In this one, the X-axis is not only lined up with the fuselage in the top view but in the side view as well. This system is generally preferred by those of us doing helicopter-flying-qualities analysis because, unlike the other two, it does not depend on a well-defined flight path and so can be used in hover. It also has an advantage in easily accounting for the elements of the stability augmentation system fixed to the structure, such as gyros and accelerometers.

In forward flight, any of the systems is valid for analysis as long as all rotations and translations are properly accounted for and the system chosen is used consistently.

Wind-tunnel analogies

The three types of axes systems can be directly related to three types of balance systems used to measure forces and moments on a model in a wind tunnel. Figure 45-2 through Figure 45-4 show this correspondence. In some tunnels, the balance system is firmly fastened to the building's floor beneath the test section and measures model lift, drag, sideforce, pitching moment, rolling moment, and yawing moment with respect to the test section's center-line (the "flight path" of the model). Thus this balance system is measuring forces and moments in "wind axes".

The balance systems of some wind tunnels are not firmly fastened to the building's structure but are suspended below the floor of the test section on a turntable that can be rotated to yaw the model. Thus, in the top view, the balance system stays aligned with the model rather than with the centerline of the test section—and the result is that the forces and moments are being measured in "stability axes".

Finally, the third, or "body axes" system, is achieved by building into the model an internal strain-gauge balance that always measures forces and moments with respect to the model itself. This system is normally used when the model is "sting-mounted" as in Figure 45-4.

No matter what system the wind tunnel uses, the data can be easily transformed with relatively simple trigonometric manipulation into one of the other axes systems as the most convenient form for analysis.

One example of the need for transformation is in determining the effect of sideslip on drag along the flight path when the data has been obtained either in stability or body axes. In these systems, the force along the fuselage centerline usually decreases as the model is yawed. Drag along the flight path, i.e. in wind axes, however, will increase. Figure 45-5 shows how this drag is actually made up of components of drag and sideforce, as measured in either of the other two systems. By combining these measurements with sine and cosine functions of the yaw angle, the wind axes drag can be calculated.

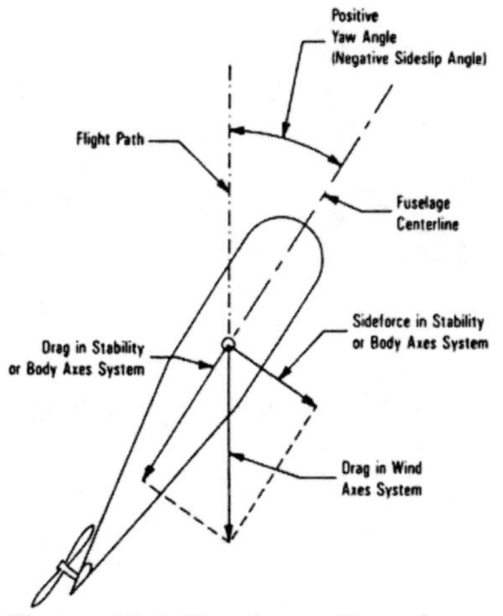

Figure 45-5 Tranformation of Forces Between Axes Systems

Degrees of freedom

Before the Wright Brothers, many people pointed out that flying would be impossible because the pilot would have to control six "degrees of freedom" with only two hands and feet. The fact that we all now know it can be done has settled the argument but going through the explanation might prove valuable if you are ever challenged by your eight-year-old nephew.

Degrees of freedom define the ways in which a body can move. For an aircraft, there are three possible linear motions and three possible rotational motions. We define the linear motions as along three axes arranged at right angles to each other. Figure 45-6 shows the orientation used by most stability and control engineers.

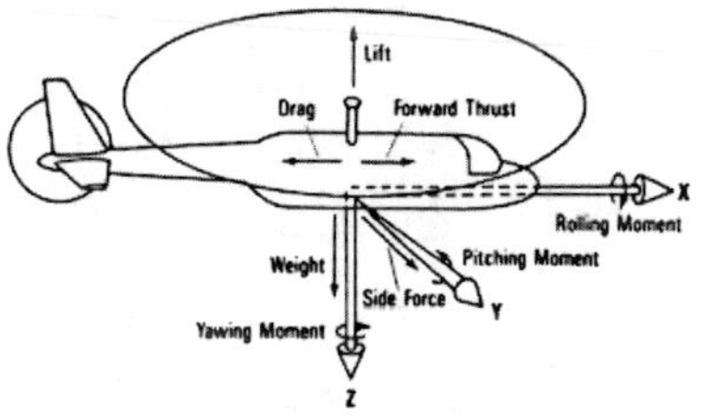

The linear degrees of freedom are described in terms of pairs of opposites: up-or-down, fore-or-aft, and right-or-left. The three possible rotational motions are around those same axes and can be described as pitch up or down, roll right or left, and yaw right or left.

Figure 45-6 Helicopter Axes System

Forces and moments

Corresponding to the three linear motions are three pairs of forces that can cause them: lift acting up and weight acting down, a propulsive force acting forward and drag acting aft, and side forces acting to the right and to the left: Similarly, the three rotational motions are produced by three moments: pitching moment, rolling moment, and yawing moment.

Vehicles with six possible degrees of freedom are relatively new in man's experience. For example, a train has only one: fore or aft, while even automobiles and boats have only two that are under the direct control of the operator. Besides flying, underwater swimming is the only other six-degree-of-freedom activity I can think of.

For a discussion of flight, let us first consider control of the airplane and then go on to a helicopter.

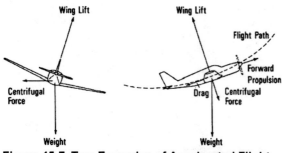

Figure 45-7 Two Examples of Accelerated Flight

Of the six degrees of freedom, the airplane pilot has direct control over only four. The three angular motions of pitch, roll, and yaw are controlled by the elevator, the ailerons, and the rudder respectively.

Of the three forces, the only one under direct control is the propulsive force, done with the engine throttle. The other two force balance conditions come as by-products: the lift can be made equal to the weight by a combination of pitching moment that controls wing angle of attack and of forward thrust that controls speed; and the two side forces are equalized using the yawing moment control to align the airplane's vertical plane of symmetry with the flight path.

Special cases

Even when the aircraft is not in steady, straight, and level flight, the three forces and the three moments must still add up to zero. But it may be that some weight and inertia effects will have to be accounted for. Any flight condition in which inertia effects play a part is called "accelerated flight."

For example, an airplane in a turn (Figure 45-7) has a centrifugal inertia force acting to the outside of the turn that must be balanced by an equal and opposite component of wing lift acting toward the center. Similarly, when the flight path is curved in an up-and-down sense, centrifugal forces known as G forces are produced in which the aircraft and everything in it seems to increase weight during pullups and lose weight during pushovers.

Top View

In the top view, an airplane is symmetric about its centerline but some flight conditions are non-symmetric and require a combination of forces and moments to acquire balance. For example, consider flight of the twin-engine airplane Figure 45-8) that has lost power in one engine.

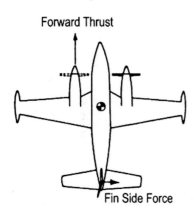

In this case, the good engine produces a yawing moment that must be balanced by a side force, created by deflecting the rudder, on the vertical stabilizer. But now the side forces are not balanced-or at least not until the pilot banks the airplane slightly to obtain an opposing side force by tilting the wing lift.

Rear View

Helicopter considerations

The helicopter is similar but different. Its pilot has direct control of the three rotational degrees of freedom by using cyclic pitch to control pitch and roll, and by using tail rotor thrust to control yaw. Instead of having direct control of the forward propulsion, however, the pilot has direct control of lift through his collective control.

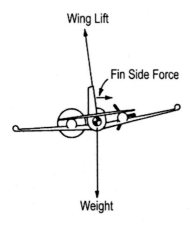

In this case, the horizontal force balance comes from a combination of tilting the rotor forward using the longitudinal cyclic pitch control and adjusting the amount of rotor thrust with the collective pitch control.

Figure 45-8 Force Balance on Twin-Engine Airplane with One Engine Out

The same type of pilot action can be used to accelerate forward by tilting the rotor until the component of the thrust in the direction of flight is more than the drag. This will produce horizontal acceleration forces that will increase speed until the drag is high enough to bring the horizontal forces into balance.

Figure 45-9 shows that balancing side forces in a helicopter flying with zero sideslip is done just as in the airplane one-engine-out case since the main rotor produces a yawing moment in one direction that must be balanced by tail-rotor thrust in the other direction which, in turn, must be balanced by tilting the main-rotor lift vector to the opposite side.

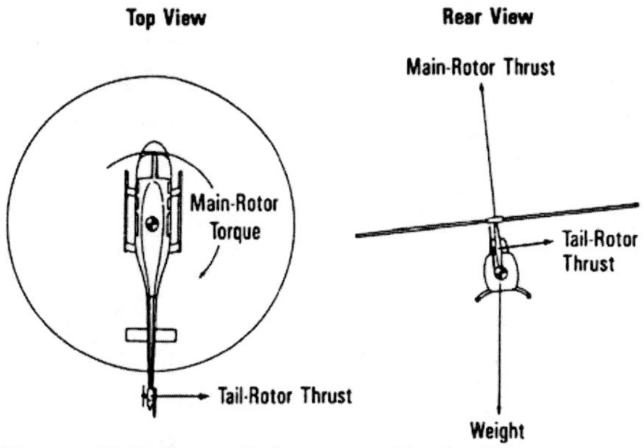

Figure 45-9 Force Balance on Single-Rotor Helicopter with Zero Sideslip

Look Ma, only one hand

Despite the fact that a pilot does not have a total of six hands and feet, he can manage to control all six possible degrees of freedom to both hold the aircraft steady and to do maneuvers.

As a matter of fact, by taking advantage of everything that one wrist can do, a helicopter can be flown with only one hand by using a sidearm controller (Figure 45-10) in which a vertical pull changes the collective pitch of the main rotor, rotation changes the collective pitch of the tail rotor, and tilting the control activates cyclic pitch.

I guess it is no great reflection on the pre-Wright nonbelievers that they didn't foresee this development.

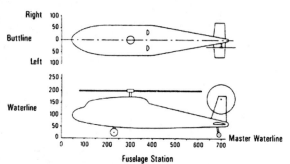

Figure 45-10 Sidearm Controller

Layout considerations

When making the first drawing for a new helicopter, the designer must decide how to orient it on his clean sheet of paper.

Working drawings for ships were once laid out full-sized in "lofts" above the shops, and we still speak of "lofting" when making drawings of aircraft-even when it is being done by a computer. One important basis of reference for the ship designers was the "waterline" which meant just what it says.

Figure 45-11 Typical Lofting Scheme

Aircraft designers also use a horizontal reference (which they too, call a waterline) but instead of straddling it with the fuselage drawing, they normally place it well below, as in Figure 45-11, so that each point on the aircraft can be said to have a positive location. Similarly, the zero fuselage station is placed well forward of the nose.

The usual unit of measurement on American helicopters is the inch. It is fairly common to locate the center of the rotor hub at an even multiple of 100 inches both in fuselage station and in waterline. Butt lines are referenced to the vertical plane of symmetry and are designated either right or left.

Orienting the side view of the helicopter fuselage with the zero waterline is quite arbitrary. If the fuselage were cylindrical, like that of a jet transport, it would be obvious that its axis should be drawn parallel to the master waterline. Except for tandems, helicopter fuselages seldom have this shape, however, and so the designer has some freedom. What usually happens is that he draws the cockpit floor parallel to the master waterline no matter what the fuselage shape turns out to be and later draws in the rotor mast tilted forward 3° to 5° in recognition of the best fuselage angle-of-attack at high speed.

Because the rotor mast is a natural reference line, it would be more convenient, for those of us who must use center-of-gravity (CG) positions and moments of inertia in our analyses, to have the mast drawn-in perpendicular to the waterline. The fuselage could then be tilted slightly noseup to achieve the same best angle.

Mast/fuselage tilt

Whether tilting the mast forward, or the fuselage noseup, it is done for the same reason. Designers of any aircraft that must fly fast use every practical method to decrease drag.

One method is to insure that the fuselage is transported through the air at its minimum-drag attitude. Figure 45-12 shows how the drag of a typical fuselage shape increases when it is not lined up with the airflow. Airplane designers attach the wing to the fuselage with just the right amount of positive "incidence" to develop the necessary lift with the fuselage at its optimum angle of attack.

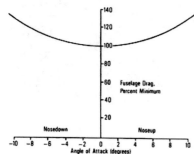

Figure 45-12 Typical Variation of Fuselage Drag with Angle of Attack

Helicopter designers use mast/fuselage tilt to do the same thing-although sometimes constraints on the pilot's field-of-view at low speed and the landing gear's arrangement for making graceful vertical takeoffs and landings might lead the designer to compromise between high-speed and low-speed considerations.

Flapping for trim

No matter what mast/fuselage tilt is chosen, it has no direct effect on rotor flapping and the resulting blade loads in forward flight. This statement is based on the balance of forces and moments shown in Figure 45-13.

Two angles are of primary importance. The first is the angle the thrust vector makes with the flight path. This vector must have the magnitude and angle such that it simultaneously supports the gross weight and

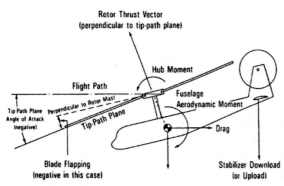

Figure 45-13 Longitudinal Trim Considerations

overcomes the parasite drag. For most situations, this thrust vector can be considered as perpendicular to the tip-path plane so that force-balance-consideration establishes the angle of attack of the rotor disc.

The other unique angle is that made by the rotor disc with the mast. This angle, which is blade flapping, is only used to satisfy the moment balance about the helicopter's CG.

Blade flapping produces two types of moment about the CG. One is a couple at the rotor hub that can be related to hinge offset (or effective hinge offset for hingeless rotors) and the centrifugal forces at the blade roots. Noseup flapping will produce a noseup couple. The other type of moment is due to the offset of the thrust vector from the CG. This is the only type of moment produced by teetering rotors.

The sum of these two moments is used to balance airframe moments caused by the aerodynamics of the fuselage and empennage, or by a CG position offset from the centerline of the mast. The sum of these external moments can be either nosedown or nose-up, and, as a consequence, the balancing blade flapping will be either noseup or nosedown. For most helicopters, the required flapping in all steady-flight conditions seldom exceeds ±4° and for some conditions will be zero.

The pilot uses his cyclic pitch control to find the exact amount of flapping that will prevent pitching either noseup or nosedown. Since the angle of attack of the tip-path plane is fixed by the consideration of balance of forces, what the pilot is actually doing with his cyclic control is adjusting the fuselage pitch attitude to obtain the correct flapping angle between rotor and fuselage to balance moments.

If it were required to minimize the blade flapping in order to prolong the life of the rotor, an adjustable-incidence horizontal stabilizer could be used to bring the sum of all external airframe moments to zero so that the rotor would have no flapping requirement. Although this sounds good on paper, it has not yet been used on any helicopter.

For a pilot-controlled system, the main drawback is the difficulty in providing the pilot with an unambiguous signal representing rotor flapping that will cue him to change the incidence in the right direction. With the increasing reliability of automatic electronic systems, the idea becomes more feasible by using longitudinal mast bending as a signal to the stabilizer actuator. Considerations for this scheme have to do with safety-of-flight in case of a runaway actuator and the necessity of nullifying the system while the pilot is deliberately trying to maneuver.

46 Main Rotor Design

"All animals are equal but some animals are more equal than others,"
-George Orwell *Animal Farm.*

All parts of a helicopter are of equal importance but main rotors are more equal than others. For that reason, designers take special care in selecting the main-rotor parameters to insure the best possible hover performance, best forward-flight performance, lowest cost, lowest weight, lowest noise, lowest vibration, etc.

Some of these goals complicate the design process because they are mutually contradictory. The design team is thus faced with conflicting requirements, which can only be handled through thoughtful compromise at each stage of the design.

Diameter

•Should be big for good hover performance.

•Should be small for low total aircraft weight and cost.

The designer's goal is to find the smallest-diameter rotor that will produce the required performance.

The critical design condition is almost always a specified hover or a vertical climb at some extreme combination of altitude and temperature. That condition is established by the customer for a military helicopter or by marketing judgment for a commercial aircraft. The basic guide for the selection is a plot such as Figure 19-1 that presents curves of power loading vs. disc loading at several values of the hover figure of merit (rotor efficiency). Figure 19-1 is specifically plotted for the usual Army design conditions of 4,000 feet and 95° F. If the figure of merit, rotor thrust, and power available to the main rotor are all known, the disc area and thus the diameter can be calculated.

The figure of merit depends on tip speed, blade area, number of blades, taper, tip shape, twist, and blade airfoil section (each to be discussed later). The rotor thrust depends on the payload, mission fuel, structural weight, and fuselage download. The power the engine can deliver to the main rotor depends on its sea-level rating and the effects of temperature, altitude, and engine deterioration with service, minus the power to run

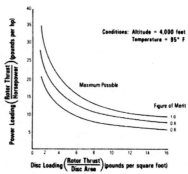

Figure 46-1 Main Rotor Hover Performance

243

the tail rotor, generators, hydraulic pumps, oil pumps, cooling fans, and losses in the main- and tail-rotor gear-boxes.

All of these factors depend upon the final configuration including, above all, which engine is actually available. During preliminary design, these variables must be estimated first and then refined by using analysis, model tests, component tests, and experience with previous helicopters. It should be no surprise, therefore, to learn that rotor diameter may change (usually upwards) during the design effort as more and more details get pinned down.

For some military designs, the maximum physical size of the helicopter, which is highly influenced by rotor diameter, is limited by the necessity to negotiate the elevators and hangar decks of aircraft carriers or to fit in transport airplanes. If for this or some other reason, the design process begets a rotor of very small size and a very high disc loading, the designer may be faced with special considerations. Disc loadings above 10 to 12 pounds per square foot may blow over ground equipment and personnel as well as "placer mine" unprepared landing sites, filling the air with gravel, clods, and bushes. The importance of these problems depends on the intended use of the aircraft.

High disc loadings also result in high rates of descent in autorotation. Tests on airplanes have shown that satisfactory deadstick landings can be consistently made by average pilots if the steady rate of descent is less than about 2,500 fpm. But at higher rates, increased pilot skills are required.

Although similar tests have not been scientifically done on helicopters, experience with some experimental ramjet-powered helicopters (with poor autorotative capabilities because of the drag of their jets) seems to verify that 2,500 fpm is a reasonable upper limit that should apply to single-engine helicopters for which the risk of a full power failure is relatively high. Whether this limit should also apply to a multiengine helicopter is a good subject for debate.

Tip speeds

• Should be high for low rotor and drive system weight and for a good retreating tip environment in forward flight.

• Should be low for low noise and for a good advancing-tip environment in forward flight.

The designer's goal is to pick the highest tip speed he can within certain constraints, one of which is noise. It is generally agreed today that tip speeds of more than 750 feet per second are unacceptably noisy and that tip speeds of less than 500 fps are "quiet." The Bell UH-1 started out with a tip speed of 740 fps and a rotor diameter of 44 feet. Later versions such as the UH-1H use a 48-foot rotor with the same rpm so that the tip speed is well over 800 fps, which partially accounts for their high noise signature. Later Bell designs such as the 206A use tip speeds of about

650. The Hughes "Quiet One" was down to 430 fps. A lower limit is set by the requirement to store kinetic energy in the rotor in case of engine failure.

Avoiding advancing-tip compressibility and retreating-tip stall also limits the choices of rotor speed. It is generally accepted that advancing-tip Mach numbers of more than about .92 will produce high blade loads due to "Mach tuck", the sudden nosedown pitching moment generated as shock waves develop on the airfoil. It is also generally accepted that for conventional helicopters at maximum speed, the tip-speed ratio (forward speed divided by tip speed) should be below about 0.5 to avoid excessive retreating-blade stall. Figure 19-2 shows how these constraints squeeze down on the available choices of design tip speed as the forward-speed goal is increased. It also shows why the maximum speed of "pure" helicopters has been about 200 knots since 1978.

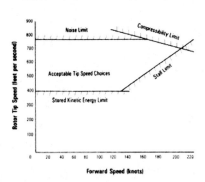

Figure 46-2 Constraints on Choice of Tip Speeds

Blade area

• Should be small (but not too small) for good hover performance as well as low blade weight and cost;

• Should be large for good maneuverability at high speed.

Just as an airplane has an optimum angle of attack for its maximum lift-to-drag ratio, a rotor has an optimum average angle of attack for its maximum figure of merit in hover. If the blade area is too high, the average angle will be less than optimum, the hover performance will be worse than it might be, and the rotor system will be heavier than it could be. Yet, if a rotor were designed strictly for hover, it would probably have too little blade area to do the required high-G maneuvers in forward flight without excessive blade stall.

The parameter governing both the hover figure of merit and the blade stall is the average angle of attack. On most rotors the hover figure of merit is maximum when this angle is about 6°.

The helicopter aerodynamicist relates the average angle of attack to a nondimensional parameter called the "blade-loading coefficient", or C_T/σ ("Cee-tee over sigma"— where the Greek letter sigma is the rotor solidity or the ratio of blade area to disc area). This parameter, C_T/σ, is equal to the rotor thrust divided by the product of blade area, density of air, and tip speed squared. It is very similar to the airplane aerodynamicist's lift coefficient (C_L), which is wing lift divided by the product of wing area, half the density of air, and forward speed squared.

(The airplane person has a good reason for using only half the air density since the product of it and the forward speed squared gives the dynamic pressure that affects every component on his aircraft.

Since the dynamic pressure at the blade tip is of no particular interest to the helicopter person, the one-half factor has not been included in the

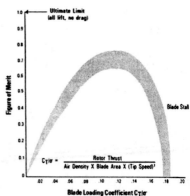

Figure 46-3   Hover Figure of Merit

Figure 46-4   Maximum Rotor Thrust Capabilities

definition of rotor nondimensional parameters except at Bell, where for many years a coefficient called "t_c" was used-which was just twice C_T/σ.)

For hover performance, the optimum value of C_T/σ is about 0.1 which corresponds to an average angle of attack of 60. The effect on figure of merit is shown on Figure 19-3.

The curve is drawn with a wide brush because other factors besides C_T/σ influence the figure of merit. By knowing the rotor thrust at hover, the air density at the specified altitude and temperature, and the tip speed, the optimum blade area for hover performance can be calculated.

The optimum blade area for hover may be too small for the required performance at high speeds, where retreating blade stall can only be prevented by increasing the blade area to lower the average angle of attack over the disc. The higher the tip-speed ratio, the lower will be the allowable value of the blade-loading coefficient as shown on Figure 19-4, where in level flight, the allowable value goes below the hover optimum of 0.1 at high speeds. This curve is also painted with a broad brush because factors other than tip-speed ratio are important, such as: parasite drag, blade twist, the airfoil maximum stall angle, and the structural dynamic characteristics between the blade and the seat of the pilot's pants.

The curve for steady turns is higher than for level flight because the nose-up pitch rate associated' with the turn requires that the angle of attack be reduced on the retreating blade while being increased on the advancing blade in order to keep the rotor precessing in the right direction. This produces a little margin below stall on the retreating blade, allowing the entire rotor to develop some more thrust before stalling. But because a lot more thrust may be required to maintain the turn, even the raised limit on C_T/σ will usually call for more blade area than is optimum for hover. The turn curve is also higher than the level-flight curve because the turn, being a short-time maneuver, can be allowed to have a higher vibration level.

The same arguments also apply to the transient pull-up but, in addition, the angle-of-attack distribution takes on a favorable pattern due to the flow being up through the rotor instead of down, which significantly reduces the angles of attack on the retreating side. Wind-tunnel tests of rotors confirm that the maximum thrust capability is little affected by forward speed with this flow orientation.

Most helicopter aerodynamicists have collections of flight-test data for their own and their competitor's previous aircraft and can use these data for this crystal-ball exercise. Once the curves have been accepted for a new design, they can be used to determine the blade area required to do whatever high load factor maneuver has been specified. For example, the capability to sustain a 1.5G turn at a true airspeed of 140 knots at 5,000 feet may be required. Having already decided on the tip speed, the tip-speed ratio at 140 knots can be calculated and the maximum allowable value of C_T/σ determined from Figure 19-4. From this, the corresponding blade area can be calculated— since the rotor thrust of 1.5 times the gross weight, the air density at 5,000 feet, and the tip speed are all known.

Add a wing?

The question of including a wing in the configuration to save on rotor-blade area is often raised during preliminary design. As a general rule, we can say that you use a wing on a compound helicopter that has a propeller or jet for forward propulsion, on an attack helicopter that needs some means of supporting external stores, on a helicopter on which the designer elects to mount engines and/or fuel tanks outside the fuselage, and on a helicopter whose maneuverability requirement is a transient one.

For a helicopter that must be designed for a steady turn or high-speed level flight, adding a wing just for this purpose is usually a bad idea. Besides producing an unwanted download in hover, the wing may actually increase the retreating tip angle of attack, leading to premature blade stall. This happens because the partially unloaded rotor must be tilted further forward to produce the required propulsive force that now must compensate for the drag of the wing in addition to the drag of the basic helicopter. This requires increased collective pitch to overcome the inflow and increased cyclic pitch to keep the rotor trimmed. In many applications, these two effects will increase the retreating tip angle of attack more than the decrease made by unloading the rotor.

Number of blades

• Should be small for low cost, low hub drag, low hub weight, and ease of storage.

• Should be large for low vibration level and ease of handling individual blades.

Once the total blade area has been selected, dividing it up into a certain number of blades is usually governed by considerations other than performance but performance may be slightly affected by the choice. With a small number of blades, the tip vortex from one blade in hover has a chance to get clear of the following blade and thus has a smaller penalizing effect.

Also, the smaller the number of blades, the larger the chord. This is beneficial from a "Reynolds number" standpoint. (Reynolds number is proportional to the chord times the velocity.) Higher Reynolds numbers result in slightly lower drag coefficients and higher maximum-lift coefficients in the range of typical rotor blades.

There is a disadvantage, however, in carrying this trend too far. If by using a small number of blades to match the required blade area, the blades come out too stubby — with radius-to-chord ratios of less than about eight, tip losses will probably be high enough to nullify the aforementioned advantages.

Conversely, if the required blade area is spread across a large number of blades, it may result in blades too slender to have enough torsional stiffness to resist the aerodynamic pitching moments they will encounter in normal forward flight. This could lead to the blades twisting into shapes not envisioned by the designer.

In forward flight, a large number of blades smoothes out the wake laid down by the rotor, thus the induced power is somewhat less than for a rotor with a small number of blades, which leaves a pulsating wake. All of these performance advantages and disadvantages based on the number of blades are relatively small and generally not "decision drivers", compared to the considerations mentioned at the beginning of this section.

Most design teams would prefer to use four blades as the best compromise between too few and too many but in some cases, a different number is chosen. For example, the Sikorsky S-56 had a five-bladed main rotor because the maximum obtainable size of the leading-edge extrusions was limited at the time (early '50s). Five blades are installed on the Hughes 500D and subsequent models, so it can use the same blade design developed for the lighter four-bladed 500C. The same reasoning accounts for Sikorsky going from six to seven blades when developing the CH-53E from the earlier versions.

Twist

• Should be high for good hover performance and delay of retreating blade stall.

• Should be low for low vibration and blade loads in forward flight.

The rotor's hover performance is best when the induced velocity (the downward air velocity generated in the process of developing upward rotor thrust) is uniform across the disc. For untwisted blades, the induced velocities are high outboard and low inboard. By twisting the blades to reduce the lift at the tip, the flow pattern can be made more uniform and the hover figure of merit can be improved by up to about 5%. Since this may represent a 20% increase in payload and since twisted blades are about as easy to manufacture as untwisted blades, there is a good reason to use twist— and all modern helicopters do.

The aerodynamic equations show that there is a nonlinear "ideal twist" that theoretically' will perfectly even up the induced velocity distribution. Starting at the tip, the blade would twist noseup at an ever-increasing

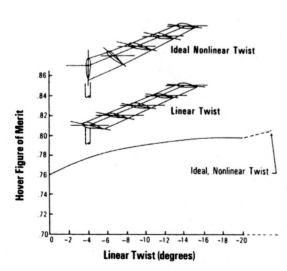

Figure 46-5 Effect of Twist on Rotor Figure of Merit

rate as you go inboard until, at the center of rotation, it would be pointing straight up.

For simplicity in manufacturing, most designers choose not to use the ideal twist. Instead they choose a linear twist in which the blade is twisted at a constant rate in terms of degrees per foot from the blade attachment point to the tip. (Linear twist is measured by how many degrees the pitch would change between the tip and the center of rotation if the blade actually went in that far. It is assigned a negative sign if the pitch at the tip is less than at the root.) Figure 19-5 shows that -20° of linear twist gives almost the full benefit of ideal twist while most of the benefit comes with the first 10° or 12°.

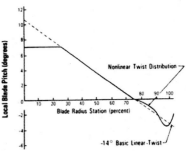

Figure 46-6   Twist Modification

A variation on linear-twist distribution is used by Sikorsky on its UH-60 Black Hawk. In hover, the tip vortex from one blade passes very close to the following blade and produces a local region of very high angle of attack, which may be enough to stall a portion of the blade just inboard of the tip. To relieve this situation, the Black Hawk blade designers have built in a sudden increase in nose-down twist in this region to improve the stall margin. This type of twist is shown in Figure 19-6.

While good in hover, high twist is bad for forward flight. This is partially due to the back-and-forth spanwise travel of the center of lift as the blade goes around the azimuth. The average angle of attack on the advancing blade is low to produce the right amount of lift to keep the rotor in trim. Twist reduces the angle of attack on the tip even further (often to negative values accompanied by corresponding downloads), meaning that the in-board portion of the advancing blade must be relatively heavily loaded. The center of lift is inboard here but moves outboard as the blade rotates to the retreating side where angles of attack are large and positive.

As the center of lift shifts back and forth, the blade is bent, resulting in oscillating forces at the rotor hub that produce vibration in the rest of the helicopter. The higher the twist, the higher are these oscillating effects. Not only does excessive twist cause blade loads and vibration, but the download on the advancing tip represents a performance penalty since substantial power is being expended there with negative benefits.

If this isn't enough to confuse you about the effects of twist, two more contradictions should be mentioned. High twist that is good for hovering out of ground effect (OGE) will usually be too high for optimum hovering in ground effect (IGE) where the inflow distribution to the rotor is different. In addition, twist that reduces the chances of retreating blade stall in forward powered flight hurts the rotor performance in autorotation. (The optimum twist for an autogyro is with the pitch higher at the tip than at the root.) Thus the decision as to what value of twist to use in a new design may depend on the projected use of the helicopter.

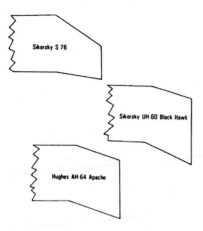

Figure 46-7 Production Main Rotor Blade Tips

Tip Shape

• Should be square for minimum cost to design, test, and build.

• Should be non-square to delay compressibility effects, reduce noise, and to introduce favorable dynamic twist.

The aerodynamics at the tip of an airplane wing in steady straight flight are complicated enough but not nearly as complex as the aerodynamics at the tip of a helicopter blade, which is subjected to rapidly varying conditions. A number of non-square tip shapes have been tried in experimental flight-testing but only a few have shown enough advantage over a straight tip to be incorporated in production designs.

Figure 19-7 shows tips used on the Sikorsky Black Hawk, the Sikorsky S-76, and the Hughes AH-64 Apache. In each case, the leading edge is swept back. This tends to delay compressibility effects because the effective Mach number is based only on the component of velocity perpendicular to the leading edge.

As with most concepts in helicopter aerodynamics, this one isn't as straightforward as it might sound. Theory and experiments show a lag in compressibility effects such that they peak after the blade enters the front half of the disc. This is where the straight blade naturally takes on a swept characteristic from the combination of rotational and forward speed —whereas the swept tip is being aerodynamically unswept. Thus the 'swept tip could suffer more than a straight tip in this region.

Flight tests show that sweeping the tip significantly reduces "Mach tuck" (the nosedown pitching moment generated on the airfoil during the airspeed build-up on the advancing side as the shock-wave moves aft of the quarter chord). But it is not yet clear whether swept tips reduce the impulse noise due to compressibility in high-speed forward flight. There is some expectation that the other source of impulsive noise, blade-vortex interaction during descents and turns, may be less —due to the spreading out of the tip vortex from a swept tip compared to the action off a straight one.

The highly swept tips on the Black Hawk and Apache also have a beneficial effect by producing "dynamic twist" in forward flight. The download on the tip of the advancing blade acting behind the structural axis tends to twist the blade noseup on the advancing side while the upload on the retreating tip increases the nosedown twist on that side. The effect also works in hover where the uploaded tips increase the twist, which is beneficial for hover performance. This blade-tip configuration also has a beneficial fallout for flying qualities, since it improves speed stability. If the helicopter starts an uncommanded increase in speed, the advancing tip, with its download, will twist up —causing the rotor to flap up in front, pitching the helicopter noseup and tending to return it toward its original trim speed.

Unfortunately, nothing comes free. Swept tips complicate the structural design of the blade and doubly so if they must be replaceable in the field when damaged. The cost of designing, testing, and building these blades is significantly higher.

Taper

• Should be zero for minimum cost to design, test, and build.

• Should be high for good hover performance.

Blade twist can be used to give a uniform induced-velocity distribution in hover but on a constant-chord blade, twist will result in a variation of the local angles of attack along the blade. Since an airfoil has one angle of attack at which its lift-to-drag ratio is a maximum, such variations are to be avoided. This can be done by combining blade taper with a twist. It is theoretically possible to obtain another 2% or 3% increase in the figure of merit over twisted, constant-chord blades.

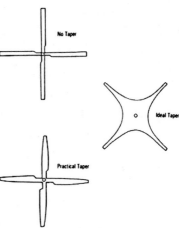

Figure 46-8 Blade Taper Configurations

Unfortunately, the ideal blade shape is one for which the chord becomes very large as you go in-board—as shown' on Figure 19-8. Fortunately, it is the outboard half that is most important, so designers often use taper only there and use straight taper at that. The usual rule of thumb is to have the chord at the 75% radius the same as it would be for a constant-chord blade.

On small helicopters, taper may be counterproductive if the blade chord at the tip comes out less than about five inches. These small chords suffer from significant drag and maximum-lift penalties associated with low Reynolds numbers even at helicopter tip speeds. An additional consideration in small-chord tips is the potential difficulty of installing weights if required to insure satisfactory autorotation entry and flare characteristics.

Root Cutout

• Should be low to minimize drag on the advancing side.

• Should be high to minimize drag on the retreating side.

A good airfoil shape can be used only so far in toward the hub before it must be modified for mechanical and structural reasons. Running it in as far as possible is beneficial in hover— and on the advancing side in forward flight— since it streamlines the spar and minimizes its drag.

On the other hand, as shown on Figure 19-9 in the reverse-flow region, the combination of high collective and cyclic pitch required to trim the rotor at high speed means that the trailing edge is acting like a scoop shovel creating a high download and a high drag. For this reason, it would be desirable to use a high root cutout by starting the full airfoil outboard of the reverse-flow region.

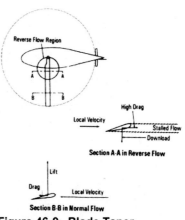

Figure 46-9 Blade Taper Configurations

Without some exotic mechanical or aerodynamic device, the designer cannot have it both ways. There is a partial solution, however, which

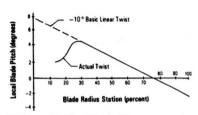

Figure 46-10 Blade Taper Configurations

Sikorsky uses on its S-76. It is the untwisting of the blade near the root, as illustrated in Figure 19-10. This decreases the negative angle of attack in the reversed-flow region while not hurting too much on the advancing side.

Rotor Inertia

• Should be high for good autorotative entry and flare characteristics.

• Should be low for minimum blade and hub weight.

Unlike most of the other parameters, the level of rotor inertia is not evident during a walk around inspection. It will show up, however, during the first practice autorotation. With too little inertia, the rotor speed will decay to an unsafe level after the power is chopped before the pilot can react by dropping collective pitch. If he does manage to survive the entry and get into steady autorotation, the landing flare will be cut short by low rpm as he raises collective to halt his downward progress.

A rule of thumb for the rotor designer is that the kinetic energy stored in the rotor at normal rpm can supply the power required to hover for at least 1½ seconds before rotor speed decays to the point that the blades stall. One and a half seconds does not sound like a very long time but tests have shown that it gives an adequate margin for average pilots.

This requirement usually means that weights must be installed in the blade tips. (Tests at Bell with external tip weights show that if the time can be increased to about 3¼ seconds, the Deadman's Curve can be completely eliminated.) Whether the requirement of 1½ seconds must also be applied to multiengine helicopters is another subject for debate—the argument hinging on how often a given helicopter will suffer — or have to demonstrate — a complete power failure.

Direction of Rotor Rotation

• Should have advancing blade on the right side to make it consistent with previous American helicopters.

• Should have advancing blade on the left side to make it consistent with previous Russian helicopters.

• May have advancing blade on either side to make it consistent with previous European helicopters.

Since many pilots have successfully learned to fly helicopters with both types of rotation, there now seems little logical reason to pick one over the other. The goal of the designer should be to pick the rotation that results in the simplest and lightest drive train between the engine and the rotor.

Rotor Hubs

Since rotary-wing flight began, the design of rotor hubs has been one of the greatest challenges. Today, the art remains in a state of flux. Many different configurations are used on production and experimental aircraft because the designers of helicopters have yet to combine features to satisfy every user's needs in one rotor hub. Among those desired features are: low weight, low drag, low cost, long life, easy maintenance, low part count, freedom from dynamic problems, adequate control power and, for military helicopters, immunity to battle damage.

Designers of rotor hubs are aware that improvements must be made but many design teams are constrained and often guided by the principle "Don't fiddle with success". Of course, this premise is based on how much time and effort has been in-vested in getting the bugs out of previous designs.

Assuming a rotor-hub designer is without the guidance of previous designs, his primary decision would be to determine how to handle the flapping, lead-lag and feathering motions. The choices in design can vary from a very loose blade attachment with rotary feathering bearings and mechanical hinges for flapping and lead-lag, to a rotor with no hinges or bearings at all.

Old Designs

Until about 1970, the two most familiar hub designs were the two bladed teetering hub used on the Bell Model 47 and the fully articulated hub with offset flapping hinges as used on the Sikorsky S-58.

The Bell hub was simple, had relatively low drag and, being stiff in-plane, needed no dampers to prevent ground resonance. It did, however, have low control moment capability and was inherently limited to two blades. While this makes the helicopter easy to hangar, it does result in a two-per-rev bounce at high forward speed since most of the rotor thrust is produced by the blades over the nose and tail.

The Sikorsky hub provided high control power and allowed for almost any number of blades but had many parts, high drag, needed lead-lag dampers and had many mechanical bearings to maintain.

Designers of the two bladed rotors do not use lead-lag hinges for two reasons: First, these hinges are not as necessary to relieve chordwise blade stresses as on multi-bladed rotors and, second, they are more dangerous because they're susceptible to ground resonance. (Ground resonance is defined as a destructive coupling of blade lead-lag motion with the aircraft rocking on its landing gear.) The first reason can be explained by the fact that most of the in-plane (back-and-forth) motion of the blades is caused by the flapping (up-and down) motion due to a law of physics called "conservation of momentum". You can observe an example of this law at an ice show. A skater will start spinning with arms outstretched and then, as he pulls his hands close to his body, he spins faster. The same thing happens when a blade flaps either up or down, its center of gravity moves in toward the center of rotation and it wants to speed up. Blade flapping takes place on a regular basis —once every revolution — and so the blade tries to speed up twice every revolution: once when it is flapping up and again when it is flapping down.

On a two-bladed rotor, this means the two blades are doing the same thing at the same time and the only restraint is from the, inertia of the engine softened by the torsional flexibility of the drive system. This restraint is soft enough that the chordwise bending moments can be successfully handled by using a moderate amount of stiffening in the root of the blade.

In a multi-bladed rotor, the blades are not simultaneously doing the same in-plane dance, so some blades are resisting the motion of other blades. This problem was solved by Juan de La Cierva, the Spanish inventor of the autogyro, when he eliminated the restraint with lead-lag hinges. Modern designers either use his idea or a flexible structure that acts like a mechanical hinge, or they put enough material in the rotor to accommodate the high chordwise bending moments with acceptable low stress levels. These latter rotors are called "stiff in-plane".

The other reason for not using lead-lag hinges on a two-bladed hub is that such a rotor would have a wide range of rotor speeds that could cause unstable ground resonance. On the other hand, rotors with three or more hinged blades are only susceptible to ground resonance over a very narrow range of rotor speeds. With suitable dampers around the lead-lag hinges and in the landing gear, they can safely get through this dangerous range.

Evolutionary Design.

Designers have been gradually making changes on the baseline hubs for many years. Bell Helicopter Textron went to a "flex-beam, door-hinge hub" on later UH-ls and AH-ls. This design locates a bit of hub flexibility where it can be used to reduce the two-per-rev bounce by using the blade's own inertia as a vibration absorber. The door-hinge design also reduces drag by making the hub significantly thinner. Unlike the earlier Bell hubs in which cyclic and collective feathering motions were done with separate bearings, both motions are done about the door hinges on the flex-beam hub.

The hub for the Bell Model 222 is also a flex-beam design but feathering is done with electrometric bearings. In addition, hub springs are installed to increase control moments, especially during low load-factor maneuvers.

On his R22, Frank Robinson has installed separate blade-flapping hinges in addition to the hub teetering hinge. This achieves the same result as the Bell flex-beam while reducing blade-root bending moments and the oscillating forces fed down to the control stick.

Variations on the fully articulated hub are on many current helicopters. The Enstrom hub is similar to the basic Sikorsky configuration, except that the controls go up the inside of the rotor shaft, not outside. Hughes has eliminated the mechanical flapping and feathering bearings by using straps that bend and twist to produce these motions.

Sikorsky, in their Black Hawk and S-76, have replaced all three mechanical hinges with a pair of bearings made of shaped layers of a rubber-like elastomeric material. These bearings deflect to allow flapping, lead-lag and feathering motions.

Bell, in its four-bladed Model 412, has also used elastomeric bearings although flapping is done with a flex-beam. This rotor has lead-lag hinges and the required damping is achieved with elastomeric dampers.

Revolutionary Designs

In 1959, Lockheed initiated the current trend to hingeless rotors (although one hingeless autogyro had been flown during the '30s and Bell had started its experimental efforts along this line in 1957). Called "rigid rotors" in the early days, they actually had considerable flexibility, thus the term is misleading and should only be applied to such rotors as the two very rigid ones on the Sikorsky Advancing Blade Concept (ABC) coaxial aircraft. The key to hingeless rotors is that cyclic pitch can be used to trim out almost all of the flapping, leaving flexibility to do the rest.

On the Lockheed Cheyenne AH-56, a thin portion of the hub was used for flapping flexibility but was stiff in the lead-lag direction. The door-hinge feathering bearing made the basic hub relatively streamlined.

Hingeless hubs are currently produced and used on the MBB BO-105, the Westland Lynx, and the Aerospatiale SA-365N Dauphin 2. The difference in configuration depends primarily on where the designer chose to introduce flexibility. All of these hubs use some sort of bearing—either mechanical or elastomeric—for feathering.

The in-plane stiffness of the Lynx and Dauphin hubs is low enough to require dampers for preventing ground resonance but the MBB BO-105 is stiff enough that it does not.

A hub that can truly be called bearingless was built as an experiment by Boeing Vertol Co. and installed on a BO-105. It relies on structural flexibility for all of its articulation. When fully developed, it should come about as close as possible to achieving those desired goals of low weight, low drag, low cost, easy maintenance, long life, low part count, freedom from dynamic problems, adequate control power, and immunity to battle damage.

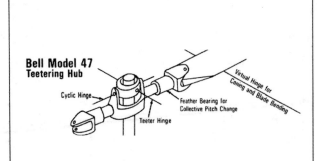

Bell Model 47
Teetering Hub

Cyclic Hinge

Virtual Hinge for
Coning and Blade Bending

Feather Bearing for
Collective Pitch Change

Teeter Hinge

Bell AH-1G
Flex-Beam, Door-Hinge Hub

Flex-Beam

Feathering Hinge

Virtual Hinge for
Coning and Flapping
Modes above
one-per-rev

Teeter Hinge

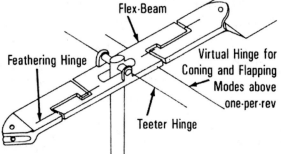

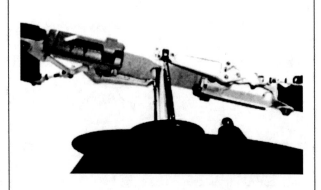

Bell 222
Flex-Beam, Teetering Hub with
Hub Spring

Elastomeric Feather
Bearing

Hub
Spring

Virtual Hinge for Coning and
Flapping Modes above
One-per-Rev

Teeter Hinge

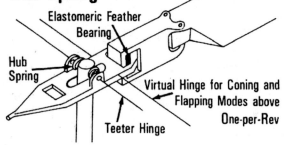

Robinson R22
Tri-Hinge Hub

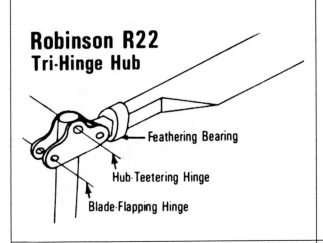

— Feathering Bearing

— Hub-Teetering Hinge

Blade-Flapping Hinge

Enstrom
Fully Articulated Hub with Internal Controls

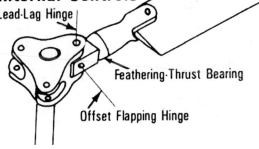

Lead-Lag Hinge

Feathering-Thrust Bearing

Offset Flapping Hinge

Hughes 500D
Fully Articulated Hub with Strap Pack

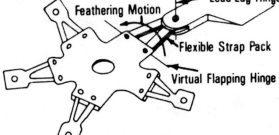

Lead-Lag Hinge

Feathering Motion

Flexible Strap Pack

Virtual Flapping Hinge

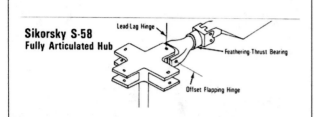

Sikorsky S-58
Fully Articulated Hub

Lead-Lag Hinge

Feathering-Thrust Bearing

Offset Flapping Hinge

Sikorsky S-76
Fully Articulated with
Elastomeric Bearings

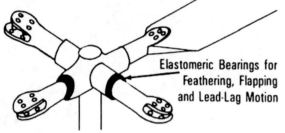

Elastomeric Bearings for
Feathering, Flapping
and Lead-Lag Motion

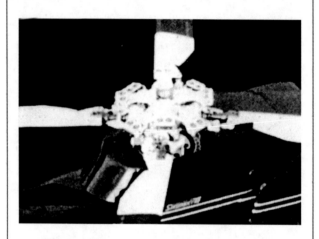

Bell 412
Soft In-Plane, Flex-Beam Hub

Virtual Flapping Hinge

Elastomeric Lead-Lag
Damper and Feather Bearing

Lead-Lag Hinge

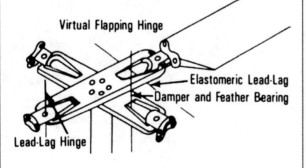

Lockheed AH-56
Stiff In-Plane, Flex-Beam Hub

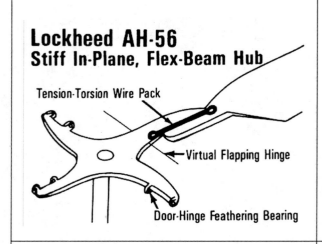

Tension-Torsion Wire Pack

Virtual Flapping Hinge

Door-Hinge Feathering Bearing

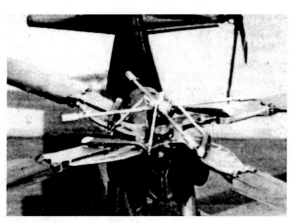

MBB BO-105
Rigid Hub with Flexible Blade Roots

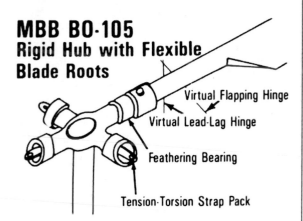

Virtual Flapping Hinge

Virtual Lead-Lag Hinge

Feathering Bearing

Tension-Torsion Strap Pack

Westland Lynx
Hingeless Hub

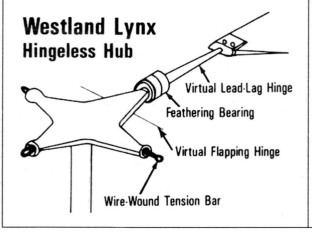

Virtual Lead-Lag Hinge

Feathering Bearing

Virtual Flapping Hinge

Wire-Wound Tension Bar

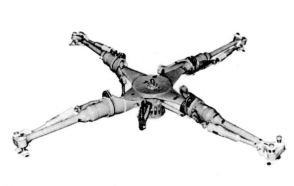

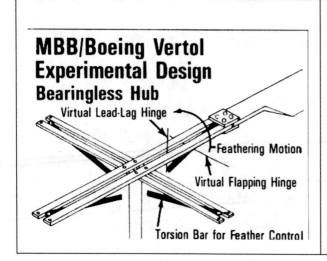

MBB/Boeing Vertol Experimental Design
Bearingless Hub

Virtual Lead-Lag Hinge

Feathering Motion

Virtual Flapping Hinge

Torsion Bar for Feather Control

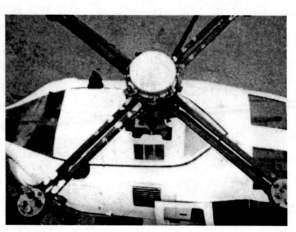

47 Tail Rotor Design

Some helicopter designs balance the main-rotor torque by using two or more rotors — while other designs eliminate the torque, applying a tip-jet drive concept. But the predominant trend over the past 20 years has been to build helicopters in which the torque from a single shaft-driven main rotor is offset by a horizontal force.

Which system?

Just how to develop that force is a decision the designer must face early in the preliminary design. Unless he invents something new, he now has the choice of a conventional tail rotor, a fan-in-fin (fenestron) or a fan-in-boom (NOTAR). The primary criteria for any system is that it must generate enough thrust to balance main-rotor torque in full power climbs with at least a 10% margin left over for directional control. In addition, it must provide adequate control in autorotation or low-speed flight in any direction and at any combination of gross weight, altitude and temperature for which the aircraft is used.

The basic advantage of the conventional tail rotors is that they require relatively little power, produce good yaw control and contribute significantly to yaw damping and directional stability in forward flight. Against these good features are the bad ones: a tail rotor is dangerous to people on the ground and to itself if swung into trees, fence posts or wires. Large helicopters circumvent these problems by incorporating tail rotors that are well above the ground but the exposed, whirling blades on smaller rotorcraft may be perceived as dangerous enough to prompt the consideration of another system.

If a design team chooses to use a tail rotor, it must then make configuration decisions. Figure 47-1 shows some of the variations.

Diameter

The first decision concerns the tail rotor's diameter. Unfortunately, there is no clear-cut guideline for this. A large tail rotor is desirable because it minimizes the power needed for anti-torque and controllability — but one with a small diameter minimizes the problems associated with weight, helicopter center-of-gravity position, and clearances to the ground and other components such as main rotor, horizontal stabilizer

Sikorsky S-61

UH-60

Figure 47-1 Tail Rotor Design Practice (Continued on Next Page)

261

Hughes 500D

Bell 205

Bell 212

and tail boom. In a thorough design effort, the smallest feasible diameter is selected as a tradeoff in which the effects of both main- and tail-rotor diameters on empty weight and performance are determined.

A survey of 17 modern helicopters shows that the ratio of tail-rotor diameter to main-rotor diameter varies from 0.15 (on the Bell 206) to 0.25 (on the Sikorsky CH-53). Tail-rotor diameters on new designs will probably fall within this range unless other considerations are overriding.

Tip speed

The next decision concerns tip speed. A low tip speed is desirable to minimize noise and compressibility effects but a high tip speed minimizes component weight and stall effects.

For its quiet four-bladed tail rotor on the 500D, Hughes selected a tip speed of 527 feet per second (fps) compared to 694 fps on the standard two bladed tail rotor. This range of tip speeds covers those used on most modern helicopters.

Blade area

With the diameter and tip speed pinned down, the total blade area can be determined. The blade area can be described as that which produces the maximum required thrust at just under blade stall. This depends somewhat on the airfoil.

The basis for the selection of the tail-rotor airfoil section is similar to that used on the main rotor. A thick, highly cambered airfoil is preferred for its maximum lift coefficient, however, at high speeds, it might run into compressibility problems. Since tail-rotor blades are almost always stubbier and stiffer than main-rotor blades, there is less problem of aerodynamic pitching moments twisting the blade into odd shapes. Thus a highly cambered, high lift airfoil, which would be out of the question for the main rotor, may be quite practical for a tail rotor.

Choosing total blade area depends on how the engine power — and thus the anti-torque force —changes with altitude. The design condition may be a vertical full-power climb at sea level, hover at the in-ground-effect ceiling or something in between. The criterion is to have sufficient blade area to prevent the tail rotor from stalling at the most critical combination of thrust required and air density.

Number of blades

Dividing the required total blade area into actual blades comes next. The fewer the blades, the cheaper the rotor is to build and maintain but if two (or even in the limit, one) require very stubby blades, high tip losses will penalize the performance. Most designers will select the number of blades based on aspect ratios (radius/chord) of five to nine.

Twist

Unless it is a very simple blade, the modern designer will probably choose to build in some twist to help the hover performance—just as he would on the main-rotor blade. Twists as high as 30° are good for hover but give high loads in forward flight and might be difficult to fabricate in relatively short blades. If twist is used, it is generally less than 10°.

Maximum pitch

The maximum blade pitch must be high enough to provide the required maneuverability in all flight conditions. But it cannot be so high that the pilot stalls the tail rotor with a high accompanying power demand while stopping a fast right hover turn (assuming he is flying in a U.S.-built helicopter with a main rotor turning counterclockwise). The most critical condition for setting the high pitch stop is usually right sideward flight at altitude.

The Army requires that their new helicopters have enough control margin to develop a 15° per second left turn while flying at 35 knots to the right (or at any other azimuth). Predicting the pitch required to do this is made difficult by some complicated aerodynamic interactions involving the tail rotor, vertical stabilizer, main-rotor wake and tail boom as discussed in Chapter 9. On the low side, the minimum tail-rotor pitch is that required to give the capability for turns in autorotation.

Pusher or puller?

Most modern helicopters use a vertical fin to augment the directional stability of the tail rotor and, for the most effectiveness, these two components should both be located at the end of the tail boom. If they are too close together, however, their mutual interference hurts both but if they are separated too far, the assembly will be heavy.

Interference in hover depends upon which side of the fin the tail rotor is mounted, i.e., does it blow air at the fin or suck air past it? Since the induced velocity "below" the tail rotor is higher than above it, the drag of the fin is higher if the tail rotor is blowing on it. This reduces the effective net thrust of the tail rotor for anti-torque purposes.

Figure 47-2 shows the power penalty associated with the relative positions of both "tractor" and "pusher" arrangements. For the American type of main-rotor rotation, the pusher is mounted on the left side of the fin and the tractor on the right.

Almost all of the tail rotors in Figure 47-1 are pushers. The outstanding exceptions are the Sikorsky UH-60 and the Bell 212. In the first case, Sikorsky designers chose to tilt the tail-rotor shaft so that part of its thrust helps lift

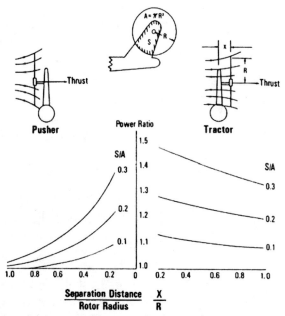

Figure 47-2   Tail Rotor Power Penalt Due to Blockage

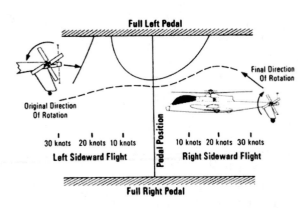

Figure 47-3 Effect of Tail Rotor Direction of Rotation on Sideward Flight Characteristics of Lockheed Cheyenne

the rear end of the helicopter. In order to provide clearance with the fin without using a very long drive shaft, the tractor configuration was chosen.

Direction of rotation

The Bell 212 configuration derives from learning late in the game about which direction a tail rotor should rotate. Over the past 20 years, several helicopter development teams have discovered that the tail-rotor rotation should have the blade closest to the main rotor going up. This minimizes the unsteadiness of left sideward flight, as the tail rotor operates in the vortex ring state. Bell chose the wrong direction when in 1954 it designed the XH-40, the prototype of the UH-1 and AH-1 series. Bell's solution 15 years later was to flip the tail-rotor installation from the left side of the fin to the right, using the same hardware. (Compare the Bell 205 and 212 in Figure 47-1.) To Bell's good fortune in this exercise, the tail-rotor blades had no twist, thus allowing for the change.

A graphic demonstration of wrong and right rotation was done during the development of the Lockheed Cheyenne attack helicopter. Figure 47-3 shows the improvement in pedal position obtained when the rotation was reversed. In left sideward flight, the pilot ran out of left pedal between 14 and 18 knots as he tried to fly in the vortex-ring state. When the direction of rotation of the tail rotor was reversed by redesigning the gearbox, the problem disappeared. (The effects of the proximity of the pusher propeller to the tail rotor had been discounted by comparing test results with the pusher on and off.) Even right sideward flight was improved by the change.

Just why the tail rotor is sensitive to direction of rotation in the proximity of the main-rotor wake is not clear. It is definitely not a ground-vortex phenomenon since, on both the Lockheed AH-56A Cheyenne and the Hughes AH-64 Apache, height above the ground had no significant effect on the left sideward flight unsteadiness. Also, it is not a vertical-fin blockage problem since on the Cheyenne, the tail rotor was located on the end of the horizontal stabilizer to clear the propeller—well away from the fin. This is another case where we would be a lot smarter if we could see air.

It is interesting to note that the Russians have apparently also learned the lesson the hard way. Their solution on the Mi-24, the "Hind", was to flip the tail rotor to the other side of the fin somewhere between the "B" and "D" versions to reverse its direction of rotation.

If steadiness in left sideward flight is not enough reason to pick the right direction of rotation, there is another reason. Recent flight tests at Westland have shown that noise in forward flight is lower if the blade on top is going back, since it is not slicing through the main-rotor tip vortices so violently. This is at least one reason why Westland reversed the direction of tail-rotor rotation when developing the WG-30 from its earlier WG-13 or Lynx.

The recommended direction of rotation is unfortunate in one respect: the tail rotor is more likely to bat rocks forward toward the fuselage when landing on unprepared ground.

Blade retention

How to attach the blades and hub to the tail-rotor shaft is a decision that has to be made early in the design process. In forward flight, the tail rotor wants to flap, something that is permitted in all designs — since inhibiting flapping by using strong structures has been found impractical.

The simplest way to permit flapping is to use a teetering hinge on two-bladed tail rotors — and on those four-bladers which are simply two teetering rotors spaced a short distance apart. (The two rotors making up the Hughes four-bladers are not at right angles primarily because the "scissors" configuration makes arrangement of the controls simpler — and there is also some evidence the configuration is quieter.)

Tail rotors with flapping hinges may have lead-lag hinges to relieve in-plane root-bending moments but do not need dampers, since no possible instability exists corresponding to the ground-resonance troubles a main rotor can get into.

A tail rotor with either a teetering hinge or individual-blade flapping hinges is usually designed with some amount of mechanical coupling that changes the pitch of the blade as it flaps. This is done either by canting the hinge — or by locating the joint between the pitch horn and the pitch link off the hinge line. Both possibilities are shown in Figure 47-4. Tail-rotor designers refer to the coupling angle as "delta-three", a term invented by autogyro engineers who identified and named several possible types of kinetic rotor couplings.

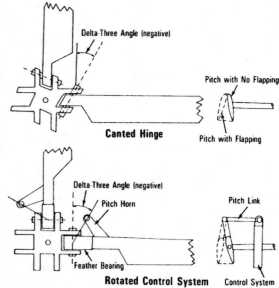

If the pitch increases as the blade flaps "up" (toward the direction of rotor thrust), then the delta-three angle is said to be positive — at least by most engineers. Both positive and negative delta-three have been used for various reasons but the negative type shown on Figure 21-4 is the most common.

There are two reasons for introducing this coupling:

1—It often simplifies the layout of the system, reducing mechanical interferences and making for shorter, lighter components; and

2—It reduces the steady and transient blade flapping primarily by changing the blade's natural frequency away

Figure 47-4 Two Methods of Obtaining Pitch/Flap Coupling

Figure 47-5 Aerospatiale Fenestron

from the resonance condition (both positive and negative delta-three angles do this).

The next generation of tail rotors are now in the test stage at most of the major manufacturers. These are hingeless and bearingless "flexbeam" rotors that use flexible spars of fiberglass or other composite materials to provide for both flapping and feathering.

The fenestron

A structure surrounding the tail rotor protects it and prevents people from accidentally being struck by a blade. There have been several such schemes but so far the only one to get into production is the fenestron. This device (Figure 47-5) was primarily developed by France's Aerospatiale for use on the Gazelle and Dauphin series. (A fenestron is a small window in French houses.)

By shaping the hole like a duct, the designers can get a performance benefit corresponding to a somewhat larger diameter — since the lips of the duct produce a low static pressure that adds to the force being generated by the fan.

Whether the force is produced by the fan or by the lips of the duct, the total force and power required to develop it are related to the energy in the fully developed wake. A normal rotor has a wake that requires some distance to contract to its final size—which is only 70% of the rotor diameter. By putting a duct around the rotor, the wake is effectively matured in the duct and undergoes no further contraction downstream. Thus the fenestron can produce the same total thrust for the same power as a tail rotor 30% larger. The benefit is even higher if the duct has a bit of divergence to expend the wake and if the comparable tail rotor suffers a blockage penalty by being too close to its supporting fin.

It is claimed that with these considerations, the fenestron fan diameter can be as small as 50% of the tail rotor it is replacing—but up to now Aerospatiale has been using even smaller fans on the Gazelle and Dauphin designs. Thus, they use more power for anti-torque than a typical tail rotor, taking power which could be used by the main rotor. For the designer, this represents a very difficult tradeoff exercise. Since it is very hard to enclose a big enough fan to replace an equivalent tail rotor, he must balance performance against safety.

It may be significant that Aerospatiale designed its latest helicopter, the AS-350, with a conventional tail rotor rather than a fenestron such as used on the two previous models. (Aerospatiale engineers have since had second thoughts and now say that a fenestron version of the AS-350 — or its twin-engined sister, the AS-355 — might still be produced.)

Size vs. power

As with the tail rotor, the larger the diameter of the fenestron, the less power it takes from the engine. A practical illustration of this is found in the development of the Aerospatiale HH-65A Dolphin for the U.S. Coast Guard. The original contract was for an off-the-shelf version of the SA-366 Dauphin 2 but it was found that the hover performance did not meet the guarantee. Aerospatiale solved that problem by increasing the diameter of the fenestron fan from 35 to 43 inches —which increases the hover gross weight by about 260 pounds.

To be effective, the depth of the duct should be at least 20% of the fan diameter, according to the theory. This means that it is difficult to streamline the thick fan for low drag in forward flight. It also means the air path into and out of the fan is torturous, so its efficiency is

Figure 47-6 Bell Ring Fin

penalized. For this reason, the fenestron is always integrated into a generously sized cambered vertical stabilizer that can take over the job of torque compensation in forward flight. This has the advantage of decreasing the loads on the blades and the drive system—thus prolonging the life of the system.

Even with the fenestron, the direction of rotation has been found to be important. Directional control problems on the Gazelle, which has the fenestron blade closest to the main rotor going down, were much reduced on the Dauphin, which reversed the rotation.

Bell Helicopter Textron has recently experimented with a "ring fin" (Figure 47-6), a kind of thin fenestron. Reports of these tests indicate that the deep duct may not be as necessary as previously believed. The interaction of the tip vortices with the ring surface apparently keeps the wake from contracting, just as the longer duct of the fenestron does. The published data show that several configurations of the ring are better than the tail rotor in specific flight conditions. However, as yet, no one arrangement has been found that is superior in all conditions.

NOTAR

Another recent experiment to eliminate the tail rotor is the Hughes NOTAR (no tail rotor). This is a controllable-pitch fan installed just aft of the transmission, blowing air down the hollow tail boom to a nozzle with a set of 90° turning vanes. The reaction against the vanes produces an anti-torque force. Both the pitch of the fan (which in the prototype is a fenestron fan from an Aerospatiale Gazelle) and the size of the nozzle opening are controlled by the pilot's pedal movements.

In addition to the nozzle reaction, another contribution to the required anti-torque force is provided by the circulation-control tail boom. This concept (Figure 47-7) makes use of the deflection of the main-rotor wake as it passes the circular tail boom. This is accomplished by a jet of air blowing from the pressurized boom through a slot on the lower right-hand side.

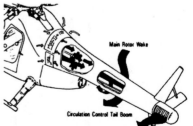

Figure 47-7 Hughes NOTAR Design

Figure 47-8 NOTAR Test Configuration

This jet of air comes out nearly tangential to the boom's surface and entrains the boundary layer on the right side—delaying its separation and bending the whole wake flow to the left. This distortion of the wake produces suction on the right side of the boom, which helps to react the main-rotor torque. As a matter of fact, the design calculations indicated that about two-thirds of the anti-torque force in hover should come from this effect. In forward flight, the rotor wake does not impinge on the boom, so the forces must come from the deflected jet and the cambered vertical stabilizer.

That things don't always go according to plan is illustrated by the test configuration shown in Figure 47-8. The "stovepipe" on the engine exhaust was found necessary to direct hot gasses away from the tail boom and the two collars at each end of the slot were used to make it work as it should.

Once that was done, the system worked very well although it is obvious that these configuration fixes cannot be considered the final solution. At this point, the NOTAR developers are exploring collapsible fences that fold at a certain forward speed or body shaping to eliminate the need for the fences. Like any development, it just takes a little engineering doing.

48 Airfoils For Rotor Blades

A speed record for helicopters was set in 1978 at 198.7 knots (368.4 km/ph) by the Soviets with the Mil A-10 —which was essentially a cleaned-up Mil Mi-24 (NATO code name: Hind).

That this record survived so long can be taken as evidence that the maximum shed of "pure" helicopters (those without auxiliary propulsion) is in the neighborhood of 200 knots, where the effects of stall on the retreating side and of compressibility on the advancing side combine to produce rapidly increasing penalties in the form of high power, excessive oscillating structural loads, and the loss of control.

In a few words, the problem is that the retreating blade is going too slow with respect to the air to produce its share of lift without stalling and the advancing blade is going too fast to avoid being festooned with shock waves with their resultant drag and pitching moment penalties.

The dilemma

The designer of a high-speed helicopter finds himself between the proverbial rock and hard place when selecting an airfoil for his rotor. To get the best performance on the retreating side, an airfoil must have a high staffing angle of attack at a moderate Mach number. This physically means an airfoil that is thick and heavily cambered.

To get the best performance on the advancing side, however, the airfoil needs to be thin and uncambered to obtain a high drag-divergence Mach number at a low angle of attack. To add to the problem, the designer wants an airfoil with low pitching moments on both sides to avoid twisting the relatively slender and limber blade into odd shapes in flight. Figure 48-1 shows several airfoils that have been, are, or may be used on helicopter rotors.

The peculiar environment of the helicopter rotor at high speed is a natural for an airfoil that can change its shape every revolution but so far the technical problems of implementing such a concept have frustrated the most inventive of the inventors. This is another challenge for future designers.

Figure 48-1 Rotor Airfoils

A little history

Without going to exotic systems, the designer of modern rotors is forced into some type of compromise with respect to airfoil thickness and camber. Small contour differences, however, can make some airfoils better compromises than others.

In the early days, airfoils were designed as pleasing shapes and then tested in low-speed wind tunnels with perhaps some later cut-and-try modifications to improve their characteristics. In the 1940s, some mathematical methods were developed that allowed designers to improve at least the low-speed performance (as, for instance, in the laminar-flow airfoils).

For many years, however, the complexity of high-speed aerodynamics kept designers from treating shock waves and their effects in analyses. By about 1970, designers could take advantage of an increased understanding of compressibility effects resulting from wind-tunnel tests; improved mathematical equations; and — above all—fast, patient, and hard-working digital computers. An airfoil can now be designed to obtain the best compromise but it still must be tested in a wind tunnel to make sure that the air treats it as the equations say it should.

More lift

On most airplanes, the ability to develop a high lift coefficient is important to minimize landing and takeoff speeds, and many airplanes use complicated retractable leading-edge slats and trailing edge flaps to obtain these goals. The helicopter, on the other hand, needs high lift coefficients at high forward speeds and on every rotor revolution just to keep flying steadily.

This is because, as the forward speed increases, the blade on the retreating side is going slower and slower with respect to the air molecules and the lift coefficient must be high to produce as much lift as on the advancing side — where relative speed is very high.

The objective of the rotor-blade designer is to get an airfoil that has the highest possible stall angle of attack (and thus lift coefficient) for operation on the retreating side — without suffering from high compressibility drag on the advancing side. So far, the gadgetry installed on airplane wings has been ruled out as impracticable for helicopter blades and so we must work with the basic airfoil shape.

A higher maximum-lift coefficient can be used to benefit either forward flight or hover. The forward-flight effect is direct, in that the maximum speed can be increased (if extra power is available) and the maximum rotor thrust can be increased for maneuvering.

If these goals have already been met, then the higher airfoil maximum-lift coefficient can be used to reduce blade chord. Any helicopter rotor designed for reasonably high forward speed has more blade area than it needs for hover. A reduction in chord will decrease the profile power in hover, resulting in better performance and a slight, but welcome, reduction in empty weight.

Types of stall

The capability of any wing or rotor blade to produce high lift is limited when the angle of attack increases to a critical point and the air refuses to follow the shape of the airfoil, separating from the upper surface. At this point, the lift either does not increase any further or it actually decreases. At the same time, the drag increases rapidly and a sharp nosedown pitching moment is generated.

Aerodynamicists working with wind tunnels have identified three types of stall that occur with simple airfoils at low speeds — and one that exists at high speeds. The three low-speed stalls depend both on the shape of the airfoil and on the Reynolds number of the flow, and are known as: thin-airfoil, leading edge, and trailing-edge stalls.

Figure 48-2 shows how each can be recognized by lift and pitching moment trends as the angle of attack is increased. It also lists the airfoil

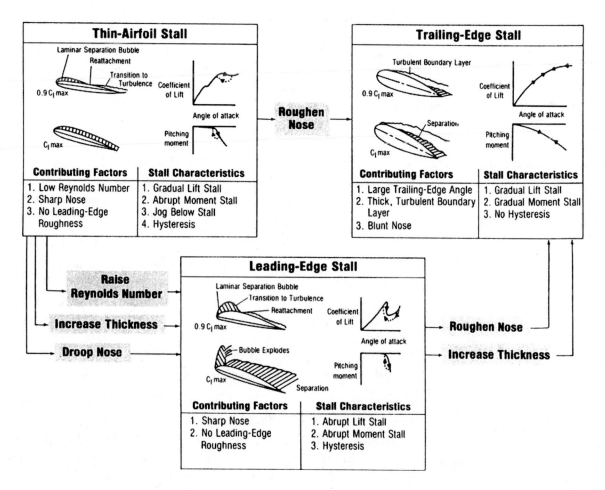

Figure 48-2   Three Types of Stall

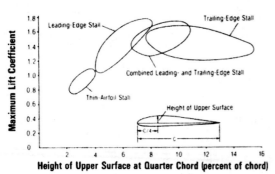

Figure 48-3 Summary of Maximum Lift Data at Low Mach Numbers

parameters that influence the type of stall and how changes in these parameters can change one type of stall into another.

Thin-airfoil stall requires that the boundary layer over the airfoil is laminar even at high angles of attack. This condition usually exists at such low Reynolds numbers that only birds and model builders are affected.

A turbulent boundary layer is actually more stable and a transition from laminar to turbulent is a condition for leading-edge stall. In this case, as the angle of attack is increased to near the stall angle, a small "separation bubble" will appear on the leading edge where the boundary layer momentarily leaves the surface and then reattaches, thus effectively producing a blunter nose shape. At a higher angle, the bubble bursts, separating the flow over the entire airfoil, as shown in Figure 48-2.

The maximum lift in leading-edge stall measured with many airfoils correlates quite well with the ratio of the height of the upper surface at the quarter-chord to the length of the chord, as shown in Figure 48-3.

Carrying this trend to its limit by thickening or cambering the airfoil will result in the separation starting at the trailing edge before the leading-edge bubble grows to a critical size. Some carefully shaped special airfoils maintain attached flow over the trailing edge to very high angles of attack, resulting in lift coefficients well over 2.0— but most airfoils that thick will have trailing-edge stall with maximum lift coefficients substantially less than 2.0.

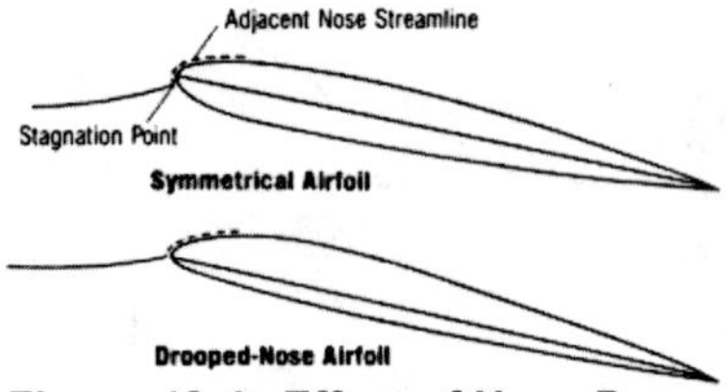

Built-in droop

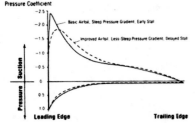

Figure 48-4 Effect of Nose Droop

A favorite method of delaying leading-edge stall and improving the maximum lift coefficients of an existing airfoil is to "droop" its nose. Figure 48-4 shows how this gives the air flowing around the nose an easier path by aiming the nose more directly into the oncoming air stream.

The basic reason that this and other nose-shape modifications work is that while air doesn't mind speeding up, it sure hates to slow down. But speeding up is necessary to generate low pressures on the upper surface to produce lift — and the slowing down is necessary to bring the speed back to the free-stream value at the trailing edge. The designer tries to make his contours such that local regions of very high velocities are avoided so that no rapid slowing is required.

When an airfoil is tested in a wind tunnel, surface pressures are measured as shown in Figure 48-5. On these plots, the rapidity of deceleration is indicated by the steepness of the pressure gradient behind the leading edge peak and the designer will try to reduce this gradient to obtain a higher stall angle of attack. With a little care, an airfoil can be designed that separates at its leading edge and trailing edge at the same time. Such

Figure 48-5 Airfoil Pressure Patterns

an airfoil is not appreciated on an airplane because the abruptness of the stall gives the pilot no advance warning and its completeness makes the loss of lift dangerous, especially if it were to occur during a landing flare.

An airplane pilot would rather have the gentle loss of lift resulting from gradual separation, characteristic of a trailing-edge stall. On a helicopter, an abruptly stalling airfoil is not so undesirable since only a small portion of the rotor is affected.

Compressibility and stall

Classic stall types — thin-airfoil stall, leading-edge stall, and trailing-edge stall — all occur at Mach numbers well below where compressibility is a factor, say, below 0.3.

At higher speeds, the stall characteristics change. This occurs at some speed beyond the critical Mach number where the local velocity over the airfoil first reaches the speed of sound. For an airfoil at a high angle of attack, the critical Mach number may be as low as 0.35.

Nothing very dramatic happens right at the critical Mach number, since the air only momentarily goes supersonic over the nose and then gracefully slows down as it progresses to the trailing edge where it must return to its original free-stream speed.

Increasing speed will produce a larger supersonic region extending along the chord and out from the surface as shown in Figure 48-6. At some higher free-stream Mach number, the local speed over the airfoil reaches a point where it has trouble slowing down. (Wind-tunnel tests show this local Mach number is in the neighborhood of 1.4.) At this point, instead of slowing down gracefully to the trailing edge, the deceleration back to subsonic speed is abrupt: through a shock wave.

At the speed where the shock first occurs, it is not strong enough to significantly change the overall flow patterns but later its effects become dramatic. In particular, the boundary layer may be so jolted by the shock wave that it separates downstream. When this occurs, we have "shock stall".

Figure 48-7 shows how the stall characteristics of the NACA 0012 airfoil change as the Mach number is increased in the wind tunnel. At the lowest speed, the stall is a sharp, leading-edge type—but as shock stall takes effect, the stall is more gentle; until at high Mach numbers the lift really doesn't reach a well-defined peak and the term "maximum lift coefficient" loses its meaning. An alternative in these cases is to define the maximum useful lift coefficient as at the angle of attack where the drag coefficient reaches 0.05— five to eight times its minimum value.

For the 0012 airfoil, the maximum lift coefficient decreases as the test Mach number is increased. This is typical of most airfoils — but not all. The VR-7, which is a 12% thick airfoil designed by Boeing Vertol, shows a maximum lift envelope that begins to decrease but then reverses at

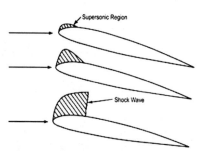

Figure 48-6 Effect of Increasing Mach Number on Supersonic Region

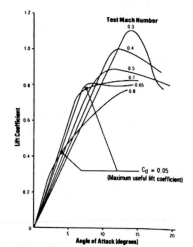

Figure 48-7 Effect of Test Mach Number on Lift Characteristics of NACA 0012 Airfoil

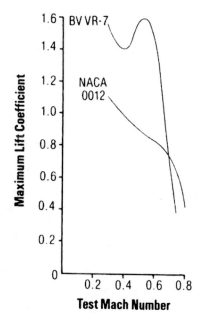

Figure 48-8 Maximum Lift Envelopes of Two Airfoils

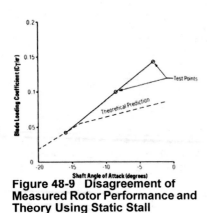

Figure 48-9 Disagreement of Measured Rotor Performance and Theory Using Static Stall Characteristics

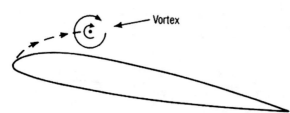

Figure 48-10 The Post-Stall Vortex Shed from the Leading Edge

about 0.4 Mach — as shown on Figure 48-8. This is due to some complex aerodynamic patterns characteristic of what have come to be known as "supercritical airfoils".

Dynamic overshoot

Early in the helicopter experience, aerodynamicists thought they could predict overall rotor-thrust limits by putting data obtained during airfoil wind-tunnel tests into their computer programs. They were surprised when complete rotors were tested in wind tunnels and continued to produce high thrust well beyond the test conditions where the computer programs said they should be in heavy stall.

Figure 48-9 shows such a comparison. There are two reasons for this relatively unusual circumstance where test results exceed the theoretical predictions.

One is that sweeping a surface either forward or aft improves its stall resistance. Of course, when the blade is straight out on the retreating side, it is unswept. But it does have aerodynamic sweep both ahead and behind that point and so can take advantage of the phenomenon in these regions.

The second reason is that the angle of attack is changing so rapidly that the boundary layer doesn't act like it does in a normal static wind-tunnel test. The airplane aerodynamicists had already discovered this during rapid pitch-up maneuvers and we were able to apply that experience to the understanding of our aircraft.

Wind-tunnel discoveries

Three effects have been identified in wind tunnels. First, the rapid nose-up pitching motion associated with the increase in cyclic pitch that the blade experiences as it enters the retreating side tends to compress the boundary layer on the nose, keeping it from separating as easily as it does with a more leisurely increase in the angle of attack.

Besides the pitching motion, the blade may be "plunging", that is, changing its angle of attack by going up and down with respect to the air, independent of pitch. If it is plunging down, the effect on the nose boundary layer is opposite that due to pitching motion and an earlier separation occurs. On a helicopter rotor, however, as the blade enters the retreating side, it is actually plunging up with respect to the local airflow due to coning and the increasing induced velocity. So both types of motion delay stall.

The second effect is due to the time it takes for the leading-edge separation bubble to burst. During this period, the angle of attack and the lift coefficient are rising, producing a small but welcome benefit.

After separation occurs, the third effect — shown in Figure 48-10—takes over. This is the shedding of a leading-edge vortex that passes back over the airfoil at about half the free-stream speed—producing high suction forces that further increase the lift coefficient. Figure 48-11 illustrates these effects on an airfoil being oscillated rapidly between 5° and 25° in a wind tunnel.

Drawing conclusions

The conclusion from all of this is that rotors do not suffer from lift stall in high-speed forward flight. The same statement is only partially true for drag and pitching moments. They do not increase very much during the boundary-layer phase on the upstroke but they go wild as the leading-edge vortex breaks loose.

When these dynamic effects are included in the airfoil data contained in the computer programs, the correlation of theory with test is much improved but still not as good as we would like. To do better, we need to find a way to instrument a blade element to measure its local angle of attack and its lift, drag, and pitching moments in various flight conditions — including rotor stall. So far, this has not been done satisfactorily.

Profile drag

The power required to turn a rotor can be traced to the dragon each blade element. This drag can be separated into different parts.

The main part of the drag is unavoidable and is due to the rotor producing thrust by moving air. The corresponding rearward tilt of the lift vectors with respect to the shaft produces a resisting force that, in hover, is called "induced drag". There is also induced drag in forward flight but it combines with another effect caused by the tilt of lift vectors due to the rotor disc's nosedown angle, required to pull the aircraft through the air. This combination of effects is known as "in-flow drag".

This discussion however, is about neither induced or inflow drag. Instead, it will cover another component, "profile drag", the remaining drag— typically about one-third of the total—caused by the energy lost as air molecules pass over the blade. One of the objectives of airfoil designers is to reduce this profile drag.

A Close look at air

Profile drag is caused by either air molecules losing velocity as they pass a stationary body or gaining velocity by being dragged along as a moving body goes by. To the aerodynamicist, the two situations are identical because all that matters is the relative velocity between the air molecules and the body.

The slowing down—or speeding up—is caused by some molecules being momentarily trapped at the body surface. When they leave, they collide with other passing molecules and slow them down, producing a "boundary layer" of slow-moving air adjacent to the surface. The

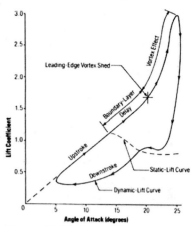

Figure 48-11 Dynamic Overshoot on Oscillating Airfoil

NACA 64A410 Airfoil

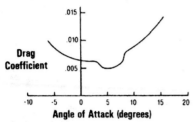

Figure 48-12 Laminar Flow Airfoil Drag Characteristics

thickness of this layer builds as the air flows along the surface. For a typical helicopter rotor blade with a 12-inch chord, the thickness of the boundary layer at the trailing edge will be about one-quarter inch.

If the surface of the airfoil is very smooth, the boundary layer will stay thin and laminar for some distance back of the nose. This is a low-drag situation since little energy is being lost in the boundary layer. Even on a smooth surface, however, a laminar boundary layer will eventually "trip" spontaneously to a turbulent layer, which becomes thicker and consumes more energy, causing higher profile drag.

Laminar flow airfoils

In addition to surface smoothness, the airfoil designer can give the airfoil a contour, which will keep the air accelerating as far back as possible. In the 1940s, this concept led NACA (the National Advisory Committee for Aeronautics, NASA's predecessor) to develop the so called laminar-flow airfoils. Wind-tunnel tests found these airfoils exhibited a "drag bucket" as shown in Figure 48-12.

By special design techniques, this drag bucket could be made to coincide with an airplane's angle of attack, thus insuring maximum cruise performance or maximum speed, depending upon the requirements of the design. Many airplanes, including the P-51 Mustang and the P-80 Shooting Star, used these airfoils.

But it was soon found bug spots, skin joints, and other surface imperfections caused an airfoil in operation to work less efficiently than the smooth-surfaced ones in a wind tunnel. These imperfections caused a premature transition from laminar to turbulent flow. So most of the expected benefits from the new airfoils were never realized except on competition sailplanes, which are carefully built and maintained.

Despite the airplane experience, laminar-flow airfoils have been found to be beneficial on helicopter blades. Instead of bug spots and skin joints (protuberances), the smooth leading edges on helicopter rotor blades are more often subject to nicks and scratches (depressions) but these do not trip the boundary layer.

Measuring drag

The profile drag of an airfoil can be measured in a two-dimensional wind tunnel in which the model extends from one wall to another. In this case, as far as the air is concerned, the model extends to infinity in both directions; the tip vortices, which would normally cause downward velocity on a real wing or helicopter blade, are too far away to have any effect. This means that only profile drag is generated.

There are two techniques for measuring drag in these two-dimensional tests. The first is to support a model on a balance system that will measure the three airfoil characteristics of interest: lift, drag, and pitching moment. The modern way of doing this is with electronic strain-gauge balances.

The other technique is to measure the loss of velocity across the wake behind the model and relate this through some simple concepts of physics to the drag. When this non-balance method is used, the lift and pitching moment are usually determined by integrating pressures on both the top and bottom surfaces. These pressures are measured at many distributed pressure orifices near the middle of the model.

Some models have been tested using both measurement techniques; however, a study of the test results poses a dilemma. In three otherwise trusted tunnels that I know of, the drag measured by the balance and the wake-survey method are substantially different. Figure 48-13 shows the difference for one tunnel. Neither I nor anyone I've talked to can satisfactorily explain why there is a difference, so suggestions would be welcome.

(Most rotor aerodynamicists use the lower curve but often feel forced to apply a "fudge factor" to make their predicted performance calculations correlate with the rotor power measured in flight test.)

Compressibility effects

When dealing with stall, we are interested in a Mach number range from 0.3 to 0.6, where the retreating blade might be operated at high angles of attack.

But for drag considerations, aerodynamicists are more interested in the Mach-number range of 0.6 to 1.0, where the advancing blade might operate — although at relatively low angles of attack. When the local Mach number over the surface exceeds about 1.4, the air suddenly slows down through a shock wave, which first appears near the "crest" or highest point on the airfoil, as shown in Figure 48-14. At this speed, drag begins to increase rapidly in what is called "drag divergence."

The speed just before the start of drag divergence is the best speed for jet transports. If you look carefully, you can see the shadow of the shock wave dancing near the quarter-chord whenever a wing is pointing directly toward or directly away from the sun.

At higher speeds, the shock wave moves further back and becomes stronger. During attempts to break the sound barrier in the late 1940s, this movement turned out to be critical. The shock wave on the horizontal stabilizer migrated back to the elevator hinge line; the elevator's effectiveness disappeared and the pilot lost all his longitudinal control. After some exciting flying by test pilots with the right stuff, the problem was finally solved, using "flying tails" in which the entire surface is moved by the control motion.

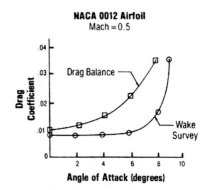

Figure 48-13   Difference in Drag Measured by Two Methods

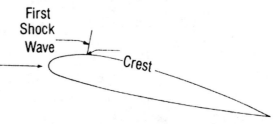

Figure 48-14   Shock Wave First Location

There are two sources of increased drag. One known as "wave drag" represents the energy the air loses as it passes through a shock wave. The other occurs when a shock causes the boundary layer to thicken. In some cases, the thickened boundary layer actually separates from the airfoil surface, causing "shock stall".

Shock waves can be photographed in wind tunnels by using special "Schlierin" optical systems, which can distinguish between dense air in the shock wave and the thinner air on each side. Another indication of a shock is the sudden change in surface pressure at the shock location. Figure 48-15 shows how the pressure distribution changes as a shock is developed by increasing the tunnel speed during the test of a NACA 0012 airfoil at a 4° angle of attack. Also shown are the drag coefficients measured at each condition. The last one is well beyond drag divergence for this airfoil at this angle of attack and reflects the shock wave location well beyond the crest.

One method of comparing airfoils is to use there-suits of two-dimensional wind-tunnel tests to plot the maximum lift coefficient vs. drag-divergence Mach number, as on Figure 48-16. By spotting various families of airfoils on trends can be determined. This presentation is most valid if all the data is from the same wind tunnel, using the same measuring techniques. The data on Figure 48-16 is from the high-speed wind tunnel used by Boeing Vertol. The trends show the effect of thickness. This is also illustrated on Figure 48-17, which shows that airfoil-thickness ratio is good for maximum lift but bad for drag divergence.

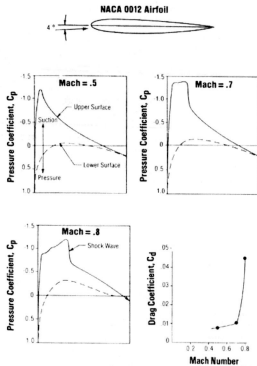

Figure 48-15 Changes in Pressure Distribution and Drag as Mach Number is Increased

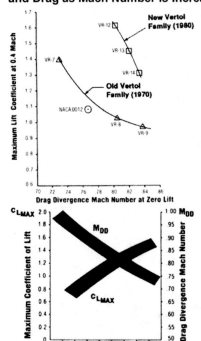

Figure 48-17 Effect of Airfoil Thickness Ratio on Maximum Lift and Drag Divergence

Supercritical airfoils

As helicopter aerodynamicists, we have sometimes been supercriticized by our supercritics because they thought we were overlooking supercritical airfoils. In defense, I will say that we have been very interested in what our fixed-wing friends have been doing in this field for years — and, although some of our design goals and constraints are different, a number of modern designs have distinctly supercritical characteristics. A typical supercritical airfoil designed for a jet transport is shown in Figure 48-18.

What is a supercritical airfoil?

One that sneers at you? No, it is an airfoil that can operate at high subsonic Mach numbers with less drag than conventional airfoils.

The flow in the supersonic region ahead of the shock wave is not uniform. It contains expansion and compression waves that reflect from the inner and outer boundaries of the region with an alternating saw tooth pattern, as shown in Figure 48-19. Going through a compression wave, the air slows down — but it speeds up through an expansion wave.

It was an understanding of this that first led to the design of supercritical airfoils by careful shaping of the nose to make the waves very distinct and position them so that, at the design lift coefficient and Mach number, the shock wave is located behind a compression wave rather than behind an expansion wave. The lower velocity just ahead of the shock decreases its strength and thus its drag penalty.

This happy condition exists only over a fairly narrow band of Mach numbers and lift coefficients. Operation outside the design region may put the shock wave behind the expansion wave and it will be stronger— rather than weaker than normal.

Peculiar airfoils

The effect on drag is shown in Figure Figure 48-20, which shows two airfoils, one considered to have conventional characteristics and the other supercritical characteristics. Incidentally, both were designed and tested long before the effects of the wave pattern were understood, and the test report could only label the results of the 66,2-215 airfoil as "peculiar".

The designer of a jet transport could take advantage of this airfoil if his design points were a lift coefficient of 0.7 and a Mach number of 0.65. With techniques now fairly well established, he can design new airfoils to have low drag at other combinations.

Compared to us, the airplane designer's task is relatively easy because his aircraft cruises in a fairly narrow band of Mach numbers and lift coefficients. We, on the other hand, put our blades through a wide range of these parameters with every rotor revolution and thus would usually operate with both the benefits and the penalties of the supercritical design.

The peculiar characteristics of the supercritical airfoils are not limited to drag. Most airfoils have a gradual reduction in maximum lift coefficient as Mach number is increased but the Boeing Vertol VR-7, which achieved its supercritical characteristics purely by accident, shows a "S" shaped curve, as you can see by looking at Figure 48-8.

The airplane people also use a trick that we can't. The airplane airfoil on Figure 48-18 has a sharply deflected trailing edge that acts like a flap and loads up the rear of the airfoil, thus allowing the wing to generate its required lift coefficient with the nose at a fairly low angle of attack.

This means that the wing can go to a higher Mach number before generating drag-producing shockwaves. It also means that the wing is generating a strong nosedown pitching moment, which must be trimmed out by the tail.

Figure 48-18 Supercritical Airfoil for a Jet Transport

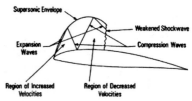

Figure 48-19   Wave Geometry at High Subsonic Speed

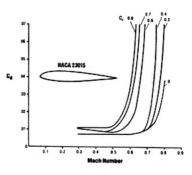

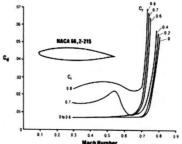

Figure 48-20   Drag Characteristics of Two 15% Thick Airfoils

Pitching moments

The pitching moment characteristics of an airfoil are more important than either lift or drag in limiting the speed of modern helicopters. If it is not the moment generated during stall on the retreating side, it is the moment generated by high speed on the advancing side that says, "this fast and no faster".

The pioneers in rotary-wing learned about aerodynamic pitching moments on their blades the hard way during the autogyro days. Following the lead of that aircraft's inventor, Juan Cierva, they all initially used cambered airfoils which, while having good lift characteristics, had healthy nose-down pitching moments.

Flight testing of autogyros in England, Germany, and America revealed that the design choice was a mistake. In a high-speed dive, the flexible blades twisted nose-down on the advancing side just as if the pilot had applied forward cyclic pitch — even if he were desperately holding the stick on its aft stop! At least one fatal accident was attributed to the failure to recover from a dive and other autogyro test pilots returned to base pale and shaken.

The lesson was well learned: avoid airfoils with high pitching moments; in fact, try to use only airfoils with no inherent moments such as the symmetrical NACA 0012 and 0015. Until about 1965, it was a brave designer who would even suggest using camber, even though blades had been made substantially stiffer by replacing wood and fabric with metal.

Simple aerodynamic theory indicates that the surface pressure on an airfoil is distributed so that no matter how much lift is being generated, the pitching moment about quarter-chord depends only on the shape of the mean line between the two surfaces.

If the mean line is straight, as in symmetrical airfoils, the moment will be zero. Thus, if a blade with a symmetrical airfoil were mounted such that its feathering bearing lines up with the quarter-chord, it should feel no aerodynamic pitching moment in flight. This is what theory says.

In practice, two effects change this ideal situation. Even a symmetrical airfoil will develop a nose-down pitching moment when it stalls and also when it is developing lift at Mach numbers above 0.5 where compressibility effects start moving the center of lift first forward and then aft from the quarter-chord.

These trends are shown in Figure 48-21. Even on helicopters with symmetrical airfoils, these effects produced high blade twisting and, with unboosted control systems, uncomfortable control stick forces. Most of these problems were solved in the '50s and '60s by stiffening the blades and introducing hydraulically boosted control systems — or at least devices that prevented rotor-control forces from being transmitted to the cockpit.

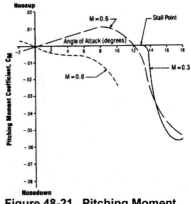

Figure 48-21 Pitching Moment Characteristics of the NACA 0012 Airfoil

Some well-known helicopters with symmetrical blade airfoils are listed in Figure 48-1.

Return of the camber

Designers knew that rotor performance could be improved by using cambered airfoils but the first steps after the early disasters were cautious. It was known that the maximum lift of a symmetrical section could be increased by "drooping" the nose. Fortunately, this forward camber has lit-tie effect on pitching moments and so could be easily accepted.

Drooping the nose of a symmetrical airfoil was only an interim step. Designers looked with envy on the fully cambered airfoils the airplane people developed. They realized, however, that the upward-bowed mean lines in these airfoils would produce a nose-down pitching moment about the quarter-chord which could generate unacceptable cyclic loads in the blades and control systems —even with the modern ways of building these components.

Therefore, they modified the airfoils by "reflexing" the trailing edge to produce a compensating nose-up moment to balance the basic nose-down moment. The designer has a choice of either incorporating the reflex as part of the basic airfoil or adding a flat tab, which then can be used for blade tracking as well.

Some other considerations

A reflexed trailing edge, either as a built-in modification or as an add-on tab, partially detracts from the high maximum-lift characteristics of the cambered airfoil because it acts like a wing flap deflected in the wrong direction. Nevertheless, the overall result is beneficial enough to pay off.

Whether it is best to deflect the tab just enough to leave a little nose-down moment or even further to produce a basic nose-up moment is not yet clear. Flight and wind-tunnel tests by Boeing Vertol and Sikorsky indicate that oscillatory loads and vibration are minimized with a nose-up moment but recent flight experience at Hughes leads to the opposite conclusion.' The exact way in which a particular blade couples its bending and twisting deflections appears the key to this mystery.

The use of a flat trailing-edge tab has a secondary benefit. As mentioned above, the theoretical position of the aerodynamic center is at the quarter-chord and wind-tunnel tests of many airfoils have confirmed the theory. They also show a trend, however, in which the center moves slightly aft if the airfoil has a small trailing-edge angle — that is if the top and bottom surfaces approach being parallel.

Tests of the Hughes HH-02 with the flat add-on tab show its aerodynamic center is at about the 27% chord instead of 25%. Since the blade must be balanced with its CG ahead of its aerodynamic center to prevent flutter, the further aft the aerodynamic center, the less leading-

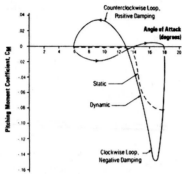

Figure 48-22 Moment Characteristics of Rapidly Oscillating Airfoil Model in Wind Tunnel

edge balance weight is required to satisfy this very important dynamic criteria.

Stall flutter

When any airfoil stalls, its center of lift moves aft and produces a nose-down pitching moment. This can lead to a series of events known as "stall flutter".

Imagine a rotor with a high angle of attack on the retreating side and relatively flexible blades. When the blade stalls, it will get a nose-down pitching moment that may be enough to twist it down and out of stall, where the moment will disappear, allowing it to spring back into stall. This cycle might be repeated several times as the blade traverses the retreating side.

This flutter will be reinforced in some cases by the blade taking energy out of the passing air in a situation of "negative damping". This moment characteristic can be traced to the shedding of the leading-edge vortex and to its subsequent passing across the chord at about half the free-stream velocity. It can be recognized in data from oscillating airfoil wind-tunnel tests when the history of pitching moment vs. angle of attack plots as a clockwise loop.

Figure Figure 48-22 shows the results for an airfoil rapidly oscillating between 6° and 18°. Until the airfoil stalls, the loop is going counterclockwise and the damping is positive. Above stall, the moment is more nose-up when it is pitching up than when it is pitching down. On a blade, this moment characteristic would try to twist the blade in an unstable direction — and if allowed to persist could eventually produce some high oscillatory loads and vibration.

Fortunately, the blade does not dwell in the high stall portion of the disc for very long and has a chance to calm down after it leaves the retreating side. Rotor designers have some control over the situation by choosing the stiffness of their blades and controls. Very stiff systems do not permit significant twisting and therefore resist flutter. Very soft systems oscillate so slowly that they only go through a part of a cycle before leaving the critical azimuth region and therefore don't produce oscillating loads but only a change of trim.

Rotors that are neither too stiff nor too soft, however, are "just right" and might oscillate several times at high amplitude, shaking the helicopter and adding to the fatigue loading.

Mach tuck

Even with a reflexed trailing edge which produces nearly zero pitching moment in most conditions, the modern cambered airfoil will still produce nose-down pitching

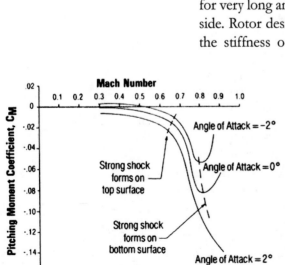

Figure 48-23 Mach Tuck Characteristics of a Modern, Cambered Airfoil

moments when it operates at high enough Mach numbers where compressibility is a factor. This is due to the changes in surface-pressure distributions that occur as shock waves are formed.

Figure 48-23 shows the "Mach tuck" characteristics of a modern rotor airfoil operating at three low angles of attack typical of the advancing tip. The origin of the sudden change is the rearrangement of the pressure distribution as strong shock waves are formed, first on the top surface and then on the bottom.

It is no surprise to find that the tuck Mach number is approximately the same as the drag-divergence Mach number. The blade tips entering the advancing side at high enough forward speed to put them into the compressibility region are operating at high dynamic pressures and are therefore very sensitive to Mach tuck. To alleviate these compressibility effects, many modern rotor blades have swept-back tips to reduce the effective Mach number.

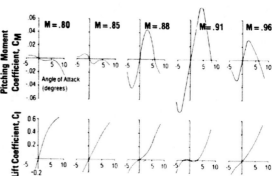

Figure 48-24   Transonic Mach Number Characteristics of NACA 0012 Airfoil

A strange phenomenon

The generation of shock waves, first on one surface and then on the other, can produce an odd characteristic over a narrow Mach-number range. The pitching moments will suddenly change from one direction to the other and then reverse again as the angle of attack is changed. An illustration of this is given in Figure 48-24.

Not only does the pitching-moment coefficient reverse in the unique Mach-number range but so does the lift coefficient at the most critical point. The phenomenon was discovered in flight on a high-speed Sikorsky helicopter, where it caused the blades to hop out-of-track every other revolution. Special design features are used to prevent this on modern rotors.

49 The Lead-Lag Hinge

When Juan de la Cierva developed the flapping hinge for his autogyro, he solved the basic problem of a rotor flying through the air edgewise by allowing it to use flapping motion. This balances the non-symmetric aerodynamics between the advancing and retreating blades.

After flying the aircraft for some time, however, a new problem became apparent. The blades began to show structural distress from back-and-forth motion in the rotor's plane. Just because the lift was balanced around the rotor did not mean the drag was also balanced.

Besides aerodynamic drag, there was a dynamic effect because the joint that was produced by the flapping hinges between the shaft and the rotor was not a constant-speed joint. So when the rotor was flapping, the blades' inertia produced oscillating dynamic loads in the rotor's plane.

When Cierva realized that the in-plane bending moment at the blade root was high enough to cause trouble, he naturally decided that if one hinge was good, two would be better. So he installed a vertical pin in the blade that gave it the freedom to move back and forth—to lead and to lag.

This eliminated the in-plane bending moment at that point and solved his immediate problem. This lag hinge may still be seen on many modern helicopter rotors with "fully articulated" rotor hubs.

Blade hinges, whether for flapping or for lagging, turn the blade into a kind of pendulum with centrifugal forces, rather than gravity, supplying the restoring moment. Figure 49-1 shows the centrifugal forces acting on the blade both in flapping and in lead-lag motion. The effects, as dictated by the geometry, are distinctly different. In flapping, the centrifugal force strongly tries to flatten the rotor disc.

On the other hand (in the top view), the in-plane centrifugal force has a relatively weaker effect in trying to straighten the blade about the lag hinge. In this case, the restoring effect is zero if the lag hinge is on the center of rotation but increases with offset (which the blade must

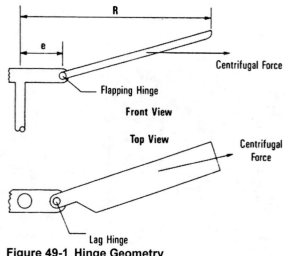

Figure 49-1 Hinge Geometry

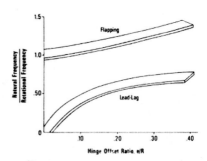

Figure 49-2 Natural Frequency Ratios

have to prevent the shaft from simply spinning in the bearing while the rotor stands still).

The differences between the effects of centrifugal force on flapping and on lead-lag motion result in differences in the motion's natural frequency. In each case, the natural frequency can be related to the rotor speed and is a function of the hinge offset ratio, as shown in Figure 49-2.

With zero hinge offset, flapping starts out in resonance (the natural frequency being equal to the rotor's rotational frequency). It then slowly increases as the hinge offset is increased because the blade's moment of inertia outboard of the hinge decreases.

Lead-lag motion starts out at zero and also slowly increases. It would reach resonance if the offset ratio went as high as two-thirds.

A blade with a lag hinge is known as a "soft in-plane blade." If the designer chooses to build a blade without a lag hinge, he has two options: use structural flexibility in place of the hinge, as on the West-land Lynx, or make it stiff in-plane, as on the Bell two-bladed rotor (see Figure 49-3). In the latter case, the in-plane natural frequency becomes much higher than the rotational frequency.

Ground resonance

Cierva's lag-hinge invention solved his immediate structural problem and allowed the autogyro's development to proceed. It did, however, plant a booby trap that later almost stopped the development. The early autogyros had no means of pre-spinning the rotor with engine power. They had to taxi awhile so aerodynamic forces could speed up the rotor prior to takeoff.

One day in the 1930s, a Kellett autogyro was completing this maneuver and apparently hit a rock with one wheel. In two seconds, the aircraft was a heap of rubble; it had literally shaken itself "to pieces.

The reason for this dramatic event was not immediately apparent. It did, however, draw the attention of two NACA (the predecessor to NASA) flutter specialists, Robert Coleman and Arnold Feingold. With some clever precomputer mathematics, they were able to explain what happened and even provide the engineering fix that would prevent it from reoccurring.

They explained in a classic paper that if, for some treason, the blades became displaced unequally about their lag hinges, the rotor center of gravity would be forced away from the center of rotation. In most flight conditions, such an imbalance will rapidly right itself as the individual blades sort themselves out.

Figure 49-3 Types of Hubs: Westland Lynx, soft in-plane (top); Bell222, stiff in-plane (bottom)

In this sorting-out process, each blade leads and lags in such a way as to spiral the combined center of gravity in toward the shaft where it belongs. The potential problem exists if the aircraft is not airborne. A gust of wind, a sudden control motion, a hard landing, or a jolt while taxiing can displace the blades. The resultant whirling motion due to the offset centrifugal force may be at just the right frequency to rock the airframe on its landing gear. Figure 49-4 illustrates the possibility.

Once that happens, the two motions get in step. Instead of spiraling gently inward, the center of gravity spirals violently outward-producing a rotating force at the rotor hub that no helicopter or autogyro can withstand. The analysis shows that a two-bladed rotor is much more susceptible to this type of mechanical instability than a rotor with more blades. For that reason, you don't see lag hinges on two-bladed rotors. Instead the mast is flexible or mounted softly to the fuselage to allow hub motion to reduce the in-plane moments.

The fix that Coleman and Feingold deduced from their equations was to add damping, both about the lag hinge and at the landing gear. Thus if you look at a helicopter with a fully articulated rotor, you should be able to identify some sort of damping device at each of these points.

Lead-lag dampers come in several configurations. The old ones were generally hydraulic dampers much like those used on door closers. Other designers chose to use friction dampers. Both types needed frequent maintenance and adjustment so designers were happy when special elastomeric materials with high internal damping became available. You will see these low-maintenance dampers on most helicopters designed in the past 15 years.

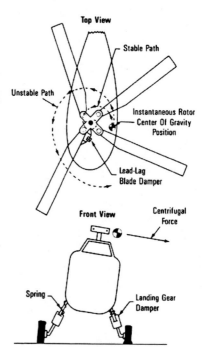

Figure 49-4 Conditions Affecting Ground resonance

Landing-gear dampers are usually hydraulic, much like the shock absorbers on your car, since they are also used to soften hard landings by absorbing energy. In addition, tires also contribute to the damping.

Another way to prevent ground resonance is to put the lag hinges so far outboard that the in-plane natural frequency is too high to couple with the frequency of the aircraft on its landing gear. This was done on the Brantly (now Hynes) design shown in Figure 49-5. Its lag hinges are about 40% of the way out the blade. No damper at either place is required to prevent ground resonance in this aircraft.

Figure 49-5 Hynes H-5 with Large Lag Hinge Offset

Air resonance

On some helicopters, a phenomenon similar to ground resonance has occurred in flight. This, naturally, is called "air resonance." It was apparently a problem on the early Sikorsky VS-300, which originally flew with dampers installed about the flapping hinges but not about the lag hinges. Hover was steady but when forward flight was attempted, a violent rocking motion started.

This was cured by switching the dampers from the flapping hinges, where they were not needed, to the lag hinges where they solved the problem. Other manifestations of the problems that lag hinges or in-plane flexibility can cause have appeared during some models' development stage in the form of pylon-whirl instability on tilt-rotor aircraft and some types of aeroelastic instabilities on hingeless blades. Fortunately, so far, these have all been problems that could be solved by making design changes.

50 Pitch-Link Loads

"The pitch-link loads are too high!" This dreaded statement prompted by looking at the data from an instrumented helicopter's early test flight is all too common.

It is common because we still do not know where all these loads come from. Therefore, the designer often does not receive the needed guidance to make the pitch links and the other rotor control-system components strong enough to indefinitely resist the fatigue loads that may be generated in flight.

What it is

The pitch link is the vertical—or nearly vertical—member that connects the blade pitch horn to the rotating swashplate (Figure 50-1). Its sole function is to make sure the blade responds to the collective and cyclic control commands corresponding to the swashplate's position.

It is generally a simple rod with self-aligning bearings at each end. This means that the pitch link carries only tension and compression loads since bending moments must be zero at each end. This simple structure makes it is easy to equip with strain gauges, and interpreting the results as loads in the control system is relatively straightforward.

Figure 50-1 Upper Control System On Schweizer 300

1. Feathering Bearing
2. Flapping Hinge
3. Pitch Horn
4. Lead-lag Hinge
5. Pitch Link
6. Rotating Swashplate
7. Stationary Swashplate

Innocent sources

How does the pitch link get loaded up high enough to surprise even experienced helicopter engineers? We know some answers, but as yet not all of them. In the first place, we know of several apparent sources that turn out to be relatively innocent.

You might think that because the blade has inertia about its feathering axis, it would mean a resisting load would be produced as the blade pitches up and down each revolution. However, a study of the dynamics, including the role of centrifugal forces acting on each blade element, shows that the cyclic feathering motion with a frequency of once per revolution actually puts the blade into resonance.

A system in resonance theoretically requires no force to keep it swinging. Therefore the oscillating pitch-link load due to cyclic feathering should be zero, although there will always be a steady force proportional to the collective pitch that is trying to force the blade toward its flat-pitch position.

The absence of an oscillating pitch-link load, due to the blade being in resonance, would only strictly be true if the rotor were operating in a vacuum. Going through cyclic pitch in air does introduce aerodynamic damping, due to the rate of pitch change, but this can be shown to be relatively small for a blade pitching through only one cycle during each revolution.

Another possible aerodynamic source is the change in the airfoil's aerodynamic pitching moment as the angle of attack changes. But most designers of helicopter blades are careful to select airfoils that have little or no pitching moment about the airfoil's aerodynamic center—the point where the lift can be assumed to be concentrated and which is on or near its quarter chord—in the normal ranges of angle of attack and Mach number where the rotor operates.

For many years, the preferred airfoils for autogyro and helicopter blades were symmetrical, such as the NACA 0012 and 0015, because they have no pitching moments. Even after designers began using nonsymmetrical airfoils to take advantage of their higher lift characteristics, they were still careful to modify them by bending the trailing edge up (reflexing) to nullify their basic pitching moment.

Additionally, the designer lines up both the center of gravity of the blade and the feathering axis on the quarter chord so that neither flapping motion nor changes in lift are expected to produce pitching moments on the blade. Thus, once again, we have failed to identify a significant source of high pitch-link loads and the designer might feel justified in saving weight in this component.

Yes, but....

Note that the above discussion was limited to "normal ranges of angle of attack and Mach number." Outside these limits, any airfoil will produce aerodynamic pitching moments either due to stall or due to compressibility effects. In each case, the result is a nosedown pitching moment as the low-pressure area on the top of the airfoil moves toward the trailing edge. Thus at high speed, we would expect to generate nosedown aerodynamic pitching moments on the advancing tip due to compressibility and on the retreating tip due to stall.

It would be nice to be able to say that the aerodynamicist could predict these accurately enough to be able to give the designer realistic loads for all the elements of the control system, including the pitch links. Unfortunately, the complicated aerodynamics in both of these regions are still not well understood.

One result of this lack of understanding can be seen on the AH-64 Apache. As first flown, the blades had straight tips. At high speeds, the loads at the hydraulic-control actuators were significantly higher than had been designed for. The problem was traced to a nosedown "spike" generated as each blade encountered compressibility on the advancing side.

Rather than redesign the actuators that had just gone through a long and expensive development and qualification process, it was decided to change the blade design by incorporating sweep to fool the tip into thinking it was at a lower Mach number. This solved the problem, though at the expense of higher blade cost.

If the retreating tip is in deep stall, as it might be in high-speed level flight or when pulling high load factors at any speed, the resulting nosedown pitching moments will also generate loads in the control system.

A typical result of flight tests on a new helicopter is shown in Figure 21-2 where cyclic loads in the pitch link are plotted against forward speed. At some speed, the loads, which in this case are attributed to retreating blade stall, are above the endurance limit. This means that they would eventually start fatigue cracks if much flying were done above the critical speed.

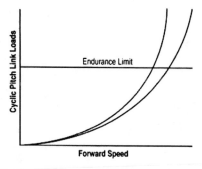

Figure 50-2 Typical Result Of Flight Test

There is another source of potential stall that primarily happens during descents or flares when one blade flies through, or close to, the trailing tip vortex shed by the blades ahead of it. The resulting high angles of attack can produce stall over a local area with resulting pitching moments. This effect adds to the "rocky road" roughness that most helicopters encounter during a landing flare.

If the blade is attached to the hub through a strap pack as on most McDonnell Douglas helicopters, or with a flexbeam as on many of the new bearingless rotors, feathering motion will produce control-system loads as these components are twisted. To minimize the steady force, it is fairly common to install the blades such that the strap pack or flexbeam is not twisted at a collective-pitch value corresponding to cruise flight.

Blade flexing

All of the above discussion has ignored the fact that the blade may not remain a straight piece of structure while being subjected to many complex aerodynamic and dynamic effects. If you have ever seen movies of a blade taken from a hub-mounted camera, you know that it does a wild dance out there.

As a matter of fact, a normal long and limber blade has more characteristics of a chain than a beam, since most of the stiffening is produced by centrifugal forces rather than by structure. A chain rotating in a plane has a natural frequency close to three time per revolution with a "mode shape" as shown in Figure 50-3, and so do most blades.

Figure 50-3 Mode Shape For Rotating Chain

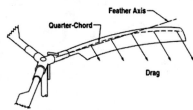

Figure 50-4 Drag Produces Pitch-Link Loads On Deflected Blade

A blade bending flapwise introduces a new source of pitch-link loads in that the drag on at least part of the blade will have a moment arm around the feathering axis to produce either compression or tension in the pitch links (Figure 50-4).

Similarly, chordwise bending offsets the aerodynamic center from the feathering axis and gives lift a chance to produce a pitching moment. At the same time, accelerations associated with flapwise bending, chordwise bending, and torsion will produce inertia forces that may couple in odd ways and will add to or subtract from the loads that get into the control system.

The challenge

You can see that the loads engineer—who should be a combination of an aerodynamicist and a dynamicist—has a difficult job if he is to accurately predict the fatigue loads that should be planned for when designing the aircraft. As far as I know, no one has yet been able to satisfactorily calculate pitch-link loads that agree with measured pitch-link loads. For that reason, the loads engineer often will try to make a logical scaling from some previous helicopter.

Historically, this has not been a very successful approach. Parts have had to be redesigned, as on the Apache, or elaborate monitoring schemes, such as the Cruise Control Indicator on the Boeing CH-47, have had to be developed to help the pilot avoid flight conditions where the loads can do fatigue damage.

The hope for this situation may be in the exploitation of some of those mysterious dynamic couplings that sometimes increase the oscillatory loads and sometimes decrease them. If by a good understanding of these effects, we can emphasize the latter while minimizing the former, we will have a better chance of not only avoiding the need for design changes after the helicopter starts its flight tests, but of actually being able to use smaller and lighter parts in the control system.

51 Considerations Of Blade/Hub Geometry

After studying the blade geometry of the main and tail rotors of the Robinson R22 and the Bell 206, Steven Fraser, an aircraft maintenance engineer in Australia, concluded that not all designers of two-bladed rotors agree as to how a blade should be attached to a hub. His conclusion generated a few questions.

Main-rotor offsets

Submitting drawings of the geometry of the two main-rotor blade attachments (Figure 51-1), Fraser asks:

• Why are the feathering axis and the center of gravity (CG) offset on the Robinson blades?

• Why does the Bell 206 have the blade-retention bolt in front of the feathering axis?

• Why does the Bell 206 manual caution "Sweep blades aft, never forward?"

I was unable to come up with good answers so I sent the letter to the designers.

About the R22, Frank Robinson wrote, "The 0.28-inch offset allows the blade centrifugal force to compensate for part of the rotor torque, thus reducing the moment carried by the pitch-change bearings.

"The 0.7-inch forward offset of the blade root places the blade root's shear center closer to the center of the pitch-change bearings for structural reasons."

Figure 51-2 shows how the centrifugal force acting at the forward-shifted CG has a forward component that opposes the rear-pointing drag force.

On the same subject, C. E. Covington, Bell Helicopter's chief of rotor system design wrote, "On the Robinson helicopter, the location of the blade CG ahead of the center of rotation is primarily to balance the steady drive torque with the blade centrifugal force.

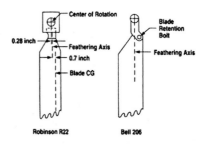

Figure 51-1 Blade/Hub Geometry

Figure 51-2 Effect Of Forward-Shifted Blade CG

"This 'torque offset,' as we call it, is incorporated in some Bell rotors, including the Model 412 four-bladed rotor, and the V-22 and XV-15 proprotors, and some tail rotors.

"The two-bladed main rotors—206, 212, UH-1, 540, and 214—have the feathering axis passing through the center of rotation and no torque offset is employed."

A long time ago

Answering Eraser's question about the location of the 206's blade-retention bolt was a bit harder, as the designers of the 206 rotor are no longer around.

"I believe," Covington explained, "it was to allow the main bolt to pass directly through the spar extrusion; this would have not been the case had the bolt been located on the pitch-change axis. [This is illustrated in Figure 51-3.]

"On the hubs with drag braces, this forward location causes a sharing of the centrifugal force between the main and drag-brace bolts; this keeps the drag-brace bolt loaded in tension, thus reducing fretting in the joints.

"I don't believe there is any aeroelastic reason for the bolt location on the 206 [which does not have drag braces], since the blade is rigidly aligned in flight by the blade bolt and the root end latches."

Blade sweep

Covington's answer to Fraser's question concerning sweeping the Bell 206 main-rotor blades is short and to the point. "The caution to sweep aft, never forward, is to avoid the possibility of a pitchup instability of a forward swept blade."

The Bell 206 blade can be swept fore or aft using the sweep adjustment nuts (shown in Figure 51-4). But on a swept-forward blade (or wing), the lift is acting in such a way as to twist the blade noseup, thus increasing its lift even more (Figure 51-5.)

If the blade were not stiff enough, it could become unstable and twist off. This "aeroelastic instability" is what Bell is trying to prevent by cautioning not to sweep the blade forward.

Tail rotors too

Also questioning the design of tail rotors, Fraser pointed out that the blades on the R22 and Schweizer Model 300 are swept forward in the direction of rotation about 3°. He asks if this is designed to reduce pedal forces and, if so, how?

Robinson responds, "The tail-rotor blade's quarter chord is forward of the pitch axis to offset part of the blade's 'tennis racket' moment and the negative pitching moment due to camber."

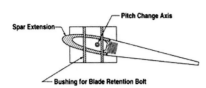

Figure 51-3 Bell 206 Hub Detail

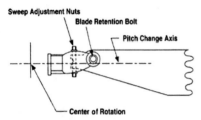

Figure 51-4 Blade Retention With Sweep Provisions

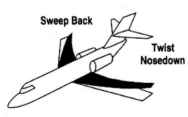
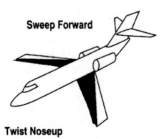

Figure 51-5 Wing Twist Coupled With Wing Bending

The tennis-racket effect (named for the feeling in the wrist when the racket is swung at an angle) is produced by centrifugal forces acting on the blade's leading and trailing edges. It causes them to want to fly at flat pitch (Figure 51-6).

Without special provisions, such as a bungee or helper spring, the pilot must exert steady pedal forces to hold the pitch required for generating the antitorque thrust.

Another factor, the R22 and the 300 use cambered airfoils on the tail-rotor blades. These airfoils produce nosedown pitching moments, which also would require compensation with pedal forces. By sweeping the blades forward slightly, the lift acting ahead of the feathering axis can overcome these effects and help the pilot hold the pitch.

But isn't forward sweep dangerous?

Why, you might ask, is forward sweep dangerous on main-rotor blades, but is used on tail blades? It is because, in contrast to main-rotor blades, tail-rotor blades are usually stubby and have sufficient stiffness to avoid instability for moderate amounts of forward sweep.

However, Bell has used a somewhat different scheme on its recent tail rotors. The OH-58D, for example, has a different alignment than previous Bell tail rotors and actually has some aft sweep.

"The OH-58D pitch-change axis," Covington explains, "is at the blade's one-third chord, so that the effective aerodynamic center (at the one-quarter chord position) helps the pilot pitch the blade up against the tennis-racket moment, acting in the same manner as the forward sweep in the R22 and Model 300 tail rotors."

The discussion above illustrates some of the subtle considerations that a rotor engineer must consider in order to produce an effective and safe design.

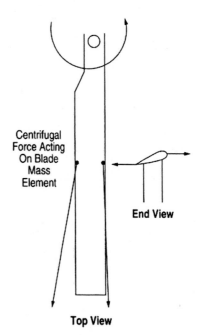

Centrifugal Force Acting On Blade Mass Element

End View

Top View

Figure 51-6 Twisting Moment Due To Centrifugal Forces

52 Blade Anhedral

As a term, "anhedral" isn't one many recognize. Yet, it's popping up more often in aeronautical circles, and it pertains to a feature that is likely to show up on more helicopters—a drooped rotor-blade tip. The feature is evident on the Sikorsky-Boeing RAH-66 Comanche mockup and the Westland Lynx Mk9. In the aeronautical world, this droop is known as anhedral.

First, dihedral

Most airplane wings are installed with a "dihedral angle," i.e. the two wing panels slope up in order to improve lateral stability. The word comes from two Greek roots for "two" and "surface."

In some airplanes—especially those with high wings—the lateral stability is already too high, and designers choose to slant the wings down instead of up. You can see this on large high-wing military transports and bombers. To distinguish this arrangement from the usual dihedral, someone— without much respect for Greek word roots— decided to call it "anhedral." The prefix "an" usually means "without."

Why use anhedral?

One effect that hurts hover performance is the tendency for the tip vortex from one blade to stay close to the plane of the rotor disc. The tip vortex does not start down immediately because the wake contracts. A comparison of the vortex pattern with and without contraction can be seen in Figure 52-1.

Wake contraction makes the older vortices force the youngest ones up toward the rotor plane. If a whirl-tower test is performed on a humid day, the tip vortices will become visible due to moisture condensation. In this condition, one can often see the tip vortex from one blade remain in the tip-path plane until the next blade actually strikes it (Figure 52-2).

Due to the vortex's close proximity, the following blade experiences changes in its local induced velocity, and this can cause such large discontinuities in the angle-of-attack distribution. These discontinuities can be large enough to force local stall—resulting in a drag penalty and decrease in hover performance.

Without Wake Contraction

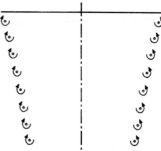

With Wake Contraction

Figure 52-1 Tip Vortex Locations

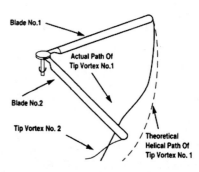

Figure 52-2 Blade-Tip Vortex Interference Effect In Hover

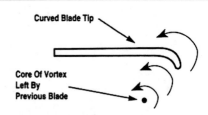

Figure 52-3 Vortex Inducing Only Tangential Velocities On Curved Blade Tip

What anhedral does

By drooping the blade tip with anhedral, the tip vortex is deposited lower and has more clearance from the following blade. This results in less disturbance of the blade's angle-of-attack distribution and better performance. Tests carried out at both Sikorsky and at Aerospatiale (now Eurocopter), show that the hover figure of merit can be increased by 2% to 4% by changing from flat tips to those with about 10° of anhedral.

For one Aerospatiale test, the rotor installed on a Super Puma Mk II had anhedral obtained with curvature. This has the theoretical advantage of further reducing the effect. If the offending vortex were located at the center of curvature (Figure 52-3), it would induce only tangential flow along the blade, with no change in local angle of attack.

In addition to improving hover performance, the anhedral tips produced a quieter rotor, as Sikorsky whirl-tower tests showed.

Climb and forward

The Sikorsky flight-test program with a UH-60 Black Hawk included vertical climbs. Data indicates that the beneficial effect of the anhedral disappeared at a rate of climb of about 1,000 feet per minute. This is to be expected, since the climbing helicopter is moving away from the pattern of tip vortices and is thus curing the problem on its own.

In forward flight, the Sikorsky flight test showed no appreciable change in performance compared to the flat tips of the standard rotor; the Aerospatiale data showed a slight improvement at low thrust levels but none at high levels.

Aerospatiale's calculations indicate that the anhedral should help when compressibility effects on the advancing tip are significant. For a straight blade, wind-tunnel tests show that the highest compressibility effects occur not right at the azimuth for maximum local Mach number (on the right side for American helicopters), but beyond it, in the second quadrant.

For a blade with tip sweep, this tendency is more pronounced. In the second quadrant, the blades become aerodynamically unswept, thus putting the highest compressibility losses in this region. Aerospatiale's analysis indicates that anhedral has an opposite effect. It is detrimental in the first quadrant but beneficial in the second, thus partially compensating for the other trends.

What's bad about anhedral?

Because centrifugal force would like to straighten the blade out, it is necessary to strengthen the blade to maintain the anhedral angle. This involves some weight penalty.

Aerospatiale also found in its flight tests that the cockpit vibration and the loads in the rotor and control system were higher than with conventional blades. High-blade loads due to anhedral were also found during some of NASA's earlier wind-tunnel model tests.

On its Super Puma testbed, Aerospatiale installed pendulum blade dampers to achieve satisfactory vibration levels. However, the weight and complexity penalties were apparently too high, since the production helicopter is without anhedral—"ananhedral" so to speak.

The anhedral factor is another illustration of the dilemma that faces helicopter designers: "Whatever helps hover, hurts forward flight and whatever helps forward flight, hurts hover."

53 Blade Strikes

Placing a moving part in close proximity to a non-moving part is the source of many an engineering problem. It is especially true in the helicopter business where engineers are motivated to make the aircraft as compact as possible.

Hub-fuselage proximity

The requirements for both the UTTAS (Utility Tactical Transport Aircraft System) and AAH (Advanced Attack Helicopter) design competitions— resulting in the Sikorsky Black Hawk and the McDonnell Douglas Apache—are a case in point. Both aircraft were designed for transport in a C-141 airplane, and then were to be prepared for flight in two hours or less. The Lockheed C-141 has an eight-foot (2.5-m)-high cargo area.

Sikorsky and Boeing competed for UTTAS, and Hughes (now McDonnell Douglas Helicopter Co.) and Bell Helicopter Textron squared off for the AAH. Each used a "kneeling" landing gear to minimize the helicopter's height, and all but Bell located their rotors low and close to the fuselage. (Bell designed an ingenious scheme for telescoping the mast into the transmission of its AH-63.)

Too close for comfort

The three companies who placed their rotors close to the fuselage all encountered difficulty. Both UTTAS prototypes were plagued by high vibration, which at least partially came from blade loads induced by the upflow of air over the front of the fuselage.

Both Sikorsky and Boeing raised their rotors by lengthening the rotor mast. They thus minimized the upflow effects, but also made it necessary to remove the rotor and transmission for C-141 transport. The Black Hawk first flown thus appeared different from the one finally delivered to the Army (Figure 53-1).

That the Apache did not suffer from the same source of high vibration was probably due to its much-narrower forward fuselage. It was found, however, that when initiating a pushover maneuver, the Apache's blades came down over the nose far enough to graze the canopy's top.

Figure 53-1 Rotor Positions On The UH-60 Black Hawk

Figure 53-2 Rotor Positions On The AH-64 Apache

To cure this unacceptable situation, the mast was lengthened first 10 inches (25 cm), and then after further testing, another six inches (15 cm). This change (Figure 53-2) forces a disassembly for transport in a C-141 (but not in the larger C-5). Also, raising the rotors on each of these helicopters reduced cockpit noise due to "canopy drumming" as the blades pass over.

In flight, the moments that accompany blade flapping will tend to move the helicopter out of the rotor's way (not always fast enough). But on the ground, the helicopter has no way to escape. So, when the rotor is up to full operating speed, inadvertent cyclic-pitch-control inputs may cause the blades to strike the fuselage. This can also happen at low rotor speeds as well, if a gust or the wake from a nearby helicopter induces high flapping.

Appropriate cyclic pitch

The amount of forward cyclic pitch designed into the control system depends primarily on the helicopter's high-speed goal. It must be enough pitch to trim the rotor aerodynamically at the maximum speed with some margin for maneuvering. The rearward cyclic pitch must be enough to trim in rearward flight and/or to make a noseup flare for a quick stop or autorotation landing.

A survey of existing helicopters reveals a range of from 20° forward cyclic pitch to 15° aft pitch. When sitting on the ground, rotor flapping will be equal to these angles if the pilot inadvertently moves his cyclic stick to the stops.

Most rotors are designed with droop stops that hold the blade up when the rotor is not turning. But being so close to the hinges, they are relatively ineffective against the large aerodynamic forces acting on the blade's outboard portion. So the blade will bend around the stop almost as if it were not there.

Therefore, to be absolutely safe, the clearance angles for fore and aft blade flapping should be at least as large as the fore and aft cyclic-pitch angles.

In the past, this rule-of-thumb has not generally been observed on the assumption that no pilot would inadvertently use full cyclic pitch on the ground. Pilots have, however, and several cases of both fore and aft blade strikes have been attributed to this cause.

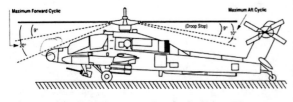

Figure 53-3 Full Forward Cyclic Striking The Apache's PNVS

The Apache has 20° of forward cyclic pitch. Although seldom used in flight, enough forward cyclic was inadvertently imposed during two ground incidents to make the blade flap down over the nose and contact the sight for the pilot's night-vision system. The problem is illustrated in Figure 53-3.

Blade clearance

Hinged, flexible blades are free to bend and flap. Centrifugal forces tend to keep them straight and nearly perpendicular to the shaft, but there are aerodynamic and dynamic forces that want to bend and move the blades. Regarding clearance between the blades and the airframe, these forces can create a critical situation when the helicopter contacts the ground either firmly or during a run-on landing.

Tail-boom strikes

Chopping off the tail boom with a blade is an all-too-frequent occurrence. Most often this type of accident happens as the helicopter makes a hard vertical touchdown or a run-on landing following autorotation. There are two contributing factors in these accidents: the blades which keep on coming down even after the fuselage has stopped; and the sudden nosedown motion, following the contact of aft-mounted wheels or the back of skids, that makes the pilot naturally want to pull the stick back to counteract it. The possible results are shown in Figure 53-4.

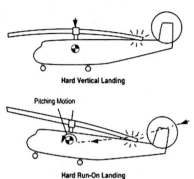

Figure 53-4 Hard Landings Invite Tail-Boom Strikes

To counteract these tail-boom strikes, designers have sometimes been forced to redesign the tail boom. An example of such a redesign was the Sikorsky S-55 (H-19), which originally had the tail boom coming straight out of the main fuselage. After a series of accidents, it was redesigned with the tail boom angled down 3° as illustrated in Figure 53-5.

Tail-boom strikes have also happened in flight. The most common scenario is during the entry to autorotation as the collective pitch is lowered. The rotor flaps forward since the advancing blade sees a greater reduction in lift than the retreating blade. The pilot overreacts to the sudden nosedown pitching moment by suddenly pulling the cyclic stick back. With this action, the rotor flaps back, but the tail boom is still rising because of the initial air-craft-nosedown motion. With insufficient clearance, a blade strike results.

Figure 53-5 Sikorsky S-55 (H-19) Tail-Boom Angles

Tail-boom strikes have also happened in maneuvering flight. In forward flight, the rotor is trimmed out approximately perpendicular to the rotor mast with forward cyclic pitch. The amount of rear flapping that can be induced with sudden full-aft stick motion corresponds to the sum of this trim value plus the maximum aft cyclic designed into the swashplate.

It is therefore possible to make the blades flap a surprising amount down toward the tail boom. Slow cyclic-stick pulls will not get the pilot into trouble because the noseup moment applied to the helicopter by aft flapping will tend to move the tail boom down out of the way.

Other incidents

Flapping to the limits of lateral cyclic pitch (usually not more than 10°) generally will not cause a blade strike unless the helicopter is equipped with long wings. But for rotors with large hinge offsets, too much lateral flapping may cause the helicopter to roll over on the ground. To guard against this type of accident, some helicopters are equipped with stick locks, which are either manually engaged or automatically activated through mechanisms that sense landing-gear compression.

Another scenario involves gusts, which are generally less of a factor than cyclic pitch when the rotor is up to full speed. But at low rotor speeds—during startup or shutdown—gusts are of concern since the blade is free to flap and bend in the absence of the stiffening effects of strong centrifugal forces. For very low rotor speeds, the aerodynamic forces are much less than at full rotor speed, and droop stops are of some value. Many rotors have spring-loaded, centrifugally operated droop stops that prevent the blades from going below the rotor hub's height until the rotor speed is near its operating value.

Despite this there have been tail-boom strikes during startups and shutdowns in a high wind or when another helicopter was landing or even taxiing nearby. The U.S. Army requires that the rotor can be safely started and stopped in 45-knot winds, while the U.S. Navy requires a 60-knot capability.

Even while parked, rotor blades may want to fly. At least one incident occurred when one large helicopter landed beside another. The recirculating rotor wake lifted the parked helicopter's blade, which then suddenly dropped against its droop stop leaving a permanent bend about two-thirds of the way out. To guard against this possibility, the designer should provide some means of tying the blades down or quickly folding and stowing them after landing.

Tail rotors, too

The tail rotor does not have a cyclic-pitch system that makes it flap more than the designers allowed for, but it does flap or teeter in response to collective pitch, sideslip, and yaw rate. Unlike the main rotor in flight, the tail rotor cannot move the tail boom out of the way as it flaps, and so tail rotors mounted on a too-short shaft have flapped enough to strike a tail boom or fin during rapid pedal inputs at high speeds.

To guard against this possibility, the designer of a new helicopter should enlist the help of an aero-dynamicist who can estimate the maximum tail-rotor flapping under the worst possible conditions.

54 Designing For Maneuverability

What makes the best helicopter for air-to-air combat? Currently, no one knows for sure. Except for some poorly documented encounters in the Middle East, there is little reference. There is, however, plenty of thinking, talking, and study on the subject.

Perhaps the most valuable experience came from a series of mock dogfights undertaken at the Naval Air Test Center at Patuxent River, Md., under the auspices of the Army's Aviation Applied Technology Directorate.

Starting in 1983, these well-instrumented tests pitted helicopters one-on-one in simulated air combat. The participating aircraft included the Bell AH-1S, OH-58, and 406; Sikorsky S-76 and UH-60; MBB BK-117; McDonnell Douglas 530MG and AH-64 Apache; and the Aerospatiale HH-65A Dolphin.

Safe dogfighting

For most tests, the weapons were fixed guns. They were pointed just as airplanes have done since 1914, when fixed-wing air-to-air combat emerged. The exception was the Apache, which had a turreted gun. Gun cameras and laser simulators, of course, were substituted for the real things.

These were simulated engagements between pilots who would be tipping brews together at the officer's club two hours later, so there was an understandable desire to make them as safe as possible. For example, to prevent accidents due to split-second inattention, the helicopters were kept 500 feet (150 m) apart and that was also the minimum altitude above the ground.

These restrictions would obviously not apply to real combat, which might well involve nap-of-the-earth flying. They were especially unrealistic if one considers unfair dogfights where one guy has some buddies on the ground with antiaircraft weapons.

As we have seen in movies, the best "gun solution" is to get on the tail of the other aircraft. You can thus shoot at him while he can't shoot at you, and the lack of side wind makes for more accurate shooting. The

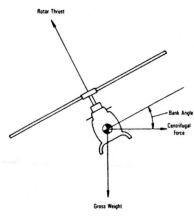

Figure 54-1 Forces Acting During Turn

dogfight then consists of quick turns and climbs to get behind and above the adversary.

In a helicopter, the best rate of climb occurs at its speed for minimum level flight power (about 50 to 80 knots). So, no matter how an engagement starts, it will degenerate to that airspeed range after the first pass. One pilot refers to the latter stages as a "knife fight in a telephone booth".

It is thus difficult to make a case for high-speed capability since even the fastest helicopter could not outrun a speeding bullet. On the other hand, quickly reaching the scene of the action may be important. It all depends on the commuting distance.

Quick turning

Except at very low speeds, most turns in forward flight are done by banking. The steeper the bank, the less time it takes to change direction. As shown in Figure 54-1, during a turn, the rotor must generate thrust to balance the centrifugal force as well as to support the helicopter's weight.

For a 60° bank angle, for example, the rotor thrust has to be twice as much as in level flight. Depending on the airspeed and helicopter, the power required to simultaneously maintain the bank angle, altitude, and airspeed will be 1.5 to four times that in level flight. Thus among the most important characteristics of an air-to-air fighting helicopter are high rotor-thrust capability and plenty of usable installed power.

The coordinated banked turn is not the combat pilot's only option. If he's sneaky, he might apply the helicopter's unique flight characteristics and cross-controls to turn without banking or bank without turning, to achieve an actual or psychological advantage over his adversary.

Rolling around

Besides sustaining a high bank angle, it is also important to be able to roll to that angle as quickly as possible. The shortest time depends both on the maximum rate of roll and maximum roll acceleration. For rotorcraft, each of these depends on different rotor parameters. As discussed in Chapter 7, the steady rate of roll is governed by gyroscopic laws as they apply to a rotor.

A little-appreciated fact about maximum roll rate is that it is essentially independent of rotor-hub type, whether it be teetering, hinged, or hingeless. This is because when a steady rate of roll is established, the tip-path plane is very close to perpendicular to the rotor shaft.

Any lateral flapping is only to generate a roll moment to overcome the small aerodynamic damping of the rest of the airframe. Any more flapping would generate a moment that would accelerate the fuselage. But no acceleration can exist if the roll velocity has already reached a steady value. For this condition, if little or no flapping exists, it does not matter how the blades are attached to the hub.

Limiting stick movement

The maximum rate of roll is directly proportional to the lateral cyclic pitch available to the pilot. This implies that a control-systems designer can make the response as high as he likes by simply providing enough swashplate travel.

There is, however, a limit to this. If the sensitivity to the control is too high, the pilot will find it difficult to hold the helicopter steady. As a matter of fact, he may even destabilize it by causing a pilot-induced oscillation (PIO) where the delay from the eye to the brain to the hand is just long enough to insure he does the wrong thing at the wrong time.

For a conventional control system with a center Stick, the limit is about 25° per second per inch of stick motion. Thus if the stick can move five inches to each side before running into the pilot's thighs, the maximum recommended rate of roll in each direction is about 125° per second. The use of a side-arm controller and possible nonlinear control laws enforced by a clever change this limitation on future helicopters.

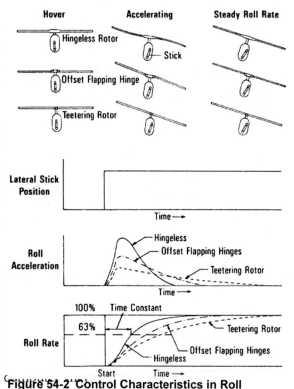

Figure 54-2 Control Characteristics in Roll

Time constants

Although rate of roll is independent of hub type, roll acceleration is not. Figure 54-2 shows the response to the same amount of cyclic pitch on three helicopters, which are identical except for their hub configurations. Although all three reach the same roll rate, the one with the hingeless rotor reaches it first. The acceleration is quantified by reference to a "time constant," which is the time required to achieve 63% of the steady rate. (Trust me. There is a good mathematical reason for picking 63%.)

Time constants for roll vary from about one half second for stiff, hingeless rotors to about one second for teetering rotors. For pitch, these time constants are three to six times as long because of the higher moment of inertia in that direction.

Decreasing the roll time constant by modifying rotor parameters can be achieved. It requires doing the same things that increase rotor damping, i.e. using high flapping hinges offset and heavy blades on a rotor placed high above the center of gravity.

The time constant is also decreased by minimizing the aircraft's moment of inertia about its roll axis. Another possibility involves quickening the control system with an electronic black box that causes the pilot's control

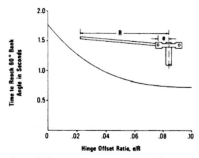

Figure 54-3 Effect of Hinge Offset on Maximum Roll Performance

motions to be delivered to the swashplate as a temporary overshoot. This is known as "control shaping."

Obviously, a small time constant is desired for maneuvering. But it isn't yet clear what maximum acceptable value it should be. Figure 54-3 shows the effect of hinge-offset ratio on the minimum time to achieve a 60° bank angle for a typical attack helicopter. As can be seen, most of the benefit is achieved with less than 5% hinge offset. This is because only the first part of the maneuver is controlled by acceleration.

The first autogyros used airplane-type elevators and ailerons for pitch and roll control. The rotor was only to produce lift and, as such, followed the airframe motion. Its flapping characteristics provided a desirable damping effect.

The magnitude of that damping divided by the airframe's appropriate moment of inertia was recognized as a useful index of damping. Later the invention of cyclic pitch made control by rotor possible, so the airplane control surfaces were eliminated.

With cyclic pitch, the rotor leads and the airframe follows. To a certain extent, this changes the importance of the inherent rotor damping. The stability -and-control engineer still uses it to predict what might happen several seconds after a disturbance; but in actual flight, the pilot usually doesn't allow appreciable uncontrolled pitch and roll rates to develop, so the exact value of this ratio of rotor damping to airframe inertia won't significantly influence his opinion of an aircraft's flying qualities.

Its significance does come in the back door, however, because its inverse (one divided by the damping ratio) is the time constant. The higher the damping ratio: the shorter the time constant.

Maneuvering at low load factors

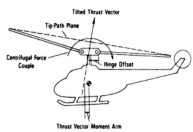

Figure 54-4 Two Sources of Control Moments

Control through cyclic pitch depends both on tilting the rotor thrust vector by tilting the rotor disc and by producing a hub moment using the centrifugal forces on the blades acting through a moment arm due to the offset as shown in Figure 54-4. Since the rotor flapping responds readily to cyclic pitch for any level of rotor thrust, the hinge offset contribution to control power will be a constant while the contribution of the thrust vector tilt will depend on the amount of thrust.

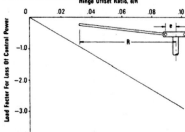

Figure 54-5 effect of Hinge Offset on Minimum Controllable Load Factor

Thus in a maneuver involving low load factors, such as a pushover, the rotor with hinge offset will maintain positive control to a lower load factor than will a teetering rotor which will lose it all at zero Gs. The result is shown on Figure 54-5 for a typical attack helicopter as the load factor at which all control power would be lost as a function of the hinge offset ratio. If the requirement were for controllable flight at minus 1 G, corresponding to a very fast pushover or even steady inverted flight, the offset should be no less than about 5% to provide an adequate margin of control.

Other considerations

As might be expected, there are some negative aspects of hinge offset. A rotor is unstable with angle of attack. The instability is such that if the rotor is hit by an up-gust, it will flap back producing a nose-up pitching moment on the helicopter that results in even more nose-up angle of attack.

Modern helicopter designers use a horizontal stabilizer to counteract this rotor instability. The more the hinge offset, the higher will be the destabilizing moment due to each degree of flapping and the bigger will be the horizontal stabilizer required to balance it. More tail area means more drag and airframe weight at the aft end where it pulls the center of gravity back - which in itself is bad for angle-of-attack stability.

Another consideration is that high hinge offset makes it easier to tip the helicopter over on the ground by inadvertently putting in too much cyclic pitch even when the rotor is at flat pitch. This possibility, of course, is a function of the landing gear tread. I know of one tip-over accident on a helicopter with less than 4% hinge offset.

Finally, very high hinge offsets are bad if they result in a bulky hub that is draggier than a hub with lower offsets.

Confidence

A pilot who has high confidence in the structural integrity of his aircraft will not be afraid to ask for all the performance the engines and rotors can provide. He will have a distinct advantage in maneuvering against an opponent who is not quite so confident. Therefore, a design goal for an air-to-air combat helicopter is: "It shall be impossible to break the helicopter in flight."

Achieving this goal would eliminate the need for monitoring gauges, warning lights, horns, and stick shakers meant to keep the pilot from doing immediate structural damage. Although such a helicopter could not be broken up in the air, continued aggressive usage would probably induce fatigue damage. High loads above the endurance limit (the threshold for fatigue damage) should be automatically recorded and made available to the maintenance officer to help him decide when fatigue-sensitive components should be replaced.

New criteria

One of the opportunities to put this philosophy into practice is in transmission design. In the past, many helicopters have been produced with "derated" transmissions and drive systems. That is, ones that were qualified for less than the engines could produce except on a hot day at altitude. This saves some transmission weight but forces the pilot to pay attention to his torque gauges during maneuvers when he has other things to worry about.

For a combat helicopter, it would seem reasonable to design the transmission to be able to transmit all of the power the engines could develop even on a midwinter day in Siberia. (I have been told that Ivan doesn't have a torque gauge to worry about.)

Similarly, today it is possible to design the rotor, the control systems, and the airframe to stand up to any air loads and to have adequate blade-to-airframe clearances within the extreme performance envelope of the helicopter. This would eliminate the pilot's concern with exceeding the V-N (velocity-load factor) and sideslip envelopes and the V_{NE} (never-exceed speed). This, of course, will involve weight penalties that might not be acceptable for helicopters intended for less aggressive roles but it would let the air-to-air pilot fight unencumbered by concerns of structural integrity.

55 Designing For High Speed

In August 1986, Westland Helicopters did what no one had done for almost a decade - it set a new helicopter speed record. For eight years prior, the record had stood at 198.7 knots, set by the Russians with a souped-up Mil Hind.

To set the new mark, the Westland team flew their modified Lynx - shown in Figure 55-1 - both ways on a 15-km course at an average speed of 216.3 knots. The fact that the old record had held for so long may be taken as an indication that 200 knots is about as fast as helicopters are meant to fly.

What was the British advantage? It appears to lie in two different areas- an innovative use of engine power and a new and unusual shape for the main rotor blade.

The Westland Lynx first flew in 1971. At the time of service introduction, its Rolls-Royce Gem engines were rated at a total of 1,800 hp on a standard day (59°F at sea level). As has been done before, the transmission was derated; that is, it was qualified to only 1,400 hp. That saved transmission weight and was based on the assumption that most operations would be at combinations of temperatures and altitudes where the engines could not develop their full-rated power.

Figure 55-1 Speed Record-Setting Westland Lynx

Excess power

During the years, the Gems were improved so that with a little special attention, two of them could put out 3,200 hp. The transmission was also upgraded and, at the time of the record attempt, could be trusted to absorb 2,500 hp-still 700 short of the engine capability.

What can you do with an extra 700 hp that you can't put into the rotor drive system? One possibility is to power a 700-hp propeller through a special auxiliary gearbox. The other possibility—and the one Westland chose-is to put the exhaust system to work.

Most helicopters are designed to hover effectively. This means getting the most engine power to drive the rotors. One way to do this is to minimize the engine backpressure by providing expanding exhaust nozzles so that nothing restricts the escape of the gases behind the power turbine. This results in a relatively low exhaust velocity that is good for hover but might actually generate a drag force at high speed.

Designers of turboprop airplanes have a different philosophy. They use convergent nozzles with high exhaust velocities that, while reducing available power at low speed, provide significant jet thrust at high speed. This was the approach used by West-land. By experimenting with different exhaust configurations, they found that by squeezing down the exit area to about 40% of what is on the conventional Lynx, it would be possible to convert the extra 700 hp into nearly 600 pounds of usable jet thrust.

This and an extensive drag cleanup combined to reduce the equivalent parasite drag to about half that of the basic Lynx. In addition to reducing the required rotor power, the auxiliary thrust allowed the main rotor to operate at a lower forward tilt, producing a more benign angle-of-attack environment on the retreating side.

The record was set in the "pure" helicopter category. Had the 600 pounds of auxiliary thrust come from a propeller or a jet engine, the aircraft would have been rated as a compound helicopter for which the unofficial record is 274 knots, set by a jet-engine-powered Bell UH-1 way back in 1964.

Designing For High Speed: The BERP blade

The other innovation was the paddle-tip blade, shown in Figure 55-2 that was developed during the British Experimental Rotor Program (BERP). Modifying the outboard 15% of the blade tips helped in both places where a rotor gets into trouble when flying fast - on the advancing and retreating tips.

Figure 55-2 The BERP Blade

The advancing tip is exposed to high Mach numbers that can result in noise, drag rise, and high pitching moments. Two geometric factors can be used to reduce these compressibility effects: an airfoil with a small thickness-to-chord ratio, and a swept leading edge. Westland used both. Some thinning came as a result of extending the chord both fore and aft of the original 12% thick blade. The rest was achieved by progressively thinning the composite structure toward the tip until a ratio of about 6% was obtained.

Air is fooled into thinking the Mach number is lower than it really is by leading edge sweep-whether it be fore or aft. The BERP tip has both, since the leading edge first sweeps forward and then aft in a curve to give more and more sweepback as the local Mach number increases. The result is that the aircraft could be flown on the record flight with an advancing tip going 97.7% of the speed of sound-undoubtedly noisy, but permissible for this special occasion.

On the other side

As forward speed increases, the angles of attack on the retreating side eventually become high enough to cause stall, as that blade tries to lift in a region of low relative velocity. Depending on the airfoil section used, most blade tips cannot go beyond 12° or 16° before stalling.

To obtain as high a stall angle as possible, it is desirable to have a thick, highly cambered section in contrast to the thin, flat section desired on the advancing side. Westland's paddle tip introduces a unique solution to this dilemma. Even though it is thin, it can go to high angles before stalling due to a vortex that is generated at the notch shown in Figure 55-3. This energizes the flow over the tip, much as happens on delta-wing airplanes, and keeps the boundary layer attached up to high angles of attack.

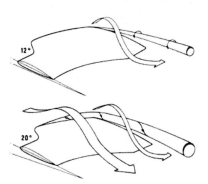

Figure 55-3 Vortex Patterns at High Angles of Attack

From a theoretical standpoint, the extra blade area in the paddle tips alone should have helped by allowing the same thrust to be generated at reduced average angles of attack. Test results published by Westland, however, indicate that this particular advantage did not, in fact, materialize. At thrust levels and speeds free of blade stall, there was no measurable decrease in collective or cyclic pitch from the baseline Lynx rotor. For conditions in which blade stall existed on the baseline rotor, however, the BERP rotor did the same job with lower control angles.

Tailoring the blade

Compared to metal blades, one advantage that composite blades bring to the aerodynamicist is the ease with which airfoil and planform shapes can be changed along the blade. This is because the composite blade is formed by compressing material in a mold that can be made with any reasonable arbitrary shape. Westland took advantage of this capability to not only form the paddle tip but to also vary the airfoil section along the basic blade as shown in Figure 55-4. From the 70% radius station to just inboard of the Mach-sensitive tip, they chose a 12% thick, cambered airfoil for its good lifting capability on the retreating side.

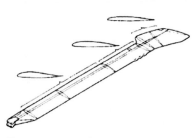

Figure 55-4 Distribution of Airfoil Sections

Such an airfoil, while having a desirable, high stalling angle, also has an undesirable, nosedown pitching moment that can lead to high control loads. This was counteracted by using an airfoil with a reflexed trailing edge inboard of the 70% radius station. The reflex produces a noseup pitching moment in this portion to balance the nosedown moment on the rest.

The stall-resistant tip, the airfoil tailoring, and the more benign angle-of-attack environment due to auxiliary propulsion, all made it possible to fly at a tip speed ratio (the ratio of forward speed to tip speed) of 0.51; just to the high side of the 0.5 value usually quoted as a maximum for pure helicopters.

56 Dynamic Inflow

Readers of technical literature for helicopter aerodynamics are increasingly encountering the term "dynamic inflow." If I had named the phenomenon for which this is used, I would have preferred "induced velocity delay," as it takes some time to feel its effects.

Delayed reaction

One of the physical laws that the helicopter obeys is: For every action, there is a reaction. For a rotor, the action is the production of an aerodynamic force, and the reaction is the resulting induced velocity in the air mass being affected. For steady conditions, the magnitude of the induced velocity can be calculated, and it is tempting to assume that, in going from one steady condition to another, changes are instantaneous. That is not a bad assumption for many situations, but it is not a good one for others.

By assuming an instantaneous change in the induced velocity, we are pretending that the acceleration of air can be infinite. This is impossible. So the analysis should account for the time it takes the induced velocity to adjust.

One of the first bits of evidence noted for this phenomenon was during some rotor whirl-tower tests done by NACA in the 1950s. Figure 56-1 shows the measured rotor thrust as the collective pitch was increased at various rates. For slow increases, the thrust increased proportionally and smoothly to the final value, but for rapid collective inputs, there was a definite overshoot of thrust.

This is because the induced flow through the rotor takes some time to develop, and for a short time, the angles of attack on the blade are not decreased by the downward induced flow.

NACA engineers developed a theory by turning the problem inside out and relating it to the mass of air that a solid disc would move with it as the disc moved through the air—a problem solved by early workers in fluid dynamics. This "apparent mass," which must be accelerated by the rotor thrust, turns out to be 64% of the air in a sphere with the same diameter as the rotor. (Some people now use a lower value for a helicopter rotor.)

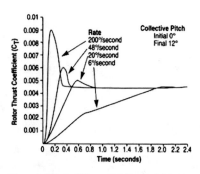

Figure 56-1 Effect Of Rapid Pitch Change On Rotor Thrust

Until this mass is accelerated to its final value, the blade angles of attack and the rotor thrust are above their final steady values. The temporary overshoot might allow a heavily loaded helicopter to hop into the air, but only briefly.

The tail rotor

The lag of induced velocity can cause real trouble for the tail rotor. Imagine a hovering helicopter turning to the right with main-rotor torque providing the turning moment (American main-rotor rotation). This is done with low collective pitch on the tail rotor.

Assume the pilot quickly reverses the turn, using fall left pedal that suddenly increases the collective pitch to its maximum. Until the new induced velocity can be established, the tail-rotor blades are working at very high angles of attack. These angles may be well over the stall angle for the airfoil.

The main result is not the loss of thrust but the very high increase in drag and thus in the tail-rotor torque. If this were the main rotor, you would expect it to slow down; but the tail rotor, with relatively low inertia, is kept up to speed by the engine. Its drive system must deliver whatever torque is required by the aerodynamic situation, which may be two or three times the expected steady value. In a number of early helicopters, the designers had not thought about this; as a consequence, tail-rotor drive shafts were twisted like pretzels.

Designing the drive system to be fully adequate in this situation, however, results in a substantial weight penalty. There are two partial ways around this. One is training the pilot to avoid making abrupt pedal inputs when stopping a hover turn. The other is to install dampers on the rudder pedals so that it is very hard for him to make abrupt pedal inputs. The latter choice is used on all Sikorsky helicopters, but as far as I know, all others rely on pilot training.

Back to the main rotor

Only recently has the delay in the establishment of the induced velocity been recognized as the source of main-rotor problems. One place this comes about is when a high-gain hover-hold system is installed in the helicopter to maintain a precise altitude using a radar altimeter. In this case, "high gain" refers to a system that tries very hard to correct for small altitude errors by using quick collective-pitch inputs.

The result may be unforeseen oscillations because of two lags. One is the lag in establishing the equilibrium-induced velocity. The other is the lag in producing the blade coning, which transfers the thrust of the rotor to the shaft.

For a normal helicopter, each lag is in the order of one-tenth of a second. Consequently, as the rotor develops its full thrust a tenth of a second after a correction from the hover-hold system, it is just in time to experience the full effect of the downward induced velocity, which decreases the thrust.

As the helicopter starts down, the hover-hold system senses this motion and increases collective pitch—quite possibly just out-of-phase with what it should be doing. This makes the situation worse or, at the least, means going through several oscillations before settling down.

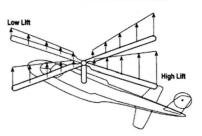

Figure 56-2 Rotor Load Distribution For Starting A Left Roll

Much recent development of the dynamic-inflow theory has been to explain why the rotor does not respond to rapid changes in cyclic-pitch inputs as quickly as the old theory said it should. Here again, the delay in developing the induced velocity and its coupling with the dynamics of blade flapping have been identified as important factors.

Imagine the pilot in a hovering helicopter is using a quick lateral cyclic-pitch input to start a roll to the left. The rotor-disc aerodynamics must be such as to generate a nosedown pitching moment to precess the rotor down to the left as a gyroscope (Figure 56-2).

The unequal thrust loading from front to back on the rotor changes the induced-velocity gradient and thus the pitching moment available to precess the rotor. At the same time, the rolling velocity that does result changes the side-to-side loading and thus the inflow gradient in this direction as well. The effect of dynamic inflow is to couple roll and pitch in ways not predicted by the earlier theories.

Figure 56-3 shows flight-test time histories for a right lateral stick input on a hovering Sikorsky UH-60. Also shown are the calculations made both with and without considering dynamic inflow. Without dynamic inflow, the calculations overpredict the roll and pitch responses, but the correlation is better when dynamic inflow is included. Some investigators have equated the reduced roll response with an effective increase in the rotor inertia, which means a decrease in its "Lock number."

In forward flight, the coupling between pitch and roll found in hover is also joined by a modulation of the induced velocity's average value and thus rotor thrust during cyclic inputs. The time delay similar to that found in hover causes a dynamic response in which the inflow can "overshoot" the final value. Both the rotor thrust and the flapping can oscillate for several cycles.

In certain cases—primarily involving bearingless rotors—the effect can decrease the stability of the rotor. Even for conventional rotors, the time lags and couplings associated with dynamic inflow can have major ramifications on the design of an automatic control system to stabilize the rotor.

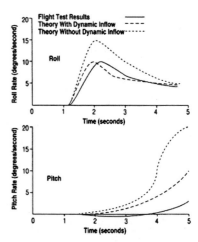

Figure 56-3 Response To One-Inch Right Lateral Stick Step Input (Sikorsky UH-60A In Hover)

57 Mysteries About Inflow And Power

Reality can often get in the way of theory. This can frustrate researchers; they much prefer to see experimental data validate their theories. When it does, the researcher can publish his findings, showing how the theory can be used to predict a system's performance.

Sometimes it doesn't work

When the correlation between theory and test results is not so good, the researcher is much like the Ring of Siam in the musical *The King and I*. He laments, "When my father was king, what was so was so. But things are different now. I am king and am not certain about things I absolutely know—is a puzzlement."

Now the investigator can either not publish, or he can put all the facts on paper and let others have an opportunity to explain the mystery. Two published papers throw suspicion on two things we "absolutely know."

Induced-velocity pattern

The first paper is by Susan Althoff, who works for the Army at the NASA Langley Research Center in Hampton, Va. Her paper, "Effect of Tip Speed on Rotor Inflow," was published in the *Journal of the American Helicopter Society*.

The long-accepted theory held up for questioning in this paper may be stated thus: The geometric characteristics of the rotor-induced flow field in for-"ward flight are independent of tip speed as long as the tip-speed ratio, the nondimensional thrust coefficient, and the attitude of the tip-path plane are held constant.

The program that inspired the investigation is an on-going project to accurately measure the induced-flow field about a rotor in forward flight. To do this the Army/NASA team has been using the laser velocimeter and a 6.5 foot (2-m) rotor in the Langley 14-by-22 foot (4-by-7-m) wind tunnel (Figure 57-1).

To give the velocimeter a clear field-of-view, the ceiling and walls of the tunnel test section are removed, leaving only the floor. In this configuration, the maximum speed of the wind tunnel is about 160 knots.

Figure 57-1 The Laser Velocimeter in Operation

319

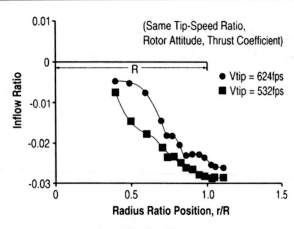

Figure 57-2 Comparison Of Induced Inflow Ratio For Two Tip Speeds (Same Tip-Speed Ratio, Rotor Attitude, Thrust Coefficient)

How do you simulate higher helicopter speeds in this tunnel? It has long been accepted that all you have to do is reduce the rotor tip speed. You are then testing at a higher tip-speed ratio (the ratio of forward speed to tip speed).

This was the approach taken by the Army/NASA team. To simulate the high-speed conditions, they chose to reduce the normal tip speed of 624 feet per second (fps) by 15% to 532 fps.

But before going to the higher tip-speed ratios this allowed, they decided to check the validity of the theory by measuring the induced-flow field at the two tip speeds. This was done by changing the tunnel speed while holding the tip-speed ratio constant—at 0.30. In defiance to the theory, the induced-flow fields were not the same!

The most striking difference was in the rotor disc's aft portion. For the azimuth position over the tail boom (Figure 57-2), the induced inflow ratio (downwash) measured just above the rotor plane was greater for the lower tip speed. In other portions of the disc there was also a difference, but not quite so pronounced.

Analysis of the data ruled out Reynolds or Mach numbers as the cause of the discrepancy. Also, by using the same reasoning that predicted the similarity of the induced-flow field, the ground (floor) effect should have not been a factor.

What is the source of the difference? I am sure suggestions will be welcome. Susan Althoffs concluding words are: "It is recommended, until the source of the difference in the measured inflow velocity is determined, that caution should be used when comparing local flow-field velocity data which have been obtained at different rotor-tip speeds."

Are flapping and feathering equivalent?

The other paper that throws doubts on a well-established "fact" of helicopter analysis was written by Desopper, Lafon, and Ceroni of ONERA (the French equivalent of NASA). The paper, presented at the 1989 European Rotorcraft Forum, is entitled "Influence of the Control Law on the Performance of the Helicopter Model Rotor."

For several years prior to 1987, rotor tests in the ONERA wind tunnel at Chalais-Meudon used a freely flapping model without a cyclic-pitch control system. In that year, cyclic pitch was added. Experimenters could thus control the flapping to more nearly represent the flight of modern helicopters.

Repeats of some of the earlier tests produced surprises. At the same thrust, forward propulsive force, and tip-speed ratio, the power required was different!

This was unexpected. Theory says that, under these conditions, the equivalence of flapping and feathering should result in exactly the same angles of attack and flow conditions at each blade element and thus no difference in power. (In theory, this statement applies only to rotors with zero hinge offset, but the ONERA rotor tested had a relatively small hinge offset of less than 6% of the rotor radius.)

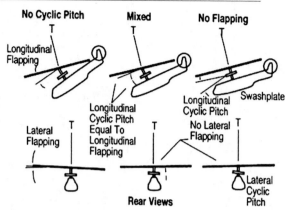

Figure 57-3 Trim Conditions For Three Control Laws

Control laws

The rotor was tested with three different control laws (Figure 57-3):

• In the first, no cyclic pitch was used, and the rotor was free to flap longitudinally and laterally to achieve its aerodynamic equilibrium, just as did those of the original autogyros or today's tail rotors.

• In the second, cyclic pitch was used to suppress all the flapping, thus making the tip-path plane perpendicular to the rotor shaft. (The French authors call this the "American law," since most American wind-tunnel tests of rotors are run in this condition.)

• The third was the "mixed law," in which the lateral flapping was suppressed by cyclic pitch. But in the longitudinal axis, only enough cyclic pitch was used to make the flapping equal to the cyclic pitch—thus taking out only about half the natural free longitudinal flapping.

Note that in an actual helicopter, the amount of flapping at any given steady flight conditions is whatever is necessary to balance the sum of the pitching and rolling moments. These moments are generated by such things as an offset center of gravity, loads on a horizontal stabilizer, or tail-rotor thrust. Thus in actual flight, the control law is mixed with both some flapping and some cyclic pitch, but not exactly as defined for these tests.

Surprisingly, when the rotor was trimmed out with the French mixed control law, the power required to develop the same thrust and propulsive force was significantly less than when it was trimmed out with the no-flapping American law. Theory says that there should be no significant difference.

The other surprise was that, with no cyclic pitch and lots of flapping (as with a tail rotor), the power required was also lower than with the no-flapping trim condition. These mysterious test results are shown in Figure 57-4.

Measurements of the pressure on the blade's upper surface indicate that there was a difference in the intensity of the unsteady transonic effects (conditions at speeds close to the speed of sound). This was especially

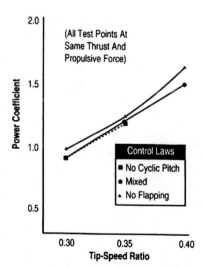

Figure 57-4 Effect Of Control Law On Power Required

evident in the early portion of the first quadrant as the blade left its downstream position.

The authors believe that this relates to the difference in power. But they don't offer an explanation of why these pressure differences should exist in the first place.

Attempts were made to reproduce the results of the power-required measurements with a computer program using lifting line theory, airfoil tables, and a simple inflow model. But they gave inconclusive results. At low speeds, there were differences, but much smaller than measured, while at high speeds—above a tip speed ratio of 0.35—the calculated results showed trends to be opposite to those measured. At these speeds, the calculated power for the rotor with no flapping was less than with the other two conditions.

The authors' conclusions end with another warning about how confidently we should accept what we absolutely know: "...the control law is a parameter that has to be taken into account."

58 Control Systems

The main and tail rotors are magnificent maneuvering devices but they must be made to do what the pilot wants. That's the job of the control system.

Most of the modern generation of main and tail rotor configurations use the same basic type of control systems, varying only in details. In spite of the fact you and I know these systems are logical and straightforward, they might appear to some to have been inspired by Rube Goldberg. The following description, therefore, is not aimed at you but is only intended to help you educate your curious friends, neighbors, and relatives.

Figure 58-1 shows the elements of the basic system, which actually consists of three subsystems: main-rotor collective, main-rotor cyclic, and directional (tail rotor). The function of the main-rotor collective system is to vary the amount of thrust the rotor produces. This is done by simultaneously changing the pitch of all the blades by the same amount in response to an up-and-down motion of the collective stick in the pilot's left hand.

The main-rotor cyclic system controls the direction of the thrust by causing the rotor disc to tilt with respect to the shaft in response to the fore-and-aft or side-to-side motion of the cyclic stick in the pilot's right hand. When the pilot moves the stick, the control linkages act on the swashplate, which is free to tilt in any direction about a large spherical bearing or a set of gimbals. The swashplate consists of tw rotating lower half fastened to the control linkages from the cockpit and a rotating upper half that follows the motion of the non-rotating swashplate through a set of bearings.

From the rotating swashplate, the motion goes up to a pitch horn on each blade, causing the pitch to be changed about the feathering bearing. When the stick is pushed forward, the blade on the right side has its pitch reduced, whereas on the left side the pitch is increased by the same amount. Thus the pitch of each blade changes "cyclically" or once every revolution.

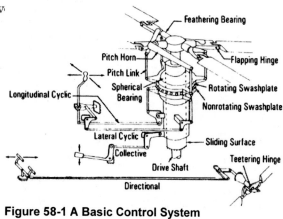

Figure 58-1 A Basic Control System

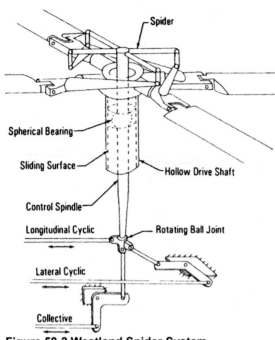

Figure 58-2 Westland Spider System

An alternative to the swashplate is the spider system used on Westland designs as illustrated in Figure 58-2. (In practice, the pitch horns are usually not made as long as shown in Figure 58-1 and 58-2. By reorienting the non-rotating swashplate clockwise, the same cyclic-pitch input can be obtained with shorter pitch horns.)

True believers only

To understand what happens following the application of cyclic pitch requires .an act of faith. If this were an airplane, with wings rigidly attached to the fuselage, you would expect the change of pitch on the right and left wings to cause the aircraft to roll to the right.

On a rotor, however, because the blades have flapping hinges —or at least flexible portions — and are rotating, the rotor disc tilts down to the front. If you are talking to a physicist, simply mention that the rotating blade is a system in resonance and "of course" its response lags the input by 90°.

(Historical note: Even Igor Sikorsky didn't believe this at first. The earliest version of the VS 300 was rigged like an airplane and was impossible to fly until the controls were modified.)

The condition of resonance also may be used to explain why such a small hand motion can result in such a relatively large reaction as the tilting of the whole rotor disc. The tilt is very fast, requiring only a fraction of a second to become equal to the cyclic-pitch change. At that point, it stops. Thus the pilot has a quick and sure control over the direction of the rotor-thrust vector — which for all intents and purposes is perpendicular to the rotor disc and follows the orientation of the cyclic stick.

The portion of the cyclic system that responds to fore-and-aft stick motion is called the "longitudinal cyclic system" because it controls the pitching motion of the helicopter. The other portion, which responds to side-to-side motion, makes the helicopter roll and is therefore called the "lateral cyclic system". This is in spite of the fact that if you only looked at the corresponding position of maximum blade-pitch change, you would be led to reverse these designations.

Cyclic pitch is used not only to tilt the rotor disc for maneuvering but also to keep the rotor trimmed as the helicopter changes speed and requires different angles of attack on the advancing and retreating blades to compensate for different air velocities. As speed is increased, for example, the stick is pushed forward to decrease the angle of attack on the advancing blade and to increase it on the retreating side.

One notable exception to the standard type of control system is that found on Kaman helicopters. On these, both collective and cyclic control are achieved by twisting the flexible blades by the forces from controllable "servoflaps" fixed to the trailing edge as shown in 58-3. When the trailing edge of the servoflap goes up, it produces a download at the blade's trailing edge and twists the blade noseup. Thus the servoflap is using reverse psychology to control the blade.

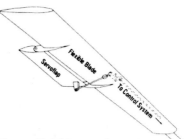

Figure 58-3 Kaman Servoflap System

Directional control

The directional control for the tail rotor is a collective system just as on the main rotor. The pilot uses it to control the thrust of the tail rotor but has no control over the tail rotor's tilt, which is allowed to find its own equilibrium position as affected by flight conditions. The control is by "rudder pedals" rigged like an airplane's — to produce a right turn when the right pedal is pressed.

On a number of modern helicopters, some tail-rotor pitch change is introduced by a linkage to the main-rotor collective-pitch control. This automatically adjusts tail-rotor thrust to compensate for changes in main-rotor torque such as occur during takeoffs.

Variations

So much for the simple control system. In practice, it usually becomes much more complicated. One of the most common complications is the addition of devices to help the pilot handle control forces. Both steady and oscillatory loads are generated in the blades by aerodynamic and inertial processes that try to move the cockpit controls unless the pilot— or something—holds firmly. On earlier helicopters, it was up to the pilot — and if he relaxed his grip with either hand, the helicopter would do a maneuver of its own choosing.

The first fixes consisted of friction and adjustable bungee cords to hold the controls so the pilot could at least momentarily tune a radio or handle a map. Pilot complaints, especially as helicopters got bigger, motivated designers to do something more sophisticated.

The airplane people had already faced similar problems and had developed hydraulic control boost systems, which with relatively small changes could be adapted to helicopters. Of course, such systems do not come cheap in terms of weight or dollars so, if possible, they are avoided. For example, the relatively small Hughes 300 and 500 helicopters do not have hydraulic systems. The Model 500, however, does have a special "un-lock" device in the longitudinal cyclic system that grounds the control to the airframe structure, except when it is actually being moved by the pilot. Collective, lateral cyclic, and directional control forces are handled with a combination of springs and adjustable friction.

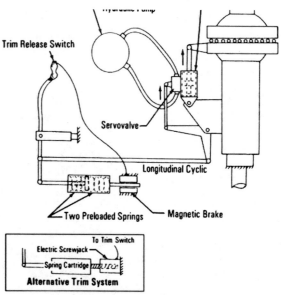

Figure 58-4 Details of Hydraulic Control System

Most larger helicopters have hydraulic systems with irreversible actuators that react control forces directly to the airframe structure near the rotor-support assemblies as illustrated in 58-4. Moderately sized aircraft can get by with only a single hydraulic system, since even with it turned off the pilot can fly the helicopter (although with some difficulty).

Larger helicopters have two or more independent systems to make sure that one is always working. A fallout of the hydraulic system is that, once installed, it is relatively easy to add stability augmentation or autopilot equipment that can move the controls with small forces.

Feel and trim

With irreversible control actuators, the pilot is only moving low-friction servo valves with his cockpit controls. He gets no feel from control motion and if he were to release a control, it might fall over due to its own weight. To remedy this, control centering and artificial feel are built into the cyclic-control system and sometimes into the pedals, while the collective system is usually equipped only with an adjustable friction device and a helper spring.

Although pilots differ in what they consider to be an optimum control feel, most modern helicopters have a longitudinal cyclic-force gradient of one to four pounds per inch, with the lateral system somewhat less in recognition of the relative strength of the arm in the two directions. This is part of what is called "control harmony".

In addition to the gradient, the control should have a definite "detent" position that requires some force to initially move or to "breakout" the control. The detent effect can be achieved by preloading two springs against each other, in a spring cartridge.

The gradient and the detent insure that if the control is moved and then released, it will go back to its original position. This is good to return to a given flight condition following a maneuver —but what if the flight condition is being changed? For this case, it must be possible to relocate the detent reference position so that, at the new trim point, the stick will again hold its position.

There are two types of trim systems on modern helicopters. On one, a magnetic brake is used to fix the feel springs' anchor point to structure. The mag brake contains a special fluid that "freezes" upon application of an electric potential and unfreezes when the electricity is shut off. When the pilot pushes the switch on his cyclic stick, the brake unfreezes and the springs quickly reset to their zero-force point.

The other trim system uses an electric motor and a screw jack to relatively slowly adjust the springs' anchor point in response to the motion of a button on top of the stick. There is not a consensus as to the best system. Some helicopters use both!

Even with irreversible controls, pilots are reluctant to let go of the control sticks any more than necessary and so both the cyclic and the collective sticks are festooned with an array of switches and buttons to allow a number of tasks to be performed with the thumbs and fingers. Besides trimming control forces, depending on the helicopter, the pilot can transmit on the radio, talk on the intercom, turn searchlights on, fire weapons, control the engines, and turn on the stability-augmentation system — all without removing his hands from the collective and cyclic.

Cockpit options

Two questions continually asked by those looking at helicopter cockpits are:

Figure 58-5 Sikorsky Experimental Side-arm Controller

1—Do the controls really have to monopolize so much valuable cockpit space?

2— Does the pilot really have to use both hands and both feet to control the helicopter?

These two questions have provided the motivation for a number of clever cockpit arrangements. One tried experimentally at Bell a number of years ago was to add a "tiller" motion to the collective control stick for directional control. It was found that sailors of small boats had no trouble with this arrangement but that landlubbers frequently forgot which way they should be moving the tiller. In recent years, the design trend has been toward the development of "side-arm" controllers (Figure 58-5), where small motions — or in some cases even small forces — are sensed electronically and used to move the servo valves on the hydraulic actuators. In some proposed designs, all the controls are incorporated in the same hand grip —using vertical motion for collective, twisting for directional as well as fore-and-aft, and side-to-side for cyclic. No production helicopter yet uses a sidearm controller for the primary control but at least half a dozen experimental installations have been studied and one, the aft-facing loadmaster's control on the Sikorsky S-64 Flying Crane, is operational.

59 Directional Stability & Autorotation Control Problems

Ever since Juan de la Cierva developed his autogyro in the early 1920s, rotary-wing aircraft have exploited the flight regime of autorotation. Compared to the other regimes of flight, it appears to be a much more benign condition. So why do some designs still have problems in autorotation?

Directional stability

Let's first consider the aspect of directional stability. On most aircraft, the fuselage shape used is basically unstable and would be most comfortable flying sideways. For this reason, some sort of device for providing directional stability is necessary.

A tail rotor is a very good directional stabilizer, but it sometimes does not provide enough stability by itself. So one or more vertical stabilizing surfaces are added. For helicopters without tail rotors, such as tandems, coaxials, and those using a Fenestron or NOTAR system, the vertical stabilizer is counted on to provide the directional stability.

These surfaces may be less effective in autorotation or steep descent than they are in climb or level flight. There are a couple of reasons for that. The first is the stabilizer's position. If it is a single surface located on the aircraft's centerline directly behind the rotor hub and fuselage, it will be more in the wake of these components in a descent than in climb or level flight. It will thus have less airflow to work with to produce forces to compensate for inadvertent sideslip.

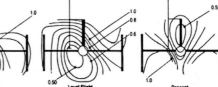

Figure 59-1 Dynamic Pressure Ratios At BO-105 Tail During Flight

Wind tunnel and flight-test measurements have shown that, for a typical single-rotor helicopter, the dynamic pressure at the stabilizer location in autorotation may be only half what it is in level flight. During level flight, the rotor swirl tends to force the wake of the hub off to one side. Figure 59-1 shows this effect as measured in flight tests by Messerschmitt-Boelkow-Blohm (MBB, now part of Eurocopter).

To avoid this situation, many designers use "end-plates" on the ends of the horizontal stabilizer, to get the vertical surfaces into clean air in all flight conditions. You can see this to an extreme on the Eurocopter BK-

Figure 59-2 BK-117 With End-Plates

329

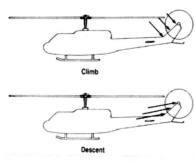

Figure 59-3 Local Airflow At Swept Vertical Stabilizer

117 (Figure 59-2), where very large surfaces were developed in flight test after first trying the smaller ones used on its little sister, the BO-105.

Another possibility is to place a ventral fin underneath the tail boom where it will be in clean air in descent. This can be seen on the latest version of the Eurocopter Super Puma.

The effect of sweep

The second reason for decreased effectiveness of a vertical stabilizer in autorotation is that the designer may have chosen to make it look good by sweeping it back. The aerodynamic effectiveness of a surface depends on its effective aspect ratio, and a swept surface suffers some loss of aspect ratio compared to an unswept surface.

If the air is approaching perpendicular to the leading edge, the aspect ratio is high, but if the air is approaching parallel to the leading edge, it is low. Thus a swept vertical stabilizer in climb has very good aerodynamic efficiency, but it will be low in autorotation. The difference can be seen in Figure 59-3.

One of the development programs that drove this fact home was the Sikorsky Advancing Blade Concept (ABC) coaxial helicopter (Figure 59-4). The vertical surfaces contained rudders for directional control in forward flight. Although the surfaces had only a slight amount of sweepback, the designers reported that they were relatively ineffective in autorotation. So, if they were to do it again, the surfaces would be swept forward instead.

Coaxials and synchropters

In autorotation, coaxials have a special problem with regard to directional control. Most of them use differential collective pitch between the two rotors to provide an unbalanced torque to use for turning maneuvers. This system works well in powered flight but not in autorotation, where its effect is reversed!

Stan Hiller's first helicopter was a coaxial. He recently told me that no one had told him about this reversal. The first time he tried to autorotate, he found himself spinning around and around even though he was using full rudder pedal in what he thought was the correct direction. It was only with a few hundred feet of altitude remaining that he decided he didn't have anything to lose by pushing with the other foot, thereby saving himself.

Synchropters have this same reversal characteristic. On the Kaman synchropters, it is accounted for by mechanically reversing the directional control system when the collective stick is put down into the autorotation position. Besides using differential torque, Kaman also uses differential longitudinal cyclic flapping to increase directional control. Kaman ensured that there would be adequate directional stability as long

Figure 59-4 Sikorsky's S-69 ABC

as there was some forward speed by using as many as four vertical stabilizing surfaces on some of its designs.

Tail shake

Another problem that is usually worse in autorotation than in other flight conditions is "tail shake." This has been a significant problem on the prototypes of a number of helicopter designs during their first test flights.

It is usually traced to unsteady airflow that arises at the main-rotor pylon or at the rotor hub, and reaches the position of the tail-rotor or empennage surfaces with high turbulence. If the frequency of the turbulence happens to match one of the empennage's natural frequencies, the resulting resonance causes vibrations that can be felt throughout the entire helicopter.

The usual cure for this is to install special pylon fairings that act as low-aspect-ratio wings. These produce tip vortices that tend to organize the flow and lower the turbulence downstream. The unsteady flow from the hub can be suppressed by the installation of a round cap—or "beanie"—that also produces vortices. Neither of these fixes should be done unless flight-test results show that they are necessary, since both add weight and drag to the helicopter.

Sometimes even these changes are not sufficient, and it is necessary to avoid resonance by adding weights, which lowers the natural frequencies of the vertical or horizontal stabilizer structure, or to raise the natural frequency with structural stiffening.

60 Stability Augmentation Systems

The goal of the helicopter designer is to make his aircraft have such good inherent flying qualities that the pilot requires no extra help. The fact that so many helicopters are flying today with just a pilot in control demonstrates that the goal can be reached — if expectations are modest. For many applications, however, such as flying in reduced visibility or while the pilot has other critical chores, the cost of providing the extra help to reduce pilot workload and improve his performance is well worth it.

Stability augmentation

Early stability augmentation systems (SAS) were primarily mechanical — such as the Bell stabilizer bar, the Hiller servo rotor, and the Lockheed gyro (as discussed in Chapter 8). As electronic/hydraulic/mechanical systems become smaller and more reliable, they took over the job— primarily because of their weight advantage and the ease with which other tasks, such as navigation, could be added to their capabilities.

The primary use of the SAS equipment is still to improve the flying qualities by damping the pitch and roll motions caused by gusts —just as the earlier systems did. This is done by installing small gyros to generate electrical signals proportional to pitch and roll rates. These signals are then used to control hydraulic or electrical actuators that tilt the swashplate in the right direction to resist the helicopter motion.

If this were done as stated, it would not only resist motions due to gusts but would also resist motions due to deliberate pilot-control motions. This would result in a helicopter with sluggish control response. To prevent this, the system must be designed to distinguish between the two types of inputs.

In many modern systems, this is done with a command augmentation system (CAS or, as a combined system, SCAS). The CAS uses an electrical signal, which is a function of stick motion to cancel out the electrical signal coming from the rate gyros. Thus, the response to control inputs can be made as snappy as you want — while still providing damping to inadvertent gust disturbances. Of course, a similar system can be installed in the tail-rotor control system to improve directional stability and control characteristics.

333

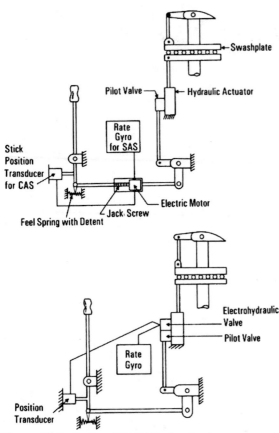

Figure 60-1 and surrounding labels: Swashplate, Pilot Valve, Hydraulic Actuator, Rate Gyro for SAS, Stick Position Transducer for CAS, Electric Motor, Jack Screw, Feel Spring with Detent, Electrohydraulic Valve, Pilot Valve, Rate Gyro, Position Transducer.

Figure 60-1   Series SCAS Mechanizations

If the system is used primarily for stabilization, it is usually set up as doing its thing without moving the cockpit controls. This is sometimes called a series system and Figure 60-1 shows two current ways of mechanizing it: one with an "extendable link" containing a motorized jack screw and the other with an SCAS electro-hydraulic valve on the hydraulic power actuator.

Since no system that relies on electrical signals can be considered wholly foolproof, the designer must use his most vivid imagination to predict failures and then figure out ways to keep those failures from being catastrophic. One way is to limit the authority of the SCAS actuator to 10% or 20% of full control throw. That way, if a gyro unit suddenly puts out a hard over signal corresponding to a 1,000° per second rate, the resulting control motion is limited and can be overridden by the pilot.

Another scheme is to use dual or even triply independent systems so that the failure of one can be at least partially compensated for by the continuing operation of the other(s).

There are conditions that, if permitted, might use up all of the limited actuator authority. These include pitch rates over a long time, as in a steady turn, and semi-permanent changes in control positions reflecting changed flight conditions. To avoid actuator saturation due to these effects, both SAS and CAS signals are "washed out" over a period of two to 20 seconds to permit the actuator to drift back to its centered position where it has maid-mum travel available to compensate for gusts or for maneuvering in either direction.

Expanding the system

While electronic stability augmentation systems for helicopters were being developed about 20 years ago, the airplane people were refining their autopilots, which had originally been developed for a somewhat different purpose: to hold course, altitude, and speed while flying from one point to another by using signals from attitude gyros, altimeters, and airspeed systems. Most of these autopilots moved the cockpit controls as well as the aerodynamic control surfaces, so that they were most effective when the pilot flew hands-off or at least did not resist the control motion. This is called a parallel system and Figure 60-2 is a typical schematic for such an installation. For maneuvering, some autopilots are turned off— either manually or with pressure-sensitive switches.

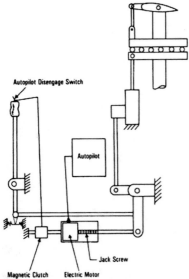

Figure 60-2 and labels: Autopilot Disengage Switch, Autopilot, Jack Screw, Magnetic Clutch, Electric Motor.

Figure 60-2   Typical Parallel Autopilot Mechanization

Once it was accepted that electric signals from rate gyros could be used 0or helicopter stability augmentation, it was not much of a step to include the autopilot functions and to develop an automatic flight control system (AFCS). The decision as to whether it should be a series system with no cockpit control motion or a parallel system with motion has not yet been settled — since both types are in operation today.

In some systems, the onboard instrumentation is combined with radio navigation and landing equipment to operate flight director displays to tell the pilot how to move his controls to achieve the desired result. In more advanced concepts, the signals go into a computer and then directly to the controls. The pilot's duty becomes primarily one of monitoring that other "pilot".

The use of a computer makes it possible to combine the signals from the various sensors to provide the best possible flying qualities in various flight conditions. This makes it a "fly-by-wire" system for all functions except for full-authority pilot inputs and these, too, may some day be done by using electronic signals generated by cockpit-control motion to replace the push rods, bell cranks, and cables used on most helicopters today. This scheme promises some weight saving but will have to be 101% reliable. I heard one pilot say, "I am willing to accept fly-by-wire as long as the wires go up the center of sturdy control rods."

61 Fly-By-Wire

The term "fly-by-wire" leaves much to the imagination and therefore generates different reactions among pilots and designers facing the idea for the first time.

To establish a base for discussion, let's first examine the older concept: "fly-by-iron." Early helicopters -and some current small ones-give the pilot direct control of the main and tail rotors through a system of mechanical linkages consisting of push-pull tubes, bellcranks, and cables connecting the cockpit controls to the appropriate rotor. Figure 61-1 shows how this works in the longitudinal cyclic system.

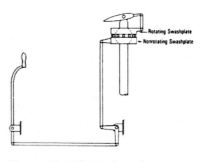

Figure 61-1 Fly-by-Iron System

With these simple systems, the controls can be easily moved when the rotors are not turning. But when they are turning, the pilot must act against sizable dynamic and aerodynamic forces. Much early design effort went toward developing refinements such as bungees, Chinese weights, and screw jacks to balance or reduce the pilot-control forces.

Fly-by-oil

At some point, as helicopters got larger, the control forces with fly-by-iron systems became too large to be handled comfortably and helicopter designers followed the lead of airplane designers by using hydraulic power for the muscle - thus introducing the era of "fly-by-oil."

Figure 61-2 shows a typical system-suitable for a medium-sized helicopter-in which the mechanical linkages from the cockpit are retained but instead of going directly to the swashplate, they go to a servo valve on a hydraulic actuator. Moving the servo valve results in the actuator extending or retracting to move the swashplate. The actuator does all the hard work while intercepting loads coming from the rotor and reacting them against structure instead of the pilot's hand.

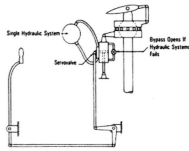

Figure 61-2 Single Hydraulic System

Only a single hydraulic system is used but it includes a bypass that opens if the system fails. This allows the pilot to control the aircraft by moving the body of the actuator but with greatly increased forces. This is similar to the power steering of your car.

On most large helicopters, the forces generated by the main and tail rotors are too large for even a strong pilot to overcome without help, so at least one more hydraulic system is added for redundancy. Great care

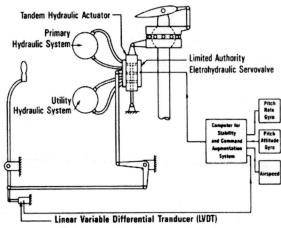

Figure 61-3 McDonnell Douglas Apache's Fly-by-Iron Dual Hydraulic Systems, and SCAS

is taken to make each system completely independent so that no one failure will leave the pilot without control.

Even though it takes only a small amount of force to move the servo valve and hydraulic redundancy exists, both the FAA and the military insist on stout control systems between the cockpit and the actuators. This is because someone getting in or out of the cockpit might inadvertently put high loads on the sticks or pedals.

Another reason is that control systems occasionally get jammed by foreign objects. The system should be robust enough so that the pilot can bend a misplaced screwdriver or crush an errant flashlight while doing whatever is necessary to maintain control.

The presence of a servo controlled hydraulic system opens the door to giving the pilot some help by artificially improving stability using gyros or other devices. Although components producing mechanical inputs were originally employed, the current practice is to use devices emitting electrical signals. These signals can be sent to a stability and control augmentation system (SCAS) computer and then to an electrically powered servo valve that moves the actuator independently of the pilot's input.

Typical of these systems is the one used on the McDonnell Douglas AH-64A Apache, shown in Figure 61-3. The servo valve controlled by the pilot can move the actuator from fully extended to fully contracted. However, the electro-hydraulic valve controlled by the SCAS computer is limited in its authority to 10% of full stroke on each side of the pilot's commands. This prevents a short in a sensor or a glitch in the computer from producing a full-stroke actuator hardover. Even the effect of a 10% hardover is minimized by monitoring the SCAS and immediately nulling its command if it is detected doing something dumb.

Note that the hybrid system has the capability of accepting signals from any type of sensor, processing them in any manner, and then using them to improve the flying qualities. Fly-by-wire advocates sometimes claim this capability exclusively for their own systems.

One type of signal going to the computer is from the linear variable differential transducer (LVDT) attached to each cockpit control. These signals improve controllability by overriding the gyro-stabilizing signals that would normally fight the pilot during maneuvers. The existence of these LVDTs leads to the possibility of true fly-by-wire.

As a matter of fact, if the Apache mechanical control system is severed in combat, a backup control system (BUCS) is automatically brought into play using the LVDT in the severed channel and giving it full authority over the appropriate actuator. By design, when the Apache is flying on BUCS, the affected channel does not accept signals from the other sensors, so control is like a pure fly-by-iron system. Since in this emergency situation the pilot is relying on a single LVDT, wire, and computer or "single-thread system," he is advised to quickly finish whatever he is doing and head home for repairs.

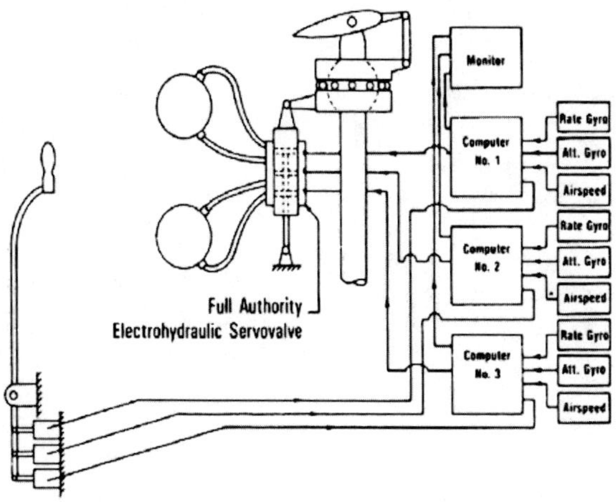

Full fly-by-wire

The Apache BUCS concept can be used as a basis for a full fly-by-wire system by not drawing in the push-pull tubes, bellcranks, and cables found in the original design. This is shown in Figure 61-4.

Now reliability becomes a major design consideration, since jeopardizing the aircraft with any single failure is not permissible. This is usually handled by using triply- or even quadruply-redundant independent systems with some sort of "voting", so that any system which is out of step with its mates will be ignored.

The control system is said to have "fail-operational" capability; that is, its performance is not degraded by a single failure. Physical separation of the various elements is also important. These considerations are of special concern to designers of combat helicopters. There is obviously a weight saving to be achieved by eliminating the mechanical elements, but the necessity of adding the redundant electronic systems at least partially reduces this saving.

Figure 22-4 Triply Redundant Fly-By-Wire System

Figure 61-4 Triply Redundant Fly-by-Wire System

Sidearm controllers

The recent thinking for such combat helicopters as the Army's proposed light helicopter, the LHX, is that, for a variety of good reasons, a sidearm controller will replace the cyclic stick and perhaps the collective lever and pedals as well. Using a fly-by-iron system with a sidearm controller does not appear possible because of the detrimental effect any free play - or "slop" - would have in a system moved with small wrist motions instead of large arm-and-leg motions.

Sidearm controllers will probably have little or no motion, but be responsive to forces instead. For these reasons, with these devices, it is quite certain that fly-by-wire is the only way to go-or is it?

Fly-by-light

Fly-by-wire can do everything the designer wants but it might also do something he doesn't want. During a thunderstorm, the wires might act as antennas and generate transient electrical spikes in response to lightning strikes or even near misses, just as a radio produces static. Radio static might only be annoying but control static could be downright dangerous. Lightning isn't the only source of electromagnetic pulses.

They can be deliberately generated by sophisticated devices in a combat situation.

To get around this, inventors have developed fly-by-light systems in which a coded series of light pulses traveling through an optical fiber carries the information from the cockpit controls and other sensors to the computer and then to the actuators.

62 Smart Control Systems

A helicopter control system should make the aircraft quickly do what the pilot wants, when he wants it-and nothing more. In this regard, the conventional helicopter control system gets a grade of B-minus.

To suit such a busy aircraft as a combat helicopter, engineers have strong motivation to raise the grade to A-plus.

Types of controls

Most man-carrying vehicles have controls the operator manipulates to achieve some desired velocity or, in engineering jargon, some desired "rate." For example, your car's accelerator governs forward velocity and the steering wheel the rate of turn. Typical of rate systems, these controls must be moved to start a maneuver and then neutralized to end it.

Not all vehicle controls are rate systems. In some cases, attitude is what is controlled. An evolutionary example of this is the passenger elevator, which started out with a rate system and usually required an operator. A modern self-service elevator, however, uses an "attitude" control in that pushing a button only once delivers you to the desired floor.

In this case, a feedback system senses the approach to that floor and skillfully reduced the rate just as the human operator used to do. This is a typical situation where increased complexity in the electromechanical components is used to reduce the "pilot workload."

It is not always necessary to have complex feedback systems with attitude control. Although a railroad train uses a rate control for distance, it uses attitude control for direction and its feedback system is about as simple as you could imagine-the pressure of the rails on the train's wheel flanges.

Besides rate and attitude controls, there is a third possibility-acceleration control. An example of this is on spacecraft, where rocket thrust produces a sustained acceleration and, upon approaching the destination, simply neutralizing the control is not sufficient-it must actually be reversed.

Time Histories Of A Desired Maneuver

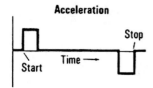

Acceleration

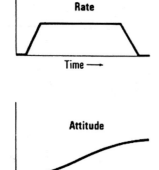

Rate

Attitude

Control Manipulation To Achieve Desired Maneuver

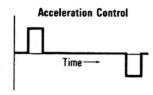

Acceleration Control

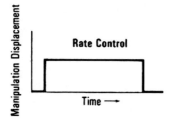

Rate Control

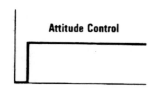

Attitude Control

Figure 62-1 Comparison of Basic Types of Control

Figure 62-1 shows the characteristics associated with all three types of control systems. First, the left side shows a maneuver described as time histories of its acceleration, rate, and attitude (or distance).

The right side shows what the operator has to do with his "manipulator" to achieve the desired maneuver.

Note that the manipulation of the acceleration and rate controls produces responses essentially directly proportional to the desired time histories. But this is not true for the attitude system. In this case, a "feed forward" feature is necessary to start the maneuver, a stability feature to hold it, and finally a feedback feature to stop it.

Hover responses

In and near hover, helicopter controls do a pretty good job of being rate systems. One of the best systems in this regard is main-rotor collective pitch. An increase in this control causes the helicopter to rapidly accelerate upward until a steady vertical rate of climb is achieved. At this point, the inflow coming down through the rotor decreases the angles of attack at the blade elements just enough to compensate for the increased pitch. When the desired altitude is reached, the collective must be returned to its hover position.

(There is a small exception to this scenario. If the original hover altitude was low enough to be in ground effect, a small increase in pitch may act as an attitude control and result in achieving higher wheel height with no further control manipulation as ground effect decreases.)

A tail rotor operates similarly to a main rotor. A change in its collective pitch will result in a hover turn at a constant rate that is stopped by returning the pedals to their original positions.

Even cyclic pitch is a rate control in and near hover. For example, a forward pitch-control input causes the rotor to process nosedown as a gyroscope so that its pitch rate-at least initially-is proportional to the longitudinal control displacement. After a few seconds, however, this changes as the tilt of the rotor causes the helicopter to translate into forward flight.

In forward flight

With translational flight comes asymmetric aerodynamics. These produce noseup flapping that eventually stops the angular rate and leaves the helicopter tilted nosedown and accelerating forward. Eventually, even this vanishes, leaving the aircraft in steady forward flight at some speed proportional to the longitudinal cyclic pitch.

(All of this is assuming that the helicopter is stable and that the lateral cyclic, the main rotor collective, and the tail-rotor collective have all been suitably and continually adjusted to keep the helicopter in trim.)

Thus the longitudinal cyclic pitch may be considered a rate system on pitch attitude for short-time response but an attitude system in the long run. At the same time, the cyclic is a short time acceleration control for translational motion, changing to a rate system in that it eventually results in a new trim speed.

In none of these systems is this response very satisfactory to the pilot and the flying-qualities engineer in that the systems are slow to settle down and usually involve some overshoots, even if the helicopter is stable.

Black boxes can improve this response or even change it from one type to another to improve flying qualities in various situations. Helicopter simulation and flight tests with various types of control systems are beginning to give us some clues here. The general conclusion is that rate-control systems are preferable for rapid maneuvers requiring gross changes in flight path or airspeed but attitude systems are preferable when only small changes are required.

Lateral cyclic pitch acts like longitudinal in hover, as it induces sideward flight. If, however, the helicopter has already been put into forward flight using longitudinal cyclic pitch, the lateral cyclic remains a rate control. A lateral stick displacement put in and held in forward flight will result in a continuous roll rate if the tendency to turn is cancelled out with the pedals.

Forward flight also changes the character of the pedal-input response from being a rate control in hover to becoming an attitude control of sideslip in forward flight.

Cross-coupling

Even though the discussion above indicates that the helicopter responds in a fairly logical manner to individual control inputs, we must admit that most of these individual control inputs also result in an unwelcome response in the other axes.

For instance, the main-rotor collective, while producing a pure rate response in hover also causes a nuisance yaw response that the pilot must cancel with his tail-rotor pedals. This, in turn, will usually cause the helicopter to roll since the tail rotor on most helicopters is above the aircraft's center of gravity.

In forward flight, these cross-couplings are even more universal, as pitch commands produce some roll and vice versa. A student, of course, learns to compensate for these odd characteristics in the process of becoming a pilot, so correct manipulation of the controls becomes second nature—at least when the view is good and he can concentrate on flying.

In more distracting circumstances, however, he would benefit if the helicopter control system would make the aircraft quickly do what the pilot wants it to do, and nothing more.

Something extra

Although a modern basic helicopter might have acceptable flying qualities without the help of avionics aids, there is always room for improvement - something to challenge the control-system designer. In particular, he looks for something that would make the control response "crisper;" that is, quicker, more predictable, and with less overshoot.

Other potential improvements include less control cross-coupling and the option to automatically hold the helicopter in a trimmed condition while the pilot attends to other duties.

For many years, helicopter engineers have used increasingly sophisticated avionics "black boxes," such as auxiliary stabilization equipment (ASE), to augment the control system—primarily to help stabilize the helicopter in an established trim condition in turbulent air. With the recent development of very lightweight and high-speed digital computers and compatible sensors, now the engineer may "highly augment" the control system to not only stabilize the helicopter but to also tailor the control responses to achieve the goals outlined above.

A model-following scheme

One way to use this increased capability is to program an ideal helicopter's equations of motion into the flight computer and have that mathematically modeled helicopter respond to the pilot's commands and to the outside environment as sensed by various instruments. Then, the actual helicopter looks at what the computer model is doing and imitates it in a follow-the-leader mode. Of course, this works best if the maneuvering computer model's capabilities are limited to what the actual helicopter can physically do.

(This technique has already been used for in-flight simulations of one aircraft by another. For example, the Space Shuttle's equations of motion while in its landing configuration were programmed into a jet aircraft to train Shuttle pilots for an actual landing where there was no option for a go-around.)

Using a model-following scheme gives the designer a wide range of flexibility. He can now change the model's "control laws" in the computer as a flight condition or task function. For a helicopter, the desired flight characteristics are different at high speed than they are at low speed - and even more different when taxiing.

The modern designer can respond to this by programming his computer to gradually change characteristics in some forward-speed range-typically 20 to 60 knots, and switch to an entirely different set of control laws when a "squat switch" is activated by putting enough weight on the landing gear to compress the oleos.

High speed

At high speed, the designer might choose to leave the basic helicopter's characteristics pretty much alone, using the augmentation only to smooth the rough edges. This is done by stabilization, response quickening, increasing damping, providing pedal-fixed turn coordination, and providing the option to hold attitude, speed, and altitude in unattended flight while the pilot does such attention-diverting tasks as reading maps or tuning radios.

The designer does not have to be satisfied with such modest goals, however. One suggested major flying modification involves separating the collective functions and the longitudinal-cyclic pitch controls in forward flight.

In a conventional helicopter, the pilot must use a combination of collective and longitudinal cyclic to change either speed or altitude without affecting the other. With suitable control laws enforced by a highly augmented control system, the designer can make the collective "manipulator" control only rate of climb as it does in hover, while longitudinal cyclic controls only forward speed without changing altitude. Whether this or other major changes are desirable can be easily evaluated using a helicopter equipped with a reprogrammable flight computer. Any advanced control system would also eliminate all undesirable cross-couplings in all flight conditions.

Low speed

At low speed, turn coordination is neither necessary nor even desirable, so this feature would be phased out at speeds below 20 to 60 knots. Instead, lateral cyclic pitch should control either sideward velocity or sideward displacement (for precision hovering), with the longitudinal pitch doing the same in its axis.

To do this right, sophisticated sensors for measuring airspeed, groundspeed, ground position, altitude, and heading must be included in the control system to provide the correct feedback information. For safety's sake, all these sensors and the flight computer must be designed so that no one failure (or two by some rules) can cause an accident.

The future

Looking into the future, we can see control systems integrated with navigation aids, incorporating preplanned maneuvers to such an extent that the pilot's primary duty is to monitor the systems.

There is a word of caution, however, coming from an investigative report on a jet-transport accident in which the crewmembers apparently put too much faith on their automatic systems. The National Transportation Safety Board report noted that increasing automation has not necessarily reduced the pilot workload—but has shifted the emphasis from controlling tasks to monitoring tasks.

There is convincing evidence, the board added, from both research and accident statistics, that people make poor monitors.

63 New Criteria for Flying Qualities

For many years, we stability-and-control engineers based the concepts used to analyze and design helicopter parts on similar work done by our fixed-wing compatriots. Starting in about 1960, we let the servomechanism engineers in on our fun, to help design automatic control systems. Suddenly, we started hearing a whole new language, with terms like "bandwidth," "cross-over frequency," and "phase margin." To understand this jargon, it is useful to look at some of the concepts they represent.

How it started

Automatic control systems have been around for a long time. Two hundred years ago, James Watt developed a fly-ball governor for his steam engine to hold its speed constant. But it wasn't until about 50 years ago that servomechanisms became a recognized field.

In a sense, the development of modern servomechanism analysis was led by electrical engineers. They worked with such devices as radios and radars, which use variable voltages.

Much of the jargon, therefore, can be related to electrical concepts. But for most of us, a mechanical analogy is helpful for understanding.

Simple system

The spring-mass-damper system (Figure 63-1) illustrates simply the physical principles of an oscillating system. It consists of an electric motor hung from a ceiling on a spring and restrained by a dashpot damper. The motor shaft is unbalanced by an offset weight, and the motor speed can be controlled by the experimenter.

For purposes of this discussion, the unbalancing mass's arm will be assumed to decrease as motor speed goes up, so the centrifugal force acting on the shaft remains a constant.

When the motor is running, the centrifugal force will cause the whole system to bounce up and down. How much? It depends on the speed - or frequency - of the motor.

It is convenient to plot the results in terms of "amplitude ratio," which in this case is measured in terms of how much the spring stretches.

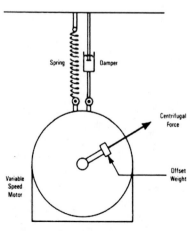

Figure 63-1 Simple Oscillating System

347

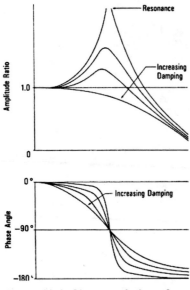

Figure 63-2 Characteristics of an Oscillating System

Figure 63-2 shows the starting amplitude ratio with the motor off; it is 1.0, corresponding to the static stretch. As the motor starts up at low speed, the oscillating centrifugal force will cause the motor's mass to alternately stretch and compress the spring.

Divide the maximum stretch by the static stretch and you have the amplitude ratio, which could also be designated as the ratio between output and input. As can be seen, the actual value depends on the level of damping in the dashpot. (You can think of changing the dashpot damping, depending on whether its working fluid is air, water, oil, or honey.)

Resonance

To investigate a unique condition, one can turn off the motor, pull down against the spring, and then let go. This will determine the "natural frequency," the frequency at which the system bobs up and down. This is primarily governed by the ratio of mass to spring rate, but also slightly by the damping.

To continue, one can fire up the motor again and slowly increase speed. Upon reaching the natural frequency, the amplitude will be at a maximum. In fact, with low damping, the system will go wild as it "resonates." Obviously damping will calm it down, and if the damping is high enough, or above the "critical damping," there will be no obvious resonance.

Figure 24-3 Bode Diagrams

At excitation frequencies above resonance, the response decreases until it finally becomes only a "dither," as the system cannot keep up with the demands placed on it. When the amplitude ratio falls below 1.0, the motor will appear to start levitating toward the no-stretch spring position.

You can demonstrate this effect for yourself on a spring-type bathroom scale. If you pump your arms up and down fast enough, you can quickly lose 10 or 20 pounds - according to the scale. Unfortunately, it is not only a temporary loss, but a false one as well. (This type of demonstration was once used to promote a device that supposedly used a directed centrifugal force to provide a direct lift capability.)

Phase

Not only is the amplitude ratio of interest, but so is the phase relationship between input and output. This is shown on the lower plot of Figure 63-2.

For very low frequencies, the mass will go up and down in phase with the direction of the centrifugal force. But as frequency is increased, the response will lag the input more and more until, at resonance, the response will be 90°, or one quarter of a revolution, behind the input. This is why a rotor blade flaps up over the nose due to an increase in lift on the right side; the blade is a dynamic system in resonance.

Note that the 90° phase lag is present at resonance no matter how much damping there is; and a blade is very heavily damped. At frequencies above the natural frequency, the response continues to lag until it gets completely out of phase and goes up when the centrifugal force points down.

Labeling scales

As in many engineering disciplines, the people working with dynamic systems have found convenient (for them) ways to present the results of their analyses. Figure 63-3 shows the same response as Figure 63-2, but replotted on "log-log" paper. The vertical axis is labeled in three ways: once as decimal values, once as 10 raised to a power, and finally as 20 times the power.

The units on this last scale are known as "decibels" or simply "dBs". In this form, Figure 63-3 is known as a "Bode diagram" after H.W. Bode, an electrical engineer working on radio amplifiers in the 1940s.

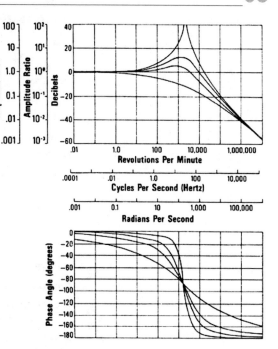

Figure 63-3 Bode Diagrams

The horizontal axis is the frequency band just like on an AM radio. For our simple system, the scale could be in revolutions per minute (rpm) or revolutions per second (rps). The latter is the same as Hertz, named after Gustav Hertz, a German physicist. The third way, labeling it in terms of radians per second, is also often used because the mathematical analysis of dynamic systems produces frequency answers directly in radians per second.

New thinking

The first several decades of helicopter stability and control work relied almost entirely on the study of time histories of rates and attitudes following step and pulse control inputs. These are known as "open loop" responses because the pilot is not using control motions to correct the helicopter but is simply going along for the ride. This, however, is not how a pilot flies an aircraft or how you drive your car. The usual real-life situation is that the vehicle operator sets goals informs of allowable errors on speed and displacement and then continually makes small control corrections to achieve these goals. This is "closed loop" operation with the human (or the automatic pilot) sensing errors and making corrections. If the task is difficult, the pilot must quickly and precisely respond to the perceived errors in order to do a good job. That is, he must "raise his gain" to do a "high-gain" task.

Bandwidth

For the most part, helicopter controls are rate command systems. That is, a deflection of any one of the cockpit controls will result in the helicopter developing an angular or a linear rate around or along the appropriate axis. At low frequencies, the rate response is proportional to the control input but at high frequencies, the helicopter cannot keep up with the control motion and so it just sits there and shakes. The frequency range over which the response (or amplitude ratio) is "flat" is known as the "bandwidth."This is the same thing the audio engineer looks for when he checks a hi-fi to frequencies as high as the ear can hear. For simple systems, the bandwidth in radians per second is equal to the inverse of the time constant. Thus if you hear that a system has a bandwidth of four radians per second, you can assume that the angular rate response to a step input would reach 63% of its steady value in a quarter of a second. Another way of defining the bandwidth is that it is the frequency at which the response is "down by 3 dB", i.e. the output is only 70% of the input. At higher frequencies, the output falls off drastically due to its logarithmic character. Physically, this means that the pilot cannot effectively control the aircraft at frequencies much above the bandwidth. Thus it may be seen that bandwidth is a logical figure-of-merit for aggressive or precision tasks where the pilot must use frequent control changes to do a good job. The new helicopter flying qualities requirements ask for bandwidths of at least two radians per second to define the minimum below which the pilot will complain that precise control is too difficult.

If high-gain flying requires the pilot to use control reversals at frequencies beyond the system's bandwidth, the response will not be as much as he expected and the lag in the response may be so long that he will find himself doing the wrong thing at the wrong time in a pilot-induced oscillation (PIO). To avoid this, the pilot must "back off" and operate at a lower frequency—one that might not produce the precision he would like for compensating for turbulence or for tracking an enemy aircraft. The highest frequency at which the pilot will be comfortable is where the system's amplitude ratio crosses the zero db line. This is known as the "cross-over frequency."

The higher the bandwidth, the crisper the system will be in responding to quick control motion, but in a helicopter, too much crispiness might get you into trouble by actually destabilizing some of the complex aeroelastic modes in the rotor or by coupling with the characteristics of the stability and control augmentation system (SCAS). In such cases, augmentation could actually reduce the usable bandwidth.

Phase margin

It is not only the fall-off of the amplitude ratio that limits the usable bandwidth. The difference between the phase at the crossover frequency and 180 degrees is the "phase margin." In theory, any margin is sufficient but if it is too small, the pilot will have to compensate by minimizing his own lag.

This may not be a problem for some flying tasks, but in others where he has other things to do such as in an intense combat situation, he may not be able to cope with an aircraft that already has a low phase margin. An accepted rule-of-thumb is that the "plant" (the aircraft and its control system) should have a phase margin of no less than 90 degrees because a reasonable value for a good pilot, considering his neuromuscular lag, is 45 degrees. This allows at least a 45 degree overall margin before PIOs rear their ugly head.

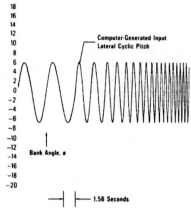

Figure 63-4 Roll Response of a Test Helicopter

Any lag in the system will decrease the phase margin. Three lags that are inherent in modern helicopters are: 1. In the rotor itself, corresponding to the time required to turn about half a revolution; 2. In the hydraulic actuators which can only move so fast; and 3. In dead spots and lost motion in the controls between the cockpit and the actuators. These add up on most helicopters to limit the bandwidth based on phase margin to about five radians per second. The clever design of the SCAS may improve this range.

Frequency domain

Studies limited to time histories obtained from step and pulse control inputs in the "time domain" will not pick up possible problems associated with rapid control reversals typical of high-gain flying so the control experts have adopted some of the techniques of the electrical and servo-mechanism engineers to work in the "frequency domain" where the Bode diagram is the primary tool. Test techniques have been developed for obtaining the open loop, frequency domain data by oscillating the appropriate control at higher and higher frequencies as shown in Figure 63-4. With a mathematical tool known as a "Fast Fourier Transform," the amplitude ratio and phase lag can be extracted from the data for the Bode diagram. Figure 63-5 was produced by this technique. It is a plot of the ratio of generated angular roll rate to lateral cyclic control input

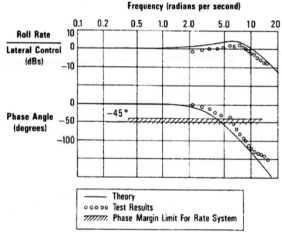

Figure 63-5 Bode Diagram for Roll Response of UH-60A

as the frequency of the control motion is increased. In this presentation, the amplitude ratio has been "normalized" on the value at low frequency to make it start out at zero db, and because the response is a rate rather than a displacement, the phase plot is already biased by 90 degrees. The "theory" line on the Bode diagram is a plot of the mathematical equation of the system known as its "transfer function." Note that from the test data, the bandwidth based on the amplitude ratio being down by 3 db is about ten radians per second but based on phase margin, the useable bandwidth would be only about five.

New specs

New specifications for helicopter flying qualities are now being written. For the first time, they will put forth requirements in the frequency domain as well as in the time domain. You will be hearing more of this strange language of the electrical and servomechanism engineers applied to our aircraft. In effect, they are saying: "What is good for an amplifier or a steam engine governor is good for a helicopter."

64 Parameter Identification

Since about 1970, a new term has entered the vocabulary of those who analyze helicopter stability and control. The term is "parameter identification" or as some people say, "system identification." What does it mean?

Starting simple

Let's start with a straightforward example. Suppose you have an object supported on a spring with a damper in parallel. If you pull the object down, let go, and then record its displacement, you will obtain a time history of an oscillation (Figure 64-1).

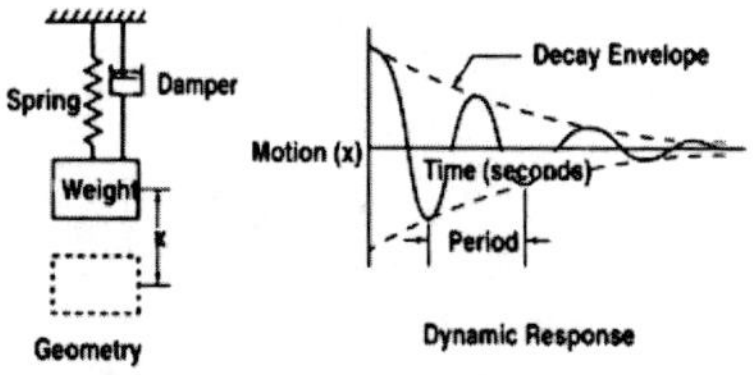

If you show this time history to someone with a little experience in the dynamics of systems, he will be able to evaluate—or identify—two parameters of the system:

• The ratio of the spring constant to the weight, and

• The ratio of the damping constant to the weight. He does this by working with the measured period of the oscillation and the rate of decay of the envelope that encloses it. If he knows the object's weight, he can tell you the spring rate, "k," in pounds per inch. He can also tell you the damping constant, "c," in pounds per inch per second.

Add complication

An airplane or a helicopter in flight obeys the same dynamic laws as the spring-mass-damper system. But the analysis is more complicated because the aircraft moves in six degrees of freedom rather than just one. It can move horizontally, vertically, and sideward, as well as rotating in pitch, roll, and yaw (Figure 64-2).

Starting from some trim condition, changes in the speed along (or the angular rate around) any of the three axes may produce changes in forces and moments in any of the degrees of freedom.

These changes would all seem to be due to the equivalent of dampers. But by looking at the system slightly differently, we can relate some of the changes to effective spring effects. Examples are the stability in forward flight of pitch provided by the horizontal stabilizer, and the directional stability provided by a tail rotor or vertical stabilizer.

Figure 64-1 Spring And Damper Weight System

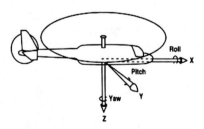

Figure 64-2 Helicopter Axes System

353

In the language of the aircraft analyst, all the change parameters are known as "stability derivatives," and they are used in a set of "linear" equations of motion.

For an aircraft in free flight with six degrees of freedom, it is theoretically possible to have 62 (36) stability derivatives. How so? Because for each motion along or around one of the three axes, a force or moment may be generated in not only the axis being directly affected but in all of the other five degrees of freedom as well. (In some rather sophisticated analyses, the rotor coning, longitudinal flapping, and lateral flapping are considered separate degrees of freedom, thus raising the theoretical number of stability derivatives to 81.)

In addition, there is another set of derivatives. They represent the forces and moments produced when the pilot moves any one of his controls: collective, longitudinal cyclic, lateral cyclic, and tail-rotor pedals. This adds another possible 24 derivatives to our collection of 36—to give 60.

Fortunately, many of the derivatives either physically do not exist or are small enough to be ignored. This leaves only about half that are really important to the analysis of flying qualities. The values of most of these stability derivatives depend on speed. In hover, therefore, even more derivatives drop out and the ones that remain have quite different values than they do in forward flight.

Estimated values of all of these stability derivatives can be obtained even before the aircraft flies. They are obtained using combinations of analysis, wind-tunnel results, and judicious guessing.

Obtaining flight-test data

However, the aircraft in flight may not behave in accordance with these initial estimates. Thus, analysts are motivated to use flight-test results to check and possibly modify the values of the stability derivatives. This is important for such things as making good simulators, providing a better analysis for correcting flying-quality problems, or even developing a sophisticated autopilot that will automatically reconfigure itself for optimum performance in any flight condition.

Flight testing is done with a helicopter that is instrumented to record accelerations, rates, and attitudes. The aircraft is first trimmed out in the flight condition to be investigated. To excite, or trigger, the various modes of response, all four pilot control-inputs may be used: longitudinal cyclic, lateral cyclic, collective, and pedals. Figure 64-3 shows several types of control inputs used.

Step, pulse, or doublet

A step control input is good for a short-time response. But for longer time histories, a pulse or doublet that represents flying through a gust must be used. The special sequence of sharp-edged pulses known as the "3211" will adequately excite both the short-period modes which damp

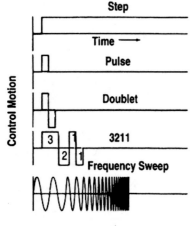

Figure 64-3 Types Of Control Inputs

out quickly and the long-period modes that might take 20 or more seconds to develop. Figure 64-4 shows how the pitch rate of an Aerospatiale (now Eurocopter) Puma at 80 knots responds to this kind of input in the longitudinal system.

To work in the "frequency domain" instead of the "time domain," one carries out a frequency sweep using sinusoidal inputs at increasing frequency.

Since it is the helicopter's basic characteristics that are desired, these tests should be done with the stability and control augmentation system (SCAS) turned off. That is, unless the helicopter is so unstable that adequate time histories cannot be obtained without SCAS.

Flight-test data can contain "noise" because the sensors pick up vibration, or the data is being taken when the air is not absolutely calm. Therefore, the data may have to be "smoothed" before analysis. A special filter to do this is known as a "Kalman Filter." Figure 31-5 shows the result of treating one test's time history with a filter.

Extracting derivatives

There are several ways to obtain the derivatives from the flight-test time histories. Each starts with a set of six equations of motion with first estimates for the 60 derivatives. The methods for extracting the derivatives may be thought of as sophisticated trial-and-error systems that attempt to curve-fit calculated results to the test data by modifying each of the derivatives.

Without going into the mathematics, we can at least name some of the techniques: Ordinary Least Squares, Weighted Least Squares, Recursive Least Squares, Deterministic Least Squares, Maximum Likelihood, Statistical Linearized Filter, and Extended Kalman Filter.

Many techniques require several passes through the data. Each pass produces better estimates. An enormous amount of calculation is required, so these techniques only became practical when high speed computers were introduced.

Several helicopters have been subjected to these techniques. Here's one discovery: The values of the final stability derivatives that make simulation satisfactorily agree with flight test-data can be more than 50% different from the original theoretical estimates.

This is most striking in those derivatives that are important in the Dutch roll mode (a combination of yaw and roll). These derivatives govern directional stability, dihedral effect, yaw damping, and roll damping.

It is evident that some of these are strongly affected by the main rotor's wake as it impinges on the tail surfaces in ways that are difficult to predict. This difficulty is what makes the parameter-identification process so valuable as the development of a helicopter matures beyond its first flight.

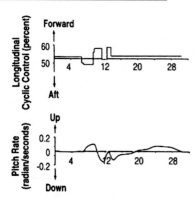

Figure 64-4 Pitch Rate Response To 3211 Control Input

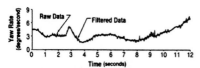

Figure 64-5 Smoothing Flight-Test Data

65 Computational Fluid Dynamics

Can the computer replace the wind tunnel? Theoretically, yes; practically, no (in my opinion).

The recent, tremendous increase in computer speed and capacity has excited the theoretical aerodynamicists, who have long known how to write very sophisticated equations for fluid flow, but haven't quite known what to do with them, except for the very simplest cases. Now with their new facilities, they have a new science: CFD-computational fluid dynamics.

Hydrodynamicists (water-flow specialists) discovered more than 200 years ago that by using the newly developed calculus and assuming water is a "perfect fluid," i.e. one that has no viscosity and is incompressible, they could study some flow phenomena.

Later, aerodynamicists used the same assumptions for a type of air flow, known as "potential flow." The basic premise is that an object going through a fluid (or held fixed while the flow passes around it) produces pressure waves that make the fluid move out of the way and then come back together after the object has passed. Potential-flow equations can also represent such phenomena as smoke rings and the flow about a rotating cylinder in uniform flow-an educational first step to understanding the lift of a wing or a rotor blade.

Yes, but...

The potential-flow equations, in their most elegant form, are known as Euler's Equations, after the Swiss mathematician, Leonard Euler (1707-1783). He simply restated Newton's Laws as applied to fluid: "The resultant force on any fluid particle must always equal the product of the mass of the particle and its acceleration, and that acceleration is in the direction of the resultant force."

Potential-flow solutions can give a good approximation as to the shape of streamlines over an airfoil or a streamline body and of lift and pitching moment, but they will not give good information on drag. Tb calculate drag, we must admit that air does have viscosity, although it is low. This is demonstrated by the observation that airplane-wing tip vortices can persist in calm air for several minutes after the airplane has passed.

357

One evident viscosity effect is the generation of a boundary layer next to the surface across which the air moves. This is due to some trapped surface molecules giving up their kinetic energy and then bouncing away to impede the progress of other molecules above the surface.

This continues out into the free stream until the effect vanishes and molecules move in streamlines unaffected by the shearing effect of those closer to the surface. How far out? It depends on how far along the surface the air has been traveling. The boundary layer may only be a quarter-inch thick at the trailing edge of a rotor blade but it may be several inches thick at the aft end of a jet transport's fuselage. The thickest boundary layer-possibly several hundreds of feet thick-is in the wind over the ocean.

Figure 65-1 shows that at the body's front, the boundary layer is "laminar" but at some distance back, it spontaneously becomes turbulent. Over very small, slow-moving surfaces (such as butterfly wings), the entire boundary layer will be laminar.

However, for most objects, such as rotor blades, the laminar flow extends back only a few inches from the leading edge. The air's loss of momentum across the boundary layer's depth, whether laminar or turbulent, results in a drag force known as "skin friction."

As long as the boundary layer is laminar, the equations governing the flow are fairly simple — some problems can be solved using old-fashioned paper and pencil mathematics. As soon as the boundary layer becomes turbulent, however, the randomness of the molecules' actions creates a situation which apparently led Theodore von Karman (Hungarian-born U.S. aeronautical engineer 1881-1963) to state, "Only God understands turbulence."

Equations

To solve the flow problem in cases where viscosity and turbulence are important, the Euler equations have been expanded into what are known as the Navier-Stokes equations, after two 19th-century physicists. These equations are so complex that there are no known general solutions. The theoretical aerodynamicist must resort to approximate methods based on statistical probabilities as empirically tailored to fit experimental data.

As if viscosity and the resultant turbulence were not bad enough, the assumption that air is incompressible is good only for low-speed flow analysis. The governing condition is a velocity ratio-the speed of the object through the standing air (or the speed of air over a standing object) compared to the speed at which pressure waves are propagated ahead of the object, which is the speed of sound. This ratio is the Mach number, named for a physicist, Dr. Ernest Mach, who worked in Austria about the turn of the century.

If the object is moving, its approach will be signaled to the molecules ahead by pressure waves propagated by the body at the speed of sound-

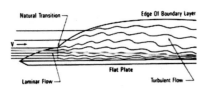

Figure 65-1 Characteristics of a Boundary Layer

about 660 knots on a cool day but faster on a hot one. If the Mach number is low, the molecules have plenty of time to move out of the way before the object gets close, just as if the air were incompressible.

If the speed approaches the speed of sound, however, the object will arrive before the molecules have moved out of the way, and if the speed is supersonic, they will be taken by surprise. As a rule of thumb, most conditions in aerodynamics can be assumed to be incompressible if the Mach number is less than about 0.5 corresponding to a speed of 550 feet per second.

Getting complicated

Thus, to study the aerodynamic conditions on a modern helicopter rotor blade, the theoretical aerodynamicist must account for compressibility and he must use the "Compressible Navier-Stokes" equations in order to adequately represent both the boundary layer and shock waves, and their possible interaction.

How complicated is this? Here is a brief description of the computing program used for the analysis of high-speed, two-dimensional airfoil characteristics at NASA:

"The approach is to solve the time-averaged, thin-layer Navier-Stokes equations with a simple eddy-viscosity model for the turbulent boundary layer. The numerical method is an alternating-direction, implicit, approximate-factorilization scheme, using scalar pentadiagonal inversion. The finite-difference approximations are solved as a series of time-like iterations with the steady state approached asymptotically."

Got that?

The computation is done by surrounding the airfoil, at a given angle of attack and Mach number, with a fine mesh grid as shown in Figure 65-2. In this case, 193 stations along the surface and 64 out from the surface were used to produce a total of 12,352 intersections.

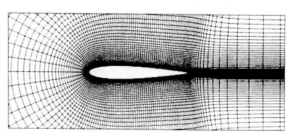

Figure 65-2 Grid System Used for Airfoil Analysis

Starting with some initial assumptions about the flow, the characteristics were calculated at each intersection. Since the characteristics at one intersection influence those at the other 12,351, the calculations are redone or "iterated."

After 1,000 iterations, the solution had converged to engineering accuracy. This all took the Cray supercomputer about five minutes. It is obvious that a three-dimensional problem done to the same detail would take many times as long.

The report's authors claim an accuracy of 5% on lift and 10% on drag and pitching moment. This is about the same magnitude as would be expected due to experimental error in a wind tunnel.

Facts of life

In engineering, there are "knowns," "known unknowns," and "unknown unknowns." The first category is easy to program on a computer and the second can be done by using "fudge factors" to make the answers agree with test data. The usefulness of CFD is generally limited to these two categories and in one sense is simply verifying what is already known. The computer's value is that, within its limits, it can be used to quickly examine the effects of changes in configurations and environmental conditions that would be very time-consuming in a wind tunnel.

Experienced engineers know that it is the third category, the unknown unknowns, that give the most trouble during any new development program, and it is here where the CFD experts will be the most-frustrated and where aerodynamic testing in the real (or almost real) world will always be required.

66 Aerodynamic Modifications

Most helicopter designs start out looking neat and clean-but as their development progresses, they often accumulate some untidy-looking external details. Most have obvious functional purposes but others cry out for explanation.

Spoilers and slats

Both the spoiler and the slat are examples of the project engineer's dilemma. While improving flying qualities, they also increase weight, drag, and cost. One of the classic helicopters, the Bell UH-1 Huey, has carried around an unsightly strip of sheet metal in the form of a spoiler riveted to the upper side of its horizontal stabilizer from the time of its early flight tests.

A helicopter, unlike an airplane, climbs and descends at a nearly level-fuselage attitude, as shown in Figure 66-1. This characteristic puts the horizontal stabilizer through a wide angle of attack range from large negative (nosedown) angles in a full-powered climb to large positive angles in autorotation.

Consequently, the stabilizer develops a download in climbs, producing a noseup pitching moment about the helicopter's center of gravity. Conversely, in autorotation, the load is up and the pitching moment nosedown. The pilot must use rotor flapping to balance these moments; so he holds the cyclic stick forward in climbs and aft in descents. If the stick travel required to go from a trim at a full-powered climb to autorotation at the same forward speed is more than about three inches, the characteristic is judged unsatisfactory.

Originally, the Huey had problems in this regard. Bell engineers first reduced the trim change by replacing the symmetrical stabilizer airfoil section with an inverted cambered section. This limited the amount of upload that could be produced in auto-rotation by inviting early stall around the relatively sharp leading edge. When this proved not quite effective enough, the spoiler was added to insure an even lower stall angle in autorotation.

Once a stabilizer stalls, either in descent or in climb, it loses its effectiveness as a stabilizing surface since changes in angle of attack are

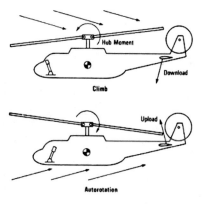

Figure 66-1 Trim Conditions in Climb and Autorotation

Figure 66-2 Fuselage Spoiler on MBB BO-105

not accompanied by corresponding changes in lift. This has resulted in degraded flying qualities for some helicopters.

The most troublesome condition has been climb, where the stabilizer is working at large negative angles. To prevent stall in this condition, several modern helicopters use fixed leading-edge slats to control the flow around the nose, thus permitting larger negative angles before stall. This fix can now be seen on the Bell Long Ranger and 222 and on the Aerospatiale Super Puma.

A spoiler is used for another purpose on the MBB BO-105. On this design, shown in Figure 66-2, the airflow separates at the bottom of the fuselage at its aft end. If left to itself, the separation point would wander back and forth, producing erratic pitching moments and flow at the empennage.

The addition of a spoiler fixes the separation point and also forces the fuselage wake down below the tail, thus producing a smoother ride. The problem has apparently not been so severe on the 105's big sister, the BK-117, since no spoiler is used on that aircraft.

Virtue of being blunt

Air molecules don't mind being pushed aside by the nose of a streamline body but they are often reluctant to close ranks after the point of maximum thickness passes by. In extreme cases, they refuse, and the result is separated flow at the trailing edge.

On a thick airfoil, the boundary-layer separation switches from side-to-side at low angles of attack. This changes the effective shape of the airfoil enough to decrease—or even reverse—the lift curve slope in this angle-of-attack range.

Since both the horizontal and vertical stabilizers on helicopters are often thick for structural reasons, they may be poor stabilizing devices in the many flight conditions where their angles of attack are small.

This may be cured by redesigning the airfoil with a blunt trailing edge so that the closure angle is more gradual and the air will stay attached. If the trailing edge is not too thick, there is not even a significant drag penalty.

A rule of thumb is that the trailing edge can be as thick as the boundary layer on one side at that point. At the speeds helicopters fly, this is about 2% of the chord. If thicker trailing edges are required to prevent separation, some drag penalty goes with it.

One such blunt stabilizer trailing edge is on the Hughes/Schweitzer Model 300 that came about by reducing the chord to minimize the up-load in auto-rotation. An even more extreme example is behind the

Figure 66-3 Very Blunt Trailing Edge on Aerospatiale Dauphin 2

fenestron on the Aerospatiale SA-365N Dauphin 2, as shown in Figure 66-3.

Figure 66-4 Trailing Edge Strip Used to Improve Aerodynamics of a Thick Airfoil Section

Another helicopter developed a thick trailing edge on its horizontal stabilizer during its flight-test program. This was the Lockheed Cheyenne, which had a pusher propeller spinning just a few inches behind the stabilizer. A few hours of flight produced fatigue damage in the original sharp trailing edge due to sonic pressure pulses. So the aft end was simply eliminated on a redesign, producing more clearance and a stouter-but blunter-edge.

An easier redesign than the physically blunt trailing edge to improve the aerodynamics of a thick airfoil consists simply of the addition of two bent-up sheet-metal strips, as shown in Figure 66-4. You can see these on the late-model Bell 222s and on the Aerospatiale TwinStar.

On the Aerospatiale Dauphin 2, a single strip is used on the horizontal stabilizer. In this form, it is a "Gurney flap", invented by a racecar driver (who had absolutely no understanding of aerodynamic principles) to make his rear "wing" hold the car tighter to the track. After it apparently helped win a race or two, a wind-tunnel test was done. Not only did the addition of the Gurney flap increase the lift coefficient (down in this case) but it decreased the drag as well!

Before this "reduction to practice", any good aerodynamicist could have explained why it couldn't possibly work. Now we can all explain why it does work.

Splitter plates, dog-house wings

The aft end of a fuselage is not the only place where erratic flow might originate. Occasionally it is found desirable to install splitter plates on the fuselage nose to help air molecules make up their minds whether to go left or right, or up or down around the nose. An example of the first was installed on the old Bell HSL tandem-rotor helicopter and an example of the latter is on the new McDonnell Douglas 500E. Relatives of these can also be seen as two strips on the forward pylon of the Boeing Vertol Chinook.

Figure 66-5 McDonnell Douglas 500E With Nose Splitter Plate (a), Doghouse Wing (b). and Beanie (c)

Both the 500E, shown in Figure 66-5, and the Chinook also have devices to control the flow behind the rotor pylon (called a "dog house" at McDonnell Douglas). These act as low-aspect-ratio wings generating tip vortices that feed high-energy air into the area behind the pylon to keep it from separating or at least to organize the air so that it is less erratic by the time it gets back to the aft end of the helicopter.

A fairing on top of the rotor hub can act as another low-aspect-ratio wing whose tip vortices organize the flow downstream primarily with the objective of reducing buffeting at the tail. These "beanies" can be seen on designs by McDonnell Douglas, Sikorsky, MBB, and Aerospatiale.

In conclusion, gadgetry added to a helicopter to make it fly better is fairly common as standards keep improving. But the goal of the aerodynamicist should be to get it right the first time.

67 Wind Tunnel Testing and Simulation

The basic idea behind wind-tunnel testing is that the effects of air moving past a stationary object are exactly the same as the effects on the same object moving through stationary air; that is, it is only the relative velocity that counts. Although some aerodynamic testing has been done by mounting a model on a moving vehicle — a car, truck, or rocket-powered sled—the wind tunnel has proven to be the most convenient, accurate, and productive aerodynamic testing device.

In using data from the tunnel, aerodynamicists depend on two fairly good assumptions:

Figure 67-1 Model of Sikorsky ACAP Used for Fuselage and Empennage Study

1—The effects on a small object are identical in character to the effects on a larger object of the same shape and thus a small-scale model can be used to determine the aerodynamic characteristics of a full-scale aircraft, and

2— The characteristics measured at one speed can be applied to other speeds by the use of nondimensional coefficients that yield full-scale forces and moments when multiplied by factors representing the actual flight velocity, the actual air density, and the actual aircraft size.

These concepts have been well known for a long time. The Wright brothers built and used a wind tunnel before their first flight.

Us and them

Helicopter engineers use wind tunnels to refine the configuration of the fuselage and empennage during preliminary design (Figure 67-1), to investigate aerodynamic-interference effects between the rotors and the airframe, to study rotor-system dynamics (Figure 67-2), and to develop improved airfoil sections for rotor blades.

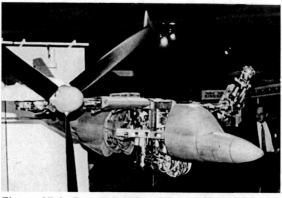

Figure 67-2 Dynamic Wind Tunnel Model of Boeing Vertol

Despite all these jobs, we still use the wind tunnel less than our fixed-wing friends. One of the main reasons is that the airplane people are always trying very hard to make their aircraft do what ours do very easily—fly slowly. They spend much of their wind-tunnel time developing flaps, slats, and effective control systems.

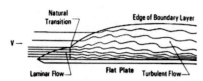

Figure 67-3 Characteristics of a Boundry Layer

Most of the rest of the time, they are trying to reduce drag. One of my Lockheed friends says, "I would sell my grandmother for a 1% drag reduction." In this endeavor, he is on firmer ground than I. He is trying to reduce drag, at least for low speed airplanes, primarily arising from two sources: skin friction and wing lift. Methods for dealing with these are fairly well understood.

A large part of helicopter drag, on the other hand, is due to air separation behind such bluff bodies as rotor hubs. So far, we have been frustrated in predicting the flow around these objects and developing fairings that reduce drag while still permitting them to work as they must. This is a standing challenge for future helicopter engineers.

A slight problem

A problem that confuses the interpretation of wind-tunnel data is caused by a small flaw in the assumptions on which such testing is justified— that small-scale models accurately represent full-scale aircraft and that the testing velocity doesn't matter. The problem is due to a change in the flow character as a parameter known as the "Reynolds number" varies.

Osborn Reynolds was a British engineering professor in the late 1800s who was concerned with how much water could be delivered by different-sized pipes. He found that the coefficient of internal resistance depended on both pipe size and water velocity, whereas the basic theory would say that it should be constant. He invented a parameter— the Reynolds number— to quantify this effect. For our purposes, it is proportional to velocity multiplied by the distance the air travels.

Flow along a surface develops a boundary layer where the air is slowed by some molecules being trapped right at the surface and affecting others a little further out. At low Reynolds numbers (represented by low velocities or small distances traveled from the leading edge), the boundary layer will be "laminar"; that is, adjacent air molecules will flow along side-by-side staying in their assigned paths as in Figure 67-3.

After achieving a certain — or critical — Reynolds number, the molecules begin jostling each other and the flow in the boundary layer becomes turbulent. This point is called natural transition and can be delayed if the air is accelerating, as it is over the nose of a rotor blade, or it can be forced prematurely by roughness on the surface.

You don't have to be an aerodynamicist to see natural transition between laminar and turbulent flow. A cigarette in an ash tray will send up a laminar smoke stream which abruptly goes through transition several inches up as it reaches its critical Reynolds number.

Effect on drag

As you might suspect, the type of flow over an object has an effect on how air travels over it and what forces it generates. Laminar flow over a surface will produce less skin friction than turbulent flow. Thus, blades

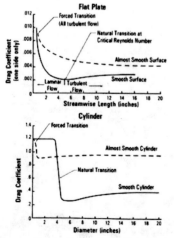

Figure 67-4 Drag Coefficients at 100 Kts

and other skins should be kept as smooth and clean as possible to avoid forced transition.

On the other hand, small bluff bodies behind which the flow separates may have more drag if the boundary layer is laminar than if it is turbulent. That is why golf balls, which travel at less than their critical Reynolds number, are dimpled. Figure 67-4 shows drag coefficients at 100 knots for a flat plate as a function of its length in the streamwise direction and of a cylinder as a function of its diameter. (The same curves would apply at 200 knots by halving the dimensions.)

The change in drag coefficient with size makes it difficult to accurately apply the wind-tunnel measurements of the drag on small models to actual helicopters. For example, a full-scale rotor mast might have a diameter of eight inches (20 cm) but only be one inch (2.5 cm) in diameter on the model. With the wind tunnel running at 100 knots, the results would overestimate the drag of this component by a factor of three. The drag of components on which skin friction is important might or might not be measured accurately, depending on the relative size and surface condition of the model and the helicopter.

Despite this general tendency to overestimate based on differences in the coefficients, the total drag measured on wind-tunnel models is almost always less than eventually proven by flight test. A contributing reason for this is that most models are built without trying to represent all of the small drag-producing items that eventually get stuck on the outside. (For example, the Lockheed AH-56 Cheyenne ended up with 12 separate external antennas of various sizes and shapes.)

Besides these external drag items, there is always air going into the fuselage and being slowed down before being dumped overboard with a loss of momentum. Not only is air being used for the basic engine supply but also for cooling the engine, the main transmission, the tail-rotor gearboxes, the cockpit, the avionics, the hydraulic system, and for ventilating the battery compartment and around the fuel tanks.

Leaky bodies

Besides this useful airflow, there is always some parasitic flow, which comes in through unsealed inspection doors and other openings, causing drag without doing anything beneficial. Many helicopter fuselages have the aerodynamic characteristics of a sieve that are never adequately represented on a model For these reasons, a wind-tunnel test of a small-scale model of a helicopter airframe can only serve as a rather uncertain data base for drag estimation. No helicopter aerodynamicist I know has ever been pleasantly surprised by flight-test results (and my airplane friends say the same).

If a wind tunnel test cannot be used to predict the absolute drag level, it can, in many cases, serve as a useful tool to investigate configuration changes designed to reduce drag by eliminating local areas of separation.

Measurements of forces and moments affecting longitudinal and directional stability are less affected by size effects and model fidelity than is drag and thus the tunnel appears to produce valid and usable data for these measurements.

Full-scale testing

For wind tunnel testing, small-scale models are useful and convenient but their less-than-full-size introduces some uncertainties into the results. Testing full-scale models or actual aircraft in a wind tunnel reduces these uncertainties.

The National Aeronautics and Space Administration (NASA) has two large tunnels for this purpose, one in Virginia with a test section 30 feet high and 60 feet wide (9 by 18 m) and another in California with two test sections: one 40 feet by 80 feet (12 by 24 m) and another section 80 feet by 120 feet (24 by 36 m).

Figure 67-5 Bell's XV-15 in NASA's 40-by-80 Foot Tunnel

(Typical other wind tunnels have test sections that range from 3 feet by 5 feet to 20 feet by 20 feet [0.9 by 1.5 m to 6 by 6 m].) Figure 67-5 shows a typical installation in the 40-by 80-foot tunnel. Because of the cost of the models and of the tunnel operation, these tests are usually only justified when investigating serious problems.

A flying wind tunnel

Even tests of full-scale models are not entirely free of uncertainties. A wing or rotor producing lift imparts a downward velocity to the air behind it. In a wind tunnel, this downward motion is stopped by the floor and this slightly changes the total airflow around the entire model. This change is accounted for by correcting data for "wind tunnel wall effects" by methods originally developed for wings and later modified for rotors.

In an attempt to avoid even these corrections and to test at higher speeds than can be obtained in a wind tunnel, NASA has recently developed the Rotor System Research Aircraft (RSRA), built by Sikorsky Aircraft. This aircraft (Figure 67-6), is — in effect — an airplane on which a test rotor can be flown while allowed to contribute various proportions of the required thrust and propulsion force.

Figure 67-6 NASA's Rotor Sstem Research Aircraft (RSRA)

The rotor is mounted to the RSRA with a six-component balance system so that its vertical thrust, forward force, side force, pitching moment, rolling moment, and torque can be measured. A unique feature of the RSRA is its ability to shed the rotor blades if serious trouble develops. This gives the crew the option of flying home as an airplane or using their ejection seats.

A dynamic concept

A type of helicopter wind-tunnel test that is becoming more common is the use of a model with a powered rotor. These models are much more expensive to build and test than those without rotors but do allow us to determine the aerodynamic interaction effects of the rotor on the airframe — and of the airframe on the rotor.

In addition, if the model rotor has dynamic similarity to the full-scale rotor (with matching stiffness and weight distributions), it can be used to investigate vibration and oscillatory load problems much more cheaply and safely than on an actual helicopter. Figure 67-7 shows one of the earliest of these models: a tenth-scale model of the Hughes XH-17 flying crane, used to investigate a dynamic problem almost 50 years ago.

Figure 67-7   Dynamic Wind Tunnel Model of the Hughes XH-17

Airfoil development

Another task the helicopter aerodynamicist assigns to the wind tunnel has to do with his continual search for a rotor blade airfoil shape with more lift and less drag. In these tests, it is desirable to match both the Reynolds number and the Mach number of the blade element in actual flight. This requires a tunnel with velocities near the speed of sound and large enough to test a model with a chord as big, or nearly so, as the actual blade.

This type of model is usually tested in a narrow "two-dimensional" test section, with the model spanning the tunnel from wall to wall to simulate the conditions from just inboard of the tip to just outboard of the root, The walls contain supports that allow the angle of attack to be changed. Figure 67-8 shows a new airfoil designed by Hughes as installed in Lockheed's high-speed, two-dimensional tunnel.

Figure 67-8   Airfoil Test Section in a Two-Dimensional Wind Tunnel

There are two ways of obtaining aerodynamic characteristics from such a test. One is to support each end of the model with balance systems designed to measure lift, drag, and pitching moment directly. The other is to measure the pressures on the model surface for lift and pitching moment and to measure the loss of energy in its wake for drag.

Often, both systems are used. There is much useful information which can be obtained only from pressure measurements, even in those installations where a balance is also used.

One of the most sought-after results of this type of test is the maximum lift coefficient at various Mach numbers. Unfortunately for the confidence of the helicopter aerodynamicist, different wind tunnels give different results — even for tests of the same airfoil contour. This is shown in Figure 67-9, which presents test data on the plain-vanilla NACA 0012 airfoil as tested in seven different tunnels. There is, as yet,

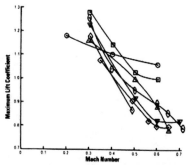

Figure 67-9   Results From Seven Wind Tunnels, NACA 0012, Max COL

no agreement between wind-tunnel engineers as to which of these tunnels (if any) are right.

Facts of life

Besides this problem, there is a further challenge in guessing how well even the best tunnel data applies to the airfoil on a blade in forward flight, considering the rapid changes in angle of attack that the blade sees during each revolution.

To investigate this, some tunnels have the capability to oscillate the airfoil at various frequencies and amplitudes. This data is then used to predict the delay in flow separation — or stall — that actually exists on the retreating side of a rotor in high-speed flight. However, even these tests do not account for the also rapidly changing Mach number and sweep angle— or the fact that the tip effects extend some distances inboard with as-yet not-well-understood consequences.

There are still enough questions about these procedures to insure job security for helicopter aerodynamicists (and tunnel operators) for years to come.

Uncertainties or not, in any wind-tunnel program, a series of good photographs of the model will prove to management and the customer that the aerodynamicist did what was expected of him.

Simulation

The other important ground test facility for the helicopter engineer is the flight simulator.

While proving very useful as a training device and for studying man-machine interface problems in the cockpit, the helicopter flight simulator faces some flying-quality problems it has been unable to solve (or prevent) before they are discovered in flight.

The goal of the simulator is to provide the same cockpit environment on the ground that the actual —and expensive—aircraft provides in the air. If this is done with high enough fidelity, the pilot's actions and reactions will be the same in either place.

Simulation got started in the '30s with the famed Link trainers used to teach airplane instrument flying. Today, the technology allows both instrument and visual flight simulation to the point where the aircrew (making only a slight disconnect with reality) can experience most effects of flight.

Both airplane and helicopter operators have found simulation a cost-effective means to teach routine and emergency cockpit procedures for instrument flight, navigation, communication, system management, and even operations into specific airports or, in the case of helicopters, oil rigs.

To move or not to move

Many training tasks can be done with the cockpit mockup firmly fastened to the floor—but motion makes the experience more realistic. So modem simulators are mounted on computer-controlled hydraulic actuators that move the cockpit to provide essential motion cues which the pilot perceives and uses to stabilize and control the aircraft.

As a minimum, motion in pitch is provided and —at increasing cost and complexity—roll, yaw, up-and-down, side-to-side, and fore-and-aft. Figure 67-10 shows a training simulator with all six of these degrees of freedom. This one also produces realistic sound and vibration in addition to a computer-generated view of the outside world.

Even limited motion is useful because our bodies are only sensitive to accelerations — or changes in velocity. Simulator designers make the actuators produce these accelerations in response to control motion or to simulate gusty air. The designers also program the simulator to continually drift back toward its center positions with motions whose accelerations are too small to be detected by a pilot busy with flying tasks.

Flight profiles that would normally result in high accelerations lasting for some time require a lot of simulator movement to be realistic. If the object is to research man-machine matching during such tasks as contour flying, the motion requirement becomes very large.

This is a feature of the Vertical Motion Simulator (VMS) operated by the National Aeronautics and Space Administration's (NASA's) Ames Research Center at Moffett Field, Calif. This apparatus can move its cab from center 30 feet (9.1 m) up and down and 20 feet (6.1 m) right and left. (Figure 67-11)

But even this large capability is not sufficient to simulate the forces on the pilot during sustained turns, pullups, or pushovers. To do this would require mounting the cab on a rotating arm so that centrifugal forces could be generated-like some carnival rides. One attempt to do this, however, led to so many false cues that it has not been tried again.

Mixed cues

Even when the VMS is able to simulate the aircraft accelerations, it is still not clear if the pilot is getting the same cues he would in the real world. I quote from a recent paper by a NASA simulation engineer:

"Unfortunately, little is known about the factors limiting a pilot's performance or the manner in which he synthesizes the information required for controlling the aircraft and, in particular, what criteria he used for selecting, rejecting, or weighing the sensations impinging on him. As a result, it is not known how much motion is required in what circumstances and for what tasks. All the complications associated with helicopters and VTOL aircraft make the need for the additional cues provided by the simulator motion system greater than in the case of fixed-wing aircraft."

Figure 67-10   Simulator with Six Degrees of Freedom

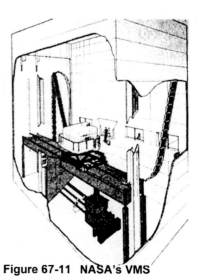

Figure 67-11   NASA's VMS

Even with an easier job, our fixed-wing friends are still having problems. For example, one of the most serious man-machine mismatches results in pilot-induced oscillations (PIO) in which the pilot does the wrong thing at the wrong time while trying very hard to do the right thing at the right time.

The control system for one of our most recent jet fighter aircraft was "optimized" on a simulator but during a high-speed taxi teat, the pilot got into a violent roll PIO and had to make an unplanned takeoff to save the situation.

Many attempts have been made with simulators to induce PIO tendencies that have occurred in flight but, so far, success has been very limited. This is apparently because the pilot, knowing he is safely in a simulator, doesn't get as excited as he would if he were facing an actual crash. Consequently, he doesn't force himself into the "high-gain" mode that causes most PIOs

Subtle aerodynamics

Problems that cannot yet be satisfactorily addressed by the simulator are those involving the subtle, yet powerful, interactional aerodynamics between the main rotor, the tail rotor, the fuselage, and the empennage. For example, we know from experience that the direction the tail rotor turns has a tremendous effect on flying qualities when the tail rotor is operating in the vortex ring state, which happens during left sideward flight.

What we do not know is how to write the equations that would allow the simulator to demonstrate these effects. In forward flight, the rotor-wake pattern, described in Chapter 22, is still beyond our ability to program and consequently, we cannot accurately predict such problems as unstable Dutch Roll.

The flying-quality problems that forced major changes in the aft ends of the Lockheed AH-56 Cheyenne, the Hughes AH-64 Apache, and the Sikorsky UH-60 Black Hawk after their first flights were not problems that could have been discovered even with today's sophisticated state-of-the-art simulation.

This is not to say, however, that simulation is not a useful tool during the development phase. It has been used successfully to improve the symbology for the head-up display (HUD) in the Apache, to investigate the acceptability of side-arm controllers, and to optimize conversion procedures on the Bell XV-15 tilt-rotor aircraft.

Perhaps simulation today is much like that of another well-known scientific discipline developed some time ago. Bart Kelley, former Senior Vice President for engineering at Bell Helicopter Textron Inc. pointed out:

"In the last half of the 19th century, thermodynamics became one of the cornerstones of physics but it played almost no part in the inventing and developing of the steam engine— only in refining and perfecting it."

Perhaps we should look forward to the art of simulation helping in refining and perfecting the helicopter.

.

68 Horizontal and Vertical Stabilizers

Designers of the first helicopters were delighted just to see them get off the ground. If they even thought about stability and control, the emphasis was always on the latter—just as the Wright Brothers had done when they developed their unstable but very controllable "Flyer." Consequently, if the early helicopters had any tail surfaces at all, they were often of minimum size; but as the helicopter grew up, so did both the horizontal and vertical stabilizing surfaces.

The reasons why

The need for these surfaces arises from the same reasons as on airplanes: a streamlined fuselage shape is aerodynamically unstable both in pitch and yaw and the addition of a wing or a rotor makes it even worse. The first to recognize that the helicopter and the airplane were similar in this aerodynamic need were engineers at NACA (now NASA) who started installing tails on their helicopters as part of the first research programs on improving flying qualities.

S-55

As a matter of course, the modern designer now sketches in a horizontal stabilizer from the first. The need for a vertical stabilizer is less clear-cut because a tail rotor alone is usually enough to stabilize the fuselage in yaw. For this reason, the vertical stabilizer in many designs is simply a streamlined fairing for the tail-rotor support structure.

Sikorsky experience

Is it interesting to follow the fortunes of the stabilizing surfaces as they were developed at several helicopter companies. Sikorsky has had the most extensive collection of tail configurations so Figure 68-1, which shows some of them, is a good place to start. The first production Sikorskys had no tail surfaces at all. A friend of mine who flew R-4s at the end of World War II said that the time required to tune the radio was, by coincidence, exactly the same time required to lose control.

S-56

Later models like the S-55 (H-19), designed about 1949, had tail surfaces but they were minimal. The same can be said of the S-58 (H-34) whose horizontal stabilizer looked like a misplaced tail-rotor mechanic's work stand. It didn't do much good but it didn't do much harm either.

S-62

Figure 68-1 Sikorsky Tails

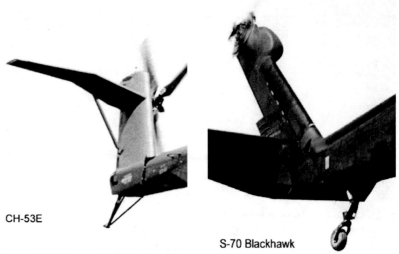

CH-53E

S-70 Blackhawk

Figure 68-1 Sikorsky Tails, Continued

300C

500C

500D

Figure 68-2 Hughes Tails

The S-56 (H-37) prototype had a reasonably sized horizontal stabilizer placed forward on the tail boom. After the first flights, the aerodynamicists were shocked at the poor hovering performance and a big part of the problem was traced to the aerodynamic download on the stabilizer. During the design, the download had been accounted for by assuming that the downwash velocity at the tail location was the same as at the rotor disc. It was known, of course, that the downwash eventually doubled in the fully contracted wake but no one at that time realized that the wake contracted so quickly, resulting in the actual download being four times (22) the estimate. The design was changed, first to a hinged surface that could be unlocked to float free and align itself with the flow in the wake at low speeds and later to a fixed, high surface opposite the tail rotor — a configuration also used on the flying crane versions, the S-60 and the S-64.

This half-tail was a Sikorsky trademark on the various models between the S-59 and the S-65. It put the stabilizer out of reach of the main-rotor wake in most flight conditions at the expense of a somewhat awkward structural arrangement. When the Sikorsky designers were developing the CH-53E from the earlier versions, they tried to break the mold by using a low, fixed surface. The result was such poor flying qualities that they once again moved the stabilizer up opposite the tail rotor for what must be one of the ugliest arrangements in modern helicopters—but it works!

The S-67 was a company-financed attack version of the S-61 and for this design, Sikorsky opted for a low, aft surface with free-floating capability at low speeds to minimize trim changes as the wake flowed over it. The results of the flight program, however, indicated that this feature was not necessary and that the flying qualities were satisfactory in all flight regimes with the stabilizer locked in its cruise flight position.

Based on this experience, Sikorsky's entry into the Army's Utility Tactical Transport Aircraft System (UTTAS) competition, the S-70 (also known as the UH-60 or Black Hawk), had a fixed, low-aft, surface. Shortly into the flight-test program, erratic trim changes at low speed made the designers realize they had been misled by the benign handling qualities of the S-67. Quickly they designed a "stabilator" (from the fixed-wing argon denoting a surface that acts both as a fixed stabilizer and as a movable elevator). Instead of letting the surface float, they elected to control it in all flight conditions by using an actuator to change incidence as a function of forward speed and collective pitch.

With this scheme, at low speed the stabilator is aligned more or less with the flow as the rotor wake passes over it. The collective input is primarily used going into autorotation to lower the incidence to minimize the trim shift that normally occurs due to the sudden upload on the tail. (Sikorsky's competitor in the UTTAS competition, Boeing Vertol, had recognized the need for the stabilator during wind-tunnel tests of a powered model of its design and so its prototype had one from the beginning.)

When Sikorsky designed the S-76, the aerodynamicists predicted that a movable stabilator would not be needed for civil operations but the Sikorsky management, nervous after the Black Hawk experience, dictated one anyway. Flight tests showed that, as on the earlier S-67, the flight characteristics were satisfactory with fixed incidence and so it was redesigned to this lighter and cheaper configuration.

Hughes searches

The Sikorsky Black Hawk experience had ramifications for other design teams and influenced the Advanced Attack Helicopter (AAH) competition that followed UTTAS by a couple of years. Hughes Helicopters, one of the two winners of a development contract (Bell was the other), had laid out its empennage design similar to the original Sikorsky UH-60 configuration with a low, aft, but fixed horizontal surface. At the time, it seemed a good idea — since it would keep people from walking into the tail rotor and could serve as a built-in work stand.

Hughes had two prototypes under construction when the engineers heard of the Sikorsky erratic trim-shift problems leading to the stabilator development. Would the troubles also apply to the AH-64? In order to find out, the Hughes engineers used an OH-6A mounted with a simple plywood stabilizer located in the same relative position with respect to the main rotor as was being built for the AH-64. It didn't take much testing of this flying test bed, shown in Figure 68-2, to prove that a change to the configuration was mandatory.

But what should the change be?

None of the options looked attractive. Stabilators as on the two UTTAS designs are complicated, structurally inefficient, and can do the wrong

AH-64 Mockup

AH-64

AH-64 T-Tail

Figure 68-2 Continued: Hughes Tails

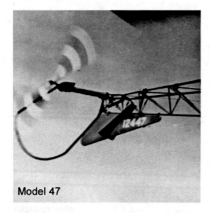
Model 47

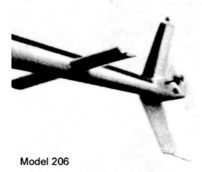
Model 206

206L

Model 222

Figure 68-3 Bell Tails

thing after a mechanical or electrical failure. A fixed surface placed well forward on the tail boom, as on most Bell designs, suffers from download in hover and because of its short moment arm must be bigger than one located further aft. A T-tail, as already used on the Hughes 500D, is structurally inefficient. Furthermore, because of its weight and location, the T-tail can introduce several modes of vibration excited in forward flight by the nearby wake of the main rotor.

After seriously considering all three options, Hughes chose the T-tail. It turned out to be a mistake; primarily for a reason not experienced before. In a high-powered climb, the download on the surface due both to the climb angle and the down-wash induced by the rotor made the AH-64 fly nose-up. This would not be a problem on most helicopters with good forward visibility but in this aircraft, the pilot has the copilot and a considerable amount of nose-mounted equipment ahead of him. This, combined with some serious vibration problems, convinced Hughes that the stabilator was not such a bad idea after all — and so one was promptly designed and built for the Apache.

Another unique tail arrangement is found on the Hughes 500C — which traces back to the OH-6A design of the '60s. On this — and on the smaller 300C — the "horizontal" surface is slanted up. This is primarily done to avoid a sudden rotor-wake impingement in transition by allowing the effect to develop gradually. This arrangement works well on helicopters with relatively low disc loadings. When the 500D was being designed, it was decided to use a T-tail, primarily because it looks better.

On this aircraft, with good forward visibility and different dynamic characteristics than the AH-64, the T-tail has proven to be satisfactory.

The tails of Bell

Bell, like Sikorsky, didn't use horizontal stabilizers on its early models (partly because they did not have streamlined fuselages) but by the time of the design of the UH-1 prototype in 1955, Bell had accepted the stabilizer's desirability. In order to minimize the trim shifts in transition, Bell, from the beginning, chose to locate the surface forward on the tail boom so that it would be in the rotor wake in hover and come out of it only after substantial forward speed had been achieved. Figure 68-3 shows the consistency of this decision — although on the Model 222 prototype an attempt was made to use a T-tail configuration, which resulted in trim-shift problems serious enough to make the designers reconsider.

The relatively modest control power achievable with the usual Bell teetering rotor has generated some secondary trim problems, especially when entering autorotation. This is due to the high angle of attack on the surface producing an upload that must be trimmed out with aft cyclic stick. Pilots object when they consider this stick motion excessive.

Bell has tackled the problem in several ways. One of the most noticeable is the use of a highly cambered surface mounted "upside down". This insures that the tail stalls with a small positive angle of attack as in autorotation and therefore cannot produce a large upload. On some models, Bell has also added spoilers and on others leading edge slats to prevent stalls in climbs. On many of their helicopters, they also change the incidence of the stabilizer by gearing it to the longitudinal cyclic-stick position. The incidence increases from a slightly negative (nose-down) value with the stick centered to positive angles with stick motion in either direction. This scheme produces the right pitching moments in both rearward and forward flight to reduce the amount of longitudinal cyclic stick displacement required to trim.

Vertical stabilizers

In most cases, the tail rotor alone is effective enough to give a helicopter fuselage directional stability without the need for a vertical stabilizer but most modern designs have both anyway.

Depending on the helicopter, the vertical stabilizer may: streamline the tail rotor support, supplement the directional stability produced by the tail rotor, unload the tail rotor in forward flight by providing some anti-torque force, support a T-tail, or stabilize the fuselage in case the tail rotor drops off completely. Figure 68-4 shows some typical installations designed to satisfy one or more of these objectives.

Dirty air

Any component mounted at the end of the tail boom operates in a poor environment because of the dirty air coming back from the fuselage and rotor hub. To investigate this on the Hughes AH-64, a flow survey was made at the empennage location during a wind-tunnel test of a powered model. The top part of Figure 68-5 shows how the local dynamic pressure was reduced compared to the clean air coming at the nose.

The bottom part of Figure 68-5 illustrates the rather chaotic flow in the wake. Both the effects of downwash and swirl are reflected, in that most vectors are pointed down and to the right. Two more features of the rotor wake are evident: the much stronger downwash behind the advancing side than behind the reverse-flow region and the beginning of the roll up of the rotor-tip vortices as evidenced by the curvature of the vectors on the right-hand side. Not only are tip vortices important in defining the flow at the tail, but the less-well-understood root vortices are also undoubtedly doing their share to mix it up.

The measurements of Figure 68-5 represent only average conditions in a flow field that also has a large amount of random unsteadiness which on several helicopters has led to a severe "tail-shake" problem. Engineers have found two ways of reducing this unsteadiness.

One is with a specially shaped, cambered main-rotor pylon fairing (first developed for the Sikorsky S-56) of which several examples are shown

Agusta 109

Astar

SA-365N

Figure 68-4 Vertical Tail Designs

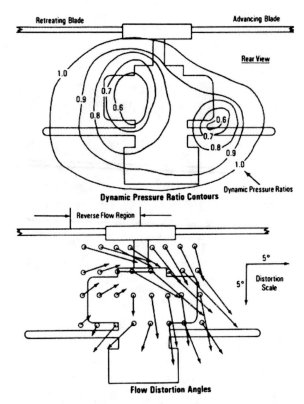

Figure 68-5 Flow Characteristics at Empennage of Hughes AH-64 in Forward Flight

on Figure 68-6 (including two used on tandem-rotor configurations to smooth out the flow at the rear rotor). This type of fairing acts like a small wing and generates a pair of tip vortices that put energy into the boundary layer, thus keeping it from separating and, in general, making the flow behave itself. It has been found that when this device is used to cure a tail-shake problem, it also reduces drag. However, if early flight tests show no evidence of tail shake, it means that the flow is already well behaved and the addition of a cambered pylon fairing will only increase the parasite drag.

The other flow calmer is the hubcap, or "beanie", installed on top of the rotor hub. This device was also first developed at Sikorsky after a serendipitous discovery that the S-61 had less tail shake when either a tank for fluid deicing or an instrumentation slip-ring assembly was installed above the hub. The action of this device is not so obvious as the cambered pylon fairing but the generation of a pair of vortices is probably again the key. Figure 68-6 also shows the beanie as installed on several familiar designs.

Ventral fins and endplates

A vertical stabilizer above the tail boom is in dirty air in level flight but in descent the situation is even worse. To improve stability in this condition, many of the designs on Figure 68-4 include a ventral fin below the tail boom whose environment improves as that of the upper fin is deteriorating.

Because of the low dynamic pressure behind the fuselage and hub, many designers now use vertical surfaces far enough outboard on the ends of the horizontal stabilizer to be in relatively clean air. An example of an endplate configuration forced by flight test results can be seen in Figure 68-7 by comparing the MBB BO-105 and its slightly larger and younger sister, the MBB/Kawasaki BK-117.

The original intent was that in the interest of commonality, the tail boom, tail rotor, and empennage would be the same for both aircraft.

The blunt cargo compartment on this type of fuselage produces a special problem for the aft end components due to the separated flow, especially in descending flight. On the BO-105, a spoiler is located around the bottom of the aft end of the pod to induce the fuselage wake to go down, thereby fixing the location of the separation point, which otherwise tends to wander around erratically —producing sudden changes in body forces and gusts at the tail

The BK-117 started out with this spoiler but ran into a tail-shake problem in descents. This was alleviated when the spoiler was removed and a hubcap was installed. Unfortunately, this configuration was shy on directional stability, so very large endplates were added.

Besides getting the vertical surfaces into cleaner air, endplates have two other aerodynamic advantages: they increase the effectiveness of the horizontal stabilizer and they place the vertical surface away from the tail rotor where it can do a minimum of interfering with the flow patterns.

Unloading

As long as the tail fin is there, it might as well be used to its fullest. For this reason, many modern helicopters have cambered or cocked vertical stabilizers that produce an anti-torque force in forward flight to help unload the tail rotor. The primary purpose is to reduce flapping of the tail rotor to minimize its oscillatory loads. The total anti-torque power required will probably be about the same, since the induced drag of the lifting surface absorbs the power that would otherwise be used to produce high tail-rotor thrust.

Flight without a tail rotor

Some recent specifications for combat helicopters have asked the designers to configure the aircraft so it could be flown home in case the tail rotor was completely shot off. By side slipping, a big enough vertical stabilizer can produce sufficient anti-torque force to do this. Unfortunately, a big vertical stabilizer area interferes with the performance of the tail rotor, especially in sideward flight.

On the Sikorsky Black Hawk, the Hughes Apache, and the Kaman Seasprite the area penalty of satisfying the requirement has proven to be unacceptable and parts of the trailing edge have been removed to improve low-speed flying qualities.

No, it's not an antenna

A somewhat unusual vertical surface is installed ahead of the rotor on the Bell 212 when it is equipped for instrument flight. The surface increases the effective dihedral while slightly reducing the directional stability. The apparent reason is to solve an unstable spiral dive problem.

Another part of the forest

Some indication of the value of a tail rotor in producing directional stability is shown by the picture of the Kaman HH-43B empennage in Figure 68-8. This helicopter had two counter-rotating rotors and so did not need a tail rotor for anti-torque force. It did, however, need an impressive collection of vertical surfaces in order to give satisfactory directional stability.

The second tail configuration shown on Figure 68-8 is for the Sikorsky S-69, the coaxial Advancing Blade Concept (ABC) helicopter, and looks like a typical tail for a 1940's airplane with slightly sweptback twin fins. A coaxial helicopter needs no tail rotor for anti-torque and in most flight

Figure 68-6 Cambered Pylon Fairings and Beanies

conditions can achieve good directional control with differential collective pitch on the two rotors to produce an unbalanced torque.

Not in autorotation, however. Here the S-69 depends on its rudders. Unfortunately, the swept back-fin configuration on the S-69 tends to align the hinge lines with the airflow in autorotation so that rudder deflection does little good. With hindsight, Sikorsky engineers have now decided that the next version will have swept-forward fins.

Figure 68-7 Evolution of an Endplate Configuration

Figure 68-8 Two Non-Tail Rotor Empennages

69 Tail-Boom Strakes

Most helicopters can satisfactorily hover and fly forward. But sometimes flying sideward is a problem. Sideward flight is not an unusual maneuver— the helicopter does it whenever it hovers over a spot in a crosswind.

There are two possible sideward-flight problems— depending on the direction of flight. In left-sideward flight (for helicopters whose main rotor turns counterclockwise when viewed from above), the tail rotor may be operating in the vortex-ring state. In this condition, the tail rotor produces erratic thrust because it is mixed up with its own disturbed wake. We have discussed this problem in Chapter 9.

In the other direction—right-sideward flight—the tail rotor might run out of thrust capability. This can usually be traced to a surprisingly high retarding force on the tail boom. This adds to the demand on the tail rotor to keep the helicopter from yawing.

Surprising forces

Why is this high force surprising? Because it is not just due to the drag of the tail boom reacting to the relatively low dynamic pressure caused by sideward speed. It is also being augmented by a "lift" on the tail boom acting horizontally to the left. This is the result of the boom's immersion in the rotor's downwash and also due to special aerodynamics.

Evidence of the problem is given in Figure 69-1, which shows the variation of tail-rotor pitch needed to hold heading on the Sikorsky UH-60 Black Hawk as it goes from hover into right-sideward flight.

Notice that at about 20 knots, the thrust requirement has a peak. The tail-rotor thrust capability and pitch range on the UH-60 is big enough to supply the requirement. But on some helicopters, they are not and the pilot will be unable to hold heading.

Above 20 knots, the rotor wake goes above the tail boom and so this adverse aerodynamic effect disappears. At even higher right-sideward speeds, the pitch requirement goes up simply because it must compensate for the increased inflow through the rotor.

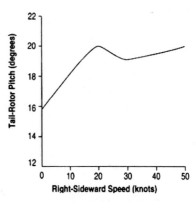

Figure 69-1 Tail-Rotor Pitch Required For Right-Sideward Flight

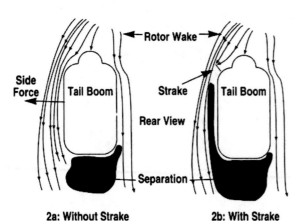

2a: Without Strake   **2b: With Strake**

Figure 69-2 Flow Patterns

Figure 69-3 Westland Sea King With Strake

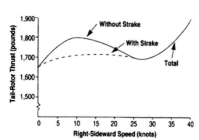

Figure 69-4 Effect Of Strake On Sea King Tail-Rotor Thrust

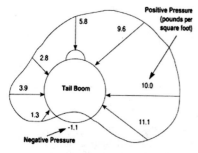

Figure 69-5 Pressures Around AH-64 Apache Tail Boom (25-Knots Right-Sideward Flight)

Circulation

Figure 69-2a shows how, at the critical speed range, a typical tail-boom shape can deflect the downwash to produce a region of low pressure and thus a sideforce to the left. This is exactly how a wing produces lift and can be associated with "circulation" about the body. (The McDonnell Douglas NOTAR system also uses circulation, but it is forced to go the other way by ejecting air from slots on the lower right side of the tail boom.)

To destroy the circulation of Figure 69-2a, a spoiler can be used to separate the airflow from the surface. In this case, the spoiler mounted on the tail boom is known as a "strake."

The effect of the spoiler/strake in eliminating the sideforce is shown on Figure 69-2b. Tests indicate that the strake's height should be 5% to 10% of the tail boom's diameter.

Reduction to practice

Tail-boom strakes can be seen on several helicopters. One of the first to get this fix was the Westland Sea King, a version of the Sikorsky S-61 (Figure 69-3). The strake much improved its directional control in right-sideward flight. Without it, the aircraft was limited to a sideward speed of only 10 knots. It is now capable of 40 knots. The improvement in tail-rotor thrust required is graphically illustrated in Figure 69-4.

You can also see strakes on EH Industries' EH-101 and McDonnell Douglas' MD 520N NOTAR. Experimental strake installations have been made on a number of other helicopters, but as far as I know, are not being included in the production versions at this time.

An exception

The effectiveness of the strake in solving the right-sideward flight problem seems to depend on the configuration. For example, early flight tests of the McDonnell Douglas AH-64 Apache revealed that the tail-rotor power exceeded the design capability of its drive system at about 20 knots to the right.

The problem was traced to a high retarding tail-boom force. But careful measurements revealed that the aerodynamic phenomenon that caused it was not low pressure on the left side produced by circulation as in Figure 69-2a.

Instead, it was high pressure on the right side. The measured pressure distribution around the Apache tail boom is shown in Figure 69-5. (There still is no good explanation for the mechanism that created these high pressures.) At the time, the fix adopted was to increase the diameter of the tail rotor by 10%. As part of a later research program, a series of strakes were tried on the Apache, but they were ineffective—as might be expected.

Tradeoffs

As so often happens, when an engineering fix provides a benefit in one flight regime, it can cause a penalty in another. The strake decreases hover performance both by its weight and by its download in hover. The download can be roughly estimated by multiplying the disc loading of the main rotor by the exposed area of the strake in the plan view.

Thus the designer is faced with a tradeoff question: Is it better to accept the decrease in hover performance, or to increase the tail-rotor capability— which might mean raising the pitch limit or upgrading the drive system?

70 Landing Gear Choices

When the designer lays out the basic helicopter configuration, he has several options of what landing gear to use and how it should be arranged.

Almost all early helicopter designers copied airplanes and installed wheels, which were mostly used to roll the machine in and out of the hangar. Engineers at Bell were perhaps the first to seriously consider skids.

Their first Model 47 (Figure 70-1, top) had four un-braked wheels with the front two castering. This made ground handling as easy as maneuvering a big market basket but two experiences led the engineers to rethink the configuration. The first was a series of forced landings during flight tests near the Bell factory in upstate New York. Usually, the only good emergency landing site was a plowed field where, unfortunately, the front wheels tended to dig in and upset the forward-moving helicopter upon touchdown.

The second experience was reported by operators in the field who often had to operate from sloping areas. After shutting down and walking away, they would sometimes turn around to find their helicopters rolling downhill. The solution was skids (Figure 70-1, bottom).

Figure 70-1 The Early Bell 47 with Wheels ... and with Skids

Skids have now become standard on almost all small helicopters. By giving up some convenience in ground handling, these helicopters gained the ability to operate from sloping or soft surfaces. Skids can also be easily equipped with floats or "bear feet" for operations on very soft sites, and are convenient places to strap external loads.

A helicopter equipped with skids moves from one spot to another on the ground by air taxiing, using special ground handling wheels, or by being carried on a dolly.

But then there are wheels

The larger the helicopter, the more difficult it is to handle on skids. For this reason, most large helicopters use wheels. This makes it possible to ground taxi like an airplane using some collective pitch to generate rotor thrust and some cyclic pitch to tilt it forward (or even backwards). Ground taxiing in this manner produces much less rotor downwash than

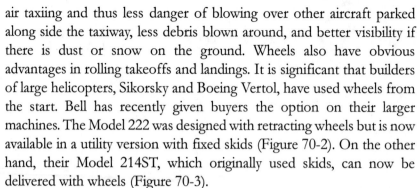

Figure 70-2 Bell 222

air taxiing and thus less danger of blowing over other aircraft parked along side the taxiway, less debris blown around, and better visibility if there is dust or snow on the ground. Wheels also have obvious advantages in rolling takeoffs and landings. It is significant that builders of large helicopters, Sikorsky and Boeing Vertol, have used wheels from the start. Bell has recently given buyers the option on their larger machines. The Model 222 was designed with retracting wheels but is now available in a utility version with fixed skids (Figure 70-2). On the other hand, their Model 214ST, which originally used skids, can now be delivered with wheels (Figure 70-3).

To retract or not to retract

If the designer wants his helicopter to fly fast, he will consider retracting the landing gear. Wheels lend themselves to this easier than skids, although skids can be retracted as was demonstrated by Bell on their prototype Huey Cobra and by Lockheed on the XH-51.

Retractable gear reduces drag but at a price. Non-retractable gear is lighter, simpler, costs less, and is more foolproof. It provides more energy absorption for unexpected touchdowns where retracting gear might not be extended. Consequently, helicopter engineers still find difficulty in deciding between the advantages of each type.

Wheel arrangement

Most skid gears look about the same but wheels can be arranged in many ways. A survey of helicopters shows that there is no true consensus on wheel placement, even among aircraft designed by each major company. This indicates the decision is being dictated by design requirements. Heavy-lift helicopters, for example, use four wheels to simplify loading but most others use only three, the single being either a tail wheel or a nose wheel.

Figure 70-4 illustrates how special requirements dictate the landing-gear arrangement. Sikorsky had equipped the U.S. Army's Black Hawk with a far-aft tail wheel to protect the back end from accidental ground strikes in nap-of-the-earth (NOE) flight. But when the manufacturer marinized the design for the U.S. Navy's Seahawk program, it had to move the tail wheel forward, so the tail boom could be folded, allowing the aircraft to fit in cramped shipboard hangars.

Incidentally, another change requested for the Seahawk was aluminum wheels in place of the lighter magnesium wheels on the Black Hawk. Magnesium has a bad reputation for corrosion in a salt-spray environment.

Preventing slip on the slope

Regardless of the landing-gear configuration, engineers must still consider the helicopter's stability while parked on a hillside or rolling deck. For example, the U.S. Army required that McDonnell Douglas

Figure 70-3 Bell 214ST

Helicopters design the AH-64 Apache so it can rest on a 15 ° side slope, or face up or down while resting on a 12° slope.

Such requirements dictate the location of the wheels with respect to the aircraft's center of gravity and to do it right, designers must make their calculations while allowing for the compression of the downhill oleo strut and tire.

Figure 70-4 Sikorsky Blackhawk and Seahawk

71 Structural Loads and Component Lives

The structure of the helicopter must be strong enough to carry all the loads to which it might be subjected—including both those once-in-a-while big ones due to extreme conditions and the repeated small-to-medium oscillatory loads experienced in normal flight. As a general rule, the big ones are important in designing the non-rotating parts of the helicopter such as the fuselage, tail boom, and landing gear. The repeated loads, which might cause fatigue damage, affect the design of the rotating components: the main and tail rotors, the gearboxes and shafting, and the rotating controls.

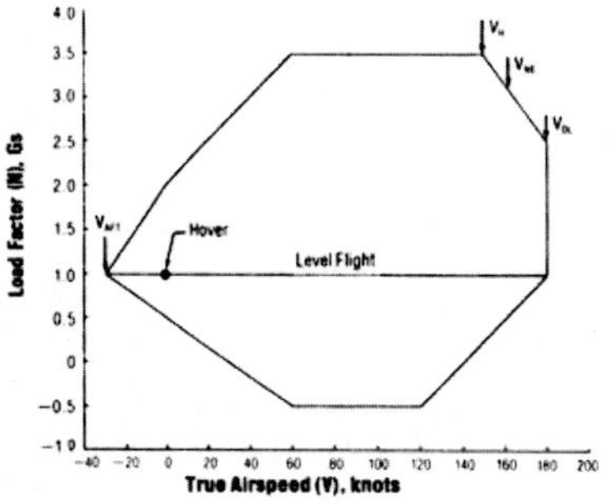

All of these loads are difficult to predict during the design process. It is a tribute to the loads engineers and designers that light and efficient — but structurally sound — helicopters can be built.

Figure 71-1 A Typical Design V-N Diagram

Envelopes

The helicopter's design is dictated by the expected use. One of the most important guidelines for the loads engineer defining that use is the diagram relating normal load factor to forward speed —the so-called V-N diagram (Figure 71-1).

The envelope limits are usually set by the customer in the case of military aircraft or by the FAA and the engineering and sales departments for civil aircraft. The corners of the envelope are usually cut off so that extremely unlikely combinations of speed and load factor do not drive the design of the structure nor the subsequent flight demonstration.

Several critical speeds are identified on the V-N diagram:

V_H — The maximum horizontal speed using the 30-minute rating of the engine.

V_{DL} — The design limit speed. This is used to calculate design loads and is also the speed the company pilots must achieve during their structural demonstration flights. For military helicopters, it is defined as 20% higher than V_H but for civil designs it can be any value above V_H.

V_{NE} —The never-exceed or redline speed. For civil helicopters, it is 90% of V_{DL}. For military helicopters, it can be any value up to V_{DL} approved by the procuring agency.

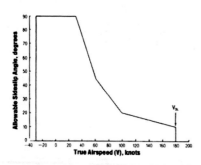

Figure 71-2 A Typical Design Sideslip Envelope

V_{AFT} — The maximum allowable rearward speed. (This is not a structural limit but is made as high as it is thought safe to test for, considering the rearward visibility from the cockpit.)

Estimating airframe loads

Another diagram needed early in the design process is the sideslip envelope (Figure 71-2). This defines the allowable right- and left-sideslip angles as a function of speed. At low speeds, sidewards (or 90° sideslip) flight is permissible but at very high speeds the sideslip angle is restricted to avoid developing excessive loads in the tail rotor and the tail boom. This restriction is justified because in normal flying, high sideslip angles at high speed are neither likely nor necessary.

During the design process, the engineer draws on several sources for estimating loads. For the air loads on the non-rotating structure, he first uses past experience on both airplanes and helicopters and later uses wind-tunnel measurements for his particular aircraft.

Usually, there are only a few airframe components designed with consideration of air loads in flight. Among them are the windshields, cockpit side windows, and doors. At high speed, the windshield is subjected to high positive pressures and the side windows and doors to high suction pressures. The latter can become especially critical during sideslips out to the edges of the envelope. There have been enough cases of caved-in windshields and blown-out doors to motivate conservative estimates of these loads.

The loads engineer gives the designer the "limit loads" which are the highest he can calculate within the design envelopes. The designer increases these by 50% to obtain "ultimate loads" for the actual design. This gives a safety factor of 1.5. The ultimate loads are later used in the structures laboratory to verify the strength of actual specimens ranging from single parts to major assemblies.

Maximum load-factor requirements

The capability of a fixed-wing aircraft to develop and/or to withstand high load factors is a primary concern for airplane designers and pilots —but not nearly so important in the rotary-wing world, for a variety of reasons.

The pilot of a fixed-wing is interested in the maximum load factor his wing can develop for two different reasons. If he is flying a fighter or an air-show aerobatic aircraft, a high load-factor capability helps him either to outmaneuver his opponent or to put on a more exciting show. On the other hand, if he is flying a transport or utility airplane, he's concerned about what load factor will damage the wings in an unplanned situation, such as a high-speed penetration into a strong vertical gust or a sudden evasive action taken to avoid a midair collision.

Fighters and aerobatic airplanes are designed with structural strength and wing area to withstand load factors of 5-to-7 Gs. Transport and utility airplane structures are designed for 3-to-4 Gs.

Maneuver requirements

So far, in the 40-some years that helicopters have been operating, no really high load-factor maneuver has been identified as a design consideration. Even such an advanced attack helicopter as the Hughes AH-64 Apache is only required to demonstrate 1.75 Gs in an operational maneuver, even though it is capable of more.

In the future, air-to-air combat might provide the motivation for more maneuverability. For example, the newest Army program, the light utility/scout/attack helicopter (LHX), is supposed to result in a machine that can do sustained turns at 2.5 Gs and pullups up to 3 Gs, still well below the requirements for fighter airplanes.

Both the FAA and the US military specify that the helicopter structure be designed to take a 3.5-G load factor but there is no requirement to demonstrate that the rotor can actually develop this in flight.

Structural difference

The airplane wing has two vertical forces acting on it (as shown in Figure 71-3): its own weight acting down and a much bigger lift force acting up. This unbalance of forces bends the wing.

All structures can take a certain amount of bending and then return to their original shape, a property known as "elastic deformation". Too much bending, on the other hand, will cause the structure to "yield" and have a "permanent set" after the load is removed.

A rotor blade is different from a wing in two respects: it is attached to the aircraft with a hinge or a relatively soft blade root— and it has an additional force acting on it: the centrifugal force trying to bend the blade down by about as much as the lift is trying to bend it up.

As a result, the blade flaps up but doesn't bend significantly when developing high thrust. And, as a consequence, the pilot need not worry about causing a permanent set while doing an extreme maneuver.

This is not to say, however, that no structural damage has been done. Experience shows that high load-factor maneuvers raise the level of oscillatory loads in the blades, hub, control system, and rotor-support structure. Usually the pilot has a sense of these loads in the level of vibration he feels. Depending on the design of the various components, the higher-than-normal oscillatory loads may cause fatigue damage that shortens the useful life of the part.

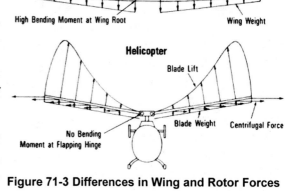

Figure 71-3 Differences in Wing and Rotor Forces

Metal fatigue

Most helicopters have parts that must be thrown away after a certain number of flight hours. On the same brand-new ship, the main-rotor blades may have an approved life of 1,200 hours, the tail-rotor blades 1,800, the main transmission 2,300, and the tail-rotor gearbox an infinite life. For exactly these same components, the lives may have been lower two years ago (or in some rare cases, higher).

The enemy of any machine is loads. Very big loads can break a part immediately but smaller loads can be just as destructive if repeated often enough — the mechanism for this slow destruction being called "metal fatigue". Almost all metals are made up of small grains that stick together with varied degrees of tenacity and the strength of the metal depends both upon the strength of the grains and of the bonds between them. These strengths, in turn, are affected by what other elements are mixed in with the base metal and how the parts are treated during the manufacturing process.

Each of the common aircraft metals — aluminum, steel, titanium, and magnesium — can be produced from many gourmet recipes calling for a pinch of chromium here and a dash of copper there to improve the strength, or the machinability, or the corrosion resistance. How the cooking is done is also important in determining the final mechanical properties and fatigue strength: in the molten stage to remove impurities; by forging and rolling in the soft state to align the grains; and by heat-treating at prescribed temperatures and times with controlled rates of cooling. Other processes such as shot peening and case hardening can be used to strengthen the outside layer of the part even more.

The application of a very high load can destroy both the bonds between grains and the grains themselves if, for example, they happen to lie in the path of a pair of tin snips. The application of very low loads will do no damage no matter how many times they are applied. But there is a range of loads between very high and very low that can cause damage to the bonds between the grains. One application of a load in this range will make the bond fail in the region of maximum stress but it will not spread beyond the local spot if the load is held.

If the load is relaxed and then reapplied, however, the damage will spread. With repeated application, these bond failures will combine into a crack that destroys the local capability to carry the load. It also throws a higher responsibility on the rest of the part, which, because of its reduced effective area, makes the crack propagate more and more rapidly until the part breaks in two.

You can demonstrate this phenomenon by bending a paper clip until it breaks. If you look at the broken surface with a magnifying glass, you should be able to see a flat, sandy-appearing area where the crack started but worked the surface down as it repeatedly closed on itself. On the other side of the wire will be a jagged surface where the grains were separated from each other on the last two or three bends.

Figure 71-4 shows a typical fatigue failure. The appearance of the jagged surface suggested to early mechanics that the metal had suddenly "crystallized" and lost its strength. Others related the sandy appearance of a static failure in such brittle materials as cast iron and thus called it a "brittle" failure.

In many fatigue failures, the part will support the load long after the crack has started. Sikorsky uses this property to identify damaged blades during the preflight inspection by pressurizing the hollow spars and then installing an indicator that shows a red flag if the pressure has been released. The usual slow propagation of the fatigue crack is the reason that such crack-detection inspection procedures as Magnaflux and Zyglo can be used to spot fatigue failures before they become catastrophic. In some non-critical components, a fatigue failure can be delayed by drilling a hole at the end of the crack to reduce the local stress concentration

A helicopter is a good fatigue machine. Many parts receive changes in loading with each rotor revolution, while others are hit only with each rotor startup and shutdown. It is the structural engineer's job to estimate how many rotor revolutions or how many startups each individual part can stand before it is likely to suffer serious fatigue damage. He then puts a flight-hour limit at which time the part will either be retired, rebuilt, or inspected—depending upon a number of factors.

It would, of course, be ideal if we could have complete faith that every part will go indefinitely without fatigue. This is gradually coming true but not quite yet. In the meantime, the engineer uses several techniques to set allowable fatigue lives in the various components that are subjected to repeated changes in stresses and his primary tool is the S-N diagram such as in Figure 71-5.

This tells him the number of cycles of loading (N) that can be sustained at a given level of cyclic stress (S) before a fatigue failure occurs. The stress that will break the part immediately is the one where N is one-fourth of a full cycle. The stress below which no fatigue failure is expected no matter how many times the load is applied is called the "endurance limit".

There are several sources of S-N diagrams. One is a collection of previous experience based on testing of many small parts —called "coupons"— made of a given material and heat-treated to a given static strength. The coupon is put in a special machine and subjected to repeated stresses until it breaks. This point is plotted on the chart and anew specimen is started at a different stress level. Fitting a curve through the various test points then gives the S-N curve for that particular metal.

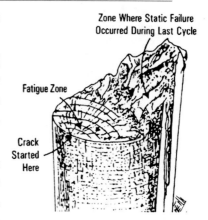

Figure 71-4 A Typical Fatigue Failure Evidence

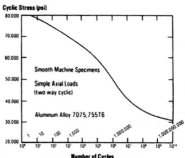

Figure 71-5 Typical S-N Diagram

One problem with this procedure is that if a test is repeated at a previously tested stress level, the second specimen will probably not fail at the same number of cycles as the first. Thus if many coupons are tested, there will be some "scatter". To be safe, the curve is faired though the middle of the test points and then dropped by an amount based on statistical probabilities and redrawn as a design curve. For application to a full-scale part, the curve is dropped even further, based on industry-wide experience. The presence of a "stress riser" such as a bolt hole, sharp corner, notch, or even a tool mark in the actual part will lower the S-N curve and many tests have been conducted to evaluate this deterioration.

Many parts are so complex that there is no way to calculate the maximum stress or to even determine its location. In these cases — ranging from a control bellcrank to a complete transmission —samples of the actual part are tested. These results are plotted in terms of the actual cyclic load, moment, or power level applied, rather than the cyclic stress. Since these parts may be expensive and each test takes along time, usually only a few specimens can be tested. The knowledge of the general shape of the S-N curve from coupon testing can be used to fair a curve through a limited number of test points but to account for the expected scatter, a penalty is assessed by lowering the curve. It is generally agreed that with one specimen, the test fatigue strength should be reduced 50% but by using more, a much smaller penalty based on a statistical analysis can be used.

Loading spectrum

Plotting the S-N diagram for a given material or part is only the first step. The second step determines what the stress levels will be in flight. Some are easy to calculate — such as those caused by the change in centrifugal force on the blade root when starting and stopping the rotor. Other cyclic loadings depend on the flight conditions. For example, loads in the lead-lag dampers are very low in hover but may be high enough to produce fatigue damage in a maneuver. There are two problems buried in this example:

1—What percentage of the life of the helicopter is spent in doing a certain maneuver?

2— How high will the loads be during that maneuver?

The answer to the first problem requires someone taking a deep breath and puffing some numbers out of the air. For a military helicopter, the customer often makes this estimate based on his mission and previous experience. For a commercial helicopter, it is usually up to the designer to make the decision — although the certifying agency can usually have some influence on what is

Type of Flight	%
Warm-up	3.3
Jump Takeoff	0.05
Hovering	8
Hover Taxiing	2
Level Flight at Transitional Speed	6
Climb at Takeoff Power	8
Level Flight at 60% of Cruise Speed	15
Level Flight at 75% of Cruise Speed	15
Level Flight at Cruise Speed	26
Level Flight at Maximum Speed	4
Tight Turn at Cruising Speed	6
Autorotation	1.9
Recovery from Autorotation	0.1
Power Flare	1.4
Vortex Ring Condition	0.1
Approach to Landing	2.5
Maneuver Prior to Landing	0.5
Landing from Autorotation	0.15

Figure 71-6 Typical Distribution of Flight Conditions

actually used. Figure 71-6 shows a typical distribution of flight conditions.

The second problem— that of load magnitude —is answered in the design stage by estimates based on previous experience and/or by computer studies of loads generated on rotors and other components in various steady and transient flight conditions.

Fatigue loads

The prediction of fixed-wing airframe loads both in steady and maneuvering flight is a fairly mature science — based on 80 years of aviation experience. Based on 40 years of helicopter experience, the prediction of oscillating fatigue loads in the rotating components is only half as good. Most of these loads are generated in the relatively flexible blades and are then transmitted to the hub, the control system, and eventually to many parts deep in the structure.

As a working helicopter engineer, I admit that my colleagues and I have a somewhat less-than-perfect understanding of what causes these uneven loads, how the blade responds by twisting and bending, and how these deflections change the uneven air loads — which we don't understand very well in the first place. This whole subject represents another real challenge to helicopter aerodynamicists and dynamicists.

(Engineers sometimes take movies of the blade motion with a camera mounted on the hub. The results are spectacular enough that no one wants to show them to the pilots.)

Because of our deficiency in understanding, we are continually working on the problem. Our tools are test helicopters, wind tunnels, and computers. We try to use the latter to duplicate test measurements and then go on to predict the loads for the new design. The computers are programmed to account for a flexible blade's modes of deflection in the best-possible picture we can draw of the local aerodynamic environment (Mach number, angle of attack, and angle-of-attack rate of change). Progress is being made.

After the prototype starts flying, strain gauges are installed at critical locations and the aircraft is flown through the complete flight envelope in a "flight-load survey that produces actual loads and moments for each of the flight conditions and maneuvers to be considered in the calculation of fatigue lives. The combination of loads and number of occurrences in each flight hour allows a "loading spectrum" as a function of stress and cycles to be generated for each fatigue sensitive component.

Estimate of fatigue lives

The existence of the loading spectrum and of the S-N diagram for a given component allows us to calculate the number of hours before the part would be expected to suffer a fatigue failure. The principle of this

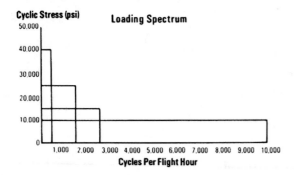

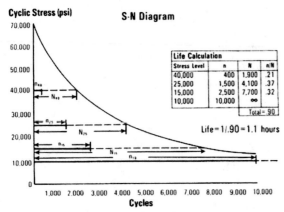

Figure 71-7 Fatigue Life Calculation

calculation is that of "cumulative damage", which accounts for the amount of life used up by each cycle of stress above the endurance limit.

Let us use for illustration a part whose loading spectrum is very simple (but severe) as shown on Figure 71-7. Also shown is the corresponding S-N diagram for the material of which the part is made. The 400 cycles at the high stress of 40,000 psi (pounds per square inch) are designated n_{40} and the allowable number of cycles at this level, 1,900, is designated N_{40}. The resulting "n-over-N" ratio is the fraction (.21) of the life used up at this stress level. Similarly, the next level of 25,000 psi results in $n_{25}/N_{25} = 0.37$, and at 15,000 psi, $n_{15}/N_{15}=0.32$. The lowest stress level in the loading spectrum is below the endurance limit and so causes no fatigue damage. The result is that only the three highest levels have caused damage but together the summations of their individual n/Ns add up to .90. Thus 90% of the fatigue life of this part will be used up in the first hour of flight and its calculated fatigue life is 1.1 hours.

The minimum retirement life is often specified by the customer. For example, the U.S. Army says that a part must go at least 4,500 hours. (Corresponding to your car going 180,000 miles without any parts breaking or wearing out.)

Increasing longevity

If a component has a calculated fatigue life that is less than desired, the engineers have several options: to change the design; to make the component bigger and stronger (and also heavier); to eliminate stress risers if that is where the crack started; to change the material to one having better fatigue characteristics; or to shot peen the part, which will lock a compressive stress into the surface that must be overcome with a tension stress before a crack can start.

Another option is to test more specimens in the lab if the calculated fatigue life is based on an S-N curve with a severe scatter penalty.

Thus, by continually working on the weak links of the design as revealed by analysis, lab tests, and flight tests, changes can be made that allow the engineers to calculate — and the authorities to bless —constantly rising fatigue lives. In certain unfortunate cases, this process may reverse if a timely inspection or an untimely accident reveals a previously undetected flaw. This will cause a review that might result in a life reduction and will certainly trigger a flurry of redesign effort.

Hierarchy of fatigue loads

All parts of a helicopter must be designed so that the loads are below the endurance limit in cruise flight. This allows some leeway for short-time excess of the endurance limit during maneuvers.

Based on the fatigue analysis, the engineers determine the progressively higher load levels that will be safe for 10 hours, one hour, and for a single application — the load limit that is two-thirds the ultimate or breaking load. These levels are used to monitor the flight tests of one of the prototype helicopters instrumented with strain gauges during a flight-load survey.

Past experience

Some helicopters have had their flight envelopes artificially limited after they started flying because of the danger of developing excessive oscillatory loads in some flight conditions. These problems existed not because the loads were impossibly high but because they were higher than had been anticipated when the parts were designed. Unfortunately, some of these parts include intricate and expensive hydraulic actuators and swashplates that are difficult to redesign, to requalify, and to retrofit. Thus, some helicopters have spent their entire life with flight limitations that 30 pounds of well-placed steel could have fixed — if the loads had been accurately predicted in the first place.

Maneuvering limits

Because of the blade's flexibility, a pilot does not have to worry about pulling the rotor off in a high G maneuver; however, he should be aware that he is usually doing some fatigue damage — but designers have foreseen this and allowed for what they consider to be a reasonable number of these events in the life of his helicopter.

Is it stall?

The high oscillatory loads and vibration in high G maneuvers are almost always attributed to retreating-blade stall— but it ain't necessarily so. In some cases, these effects build up long before any actual stall occurs. This is apparently due to a redistribution of the uneven airloads over the disc, causing an increase in the dynamic bending and twisting response of the blades.

In other cases, retreating-blade stall does play a part; however, it is not the loss of lift or the increase in drag that are important. Instead, the nosedown airfoil pitching moment twists the blades and generates loads in the hub and control system as the blade goes in and out of stall from one side of the disc to the other. Thus, when selecting an airfoil for its retreating-side characteristics, the airfoil that goes to the highest angle of attack before producing a big pitching moment should be chosen over the one that can only boast of the highest maximum-lift coefficient (see Figure 71-8).

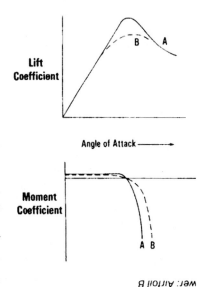

Answer: Airfoil B

Figure 71-8 Which Airfoil is Best?

Limiting by instability

Besides stopping when the vibration gets high, the pilot may decide it wise to limit his load factor because he feels his helicopter losing maneuver stability as it takes less and less aft stick to produce an increase in rotor thrust—until he reaches the point where his aircraft will try to pitch up (or "dig in" as some pilots say) all by itself. This is sometimes blamed on blade stall but it is more likely due to the basic nature of the rotor, which is unstable with angle of attack.

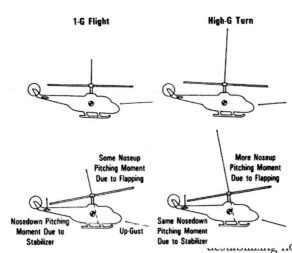

Figure 71-9 Loss of Angle-of-Attack Stability in High-G Maneuver

Figure 71-9 shows the helicopter in level flight and in a high-G turn (or a pullup) first in steady conditions and then as it encounters an up-gust. In each case, the rotor flaps back about the same amount and so the thrust vector passes ahead of the CG the same amount. But in the high-G turn, the larger rotor thrust produces a larger destabilizing noseup pitching moment. The stabilizing nosedown effect of the horizontal stabilizer, on the other hand, is the same in each case. Thus, at some high level of rotor thrust, the helicopter that might be quite stable in 1 G flight will become unstable. The presence of blade stall only accelerates this process. (Note: electronic stability and control augmentation systems [SCAS] can be used effectively to help out in this situation.)

Even after the helicopter becomes unstable and even if it has appreciable blade stall on the retreating side, it will still respond to cyclic-pitch inputs. However, to avoid getting into a very nose-high attitude, these inputs should be prompt. The usual recommended action to avoid trouble in this situation is to lower the collective pitch to reduce rotor thrust.

What is the maximum?

The maximum load factor a rotor can produce aerodynamically is usually considerably higher than the pilot is willing to use. Model rotors tested in wind tunnels have generated thrust levels corresponding to 3 or 4 Gs without reaching their aerodynamic limits. They were stopped by mechanical limits corresponding to the allowable travel of the model's control system. I believe that these models could have gone up at least another 50% before fulfilling their aerodynamic potential.

Giving the pilot full use of this capability is one of the current challenges of the helicopter designers.

72 Designing Reliable Helicopter Structural

One goal of designers is to make helicopter Structural components so they do not fail for a long, long time under normal usage. This is called "reliability." The request for proposal (RFP) for the RAH-66 Comanche contract specified that for a design life of 4,500 flying hours, the chance for a catastrophic failure in any major structural component should be less than one in a million.

Kenneth Amer of the Rand Corp. gave a paper before the American Helicopter Society in 1988 in which he discussed the problems associated with this ambitious goal and presented some promising alternative solutions. The following is from his paper.

Safe-life or fail-safe?

To achieve a high standard of reliability, the designers of structural components often have a choice in their design philosophy. One is called "safe-life," and if it is followed in the case of the RAH-66, each component will have a 999,999 chance out of 1 million of surviving 4,500 hours of flying.

The other approach is "fail-safe," and it relies on backup or "redundant" load paths to prevent a complete failure even if one part breaks. All structural components of modern jet transports are designed using the fail-safe philosophy, but it has not yet been required for helicopters.

Helicopter designers have generally used the safe-life approach. This has applied not only to components that were difficult to make redundant, such as rotor masts, drive shafts, and pitch links, but also to the basic aircraft structure.

On systems, however, they have gone to the failsafe approach whenever they design a multiengine helicopter or install two hydraulic systems. Even more redundancy is being built into fly-by-wire control systems where three or even four independent systems are provided.

In some designs, the decision to use the fail-safe route with redundant load paths has been dictated by other considerations, such as the possibility of combat damage. This was a prime driver in the decision to make the McDonnell Douglas Apache blade using four spars (Figure 72-1).

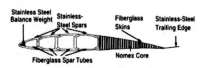

Figure 72-1 Apache Tail-Safe Blade Design

401

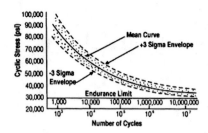

Figure 72-2 Typical S-N Curve

Fatigue and uncertainty

For most structural and many mechanical parts in a helicopter, the primary Consideration in achieving high reliability goals is the part's vulnerability to fatigue damage. This occurs progressively when a part is subjected to high loads many times. The first application of a high load doesn't break anything, but starts a tiny crack that grows with each subsequent application of load above a certain threshold value. This value is called the "endurance limit."

When the part's strength drops to a point too low to carry the load, it fails. You can demonstrate this to yourself by bending a paper clip until it breaks.

But uncertainty emerges here. Parts that appear to be identical will have different vulnerability to fatigue damage. This happens because of small differences in the composition of the basic material, in how the parts were handled, and in how they were fabricated.

Consequently, when the designer calculates how strong a given part must be, he assigns a probability to the strength. It is based on knowledge acquired by industry-wide fatigue testing of many "coupons" of the material to be used; for complicated assemblies, several specimens of the proposed design are tested. The results, depicted in an "S-N Diagram," are presented as the stress level maintained during the test vs. the number of cycles the specimen withstood before failure (Figure 72-2). The scatter of the test points depicts the uncertainty.

Playing the odds

Statistical theory says that for most physical phenomena, the probability of occurrence can be represented by a "normal-distribution curve" shaped like a bell (Figure 72-3). Here it was generated by dividing the test data of Figure 72-2 into individual vertical slices with a small but finite width, and then dividing each slice into segments of stress level that cover the entire scatter band.

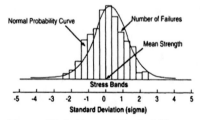

Figure 72-3 Normal Probability

The curve is then generated for each vertical slice by plotting the number of test points that fall in each segment. The more test points there are, the more accurate this procedure is. But even for only a few points, a reasonable curve can be drawn based on an understanding of probability theory. (Teachers use this when "grading on the curve.")

Some test specimens plotted on the left-hand portion would fail under a relative small load and some plotted on the right-hand side would not fail until the load was increased to a high level. Most would fail due to loads represented by the middle of the bell curve.

By applying some statistical techniques to the plot, the probability of failure can be represented in terms of the standard deviation (or "sigma") above and below the most likely value. In fatigue analysis, the "three sigma" values are significant, since they represent the limits below and above which one part out of a thousand would break.

For conservatism's sake, the lower three-sigma line is usually plotted on the S-N curve and is currently used for design guidance for fatigue strength.

With the RAH-66 requirements, this is not conservative enough. To achieve a one-in-a-million failure rate, the -5 sigma limit would have to be applied to the S-N curve, and the part must be designed so that the stress level stayed below that boundary. This means that the part is bigger and heavier than if it had been designed to the -3 sigma boundary.

What? Another uncertainty?

Another uncertainty is concerned with how well the loads in flight are known. The design should be such that no loads over the endurance limit are ever experienced in hover or steady forward flight. On the other hand, maneuvers and hard landings may result in loads high enough to cause fatigue damage. How is a designer to predict what a given pilot might do?

Here again the probabilities are examined. By now, enough helicopters have been flown to build up a data bank that can be used to guess at how many times an hour a given helicopter type might make a specific maneuver.

The loads engineer translates these maneuvers into predicted loads on the part and presents them to the designer; the calculations are again plotted as a bell-shaped curve. The curve reflects the uncertainty of the loading spectrum; it will be more severe, for example, if a specific aircraft is primarily used for nap-of-the-earth training rather than as a VIP transport.

When the two curves representing strength and load are plotted together (Figure 72-4), the desirable result would be that they would never overlap. In that case, no part would ever fail due to fatigue damage. The penalty for designing to this condition, however, is that each part would be significantly over designed and thus very heavy—an unacceptable situation for a helicopter.

The aim of the designer is to accept just enough overlap to meet the reliability criteria specified by the military customer or by a civil certificating agency such as the FAA.

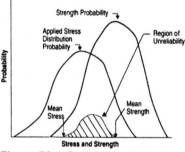

Figure 72-4 Reliability Analysis

Making choices

In achieving the desired reliability, designers of many structural parts have the option of choosing which philosophy will produce the lightest result.

With safe-life, each part must be made so strong—and heavy—that it will not have a fatigue failure during the specified life of the helicopter. With the fail-safe design, some failures can be accepted since the load can be safely carried for a while by the remaining load paths.

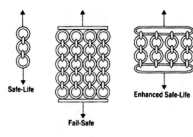

Figure 72-5 Reliability Options

Figure 72-5 illustrates design philosophies. The safe-life example is made up of stout, single links in series, each of which carries the design load safely. The fail-safe assembly is made up of four chains with weaker links but any two can carry the load.

If these were helicopter parts, the safe-life assembly would be periodically inspected for fatigue cracks leading to future failures. This would be done through careful visual inspection or using special techniques that spot small fatigue cracks through magnetic or dye-penetrant methods.

The inspection for the fail-safe assembly, on the other hand, looks for complete failures, which should be relatively easy to detect. (One inspection of the transmission on the Robinson R22 involves simply counting the belts.)

Weight tradeoff

For the reliability required of the Boeing Sikorsky RAH-66 Comanche, a fatigue-critical part must be designed to the -5 sigma boundary on the S-N curve for safe-life. Combining this with a -1 sigma increase in the loading spectrum results in a reliability parameter which can be translated into the ratio between mean strength and mean stress.

Amer shows that for the required reliability of one-in-a-million, this ratio must be 1.65, which is the equivalent of taking a 65% degradation on the mean S-N curve. The equivalent penalty for the current one-in-a-thousand failure rate is only 35%. Thus the part designed to the new requirement will be 22% heavier than one designed to the -3 sigma requirement.

Amer also showed that if the design for the new reliability criteria is a fail-safe structure with four redundant load paths (any of two which could support the load), the strength need be based on only a 1-sigma degradation of the S-N curve. The resulting mean-strength-to-mean-stress ratio of 1.14 would produce a structure that would actually be lighter than using the current practice with the 3-sigma penalty.

Amer admits that not all assemblies could be designed fully fail-safe, but he contends that a combination of safe-life and fail-safe designs (Figure 72-5) could be practical in many situations. As a matter of fact, Amer proposes what he calls an "enhanced safe-life" design in which the components of such an assembly that cannot be made fail-safe are designed to a -6 sigma criteria. This would ensure for them a nearly infinite fatigue life.

Assuming that these parts are only 20% of the assembly by weight, he calculates that there is still a weight saving over current practice and a very much-improved reliability.

Cost considerations

The practical result of following Amer's suggestions should be a saving not only in weight but also in cost. One of the primary benefits would be related to spares.

The safe-life approach requires that all parts be scrapped when their design life is up, even though some might still be good—but there is no way of knowing which. It is also probable that one helicopter in the fleet would have experienced a catastrophic failure before its calculated service life was up.

On a helicopter designed under the fail-safe philosophy, some 8% of the parts would have already safely failed and been replaced in the 4,500 hours. All the others would be ready for more flying to be replaced only "on-condition."

Even the helicopter designed for enhanced safe-life could continue flying since its fail-safe parts are on-condition and its safe-life parts are designed for a nearly infinite fatigue life. Amer also projects significant cost savings in laboratory fatigue testing, analysis, and inspection.

73 Airspeed Systems

Both airplane and helicopter pilots rely on their airspeed indicators while setting up the speed for best performance in climb, cruise, and glide; observing structural limitations; and solving navigation problems. In addition, the airplane pilot relies on his airspeed system to help insure safe takeoffs and landings, in much the same way the helicopter pilot uses it to avoid the "deadman's curve" during operations out of restricted areas.

Airplane-type airspeed systems

The conventional airspeed system uses the difference between the *total* pressure (developed by stopping air dead in its tracks) and the *static* pressure (the ambient pressure for the altitude and temperature). This difference is called the *dynamic* pressure and is proportional to the square of the airspeed. For instance, the dynamic pressure at sea level and 50 knots is 8.5 pounds per square foot; while at 100 knots it is 34 pounds per square foot.

Figure 73-1 shows a typical system consisting of a forward-facing pitot tube that stops the air, a static port positioned so as to ignore local airspeed, and a bellows-like pressure cell plumbed to total pressure inside and static pressure outside. As the cell expands due to the pressure difference (the dynamic pressure), it operates the needle on the face of the indicator.

The pilot sees the *indicated airspeed* (IAS) but, because the system is not perfect, there is almost always a correction added or subtracted to give the *calibrated airspeed* (CAS). (This is much like making allowances for your car speedometer to account for the dial markings not being placed exactly right or your tires being slightly larger or smaller than the system was designed for.)

Since the total pressure is proportional to the kinetic energy being trapped by the pitot tube, its value will be proportional to the density of the air and to the square of the *true* airspeed (TAS), which is the calibrated airspeed corrected for air density. If the air density were always the same as it is at sea level and 59° F, the calibrated airspeed would also be the true airspeed. At lesser densities found at higher altitudes and/or

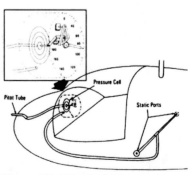

Figure 73-1 Typical Airspeed System

Sikorsky S-61N

Pitots

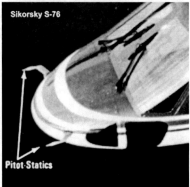

Sikorsky S-76

Pitot-Statics

Pitots

Sikorsky UH-60

Figure 73-2 Airspeed System Examples

higher temperatures, the calibrated airspeed is lower than the true airspeed.

Even with this error, the CAS is a useful parameter, especially for airplanes where the wing stalls at the same calibrated airspeed regardless of air density. On helicopters, parasite drag and the air-loads on the non-rotor components are also related to the square of the calibrated airspeed. For navigation purposes, CAS must be converted to TAS by consideration of air density and then to ground speed by consideration of winds.

A basic problem with the conventional airspeed system is that if the pressure cell is strong enough to withstand the dynamic pressure at high speed, it is too stiff to react at low speeds. For airplanes, this is accepted by not expecting the indicator to do anything intelligent below about 40 knots —where the airplane can't fly anyway.

However, this is an operational speed range for the helicopter — and no airplane-type system is satisfactory over the entire helicopter speed range including rearward and sideward flight. Despite this, all current-production helicopters are equipped with airplane-style airspeed systems.

Trial by error

Getting a conventional system to work accurately in various flight conditions, even above 40 knots, usually requires fairly extensive trial-and-error procedures during the flight-test development. One of the problems is locating the pitot tube and the static ports. On airplanes, the pitot tube is usually mounted out in front of the leading edge of the wing, which allows it to sample the oncoming air before the flow is disturbed by the rest of the aircraft.

A helicopter designer usually does not have this option. Even if his aircraft has a wing, it is always too short to be out of the rotor influence, which, especially at low speeds, significantly adds velocity to the air stream under it. Many designers find the fuselage nose the best-available position but this may be denied if the nose is also used for a movable sight turret as on the Hughes AH-64 attack helicopter.

(Since the pitot tube is usually heated for anti-ice protection, it poses an unusual situation on helicopters with heat-sensitive sighting systems. If that heated pitot is within the sight's field of view, it looks like the sun! For this reason, the pitots on the Apache have been installed far outboard on the wings.)

Figure 73-2 shows a number of pitot installations on familiar designs. In any case, pitot tubes do not have to be strictly aligned with the oncoming flow. Most tubes will tolerate misalignments of 15° to 20° before starting to read low.

Static ports are usually drilled perpendicular to flat surfaces parallel to the streamwise direction where the adjacent velocity is constant and the surface pressures can adjust to the ambient pressure. The static port can be integrated with the pitot tube, in which case the assembly is known as a pitot-static tube (note the Agusta 109A in Figure 73-3). Static ports can also be placed somewhere on the fuselage. A stroll through the tie-down area of your local airport will show a variety of installations on both airplanes and helicopters.

If the static port is on one side of the fuselage, it is generally connected to one on the other side to balance the effects of sideslip. To make fuselage mounted static ports read correctly in climbs and descents, it is sometimes necessary to strategically locate small bumps to speed up, or small dams to slow down the air coming from directions other than straight ahead.

These techniques may also be used to compensate for an inherent error in the total pressure if no interference-free location for the pitot tube can be found. Such fudging must be done with care, however, since the same static ports are almost always used as the source for the altimeter.

Extending the boom

Finding acceptable locations and configurations for pitot tubes and static ports can be a very time-consuming process. Most flight-test programs start out using a temporary system mounted on an instrumentation boom as far ahead of the nose as is practical. Usually this consists of a finned pitot-static tube fastened to the boom with a universal joint to allow it to align itself with the relative wind and provide the most beneficial environment possible. Rotary transducers on the boom are used to provide a means of measuring angles of attack and sideslip. Figure 73-4 shows an example fitted to the Bell OH-58.

The development of a permanent ship's system can then be done by giving the pilot two airspeed indicators to compare — one driven from the instrumentation boom and the other by the potential pitot and static port locations on the helicopter. Both systems can be calibrated using several methods, the simplest being to time the flight between two known points — in both directions to account for wind. This is good for level flight but to check a system in climbs and descents, formation flight with another aircraft having a fully developed and calibrated airspeed system may be required.

How did that system get calibrated? Glad you asked. It's done by using a trailing bomb, which is a pitot-static system in a streamline package that can be lowered by cable to insure operation in undisturbed air far below the aircraft. In turn, the bomb has been calibrated in a wind tunnel that has been calibrated by a special National Bureau of Standards instrument that has been calibrated

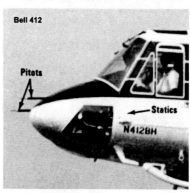

Figure 73-3 More Airspeed System Examples

Figure 73-4 Flight test boom on a Bell OH-58

by scientifically unimpeachable methods. Satisfied? The search for acceptable locations sometimes extends into the production run. Sikorsky has recently developed the U.S. Navy SH-60B Seahawk from the Army UH-60A Black Hawk and in the process found it desirable to relocate both the pitot tubes and the static ports.

Alternate systems

The conventional airspeed system has been accepted by the helicopter industry but there is still a general feeling of, "Wouldn't it be nice if we knew how fast the helicopter was going in any flight condition?" It sure would — and a number of people have attempted to fill the need, especially for flight at low speed.

The best way would be to paint an air molecule red and then observe its direction and how long it takes to get there. Columbus used a version of this by spitting over the bow of the *Santa Maria* and then using his pulse rate to time the traverse to the stern. (Of course, he then falsified his log so that his sailors wouldn't know how far from home he was taking them.) A couple of experimental versions of this have been recently developed, using a small bundle of ionized air molecules instead of spit.

Several prototype systems use the difference in dynamic pressure between the advancing and retreating blade tips. Because of the high tip speeds involved, the pressure transducer installed on a small tip-mounted pitot tube can send a sinusoidal (waveform) electrical signal to a processor that can analyze its magnitude and phase to generate the airspeed and direction of the helicopter's flight path. This system has not been installed on any production helicopters but does look promising. A version of the system installed on the U.S. Coast Guard HH-65A Dolphin (Figure 73-5) is the Pacer Systems Inc. OADS (Omni Airspeed and Direction System), which doesn't use the helicopter rotor but has a small motor-driven beam with a pair of Venturi tubes.

Another system in Figure 73-5 is used on the Bell AH-l Cobra. This is the Marconi ADS (Air Data System), which is essentially a conventional pitot-static system on a swiveling mount deliberately placed in the rotor downwash to measure its magnitude and direction as an indication of how fast and in what direction the helicopter is moving. The Army flight test organization has found this system very useful in setting up true hover and vertical-climb flight conditions.

Both of these omni-directional systems are complicated, draggy, and expensive. There is certainly a fortune waiting for anyone who can come up with a better way.

Pacer OADS
(HH-65A)

Marconi ADS
(Bell AH-1)

Figure 73-5 Two Low-Speed Airspeed Systems

74 Icing and Deicing

In many technical fields, the helicopter lags the airplane by 20 to 30 years. This isn't for want of trying but because, both in configuration and self-made environment, rotary-wing aircraft are much more complex than their fixed-wing cousins.

Aircraft deicing is certainly one of these lagging fields. Whereas many airplanes can effectively detect and remove ice from critical components, very few helicopters (outside of the Soviet Union) are so equipped. The reason is because icing conditions are encountered so rarely in normal helicopter operation that it is hard to justify the weight and expense of systems that on any one helicopter may never be needed. (Note: in Europe, icing conditions appear to be more prevalent than in the United States.)

On the other hand, during those times when icing is a factor, the presence of ice protection may save the aircraft and all aboard — or at least permit a flight to be completed that would otherwise have to be aborted. The philosophy here, of course, is similar to that which dictates carrying fire-extinguishing systems around.

Flight limitations

A review of helicopter flight manuals gives a pretty consistent picture: "Flight during icing conditions is prohibited" (Hughes 500D); "Flight into known icing conditions is prohibited" (Boeing Vertol CH-46E); "Continuous flight in light icing not recommended" (Bell AH-1G); "The helicopter is restricted from flying in moderate or heavy icing conditions. Flight in light icing conditions is limited to 30 minutes duration, due to the probability of damage from shedding ice" (Sikorsky CH-53E).

The severity of icing depends both on temperature and the "liquid water content" of the air — that is, on how many grams of water there are in each cubic meter. In practice, the airplane people define severity by the distance traveled while picking up half an inch of' ice on a small probe. If 40 miles are required, the icing is "light". If only 10 miles are needed, then it is "heavy icing".

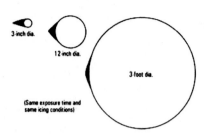

Figure 74-1 Effect of Object Size on Ice Accumulation

Ice formation

Even at below-freezing temperatures, it is possible for water droplets in the form of fog, drizzle, or ram to remain in the liquid state as long as there is nothing for the first ice crystal to form on, such as a speck of dust. When an aircraft flies by, it provides the required foreign body and the "super-cooled" droplets will freeze to any surface on which they impinge.

Naturally, it is the forward-facing surfaces that receive the brunt of the impingement, especially on the very leading edge of a component at the "stagnation point", where one streamline of air is brought to a complete stop. Further back, the airflow is parallel to the surface and so diverts most of the droplets. Small objects are more efficient in picking up ice than larger ones.

Figure 74-1 shows the results of exposing three cylinders to the same icing conditions. The reason for the significant difference is that the larger the cylinder, the more warning it projects ahead to distort the approaching flow field and to deflect the oncoming droplets to either side. Since blade leading edges are similar to small cylinders, they are efficient catchers and the smaller a blade, stabilizer leading edge, or inlet lip, the more sensitive it will be to ice.

Engine protection

One of the most serious potential problems concerns the engine installation. A turbine engine may be prone to compressor stall if large distortions of the air coming into it produce regions of very high local angles of attack on some of the blades. If the separated-flow region becomes too large, the airflow through the engine decreases to the point where the fuel-air ratio in the combustion chamber is too rich to burn and the engine flames out.

Designers work hard to shape the engine inlets to obtain the most uniform flow in all flight conditions but the accretion of a blob of ice on an inlet lip or on a screen may completely undo their efforts. In some installations, the inlet duct has bends or a plenum chamber where wet snow can be trapped.

And, as if these possibilities weren't bad enough, if that chunk of ice or wad of frozen snow should come loose before it has become large enough to cause a flameout, it may still cause physical damage to the compressor blades as the engine tries to gulp it down.

Part of this latter problem has to do with the nature of ice, which can be either brittle or tough —depending on the temperature. For example, ice cubes right out of the freezer are brittle but they toughen up as their temperature rises to the melting point. This phenomenon once caused some red faces at a major turbine-engine manufacturer. A press tour of the plant was planned and the test-cell people had successfully practiced for their part by throwing handfuls of fresh ice cubes into the intake of their new engine. As usually happens, the tour group was delayed and the bowl of ice cubes sat at room temperature for some time. They say the result was an unexpected exploded view of the engine.

To avoid such problems, one current technology for engine-inlet protection involves burying electric heating blankets in the skin of the inlet leading edges and other critical locations to prevent ice from forming. Alternate methods include ducting hot compressor bleed air between double skins to keep the surfaces warm. These systems are modeled on those used in airplanes and, as such, are not so much of a challenge to the designer as that required to protect the rotor blades.

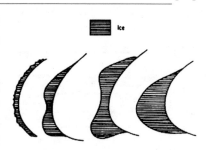

Figure 74-2 Leading Edge Shapes Observed in Icing Tests

Carburetors of reciprocating engines can ice up even in clear air if the humidity is high enough. The pressure drop as the air enters the intake may lower the temperature enough to first cause the moisture to condense and then freeze. Under conditions of very high humidity, carburetor icing can occur at outside temperatures as high as 38° C (100° F). To prevent this, the pilot is given a *carburetor heat* control that ducts warm air from around the exhaust manifold to the inlet. Turbine inlets can experience similar clear-air icing but because the pressure drop is less, the critical temperature is below about 8° C (46° F).

The problem with rotor Ice

Just as in the engine inlet, ice on the main- and tail-rotor blades can have bad effects while building up and possibly catastrophic effects when it breaks loose. Since the blades are going faster than any other part of the helicopter, they encounter more droplets per second and, because of their collection efficiency, accrete ice at a faster rate. On the other hand, compression of the air at the stagnation point on the leading edge of the blade raises its temperature — as much as 22° C (40° F) at the very tip. For this reason, tips often remain free of ice while it builds up on inboard sections.

Ice degrades the aerodynamic characteristics of the blade airfoil by forming irregular shapes that increase drag and decrease maximum-lift capabilities. Figure 74-2 shows some of the odd lumps and bumps that ice has been observed to construct on airfoils during tests in icing and wind tunnels.

The power increase due to the higher drag may give an alert pilot the first indication of ice. The degraded aerodynamic characteristics will also jeopardize the ability to autorotate in case of an engine flameout. Autorotation with ice on the blades puts the helicopter into a multiple bind:

Bind 1—Because the power required is higher, the autorotative rate of descent must be higher to produce that power from the loss of potential energy. This gives the pilot less time to get the engine restarted if that is in the cards.

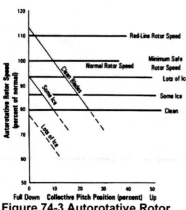

Figure 74-3 Autorotative Rotor Speed Trends

Bind 2— Because the rate of descent is higher, the collective pitch required to maintain normal rotor speed is lower. If the designers did not foresee this possibility, the collective downstop may be too high to get the rotor speed up to a desired level. Figure 74-3 shows the trend.

Bind 3—Because the maximum-lift capability is lower, the safe minimum rotor speed will be higher. With lots of ice, the minimum safe rpm may actually be higher than the rpm on the downstop.

Bind 4—Because the drag is higher, the ability to build up excess rotor speed in a cyclic flare will be lower.

Bind 5—Because the maximum lift is lower, the load factor that can be generated in the final collective pull will be lower.

Blade ice will eventually be shed because of centrifugal forces, airloads, blade flexing, or flying into warmer air. When it does, it often goes from one blade at a time or "asymmetrically" so that the rotor goes out of balance and out of track. This can produce severe vibration in the cockpit and damaging cyclic loads in the main- and/or tail-rotor support structures. At the same time, damage to the tail rotor may result from ice thrown off the main rotor or vice versa.

Blade protection

I was once told that the early Russian Mil helicopters had blades constructed from metal spars and wooden ribs like the early Sikorsky's —but with sealskin coverings instead of doped aircraft fabric. The seal skin was kept pliable and ice-free by periodically swabbing with walrus oil.

Perhaps because of the current shortage of walrus oil, almost all rotor deicing systems — including those on recent Russian helicopters — now use electrical heating blankets. These are built into the leading edges with heat supplied through slip rings at the rotor hub from a generator mounted on the transmission. The blankets are divided into zones and each is periodically heated. This melts the bond between the skin and the ice that has accumulated since the last heating cycle, allowing centrifugal forces to fling the ice off. Corresponding zones of every blade are heated at the same time to minimize possible unbalance. The interval between heatings of any one blade segment is determined by the icing severity measured with an ice detector, sometimes mounted in an engine inlet to ensure a flow over it even in hover. It is generally accepted that ice can be allowed to build up to about a quarter of an inch halfway out on today's blades before it becomes dangerous. By popping the ice off quickly from the leading edge, there will be little water to run back and freeze on the trailing edge. This deicing system takes much less power than would an anti-icing system that would try to continuously keep the whole blade above freezing. Of course, on some experimental pressure-jet helicopters, the effects of an anti-icing system come free, as surface temperature of the blades can run at several hundred degrees.

Proof of the pudding

A big problem in the development of any ice-protection system is proving that it works after it is installed. Sending the test aircraft out to look for natural icing conditions of various kinds and severities could take years. For this reason, two artificial icing flight-test facilities are now in operation. One is operated each winter by the Canadians in Ottawa and consists of a tower — shown in Figure 74-4 — that sprays a cloud of water from calibrated nozzles to give the desired droplet size and cloud density. A helicopter hovering downwind can stay in the cloud until it demonstrates that its system is working or until a dangerous amount of ice builds up. The procedure is relatively safe since a landing can be made quickly. It also gives the engineers a chance to observe the ice formations close up before they melt. The limitation of the tower is that it does not simulate forward flight. That limitation is not a factor with the other facility. A U.S. Army Chinook called the "Helicopter Icing Spray System" (HISS) emits a cloud from a 60-foot-wide spray bar, as shown in Figure 74-5.

Figure 74-4 Ottawa's Spray Rig Generates Icing Cloud for Aerospatiale Puma

Looking for Mr. Goodsystem

No one likes the cost and complexity of an electrical deicing system, nor the weight of its electrical generator. Therefore high motivation persists to find other methods of ice protection and a large number have been tried in the past. One is to try breaking the ice up with blade bending induced by sudden cyclic, collective, or rotor-speed changes. This seemed to work in hover on the hingeless Lockheed Cheyenne attack helicopter at the Ottawa spray rig but has been less than successful on other rotor designs. In forward flight, this method has often led to severe asymmetrical shedding and resultant high vibration.

Another approach that was once used on propellers is to allow antifreeze fluid to run out the blades through holes in the surface from a distribution system at the hub. Engineers have tried it but were soured on the idea for two reasons: there is difficulty in getting uniform distribution all the way, out, and all those holes affect blade fatigue life.

"If we could only coat the blade with something that ice wouldn't stick to, we would be in like Flynn." That has been the motivation behind many experiments. Except perhaps walrus oil, no one has yet come up with that magic paint, paste, or tape that would be "ice phobic" yet could still stand up to the erosive effects of dust, sand, and rain. There is a fortune waiting for the person who does.

Figure 74-5 US Army HISS Provides Icing Cloud to Test Bell's 412

75 The Turbine Engine and the Helicopter

The marriage of an engine and a helicopter airframe is like most marriages — it requires some minor and some major adjustments from both partners to make it work. Most of the time, satisfactory adjustments can be made early but sometimes idiosyncrasies just have to be lived with.

Keep it clean

Because of the high speed and small size of a turbine engine's rotating parts, items more solid than a molecule of air can do damage. Big items, such as screwdrivers and rocks, do their damage quickly, leading to a sudden engine stoppage. Smaller items, such as grains of sand, do it more slowly— with the evidence being a gradual loss of performance. The goal of everyone who designs, builds, maintains, or flies helicopters is to assure that only air and fuel molecules reach the sensitive parts of the engine.

One solution common to most designs is locating the engine intakes as far above the ground as possible in the expectation that most objects stirred up by the rotorwash will stay low. Some helicopters use screens to keep large and medium-sized foreign objects out.

Smaller particles, such as sand and dust, present a more-difficult challenge normally overcome by ducting the air through a filter. Originally, these filters used a maze design somewhat like the air cleaner on your automobile. Turbine engines, however, gulp prodigious quantities of air and maze filters result in a significant performance (installation) loss by reducing the energy coming into the compressor.

Typical Centrifugal Tube

A better design now widely used causes the air to pass through tubes with swirl vanes that throw the particles to the outside where they can be collected and dumped overboard (Figure 75-1). This arrangement is called a centrifugal particle separator and is used not only on helicopters but also on heavy construction equipment. Installation losses are smaller than with the maze variety but are still significant. For this reason, some helicopters

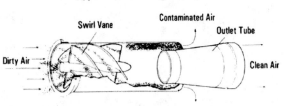

Figure 75-1 Centrifugal Particle Separator on Hughes 500

417

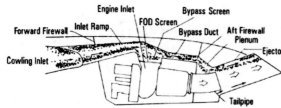

Figure 75-2 Bell 222 Integral Particle Separator

give the pilot the option of using the particle separator only for operations where the air is really dirty.

Another particle separator arrangement is shown on the Bell 222 in Figure 75-2. By forcing the air to make a sharp turn before entering the engine, particles with more momentum than air are forced to the outside of the duct where they can be separated out. The recent trend is to incorporate the separator as an integral part of the engine.

Exhaust reingestion

More than foreign objects should be kept out of the engine intake. Hot exhaust gases can also cause trouble.

Typically, a 1°C increase in outside air temperature reduces the power capability of a turbine engine by about 1%. An engine breathing its own hot exhaust gases "thinks" the day is hotter than it is and reaches the turbine temperature limit at a lower fuel flow and horsepower than it should.

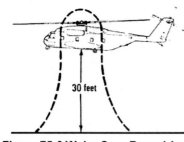

Figure 75-3 Wake-Core Boundries (CH-53 IGE)

Measurements on an early prototype of the three-engine Sikorsky CH-53E showed temperature increases as high as 30°C (54°F) when the aircraft hovered at a wheel height of 30 feet. This was at least partially due to the large blade-root cutout—30% of the radius—which produced a large wake core, or region of relatively dead air, when hovering in ground effect (Figure 75-3). Since the engines exhausted into this core and also used it as a fresh-air supply, it's not surprising they experienced a high temperature rise.

Sikorsky has since reduced this from 30°C to 10°C (18°F) by increasing the engine exhaust velocity so that it propels the hot gases out of the core and into the rotor wake. This was done somewhat reluctantly, since an increase in exhaust velocity (accomplished by reducing the size of the tailpipe opening) comes at the expense of higher backpressure — which causes another well-defined power loss.

An even more severe condition for reingestion than hover was found during low-speed, low-level tests of the Boeing Vertol YUH-61 UTTAS prototype. The ground vortex entrained the exhaust and led it directly to the intake (Figure 75-4). Sudden temperature increases of as high as 60°C (108°F) were enough to cause compressor stalls. I have not heard of this on other helicopters but the flow conditions are common enough that it is certainly a potential for any design.

Play it cool

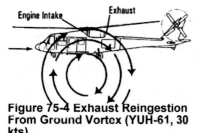

Figure 75-4 Exhaust Reingestion From Ground Vortex (YUH-61, 30 kts)

On a modern battlefield, any concentrated source of heat is a potential target for sophisticated heat-seeking missiles that "see" infrared radiation. For this reason, it is important to shield and cool any hot spots on military helicopters.

Since the engine exhaust system is the primary heat source, it is common practice to provide an exhaust duct with a sharp enough bend to hide the hot engine components. In addition, the insides of the duct are often painted with a special black paint to suppress radiation. Another practice mixes the exhaust gases with a flow of cool air to lower the "IR signature" of the exhaust plume (Figure 75-5).

Torsional oscillations

A modern turboshaft engine incorporates a governor to keep the rotor turning within a narrow rpm range, no matter what power is required. The governor does this by sensing the error between the actual and the desired (100%) rpm and then increasing or decreasing the fuel flow as appropriate.

Figure 75-5 Exhaust Cooling Installation - Hughes Apache

Sometimes, a governor that works very well in controlling an engine in a test cell will give trouble when installed on a helicopter. This is because a helicopter rotor mounted on a drive train of finite flexibility has a torsional natural frequency of two to four times per second—or two to four Hertz. That's low enough for the engine governor to mistake the natural oscillations for the type of rpm changes it was designed to prevent. A poorly matched governor might zig when it should zag and make the situation worse by driving the oscillation to larger and larger amplitudes.

This type of engine/rotor incompatibility is a possibility on all turbine-powered helicopters. It first became evident in the Bell YH-40, the prototype for the UH-1 series, where it was cured by desensitizing the governor with a deadband — so it could not respond to small errors in rotor speed. Later governors handle the problem with more sophistication, although even in very recent development programs the problem has called attention to itself and had to be addressed with changes to the engine's governor; usually involving a reduction in sensitivity that hurts the ability to respond rapidly to changing power demands.

A test pilot looks for the oscillation by rapidly pulsing the collective pitch at the predicted natural frequency— that is, exciting the system in resonance— and then observing the rate of decay for the oscillations after he stops moving the stick. Both the FAA and the military insist that helicopters be proven free of mechanical instability before acceptance. As far as I know, this particular problem has never been encountered in production helicopters.

Rotor rpm droop

When a turbine engine is operated at a low power level, its gas generator— consisting of the compressor and its turbine—is turning at something less than full speed, even if the rotor and the power turbine are up to their design speeds. If a sudden demand (a jump takeoff, a recovery from a practice autorotation, or the final transition to hover at the end of a quick stop) is put on the engine, the gas-generator speed must be increased to produce the new power level. If it does not accelerate rapidly enough, power available will lag behind power required and the rotor speed will decrease to make up for the deficiency — at the expense of stored rotor kinetic energy. The amount of rpm decrease is known as "droop".

A certain amount of droop is necessary for the engine governor to work, since rotor speed is the signal it normally uses to adjust the fuel flow. For a sudden power demand, however, the governor may not be able to call for enough fuel flow soon enough and the droop may be so large as to slow the rotor to a dangerous level before the engine can recover. The faster the maneuver, the larger the droop.

Trying to decrease the droop by increasing the "gain" of the governor can lead to unstable oscillations (as discussed earlier), so this potential is limited. Another scheme, now common practice, is to use an "anticipation" signal in the form of collective stick motion to increase the fuel flow even before the rpm droops. This is analogous to the accelerator pump in the carburetor of your automobile being actuated when you step on the gas pedal. While not eliminating droop entirely, this usually reduces it to an acceptable level.

Another possible rotor droop situation is when the helicopter requires more power than the engine is designed to produce even with the gas generator already up to full speed. Such situations include the failure of one engine of a twin-engine helicopter and high-speed, high-load maneuvers.

Most turbine engines are protected by a device that limits the fuel flow at a preset maximum turbine temperature or "topping" limit. If the helicopter is asking for more power than this limit allows, it will feed upon its own rotor kinetic energy by slowing down. Some engines minimize this type of droop by switching to a contingency rating that allows higher-than-normal maximum power for a short time. In any case, the pilot must decrease his demands on the engine to prevent excessive rotor rpm droop or excessive overtemp operation.

76 Modern Turboshaft Speed Governing

For many good reasons, helicopters are designed to fly with the rotor speed in a fairly narrow range. It is therefore nice to have some kind of engine-speed governor, either automatic or human.

Different governors

In the case of most piston-engine helicopters, humans play a role. A linkage between collective pitch and the throttle controls speed somewhat, but the pilot uses the twist grip on the collective lever for fine tuning. Because the load-speed-fuel interactions on a piston-engine are so complex, designing an automatic system that senses rpm and then uses adjustments in the throttle setting to hold a fixed value has long been a challenge. But such a system is now available on Robinson helicopters.

On a turboshaft engine, however, it is relatively easy to design an "isochronous" governor that can hold the output turbine speed close to a desired value. This is because the turbine speed is affected directly by fuel flow into the burners.

Speed governors have been installed on turboshaft engines since the very first applications in helicopters. The first were simply variations of the mechanical fly-ball governors developed for steam turbines. In some situations, they were not fully satisfactory.

On the Bell UH-1 prototype, the XH-40, the Lycoming T53 engine's governor tended to go out of phase with the torsional oscillations of the rotor on the long shaft. It therefore did the wrong thing at the wrong time. It pumped more fuel when it should have been giving less, and thus drove the entire system into an ever-increasing oscillation. This was eventually fixed by incorporating a "dead-band" in the governor which prevented it from making corrections to very small deviations from the desired rpm.

Electronic help

The designers of the second-generation engine-control systems—used on such modern engines as the General Electric T700—made significant improvements based on the newly maturing science of electronics. These systems consist of two major components: the hydraulic mechanical unit, or HMU, and the electronic control unit, or ECU.

The HMU is the muscle. It contains the fuel pump and all the necessary devices needed to start and shut down the engine, and to control the gas-generator speed.

The ECU is the brains. It tells the HMU how to adjust the fuel flow to keep the output turbine at the right speed. It protects the turbine from overheating, and in multiengine helicopters, provides torque matching. Instead of using a fly-ball governor, the ECU works with an electrical signal from a tachometer on the output-turbine shaft.

The dead-band used in the earlier units to control the unstable oscillations is replaced by a "notch filter" in the ECU circuitry. This filter retards the engine control's action at the drive system's natural frequency, which is generally two to four cycles per second.

Even then, it's sometimes been necessary to desensitize the system by lowering the "gain" to avoid the oscillations in all flight conditions. This, of course, means that the governor cannot hold the rotor speed quite as close to the desired value as it could before the gain was reduced. Figure 76-1 shows how the torsional oscillation on the CH-53E was unstable before this fix was incorporated.

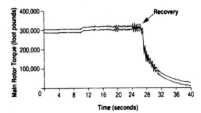

Figure 76-1 CH-53E Rotor/Drive System Torsional Oscillation

Rotor droop

Helicopters with these governors have also encountered another problem: in some maneuvers, the rotor speed droops to an alarming level. One such maneuver is the power recovery from a practice autorotation. Imagine a helicopter descending in autorotation at low collective pitch for some time, with the rotor turning faster than the 100% speed the governor has been asked to hold—that is, with the "needles split."

For this condition, the engine thinks it's been dismissed for the day and goes to an idle state. Very little fuel is being burned and the gas generator is running at significantly less than its normal operating speed.

Now the pilot tries to return to normal flight. He suddenly applies power by pulling up the collective stick. Initially, the demanded power will come from the main rotor's stored kinetic energy, and this causes the rotor to slow down, as shown by the solid line in Figure 76-2.

The engine control will not be aware of this slowdown until the rotor speed passes through the 100% level, its reference setting. At this point, it will recognize the difficulty and start calling for more fuel flow. But the engine can only swallow fuel so fast before the compressor will stall or "surge."

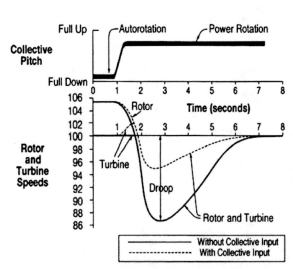

Figure 76-2 Rotor Speed Droop During Recovery From Practice Autorotation

The quickest the engine can respond without experiencing this difficulty is called its "acceleration schedule." It was determined by the engine manufacturer during many hours of test-cell work. Thus even if the engine can be run up to the acceleration schedule, there will be a finite time when the engine cannot generate enough torque to speed the drive system back up to the desired level.

The solid line on Figure 76-2 illustrates the lag and the subsequent "rotor droop" which, if large enough, would jeopardize the rotor's ability to maintain flying thrust.

On the McDonnell Douglas Apache and the Sikorsky Black Hawk, this problem is partially solved by sending an "anticipation signal" from the collective-stick motion, both from its position and from its rate. This signal forewarns the engine of the upcoming power demand, and changes an otherwise undesirable characteristic of more than 10% droop into an acceptable one with about 5%, as shown by the dotted line on Figure 76-2.

FADEC

Modern engine-control system designers are making even bigger improvements. The above-mentioned governors use analog technology in their electronic circuits. But analog computers are limited in their accuracy because of the build-up of tolerances inherent in their many electronic components. Thus the gain—or tightness—that they're capable of is limited.

The next-generation control systems use digital technology where even small variations can be almost eliminated. For example, the turbine speed is determined by accurately counting pulses from a magnetic pickup. In some systems, not only the turbine speed but also the rate the speed changes serve as a signal to the fuel control.

Digital technology led to the development of fall authority digital electronic control (FADEC), which will be on the engines being developed for the next generation of helicopters such as the Boeing Sikorsky RAH-66 Comanche. These engine-control systems will safely run closer to the conditions that might trigger unstable torsional instabilities or compressor stall, without encountering them.

Adaptive too

With some additional sophistication, designers promise, the engine controls can be made adaptive. That is, their characteristics might be changed to allow them to do such things as:

• Optimize the rotor speed for minimum fuel consumption in cruise flight as changes in weight, air temperature, and air density occur (only down to a safe rpm limit, of course);

• Increase rotor speed to help develop more thrust in a maneuver requiring a high load factor; or

423

• With the right inputs, intelligently reconfigure themselves at the first sign of compressor stall or of unstable torsional oscillations, to suppress these problems while operating right up to the edge of the cliff—even with engine deterioration.

All of these projected improvements will mean that in the future the pilot can get the maximum performance from his engine in both normal and extreme flight conditions without having to monitor it as closely as he does now.

77 Engine Snow Protection

Unexpected technical problems challenge almost every new engineering program. It's the curse of the "unknown unknowns." Sometimes the problems are serious enough to be fatal to the program. At the very least, they result in schedule slips and cost overruns that make the management and customer bite their fingernails.

Helicopter engineers face these problems like all other engineers. The following account of the successful solution of a real problem can be taken as typical of how engineers earn their paychecks.

A chilling example

The problem was on the Aerospatiale (now Eurocopter) HH-65A Dolphin, which the U.S. Coast Guard began procuring in the early 1980s as its Short Range Recovery helicopter.

Since snowstorms can't be ruled out during a rescue, the Coast Guard required that the aircraft must have "unrestricted operation in falling and blowing snow." Therefore, the Dolphin was equipped with a state-of-the-art engine-intake anti-ice system. But during the demonstration tests, a few cases of engine surge were unexpectedly encountered.

The problem took two years to correct. How it was solved was reported by John Murphy of Aerospatiale Helicopter Corp. at the 1988 American Helicopter Society Forum in a paper entitled, "Dolphin Eats Snow."

The first task was to determine just what the problem was. In the HH-65A's two Textron Lycoming LTS 101-750s as first installed, the air entered forward of the rotor mast and reached each engine by making a right-angle turn at the engine scroll (Figure 77-1).

To research the difficulty, the system was set up in Lycoming's test cell, and windows were installed in the ducting. When fresh snow was gently thrown into the intake, some of it piled up in the turn at the engine scroll. The snow would then come loose, and go through the engine in lumps at unpredictable times.

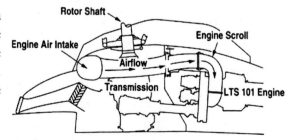

Figure 77-1 HH-65A's Original Inlet System

When this happened, the airflow to the compressor was so affected that the engine surged with an audible "bang" and there was the possibility of damage to the compressor.

Melt the snow

The first attempted fix was to try to melt the snow with electric heating pads. Several modifications were made, but they did not do the job. Engineers found that the snow took a finite time to melt, and even as it was doing so, fresh snow was piling up on top of it. Also, it was impossible to increase the heat without damaging the scrolls, which were made of polymide plastic.

Since heating failed to fix the problem, the next step was to try to modify the internal contours of the scroll. The idea was to increase the air velocity in the regions where the snow piled up. Flights in the French Alps and tests in the Climatic Hangar at Eglin AFB in Florida subsequently showed that the modified contours didn't work either.

A more successful approach was to replace the engine-supplied scroll with an aircraft-supplied "plenum chamber" that had a much larger volume and enclosed the engine accessory gearbox (Figure 77-2).

Even this was not straightforward. Some heating had to be supplied to critical areas, and deflectors, drains, and insulation modifications had to be made. This solution was also expensive since it involved changes to the engine.

Several alternate solutions were investigated. The team even returned to scroll-heating schemes both with compressor bleed air and with electrical spray mats. Neither proved practical.

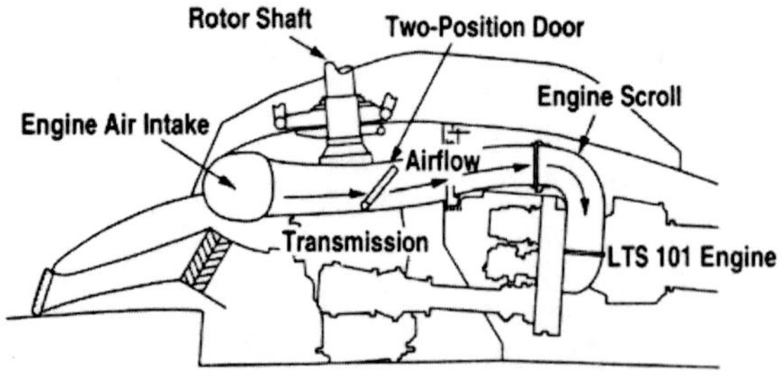

Try a different inlet

Another promising solution investigated an alternate inlet (Figure 77-3). For this, the air is taken from the main-rotor gearbox compartment during operation in snow, with the normal intakes being used in all other conditions. The air going to the engine is pre-warmed by the oil coolers and by the gearbox itself.

This scheme was tested not only in the Climatic Hangar, but in Montana, Wyoming, and Michigan. (Engineers must be prepared to travel when faced with a problem involving cold weather operation.)

The results were "generally satisfactory," though there were a few loose ends to be worked out if this system was to be chosen.

This solution was less expensive than the plenum chamber, because the engines would not require modification. But there was a safety-of-flight

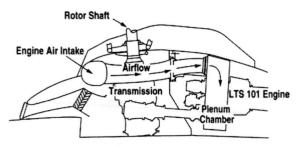

Figure 77-2 Modified Inlet System With Plenum Chamber

Figure 77-3 System With Alternate Inlet

concern: The engines might suck in oil or hydraulic fluid should a malfunction occur in the gearbox compartment.

Following tradeoff studies, the plenum chamber was chosen by Aerospatiale and approved by the Coast Guard. Tests subsequently had to be conducted to prove that the modification would indeed work. This involved looking for the right kind of weather through Colorado, Wyoming, Minnesota, and Michigan during the winter of 1984-85.

The tests were satisfactorily completed and the plenum-chamber system is now standard on all HH-65s.

78 Helicopter Noise

Compared to a quarter-horsepower vacuum cleaner, a 1,000-shp helicopter is quiet—but not quiet enough. Designers have the prime responsibility for improving the situation—but pilots also have some opportunities to hold the noise down. To control noise, one must understand where it is coming from. There are not only several distinct sources of helicopter noise but what you hear depends upon where you are.

Rotor noise in hover

For example, if you were to sit on the hub of a r turning at flat pitch on an electrically powered whirl tower, you would hear only a steady "swoosh" as the blades swept through the air. This noise is made primarily by the air molecules that have been brought up to speed in the boundary layer of the blades and then dumped off the trailing edge with much bouncing and jouncing. This is similar to the air noise you hear in a high-speed car. As blade pitch and blade lift are increased, tip vortices are formed that spin like a whirlpool and can change the noise characteristics from a "swoosh" to a "roar". Part of this change is caused by the gusty inflow generated by a hovering rotor. Neither the turbulent-air noise nor the vortex noise has a discrete frequency. For this reason, they are called broadband or "white" noise to compare them to white light, which contains all frequencies—or colors—of the spectrum.

Getting off the hub and standing somewhere near the rotor would give a different impression of the noise characteristics. Now you would be aware of "rotational noise,' in which you could hear each blade passing by and also multiples—or higher harmonica—of this frequency.

The higher the rotor rpm and the more blades the rotor has, the higher the blade-passage frequency will be. Our ears are more sensitive to high than low frequencies. Thus, a small fast-turning tail rotor with four blades maybe perceived as making a louder noise than a slower-turning main rotor with two blades—even though the tail rotor is disturbing less air and radiating small pressure pulses. Carried to an extreme, a siren can produce a high level of "perceived noise" with relatively little power.

Measuring noise

This is a good place to discuss how sound is measured. Sound travels through the air as a series of expansion and compression waves, much like ripples on a pond. The change in pressure from peak-to-trough of these waves causes a deflection of your eardrums and you hear a sound. The number of waves per second is the frequency, or "pitch," of the sound. Unless you are listening to a tuning fork, most of what you hear is coming at many different frequencies with amplitudes continuously changing.

Noise scientists (who call themselves "acousticians") use calibrated microphones and recording equipment to measure the sound pressure produced by the oscillating waves passing a given point. Instead of reporting the pressure in absolute units of pounds per square foot, the acousticians prefer to compare the ratio of their measurements with a standard low level that moat people can just barely hear. The units of this ratio are called decibels or, simply dBs. Normal speech is about 70 dB and noises that get our attention go up from there—with about 140 dB starting to cause physical pain.

To be able to plot both soft and loud noises on the same piece of graph paper, the dB scale is "logarithmic". That is, doubling the measurement from 70 dB to 140 dB does not represent doubling the loudness of normal speech but something much higher. Each 6 dB increase *doubles* the loudness from the previous level, so that by the time it gets to 140 dB, it is about 130 times as loud as normal conversation. (A good cocktail party gets up to 110 dB.) Because of the ear's sensitivity to high frequencies, the acousticians have developed a compensating correction to the sound levels measured by their equipment The result is a "perceived sound level" or "weighted noise" that decreases the measured values coming from low-frequency sources such as bass drums and increases the values from high-frequency sources such as piccolos. (Remember how clearly you can hear the piccolo above the rest of the band in *Stars and Stripes Forever,* even when it is being played by a 90-pound high-school girl?)

Noise in forward flight

Now, getting back to helicopters, we have already seen how you would hear rotational noise at blade-passage frequency while standing near a rotor whirl tower or a hovering helicopter. If, Instead, the helicopter is flying over, the rotational noise is still a factor but you might also hear another characteristic called "blade slap" or "impulsive noise". There are two possible sources for this. In one case, the advancing tip is going fast enough to appreciably compress the air ahead of it. This causes shock waves that project strong pressure waves ahead of the tip like stones from David's sling. At short distances, the "crispness" of these impulses is especially annoying. Farther out, the noise degenerates to a series of thuds that can be heard for miles.

The other type of impulsive noise is "blade-vortex interaction" which, as the name implies, is due to a blade running into—or at least near—the trailing tip vortex left by a preceding blade. In most flight conditions, the tip vortices and the blades keep away from each other—but if the helicopter has a slight rate of descent or is rolling into a turn, this separation may not be maintained. The flow pattern around the vortex induces sudden changes in the angle of attack and velocity on the blade, causing local stall and possibly shock waves. What counts here is the rate of pressure change. Slowly pressing your palm against a tabletop is silent—but slapping the table is noisy even if the final "slap" pressure is the same as the "press" pressure. This type of blade slap is generally projected down and forward, and to the untrained ear sounds the same as that caused by high-speed compressibility.

Figure 78-1 Typical Forward Flight Sound Footprint

All of this forward noise projection results in a sound pattern on the ground in which lines of constant sound levels form a "footprint" as In Figure 78-1. This is important in military operations in terms of detectability and in commercial operations in terms of good neighborliness. Of course, both of these situations are influenced subjectively by the "ambient" noise level existing in the vicinity of the listener. Flying a helicopter over a freeway during rush hour will attract much less attention than over a residential neighborhood Sunday at 8 pm.

Interior noise

If you are riding in the helicopter, you get a somewhat different impression of the noise characteristics. The rotor rotational noise is much reduced, since you are closer to the eye of the sound pattern.

You may, however, hear a similar noise due to each blade's pressure pulse impinging on the fuselage. In some helicopters, this takes the form of "canopy drumming" and can be not only heard but also seen as rattling of thin window and skin panels. Impulsive noise due to advancing blade compressibility can never be heard in the cockpit and impulsive noise due to blade-vortex interaction may not always be heard. Thus, a quiet cockpit is no assurance that you are not causing a problem on the ground.

Quieting the helicopter

For the designer who wants to minimize external noise, the moat promising method is to choose low tip speeds for both the main and tail rotors. This choice will reduce the perceived rotational noise and minimize compressibility noise, especially if the blades have thin and/or swept blade tips. The dilemma, however, is that lowering the tip speed requires more blade area and, thus, a heavier rotor to develop the same performance. Weights of the transmission and drive shaft also increase, due to lower rpm and higher torque. The resulting design is always a compromise between high performance and low noise, with customer

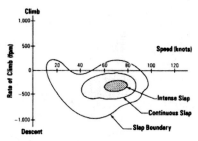

Figure 78-2 Blade-Slap Boundries for Bell 212

requirements and competitive pressure playing significant roles in arriving at the final design decisions.

There has been some research done recently on modifying the characteristics of the tip vortex by special tip shapes or by injecting jets of air. The objectives of the modifications are to either spread out the vortex and make it less intense, or to move it out of the way of the following blades. At this writing, vortex modification is promising but has not yet had an effect on production rotor designs.

The pilot also has some control over external noise, especially with respect to blade slap due to blade-vortex interaction. Figure 78-2 shows the result of a test program that measured blade slap in various flight conditions. For this program, microphones were mounted on the outside of a Bell Model 212. The measured noise characteristics may not be exactly the same as would be heard on the ground but can still be used for guidance. It may be seen that the worst flight condition for blade slap on this helicopter is 75 knots with a rate of descent of 300 fpm. Avoiding this condition when making a landing approach will minimize the blade slap both for ears on the ground and in the helicopter.

Internal noise can be controlled by the designer through the use of a wide range of techniques, including quieting such noise sources as gearing and pumps; avoiding metallic paths between rotating parts and the passenger compartments; changing the "rattling" characteristics of sheet-metal panels and equipment by stiffening, softening, or damping, and by adding sound insulation as a last resort.

In all regards, helicopter noise is an important factor in the general public's acceptance of these otherwise quite neighborly aircraft. The study is complicated enough that it promises to provide job security for a number of people into the foreseeable future.

79 Helicopter Noise Research

In any scientific field, some research is known as "basic" and some as "applied". The pure scientist doing basic research is satisfied to know why things are as they are. But the engineer doing applied research is continually asking, "How does that help me improve my product?"

NASA/AHS Rotorcraft Noise Program

A project involving helicopter noise used both basic and applied research. The basic research tried to resolve where noise comes from, while the applied research attempted to answer the question, "Are there ways to make helicopters quieter?"

This effort began when the Federal Aviation Administration (FAA), in response to public pressure, proposed a new set of stringent helicopter noise rules. These rules, similar to the ones the agency was adopting for fixed-wing aircraft, would have made designing new helicopters a headache, since the rules were based on vague ideas of where helicopter noise comes from and what the design factors are.

In a panic, the manufacturers, acting through the American Helicopter Society (AHS), began a joint five-year effort with NASA. They convinced the FAA to postpone its rulemaking until a more logical base for predicting noise could be prepared. At the same time, the FAA began a detailed survey of just how much noise could be tolerated under helicopter routes and around heliports.

The four major U.S. helicopter companies already had some noise-research programs underway. These were incorporated into an overall plan, which comprised four main categories of effort: noise prediction, testing and database, noise reduction, and criteria development.

Noise prediction

One of the program's main objectives was to develop methods so the engineers can "design-to-noise." After all, without some means of translating design parameters into noise characteristics, they have no good way of doing this.

NASA had developed a computer program for helicopter-noise prediction called "ROTONET." One of the tasks of the experts in the

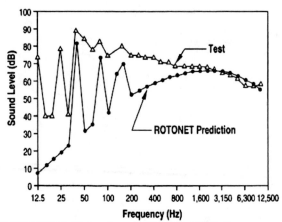

Figure 79-1 Noise Levels For MD 500E Flyover Test Vs. Predicted

various organizations was to compare their test results with the computed predictions. Figure 79-1 shows a comparison of the ROTONET prediction with actual test data for an 80-knot fly-over by a McDonnell Douglas MD 500E. The correlation is only so-so; the analysts believe that much of the discrepancy is caused by the difficulty of accurately modeling the tail rotor as it works in the disturbed wake of the main rotor.

This condition relates to the one responsible for the distinctive "blade slap" that you hear when one blade of the main rotor runs into the tip vortex left by a previous blade, as might happen in a descent to a helipad or when rolling into a tight turn. It is known as "blade-vortex interaction" (BVI) by the acousticians.

Several industry teams were trying to write the equations that govern the sudden change in pressure that causes the noise in this phenomenon. Figure 79-2 shows a more-or-less satisfactory correlation. In this case, the computer program used is appropriately called "WOPWOP."

In addition to the BVI noise, NASA also identified a similar phenomenon caused by one blade simply passing through the turbulent wake of another. This, they decided to call "blade-wake interaction" (BWI) noise. It is not as severe as BVI, and according to the wind-tunnel measurements, it is, surprisingly, more likely to be encountered during a low-speed climb than in a descent.

Besides BVI and BWI noises, there is another impulsive noise—one caused by compressibility. You hear this when a version of the Bell UH-1 with the big, 48-foot (14.6-m)-diameter rotor comes toward you. The rotor's tip speed is high enough that the advancing blade is generating a series of pressure waves or "sonic booms." These booms go forward and down to let you know without question that the helicopter is coming.

No recent designs use such high tip speeds, and as a result, none are quite so noisy as the UH-1. Still, the basic research in that helicopter's rotor may well assist in the applied research to reduce noise in future designs.

Testing and database

Another of the program's four major categories was testing and database. To develop this database, each source of helicopter noise was to be carefully measured under various flight conditions.

While the ear is a pretty good instrument for rough noise research, it can be confused by noise coming from various sources. Using sophisticated instrumentation, an acoustician can investigate and record characteristic noises as they come from the main rotor, the tail rotor (or the interference between the two), the engine, or the drive system. Each source puts out different signals depending on the flight condition.

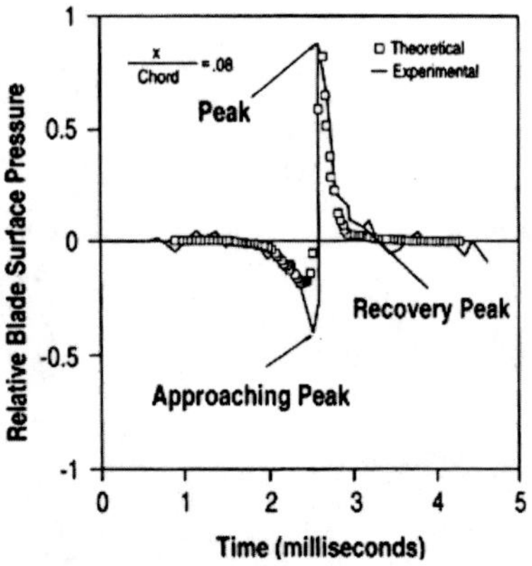

Figure 79-2 Surface Pressures On A Blade During Blade-Vortex Collision; Relative Blade Surface Pressure

One of the main objectives of the program was to carefully measure each source under various flight conditions as a base for the theoretical work.

Calibrated microphones and recording equipment measure the sound pressure produced by the oscillating waves passing a given point. Instead of reporting the pressure in absolute units of pounds per square foot, the acousticians measure it on a ratio basis, expressed in decibels (dBs). The standard "low" is at a level that most people can just barely hear.

Because we hear high frequencies better than low, the measurements are usually weighted toward the high-frequency end to give a modified scale of "perceived noise level" (PNL) or, in another form, dBA. The system is logarithmic so that an increase of 6 dB represents a doubling of loudness. Normal speech is about 70 dB. Noise that is objectionable starts at about 90 dB and becomes painful at 140 dB.

Concentrating on the main rotor as a source of annoyance, McDonnell Douglas Helicopter Co. equipped an MD 500E with an engine muffler and a low-speed tail rotor; this minimized noise sources other than the main rotor. Main-rotor noise in hover and in forward flight was measured during whirl-stand tests and flight tests.

Model rotors were also tested in rooms and wind tunnels specially treated to eliminate echoes, so that the sound measured is the same as if the rotor were far away from walls and obstructions. One result of these "anechoic" tests was the discovery that main rotors smaller than 2.5 feet in diameter did not reproduce the noise characteristics of full-scale rotors, and they should not be used for research.

During its wind-tunnel tests, Sikorsky Aircraft did extensive work with main-rotor/tail-rotor/empennage interference. The manufacturer found that the "tractor" position of the tail rotor— as on the Black Hawk—is quieter than the pusher position used on almost all other helicopters. This is because the flow coming into the tail rotor is "cleaner."

One of the favorite wind tunnels for rotor-noise research used by both companies and NASA is Holland's DNW (Duits Nederlandse Wind Tunnel). Up to 26 microphones can be placed around the test section to measure the noise propagation in all directions in a variety of flight conditions.

This data is especially useful to the analysts when taken concurrently with pressure measurements on the blades.

Noise reduction

During research to reduce noise, McDonnell Douglas flew the special MD 500E to investigate what happens if the rotor is slowed down. This was done by using a special engine governor.

Slowing the tip speed from 700 feet per second (fps) to as low as 510 fps made a significant difference in the noise of an approaching MD 500E

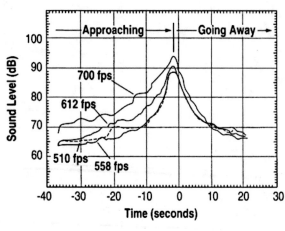

Figure 79-3 Helicopter Noise At Various Rotor Tip Speeds MD 500E During 80-Knot Flyover

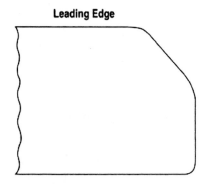

Figure 79-4 Sikorsky's Quiet Tip S-76 Tail-Rotor Blade

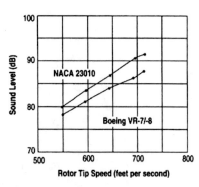

Figure 79-5 Effect Of An Airfoil Shape On Sound Level

(Figure 79-3). Going away, the change in rotor speed made little difference.

The experimenters were pleased with the results, but pointed out that lowering the tip speed also reduced the chance of making a safe entry into autorotation in an emergency. They suggested that if this scheme were used, the helicopter would require some auxiliary means of supplementing the rotor inertia. (It is not clear whether this recommendation applies to a helicopter with more than one engine.)

Sikorsky's noise-reduction research used wind-tunnel models with various blade-tip shapes for both main and tail rotors. By spreading out the tip vortex, a significant reduction in main rotor-blade/vortex interaction noise was obtained. In addition, a tip shape was found for the tail rotor that reduced its noise signature (Figure 79-4).

For its part, Boeing Helicopters discovered that the type of airfoil had an effect on noise. Figure 79-5 shows the difference in noise between a rotor with the old NACA 23012 airfoil and a second-generation Boeing rotor with the VR-7 and VE-8 airfoils. It is not clear how this conclusion applies to the slab-sided airfoils that have been used on all recent rotor designs.

NASA experimented with ways of reducing blade vortex interaction (BVI) noise by using active control—a variation of Higher Harmonic Control proposed for reducing vibration. The results indicated that this could reduce the BVI noise by up to 5 dB.

NASA also looked at ways of reducing internal noise by introducing an audio system that produced equal and opposite sound waves to those coming from the helicopter. (This "noise-canceling" concept is already being used in some earphone systems.)

Criteria development

The final task to develop criteria was assigned to the FAA. The agency surveyed existing helicopter operations and studied the results from the program's participants to develop a set of helicopter-noise regulations to replace those it had prematurely proposed.

Presumably, by the time the regulations are official, the engineers will know enough to "design-to-noise" for all their future projects.

80 Helicopter Vibration

Of course your helicopter shakes!

The reason for this dogmatic statement is that most of the time the rotor is going through the air in an unnatural state—edgewise—and the blades are subjected to rapidly varying aerodynamic environments during each revolution. The use of flapping hinges, lead-lag hinges, and cyclic pitch tend to cancel out the big effects of this unsteady situation but smaller disturbances still come through as periodically varying forces and moments applied to the structure holding the blade to the hub. In addition, the top of the fuselage and the empennage may get slapped by the downwash from each passing blade.

A big job of the designer is to find ways to minimize the effects of these various oscillating forces and moments on the rest of the helicopter—especially wherever a person or a piece of sensitive equipment is located.

Safety in numbers

One of the most effective ways to minimize vibration is to use as many blades as possible. This cuts down on the effect of an individual blade and allows an up-force from one blade to be played off against a down-force from another to smooth out the net oscillations coming down to the rotor support structure. Presumably, an infinite number of perfectly matched blades could be used to produce a rock-steady set of forces and moments just as a wing does for an airplane. For the same type of construction, each blade costs about the same to build, whether it is for a two- or 10—bladed rotor. So, the designer who tries to achieve a smooth-riding helicopter with many blades must also consider the economics of his choice.

Facing the hard facts of life and having chosen a finite number of blades for his rotor, he still has several things he can do to minimize the less-than~ optimum results of his choice. One of the most obvious is to try to make all of his blades as nearly identical as possible in contour, weight distribution, and stiffness. (Identical lead-lag dampers are also important.)

Avoiding trouble

The next step is designing to avoid resonances.

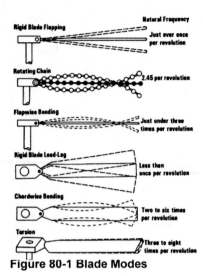

Figure 80-1 Blade Modes

This applies to both the blades and airframe components—and is easier said than done. Each part of the helicopter has a certain unique natural frequency just as each string of a piano has its own natural frequency that determines its pitch. If any component (blade, fuselage, tail boom, empennage surface, seat, instrument panel, window, etc.) is continuously shaken at or near its natural frequency, it will respond, rattle, or bounce at high amplitude. (It only takes a few pounds of force to push a child high in a swing when the force is applied at the swing's natural frequency.)

A blade with a flapping hinge is in. or near, resonance with the aerodynamic forces that occur once per revolution. This type of resonance is acceptable, since it is self-curing by a process in which any big flapping motions reduce the aerodynamic imbalances that caused them in the first place. The same thing cannot be said about other potential resonance conditions that a blade might encounter.

If you hit a blade with a hammer (soft, of course), you can make it "ring" at its various natural frequencies—depending upon whether your blow excites flapwise bending, chordwise bending, or torsion. Figure 80-1 shows possible mode shapes for these various responses.

No matter how much flapwise stiffness the blade has when it is standing still, it acts much like a chain when it is up to speed. If you whirl a chain around your head and someone raps it with a stick, the chain will oscillate at its centrifugal-force-governed natural frequency which is just under 2½ times per revolution with the mode shape shown in Figure 80-1. The corresponding flapwise bending mode of a rotating blade is nearer three per rev, due to its structural stiffness. Since there are some aerodynamic excitations that peak three times per revolution in forward flight, most rotor blades are close to being in flapwise resonance at "3P" and therefore respond at fairly high amplitudes.

Figure 80-2 is a plot of the most important natural frequencies of a typical blade as affected by rotor speed. Whenever a natural frequency crosses one of the lines representing a rotor-speed ratio, there is a possibility of a resonant condition provided that there are sufficient aerodynamic forces at that frequency to get it going. In forward flight, the aerodynamics repeat themselves every revolution but contain peaks and valleys that correspond not only to 1P but also to multiples of rotor speed as high as you can imagine (although it is the lower ones that contain the most energy).

The rotor in Figure 80-2 is in fairly good shape at 100% rpm but could get rough at 79, 89, 96, 110, and 119%. This is similar to a reciprocating engine that usually has one or more rpms to avoid because it runs rough there.

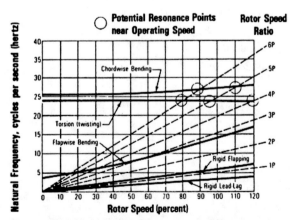

Figure 80-2 Main Rotor Blade Natural Frequencies for Typical Articulated Rotor

Blade resonance not only leads to high vibrations in the airframe but also to high blade stresses. For this reason, as much care must be taken in designing a tail-rotor blade as a main-rotor blade. The designer does have some control over natural frequencies by judicious selection of local weight and stiffness modifications.

Fuselage response

Whether in resonance or not, the blades will transmit some oscillatory loads to the fuselage.

One of the most common is at 1P and is caused by a rotor that is out of balance or out of track. Another oscillatory load comes down the shaft at a frequency corresponding to the number of blades per revolution. Helicopters with three-bladed rotors are especially sensitive to this since the blades are near resonance at 3P and thus go up and down in unison to put a plunging force into the rotor shaft.

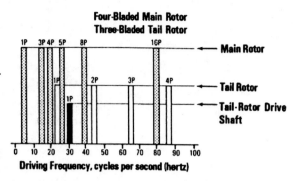

Figure 80-3 Driving Frequencies for Typical Helicopter

Other oscillatory loads associated with blade flapping and lead-lag motion are sensed at the fuselage at frequencies corresponding to the number of blades per revolution. The main rotor is not the only possible source of vibration since the tail rotor, unbalanced cooling fans, and out-of-balance drive shafts can also be source of trouble.

Resonances in the airframe components at the various excitation frequencies are fairly common when a helicopter first flies. It is not yet possible for the dynamicist to successfully guide the designer in his placement of stiffness and weight elements to obtain an absence of the coincidence of structural natural frequencies with frequencies of possible exciting forces. The late Bob Wagner used to give guidance to the designers by telling them to design everything *in* resonance as a way of ensuring that everything would be *out* of resonance when it was built. If this design philosophy doesn't work, local stiffening (or softening) or redistribution of fixed weights might have to be used.

Avoiding all of the troublesome frequencies is like trying to throw rocks through the gaps in a picket fence. Figure 80-3 shows a typical batch of frequencies that could produce high vibration.

In some cases, a resonance might exist but not be much of a problem. For example, a fuselage may be primarily excited by a rotor to bend vertically in a hump-backed mode as shown in Figure 80-4. Two points, known as "nodes," do not move. If the only seats are on or close to anode, then the crew or passengers will experience a smooth flight — even though parts of the fuselage behind and ahead of them may be getting a rougher ride.

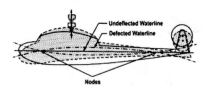

Figure 80-4 Flexible Fuselage Subjected to Oscillating Plunge Forces from Rotor

Trying to tame the rotor

In some cases it is possible to stop—or at least reduce—the oscillatory rotor loads in place. One approach is to use a vibration absorber mounted on the rotor head. One of the most familiar is the "bifilar" absorbers used on some Sikorsky helicopters. These consist of hinged weights designed to swing on their pivots in the right way to eliminate oscillating inputs. Something similar is used on automatic washing machines to balance the basket during the high-speed spin cycle.

Some designers, with stars in their eyes, are now working on systems to wobble the swashplate in such a manner as to smooth out the unsteady aerodynamics at the blade. These systems, which are generically called "higher harmonic control systems," have shown some promising trends in wind-tunnel tests. Yet another way is to install the rotor and its support system on soft mounts that pass steady loads but inhibit vibrating loads. Such systems have to be tailored to the troubling frequencies and, since there may be more than one, the design is usually a compromise.

Passive vibration absorbers

In some helicopters, resonance is used to solve a vibration problem. This is done by installing in the fuselage a mechanism in which a spring-mounted weight is deliberately tuned to be in resonance with the troublesome rotor frequency. If the design is right, the weight, as it shakes up and down, will put back into its support structure an oscillating force that is equal and opposite to whatever is causing the shake. This is an old technique first developed to minimize the vibration of high-speed steam turbines as they became unbalanced in service.

A vibration absorber is like the portrait of Dorian Gray. Out of sight in a closed box, it absorbs all the bad stuff while the rest of the helicopter flies calmly along.

If the designer is clever, he may not have to use extra weights for his vibration absorbers. Sikorsky has used batteries and Bell has developed the Noda-Matic system that allows some models to use the transmission as the moving weight.

Roughness in the landing flare

A takeoff is usually smooth but a landing through the same speed regime is almost always rough. The reason for this difference is that, in a typical landing approach, the blade-tip vortices will initially be going up from the rotor due to the rate of descent —but when the helicopter comes to a hover, the vortices must be going down. Thus, at some point during the landing, the tip vortices will be in the plane of the rotor where they will be struck by each blade in turn. Each vortex acts as a small but powerful whirlwind and causes abrupt changes in the local angle of attack as the blades pass over, under, and through them. It is no wonder then that this "rocky road" makes the rotor impart high oscillatory loads down the shaft, until the helicopter slows to a condition where the tip vortices are blown down free of the rotor.

There is a landing technique that the pilot can use to minimize the shakes. It is primarily aimed at getting the vortices to pass through the rotor quickly at high speed—since there they are spread out more than they will be later. The technique consists of doing a moderate flare at about 50 knots and continuing to a hover with a gentle flat deceleration using collective to hold altitude or if possible to make a slight climb. And, of course, a landing into the wind will produce less shaking than a downwind landing.

After all this discussion, it should come as no surprise to learn that more than half of the problem-solving types in a helicopter engineering organization are employed in trying to give you a smoother ride.

81 Vibration Sources

Yes, helicopters do vibrate, some with more gusto than others. An aerodynamic sleuth looking for the source of most vibration during forward flight would locate it at the main rotor. Looking further, he would trace the vibration to the uneven aerodynamics on each blade as it goes around.

This occurrence of uneven aerodynamics causes the blade to exert a force on the hub that has both steady and oscillating components. The way the components from each blade combine to produce a response in the fuselage depends upon three factors:

• The nature of the force—whether it acts vertically, which would make the helicopter plunge up and down, or acts in a way that would try to rock the aircraft;

• The frequency of the oscillating components; and

• The number of blades in the rotor.

What vertical forces can do

Figure 81-1 shows a calculated time history for two revolutions of a single blade's lift on a typical helicopter in steady forward flight. For this example, the average lift per blade is assumed to be 1,000 pounds (454 kg). In a flight-test program, a similar trace could be obtained by installing strain gauges that measure the bending moment on one arm of the hub inboard of the flapping hinge (Figure 81-2). This bending moment can be "calibrated" to represent blade lift.

Although the time history of Figure 81-1 looks somewhat random, it is actually composed of several distinct components as shown in the lower part of the figure. Superimposed on the steady value are "harmonics." In steady, forward flight, the aerodynamic and dynamic loads on each blade are the same as in the previous revolution. Therefore, the oscillating parts must have frequencies equal to the rotational frequency of the rotor or of some multiple of the rotational frequency.

In this simplified case, the frequencies consist of one at once per revolution—which is usually referred to as IP—and others at 2P, 3P, 4P, etc. Each harmonic has its own amplitude and phase relationship. In an

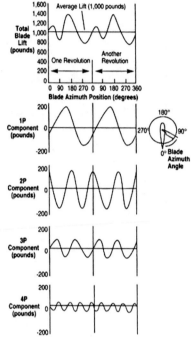

Figure 81-1 Time History Of Lift Of Single Blade

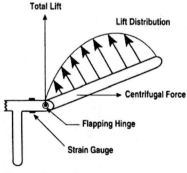

Figure 81-2 Strain Gauge Locations For Measuring Single Blade's Total Lift

443

actual strain gauge output, as recorded by an oscillograph or by more modern data-acquiring methods, components as high as 10P or 12P could be identified because the unevenness of the air load theoretically contains components as high as you want to count. The method an engineer would use to find these higher harmonic's amplitudes and phase relationships is called "Fourier Analysis."

By the way, Figure 81-1 shows an interesting effect that is true for all rotors in forward flight:

The blade lifts the most when it is passing over the nose and least when it is on the retreating side. While the lift varies around the azimuth, the center of lift on the blade changes in the opposite way so that the rotor is trimmed with no aerodynamic pitching or rolling moments.

From blade to fuselage

To determine how the lift comes down into the fuselage, we must total the contribution of each blade on the rotor. The sum of the steady parts represents the rotor thrust and naturally has nothing to do with vibration. Whether each of the other components produce vibration or not depends on the number of blades in the rotor.

For example, let's look at the IP oscillating lift force on each blade as it applies to a two-bladed rotor. In this case, whatever blade No. 1 does, blade No. 2 on the other side of the rotor will do the opposite and provide a canceling effect. Thus an IP vertical oscillating force on a two-bladed rotor does not produce any vibration. This argument can be easily extended to any rotor with an even number of blades, and with a little trigonometry, can apply to rotors with odd numbers of blades. Hence, we can see that any rotor on which vertical forces change once per revolution will not produce fuselage vibration.

Twice per revolution

A vertical 2P oscillating force (twice per revolution) on a two-bladed rotor draws a different conclusion. In this case, the two blades are doing the same thing at the same time and therefore their contributions reinforce each other. The fuselage will thus be subjected to a vibrating load with a frequency equal to twice the rotor speed. For instance, on the two-bladed Robinson R22, this oscillation is at about 18 Hertz (cycles per second).

Conversely, on a four-bladed rotor, loads at 2P are canceled; while one pair of blades is doing one thing, the other pair is doing the opposite. So no vibratory loads are sent down the shaft. This can also be shown for rotors with three or any other number of blades above two.

Regarding vertical 3P oscillating forces, only a three-blade rotor will generate a vibration; all other rotors will "filter out" these loads. Perhaps the general rule is evident now. Vertical oscillating forces at each blade can only produce vibration in the fuselage when the oscillation's frequency is equal to the number of blades.

The amplitude of the loading components with high frequencies is usually less than for those with low frequencies. Hence, a helicopter with a large number of blades will vibrate less than one with a small number. When, for example, the four-blade McDonnell Douglas Model 500C was changed to the five-blade D model, vibration was reduced substantially.

I should point out that not only will a 2P blade vertical oscillating force produce vibration on a two-bladed helicopter, but so will multiples of 2P such as 4P and 6P. By the same reasoning it can be shown that helicopters with three-bladed rotors will respond to 6P and 9P as well as to 3P, and four-bladed rotors to 8P and 12P. The results of the discussion above are summarized in Figure 81-3.

Rock and roll

The above discussion covered blade forces that create vertical vibration. The blade, however, can also transmit forces to the hub that try to rock the helicopter back and forth or from side to side. These produce fuselage vibrations differently than do vertical forces.

One possible source of this type of force is the lift acting through an offset flapping hinge (Figure 81-4). Also acting through the flapping hinge are inertial forces associated with blade flapping. Similarly, blade drag and the inertia force (due to in-plane motion) act through the lead-lag hinge.

Any of these forces from a single blade would produce a bending moment in the rotating drive shaft. Strain gauges placed as in Figure 24-4 could measure the bending moment from forces acting at the flapping hinge; gauges on the other axis would detect forces at the lead-lag hinge.

Figure 81-5 shows a time history of this bending moment for two revolutions of a single-bladed rotor. The large IP component might be associated with noseup flapping; other effects cause the higher harmonics. A positive value represents a moment that is trying to bend the shaft toward the single blade. Just as for the vertical forces discussed above, this bending moment has both steady and oscillating components.

The steady doesn't count

First, let's dispense with the steady component. For a single-bladed rotor, the steady component would produce a whirling moment in the fuselage with a frequency of once per revolution—or IP. With two or more identical blades, however, symmetry eliminates this moment; thus it can be ignored for helicopters as we know them. (This may be an issue, however, if the blades are not identical, just as an unbalanced tire produces vibration in a car.)

Harmonic Of Single Blade Vertical Force	Number Of Blades						
	2	3	4	5	6	7	8
1P	—	—	—	—	—	—	—
2P	2P	—	—	—	—	—	—
3P	—	3P	—	—	—	—	—
4P	4P	—	4P	—	—	—	—
5P	—	—	—	5P	—	—	—
6P	6P	6P	—	—	6P	—	—
7P	—	—	—	—	—	7P	—
8P	8P	—	8P	—	—	—	8P

Figure 81-3 Frequency Of Fuselage Response To Vertical Forces

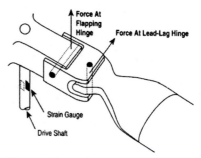

Figure 81-4 Blade Forces That Produce Shaft Bending

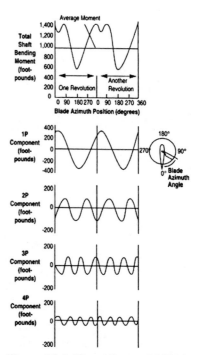

Figure 81-5 Time History Of Shaft Bending Moment Due To Single Blade

The oscillating components

How do the oscillating components of the shaft-bending moment produce pitching and rolling moments in the fuselage? Let's take the IP component first, which we said might come from the rotor flapping noseup.

When the blade is over the tail, the positive value of shaft-bending moment means the blade is trying to pitch the helicopter noseup. And when the blade is over the nose, the negative value means that it is also trying to pitch the helicopter noseup. This comes about mathematically by multiplying the shaft-bending moment by the cosine of the azimuth angle. Thus, although the IP component always cancels itself out when vertical forces are concerned, it adds to itself when dealing with forces that try to bend the rotor shaft.

If the rotor had two blades, their combined IP components would produce a shaft-bending moment that has a noseup direction. But this moment would also vary at 2P, since it would simultaneously go to zero on both blades when blade No. 1 passed through about 120°. This is only true for a two-bladed rotor.

Rotors with three or more blades have "polar symmetry" and produce only the constant portion of the fuselage moment with no oscillating component. In the example illustrated by Figure 81-5, the rotor would be trying to pitch the helicopter up and roll it to the right.

This might be required to balance some external nosedown and left-roll moments. These moments could be caused by several factors:

• An offset center of gravity,

• Aerodynamic moments of the fuselage or anti-torque system, or

• The result of the pilot using the longitudinal and lateral cyclic pitch to maneuver.

The average value of the moment acting on the fuselage will be proportional to the number of blades in the rotor.

Now about 2P

The shaft-bending moment that is occurring at twice per revolution, or 2P, may or may not result in fuselage vibration. It all depends on the number of blades.

For example, with a two-bladed rotor, when blade No. 1 is over the tail, it would be bending the shaft away from it; this would result in a nosedown pitching moment. But blade No. 2, over the nose, would also be trying to bend the shaft away from it, thus canceling the effect of blade No. 1. For two blades, therefore, the shaft-bonding's 2P component will produce no fuselage vibration.

This conclusion also applies to four-bladed rotors, but not ones with three blades. In such a case, the blades will be out of phase and produce a 3P vibration response in the fuselage.

For any rotor with more than three blades, the 2P component is canceled out so that no fuselage vibration can be blamed on this factor.

Putting it all together

As we progressively think about more blades and higher harmonics, the situation becomes too complicated to be solved by intuition. But trigonometry can produce the results summarized in Figure 81-6. This shows that a two-bladed rotor can transmit many harmonics of shaft bending into the helicopter to make it shake at multiples of 2P. Therefore, if any of the equipment or structural elements respond easily at frequencies corresponding to 2P, 4P, 6P, 8P, etc. of the rotor's rotational frequency, we can expect that equipment or structural element to shake, rattle, and roll.

As we add blades to the rotor, more and more of the rotating harmonics are canceled out in the rotor itself and never get down into the fuselage. It is also evident that, as was true with vibration produced by oscillating vertical forces, the fuselage response will always be at a frequency corresponding to the number of blades or to a multiple of this number.

Harmonic Of Single Blade Rocking Force	Number Of Blades						
	2	3	4	5	6	7	8
1P	Steady,2P	Steady	Steady	Steady	Steady	Steady	Steady
2P	—	3P	—	—	—	—	—
3P	2P,4P	—	4P	—	—	—	—
4P	—	3P	—	5P	6P	—	—
5P	4P,6P	6P	4P	—	—	—	—
6P	—	—	—	5P	—	7P	—
7P	6P,8P	6P	8P	—	6P	—	8P
8P	—	9P	—	—	—	7P	—

Figure 81-6 Frequency Of Fuselage Response To Hub Rocking Forces

82 Vibration Criteria

Vibration is a natural consequence of flying a helicopter rotor edgewise through the air. High levels of vibration contribute to crew and passenger discomfort, equipment failures, and structural problems. So the rule makers have long attempted to write specifications on the amount of vibration that will be allowed. Although these specifications have not always been met, they remain as goals for the ultimate quest of the "jet-smooth ride."

Shaking the body

The human body is not sensitive to all frequencies in the same way. Very low frequencies, such as those of a ship in rough water, cause motion sickness. Increasing frequencies start getting into the range where body parts will shake at their natural frequency—or resonate—causing discomfort.

The lowest of these frequencies has been identified as that corresponding to the upper chest organs—the lungs and the heart—bouncing vertically on the diaphragm as a spring. The range of this frequency for most people is from 4 to 7 Hertz (cycles per second).

For the helicopters flying today, this just happens to be the range which corresponds to a once-per-revolution (IP) oscillating force coming down the shaft caused by an unbalanced rotor or by out-of-track blades. This is why maintaining good track and balance is such an important factor in helicopter operations.

Another possible critical vibration range for humans is at about 12 Hertz. It corresponds to the spine in compression using the pads between the vertebrae as springs. But this is usually attenuated by the characteristics of the seat cushion.

Tests on shake tables have indicated that humans are more sensitive to up-and-down vibration than to fore-and aft or side-to-side motions.

The literature on helicopter vibration that I've consulted also mentions that the hands and feet have their own critical frequencies for maximum discomfort, but no frequency ranges are mentioned.

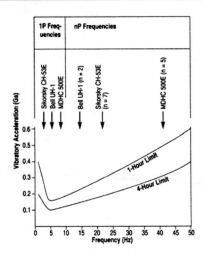

Figure 82-1 Human Body Tolerance To Vibration

The designer cannot do much about the IP vibration except to provide means for adjusting the balance and tracking in the field. The vibration frequencies that the designer can possibly minimize are those corresponding to "blade passage" and its multiples.

The discussions in the previous chapter show how only vibrations corresponding to these frequencies can get down into the fuselage. The designer tries to minimize these vibrations by avoiding structural natural frequencies corresponding to the oscillating forces generated by the rotor, and by using various methods of absorbing vibration or of isolating it.

The "nP" frequency

Blade passage frequency depends on the rpm and the number of blades. It is usually referred to as "n/rev" or as "nP." Since most helicopters have about the same tip speed, the rpm is low for large rotors and high for small ones.

Thus the lowest nP frequency would be for a large two-bladed rotor and the highest for a small multi-bladed rotor. This puts the Bell UH-1 at one end and the McDonnell Douglas MD 500 at the other.

Figure 82-1 shows the discomfort level of vibratory acceleration measured in Gs as a function of frequency. These results depict my interpretation of the somewhat confusing results published by a number of researchers. It is meant to represent the maximum vibration level at which the pilot could maintain proficiency. It is a higher level than what a passenger would like while trying to write or drink a cup of coffee.

Since the pilot can tolerate higher vibration for a short time than for a long time, both a one-hour and a four-hour limit are shown.

For frequencies above about 10 Hertz, the amount of vibration required to cause discomfort rises until, at some high buzzing frequency, you can take relatively high Gs. The report on one flight-test program involving the Bell UH-1H, stated that 0.3 Gs at 7.2 Hertz was "tolerable only for a short period of time," but that the same 0.3 Gs at 32 Hertz was "hardly noticeable." (The first point occurred at low rpm on the ground at the 2P blade-passage frequency and the higher one in flight at 6P.) Also shown on Figure 82-1 are the IP and the nP blade-passage frequencies that define the ranges for several modem helicopters.

Requirements and goals

The original specifications for both the UTTAS and AAH programs—which subsequently yielded the Sikorsky Black Hawk and the McDonnell Douglas Apache—called for the maximum allowable vibration to be less than 0.05 Gs at frequencies at blade passage and below. Above this range, the vibration limit was raised as shown in Figure 82-2 (between the one- and four-hour limits of Figure 82-1).

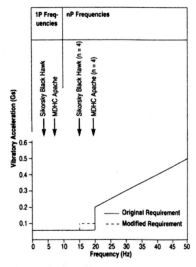

Figure 82-2 Vibration Criteria For Black Hawk And Apache

None of the four competitors in the two flyoff programs could meet the stringent 0.05 Gs at blade passage, so for the production Black Hawk and Apache, the limit was raised to 0.10 Gs at blade passage, but kept at 0.05 below this frequency. Thus the designer was relieved of his problem, but the maintenance officer in charge of track and balance was not.

Just because we humans can take high vibration at high frequencies does not mean that equipment and structural components are happy under those conditions.

To be really good, the ultimate goal as stated by some dreamers is to get the maximum vibration level down to less than 0.03 Gs for all frequencies. That would truly be a "jet-smooth ride."

83 Higher Harmonic Control

Most helicopters shake. It is just a fact of life that when a rotor is flying through the air edgewise, it is subjected to air loads that change many times a second as the blades go around the azimuth. Each blade responds by producing unsteady loads at the hub. These loads are then transmitted down into the rest of the helicopter. There have been many schemes for minimizing the resulting vibration where people or sensitive equipment are located. These include:

•Using a large number of blades,

• Isolating the fuselage from the rotor using devices made of rubber, hydraulic dampers, or even more exotic mechanisms, or

• Using special "vibration absorbers," either at the rotor hub or in the fuselage.

Each of these methods can be seen on helicopters flying today, but none of them are entirely satisfactory.

Searching for a solution

Helicopter engineers have long recognized that to minimize the blades's unsteady content, it should be possible to modify the characteristics of the air loads on them. The hope for doing this lies in the field of higher harmonic control (HHC).

A conventional helicopter uses a swashplate to introduce cyclic pitch into the rotor hub. Because the swashplate is rigid, each blade goes through one cycle of pitch change each revolution. The change can be represented by a smooth sine wave, or a "first harmonic." Even though the pitch change is smooth, the variation of local velocity and angle of attack, caused by effects other than cyclic pitch, make each blade's airloads anything but smooth. This lack of smoothness eventually results in vibration.

What, the dynamicist asks, would happen if, instead of the cyclic pitch being a smooth sine wave, one could modify it to compensate for all those other effects?

That question leads to the concept of higher harmonic control. The simplest method involves wobbling the swashplate each time a blade

453

passes over a certain point. This action introduces a variation on top of the normal once-per-revolution motion. That means that in terms of harmonics, the frequency is three times per revolution for a three-bladed rotor or four times for four blades, etc. The wobbling can be in the collective system or in either the longitudinal or lateral cyclic system, whichever does the job best.

In the HHCs being proposed, the amplitude and phase of this additional pitch change is to be controlled by a computer; It receives signals from strategically located accelerometers, and tries to do whatever is required to make them stand still. With this system, the mechanisms for moving the swashplate are in the nonrotating control system. There it is relatively easy to get power to the actuators that are doing the work.

Countering this advantage is the limitation that the blades are forced to move in some sort of a regular sinusoidal way. It may be shown that if they could move in a more arbitrary Way, the effectiveness of the system would be improved. This might be done by putting the necessary actuators at the root of each blade in the rotor hub, providing individual pitch control in the rotating system. With this scheme, the blade pitch-motion can be optimized, but the designer has the nagging problem of getting power to the actuators.

Testing the concept

Figure 83-1 Hughes Four-Bladed OH-6

Over the past decade, both systems have been tested in wind tunnels and briefly evaluated in flight tests of specially equipped helicopters. One of the first of the flight-test programs was done on the four-bladed OH-6 (Figure 83-1) by Hughes Helicopters (now McDonnell Douglas Helicopter Co.).

This helicopter was equipped with a hydraulic control system (not normally in the OH-6) and a set of high-speed actuators to apply a four-per-rev pitch variation on top of the normal one-per-rev cyclic pitch. Flight testing involved changing the amplitude and the phasing of this additional control input, and measuring the vibration level in the cockpit.

By using the lateral actuator to make the pitch dip by only a one-third of a degree just before it reached a position over the tail boom (330°), vertical and lateral vibration levels could be reduced (Figure 83-2). Those levels are less than half of their values with the system turned off. It may also be seen that with the wrong phasing of the HHC, the vibration was increased rather than decreased.

A mystery

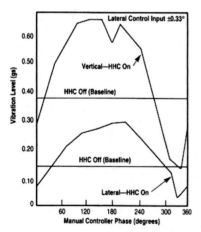

Figure 83-2 Effect Of HHC On Vibration

After the Hughes dynamicists looked at the vibration data, someone also noticed that when the system was turned on, the engine power required to fly both in hover and in forward flight seemed to be slightly less than when it was turned off. This was completely unexpected.

The perceived benefit was not on really firm ground though, because the flight-test conditions were not as strictly governed as they would have been if the prime objective was measuring performance. A second flight-test program was planned, but unfortunately due to factors having nothing to do with the HHC system, these tests were never performed. As of right now, there has been no definite verification of the power effect.

Motivation

Engineers and customers look very carefully before they add a complicated and expensive HHC system to an already complicated and expensive aircraft. The Hughes experience, again, provides a good example. The four-bladed main rotor of the OH-6 and its derivative, the Model 500C, needs some help from blade-mounted "pendulum vibration absorbers" to keep the passenger cabin quiet. (You can also see these on the Eurocopter BO-105). But when the five-bladed Model 500D was flown, these vibration absorbers were not needed. Thus there is little incentive to equip the 500D (or E or F) with any higher harmonic control system.

When the four-bladed AH-64 Apache was designed, vibration problems like on the OH-6 were expected. So the prototype Apache was equipped with similar blade-mounted pendulum absorbers. During flight test, however, it was found that these were not required, so the Apache flies today without any special vibration-reducing devices. And there is little motivation for equipping this helicopter with a HHC system.

This is in contrast to the Sikorsky UH-60 Black Hawk, with a four-bladed rotor that is quite similar to Apache's. The UH-60 needs several hundred pounds of special vibration absorbers both at the rotor head and in the fuselage. It might be a logical candidate for the installation of a lighter HHC system.

84 Spiral Dives And Dutch Rolls

Because a flying aircraft can move in six degrees of freedom—linearly in three directions and rotation-ally in three—it has the opportunity to do some fancy maneuvering. This can be done intentionally as directed by the pilot or unintentionally as dictated by the laws of physics.

Two of the unintentional maneuvers which have sometimes been problems for both airplanes and helicopters go by the names of "spiral dive" and "Dutch roll."

Spiral dive

A spiral dive is one of the possible unstable motions that an aircraft might tend to do by itself if the pilot were to lock the controls. The motion is illustrated very well by the term, spiral dive, in that after being disturbed, the aircraft starts a turn which gradually becomes steeper and steeper with a faster and faster dive speed.

In the jargon of the flying-qualities analyst, this is a "non-oscillatory divergence." It can be traced to a mismatch of the characteristics which contribute to the rolling and yawing moments. Specifically, the flying-qualities engineer will attribute it to too little dihedral effect and/or too much directional stability.

Dihedral

To explain this, we should understand what dihedral effect is. If an aircraft flying straight and level runs into a gust that rolls it over slightly, the force of gravity will make it slide down toward the low side, resulting in a sideslip.

Airplane designers take advantage of this situation by using dihedral—slanting the wings up. The result is that the wing facing the oncoming air is at a higher angle of attack than the other wing. This generates a rolling moment proportional to the sideslip angle, which then restores the airplane to a "wings level" attitude. This is why free-flight model airplanes can fly without any pilot to keep them upright.

While most helicopters do not have wings, the rotor happens to be an effective source of dihedral effect. But despite the fact that rotor coning appears to look like wing dihedral, coning does not generate a rolling

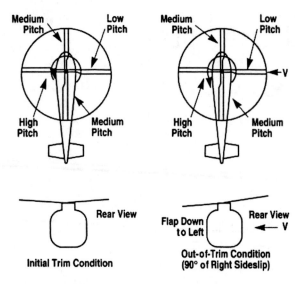

Figure 84-1 Dihedral Effect From The Rotor

moment. Any moment from this source would be the result of flapping a quarter of a revolution late, i.e. a pitch instead of a roll.

A dihedral "effect," however, can be traced to another consequence of blade flapping. Imagine that a helicopter is in forward flight with no sideslip and with the rotor trimmed perpendicular to the shaft with cyclic pitch (Figure 84-1).

If the flight direction were suddenly changed so that the helicopter was flying to the right without changing the fuselage heading or control settings, the blade over the tail would become the advancing blade and the one over the nose the retreating blade. Since the cyclic pitch no longer corresponds to trim conditions, the rotor would flap down on the left side because of the asymmetrical velocity distribution—thus producing a rolling moment to the left.

In practice, sideslip angles are less than the 90° used for this illustration, but the trend is the same—the helicopter tends to roll away from the approaching wind, giving evidence of a positive dihedral effect. During flight test, the magnitude of the dihedral effect is judged by how much lateral stick displacement is required to maintain roll equilibrium during deliberate sideslips.

Directional stability

Besides dihedral effect, the other consideration in the study of spiral dives is the directional stability produced by the weather-vane effect of the tail rotor and vertical stabilizer in trying to keep the fuselage pointed into the oncoming wind, i.e. suppressing sideslip. If the aircraft possesses too much directional stability, its nose will always be forced into the oncoming airflow and little sideslip will develop. With little sideslip, the dihedral effect is ineffective and after a disturbance, the aircraft will simply keep rolling into a turn, which will then develop into a spiral dive.

This type of instability is often evident on the first flight of a free-flight model airplane and is cured by reducing the area of the vertical stabilizer or by increasing the dihedral of the wing.

Both benign and dangerous

Most full-scale airplanes are characterized by a slightly unstable spiral dive. If the pilot has a good view of the ground and the horizon, this is no problem because he instinctively does the right thing to keep the aircraft heading in the right direction and the wings level.

It might, however, be a problem when flying in poor visibility. The motion develops so gradually that the pilot is often unaware that his airplane is deviating from straight flight. In the air if the pilot is without good visual cues or training in instrument flight, it is difficult to know whether the flight path is straight or is a circle of large radius. Even the increase in the centrifugal force might be too small to warn the pilot.

A number of airplane accidents have been attributed to inexperienced pilots getting into a spiral dive in a cloud and inadvertently attaining such a high speed that when they realized what was happening and pulled up to stop the dive, they pulled the wings off. I know of no such accidents with helicopters.

Figure 84-2 Bell 212 With Vertical Destabilizer

The U.S. military allows the airplanes it purchases to have slightly unstable spiral-stability characteristics. The military is satisfied if a fighter does not double its bank angle in more than 12 seconds or a transport in more than 20 seconds.

The FAA requires helicopters that are certificated for instrument flight rules (IFR) to not be subject to spiral dives. You can see the result of this policy on the Bell 212 (Figure 84-2). Before it could be certificated for instrument flight, it had to be modified to decrease its directional stability by the addition of a vertical "destabilizer" ahead of the rotor.

Dutch roll

The other side of the lateral-directional coin is the oscillation called "Dutch roll." If an unstable spiral dive can be caused by too little dihedral effect and/or too much directional stability, an unstable Dutch roll can be caused by the opposite combination.

Dutch roll is an oscillation involving mostly roll and sideslip. It got its name years ago by its resemblance to the sight of a Dutch couple skating arm-in-arm down a frozen canal.

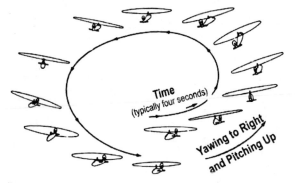

Figure 84-3 Dutch Roll Action (Slightly Unstable)

The Dutch roll can be prompted by flying through a gust or by a twitch of a rudder pedal. Following the input, the oscillation will have a period of two to four seconds no matter how large or small the aircraft.

It may be well-damped, in which case it will soon disappear. Or the oscillation may be unstable, in which case it will build up to higher and higher amplitudes until the pilot or the autopilot takes action to suppress it. Figure 84-3 shows a helicopter going through one cycle of a mildly unstable Dutch roll.

You can see the evidence of Dutch roll when flying in a jet transport. Watch a speck on the window against the horizon and you will see the speck "move" up and down every two to four seconds.

If you sit behind the wing, you can also see the inboard ailerons moving to suppress this motion. The autopilot makes them go up and down every two to four seconds in response to the detection of the change in bank angle.

From the cockpit, you would also be able to see an accompanying left-to-right motion. For fighter aircraft with fixed guns, this type of movement makes accurate shooting difficult.

Helicopters are different

With airplanes, Dutch roll involves roll and sideslip but not forward speed nor angle of attack. Thus the airplane analyst can work with only the three equations of motion commonly known as the "lateral-directional subset." This consists of only the equations for rolling moment, yawing moment, and sideforce. He can ignore the "longitudinal subset" consisting of the equations pertaining to lift, drag, and pitching moment because in the symmetric airplane it is not "coupled" with the lateral-directional subset.

The helicopter analyst is not so lucky. The two subsets are coupled by the fact that a change in rotor angle of attack will produce a change in the rotor torque and thus in the yawing moment. The helicopter analyst is advised to use all six equations of motion for his studies.

At low speeds, the subset coupling will be stabilizing; it will tend to damp out the oscillating motion as an increase in angle of attack puts the rotor closer to autorotation and reduces the torque. At high speeds, however, the effect is destabilizing; with high collective pitch required to maintain trim, an increase in rotor angle of attack will increase the torque. At high speed, the Dutch roll oscillations might build up to higher and higher amplitudes until the pilot intervenes.

And pilots instinctively do intervene in their quest to remain "wings level." I know of two helicopter designs that had quite unstable Dutch roll oscillations at high speeds if flown with the controls locked and the stabilization augmentation system (SAS) turned off. Experienced test pilots flew for many hours, never noticing the instability until they were asked to turn off the SAS, place a small disturbance into the control system and then freeze the controls to see what the helicopter would do. They were surprised to discover unstable Dutch roll characteristics.

Dutch roll criteria

Because of the pilot's wings-level instinct, moderately unstable Dutch roll characteristics are not considered objectionable—providing the horizon is visible. In poor visibility, however, such a condition might lead to an inexperienced pilot becoming disoriented. Thus both military and civil authorities require stable Dutch roll characteristics for aircraft that are to fly through the clouds.

Dutch roll can be easily stabilized with a simple gyro-driven black box in the control system providing a small amount of artificial damping in either roll or yaw. The McDonnell Douglas MD 520N with the NOTAR system uses such a device to move one of its rudder surfaces to provide yaw damping.

Something that decreases the stability of the Dutch roll mode is too much dihedral effect. If the aircraft gets into a sideslip condition, dihedral effect causes the aircraft to roll away from the approaching wind. With too much dihedral, the aircraft will overshoot the "wings level" attitude, sideslip the other way, and then return with ever-increasing oscillating amplitude.

Dihedral that is in addition to the positive dihedral produced by the rotor comes from any vertical surface located above the aircraft's roll axis. When the Sikorsky S-76 prototype showed evidences of a bothersome unstable Dutch roll, the designers reduced the dihedral effect by cutting 15 inches (38 cm) from the top of the vertical stabilizer.

In a similar situation, Bell's 222B engineers decreased dihedral by increasing the vertical surface area below the roll axis; they installed fences under the landing-gear sponsons.

Other effects

Engineers have difficulty predicting analytically whether the Dutch roll on a new design will be stable or unstable. They are frustrated because they don't really understand the exact flow conditions at the back end of the helicopter. Here the aerodynamic environment at the tail rotor and empennage are influenced by the disturbances produced by the main rotor and fuselage.

Evidence of how relatively small configuration changes can change the Dutch roll stability was found during the flight test of the Hughes (now McDonnell Douglas Helicopter) YAH-64 in its original configuration with the "T-tail." Figure 84-4 shows that with the helicopter's SAS off, Dutch roll was unstable without endplates on the horizontal stabilizer but stable when small canted endplates were installed. The dramatic change in stability was much more than could be predicted by any known analytical method and must be attributed to some peculiar flow conditions in the main-rotor wake.

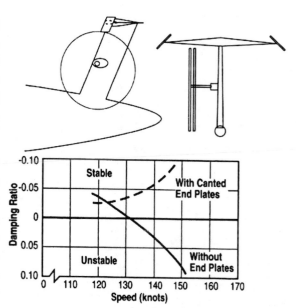

Figure 84-4 Dutch Roll Stability Of The Original AH-64 (With And Without End Plates)

85 Crashworthiness And Escape

Most fast, man-carrying vehicles are high-energy devices. The helicopter fits this description better than most. When flying, it has potential energy associated with its height above the ground. It also has kinetic energy—that of forward speed and that stored as rotational energy in its rotor.

Almost always, the pilot has good control of these various energy types, but on those rare occasions when he loses control, the result may well be a crash.

Even though a crash is a rare occurrence, the designer—being a realist—must take it into consideration and try to make certain that its detrimental effects are as minimal as possible. That is, he must make an effort to make his helicopter "crashworthy," while at the same time being careful to do it within a reasonable budget of weight and cost.

The use of "crashworthy" is perhaps an unfortunate choice of words. It seems to promise more than it can deliver. A recent attempt to change the semantics has been prompted by the legal departments of aircraft manufacturers who suggest replacing "crashworthy" with "crash resistant."

Design conditions

There are, of course, many possible impact conditions for a crashing helicopter. One of the most stringent, used as a recent design requirement by the U.S. military, is an injury-free crash with a vertical touchdown at 42 feet per second (fps) (12.8-mps)—the equivalent of a free fall from 28 feet (9 m). This is much more severe than most civil requirements of only 10 fps (3 mps).

The design problem is to somehow absorb the crash energy before it is applied to the crew and passengers, while at the same time making sure that the structure around them does not collapse and that they are protected from flying objects or from striking anything that might cause injury.

Apache solutions

On the McDonnell Douglas Apache (Figure 85-1), the energy absorption is first done as the "trailing arm" landing gear is forced up.

Figure 85-1 McDonnell Douglas AH-64 Apache

463

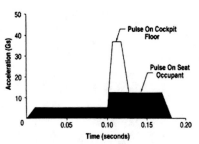

Figure 85-2 AH-64 Apache's Acceleration During Vertical Crash At 42 FPS

Special diaphragms in the oleo shock strut are punctured and fluid is squirted through the resulting orifices to provide a damping action. If this is not enough, the fuselage's bottom collapses, absorbing more energy. Finally, the crew seats "stroke" as the occupants are lowered to their final position.

Figure 85-2 shows the chain of crash-energy attenuation provided by the landing gear, the fuselage crushing, and the seat stroking during a crash with the specified 42-fps vertical touchdown velocity. The landing gear and fuselage crushing result in a 37-G acceleration at the cockpit floor and the crew seats reduce this to a livable 13 Gs for the occupants.

The Apache's forward fuselage is built with two keel-like structural members serving as skids in case of a crash with forward speed. This prevents the nose from "plowing in" and also provides space for the turreted gun to be forced up into the lower fuselage without entering either cockpit.

For crashes in which the Apache might roll over, the designers have made use of the sturdy transparent blast shield between the two cockpits as a "roll bar" and a stationary rotor pylon securely fastened to basic structure.

As part of his concern about crashworthiness, the designer must guard against the possibility of the crew or passengers being trapped by doors or canopies that cannot be opened after being deformed. The usual solution is to provide explosive devices that can blow a door off or create a new exit where none existed before.

Ditching

Not all crash landings are on land. Helicopters intended for operation at sea must also be capable of being safely ditched. This means that not only must the structure be strong enough to withstand the impact loads on contact with the water, but the helicopter must float upright and remain watertight in specified sea states long enough to ensure rescue.

For the unfortunate cases where the helicopter sinks, provisions must be made for quick emergency egress and for taking along all the equipment that is required for survival at sea.

Emergency exits should be clearly marked with lights and be big enough that they can be used by people wearing immersion suits and life preservers. One set of tests resulted in the interesting observation that if the exits appear too large, two people would try to go through at the same time with the result that both would become trapped.

Jump!

There may be situations in which the crewmembers wish that they did not have to depend on crashworthiness but could get out before impact. Since World War I, fliers have had the option of wearing parachutes to give them a chance of surviving if something goes wrong in the air.

Most helicopter pilots do not take advantage of that option. There are three reasons for this decision. The first is that the rotor's proximity makes it very difficult to find a safe escape route. The second is that the helicopter is often flying too low to give a parachute time to open, and the third reason is that the helicopter carries its own "parachute" in the form of its rotor, which in most cases can provide for a safe landing through autorotation.

Despite these reasons, helicopter test pilots that I have observed will usually take a chute along if the test plan calls for flying at altitudes of more than a couple of thousand feet— and several have actually been glad they did. John Wheatley, who was at NACA during the 1930s when it was evaluating the Pitcairn autogyro, says that he was the second person to ever bail out of a rotary-wing aircraft. He would have been the first, but the pilot beat him to it!

For many modern test programs, more exotic means than just jumping overboard are provided. NASA's Rotor System Research Aircraft (RSRA) was designed with upward ejection seats that would be used after the rotor blades were jettisoned by explosive charges cutting through each blade root. The Lockheed Cheyenne prototype was equipped with a downward ejection seat for flight-test conditions deemed to have an element of danger.

Upward ejection for the crew is a flight-test feature of the Bell Boeing V-22 Osprey—a relatively easy choice since the rotors are never above the cockpit. Of course, when this aircraft is carrying passengers, it will have to abide by the rule that has always applied: "Either everybody has a parachute or nobody does."

86 Tip-Driven Rotors

Two of the most troublesome components in most helicopters are the transmission and the antitorque system. Getting rid of either or both to save weight and development headaches has long challenged helicopter designers.

One of the most obvious answers is the tip-driven rotor. This has been tried a number of times, so far without much lasting success. There are those who think it should be reconsidered.

We can trace the principle back 2,000 years to Heron of Alexandria, who used it to make a steam-powered whirligig. By shooting gases out an aft-facing nozzle at the blade tip, a rotor can be made to spin like a rotary lawn sprinkler.

A variation of the scheme was first applied to helicopter designs in the 1930s when blade-mounted propellers were used to pull the rotor around. This configuration was also used in the da Vinci, a man-powered helicopter developed by the students at the California Polytechnic University at San Luis Obispo (Figure 86-1).

It was not until after World War II, however, that the more direct approach of using jet propulsion in one form or another was developed to an almost successful conclusion.

Jets from Germany

The development of the pulsejet and the ramjet for use on German fighters and "buzz-bombs" paved the way for their use on rotor-blade tips. Both of these simple propulsion systems work best at high subsonic Mach numbers, and since designers also choose high subsonic Mach numbers for rotor-tip speeds, the marriage was obvious.

It was not long after World War II ended that a number of small experimental helicopters with pulsejets or ramjets were flying in Europe and in America.

The first was McDonnell's Little Henry (Figure 3-2). It had two ramjets of 10-pound thrust rating (about 13 hp each at

Figure 86-1 Blade-Tip Propellers on the Da Vinci

Figure 86-2 Ramjet-Powered McDonnell Little Henry

full tip speed) and an empty weight of only 285 pounds (130 kg).

It was built under an Air Force contract and designated the XH-20. The project began in 1946 and continued for about five years, taking it through an extensive, but fruitless, flight-test program. Little Henry may now be seen hanging from the rafters in the Air Force Museum at Wright-Patterson AFB in Ohio.

Another ramjet-powered helicopter was the Hiller XHJ-1 Hornet, first flown in 1950. The two 40-pound thrust engines were similar to Little Henry's because they were designed by the same engineer. Each ramjet was fed by fuel lines through a rotating seal in the hub from a tank in the fuselage. A typical public relations shot of the time is Figure 86-3, showing the "commuter of the future" leaving for work in his ramjet-powered Hiller Hornet.

Challenges

As might be expected, the development of these aircraft involved some interesting engineering challenges. For example, the high centrifugal forces at the rotor tips caused the red-hot ramjets to deform from their original round cross-sections to egg-shaped, thus changing their aerodynamic characteristics.

Sometimes just getting the aircraft going was a problem. A ramjet has to be brought up to a fairly high speed before it can be started. On the Hornet, this could be done by hand swinging the rotor up to about 50 rpm or by using an auxiliary drive from a two-cycle gasoline-powered ground unit.

I've been told that sometimes the spark plugs on the Hornet prototype failed to ignite the fuel being pumped to the jets, so the test engineer would try to light them by throwing matches into the intakes as they whizzed by. If this didn't work right away, there was soon a path of raw fuel on the ground, which if ignited by an ill-tossed match, suddenly became a ring of fire from which the only escape was by helicopter!

Versions of the Hiller XHJ-1 were evaluated by the U.S. military. The H-32 variant was tested by the Air Force and Army, and the HOE-1, by the Navy. As a condition of the military contract, Hiller was to obtain FAA certification for both the ramjets and the aircraft.

The ramjet was certificated in 1954 after a 150-hour test. But the FAA objected to the Hornet's very high rate of power-off autorotative descent (due to the drag of the ramjets) and so refused to certificate it.

Figure 86-3 Ramjet-Powered Hiller Hornet

Despite this setback, about 15 aircraft were delivered to the Army, Air Force, and Navy. Operational tests showed that the ramjet's high fuel consumption severely limited the helicopter's usable range and endurance. Also, its hot-weather performance was only marginal at best. These basic problems spelled the end of the project.

Although the Hiller Hornet was never certificated, another ramjet-powered helicopter was. This was the Dutch Kolibri (Hummingbird) developed by a team headed by Jan Drees, who later came to America to work for Bell. About 25 of these helicopters were built and were used extensively in agricultural work.

Figure 86-4 Pulsejet-Powered Jet Jeep

Without a heavy transmission and an antitorque system, a helicopter such as the Kolibri can carry a very high payload in relation to its empty weight. It therefore is a very effective load carrier for operations where it can be frequently refueled.

The pulsejet

Helicopters with pulsejets were also developed. A ramjet is just a shaped "stovepipe" in which air is compressed by ram effect before fuel is introduced for burning. A pulsejet, on the other hand, has a set of tuned louvers in the intake, which open and close as the fuel is burned in cycles. This gives them a higher fuel efficiency and allows them to be started from rest with just a shot of compressed air.

Pulsejets were used on the Jet Jeep built in the early 1950s by the American Helicopter Co., of Manhattan Beach, Calif. (Figure 86-4). Their plant was about seven miles (11 km) from the Aircraft Division of Hughes Tool Co. where I was working at the time. Even inside the Hughes engineering building, we could hear American Helicopter testing their Jet Jeep. At that distance, it sounded like an angry bumblebee, and of course it sounded louder to its immediate neighbors.

Hydrogen peroxide rockets

A quieter system of the time took advantage of the fact that when a stream of 95% pure hydrogen peroxide is squirted onto a silver screen, it decomposes into high pressure steam and oxygen. The designers of torpedoes had been using this for many years.

When applied to helicopters, this propulsion scheme resulted in the rocket-powered Pin-Wheel, built by Rotor-Craft, also in Southern California (Figure 86-5).

This helicopter flew with a loud hissing sound, but not for long. Its fuel tanks could hold enough hydrogen peroxide for only a few minutes of flight—which perhaps was just as well since the fuel cost was about $10 a minute (in 1950 dollars).

Figure 86-5 Hydrogen Peroxide-Powered Pin-Wheel

A further disadvantage that prevented this type's development was that hydrogen peroxide of this purity is quite dangerous if spilled. It is extremely reactive to organic compounds such as skin and clothing.

469

Figure 86-6 Doblhoff WN342

Figure 86-7 Fairey Rotordyne

Figure 86-8 McDonnell XV-1 Convertiplane

At least one attempt was made to install turbo-jets on blade tips. On paper, this system could be shown to provide good fuel efficiency while being quieter than either ram or pulsejets.

Hiller made a ground test rig using a two-bladed rotor with two small turbojets. The project did not come to a logical conclusion apparently because of problems associated with the jet engines, which were not specifically designed for operation in high centrifugal force fields.

The pressure-jet

None of the foregoing tip-jet systems now seem to be candidates for helicopters of the future. There is another type, however, that periodically gets the attention of designers.

The pressure-jet rotor was first developed in Austria during World War II by a team headed by Friedrich Von Doblhoff. His WN 342 is shown in Figure 86-6.

The pressure-jet rotor is truly like a rotary lawn sprinkler. In the WN 342, an engine-driven air compressor, located in the fuselage, fed air through the hollow rotor blades and into aft-facing nozzles at the rotor tips.

The compressor, though, was not powerful enough to supply all of the air-power necessary to fly. So fuel was mixed with the air in a fuselage plenum chamber and then ignited at the tip nozzles. This method provided extra thrust by afterburning.

The tip-propulsion system was only supposed to be used for takeoffs and landings. Once in the air, the WN 342's engine power was to be disengaged from the compressor and routed to a propeller. This way the aircraft could be flown as an autogyro with no air or fuel going to the rotor.

As with all World War II helicopter projects, this one was too late to have any affect on the war. But afterward, members of the Doblhoff team scattered to England, France, and the United States, and each country soon launched ambitious pressure-jet helicopter projects.

In England, the primary result was the Fairey Rotordyne. This large, transport, compound helicopter (Figure 86-7), generated a lot of excitement as the much sought-after replacement for the DC-3. The Fairey company decided that 25 orders were needed to start production, but when only 20 could be obtained, the project was dropped.

Doblhoff, who came to the United States, was instrumental in the designing of the McDonnell XV-1 Convertiplane (Figure 86-8) for an Air Force competition. He also consulted in the design of the XH-17 Flying Crane (Figure 86-9) which was started at Kellett but sold to Hughes when half-finished. These two pressure-jet helicopters flew but never advanced beyond the prototype stage.

All of the helicopters described above used tip burning like the original Doblhoff WN-342 and were almost as noisy as those powered by pulse or ramjets. When the Rotordyne was demonstrated at airshows, its takeoffs were timed to coincide with the fly-bys of jet fighters so that its noise was masked. In Figure 86-10 measured sound levels for the XV-1 and the Rotordyne in tip-burning flight are compared to the much quieter turboshaft-powered helicopters.

One pressure-jet helicopter, however, used a compressor large enough to provide sufficient airflow to fly without tip burning and thus was relatively quiet. This was the French Sud Aviation Djinn (Genie) (Figure 3-11). The Djinn was so successful that it went into a production run of almost 200— mostly for the French army. Within the past few years, an American company, Voljet, has proposed to develop a similar helicopter.

Hot and warm

Hughes Helicopters used a variation of the pressure-jet for its XV-9 hot-cycle testbed in the 1960s (Figure 3-12) but instead of using an air compressor, Hughes simply sent the exhaust gasses from two jet engines out the rotor blades.

This is a simpler propulsion system than using an air compressor, but it did present the challenge of operating the rotor with gas temperatures of about 1,300°F (700°C) going through a rotating seal and out the blades. It is obvious why this was called a hot-cycle system! Noise measurements of the XV-9 showed it to be even quieter than comparable helicopters with turboshaft engines.

Even though they demonstrated the system's feasibility on the XV-9, Hughes engineers (now McDonnell Douglas Helicopter engineers) have been proposing that their next design—for a Heavy Lift Helicopter— would be a "warm-cycle."

This would use a cooler mixture of compressed air and exhaust (only SOOT [425°C]) from jet engines with about a 1.5 bypass ratio. This system can offer moderately good fuel efficiency; although because of some basic laws of physics, not quite as good as turboshaft-powered helicopters. A secondary advantage is continuous blade deicing.

However, what the pressure-jet lacks in fuel efficiency, it should be able to make up in its ability to operate without a heavy transmission. In very large shaft-driven helicopters, the ratio of transmission weight to gross weight grows faster than the rest of the structure. It thus becomes a prohibitive penalty for very large machines. The propulsion system on a pressure-jet helicopter, on the other hand, should follow the same trend as the rest of the structure.

It is this difference that encourages the pressure-jet enthusiasts to keep hoping that someday the need for a VERY LARGE helicopter will allow them to proceed with their dreams.

Figure 3-11 French Djinn

Figure 3-12 Hughes XV-9A

Figure 86-9 Hughes XH-17 Flying Crane

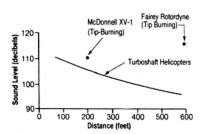

Figure 86-10 Noise Levels of Tip-Burning Pressure-Jet Helicopters

87 Which Do You Tilt: Wing Or Rotor?

Tiltrotor or tiltwing? It's a good question to ponder. Both represent a new type of aircraft. Each uses different, and innovative, engineering to achieve its vertical-to-horizontal-and-back flight.

Engineering innovation plays an important role in the development of any new class of vehicles. As an industry matures, however, the accumulated experiences of successes and failures tend to make innovation less and less evident. As proof of this, notice that today almost all automobiles and all jet transports look about the same.

Right now, the high-speed rotorcraft industry is still immature, and so designers have not yet achieved a consensus as to the best configuration. We are still proposing different ways of achieving the same goal, as is evident in the tiltrotor and tiltwing designs.

Requirements and challenges

The two basic requirements for any aircraft to safely takeoff and land vertically are:

• The vertical lifting force must be equal to the aircraft weight.

• The aircraft must be controllable in all flight conditions.

If the aircraft it is also required to have a high-speed capability, the designer must find some solution other than the conventional helicopter rotor, which runs into a speed barrier at about 200 knots. This challenge has inspired a number of inventors over the past 50 years.

Boeing engineer John Schneider, in a 1983 survey of vertical-takeoff aircraft with high-speed capabilities, identified a rather prodigious number of prototypes that had flown or at least reached the hardware stage. They included 21 with rotors, 12 with propellers, 11 with ducted fans, and 18 with jet engines.

A little history

The tiltrotor concept was the brainchild of Mario Guerierri who got together with Bob Lichten, then working at Kellett, to form Transcendental Aircraft in the early 1950s. They built and flew the Model

Figure 87-1 Hiller X-18

Figure 87-2 Canadair CL-84

Figure 87-3 Bell Aircraft X-22A

1-G, but after it crashed due to dynamic rotor/wing problems, Lichten went to Bell where he headed the XV-3 tiltrotor project.

Another Kellett designer, Bill Cobey, bought out Guerierri's interest, rebuilt the Model 1-G as the Transcendental Model 2 and flew it briefly in 1956.

At Bell, Lichten's XV-3 went through a long development phase which culminated in full conversions to the airplane mode and eventual flight testing by the U.S. Air Force. This proved that a piston-engine helicopter could indeed be converted into a moderately fast airplane but the price in extra weight and cost was high.

This did not completely discourage the enthusiasts at Bell. Seeing the benefit of the newly developed turbine engine for their purposes, they went on to develop the XV-15 and with it established the experience base necessary to go into the V-22 Osprey project.

Other companies in the exciting 1950s and 1960s had not neglected the challenge. Vertol (now Boeing Helicopters) built the VZ-2 tiltwing testbed, which made the world's first complete transition from hovering to forward flight in 1958. (Within just a few years, there were a total of nine military-sponsored "VZ-X" contracts for small test beds with vertical-takeoff capability.)

Vertol also carried out investigations of tiltrotors with both analysis and wind tunnel models. This work, along with a contract to design and build composite rotor blades for the Bell XV-15, gave Boeing the background necessary to become a partner with Bell Helicopter Textron on the V-22.

Curtiss-Wright built two tiltpropeller aircraft, the twin-propeller X-100, and then the quad-propeller X-19A. Another manufacturer, Hiller, built and flew the X-18, a tiltwing modification of the Chase C-122 transport airplane (Figure 87-1). Hiller then cooperated with Vought on the much larger four-engine XC-142A. In Canada, Canadair built and demonstrated two of its CL-84 Dynavert tiltwing aircraft (Figure 87-2).

Bell Aircraft, in upstate New York, in competition with its Texas cousin, used four big swiveling ducted fans on its X-22A (Figure 87-3). In forward flight, the ducts became the wings. In the hands of the Cornell Aeronautical Laboratory, this aircraft with a programmable autopilot became a valuable variable-stability research aircraft for investigating flying qualities. Also using the same technique, Ed Doak, in California, flew his VZ-4 with two ducted fans mounted on the ends of a long wing.

Many of these programs were moderately successful, but none resulted in production contracts. Perhaps the time was not yet ripe.

Today's contenders

Except for the Harrier direct-lift fighter and its Russian counterpart, the Yakovlev Yak-38 Forger and the experimental Yak-141 Freestyle (first seen by Western audiences during the 1992 Farnborough airshow in

England), the only two configurations currently in the news are the tilt-rotor and the tiltwing.

A European consortium is working on the Eurofar tiltrotor, but the tiltrotor program that we know best is the Bell Boeing V-22 Osprey. A tiltwing project was the TW-68 once proposed by the Japanese Ishida Group in conjunction with Dual Mode Air Vehicle, Inc. of Arlington, Texas (Figure 87-4).

Figure 87-4 Ishida TW-68

The difference between these two designs is twofold. The V-22 keeps the wing fixed and tilts only the engine/rotor assemblies mounted at the wing tips, whereas the TW-68 tilts the entire wing with the engine/propeller assemblies firmly attached.

The other difference is low-speed control. The V-22 gains low-speed control using rotors with flapping hinges and cyclic control systems that cause the rotors to flap to produce control moments in hovering flight, just as a conventional helicopter does.

The longitudinal flapping of the two rotors together is used for pitch control and differentially for yaw control. The primary roll control is done with differential rotor thrust, but is supplemented with lateral rotor flapping to minimize the bank angle while hovering in a crosswind.

On the other hand, the propellers on the TW-68 are rigid, and do not have cyclic pitch. They are therefore simpler and should cost less. They should also be easier to maintain than rotors with flapping blades and cyclic-control systems.

Note that there is no inherent reason why a tiltwing aircraft could not use rotors instead of propellers or why propellers could not replace the rotors on the tiltrotor configuration. If these alternatives are ever developed, we may find that "tiltrotor" and "tiltwing" are not the designations we want to use.

Bob Lichten, the XV-3 developer at Bell, did not like to call the aircraft a tiltrotor. He said that gave the impression of something about to fall over. He preferred the term "proprotor."

Arguments

The proponents of the tiltrotor and the tiltwing aircraft have long had disagreements about the relative advantages of their particular configurations.

Historically, tiltwing aircraft with propellers have had higher disc loadings than the tiltrotor aircraft, although there is no law that says that this has to be so. In the case of the two aircraft now being considered, the V-22 has a disc loading of about 20 pounds per square foot and the TW-68, about 29. This means that the TW-68 should take somewhat more power per pound of weight to hover.

Except, argue the tiltwing proponents, one of the advantages of their configuration is that its wing produces essentially no download in hover, since it is always aligned with the downwash from the propellers.

On the other hand, the fixed wing of the V-22 creates a substantial download in hover and thus requires extra rotor thrust and power. This has motivated the engineers on both the XV-15 and the V-22 projects to investigate ways of decreasing this penalty.

As a counterargument, the tiltrotor proponents will tell you that on their tiltwing competitor, the entire wing/engine/propeller assembly must be mounted on a structurally inefficient hinge—with an expected weight penalty over that of the mechanisms just required to tilt the engine/rotor assemblies.

It should be recognized, however, that the military V-22 has almost the same weight penalty, since the wing assembly is mounted on a vertical pivot to allow it to be aligned with the fuselage for storage on small ships. This would not be a feature of a civil tiltrotor.

Another argument of the tiltrotor enthusiasts is that by using the rotors for longitudinal control, their configuration does not suffer the power penalty and mechanical complexity of the horizontal ducted fan that the TW-68 designers use.

They also point out that obtaining directional control with differential longitudinal flapping is a well-established method identical to that used on tandem-rotor helicopters, whereas the tiltwing's use of differential flaps in the propeller slipstream close to the ground is relatively unproven.

Other effects

The disc loadings of these two aircraft are both high by current helicopter standards. They therefore create hurricane-like downwash: being almost 80 knots for the V-22 and more than 90 for its competitor. This means, of course, that the surface they hover over should be pretty well packed!

High disc loading also brings a high rate of descent during autorotation should all engines quit. What's more, the rotors/propellers can store only a small amount of kinetic energy, inhibiting the ability to make a safe landing flare from autorotation.

The hope here is that with two or more engines, there will never be such a thing as a complete power failure. (A hope, incidentally, shared by the designers and operators of most large multiengine helicopters.)

Other choices

The V-22 tilts both its rotors and engines. But an aircraft could be built which has engines fixed in place and tilts only the rotors, as was done on the single-engine Bell XV-3. Such a design would seem appropriate for aircraft that must operate where a downward pointing hot exhaust might melt an asphalt surface or start a grass fire. The Eurofar tiltrotor design avoids this problem by only tilting its proprotors, leaving the engines horizontal.

Also, the ducted fan on the TW-68's tail could be replaced by cyclic pitch on the propellers. This was demonstrated to work on the Vertol VZ-2's rigid propellers by putting the maximum pitch in 90° ahead of where it would be on a flapping rotor.

In conclusion, it will be some time before the high-speed rotorcraft industry is mature enough to have converged on one mutually accepted configuration. In the meantime, the designers are not restricted in their use of innovation.

88 Tandem Rotor Helicopters

For many years, it was apparent the helicopter industry couldn't decide which rotor configuration was best and experimented with many besides the main-/tail-rotor configuration considered standard today. Most of these other configurations used self-balancing ways of compensating for main-rotor torque. They included rotors arranged in tandem, side-by-side, coaxial, in combinations of three and even four, and some with tip-jet power. Of these alternate configurations, the tandem undoubtedly gave the main-/tail-rotor configuration the most competition.

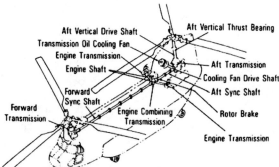

Figure 88-1 Arrangement of Chinook Components

Tandem configurations

Before going into the relative advantages and disadvantages of tandem-rotor helicopters compared to their main/tail-rotor cousins, we should describe some of the tandem's significant features. Figure 88-1 shows a typical modern tandem helicopter, the Boeing Vertol Chinook, and the arrangement of its components. Two rotors turning in opposite directions are driven by the same drive system to insure that they always have the same rpm and, like an eggbeater, to keep them from hitting each other.

Figure 88-2 demonstrates how longitudinal control through fore-and-aft motion of the control stick is achieved by differential collective pitch to change the relative thrust of the two rotors. On most modern tandems, a trim control for longitudinal cyclic pitch adjusts the tilt of the tip-path planes to reduce rotor flapping. This insures adequate fuselage-blade clearance and minimizes the oscillatory forces coming from the rotor hubs.

Roll control by sidewise motion of the stick is exactly the same as it is on main tail-rotor helicopters —lateral cyclic pitch tilts the two tip-path planes in the same direction to produce a rolling moment about the center of gravity (CG). The same lateral cyclic pitch is used to obtain directional control in response to pedal motion but, in this case, the two tip-path planes tilt in opposite directions, producing a yawing moment about the CG with the two rotor-thrust vectors.

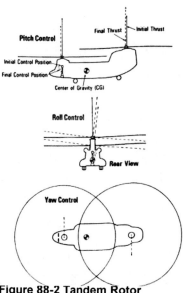

Figure 88-2 Tandem Rotor Helicopter Controls

The capability to tilt the rotors laterally both together and differentially gives the pilot flexibility in how to make turns. For example, a hovering turn can be done about the CG using only differential tilt controlled by the pedals. Or, a turn may be made about the cockpit using a combination of pedal and lateral stick to nullify the tilt of the front rotor while doubling that of the aft rotor. This type of maneuver can cause the aft rotor to achieve significant translational lift, thus requiring aft stick to keep the helicopter level.

Tandem advantages

On paper, it is fairly easy to show that the tandem arrangement should be superior to the main tail-rotor configuration —especially with regard to lifting capability — since a tail rotor absorbs 10% to 20% of the engine power that otherwise could be used by the main rotor. On a tandem, the torque-balancing task is done automatically and at little expense by the opposite-turning rotors. Thus, the full engine power can be used to produce lift.

Another advantage cited by tandem designers is a lighter drive system. Since all rotor designers chose about the same tip speed, the smaller-diameter rotors on a tandem turn at a higher rpm than a larger, single main rotor with the same lifting capability. This results in less speed reduction between the engine and the rotor and in less torque —both effects that can be shown to reduce the total drive-system weight. Tandem enthusiasts tell me their studies indicate that below 20,000 pounds (9,070 kg) their configuration can't compete with the main/tail-rotor helicopter but that above 70,000 pounds (31,750 kg), the tandem has a clear-cut advantage. This leaves the 20,000-to-70,000-pound regime up for grabs. However, other people dispute these conclusions.

Also, main/tail-rotor configurations have trouble handling big shifts in the position of the CG. Unless the CG is almost under the main-rotor hub, the pilot cannot trim the helicopter in steady flight. Tandem configurations, on the other hand, have a natural capacity to unevenly divide the lifting chore between the aft and forward rotors, thereby handling a wide range of CG locations.

And finally, designers of tandems only have to design one rotor — and then reverse the drawing for the other— instead of designing two completely different rotors.

Tandem disadvantages

Up against these advantages are some not-so-good factors. All helicopter fuselages are directionally unstable. If allowed to find their own preferred way of flying through the air, they would all turn broadside. On main/tail-rotor configurations, the tail rotor located way behind the CG acts like the feathers on an arrow to keep the fuselage pointed into the wind and, if that is not enough, vertical stabilizers can be used.

A tandem does not have the stabilizing benefit of a tail rotor, plus its aft end is not as far behind the CG — so the fin effect of the aft pylon is usually comparatively weak. Marginal directional stability has been a problem on all tandem-rotor helicopters. The tandem's desire to switch ends at high speed has led to some scary moments in flight and, in at least one case, to the abandonment of an otherwise promising prototype-development program.

Magnifying the problem of low directional stability, most tandems also have sluggish directional control because of their high moment of inertia about the vertical axis. This is due to the high weights at each end of the fuselage as compared to a conventional rotor configuration where most of the weight is concentrated near the middle of the fuselage. (Some people say the directional stability and control deficiencies of a tandem-rotor helicopter are nothing that a good tail rotor couldn't fix.)

In some situations, the lack of strong directional stability is an "enhancing" characteristic since it makes the tandem relatively insensitive to wind direction while landing on a ship or maneuvering close to obstacles on a gusty day.

Flying one rotor behind another in forward flight has a couple of disadvantages. First, as shown in Figure 88-3, the rotors are working on the same relatively small air mass and must impart more total energy to it in order to produce lift. This shows up as increased induced power (the power associated with developing rotor thrust in the passing air). A tandem in sideward flight, on the other hand, works with a larger mass of air and requires less induced power than for a conventional rotor configuration. This can be used to obtain better climb performance by flying sideward at speeds below which the fuselage drag begins to eat up the advantage.

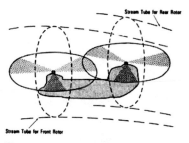

Figure 88-3 Overlapping of Affected Stream Tubes

Another problem has to do with longitudinal stability. To get a stable nosedown pitching moment when the angle of attack increases due to an up-gust, the rear rotor must be relatively more powerful than the front and the unstable fuselage. The problem is added to because as the front rotor's lift increases with the greater angle of attack, so does the downwash behind it. Thus, the aft rotor has a harder time developing a stabilizing influence than if it were operating in clean air.

Achieving inherent stability could be done by locating the CG ahead of the midpoint between the rotors, giving the rear rotor a longer moment arm. This requirement would tend to negate the advantage of the "unlimited" CG position discussed earlier. In practice, artificial stability augmentation systems incorporating gyros feeding signals to the controls compensate for the lack of stability. Without these black boxes in both the longitudinal and directional control systems, tandem-rotor helicopters have poorer handling qualities than their competition and thus need more complication and reliability in their auxiliary stabilization systems to achieve the same degree of pilot acceptance.

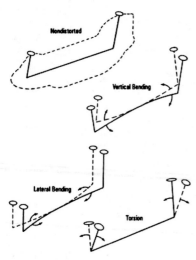

Figure 88-4 Some Fuselage Bending Modes

Finally, while vibration is a problem for all helicopters, the tandem's rotor at each end gives it more than its share. Figure 88-4 shows some of the possible ways —or modes — that can be excited by the oscillating forces and moments coming from two rotors. There are several ways of reducing vibration but the dynamic engineers have had only partial success in solving the problems of *any* helicopter and those working on tandems, in general, have come up second-best.

89 Coaxials and Synchropters

The neatest solution to the unbalanced-torque problem in a shaft-driven helicopter is to turn one half of the rotor in one direction while turning the other half in the opposite direction. This results in the coaxial helicopter, which would seem to have many advantages over those with tail rotors.

The list of helicopter pioneers who tried to make these advantages work in early projects includes Igor Sikorsky, Arthur Young (who developed the first Bell), and Stanley Hiller. They each had coaxial helicopters at one time but eventually decided they could not live without a tail rotor. Today, the only coaxials being flown are the Sikorsky ABC (Advancing Blade Concept) experimental aircraft and those being built by Kamov in the USSR (Figure 89-1).

Figure 89-1 Two Current Coaxial Helicopters

Coaxial pluses and minuses

The coaxial-rotor helicopter shares with the tandem and the synchropter (such as the Kaman H-43 Huskie) the major advantage of no tail rotor. This means all the engine power can work to produce useful thrust, there is no need for the extra weight and complexity required to drive the tail rotor, and ground clearance is not as critical. Compared to helicopters with tail rotors, the coaxial configuration has everything desirable in a helicopter: efficient use of installed power, low structural weight, ground safety, and compactness (except, perhaps, vertically).

However, although a tail rotor is unnecessary for antitorque on these aircraft, it is sorely missed in its role as the source of directional control. The most common method of obtaining directional control on coaxials is to produce a difference in torque between the two rotors by increasing collective pitch on one and reducing it on the other. Figure 89-2 shows what this does at the rotors.

Differential collective pitch is controlled by the rudder pedals. If the gearing is right, the total rotor thrust will remain a constant while the unbalanced torque will produce a yawing acceleration in one direction or the other. Once the desired yaw rate is established, the pedals can be nearly neutralized; now, only enough unbalanced torque is needed to overcome the fuselage aerodynamic damping.

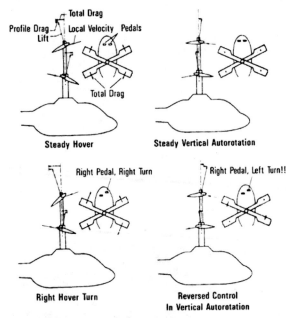

Figure 89-2 Directional Control with Differential Thrust

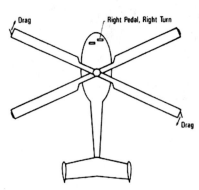

Figure 89-3 Directional Control with Tip Vanes

Backward autorotation, maybe

The system works well in powered flight but not in autorotation, where it either doesn't work at all or else works backward! Figure 89-2 shows why this is true. This trait has led to some remarkable aerodynamic and mechanical innovations.

One partial solution is to provide one or more vertical surfaces with movable rudders connected to the rudder pedals to at least provide positive directional control when the aircraft has some forward velocity. This has been used on the Sikorsky ABC coaxial helicopter but even here it was found that it is easy to go wrong.

The vertical fins on this aircraft have a slight sweepback and, as a consequence, the rudder hinge lines are also tilted back. In autorotation, the airflow is nearly parallel to the hinge lines and, because of this, rudder deflections are ineffective in producing directional control. The Sikorsky engineers have decided that, next time, their rudders will be swept forward.

Another solution to the problem was incorporated in the Gyrodyne DASH (drone antisubmarine helicopter) remotely controlled torpedo carrier. This coaxial helicopter evolved from the one-man RON-1. Movable drag vanes, shown in Figure 89-3, were installed in each blade tip of the two-bladed rotors and connected to the pilot's rudder pedals in such a way that when a turn was desired, the vanes on one rotor were deployed to increase its torque while leaving the vanes on the other rotor in their streamline position.

Although producing positive directional control in all flight conditions, this concept has a disadvantage. Even in their streamline positions, the vanes produce some drag, resulting in a power penalty that the engine must overcome.

A variation of this scheme has been tried on some experimental prototypes. It uses brake shoes to grab either one or the other of the coaxial drive shafts in order to turn the fuselage. This may be the eventual solution but mechanical reliability and failsafe considerations might make it difficult in the long run.

Power concerns

If, despite the directional-control problem, the designer elects to use the coaxial configuration to save on antitorque power, he is handed one additional aerodynamic advantage and also an aerodynamic disadvantage. The advantage is found in the absence of swirl in the wake due to the antiswirl role of the lower rotor.

A single rotor generates a wake with a swirl in the same direction as rotor rotation. The energy associated with this swirl represents a power loss. It is fairly small for rotors with relatively low disc loadings but becomes significant as disc loadings go above 10 pounds per square foot, as modern trends seem to be taking them. The lower rotor of the coaxial configuration takes out most, if not all, of the swirl put in by the upper rotor, thus eliminating the power loss.

The aerodynamic disadvantage appears if there is a significant separation between the upper and lower rotors. Figure 89-4 shows how, in this case, the lower rotor operates in a perpetual "climb" condition in the maturing wake of the upper rotor.

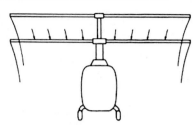

Figure 89-4 Lower Rotor Downwash Environment

The farther the two rotors are apart, the harder the lower rotor must work to develop its share of the thrust. Tests on a coaxial with the rotors spaced about one-quarter radius apart shows that the penalty due the lower rotor "climb" power just about cancels out the power saving due to its antiswirl contribution

Synchropters

Like the coaxial, the synchropter has two closely placed rotors turning in opposite directions. But unlike the coaxial, which has both rotors on one shaft, the synchropter has its rotors mounted on separate shafts at the same height above the fuselage. When they rotate, the rotors intermesh like an eggbeater.

This configuration was invented by Anton Flettner in Germany just before World War II. Flettner's chief of aerodynamics and dynamics was Dr. Kurt Hohenemser, who moved to the United States after the war. Hohenemser worked for McDonnell Aircraft when it was first developing helicopters in the 1950s and then became a professor at Washington University in St. Louis, Mo.

World's first production helicopter

Hohenemser recalls working with the German design team. He said the team members considered several other configurations before selecting the synchropter concept. They rejected both the main-rotor/tail-rotor and tandem concepts as being too complicated.

Flettner's FL-282 was the world's first production helicopter, beating Sikorsky's R-4 by several months. Its development program included the first wind-tunnel tests of a powered-rotor model and later a full-scale wind-tunnel test. A total of 24 FL-282s were built before Allied forces bombed the factory during the closing months of the war.

The synchropter configuration had also been adopted by Kellett Aircraft Corp. in the United States. It built two experimental prototypes: the XR-8, which first flew in 1944, and the twin-engine XR-10, which flew three years later. The XR-8 looked like a giant tadpole with rotors, while the XR-10 looked like a tadpole with rotors and an engine nacelle on each side. Neither entered production.

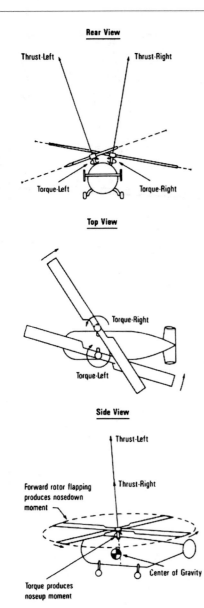

Rear View

Thrust-Left Thrust-Right

Torque-Left Torque-Right

Top View

Torque-Right

Torque-Left

Side View

Thrust-Left

Thrust-Right

Forward rotor flapping produces nosedown moment

Center of Gravity

Torque produces noseup moment

Figure 89-5 Forces and Moments Acting on a Synchropter in Powered Flight

But, in the 1950s and 1960s, Kaman Aircraft Corp., Bloomfield, Conn., (now Kaman Aerospace) built about a hundred HTK and HOK synchropters for the U.S. Navy and about 300 HH-43 Huskie synchropters for the U.S. Air Force. In 1956, during the Navy's utility-helicopter competition, Kaman submitted two proposals, one for a synchropter and one for a main-rotor/tail-rotor configuration. The latter proposal won and became the HU-2K, eventually evolving into the SH-2F Seasprite. That effectively ended any further synchropter development.

Advantages

The synchropter shares with the coaxial the efficient use of engine power and compactness allowed by the absence of a tail rotor. It is even more compact than the coaxial, since the two rotors are at the same height rather than one above the other on the same shaft. Blade clearance is obtained by careful synchronizing rather than by vertical displacement.

In addition, the synchropter has an inherent design feature that improves its longitudinal stability. Because the two rotors are tilted outwards, a small part of the rotor torque becomes a pitching moment, as shown in Figure 89-5.

When the direction of rotation is such that the blades approach each other over the tail boom, the pitching moment is noseup and the helicopter has to be trimmed with the tip paths tilted forward to provide a compensating nosedown moment. This orients the thrust vectors of the rotors behind the center of gravity, so when an up-gust increases rotor thrust, a stabilizing nosedown pitching moment is generated. Despite this inherent rotor stability, all the synchropter designs included large horizontal stabilizers when most other helicopters had small ones.

Disadvantages

Although the absence of a tail rotor provides the synchropter's main advantage, it also provides its main disadvantage: weak directional stability and control. On the Flettner helicopters, directional control was achieved with differential collective pitch, like the coaxials. This system was adequate in powered flight but it reversed in autorotation.

Therefore, a vertical fin with a rudder was used to provide positive directional control-at least when the aircraft had some forward speed.

Kaman added differential lateral cyclic pitch, which helped a little in all flight conditions but, to boost the level of directional stability to a desirable level, the manufacturer kept adding vertical stabilizers. It started with a single surface on the early prototypes and finally ended up with four vertical stabilizers on the Air Force HH-43B Huskie rescue helicopter (Figure 89-6).

Another problem was the difficulty in designing rotors with more than two blades. On its XR-8 and XR-10 prototypes, Kellett Aircraft attempted to intermesh three-bladed rotors; however, flight tests found that the blades occasionally grazed each other during maneuvers. The Kellett engineers promptly (although probably not too proudly) claimed to have the only self-stropping blades in the helicopter industry.

Because the blades slanted down to the side, head clearance was a concern. Hohenemser says it was impossible to approach the FL-282 from the side with the rotors turning. And with the rotors stopped, the blade tips were so close to the ground that Herman Goering, Adolf Hitler's commander of the Luftwaffe, gave one kick when he was inspecting the project. Even the much larger Kaman HH-43 had a prominent warning painted on each rotor pylon: "Approach From Front."

Figure 89-6 The U.S. Air Force's Kaman HH 43 Huskie

The synchropter may be an idea whose time has come and gone. On the other hand, it may have been ahead of its time and just the right configuration for some future helicopter requirement.

90 Antitorque Schemes For Compound

Helicopters

A continuing concern of rotorcraft engineers is how to maintain the vertical-takeoff capability, but fly faster than conventional helicopters.

One of the most popular concepts involves adding a wing and a forward propulsive device' to a "pure" helicopter to produce a "compound helicopter." In a sense, the result is an airplane with a very good low-speed lifting capability. By thus bypassing some of the rotor's high-speed limitations, it appears possible that speeds of at least 300 knots could be feasible.

In the early 1960s, the U.S. Army gave research contracts to each of four helicopter manufacturers to convert one of their conventional helicopters into a compound by adding a wing and one or two jet engines. Sikorsky, Bell, Kaman, and Lockheed all flew their versions, with Bell flying the fastest at a speed of 274 knots.

This work was in preparation for the attack aircraft known as the Advanced Aerial Fire Support System (AAFSS) that the Army was then planning. The military branch wanted a speed of at least 220 knots, which was about 50 knots faster than the demonstrated helicopter speed capability at the time.

The jet engines were quick and easy installations for demonstration of the concept. But they were not practical for the new aircraft because of their high fuel consumption. (It was before the days of the high-bypass jet engine.) For instance, the jet engine on the Lockheed XH-51 Compound would suck the fuel tank dry in six minutes!

For that reason, all the engineering teams that were preparing to enter the AAFSS competition decided to use propellers, which at 220 knots could be made quite efficient.

What do you do with torque?

Several teams were planning tilt prop/rotors or tiltwings where torque was balanced by symmetry. Other teams, however, were faced by the torque problem because they chose to develop variations of the single-main-rotor configuration. All these teams investigated the possibility of eliminating the tail rotor by using the propeller to generate the required antitorque moment.

At Lockheed, where I worked at the time, we investigated two possibilities. The first was to use two propellers mounted on the ends of the wing and operating one in reverse pitch during hover and low-speed flight. This scheme was discarded when calculations showed that to produce the required anti-torque moment, the wing would have to be longer than was compatible with ground clearance during slope landings or rotor clearance during maneuvers.

Figure 90-1 Lockheed's XH-51A and Cheyenne

The other proposal was to use a pusher propeller and put turning vanes in its wake, thus producing a sideforce similar to that normally generated by a tail rotor. This proposal got as far as wind-tunnel tests. Although it worked as required for the hover condition, the flow broke down when the testing simulated left sideward flight before getting to the 35-knot Army requirement.

The scheme was abandoned, and Lockheed chose to incorporate a conventional tail rotor on its design, which won the AAFSS competition as the AH-56 Cheyenne Figure 90-1).

Perhaps this was giving up too easily, since another team actually got the turning-vanes system into the air. Piasecki Aircraft built and flew the 16H-1 Pathfinder (Figure 90-2), with a "ring tail" incorporating turning vanes in a duct behind a pusher propeller. I do not know whether its left sideward flight performance was satisfactory.

Figure 90-2 Piasecki's Pathfinder

Other approaches

Sikorsky tried to make one device do everything by using a swiveling tail rotor. It was positioned as a tail rotor in hover and as a pusher propeller at high speed, using a movable rudder to provide the antitorque moment. This system was flown on a modified S-61. It was satisfactory in hover and in high-speed flight. But as might be expected, the transition when the rotor was being swiveled between the two positions was troublesome. I recently saw another proposal for a single-rotor compound helicopter. It uses wings that swivel differentially in the rotor downwash during hover and low-speed flight to produce the required antitorque moment and directional control. In forward flight, the antitorque force is provided by a rudder.

The basic concept is not much different from that used on the McDonnell Douglas NOTAR system, which uses aerodynamic forces on the tail boom to do the same job. The NOTAR, however, has a backup system provided by the airflow ejected through a quick-reacting turning nozzle at the end of the tail boom.

The examples above simply illustrate that engineers can usually find several ways to meet the challenges that arise on the "cutting edge of technology."

91 Stopping a Rotor in Flight

In this era of fast transportation, engineers have searched for ways to make helicopters fly very fast. Sometimes these specially designed schemes involved stopping rotors in flight.

This, in turn, introduces design problems that become major engineering challenges. Can they be satisfactorily met?

For a hovering aircraft, a rotor is a very effective device. In forward flight, however, a rotor going edgewise through the air and having to do both the lifting and propelling jobs starts to lose its effectiveness. At around 200 knots, it simultaneously runs up against some basic limitations caused by stall on the retreating side and by compressibility effects on the advancing side.

Over the past several decades, designers have suggested several ways of making rotorcraft overcome this speed limitation. One approach is to add a wing to take over the lifting duties and a jet engine or propeller to provide the push. This produces a "compound helicopter." Speeds approaching 300 knots were demonstrated by several experimental jet-powered compound helicopters in the 1960s and '70s during a U.S. Army-sponsored program. One of these, the Lockheed XH-51 compound, is shown in Figure 91-1.

Another approach is to convert the rotors into propellers as in Bell's XV-15 tilt-rotor. Speeds up to 400 knots should be possible with this configuration before running into propeller-type compressibility problems.

To go faster, the aircraft must become a non-rotor-craft machine by stopping the rotor in flight but what do you do after you stop a rotor? One possibility is to fold the blades into a compact bundle and then let them trail or stow them like landing gear, while a wing and propellers, or jet engines, provide the lift and thrust.

Figure 91-1 The Experimental Lockheed XH-51 Compound Helicopter with Wing and Jet Engine

Although never going as far as building a prototype, much serious engineering effort was expended by several companies in the late '60s for the Army Composite Aircraft Program. (This was before the word, "composite," was taken over by the materials people. Back then, it simply meant an aircraft that was both a helicopter and an airplane.) Figure 91-2 shows a Lockheed composite proposal.

The other thing you can do after stopping a rotor in flight is to make it into a wing. If the very modern X-wing configuration pops into mind at this point, it isn't surprising-but the idea goes back almost 50 years. Back then, Gerald Herrick of Pennsylvania built a biplane whose upper wing was mounted on a central pivot so it could be unlocked to become an autogyro rotor in flight. This procedure was demonstrated over 100 times but the reverse transition of stopping it in flight and converting back to a wing was just never accomplished despite good intentions. Figure 91-3 shows the Herrick Convertiplane in its autogyro mode.

Problems

Figure 91-2 Lockheed's Proposal for a "Composite" Aircraft had a Rotor That Could Be Stopped, Folded and Stored.

Whether stopping a rotor to fold it or to make it into a wing, some rather formidable technical problems must be overcome.

When the rotor is turning at full speed, the blades are so stiffened by centrifugal forces that aerodynamic loads can't bend them much. Compensating for the loss of centrifugal stiffening during the stopping process is the primary challenge to aircraft designers. It is especially critical for a slowly turning blade pointed forward because of the phenomenon known as "aeroelasticity instability."

To understand this, let us look at what the airplane people have done with swept wings. The primary reason for sweeping a wing forward or back is to relieve compressibility effects as the airplane nears the speed of sound - about 600 knots. This is because these effects are only a function of the air-velocity component perpendicular to the leading edge. Sweeping the wing - either forward or back - fools it into thinking the airplane is flying slower than it really is.

Sweepback has been the preferred method because it provides a significant amount of automatic gust alleviation as the geometry causes the wing to twist nosedown when it is being bent up by an upward moving gust. Figure 91-4 shows this effect. You can demonstrate this structural coupling using a yardstick or other long, thin piece of flexible material.

Figure 91-3 The Herrick Convertiplane with the Upper Wing Acting as an Autogyro Rotor.

Aileron reversal

If sweepback is good for gust alleviation, it seems obvious that sweep forward is bad and will accentuate the effects of gusty air. Why then do airplane designers even consider it?

It's because every coin has two sides. The flexibility that accounts for gust alleviation in a sweptback wing also accounts for a reduction in roll control.

The Boeing B-47 bomber was the first large aircraft extensively flight tested with a flexible sweptback wing. A dramatic piece of test data obtained during that program is a film made by a camera mounted over the pilot's shoulder with the control stick, the airspeed indicator, and the horizon in the field-of-view.

The first sequence, at a fairly low speed, shows the stick being moved left and the horizon rolling to the right as any pilot would expect. The second sequence at a higher speed, again shows the stick moving left but the horizon stubbornly staying put. On the last sequence, at an even higher speed, the same left-stick input made the horizon roll to the left!

The reason for this control reversal was that the ailerons placed near the wing tip - where ailerons had always been placed - were twisting the wing. At low speeds, the twist was small but at high speed, it was not.

When the pilot moved the stick left, the left aileron moved up, decreasing the lift on the left wing tip. At low speeds, this produces a left roll.

At the same time, however, the download on the aileron was twisting the left wing nose-up thus increasing its lift. At low speeds, this latter effect was small - but at the aileron-reversal speed demonstrated in the second movie sequence, it was just enough to cancel the normal aileron effect and at higher speeds, it overpowered it.

The next time you are on a jet transport, notice that the ailerons at the wing tips are only used at low speeds and that at high speeds, only the inboard ailerons-which can not twist the wing very much-are used for roll control. Inboard ailerons are satisfactory for maneuvering jet transports at high speeds but are not satisfactory for high-performance fighters.

Of course, a fighter's wings are not nearly as flexible as those on a bomber or transport, so the aileron-reversal problem is less-but another phenomenon also exists that reduces roll control on a sweptback wing. The boundary layer of low energy air builds up on the wing's inboard portion and slides out and back toward the wing tips. Thus the ailerons are working with air that is not as clean as it might be.

How about forward sweep

This and the adverse twist effect has prompted designers to look at swept forward wings, as on the Grumman X-29A which puts the ailerons in a more-favorable clean air environment.

But forward sweep introduces a couple new problems. As shown in Figure 91-4, the angle of attack increases on a swept forward wing as it is bent up-just the opposite of the effect on the sweptback wing. At all flight speeds, this produces a rougher ride through gusty air by amplifying the change in air load. But this is not the end. At high speed, the wings will become aeroelastically unstable.

This is the speed for "wing divergence" where the increase in lift is more than the wing stiffness can oppose and the wings will either break off and let the fuselage do its own thing or they will produce such a large

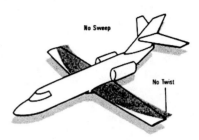

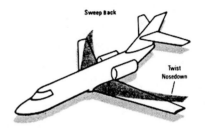

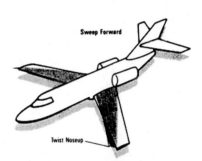

Figure 91-4 The Coupling of Wing Twist with Wing Bending

nose-up pitching moment that the aircraft will go into an unplanned loop.

Locking the hinges

With the disappearance of centrifugal force as the stoppable rotor slows down, the natural stiffening effect is lost and either the flapping hinges have to be locked or the rotor has to be built without hinges and with more stiffness than a normal helicopter blade. As the blade swings into the forward portion of the advancing side, it becomes a swept forward wing subject to the aeroelastic divergence phenomenon.

The situation worsens as it crosses the nose because here it is not only swept forward but is being carried backward through the air. This introduces another aeroelastic problem. On any surface, whether a wing or rotor blade, the air load is distributed such that the effective center of lift is about a quarter of the chord back from where the air molecules first encounter the surface.

For this reason, designers of wings and conventional rotor blades place most of the structure in the chord's first half. Often, the second half is not much more than an aerodynamic fairing. This is an attempt to put the "elastic axis" as close to the aerodynamic center as possible so that the air load only bends the structure without twisting it.

When the blade of a rotor being stopped in flight is going backwards through the air, its center of lift and its elastic axis do not coincide. Its aerodynamic center will be ahead of its elastic axis. Therefore, an up air load will tend to twist the blade to a higher angle of attack thus increasing the air load even further. Thus the blade is susceptible to another type of aeroelastic instability where it might twist off if subjected to an up gust as the air load increases faster than the torsional stiffness can resist it.

Therefore blades intended to be stopped in flight need both high-flapwise and high-torsional stiffness to prevent the two types of aeroelastic instabilities that gang up when the blade is pointed forward on the retreating side during the low-rpm times.

The X-wing blades/wings will have to be stiff enough to stay stable at the highest flight speed. For stopped-rotor aircraft on which the blades are to be stowed, however, it is only necessary that they be stable at the conversion speed-typically 100 to 150 knots. In either case, the blades are something else.

92 A New Look At The Autogyro

There's been speculation about the use of the civil tiltrotor aircraft as a city-center-to-city-center transport. I believe, however, that if the civil tiltrotor reaches fruition, it may face competition from aircraft that are less expensive to buy and operate.

The helicopter, though slower, will be competitive on short trips (perhaps up to 100 miles) and the STOL (short takeoff and landing) airplane will be competitive for those legs providing block-long chunks of concrete at each end—as would be true for vertiports having 10 or 20 loading gates. For in-between operations, a modern-day autogyro might be just the ticket.

An autogyro?

The autogyros of the 1930s with jump-takeoff capability could fly out of a fenced-in tennis court. Landings almost as short were demonstrated with ground rolls of less than the aircraft's length.

Despite this spectacular performance, the autogyro's development came to a stop 50 years ago because it couldn't hover. But now, for those air transportation tasks requiring short-field operation but not hovering, it deserves a second look. It has some apparent advantages.

The autogyro is mechanically simpler than either a helicopter or tiltrotor, so its payload-to-empty-weight ratio is higher than either. For the same reason, the autogyro's maintenance expenses should be less.

Its fuel economy should be better than the helicopter's even after accounting for propeller efficiency. This is because the rotor in or near autorotation is significantly more efficient than in the "propulsive" helicopter mode since more of the blade elements are operating at or near the angle of attack for the airfoil's maximum lift-to-drag ratio.

A rotor's speed capability is higher if it is flown in an autogyro mode than in a helicopter mode. This is primarily because, for the same thrust and tip-speed ratio, the angle of attack on the retreating tip is less (Figure 92-1). Helicopter rotors run up against a fairly well defined stall boundary at about 200 knots when their tip-speed ratio reaches about 0.5. But the old autogyros of the 1930s regularly cruised at this tip-speed ratio. Thus

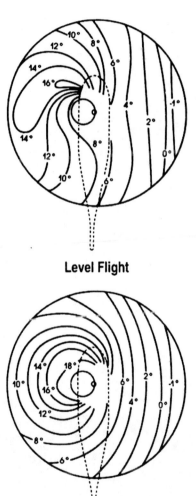

Level Flight

Autorotation

Figure 92-1 Angle-of-Attack Distribution

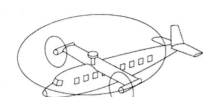

Figure 92-2 A Possible Interurban Autogyro

an autogyro based on modern technology could have a maximum speed of 250 to 300 knots before running into serious blade stall.

Fixing a control problem

By the time autogyros got developed (just before World War II), they were using cyclic pitch for longitudinal and lateral control just as helicopters do today. The cyclic-control system doesn't depend on forward speed, and thus pitch and roll control are effective as long as the rotor is turning.

For directional control, however, these autogyros still depended on the rudder, leftover from the airplanes. They therefore sometimes suffered from a lack of adequate directional control during slow-speed operations, especially during the final seconds of a short-field landing. Some of these landings resulted in rotor-splintering rollovers as the aircraft touched down with more sideslip than full rudder deflection could eliminate.

I suggest that the new-age autogyro should have some positive means of directional control, either with a small tail rotor or by the use of differential pitch in propellers mounted at the ends of a stub wing. This configuration might look something like the sketch in Figure 92-2.

An advantage of this proposal is that by providing a means for producing some antitorque moment, the rotor could stay coupled to the drive system at all times. This gives the designer the opportunity to use the engine governor to maintain a constant rotor speed. But it would also help improve the landing and takeoff performance if the rotor could accept some power during these critical maneuvers. Of course, the aircraft would no longer be an autogyro; it could more properly be called a "non-hovering compound helicopter."

One thing the old autogyros did not have was a high rate of climb. Even though rotors are efficient, propellers are not. Designers of new autogyros would have to provide enough power to satisfy the FAA requirement for a rate of climb of at least 100 feet per minute following the loss of one engine.

Other ways to do it

A shaft-driven rotor is not the only option the designers have for this type of aircraft. The McDonnell Aircraft XV-1 convertiplane (Figure 92-3) was a "hovering autogyro" using a pressure-jet rotor. It first flew in 1954.

Figure 92-3 McDonnell's XV-1 With Pressure-Jet Main Rotor

With this system, the engine either drives a compressor to supply air to the hollow rotor blades in the helicopter mode, or it powers a propeller for forward flight as an autogyro. Antitorque is not required for a tip-jet powered rotor but the XV-1 still had small fans at the end of its twin tail booms for directional control.

The discussion above is not meant to detract from the obvious potential of the tiltrotor aircraft, but to show that there are two starting points for the process of meeting a need in the air-transportation field. One is to find more missions that a given aircraft can do and the other is to find the best aircraft suited for a given mission.

93 Attempts To Revive The Autogyro

During the 1930s, the autogyro, with its freely spinning rotor being pulled though the air by a propeller, was relatively successful. Several hundred were built and flown worldwide. Although used in a variety of useful roles, there was something missing—the ability to hover. Hover was what the military customer needed and was willing to pay for.

Second thoughts

Thus the autogyro was displaced by its younger, hovering brother, the helicopter. The question since then has been, "Should the idea of the autogyro be given another chance?

The characteristics of the autogyro place it in the gap between airplanes and helicopters. It is simpler than a helicopter but not so simple as an airplane. On the other hand, it can fly slower than an airplane but not as slow as a helicopter.

Autogyro enthusiasts believe that for many types of flying, the compromise between the two characteristics is favorable for their aircraft and warrants giving aviators a choice between the airplane, the autogyro, and the helicopter to match their needs. Since the late 1950s, these enthusiasts have tried to fan the embers into a flame several times, but with the exception of the small homebuilt Bensen-type gyrocopters used for thrill flying, no one has succeeded in keeping it burning.

Kellett KD-1A

An attempt was made by Kellett starting in 1958. Kellett had been one of the most successful producers of prewar autogyros, but had gotten out of the field to devote full efforts to the development of military helicopter designs which, while interesting, had not resulted in any production contracts.

It was probably with a certain amount of desperation, therefore, that the Kellett management hit on the idea of putting a 25-year-old autogyro design back into production to take advantage of the swing to aircraft for doing chores around the farm. Although they had formerly produced many autogyros, at this time they hadn't one on hand.

Figure 93-1 Kellett KD-1A In Airmail Role

To avoid having to build a prototype from scratch, they located one of their old ships in the collection of a Pennsylvania farmer who had acquired a number of autogyros and other interesting aircraft. Kellett prevailed on the farmer to part with his XR-3 so they could rework it into the KD-1 configuration (Figure 93-1), which had been certificated in 1935.

This aircraft, with its 225-hp Jacobs radial engine, was then recertificated by the FAA. Gross weight was 2,200 pounds (1,000 kg) and the speed range was 20 mph to 120 mph. With provisions for a 17-cubic-foot (0.5-m3) hopper in the front cockpit, it was dubbed the "Cropmaster."

Actually, Kellett had been able to achieve a vertical takeoff of sorts with the autogyro. Just before the war, Kellett had developed "jump-takeoff" capability in which the rotor was spun up to overspeed at flat pitch on the ground and then simultaneously declutched and given a shot of collective pitch to make it produce high thrust. This caused the autogyro to spring vertically from the ground while the propeller pulled it into forward flight.

If all went well, the necessary flying speed of 20 mph would be achieved just before the rotor rpm decayed to a dangerous level. Although this capability had been provided on some of the later Kellett

In 1940 autogyros, it was decided to restart production with the KD-1 design as certificated in 1935 without jump takeoff and to reintroduce this desirable feature in later versions.

A price of $27,500 was set and a goal of 50 orders was established to justify a production line. During 1959 and 1960, many demonstration flights were made and at one time 100 firm orders were on the books. The company, however, was having financial difficulties and as a result, Kellett reluctantly withdrew from the autogyro field forever.

Umbaugh U-18

Raymond E. Umbaugh had been in the farm-supply business and, as a sideline had been a dealer in Bensen Gyrocopters. He teamed up with Gilbert DeVore, a rotor-wing expert formerly with the Civil Aeronautic Administration (and incidentally still active as a manufacturer of aircraft and heliport lighting systems—DeVore Aviation Corp.) to design a larger version of the Bensen ship.

Figure 93-2 Umbaugh U-18 In Final Triple-Tail Configuration

The result was a two-place, tandem-seat aircraft grossing 1,800 pounds (800 kg) with a 180-hp Lycoming HIO-360 engine turning a pusher prop. Top speed was about 100 mph and the machine had jump-takeoff capabilities (Figure 93-2).

Umbaugh Aircraft Corp., of Ocala, Fla., was organized in 1958 with DeVore acting as the chief engineer. A prototype was built, a price of $10,000 set, and an extensive marketing effort started. Like the Kellett autogyro, one of the prime uses of the U-18 was seen to be in the agricultural market, but other expected uses included transmission and pipeline patrol, construction liaison, and Sunday joyriding.

Umbaugh's method of booking orders was more aggressive than Kellett's. He divided the country into 100 districts, found a distributor for each and assigned them a quota of 100 ships apiece. Thus he had an instant backlog of 10,000 orders. By accepting deposits of $1,500 for individual orders, $20,000 from dealers, and $80,000 from distributors, he amassed nearly $2.5 million.

But no matter how good the technical design and how innovative the marketing, it also takes some good business practices (and some amount of luck) to shepherd a new product from drawing board to the marketplace. The following sequence of events highlight almost 15 fateful years in the life of the Umbaugh U-18:

• April 1958—U-18 project publicly announced.

• February 1959—Prototype built, production to be done by Colonial Aircraft Corp., of Sanford, Maine.

• August 1959—No! Production to be done by Fairchild Engine and Airplane Corp., of Hagerstown, Md.

• February 1960—V-tail replaces T-tail

• May 1960—Fairchild builds five preproduction aircraft for $300,000.

• June 1960—Triple-tail replaces V-tail.

• July 1961—Umbaugh severs relationship with Fairchild following disagreement about costs for subsequent production aircraft.

• September 1961—FAA certificates the U-18.

• October 1961—Umbaugh moves operation to Florida.

• March 1962—Distributors begin complaining.

• December 1962—Bankruptcy.

• January 1964—Air and Space Corp., Muncie, Ind., buys the company.

• September 1968—Air and Space Corp.'s plant put up for sale.

• November 1985—Don Farrington of Paducah, Ky., buys the U-18 inventory, renames the ship the Air and Space 18-A, sells some and uses others for training.

McCulloch J.2

The next big autogyro program featured the McCulloch J-2 (Figure 93-3). The rotor for this design had a long and interesting evolution. In 1949, Drago K. Jovanovich designed and built a small helicopter with tandem, three-bladed, 23-foot (7-m)-diameter rotors in Philadelphia. Having no way of getting the design into production by himself, he interested Robert P. McCulloch, the world's chain-saw king at the time.

Figure 93-3 The McCulloch J-2

(Later, McCulloch added some very successful oil investments and single-handedly developed Lake Havasu City, Ariz.)

McCulloch brought Jovanovich and his helicopter to the chain-saw factory near Los Angeles airport, assembled a team of experienced rotary-wing engineers, and proceeded to redesign the JOV-3 for production while changing its designation to the MC-4. This helicopter was certificated in 1952 but, like many other projects, the makers decided that it could not be produced to provide a reasonable return on investment.

Sometime after that decision was reluctantly made by McCulloch, the Aircraft Division of Hughes Tool Co. was looking at the possibility of a small single-rotor helicopter as a commercial project following the cancellation of the big XH-17 Flying Crane. Their design studies led to a three-bladed rotor with a diameter of 23 feet (7 m). Hughes engineers suggested a development shortcut which involved acquiring the license to use the certificated Jovanovich/McCulloch rotor design. This suggestion was acted upon and the project became the Hughes Model 269, which is still in production by Schweizer Aircraft as the Model 300C.

Another try

In the meantime, Jovanovich had acquired the entire ML-4 project including the prototype aircraft and the McCulloch tooling. He renamed it the Jovair 4-E Sedan. He also used the same rotor in the design of a small autogyro, which he called the Jovair J-2. In the process of trying to raise money for his line of aircraft, he again contacted Bob McCulloch. McCulloch was not interested in the helicopter that had once been his—but was intrigued by the simpler autogyro. Thus for Jovanovich, lighting struck twice as McCulloch decided to get back into the rotary-wing business with a Jovanovich design. Of course, the Jovair J-2 immediately become the McCulloch J-2.

The J-2 configuration was very similar to the Umbaugh U-18. It used the same 180-hp Lycoming engine and weighed nearly the same. The obvious configuration differences were side-by-side seating in the cockpit, a wing containing fuel tanks, and twin tail booms instead of one.

By 1972, 110 aircraft had been built but, at a price of $19,950, only 46 had been sold. This disappointing sales picture, along with a couple of rollover accidents, cooled McCulloch's enthusiasm and he withdrew his support, ending the project.

The inventory was sold to George Morton, who changed the name to Aero Resources. Not much has been heard from this aircraft since then— except that one ship turned up in Phoenix, Ariz., where it was converted into the prototype for the Nagler "Honcho" helicopter by installing a pressure-jet rotor.

Epilogue

One of the most serious design deficiencies of these autogyro aircraft was the lack of adequate directional stability and control at low speed. You may have gotten a hint of this in the several tail changes for the Umbaugh and the mention of rollover accidents with the McCulloch.

A number of autogyros, including Kelletts, were lost when a touchdown was made with too much lateral drift. Future autogyro designers should consider a small tail rotor or some sort of rotor brake/clutch to solve this problem.

Recently, pioneer autogyro test pilot George Townson published a book entitled, Autogiro, the Story of the Windmill Plane. Although admittedly biased, his concluding remarks are thought provoking.

"What would the future autogiro be if it employed already-tried techniques? It could take off vertically, fly slowly—as slow as zero mph—and land vertically. Adding simple also-tried devices, it could perform limited hovering with rotor-tip drive jets. There is no reason to believe that autogiros could not be built to carry payloads equal to the loads carried by the largest helicopters. There is no apparent limit to the possibilities."

Is it time to give the autogyro another try?

94 Low Observables

In warfare, surprise is often an important element. One aspect of achieving surprise, of course, is to remain undetected as long as possible. This capability is now known as "stealth." Come to think of it, it is also an important element in the "fly neighborly" program.

Sight

We observe with our natural senses—sometimes augmented- and with any artificial senses that we can muster. Sight is probably the most valuable natural sense in detecting a helicopter so if we are to frustrate the adversary, we should try hard to make our helicopters invisible.

To this end, small size is one of the most obvious beneficial characteristics although it is one that only the people specifying the payload capabilities of the new helicopter have much control over. A camouflage paint job that makes the aircraft blend into the background is good as is a dull surface to minimize sun reflections. In this respect, the canopy surfaces provide challenges to the designer. A polished sphere on a sunny day would be very observable to someone between it and the sun since from many directions, the sun would be reflected as a "glint" from the mirrored surface. On the other hand, a shiny flat plate would produce a flash only to one position-although a strong one. The U.S. Army decided several years ago that the one-position flash was better than the omnidirectional glint and so they decreed that their helicopters would no longer have curved canopy panels. The decision came during the development of the Hughes (now McDonnell Douglas) AH-64 'Apache "It had been designed with pleasingly rounded canopy panels but at the insistence of the Army, it was redesigned with flat panels even in the face of a predictable increase in drag. Besides this penalty, these panels, at first, had another problem. As stretched diaphragms, they picked up the air pulses from the passing blades and gave the pilot the impression that he was a prisoner in a bass drum. It was even called "canopy drumming." A compromise was reached. The top panels were stiffened and the side panels took on the small curvature that you can see on the production Apaches such as the one in Figure 94-1. You can also see the same transition from rounded to flat panels on the Bell AH-1 series for the Army starting with the "S" version. Some

Figure 94-1 Canopy Panels on the AH-64 Apache

Figure 94-2 Canopy Panels on Cobra Models

Army pilots have complained, however, that this change has sacrificed some of their field-of-view. Perhaps because of this, the Marines have stuck with the more sexy-looking rounded canopy panels even on their latest AH-1W Cobras. Figure 94-2 shows the comparison.

Another aspect of seeing a helicopter is that "blade flicker" might draw the observer's attention from a distance where it might otherwise have gone unnoticed. This is because the eye and brain combination are sensitive to regularly repeated clues at certain frequencies that happen to be where main rotors operate. If you want to make a helicopter very visible from a distance, paint one blade white and the others dull black. (This sensitivity to visual frequencies has been reported to lead to hypnotic states in certain pilots flying certain helicopters.)

Yet another visual means of detection is a dust or snow cloud that a hovering or slow-moving helicopter close to the ground might produce. Studies have shown that the size of the cloud is dependent only on the gross weight of the helicopter and not on its disc loading as might be thought. The disc loading only affects how big the particles that can be dislodged are, but any particles larger than snow flakes or dust will stay close enough to the ground that they will not become part of the telltale cloud. On the other hand, a cloud may be just what the tactical situation calls for, and so a combat helicopter may be equipped with a smoke-screen generating system.

Sound

Sound is another powerful detection clue. The fact that the helicopter puts so much energy into the air at frequencies that the human ear can hear is the basic problem. At short range, the ear's increasing sensitivity to high frequencies make a fast-turning tail rotor or a Fenestron fan seem to be noisier than a main rotor even though it is putting far less energy into the environment. At long range, it is usually the main rotor that is heard; especially if the advancing tip is throwing shock waves ahead of it when going fast enough to experience compressibility effects or if one blade passes through or close to the tip vortex shed by a preceding blade. In each case, the observer on the ground hears an impulsive noise often referred to as "blade slap" that can carry for miles. So far the only known cure for these effects is to select a low tip speed during the design. Most designers now would limit the design tip speed to the neighborhood of 700 feet per second whereas twenty years ago they would go as high as 800 feet per second. By going to a lower tip speed, the helicopter becomes quieter but the rotor and drive system become heavier-nothing comes easy.

Radar

Since World War II, the accepted way to detect an aircraft at long range has been radar. The best radar targets are large metal aircraft with many surfaces intersecting at right angles. Thus the best way to design a helicopter which is hard to detect with radar is to make it small, to use nonmetallic materials, and to avoid surfaces intersecting at right angles. Composite materials might seem to be the answer: they are non-radar reflective, but they may also be radar transparent and let the signals go right through to be reflected from metal parts underneath. Composite parts also have a special problem in that they are more vulnerable to being damaged by lighting strikes than if made of metal; so to protect them, many designers include metal meshes in the lay-up to provide circuits to basic metal parts such as the transmission. These meshes in turn, become radar reflectors.

A similar dilemma faces the blade designer. Although composite blades have many good features, resistance to leading edge erosion is not one of them. For that reason, most blades that are expected to last for any length of time in an environment where abrasive sand might be present will probably be equipped with metal anti-abrasion strips that are very good radar reflectors. One possible suggestion for this is to have two sets of blades: one for peacetime and one for combat where a blade life of only a few hours may be sufficient.

Recently, materials have been developed that will absorb radar energy to prevent it from being reflected back to the receiver. These can be applied to surfaces to reduce the "radar cross-section" though with a penalty in weight and cost. This and special shaping are the elements of "passive" protection. There is also active protection involving sophisticated "radar jamming" equipment that can detect when the aircraft is being "painted" by a gun or missile radar and can send out a false signal that will tell the enemy, "I'm over there". At the same time, a radar warning receiver (RWR) tells the pilot that he has been observed and from what direction the signals are coming to give him a chance to make an evasive maneuver.

Another system that might be classified as both active and passive is a dispenser that fills the sky full of "chaff consisting of long ribbons of aluminized Mylar film whose reflections look like a helicopter that has suddenly come to a hover or that completely fill up the radar screen and lets the helicopter escape in the cloud.

From an operational standpoint, nap-of-the-earth flight provides some protection from conventional radar because of the "ground clutter" coming from all the other things that reflect radar. The radar people, however, have developed a special type using Doppler principles that picks up only on things that move. Depending on the threshold of velocity set to trigger this radar, the helicopter may or may not be detected unless the signals from its fast-moving blades are what give it away.

Figure 94-3 The Apache Exhaust System

Infrared

The human eye has the ability to see only part of the frequency spectrum that is out there. We can see from the short violet waves to the long red waves but nothing on either side. Some creatures have more capability. Many snakes have special sensors that can accurately locate sources that are giving off waves at frequencies in the infrared, or heat range. We have learned to do this artificially starting with the "sniper-scope" of the Korean War developing into forward-looking infrared (FLIR) and then into the pilot night-vision system (PNVS) used on the Apache. These systems sense the temperature differences between objects and electronically produce a visual image. For natural features, they work best after a sunny day before things have had a chance to cool down and worst just before dawn on a snow-covered landscape where almost everything is at the same temperature. Of course, people or operating machines will almost always be at a different temperature than the background and so will stand out.

Heat-seeking, or IR missiles use the same temperature differences to home in on a source of heat such as a turbine exhaust pipe. For that reason, to be low-observable to these missiles, many helicopters include methods for both shielding the hot parts of the engine from direct viewing and for cooling the engine and exhaust plume by passing great quantities of air through and around them. Figure 94-3 shows the Apache exhaust system which was designed to do this while also giving the missile no chance to see into the engine compartment looking for hot parts.

In addition to concern about hot engines, designers must consider that gun barrels get very hot during firing and therefore must have some way of rapidly dissipating heat before they become targets.

Figure 94-4 An IR Jammer Installed on the AH 1 Cobra

Another means of protecting the helicopter against IR homing missiles is to use an infrared jammer. These operate by generating an intense but flickering IR signal that is intended to confuse the on-coming missile into thinking that it is slightly off track and therefore cause it to pass harmlessly by. A jammer installed on a Cobra is shown in Figure 94-4. How effective is this device? Time magazine in its Dec. 14,1987 issue shows a photo of a Mil Hind in Afghanistan. It appears to have an IR jammer installed above the engines just as an American helicopter would have. The photo caption claims that "Heat-seeking missiles [U.S.-supplied Stingers] have neutralized the lethal choppers."

As a last resort, the helicopter might fire off decoying flares from the same dispenser used for the radar-confusing chaff. The original idea was that the flare would appear to be a hotter target than the helicopter and the missile would home in on it instead. In the continuing game of one-upmanship, the missile designers have been able to make their sensors remember the IR frequency signature that first attracted their attention and to ignore any other signature. So the flare designers have had to tailor their devices to give off the same signature that their helicopter has-only hotter.

Electromagnetic radiation

Finally, on today's modern battlefield, a helicopter may be detected by signals that it sends out in the electromagnetic range. These include such deliberate transmissions as radio signals for communication and radar signals used for sensing altitude and ground speed or for active target search. Even using radar jamming to confuse a missile may signal the helicopter's location to a battlefield surveillance system.

Radio silence has been practiced for years to minimize detection due to communication, but one method allows the pilot to talk or use a keyboard, temporarily stores the message, compresses it, and then sends it out as a brief burst to a receiver that can reconstitute it. The hope here is that the transmission time will be too short for a surveillance device to get a lock on the aircraft.

There may also be detectible non-intentional transmissions from such rotating electrical machinery as generators and motors. Thus it may be seen that both the pilot and the designer have to take precautions to hold give-away signals to a minimum.

95 Windmills

Even though helicopter rotors and windmills operate under different flow conditions, when designed for optimum performance they look almost identical. No wonder, therefore, that many rotor engineers see the windmill field as a worthy challenge for their efforts.

The rotor of a hovering helicopter produces a force (thrust) in a direction opposite the airflow and requires a driving torque. A windmill, on the other hand, produces a force (drag) in the direction of the flow and generates a torque that can be made to do something useful such as grinding grain, pumping water, or generating electricity.

Technically, the word "windmill" applies to the entire system-including the millstones, the pumps, or the generators. The rotating aerodynamic part is properly referred to as the "turbine" and this is the appropriate word to use in discussing any rotating device extracting energy from the passing flow whether it be in air or in water.

Figure 95-1 A Typical Farm Water-Pumping Windmill

Two types

There are two types of horizontal-axis wind turbines that you might see in America: the multi-bladed, high-solidity farm type of Figure 95-1 and the more-modern two- or three-bladed, low-solidity turbine shown in Figure 95-2. (Solidity is defined as the ratio of blade area to disc area.) It is interesting to note that- the original Old World windmills appear to fall in between these two styles.

Aerodynamically, they are not very different. Each relies on absorbing energy from continuous bundles of air, giving them a chance to react to several blade passages. Grandpa's windmill turned slowly but had lots of blades to accomplish this. The modern wind turbines have only two or three blades but come around so fast that, to the passing air, there appears to be many blades. Thus little air "leaks" through, even though the solidity is low.

Design considerations

The energy produced by a wind turbine is a function of how much it slows the flow passing through it. If it does not slow the air at all, no energy will be produced. If, on

Figure 95-2 Modern Windmills in a California Mountain Pass

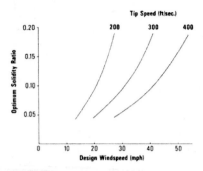

Figure 95-3 Designer's Choices for Tip Speed and Solidity

the other hand, it were to completely stop the flow like a solid disc, it would again produce nothing.

From momentum considerations, we can demonstrate that the most power can be absorbed if the air is only slowed to two-thirds of its original speed. (This is less effect than a bushy tree, in case you are worrying about the effect that the large turbine farm in Figure 95-2 has on the environment.) Under these conditions, the maximum energy that can be absorbed is about 60% of the original amount in the stream tube approaching the disc. This corresponds to a Figure of Merit (measure of efficiency) of 1.0 for a hovering rotor.

To get the best performance, the modern wind-turbine designer selects a combination of tip speed and solidity that makes the blade elements operate at their maximum lift-to-drag ratio-just as does the designer of a modern helicopter rotor. The tip speed chosen is five to 10 times the design wind speed and the best solidity is as shown in Figure 95-3. Since the wind speed is beyond his control, the designer must make an educated guess based on previous wind surveys on the intended site-literally pulling a value out of the air.

Similar to helicopter blades, the wind turbine is most efficient if the blades are twisted. A helicopter blade that is twisted to improve performance in hover and forward flight has twist in the wrong direction for best performance in vertical auto-rotation. If, however, the helicopter were descending upside down, the twist would be in the correct direction. This is also the right sense for the twist of a wind-turbine blade with values as high a 30° being desired.

Taper can also be beneficial in optimizing the aerodynamic characteristics, so a wind-turbine blade designed to take advantage of all the aerodynamic niceties would be both twisted and tapered. But, just as in the helicopter industry, these blades cost more to build and so many are both untwisted and untapered. The turbines of Figure 95-2, however, have an aerodynamic refinement in terms of blade endplates that are meant to slightly increase the effective radius.

Holding speed

For any reasonable wind speed, the tip speed can be held constant by a control system that adjusts the blade's pitch as wind speed and the power being generated vary. Generally, the pitch at the three-quarter radius station is in the neighborhood of 2°. Holding a precise turbine speed is important when feeding electricity into the power company's 60-cycle network.

Other schemes allow operation at variable turbine speeds but require additional electrical equipment to synchronize the final output. When the wind dies to a point where the turbine cannot generate a reasonable amount of power, it is automatically disconnected from the grid. And, to prevent damage in winds high enough to cause overspeeds, most are

equipped with a brake or feathering mechanism that automatically comes into play.

Downwind or upwind?

Obviously, the most efficient position for the turbine disc is broadside to the wind. To accomplish this, designers use various pivoting techniques. Some turbines are meant to operate behind their supporting towers. This allows the weathervaning effect of the drag force to keep the axis aligned with the flow but may produce oscillating fatigue loads as each blade penetrates the tower's "wind shadow."

Figure 95-4 Darrieus Wind Turbines

Others operate upstream of the tower and may use a trailing vane like Grandpa's or some basic rotor dynamics involving a natural tendency to equalize the lift in the upwind and downwind blades to keep it in place. The mechanics of this are essentially the same as those that produce blade flapping on a helicopter rotor in forward flight.

Besides the well-known horizontal-axis turbines, another type has been developed - the vertical-axis turbine or Darrieus rotor shown in Figure 95-4. This type has the advantage of having its critical machinery conveniently at ground level and being able to accept the wind from any direction. The lack of height, however, is a disadvantage, since much of the turbine is down in the earth's boundary layer where wind energy is lower.

96 Helicopter Development: The First 50 Years

When tracing the source of the helicopter concept, it is customary to harken back to that Renaissance genius, Leonardo da Vinci, who sketched a continuous ramp device apparently based on the Archimedes' Screw, which since ancient times has been used to lift water. It can be contended, however, that Leonardo was preceded by a much earlier genius, as documented in the Jerusalem Bible: ".... and God's Spirit hovered over the water."

However, the idea of the helicopter—and all aviation—long lay dormant while civil engineers built roads and bridges, architects raised palaces and cathedrals, and mechanical engineers developed clocks and printing presses. Aeronautical engineers developed windmills and sails for ships, and they watched the birds while thinking, "I wish I could do that."

Sikorsky's explanation

Igor Sikorsky, who besides being a talented inventor, had an intense appreciation for the mystic. He pointed out that the ancient Egyptians had the materials and the construction techniques to fly kites, to float hot-air balloons over the Nile, and to launch hang-gliders from the pyramids. They apparently, however, did not even do so much as fold a papyrus airplane.

Sikorsky's conclusion was that ideas come to practical fruition only when their time is ripe. The time for human flight came in the late 1700s when the Montgolfier brothers began flying around France in balloons. From that simple beginning, aviation has grown exponentially. Today, not even the sky is the limit.

The start of aviation

After the balloon, two winged aircraft captured the imagination of dreamers of flight: the ornithopter and the glider.

An ornithopter has wings that flap like those of a bird. To early inventors, it appeared that only small technical problems stood in the way of successful man-carrying aircraft. Many demonstrated that the problems could indeed be solved on a small scale, and model orinthopters flapped across lecture halls and in front parlors, but none ever carried a person.

Gliders were built by more-realistic inventors, such as Otto Lilienthal and Octave Chanute. We now call their aircraft hang-gliders—a type that had limited success then, but 70 years later come to full fruition wherever a steady wind blew uphill.

The birth of the helicopter idea

While orinthopters and gliders were receiving attention, other talented people were inventing the helicopter. They realized that to fly from my backyard to your backyard, vertical takeoffs and landings would be required. The idea of the two-mile-long runway had not yet come.

The inspiration for the helicopter probably came originally from the Chinese top that appeared in Europe in the 14th century, but the development of the screw propeller for marine propulsion undoubtedly gave many helicopter designers a more current starting point. Helicopters, just as orinthopters, became successful on a small scale.

Sources of power ranging from the energy in a bent bow, to clock springs, to ingenious small steam engines made short vertical flights possible. But there was no sign of stability or control, so important for man-carrying vehicles. One of the early experimenters, Ponton d'Amecourt, coined the word "helicopter" from two Greek roots: *helico* meaning spiral and *pteron* meaning wing.

The young Wright brothers made several model helicopters, but gave them up for their kite and glider experiments. Later Wilbur was quoted, "The helicopter does, with great labor, only what the balloon does without labor."

In the beginning decade of this century, automobile development resulted in improved powerplants and made it finally possible to consider real, full-scale helicopters.

It is not clear who should get the credit for the first helicopter flight. Was it Louis Breguet, the scion of a famous French watch-and-clock making family?

He claimed it for his 1907 multi-rotor helicopter (Figure 96-1). The craft had no control system so Breguet stationed a man at each of the four comers for stability.

In later years, after he had become a successful builder of airplanes, he recounted the results of the brief helicopter tests. He told how the four men had to hold the aircraft down. Two of these, who were still with him, would

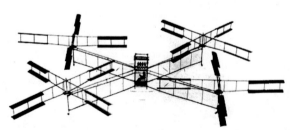

Figure 96-1 Louis Breguet's Multirotor Helicopter

smile and nod their heads, but when the old man was out of earshot, they would say, "We were really lifting up."

Was it Paul Cornu, another Frenchman? His attempt was also in 1907, and he, too, claimed to have been airborne for several seconds in his tandem-rotor helicopter (Figure 96-2). Later helicopter engineers have doubted that his machine had enough power to fly.

It is true that Cornu never could produce a photograph showing light under the wheels or an affidavit signed by 60 witnesses—as he had for some model flights the year before. At any rate, 1907 seems to be a good one to proclaim as the start of the helicopter era.

A couple of years later, young Igor Sikorsky tried to fly a rotary-wing aircraft and failed in his native Russia. Tests of his second machine (Figure 96-3) in 1910 showed that it could almost lift its own weight but no more.

Figure 96-2 Paul Cornu's Tandem-Rotor Helicopter

In his book, The Winged S, Sikorsky wrote "I had learned enough to recognize that with the existing materials, and—most of all—the shortage of money, and the lack of experience of the designer, I would not be able to produce a successful helicopter at that time.

"Realizing all of this, I decided to enter—temporarily—the fixed-wing field and so started to build my Airplane No. 1." Like Breguet, he successfully followed this "temporary" detour for 30 years before finding his way back to the true path.

The honor for the first well-documented helicopter flight goes to Jens Ellehammer of Denmark. He demonstrated his helicopter in 1913 in Copenhagen—and had enough foresight to have both a cameraman and His Royal Highness Prince Axel as a witness. The Prince then issued an official statement that he had indeed seen this strange-looking aircraft "rise by its own power."

No matter who gets the credit, each effort served to advance the art. They were all well-covered by the press of the day, and the accounts inspired inventors all over the world. By the early 1920s, there existed half a dozen machines on both sides of the Atlantic that could skitter a few feet above the ground and go approximately in the direction the pilot desired.

Lucky breakthrough

One of the biggest technical breakthroughs in rotary-wing design came to light in postwar Spain, of all places. Juan de la Cierva was a young aviator who had built gliders and airplanes, including a three-engine bomber. On its second flight, the bomber crashed in a low-speed stall, ending a promising fixed-wing career for Cierva. It did not, however, stop his aviation career.

As he thought about the problem of low-speed stall, an idea came to him—an idea whose time was ripe. Instead of depending on the forward speed of the entire aircraft

Figure 96-3 Igor Sikorsky's Second Helicopter

Figure 96-4 Juan De La Cierva's Autogiro With Braced Rotor

for lift, what if the wing was rotated so that it had speed with respect to the air at all times? This, of course, was characteristic of the helicopter, but Cierva saw it somewhat differently.

He had observed that windmills kept rotating even when the wind approached them edgewise instead of straight on and that a significant force could be developed along the axle in this case. With some simple models, he demonstrated that a windmill rotor could replace a wing and develop enough lift to support the aircraft with much less forward speed.

Keeping the rotor spinning in a gentle edgewise breeze without turning it with an engine is called autorotation, and Cierva dubbed his new rotary-wing aircraft the Autogiro (Figure 96-4). (Capitalized and spelled with an *i*—as Autogiro—is Cierva's trademark. Not capitalized and spelled with a *y*— as autogyro—is the convention used here.)

It was not an immediate success.

On the first takeoff attempt, the autogyro rolled over on its side and thrashed the rotor into splinters. Cierva rebuilt the aircraft and experienced the same disappointing result.

With hindsight, the difficulty is not hard to analyze. When a rotor travels edgewise through the air, on one side of the disc the blade is going upwind and on the other side, downwind. This difference in relative air velocity also produces a difference in lifting capability.

Cierva had realized this and had made some provisions for compensation, but obviously not enough. The inadequate provisions were based on experience with the model autogyros, which had flown successfully with no tendency to roll over.

One night, he had taken his wife to see "Aida," but he couldn't keep his mind on the opera. (It might have been different if the opera had been one of those classic aviation works like "The Flying Dutchman.") As he mused about his autogyro problems, he had a flash of inspiration. Suddenly, the difference between his full-scale aircraft and his model was apparent—it was the difference between rigidity and flexibility.

Be flexible

On the aircraft, he had obtained structural integrity by rigidly bracing the blades with wires— just as airplane wings were braced in those days. On the other hand, the model was built with flexible rattan spars, since this type of construction was adequate for model size.

As the rigidly braced autogyro taxied down the runway toward a takeoff, the airspeed seen by one blade changed during each revolution. Since each blade had the same pitch setting—and, therefore, angle of attack— the difference in velocity produced more lift on the blade going upwind, or "advancing," than on the retreating blade. An unbalanced rolling moment was generated, followed by general self-thrashing.

But on the model, the flexible rattan spars could bend up and down. Thus the advancing blade, which had high lift, began to flap upward. As it did, it was also being rotated toward the nose, where the velocity was reduced to the mean value. The retreating blade was undergoing a similar experience except that it was flapping downward as it rotated to a position over the tail.

This flapping produced a climbing condition on the advancing side, decreasing its angle of attack, and created the opposite effect on the retreating side. Flapping equilibrium came when the model's rotor had an angle of noseup flapping just sufficient to compensate for the airspeed difference at each azimuth of revolution. In this condition, the rotor was tilted fore-and aft, and the lift distribution was balanced.

When the opera was over, Cierva knew what he had to do—add flexibility to his full-scale rotor. The simplest solution, he decided, would be to install mechanical hinges allowing the blades to flap just as they had on the model. With this technical breakthrough, Cierva, who had only wanted to develop a non-stalling airplane—not a helicopter— provided the base on which all later helicopter designers would build.

The maturing of the autogyro

While embryonic helicopters struggled through development, their autogyro cousins were filling the airways during the 1930s. With its freely spinning rotor being pulled through the air by a propeller, the autogyro was relatively successful.

Several hundred were built and used worldwide between the two World Wars despite such remarks as "An autogyro is an aircraft that flies with no visible means of support."

Although used in a variety of beneficial roles, something was missing. This emerged from a defense of the autogyro by Harold Pitcaim, one of the most successful of its U.S. builders, just before World War II.

"Slowly, methodically, Pitcaim laid out his analysis of the issues and reasons that, in the long run, the Autogiro had more to offer the average flying citizen than did the helicopter," noted Frank K. Smith in *Legacy of Wings*.

Pitcaim reviewed the ease of maintenance, saying that since the autogyro rotor didn't have to provide both lift and thrust, there were fewer operational problems. Stating that helicopters required many hours of maintenance for each flight hour, he argued that autogyros could be flown for hundreds of hours with only routine periodic maintenance.

He also stated the autogyro "was easier to fly, simpler for the fixed-wing pilot to transition to, could do everything a helicopter could do except hover in still air, and people did not need that, except in special cases."

Figure 96-5 Harold Pitcairn's PA-36

The only problem in this argument was in the phrase "except hover." Hovering was what the military customer needed and was willing to pay for. The last Pitcaim autogyro, the PA-36 Whirlwind (Figure 96-5), was a beautiful aircraft. It did everything an autogyro was supposed to do, but time had passed it by. Only one was built, and it was cut up for its aluminum scrap value during World War II.

Besides the flapping hinge, the autogyro bequeathed to the helicopter a means of controlling the tilt of the rotor-tip path plane and thus the rotor-thrust vector. This system, called "cyclic pitch," is used on all modem helicopters.

The helicopter age dawns

During the time the autogyro was enjoying its limited success, helicopter engineers were not idle. Yet, it must be noted that in 1928, helicopters were still struggling to stay aloft for more than 10 minutes. That year, a Cierva autogyro flew from London to Paris at more than 100 miles per hour— but, again, it couldn't hover.

Figure 96-6 Anton Flettner's Kolibri

By the late 1930s, several helicopters could hover and even fly from point-to-point at reasonable speeds. Two of these designs were by Louis Breguet in France and Igor Sikorsky in the United States— the two successful fixed-wing builders who three decades before had shelved their youthful helicopter efforts. In Germany, Heinrich Focke and Anton Flettner were also flying practical helicopters.

World War II gave the autogyro its final opportunity. The military forces in every nation tried to use them for liaison, artillery spotting, and other duties. The Germans used captive autogyro kites towed by surfaced submarines to extend their viewing horizon, and even the Japanese built more than 200 for antisubmarine warfare.

As a general rule, however, the autogyro proved to have too limited an operational envelope. And, based on the success of recent experimental helicopter prototypes, the military clamored for an aircraft that could hover.

During World War II, military helicopters were developed and production lines were established in Germany and the United States. In both cases, however, they came too late to have much effect on the war. Twenty-four Flettner 282 Kolibris (Figure 96-6) were built before the factory at Munich was destroyed by Allied bombers.

On the other side of Germany, at Berlin, Focke got his Fa 223 (Figure 96-7) into production with an order to produce 400 a month, but had only finished nine when the Russians overran his underground factory and took 30 off the assembly line. Of the nine delivered, only three survived the war.

Figure 96-7 Heinrich Focke's Fa 223

Sikorsky, in the United States, had no such problems. Starting in 1943, he delivered more than 400 R-4s, R-5s, and R-6s to the Allied forces (Figure 96-8). A few saw combat action in the closing months of the Pacific War, but the others were being used for training and development of tactics when victory came—and their immediate reason for being vanished.

Mass production quickly came to a stop at the end of the war, but the idea of vertical flight had caught the imagination of many inventors. Hundreds of prototypes of all sizes and types were built, and many even got high enough to have their pictures taken in the air.

Figure 96-8   Igor Sikorsky's R-5

A trial marriage

One of the most exciting concepts at this time was the marriage of the new field of jet propulsion with the helicopter. Rotor-blade tips travel in the high subsonic-speed range where jet engines are relatively efficient.

By mounting the powerplant at the blade tips, designers could take advantage of this matching, and at the same time, eliminate the heavy and complex transmission required to transmit torque from the engine to the rotor. It also eliminated the tail rotor required to balance that torque.

The resulting reduction in empty weight appeared to allow an order-of-magnitude improvement in the payload-carrying capability of helicopters. This was especially true when very large helicopters were considered. In 1945, paper studies "proved" that the square-cube law as applied to helicopters with mechanical transmissions would limit these aircraft to a gross weight of about 5,000 pounds (2,300 kg).

Figure 96-9 McDonnell's "Little Henry"

All types of propulsion schemes were used, including rockets, ramjets, pulsejets, turbojets, and compressed air or exhaust gasses generated in the fuselage and ducted out to tip nozzles (pressure-jets).

Sizes ranged from the tiny McDonnell ramjet powered "Little Henry" (Figure 96-9) to the giant pressure-jet Hughes XH-17 (see next chapter). At least two of the tip-driven aircraft, the Dutch Kolibri and the French Djinn (Figure 96-10), actually went into production. All others were limited to one or just a few experimental prototypes.

As a class, all the jet-powered helicopters had very poor fuel efficiency, and most of them were also very noisy. To counter these two disadvantages, the designers had two arguments:

• Since jet engines can bum anything, the price of fuel will always be low, and

• People become accustomed to noisy machines. It is not necessary to discuss how these two arguments have fared since then. It should also not be necessary to point out that the upper limit of 5,000 pounds has

Figure 96-10 Sud Aviation's Djinn

long been passed by shaft-driven helicopters. The Russian Mil Mi-26 weighs 123,000 pounds (56,000 kg) when fully loaded.

A turbopower boost

Although the tip-jet scheme came to naught, by 1957 the development of jet engines for fixed-wings resulted in a benefit for helicopters—the turboshaft engine. It was equal in development value to the introduction of flapping hinges.

By placing a turbine behind the jet, the turboshaft engine, which converts jet energy to mechanical energy, was invented. This allowed a straight substitution of a turboshaft for a reciprocating engine. Unlike the tip-jet schemes, the turboshaft's specific fuel consumption is as good or better than the engine it replaced.

In addition, its weight is much less. A modern reciprocating engine weighs about a pound per horsepower, but a modern turboshaft weighs less than a third of this. This is very important to the helicopter which is more weight-sensitive than airplanes.

An increase of weight in an airplane can usually be compensated for by increasing the length of the runway another few thousand feet, but an increase of weight in a helicopter reduces its ability to make a vertical takeoff. Unfortunately, the cost comparison between reciprocating and turboshaft engines is not so rosy.

How many rotors?

Besides the question of what kind of powerplant is best for helicopters, designers also struggled with the questions "How many rotors?" and "How should they be arranged?"

A single shaft-driven rotor produces a torque that must be balanced in some way to keep the fuselage from revolving. The most straightforward way to do this is to use two rotors rotating in opposite directions. This results in helicopters with coaxial, synchropter, tandem, and side-by-side rotor configurations. Variations that flew in the first 50 years even included helicopters with three and four rotors.

Despite the obvious advantages of these self-balancing schemes, most recent helicopters have used a tail rotor to provide good directional stability and control. It is this last advantage that makes most designers accept the power penalty associated with the tail rotor.

The 50 years between Breguet's and Cornu's experiments in 1907 and the dawn of the turboshaft age in 1957 saw the helicopter undergoing major revolutionary changes. By the end of that period, however, many helicopters had configurations that still do not look particularly dated. Comparing the Sikorsky S-62 (Figure 96-11), which first flew in 1957, and the EH Industries EH-101 that first flew in 1987, the two aircraft look remarkably similar. What happened in those 30 years? That's another story.

Figure 96-11 1957 Sikorsky S-62

97

The Hughes XH-17 Flying Crane

Looking back at it, the idea seems preposterous for its time—a giant flying-crane helicopter being seriously considered only six years after Igor Sikorsky first flew his little VS-300. Nevertheless, such a far-out project did get started and almost advanced the state-of-the-art of very big helicopters by 20 years.

Necessity—the mother of invention

As with many projects, the initial spark was provided by someone who saw a promising new solution for a nagging old problem: getting heavy army equipment—tanks, trucks, and artillery—across a river. The perceived solution was the jet-driven helicopter rotor.

Figure 97-1 Hughes XH-17 Flying Crane

At the end of World War II, it was clear that the small helicopters Sikorsky and others were designing and building could be used to transport soldiers and light equipment. But it could be also be "proven" that the square-cube law would prevent such helicopters from carrying anything heavier than a jeep, primarily because the weight of the transmission required to handle the necessary torque would be prohibitive.

Thus the only possible configurations for large helicopters appeared to be those without transmissions—that is, those whose rotors were driven by power sources mounted in the rotor itself rather than being installed in a non-rotating fuselage.

This idea was not new. It had been tried in the 1920s and 1930s by several helicopter designers who had mounted airplane engines with propellers partway out on the rotor blades—without much success, needless to say.

Flames at the blade tips

The first successful development of a transmissionless helicopter was made in the 1940s by Frederick Doblhoff, an Austrian engineer designing a rotorcraft for the German army. His rotor was driven by air pumped from a compressor in the fuselage out to the tips of the rotor blades where it squirted out like water from a lawn sprinkler.

The compressed air did not carry enough energy in itself so kerosene was burned in tip nozzles to provide the required thrust. Reports of the Doblhoff Model WNF 393 V4 pressure-jet helicopter became available in America at the end of the war and were studied with interest by a number of organizations.

Doblhoff, himself was brought to this country by the Air Force to work at the engineering center at Wright Field in Ohio. He was later released to join McDonnell Aircraft where he adapted his rotor design in the development of the XV-1 convertiplane and the Model 120 helicopter.

One of the organizations that studied the pressure-jet rotor was Kellett Aircraft of Philadelphia. Kellett had been the most successful builder of that relatively unsuccessful aircraft, the autogyro, but the company saw that helicopters were the aircraft of the future and so was ready and willing to take advantage of the German ideas. After developing the synchropter XR-8 and XR-10 helicopters based on Anton Flettner's design concepts, Kellett engineers studied the application of the Doblhoff rotor to a large flying crane. Kellett's chief engineer, Lee Douglas, met with Dave Prince, General Electric's vice president for advanced propulsion systems, and worked out a design concept as well as a working relationship for the two organizations.

The project gets started

At that time, the Air Force was responsible for developing and buying all aircraft for the Army, so the next step was a presentation to the Air Force Research and Development Command at Wright Field. This presentation and subsequent negotiations resulted in a July 1946 contract to Kellett to design, build, and test the XH-17—as it was designated by the Air Force.

The design goal was a payload of 20,000 pounds (9,000 kg) and a range of 50 miles (80 km). The contract was to be done in two phases. The first was to be a ground demonstration of the rotor and power plant to show that sufficient thrust could be developed by a rotor that would stay together. The second phase was to be the installation of a cockpit and the helicopter control systems required to convert the ground testbed into a flying machine. Fred Doblhoff was loaned by the Air Force as a consultant and made significant contributions to the project.

A two-bladed rotor configuration was selected. It had a diameter of 130 feet (40 m) and was designed for a helicopter weighing 40,000 pounds (18,000 kg). This resulted in a relatively low disc loading of 66 tons per acre (3 pounds per square foot). The blade was almost six feet wide and the airfoil was a thick NACA 23018, which gave sufficient room for the air ducts that ended in four burners in the trailing edge of each tip.

Design details

To avoid flutter, a rotor blade must carry ballast in its leading edge to ensure that its center of gravity is ahead of its aerodynamic center. Most blades are ballasted with a continuous balance bar in their leading edges, but to save weight the XH-17 had a concentrated weight supported by a boom extending from the leading edge of each blade (Figure 97-2).

The blade was fabricated of extruded aluminum tubes supported with ribs and covered with aluminum skins. It was supposed to be bonded together, but adhesive technology was not far enough advanced to provide satisfactory bonded joints, so the blade was redesigned and built as a riveted structure.

Figure 97-2 Hughes XH-17's Leading-Edge Blade Weights

The hub configuration was based on the Doblhoff design. A central Y duct carried the air through the hub to each blade. The blades, which weighed about 5,000 pounds (2,300 kg) apiece, were mounted to the hub on flapping bearings at about 3.5% of blade radius.

Centrifugal loads were carried from one blade to another by two tension-torsion straps that also supplied the chordwise stiffness needed to prevent ground resonance on a two-bladed rotor. These straps allowed the feathering bearings around the ducts to be designed to provide only rotary motion without carrying axial loads, as most feather bearings did at the time.

Power was supplied by two General Electric TG-180 jet engines modified to act as compressors. Normally this engine had 11 stages of compression. For this application, the last several stages were removed and a scroll duct was attached to pick up the compressed air and direct it to a plenum chamber connected to the rotor by a rotating seal.

This setup could deliver about 1,000 horsepower when ejected at the blade tips. This was less than required, so jet fuel was delivered from a tank in the fuselage through a rotating seal to be burned at the nozzles in the blades' tips. With maximum tip burning, the XH-17 rotor could develop about 3,500 horsepower.

This scheme differed from Doblhoff's solution to the problem of delivering fuel to the burners. He had atomized the fuel in the plenum chamber thus neatly eliminating the rotating fuel seal—but at the same time setting up an explosive situation.

The rotor-control system was unique in that the swashplate and the three massive hydraulic actuators were mounted above the rotor head. The whole rotor was perched about 20 feet in the air on a stilt-like four-legged landing gear.

Things go wrong at Kellett

In 1949 the XH-17 design was completed and fabrication had started when Kellett was forced into bankruptcy. Like many aircraft firms just after World War II, Kellett had felt a need to diversify into the civilian market and had ambitiously chosen refrigerators, freezers, and office furniture. Development problems and material shortages soon overcame the company's limited financial resources and it found itself unable to meet commitments for delivery and financing of these new product lines.

The bankruptcy court appointed trustees who tried to negotiate the sale of Kellett to Fairchild Aircraft Co. This maneuver was, however, considered unacceptable by the Kellett family who would have lost their company by this sale. An alternate solution was to sell the XH-17 as a separate transaction.

Across the country in California, the Aircraft Division of Hughes Tool Co. had been unsuccessfully trying to get back into the aircraft business ever since work on the giant flying boat and the F-11 observation plane had stopped about 1946. During this time, the Hughes engineering team had submitted competitive bidding proposals on fighters, bombers, flying boats, and even missiles—without any notable success.

To find ways to use his engineering team to best advantage, Howard Hughes met with an Air Force general to discuss the situation. It was during this meeting that he was told about the XH-17 project and Kellett's willingness to sell it to avoid bankruptcy. Hughes immediately commissioned a prestigious Philadelphia law firm to negotiate the purchase. Within days, Wallace Kellett had $250,000, which solved his financial dilemma, and Howard Hughes had a helicopter project for his engineers (much to their surprise).

The partially completed helicopter was loaded onto railroad flat cars and shipped to Hughes' plant in Culver City, Calif., where it was set up in the "Cargo Building"—the largest wooden building in the world, where the largest wooden airplane in the world (the Spruce Goose) had been built. Along with the blades came Nick Stefano, and eight other key people of the Kellett XH-17 project team.

The new helicopter engineers joined with the airplane engineers of the Hughes organization, and the combined team completed the detail design and then the fabrication of the parts necessary for the Phase One ground tests. Howard Hughes had paid close attention to the technical details of his fixed-wing aircraft, but left the helicopter engineers strictly on their own.

Talk about pulling pitch!

Ground testing started in March 1950 and by June, 10 hours of rotor time had been accumulated when a near-catastrophic accident occurred. The swashplate failed and permitted the blades to go suddenly to full pitch. This produced a rotor thrust of more than 100,000 pounds, which damaged blade-retention components and the upper airframe structure.

Many parts were beefed up during the resultant redesign. The new swashplate required three of the biggest aluminum forgings made up to that time, and the hub bearing was changed from a roller bearing to a double-row ball bearing.

Even before the repairs had been completed, the Air Force agreed that the conversion of the testbed into a flight vehicle could be started. Since this had been planned from the beginning, it proceeded with a minimum of fuss. A tail boom carrying a two-bladed tail rotor from a Sikorsky H-19 and a horizontal stabilizer were installed. The tail rotor was not needed to balance main-rotor torque as on most helicopters, but was to be used for directional control and to balance the effects of friction in the main-rotor bearings and rotating seals. Tail-rotor power came from an auxiliary transmission driven by the main rotor.

Figure 97-3 Heavy Lifter

Besides the tail rotor, other components came from existing aircraft. The cockpit was from a Waco cargo glider and was installed complete with tow hook. The front landing gear struts and wheels were from a B-25 and the rear gear from a C-54, and a B-29 bomb-bay tank served as the fuel cell.

First flight

Finally, on Oct. 23, 1952, all preliminary tests had been completed and the XH-17 was ready for its first flight. Gale Moore, who was a pilot for Hughes Aircraft Co. (which was a separate company by that time), was "borrowed" to fly the helicopter. Howard Hughes appeared for the first flight and had his picture taken with the key personnel. Even though he was subsequently to spend millions on the development of the Models 300 and 500, this was apparently the last time he was seen at his helicopter company.

The first flight, for about a minute, got to an altitude of about a foot—not untypical. The reason for ending the flight was not the main rotor but the tail rotor. The pilot found the pedal forces required to keep the fuselage from rotating due to bearing and seal friction effects were higher than he liked.

This was because the tail rotor was being used in the opposite sense than when installed on the H-19. This was quickly fixed by the installation of weights that, under centrifugal force, acted to relieve the pedal forces.

Subsequent flights came with fair regularity. The rotor turned at 88 rpm and had a tip speed of 600 feet per second. This meant that the blades were always visible and did not become a blur as they do on smaller helicopters. Many spectators at a distance observed an optical illusion in which the two blades seemed to open and close like a huge pair of scissors.

The predominant noise characteristic was from the tip burners, which produced a wop-wop-wop as they pointed at the observer, who also noticed the flame in the burners flashing at him at the same frequency.

Most flights were made straight down the runway of the Hughes Airport at fairly slow speeds with a fire truck tagging along. Examination of the oscillograph traces from the blade and hub strain gauges in these flights showed that unexpectedly high stresses were being generated at a frequency corresponding to exactly three cycles for each blade revolution or "3P," as the dynamics engineers say.

The measured stresses were not high compared to the capability of aluminum being pulled apart on a laboratory testing machine, but they were high with respect to the fatigue capability of aluminum—that is, its ability to withstand repeated cycles of change of stress.

Fatigue failures had been around for a long time but were not well understood by the general public. When the rear axle of a car failed and the break showed a grainy texture, the mechanic would say, "The steel suddenly crystallized and lost its strength." In aviation, intense interest was focused on fatigue by the disastrous in-flight failure of the pressurized fuselage of the British Comet jet transport in 1955.

Metal fatigue is the result of an accumulation of damage due to repeated stresses above a certain threshold level, called the "endurance limit." The damage is in the form of a crack that usually starts at a "stress riser"— which can be a hole, a notch, a sharp edge, or such a seemingly small item as a scratch, a tool mark, or an imperfection in the base metal. Once the crack starts, it propagates at a rate that is proportional to the amount the endurance limit is exceeded, until the part can no longer carry the load and breaks suddenly.

Breaking a paper clip by repeated bending is a demonstration of the process. The section that breaks last often exhibits the grainy texture that led to the crystallization explanation, but the origin of the failure can usually be seen as a section of smooth surface that resulted when the fatigue crack repeatedly opened and closed on itself.

The structure engineers knew all this, and realized that the XH-17 blade design, with stress risers at each rivet hole, had a very poor fatigue tolerance to the high oscillating stresses being generated at a rate of almost 16,000 cycles per hour!

During the design phase, the NACA scientists at Langley Field in Virginia had been interested enough in the dynamic phenomena associated with this type of helicopter to build a one-tenth scale model of the XH-17 (Figure 97-4) powered with compressed air, primarily to investigate whether the type of unstable oscillation known as "ground resonance" could occur in flight as well as on the ground.

The hover tests of the XH-17 model showed no sign of resonance, but had shown a tendency for the blades to oscillate at 3P. When these same oscillations were experienced in forward flight, the model was installed in the return passage of the Langley 30-by-60-foot wind tunnel and the flight-test experience was duplicated.

Figure 97-4 NACA's One-Tenth Scale Model XH-17

A whirling chain of events

Since it was not practical to redesign the blades at this point, the engineers sought ways of first understanding and then reducing the oscillating stresses. Oscillations at three times each rotor revolution are not uncommon in rotor blades.

If you whirl a length of chain around your head and then someone gives it a sharp vertical rap at the end with a stick, the chain—which gets all its stiffening from centrifugal forces—will oscillate at its natural frequency, which is exactly the square root of 2π or 2.51P. (The details of the solution would be called elegant by a mathematician who uses Bessel Functions to arrive at the answer.)

A rotor blade is not too different from a chain in that no matter how stiff it may appear when standing still, most of its effective stiffness when rotating comes from centrifugal forces. Of course, any additional structural stiffening raises the natural frequency.

It is not surprising, therefore, that one of the natural frequencies of a rotor blade is close to three times the rotational speed, or 3P, and if it is somehow excited at this frequency, it will oscillate at high amplitude.

When a rotor is in forward flight, the aerodynamic asymmetry will produce exciting forces at each integer multiple of rotor speed. For example, the high drag on the advancing tip produces IP excitation. The fact that the blade lift is higher over the nose and tail than to either side produces 2P excitation. The source of the 3P is a little more subtle but can be traced to the effects of cyclic pitch and flapping required to trim the helicopter in forward flight.

For the low forward speeds at which the XH-17 was flying, it was surprising to aerodynamicists at the time that the 3P input was so significant. They now have a little more respect for the effects that even very low forward speeds can have in messing up the inflow patterns though the rotor, and the thought of getting high aerodynamic fluctuations is more readily accepted.

Studies made of blade motion with a hub-mounted camera showed not only 3P blade bending but a corresponding twisting motion that amplified the deflections. These observations led to some detailed analysis of how to change the dynamic characteristics of the blade to make it less sensitive to aerodynamic excitations by installing concentrated weights at various positions along the blade. The analysis was backed up by making similar studies with the wind-tunnel model.

The final result of the analysis and model test was the installation of a 300-pound block of steel in the inboard portion of the balance boom of each blade. The weight at this location increased the centrifugal stiffening and raised the natural frequency of the first flapwise bending mode.

It also had an additional beneficial effect on reducing the coupling of blade twist with blade bending. Flight tests made with this fix showed a 35% to 45% reduction of blade stresses, but by this time it was only of academic interest.

In December of 1955, all flying stopped since the predicted fatigue life of the blades was nearly used up. During the program, the aircraft had flown at a maximum gross weight of 50,000 pounds (23,000 kg) and had achieved a top speed of 70 mph.

Figure 97-5 XH-28 Mockup

The ultimate flying crane?

Embedded in the XH-17 program was a design study for the ultimate flying crane. In 1951, based on glowing predictions for the XH-17, the Air Force awarded Hughes a contract for the XH-28 (Figure 97-5). Its specific design mission was to carry the Army's 52,000-pound (24,000-kg) Sherman tank for 50 miles.

The design was based on the XH-17 with several significant changes, including going from two to four blades and greatly increasing the installed power to handle a design gross weight to 116,000 pounds (53,000 kg). Most important of all, the XH-28 would use bonded titanium for the blades with a minimum of stress risers.

By August 1954, the project had progressed through preliminary design and well into detail design, which included tests of the blade ducts, wind-tunnel tests of the fuselage, and construction of a full-scale mockup.

Then came the money crunch, and just as a severe financial crisis had been responsible for Hughes getting the XH-17 project, another resulted in the loss of the XH-28. The Korean War turned Air Force procurement funds toward production of fighters and bombers, and the Army was asked to take over the financial support of the XH-28.

But the Army had funding problems of its own and decided that it would rather spend its limited budgets on many small helicopters rather than on a few giants. That was the end of the Hughes XH-28 and of flying-crane helicopter development in the United States until Sikorsky unveiled its relatively small 40,000-pound S-64 in 1963.

98 The Lockheed Experience

It was a dream—to build a helicopter that anyone could fly. Yet, such dreams inspire engineers, and following World War II, Lockheed found reasons to give its engineers plenty of encouragement.

During that postwar era, all of the aviation crystal balls predicted swarms of aircraft, but a shortage of runways. In response to this picture, Lockheed embarked on a series of VTOL studies that soon resulted in four flying test beds:

- A propeller-driven tail sitter for the Navy;

- The augmented-jet Hummingbird;

- A "Flying Framework" with six jet engines; and

- A hingeless-rotor helicopter.

The first three projects were relatively short-lived, but the helicopter activity lasted for 15 years—and has influenced work at other helicopter manufacturers ever since.

In the beginning

The sparkplug of the Lockheed helicopter effort was Irven Culver who, though largely self-taught, has the unique capability to intuitively understand complex physical situations and to produce designs that take advantage of those situations. Irv, as he is known to those who worked with him, reasoned that conventional helicopters were too unstable for easy flying and could use some help from the inherent feature possessed by all rotating systems—gyroscopic inertia.

The obvious way to do this was to attach the blades directly to the hub without teetering or flapping hinges, making the rotor into a big gyroscope. This resulted in a hingeless rotor, somewhat misleadingly referred to as a "Rigid Rotor" in the early days. (A less alliterative description involves "flexible blades cantilevered from a hub.")

The use of a hingeless rotor was an innovation but not really a first. The first autogyro built by Juan de la Cierva in the mid 1920s had a hingeless rotor, but forces due to aerodynamic asymmetry rolled it over, prompting Cierva to introduce flapping hinges. The later invention of cyclic-pitch control for autogyros opened the way for removing the hinges, and a hingeless rotor on the Wilford Gyroplane had been briefly tested in the 1930s. Stanley Hiller's first coaxial helicopter also had hingeless rotors.

(A note about nomenclature: By eliminating the flapping and lead-lag hinges, the Lockheed concept yielded a "hingeless rotor," but it still had feathering bearings. Recent designs have also eliminated these bearings and can properly be called "bearing-less rotors.")

Let's build a model

Most modern aircraft projects use wind-tunnel models to help refine the design, but these are of limited use when it comes to studying dynamic stability and control. Culver and the Lockheed team decided that a radio-controlled, free flight model would be much more valuable, and they were not deterred by the fact that no radio-controlled helicopter model had ever flown.

Their model had a five-foot-diameter, two-bladed rotor with fixed collective pitch. Thrust was varied by changing the speed of the McCoy 60 model-airplane engine, which turned the rotor through a combination belt-and-gear drive with an 8:1 reduction ratio. The radio control was a simple on-off system using two channels each for pitch, roll, and throttle.

The tail rotor had four sheet-aluminum blades and was driven with a belt from the main gearbox. It also had fixed collective pitch, so a special technique had to be developed to find its correct thrust for balancing the main-rotor torque. This involved mounting the model on a turntable and running the engine up to takeoff power.

Between runs, the tail-rotor blades were twisted by hand until the model did not rotate the turntable. When this adjustment was satisfied, the operator pulled a lanyard that released the hold-down latches, allowing the model to take off vertically.

The configuration for the first flight attempts was simply a hingeless-rotor helicopter with direct cyclic-pitch control. It was soon discovered that in model size this configuration was too lively to fly by remote control. Late one discouraging day, Irv and his team agreed to add a separate stabilizing gyro.

The nest morning, Irv came in and said, "By the way; the blades must be swept forward, 'to prevent the gyro from diverging." He was right, as subsequent (deliberate) tests showed. The forward blade sweep provided for flapping-moment feedback to the gyro, which became an important element in the concept. With the gyro and the swept-forward blades, flying was easy and gave the confidence required for the nest step—a full-sized prototype.

A semi-skunk works

In July 1958 the team that had designed the model was expanded to five engineers and given a walled-off corner of the experimental flight-test hangar. Their assignment was to design and super-vise the building of a two-place helicopter, using the "Skunk Works" approach proven so successful in the rapid development of the Lockheed P-80 jet fighter just a few years before.

The new project was designated the CL-475 (the 475th preliminary design of the Lockheed California Co.). The two-bladed rotor was essentially the same design as had been flown on the model. The blades were made of wood and had a fixed collective pitch of 7°. Thrust modulation was obtained by changing the rotor speed. Cyclic pitch was achieved through a single spanwise hinge similar to the early Bell rotors.

The CL-475's gyro consisted of a double "lollipop" attached to the blades, making the affair look much like a Hitler servo-rotor. Below the rotor was a conventional swashplate, but instead of solid pitch links, springs connected it to the gyro allowing precessional forces to be transmitted for control.

The fuselage was fabricated primarily of steel and aluminum tubing and covered with fabric— just like a Piper Cub—but the cabin was of molded fiberglass. Power was supplied by a 180-hp Lycoming piston engine working through a Bell Model 47 gearbox. The tail rotor had wooden blades, twisted straps for feathering, and a gyro to help with yaw damping.

As an integral part of the development, Lockheed built a rotor whirl stand using a Mack truck engine and the rear end from a Buick. The rotor was mounted on a framework that was gimbaled so that it was free to pitch and-roll. A cockpit mounted on the device allowed engineers to get a feel for the control characteristics.

In November 1959, just five months from the project's start, the CL-4-75 was put on a covered trailer and taken to a remote corner of Rosamond Dry Lake near Edwards AFB for its first flight. At -that time, Lockheed had no helicopter test pilots, so an conventional helicopters) reported that the ship was "kind of rough." To find out how rough, Irv Culver took a short ride. After landing, Irv was visibly shook up and decreed, "Keep that thing on the ground until we solve that vibration." That turned out to be the beginning of the end for two-bladed hingeless rotors.

Three- and four-bladed wooden rotors were quickly built and tested with much better results. For six months, test flying proceeded under tight Lockheed security, and the good stability and control characteristics soon began to show themselves.

Case in point: Once, an engine problem cut short a flight several miles across the dry lake from the staging base. By the time the engine was fixed, the pilot had left; so instead of towing the CL-475, one of the mechanics (who had a fixed-wing license, but no helicopter time) got in and flew it back. You might say that whereas Bell and Hiller had used gyros to supplement the pilot, Culver's system made the pilot supplementary.

As the success of the first flight program became evident, Lockheed began to devote more and more resources to the project. Gradually, the effort became less of a Skunk Works job and was consolidated into the mainstream engineering organization.

Culver remained as the technical guide, but the administration and budget control were taken over by the Advance Design Division, which was following the Electra turboprop transport and the F-104 fighter at the same time.

Engineers with previous rotary-wing experience (including me) were recruited to work in the existing aerodynamics, design, dynamics, stress, and flight-test departments. Lockheed finally sent one of its own test pilots through helicopter flight school.

By mid-1960, the flight-test operations had been moved closer to Burbank. The farm fields near the Rye Canyon research facility became the test area. Since this was close to a busy highway, sketches and photographs of the CL-475 soon began appearing in local newspapers and aviation magazines.

Figure 98-1 The CL-475

By this time, the CL-475 had evolved through a series of rotor configurations. It now had a rotor with three aluminum blades. The gyro had become a ring, fastened directly to the swashplate, and the springs had been moved from the rotating system to the non-rotating portion of the control system (Figure 98-1).

With some reluctance, the simple, fixed collective, variable rpm concept for thrust modulation had been dropped in favor of the more conventional variable collective pitch and fixed-rpm system. The newly hired aerodynamicists had pointed out that only a limited flight envelope could be achieved with the original system, and the dynamicists had pointed out the dangers from a resonance standpoint of operating over a wide rotor-speed range.

At this point, pilots from the military, FAA, and NASA were invited to fly the helicopter. The CL-475 was somewhat underpowered, but the visiting pilots could do all of the conventional helicopter maneuvers. In addition, they could trim up and fly hands off for a considerable period of time—something which could not be done on any of the operational helicopters of the day.

As a matter of fact, some found the handling qualities almost too good. One Army pilot asked, only half-jokingly, "If you have a bird that any private or general can fly, who needs me?"

As a milestone in the field of hingeless-rotor helicopters, the CL-475 has been given to the Smithsonian Institution for eventual display in the Air and Space Museum.

The XH-51A

In 1961 Lockheed submitted its new rotor concept on a design for the U.S. Army's Light Observation Helicopter (LOH) competition. Although Army pilots had flown the CL-475 and had filed favorable reports, the competition evaluators were not about to go too far out on a limb by awarding Lockheed a winning position. Instead they opted for three rather conventional LOH designs from Bell, Hiller, and Hughes.

Figure 98-2 The XH-51A

The military was impressed enough, however, to award Lockheed a consolation prize in the form of a joint Army/Navy contract to design, build, and test a new research helicopter. This aircraft was to be somewhat bigger and faster than the LOH requirements. The result was the XH-51A (or CL-595) (Figure 98-2). Instead of being built like a Piper Cub, it represented jet-age technology.

Since high speed was a major goal, the head of the design department set the tone by decreeing, "Make it look fast." The result was a streamline fuselage with flush riveting, a retracting-skid landing gear, control rods inside the rotor shaft, and a flush engine-air inlet.

The design did indeed look fast, provided you did not let your eye wander above the fuselage to the rotor system. From an aerodynamicist's standpoint, the hub was a nightmare—but then, as now, the aerodynamicist had little guidance for the rotor designer except to say, "Make all parts small." That bit of advice is generally in conflict with the wishes of the stress and dynamics specialists.

Two XH-51As were built under the initial Army/Navy contract. The design had a three-bladed rotor like the CL-475 and was the first application of the production version of the 500-shp Pratt & Whitney PT-6B turboshaft engine. The gross weight was 4,000 pounds (1,814 kg) and the cabin was big enough for two in the front and three in the back.

An early test of the new rotor system involved installing it in the NASA's 40-by-30-foot wind tunnel at Moffett Field, California for preflight verification. It was probably a good idea, because the rotor came apart early in the test when a leading-edge balance weight squirted out of one blade.

An examination of the wreckage revealed that the bonding material used to glue the bar to the leading-edge skin had taken hold over only about two square inches. From then on, strict attention was paid to quality control and mechanical fasteners were added to hold parts together even if the adhesive bond failed entirely.

In late 1962, the XH-51A made its first flight and soon confirmed the good stability and control demonstrated earlier on the CL-475. Speeds of 140 knots were achieved within four months of first flight.

Curing the shakes

Lockheed's helicopters were more stable and maneuverable than others of their day, but the hingeless-rotor machines did share a common characteristic—they shook! With three blades, they shook especially hard, primarily because on any rotor blade the inherent natural frequency of one of the bending modes is always close to three times the rotor speed.

On a three-bladed rotor, this means that the blades will bend up and down in unison three times each revolution like the ribs of an umbrella being opened and closed. This is particularly bad if one of the natural frequencies of the fuselage is also close to three-per-rev—which it was. On a four-bladed rotor each blade is bending up and down three times per revolution, but they are slightly out of step with each other and so the shaking transmitted to the hub is not so severe.

This understanding eventually led Lockheed to add a fourth blade to the rotor—but not before trying other things first. One was an attempt to stiffen the fuselage with a dorsal fin under the tail boom. Also, the engineers tried to lower the natural frequency of the blades by installing tension cables from root to tip and by installing concentrated weights at strategic locations inside the blades. None of these proved practical.

The most successful solution before going to four blades was to mount the entire cabin on springs fastened to the keel beams of the fuselage—effectively isolating it from the three-bladed rotor.

The first two prototypes were flown for a couple of years in both Lockheed's flight-test program and later in a joint Army/Navy evaluation at the Navy's Patuxent River flight-test center in Maryland.

Not only were excellent flying qualities demonstrated, but the ability to trim with large center-of-gravity offsets was dramatically shown with a flight-test engineer perched at the end of a 15-foot, side-mounted boom. Another demonstrated advantage over conventional helicopters was the ability to maintain good pitch and roll control even at zero load factors.

These demonstrations whetted the appetite of NASA; so it ordered an XH-51A to use for its basic flight research into hingeless-rotor characteristics.

Because of the favorable test results, Lockheed saw the possibilities of a successful commercial venture. Consequently, it built two of the four-bladed helicopters for the company, and in 1966 carried them through FAA certification as the Lockheed Model 286.

After the award of the type certificate, Lockheed had to decide whether to put the design into production. On the positive side was a tremendous interest in the aircraft—fed in part by some spectacular airshow demonstrations of aerobatics that included loops and rolls. On the negative side was Lockheed's lack of dealership and support organizations for non-airline and nonmilitary business.

Robert Gross, who as Lockheed board chairman had promoted the helicopter effort as the start of a new air age, had recently died. Without his strong support, the new management took a cautious approach and said, "Sell it to the military;" so the Model 286 was reconfigured for antisubmarine warfare missions. Despite a high asking price, the marketing effort appeared to be paying off when the Royal Netherlands Navy agreed to order 12 aircraft.

The timing was terrible. Corporate management had just been advised of major losses in Lockheed's shipbuilding, missile, and transport divisions. They need six months to sort out the situation, but the customer could not wait. The plans for Model 286 production were killed.

The two remaining Model 286 demonstrators were used for personnel transport around Southern California for several years and then eventually sold in a non-flying status. After passing through several hands, they were both destroyed in a hangar fire in central California in 1988.

Compounding

As a logical step in the development of high-speed helicopters, the Army in 1963 contracted with several helicopter manufacturers to each convert a pure helicopter into a compound helicopter. Sikorsky used a S-61, Kaman a UH-2, Bell a UH-1, and Lockheed the XH-51A (Figure 98-3).

All of the conversions were done by adding a wing and one or more jet engines. The result of this modification is that the rotor is relieved of most of its lifting and propulsive duties. This eliminates retreating blade stall, which is the most serious limitation to high-speed flight.

Figure 98-3 The Compound XH-51A

One of the big advantages of the hingeless Lockheed rotor over the other rotors used in this program was that it needed no airplane control surfaces. Even with the rotor fully unloaded, it had a high level of control power due to its hingeless design.

The jet engine selected was a 2,600-pound-thrust Pratt & Whitney J-60 in a nacelle salvaged from a wrecked Saberliner. It was mounted on the left side of the fuselage and the wing was tailored to fit. The pilot flew from the right seat, and a pod on the right wingtip contained a battery and flight-test equipment to counteract the weight of the jet.

The jet was satisfactory for experimental flying. But considering that it could suck the fuel tank dry in six minutes of full-thrust operation, it is easy to see why it was not operationally suitable.

Figure 98-4 The AH-56A Cheyenne

Since speed was the objective, setting speed records became a game between the various compounds. At the end of the program, the Bell UH-1 Compound with two jet engines was the slight winner with a speed of 274 knots followed by Lockheed at 263 knots.

The Lockheed XH-51A compound was also used by the Army in a helicopter-detectability study, during which the machine was flown in the nap-of-the-earth at various speeds over broken terrain as scattered observers recorded when they first became aware of its presence. A Model 286 flying at a lower speed was also used in this study. It is not clear what the Army gained from this project, but Lockheed got some spectacular movie footage from both the ground and the cockpits.

The primary result of the entire compound-helicopter program was that the Army obtained enough verification of the concept to include it in its plans for a new aircraft program that eventually resulted in the Lockheed Cheyenne (Figure 98-4).

The Cheyenne

In 1964, the Army sent out a request for proposal (RFP) for an Advanced Aerial Fire Support System (AAFSS). Its primary mission was to provide armed escort for the Army's Boeing Chinook transports (while making quick sorties from the line of flight) and to clear landing zones of enemy opposition, ranging from individual troops to tanks.

To do this effectively, the Army reasoned that the aircraft would have to have performance characteristics on the remote edge of the state-of-the-art. A dash speed of 220 knots, which at that time had only been achieved by jet-assisted compounds, was the most critical requirement. A second requirement was for a hover capability at 6,000 feet and 95°—coincidentally just like a summer day in Cheyenne, Wyo. The third requirement was a ferry range of 2,100 nm, which could take it from California to Hawaii—the longest overwater hop envisioned in a wartime situation.

A crew of two was to handle the flying duties as well as the weapons, which were to consist of TOW antitank missiles, folding-fin rockets, a 30-mm fast-firing cannon with a wide field of fire, and a turret-ed 40-mm grenade launcher (to be quickly interchangeable with a 30-caliber machine gun). The Army also specified that the aircraft should be single-engined—a decision based on a tradeoff evaluation between cost and safety at that time.

The Army saw the airframe as only part of the Advanced Aerial Fire Support System. It also had quite ambitious plans for large advances in fire control, navigation, communications, and even automatic terrain following and formation flying; only some of which have been achieved up to now. The RFP went out to 148 organizations and 12 responded with preliminary designs.

Lockheed bids

Lockheed's proposal was based on scaling the rotor/control gyro concept used on the 4,000-pound XH-51A up to one suitable for the 18,300-pound AAFSS. The engine selected was General Electric's T64 turboshaft rated at 3,400 shp. (During the program, this powerplant was uprated to 3,925 shp.)

Figure 98-5 Tail Pusher Prop on AH-56A Cheyenne

An efficient propeller, instead of a fuel-hungry jet, was to be used for forward thrust. At the beginning of the preliminary design, a decision of where to put the propeller was up in the air—as was the possibility of using more than one. Layouts were made with propellers on the nose, over the wing, at the wing tips, around the tail boom, and at the back end. Even a tandem-rotor helicopter was given serious consideration.

One idea that got as far as the wind tunnel was a pusher propeller with turning vanes to replace the tail rotor. It worked satisfactorily in hover and forward flight—but in rearward and left sideward flight, it just couldn't cope. Finally, a tail pusher propeller with a conventional main/tail-rotor configuration was selected as the "least-worst" compromise (Figure 98-5).

The crew was seated in tandem, with the copilot/gunner in front on a seat that could swivel 220° to each side, as would the telescopic sight just below him. This sight had a laser rangefinder, 1.5-, 4.25-, and 12-power telescopic magnification, and infrared night-vision capability.

The copilot had a full set of flight controls that could be folded away when he was operating the weapons. The pilot had a helmet sight with which he could aim either of the turret-mounted guns, while the copilot fired the other one. The navigation system employed an inertial platform and Doppler radar with linear motion compensation.

The canopy had generously curved panels for streamlining and rigidity. (This was before the Army began insisting on flat canopy panels to reduce sun flashes.)

Lockheed's design could be described as an airplane with a very effective lifting device for low-speed flight . As an airplane in high-speed flight, the rotor could be completely excused from its lifting role as the wing took over. But because of its hingeless characteristics, the rotor could still be effectively used for pitch and roll control—even with little or no lift.

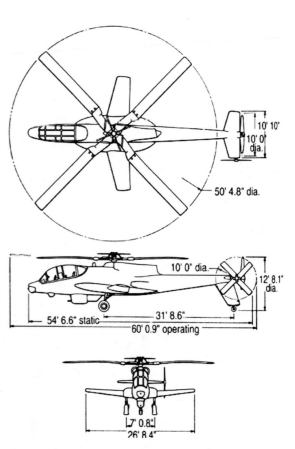

Figure 98-6 Three view of Cheyenne

Don't unload the rotor

Analysis shows, however, that it is a mistake to unload the rotor completely. The wing/rotor combination has the least induced drag operating as a biplane with the rotor carrying some lift, since its "wingspan" makes it a more efficient lifting device than the shorter wing. The amount of rotor/wing lift sharing was determined by the pilot's setting of the collective pitch. Flight tests showed that at high-speeds, the rotor could carry as much as 30% of the aircraft's weight without suffering from blade stall.

The main rotor -was right up-to-date—for the date. It had a titanium, flat "door-hinge" hub for low drag. Centrifugal forces were carried with wire-wound tension-torsion packs. The blades were formed out of stainless-steel spars and outer skin with a honeycomb core. They tapered linearly in thickness from 12% at the root to 6% at the tip and used a "droop snoot" airfoil. Twist on these blades was -5°.

To avoid compressibility penalties at high forward speeds, the main- and tail-rotor tip speeds were modest at 650 feet per second (fps), but the propeller had a tip speed of 900 fps and was the main source of noise on this aircraft.

At the tail

The Hamilton-Standard pusher propeller had three steel-spar fiberglass blades and was driven directly from the main transmission with a large thin-walled tube turning at propeller rpm; it was designed to accept as much power as the engine could develop. There was no way of disconnecting the propeller from the drive system, since the tail rotor was also powered from the same source.

The pilot controlled the propeller pitch with a twist grip on the collective lever. In hover, it was normally set to flat pitch to conserve power, but it could be made to produce positive or negative thrust. Operating the propeller in this manner could be used to change the hover attitude of the fuselage as much as 10°—a valuable feature for aiming rockets.

An advantage often claimed for this type of configuration is that the propeller can be used for high forward acceleration from hover. This has to be taken with a grain of salt. The Cheyenne propeller could develop about 2,000 pounds of static thrust, thus providing an acceleration of about 0.1 G. Tilting the main rotor by 45°, on the other hand, could provide an acceleration of 1.0 G and would be a more likely pilot option.

One of the problems inherent in the compound helicopter configuration is that when entering autorotation at high speed, the wing tends to produce so much lift that the rotor is starved for the necessary thrust to keep it spinning. All of the jet-powered compounds had special devices to reduce wing lift when going into autorotation to avoid this problem.

The Cheyenne needed no such provision. Instead, the pilot could reduce the pitch of the propeller— thus converting it into a windmill that could extract energy out of the passing air stream. This could keep the entire drive system turning until the aircraft had slowed down to about 80 knots, at which speed it was in conventional autorotational descent. Putting the propeller into negative pitch in flight was also a spectacular way to produce a rapid deceleration, without the usual noseup flare, a maneuver which might be useful in air-to-air combat.

The tail rotor was conventional. To clear the propeller, it was mounted on the left tip of the horizontal stabilizer and was driven from a gearbox in the propeller drive system. The tail-rotor blades were untwisted and used a 6% thick airfoil.

The main landing gear retracted (almost) into the fuselage sponsons, and a tail wheel was chosen instead of a nose wheel to minimize interference with the weapons and the sight.

Lockheed wins!

From the 12 proposals received, the competition evaluators chose two companies to continue with contracted design studies. One was Lockheed and the other was Sikorsky, which had proposed a winged helicopter with a powerful tail rotor that could pivot 90° to serve as a pusher propeller.

The design studies took six months and then each company made a formal proposal to develop their concept by building and testing 10 developmental prototypes. Despite Lockheed's lack of helicopter production experience, the Army's Source Selection Board chose Lockheed over Sikorsky based on the anticipation of lower costs, earlier availability, and less technical risk.

The AH-56A program was officially underway in November 1965 with a goal of one year until rollout. The projected flyaway cost for production vehicles at the time was $1.5 million.

Lockheed had considerable experience in designing and building both large and small experimental aircraft, so a team was rapidly put together around a nucleus of helicopter people augmented by others selected from the various fixed-wing projects. The entire rotary-wing effort was moved to a pair of hangars that were leased at the Van Nuys, Calif., airport, 10 miles west of Lockheed's main plant in Burbank.

A large, rotor whirl tower was built in a natural bowl at Rye Canyon so that the rotor's structural integrity and hover performance could be checked before being installed on the aircraft.

The first Cheyenne off the line (1001) was the ground-test vehicle (GTV). It was tied down in "Fort Cheyenne," a circular stockade built of two heavy plank walls holding eight feet of gravel between them—just in case anything happened. Here, the GTV spent many hours running to check out the drive system.

The next ship off the line (1002) was the first flight-test vehicle. It lifted off for the first time in September 1967. Considering the complexity of the aircraft, initial flight-testing went very well. Of course, as the flight envelope was expanded through cautious testing, some technical problems were encountered—but were generally systematically surmounted as in any well-run helicopter development.

Solving problems

One of the problems was an offshoot of the high control power of the hingeless rotor. A pilot could tip the aircraft over on the ground if he inadvertently moved the control stick while doing something else in the cockpit. This was fixed by engaging a heavy stick-centering spring whenever the ship was heavy on its landing gear.

Another ground-only problem caused a rollover accident following an autorotational landing. This occurred as the rotor was slowing down and passing through about 70% of its normal speed. At this point, the inplane natural frequency of the blade was in resonance with twice the rotor speed—or 2P. At the same time the pilot was holding some cyclic pitch to make the rotor flap once per revolution—or IP. The combination of inplane and flapwise bending moments generated an upsetting processional moment on the gyro.

After analyzing what had happened, the engineers dubbed this the "IP X 2P" phenomenon. It was partially solved by the spring-centering device described above and completely solved by a modification of the control system (to be described later) that isolated the gyro from the inplane moments.

Sideward flight

Another problem was the inability to maintain steady left sideward flight in the 10-knot to 30-knot range. At this speed, the tail rotor operated in the "vortex-ring state," and its erratic thrust variations were accentuated by the interference from the wake of the main rotor. The cure was to reverse the tail rotor's direction of rotation so that the blade closest to the main rotor was going up rather than down. (At about the same time, this change was incorporated for the same reason on a number of other helicopters, including the Bell UH-1 and AH-1 and the Russian Mil Hind. Even today there is no good explanation for the phenomenon.)

A much more serious problem concerned the fact that the rotor was "talking" to the gyro in flight in ways not seen on the smaller Lockheed helicopters. According to simple theory, the gyro was supposed to respond only to gust-caused attitude changes, pilot inputs, and rotor moments due to flapwise blade bending. Two other gyro inputs were soon identified: cyclic variations of aerodynamic pitching moments on the airfoil section, and drag and inertial forces near the tip acting through a moment arm provided by outboard flapwise blade bending.

These extraneous inputs worked against the inherent stability of the rotor and gyro system in some flight conditions. One of the results was a loss of maneuver stability at high speeds, as evidenced by an unstable pitchup tendency that occurred when the pilot tried a pullup.

A separate but related effect of the unwanted gyro motion was the so-called "half p hop," which also manifested itself at high speeds. This was a variation of rotor thrust which occurred every other revolution.

It led to the fatal crash of ship 1003 in March 1969 when the hop became so bad that it caused the pilot's left arm to operate the collective lever to an ever-increasing amplitude against his will. This uncontrollable action continued until the divergent flapping motion caused a blade to come crashing down through the canopy roof.

Subsequent investigations with a Cheyenne seat mounted on a shake table told the story. The dynamics of the seat and the pilot's left hand on the collective lever set up a classical resonance situation at the exact frequency of the half p hop.

As a result of this accident, Lockheed incorporated a collective pitch lock, stiffened the blades and control system, and changed the rotor geometric parameters to stabilize the half p hop. It also brought about a policy of doing envelope-expansion flight from the front cockpit where the swiveling gunner's seat was replaced by a downward ejection seat.

Cure Notice

The accident triggered an action within the Department of Defense (DoD) and in less than a month, DoD gave Lockheed a "Cure Notice" that essentially said: "Cure all of your technical problems or else."

The "or else" was the cancellation of the production contract for 375 helicopters for which the long-lead items had already been ordered and the first production fuselage was in the jig. DoD cited problems already in the process of being solved, those recently identified but not yet worked on, and potential problems that could only have been anticipated by looking into a crystal ball. Lockheed had 15 days to prepare a response.

In a flurry of activity, Lockheed engineers documented the fixes in progress, invented solutions for the new problems, and rationalized why there would be no other surprises. The answering document, however, wasn't convincing enough and the production contract was canceled—while leaving a reduced-scope development contract in force.

(It was a dark time for Lockheed. The USAF's giant C-5A transport, the L-1011 transport, and the shipbuilding programs were also in trouble. This was the climate that also killed the Model 286 production plans.)

To monitor the remaining Cheyenne program, the Army appointed a blue-ribbon committee of government and industry specialists to offer constructive criticism. One of their recommendations was to test the

AH-56A in NASA's 40-by-80-foot wind tunnel. Besides dynamic investigations, it was expected that good information on fuselage drag and on the forward flight performance of the main rotor, tail rotor, and propeller could be obtained.

As a result, Aircraft 1010 was modified to permit its being mounted on a three-strut support at the landing-gear attachment fittings. Fuel was supplied to the engine from a tank below the tunnel floor. Electrically operated actuators were installed in the control system and two test pilots were assigned the job of "flying" the ship—one to control pitch and the other roll.

The pilots were given displays of rotor-shaft bending in pitch and roll to use in judging how much cyclic pitch to use. They also had the total lift and drag from the wind tunnel balance to use in adjusting the collective pitch of the main rotor and the propeller to put the aircraft into a "trimmed flight" condition. Shakedown runs without the rotor blades installed were first made to check test procedures and to identify any resonances in the support struts that might be excited by operational rotor speeds.

Following this checkout, the blades were installed and expansion of the test envelope began. At about 80 knots, and as the rotor thrust was being increased to a planned test value of 20,000 pounds, the rotor began to flap back, indicating that the stabilizing blade-bending feedback to the gyro was being overpowered by other unstable effects.

It is still somewhat controversial whether the pitch pilot could have suppressed the rearward tilt with prompt control motion, but he did not and the flapping quickly became divergent as the blades sliced into the tail boom. An observer saw the light-green zinc chromate primer on the inside of the tail boom skin suddenly contrasting against the olive drab paint on the outside.

This artistic display lasted only the fraction of a second it took for the blades to saw all the way through the boom. The entire helicopter then disappeared down the tunnel with a flash of flame and a loud noise as one of the 20-pound tip weights from the rotor was flung through the upper part of the control room. Ship 1010 was found upside down and considerably battered at the first set of tunnel turning vanes.

A tunnel-only accident

The analysis of the accident showed that the same blade-pitching moments (later identified as being primarily nose-down airfoil section moments due to retreating blade stall) and tip-deflection effects that accounted for the pitchup tendency in high-speed flight had also shown up in the tunnel at only 80 knots.

The phenomenon was more serious in the wind tunnel, since the fuselage was held firmly and could not be moved out of the way by rotor moments, as it would be in flight. Also, the cues to the pilot watching the tunnel instrumentation were much weaker than he would have gotten from the seat of his pants.

Thus an accident happened in the wind tunnel that would not have happened in flight. On the other hand, the accident involving half p hop on 1003 could not have been duplicated in the tunnel, since the supports would have prevented the plunge motion that was the key to that tragic event.

The need to understand the rotor and gyros's complex dynamics prompted development of a very sophisticated computer program that could predict the in-flight forces on the blades and their deflections under these loads. The program went through several phases of growth before final verification. Dubbed REXOR, it was used for several years by military and NASA engineers to investigate the rotor dynamics of new designs.

Long before the two accidents, design studies had been started to solve the unstable gyro-feedback problem. These resulted in the gyro being moved from the top of the rotor to below the transmission. It was also made smaller and lighter and was provided with a feedback path that could only sense the blade-root bending moments on which the original concept had been based.

Known as the Advanced Mechanical Control System (AMCS), this gyro design controlled the blade cyclic pitch through irreversible servos. (An Advanced Electronic Control System was also being designed just in case the AMCS didn't work.) One of the prototype airframes was equipped with AMCS and put through an extensive flight-test program both by Lockheed and the Army.

Everything is fixed

By November 1970, the program had been completed to everyone's satisfaction. Not only had the flying qualities been verified with no bad characteristics, but several other impressive milestones had been passed: Cheyenne had flown to 215 knots in level flight and to 245 knots in a dive; high-speed maneuvers had included pullups to 2.6 Gs and pushovers to -0.2 Gs.

High control power, quick response times, and low cross coupling provided the aircraft with excellent handling qualities. Pitchup tendencies and rotor-blade contamination of control characteristics had been eliminated. Other features of the hinge-less rotor—namely, wide center-of-gravity range, control capability at low load factors, and low tip excursions during maneuvers—had been preserved with the AMCS control system.

Tests at the Army's Yuma Proving Grounds showed that the weapon accuracy was excellent. The first shot from the 30-mm cannon could consistently hit a 10-inch bull's-eye at a range of two miles. The Hughes Aircraft TOW missile system also lived up to its advanced billing.

A typical demonstration of the combined automatic navigation and fire-control system consisted of peeking over the brow of a hill, acquiring a target in the gunner's sight, dropping back behind the hill, flying up the valley three miles, and then popping up again with the sight still dead on the target—all without the gunner having touched a thing.

Not to be

With the dynamic problems solved and the other systems working well, Lockheed was ready for the production contract to be reinstated. It wasn't that simple, however. From the start of the AAFSS program, the Army had a problem within DoD. Close-air support of ground troops had always been an Air Force mission and the Air Force was busily preparing for its own design competition—which eventually resulted in the Fairchild A-10 jet. For the Air Force, the problem was aggravated by the potential high speed of the Cheyenne and its ability to make strafing runs—strong points reserved for the A-10.

In addition, Lockheed's projected costs for a production run had increased substantially, from $1.5 million in 1966 to well over $3 million in 1971. In response to these factors, the Army was already contemplating a new set of requirements for a helicopter to do its attack mission.

The most dramatic change was a new concept of the attack helicopter's role in combat. Based on Vietnam experience, the service decided that high speed was not essential. For this reason, the 145 knots of a conventional helicopter (which wouldn't step on Air Force toes, incidentally) became the speed requirement. Also since survivability was a prime consideration, the doctrine that two engines are better than one had been accepted.

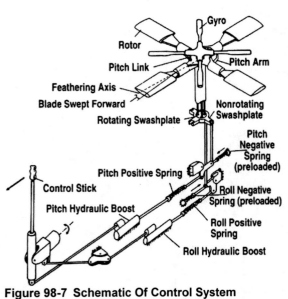

Figure 98-7 Schematic Of Control System

When Lockheed heard of the new ground rules, it proposed a twin-engine, propellerless Cheyenne— but it was too late. The Army had decided to start from scratch with the Advanced Attack Helicopter (AAH). That competition began in 1973 and although Lockheed submitted a best-effort proposal, the two development contracts went to Bell for the AH-63 and to Hughes for the AH-64—the eventual winner.

The remaining Cheyennes were either scrapped, used for vulnerability studies, or sent to museums. One is on display at the Army's Transportation Museum at Fort Eustis, Va., and another at the Army's Aviation Museum at Fort Rucker, Ala. Many Cheyenne engineers went to other rotorcraft manufacturers—taking with them the valuable lessons learned.

Lockheed's helicopters were unique in their combination of stability and control characteristics that gave an extraordinary good machine-man matching. The key to this was in the rotor and control system shown schematically in Figure 98-7 as it was installed on the XH-51A.

Stability

The stability of the aircraft is illustrated in Figure 98-8 as a sequence in which the trimmed helicopter in hovering flight experiences a sudden disturbance applied to the fuselage, tilting it nose-up. The gyro, with its high rotational inertia, tends to stay fixed in space—since it is only loosely anchored to the aircraft through a pair of soft spring assemblies.

Each assembly consists of a positive spring that tries to restrain the gyro and a preloaded "negative" spring that tries to upset the gyro. By a careful matching of parameters, the two can be made to give essentially no resistance to stabilizing gyro motions—while allowing precession forces to be applied as the result of control inputs from the pilot acting on the positive spring.

Since the gyro is attached directly to the control system, it introduces cyclic pitch into the rotor blades. The resultant flapping bends the tip-path plane into an S-shape, producing a rotor moment that is in the direction to force the rotor shaft back into its original hover position.

When this is achieved, there is no more cyclic pitch and thus no more rotor moment. The result is that the helicopter is essentially locked to the horizon (as represented by the gyro) by a big spring (as represented by the rotor).

This analogy is good for short-time motions but should be modified to explain the effects of changes in trim. The reason for the difference is the deliberate feedback of a small portion of the blade-bending moments to the gyro.

This is accomplished by sweeping the blades slightly forward so that an upward component of blade bending becomes a blade noseup torsional moment and acts on the gyro to process it in the direction of reducing the bending moment.

The main reason for this feature is to provide the ability to trim the rotor at high forward speeds where large cyclic pitch is required to equalize the lift between the advancing and retreating sides of the rotor—but little or no moment is required to balance the effects of external aerodynamics or center-of-gravity offsets.

For short-time disturbances, the natural position of the gyro is where it was at the beginning of the disturbance. For longer periods, the natural position of the gyro is where it produces no blade bending and thus no rotor moment—unless deliberately held off this position by the pilot.

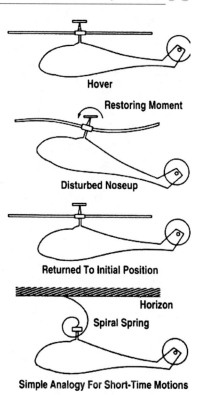

Figure 98-8 Illustration Of Stability

Control

The gyro-controlled rotor makes the helicopter very stable but would not ensure good flying qualities if the aircraft were so single-mindedly stable that the pilot could not maneuver it. Making the helicopter maneuverable is the other outstanding characteristic of the Lockheed system.

Looking at Figure 98-7, note that moving the control stick forward compresses the positive spring in the pitch system, putting an up force on the left-hand side of the non-rotating swashplate. This force is transmitted up to the gyro, causing it to process nose-down. The spring assembly in the roll system would try to oppose this motion, except that the near balance of positive and negative springs gives the assembly a very soft spring rate.

The nose-down precession of the gyro carries the swashplate with it and produces the same change in blade pitch as it would on a conventional helicopter, with a resultant nose-down blade flapping and pitching motion which the pilot wanted when he pushed forward on the stick.

Because of the large effective hinge offset produced by the hingeless-rotor design, the moment produced at the top of the mast is larger than can be achieved with conventional rotors. This gives a high value of control power, but one moderated by the stabilizing influence of the gyro. The result is a very quick attainment of a constant pitch or roll rate directly proportional to stick displacement with little cross-coupling—one of the most desirable types of control response in any manned vehicle.

The Advanced Mechanical Control System (AMCS) was the result of learning that the gyro should not be subjected to extraneous moments. It used a high-speed gyro buried in the structure below the rotor. A special feedback path was used that could only transmit flapwise bending moments to the gyro. This returned the system to its original concept by eliminating the upsetting effects of airfoil pitching and inplane bending moments.

(My thanks to Al Yackle, former Lockheed design engineer, who contributed his memories to this story.)

99 Attack Helicopters*

*Reprinted from Vertical Flight: The Age of the Helicopter, Eds. Walter J. Boyne and Donald S. Lopez (Washington, D.C.: Smithsonian Institution Press 1984), 133-143, by permission of the publisher. Copyright 1984 Smithsonian Institution.

Not long after helicopters began to be shot at in combat, aviators started to improvise defensive shoot-back-to-keep-enemy-heads-down capabilities. This was first done with handheld weapons, but normal evolution brought the development of weapons that the pilot could fire by aiming the helicopter. The French began this development in their battles with Algerian rebels in the 1950s.

Figure 99-1 Bell Sioux Scout

Once the defensive capability had been provided, it was only logical to see the possibilities of using these wonderfully maneuverable aircraft for supporting ground forces, for escorting other helicopters, and for independent attack missions. This was done first by installing guns and rocket launchers on helicopters that had been designed for other purposes. Later, machines whose narrow fuselage configuration clearly identified them as attack helicopters were developed. It is this latter type that is the subject of this discussion.

In the United States, the development of the attack helicopter has had two purposes, one for escort and for soft-target suppression, as in the jungle warfare in Southeast Asia; the other was to establish the capability to find and destroy heavy armor such as tanks, for which the most likely theater of operation was Europe.

The first purpose was satisfied by quickly modifying existing helicopters into suitable attack configurations; the second is being met by developing new helicopters with advanced characteristics.

The Bell Sioux Scout

The first example of a helicopter modified for the attack mission was the Bell Sioux Scout, a redesigned Model 47 with a 260-hp piston engine (Figure 99-1). The Scout was built as a testbed to study a need then beginning to be recognized in Vietnam.

For this helicopter, first flown in 1963, several innovations were developed that became standard features on many subsequent attack

Figure 99-2 Bell AH-1 Prototype

Figure 99-3 Bell AH-1G Cobra

Figure 99-4 Bell AH-1J Twin-Engine Cobra

Figure 99-5 Bell AH-1T Twin-Engine Cobra

helicopters. A two-man crew sat in tandem in a narrow fuselage, each man having the best possible field of view. The copilot-gunner was in front and the pilot above and behind him.

A machine gun was mounted in a turret in the nose. The copilot-gunner aimed the gun using a telescopic sight. His turret control was located where a cyclic stick would normally be, but since he was sometimes expected to serve as copilot, he was given a short cyclic stick located to his right as a side-arm controller.

By using a twisting motion of the hand, he could also use this stick as a directional control. This eliminated the need for rudder pedals, but pilots had trouble controlling direction precisely with this system, which has not since been used by Bell Helicopters.

The Huey Cobra

With the Sioux Scout experience behind them, Bell embarked on a similar program as a private venture by modifying its much more powerful UH-1B, nicknamed the "Huey." The heart of the helicopter—the rotors, the engine, and the drive system—was saved, and a thin fuselage was designed around it. The design work was begun in early 1965, and the first flight was made the following September.

The original speed goal was 175 knots. To achieve this, the first prototype was built with retracting skid landing gear (Figure 99-2). On later versions, however, a fixed skid gear was used. This decision was made because, although the retractable gear had less drag than the fixed gear and did increase airspeed, the offsetting weight-to-performance penalty was too great.

A compensating drag-reduction feature was the elimination of the rotor-mounted stabilizer bar that had been a feature of all previous Bell designs. Instead, a stability and control augmentation system (SCAS), consisting of a "black box" with gyros and solid-state electronics, was used to achieve even better handling qualities.

It was the right aircraft at the right time. The U.S. Army placed an order for 529 of the AH-1G "Cobras" (Figure 99-3). By August 1967, the first of them was in action in Vietnam.

The U.S. Marine Corps procured and used a few AH-1Gs, but as an "army" aircraft, it lacked two important features for amphibious operations: twin-engine reliability for operation over water and a rotor brake to keep the rotor from wind milling when tied down to the deck of a ship.

These deficiencies were remedied in the AH-1J Sea Cobra with 1,290-shp Pratt & Whitney T400 twin-pac engines and with a rotor brake (Figure 99-4). The Marines began taking delivery of this design in 1969.

During the early 1970s, Bell built two testbed Model 309 King Cobras—one single-engine Cobra and one twin-engine Cobra—for increased payload and higher performance. The King Cobra was evaluated by the Marines and became the forerunner of the Marine AH-1T (Figure 99-5)

The first Blackhawk

The obvious need for attack helicopters during the Vietnam conflict encouraged Sikorsky to try to duplicate the Bell Huey Cobra program by modifying an existing cargo helicopter. For a prototype, they combined the rotors and drive system of the S-61 with an airframe consisting of a new fuselage and a generous wing to help the rotor in maneuvers and to carry external stores. The wing included dive brakes, which could be used to decelerate quickly or to assist going into autorotation at high speed.

Figure 99-6 Sikorsky Blackhawk

Power was supplied by two General Electric T58 turboshaft engines rated at 1,500 shp. The fuselage, while narrower than that of the S-61 could still carry eight fully equipped soldiers. The resultant design was designated the S-67 Blackhawk (Figure 99-6).

Design work was begun in August 1969 and the first flight was made just a year later. During the next four years, the aircraft demonstrated its capabilities. In the process, it set an official speed record of 192 knots. It was one of the first helicopters to do loops, rolls, and "split Ss" as part of routine public flight demonstrations.

Sikorsky obtained several government contracts to evaluate specific S-67 features, but customers were not attracted. The effort ended with the crash of the prototype in 1974. The program was over, but the name, Blackhawk, was saved for use on a later Sikorsky helicopter—the Army's H-60 utility transport (which is the Black Hawk).

The tankbusters

The year 1962 saw both the beginning of the American involvement in Vietnam and the U.S. Army's Howze Board report recommending that the Army develop an attack helicopter to provide close-in support and antitank capabilities. For this mission, the Army staff" recommended procuring an interim attack helicopter, such as the Bell Sioux Scout, based on an existing off-the-shelf design.

The secretary of the Army, however, rejected this approach and directed the staff to lift its sights to a more advanced system. Thus in 1964, a request for proposal (RFP) was issued for an Advanced Aerial Fire Support System (AAFSS).

Besides seeking out and destroying enemy tanks, the AAFSS was expected to provide armed escort for the Army's Boeing Chinooks, while making quick sorties from the line of flight, and to clear landing zones of opposition.

To do this effectively, the aircraft required performance on the remote edge of the state-of-the-art. A dash speed of 220 knots, which at that time had been achieved only by jet-assisted compound helicopters, was the most critical.

A second requirement was hover capability out of ground effect at 6,000 feet at a temperature of 95° F. This was expected to cover the worst possible combinations of altitude and temperature that the aircraft would see in worldwide operations.

The third requirement was for a ferry range of 2,100 nm, which would allow the aircraft to fly from California to Hawaii—the longest overwater flight envisioned in a wartime situation.

A crew of two was to handle both the flying and the weapons, which were to consist of TOW antitank missiles, a 30-mm fast-firing cannon with a wide field of fire, and a 40-mm grenade launcher that was to be readily interchangeable with a 7.62-mm machine gun.

The Army also specified that the aircraft should only have a single engine—a decision based on an evaluation of the trade-off between cost and safety at the time. The Army saw the airframe as only part of the AAFSS. The service also had ambitious plans for large advances in fire control, navigation, communications, and even automatic terrain following.

The Cheyenne

The request went out to 148 organizations, and 12 responded with preliminary designs. From these, two companies were chosen to continue with contracted design studies. One was Lockheed. The other was Sikorsky, which had proposed a winged helicopter with a powerful tail rotor that could pivot 90° to serve as a pusher propeller.

The design studies took six months. Each company then made a proposal to develop its concept by building 10 preproduction prototypes. Lockheed won, and the AH-56 Cheyenne program was officially underway in November 1965.

Because of the aerodynamic limits on helicopter rotors, the 220-knot speed goal was too high for a conventional helicopter, so the AH-56 was designed as a compound helicopter. This means simply that it was an airplane with a wing and a propeller to which an effective lifting device—the rotor—had been added for flight at hover and low speeds.

At high speed, the wing and propeller provided the necessary lift and propulsion force. The main rotor was used in conjunction with the tail rotor to provide pitch, roll and yaw control, and to replace the aerodynamic controls found on conventional airplanes (Figure 99-7).

Lockheed had entered the helicopter field only a few years before, with a radical concept involving the combination of a hingeless rotor and a rotor-mounted control gyro. This gave excellent flying qualities on two small helicopter designs. It was primarily this radical concept that

Figure 99-7 Lockheed AH-56 Cheyenne

attracted the attention of the AAFSS Source Selection Board of the Army.

On the Cheyenne, however, two years of flight test showed that the rotor-mounted control gyro, while working well on small helicopters, could not be used satisfactorily on this larger machine. The technical problems were eventually solved by moving the gyro to an interior location. The Cheyenne then demonstrated level flight at 215 knots, a dive speed of 245 knots, and high-speed maneuvers.

By November 1970 a successful flight-test program had been completed, but in the meantime political, financial, and military considerations had combined to create an unhealthy climate for the Cheyenne. The Army was contemplating a new set of requirements for a helicopter to undertake the attack mission. High speed was not deemed essential, and the conventional helicopter's 145-knot speed became the new cruise-speed requirement. Also, Army doctrine now called for two engines, to improve aircraft survivability in combat.

Lockheed proposed a twin-engine, propellerless Cheyenne, but the Army had decided to start from scratch with the Advanced Attack Helicopter (AAH). The competition began in 1973, and although Lockheed submitted a proposal, the two development contracts went to Bell and to Hughes. (A more detailed discussion of the Cheyenne program is in Chapter 39.)

The Apache

The Bell AH-63 and the Hughes AH-64 were designed to meet the AAH requirements. The primary mission was to find and destroy tanks with as many as 16 guided missiles. Neither bad weather nor darkness was to detract from the mission capability.

In addition to the missiles, the aircraft was to have a turret-mounted 30-mm cannon for targets less well armored than tanks and the ability to carry up to 76 2.75-inch folding-fin unguided rockets. A limitation on size was that two of the helicopters were to be transportable in the nine-foot-high cargo compartment of the C-141 transport airplane.

The performance goals represented a relaxation from those for which the Cheyenne had been designed: a cruise speed of 145 knots instead of a dash speed of 220; a hot-day hover altitude of 4,000 feet instead of 6,000 (although a power margin for vertical climb was also required for the AAH); and a ferry range of 800 nm instead of 2,100.

On the other hand, the potential for survival in combat was to be improved with two engines instead of one, with all components designed so that minimum damage would be done by a 23-mm shell and no single 12.7-mm (50-caliber) round could cause enough damage to prevent safe flying. In the case of a crash, the crew was to be able to survive a vertical impact of 42 feet per second, or 29 miles per hour.

Figure 99-8 Bell's AH-63 For AAH Competition

While both of the candidate helicopters were designed to meet the same requirements, their physical appearance—reflecting the design philosophies of Bell and Hughes at the time—were quite different. Bell used the two-bladed main and tail rotors as it had on the Huey series (Figure 99-8) while Hughes put four blades on each. Bell used a tricycle landing gear with a nose wheel, while the Hughes design had a tail wheel.

Bell mounted the machine-gun turret in the nose with the sight on the belly, while Hughes reversed the placement. In each aircraft, the crew was seated in tandem, but Bell chose to put the pilot in the front seat instead of the rear as it had in its Huey Cobras—and as its Hughes competitor did.

Apache AH-64 With Stabilator

A significant difference that could not be determined by looking at the two designs was the approach to development—and later to production. Bell relied on its own extensive manufacturing experience and capability to make most of the components itself. Hughes chose to do the preliminary design of the components, but to team with firms of proven expertise in the various fields for the necessary development testing and building. In the process, Hughes acted as the responsible integrator of systems and the assembler.

Each company built a ground test vehicle (GTV) for testing the drive and control systems, and two flight-test aircraft. The first Bell flight ship was lost in a landing accident, so the ground-test vehicle was converted to take its place.

The Army accepted all four flight prototypes and tested them extensively for four months at Edwards AFB in the California desert. In December 1976, the Army declared the Hughes AH-64 to be the winner. Even as the loser, the Bell AH-63 served a useful purpose. One was used in a controlled crash test to demonstrate that helicopter designers could indeed make a crash at 42 feet per second survivable.

As the winner, the AH-64 was ordered into Phase Two, in which three more test aircraft were built for development of the airframe and its associated systems. At this time, the Army changed the primary weapon system from the wire-guided TOW missile to the laser-guided Hellfire. The goal of the Phase Two development contract was to integrate all the necessary systems into the helicopter before ordering it into production.

The airframe was nearly in its final form except for some details that were changed as problems came to light in flight tests. Two changes, obvious to even casual observers, were made:

• The main blades tips were swept back, and

• The horizontal stabilizer was changed from a fixed surface on top of the fin to a movable surface at the bottom.

The first change was prompted by higher-than-anticipated blade loads at high speed caused by operation of the advancing tip at high Mach numbers. Sweeping the tip relieved this aerodynamic problem, just as sweeping the wings of a jet aircraft allows it to fly faster.

The horizontal stabilizer was changed from a T-tail to a stabilator configuration to minimize an unfavorable interference between the main-rotor downwash and the surface that had caused high dynamic loads in forward flight (Figure 99-9).

Figure 99-9 Apache AH-64 With T-Tail (above) and stabilator (below)

A bigger task than modifying the airframe was the integration of the sophisticated avionics systems for fire control, navigation, night vision, and communications. As in many modern military aircraft, the investment in these systems was considerably more than in the basic airframe that carries them to where they are to be used.

During the Phase Two program, extensive tests of the helicopter and of all the systems using the GTV and the five flight aircraft were made. Both Hughes and Army pilots and engineers participated in these tests, which included many hours of high-power running on the drive system, blade-deicing tests in the middle of Minnesota winter, air-conditioning tests in the middle of an Arizona summer, live firing of all weapons, night and bad-weather flying, and two months of remote-base operation with maintenance done exclusively by Army personnel.

Fulfillment of the Phase Two development contract in 1982 led to the award of a production contract for 11 helicopters in the first year's purchase. At that time the helicopter was given its Indian name, "Apache" (Figure 99-10).

To produce these and subsequent aircraft efficiently, the Army and Hughes agreed that a new factory was needed, since the Culver City plant was busy making the Model 500 civil helicopters and did not have enough capacity to set up a modern assembly line for the Apache. A site at Mesa, a suburb of Phoenix, Ariz., was chosen and a new plant was built.

The first production airframe structure was delivered by Ryan Teledyne, its builder, in March 1983, and the first flight was made the following January.

The Hind

A competitor of the Apache in future confrontations (or for customers) is the Russian Mi-24 Hind in its D or E configuration (Figure 99-11). This helicopter went into operation as an assault aircraft in about 1980 and saw extensive use in Afghanistan.

Figure 99-10 McDonnell Douglas AH-64A

Figure 99-11 Mil Mi-24 Hind

It is a relatively large helicopter weighing about 22,000 pounds. One reason for this size is that it is configured to carry eight to 10 fully equipped soldiers in addition to its armament. It is technically advanced, with fiberglass main rotor blades and a retractable landing gear.

Since then

The text above was written in 1984. Since then, more than 800 Apaches have been built. A new version carrying the Longbow radar system is in test, and this radar will be aboard the new AH-64D Longbow Apaches.

The Army's desire for a small scout/attack helicopter, once called the LHX program, is being met by the development of the RAH-66 Comanche. Boeing and Sikorsky are teamed to develop this aircraft and the first prototype is being assembled.

The Russians have developed two new attack helicopters. The Mil-28 Havoc is discussed in Chapter 36. The other helicopter is the coaxial Kamov Ka-50. While all other attack helicopters have a crew of two, the Ka-50 is a single-pilot aircraft.

The tradeoff between one-and two-man crews was a central issue in planning for the Comanche. The single-pilot helicopter can be made lighter, less expensive, and less demanding on the pilot pool. But the job of looking for targets, managing weapons and communications, and recognizing enemy threats while flying nap-of-the-earth was thought to be too much for one person, even with the aid of sophisticated flight control and weapon management systems.

100 The Mil Mi-28 Havoc

As a result of their glasnost policy, the Russians showed off their Mil Mi-28 attack helicopter, which bears the NATO name of "Havoc," at the 1989 Paris Airshow. As a former aerodynamicist for McDonnell Douglas Helicopter Co., I couldn't help but compare the Havoc with the U.S. Army's antitank helicopter, the McDonnell Douglas AH-64A Apache.

My first impression was that the Mi-28 looks a lot like the Apache. It could well be called the "Apachesky." My second impression was that the Pentagon's intelligence-gathering system must be pretty good; the Havok looks almost identical to the sketches that accompanied the evaluation of Soviet airpower several years ago. (It may be significant that both the Mi-28 in the sketch and the one exhibited at Paris are designated with the number "32." Perhaps this is the aircraft we were meant to see.)

Similarities and differences

When two aircraft are designed to the same mission requirements, designers make similar choices. Figure 100-1 shows the two aircraft on the ground. Several similarities between the Apache and the Havoc are obvious:

- Tandem cockpit for the two-man crew,

- Chin-mounted gun turret,

- Rockets and missiles mounted on two store stations on each wing,

- Forward main wheels,

- Tail wheel,

- "Trailing-arm" main landing gear,

- Forward avionic bays,

- Front-drive turbine engines, and

- Double two-bladed tail rotors.

On the other hand, you have to expect some differences. Some that stand out include:

- Five main-rotor blades vs. four,

Figure 100-1 The Two Rivals: AH-64, Top; Mi-28, Bottom.

Figure 100-2 Main-Rotor Head (AH-64, Top; Mi-28, Bottom)

Figure 100-3 Tail Pylon

• Direction of main-rotor rotation,

• Step-down canopy,

• High horizontal stabilizer vs. low stabilator,

• Size of the forward avionic bays,

• External debris deflectors vs. internal particle separators, and

• Turret-mounted ammunition bins vs. internal ammo bay.

The similarities lead one to suspect that in about 1977, when the Mil team started the design work, it was much influenced by the Apache, which had been started been started five years earlier. Most differences between the two aircraft seemingly relate to features that the Mi-28 inherited from the earlier Mi-24 Hind helicopter.

A look at the details

Regarding cockpit canopies, Apache pilots are not particularly happy with the field-of-view from either the front or rear cockpit. Havoc pilots might be a little happier because their faces are closer to the glass, even though the window frames appear to be quite wide.

The Mil designers swapped the blown-bubble canopies of the Mi-24 for flat panels. The reason is apparently to make use of thick bulletproof glass.

The Apache's glass canopy panels, which are not bulletproof, have a slight bulge. This is a compromise between curved panels, which can create an omnidirectional sun glint, and thin panels, which can vibrate to produce "canopy drumming" and create a unidirectional sun glint. One of my pilot friends calls the latter phenomenon the "searchlight effect." Comparing the rotor heads (Figure 100-2), although the Mi-28 rotor head looks almost identical to that of the 20-year-old Hind, I've been told the structure and the hinging arrangement have been improved significantly. One holdover from the older technology, however, is the hydraulic lead-lag damper on each blade. Most Western helicopter designers have gone to elastomeric dampers.

The Havoc's hinge offset appears to be more than the Apache's—about 6% compared to 4%. This should give slightly crisper handling in maneuvers at the expense of higher loads in the hub.

The "pot" on top of the Havoc's rotor hub encloses the electrical deicing system's slip rings. But cables to the blades were apparently left back at the Mil factory. The Soviets must have felt that they weren't needed in Paris in June.

Loads in any helicopter's blade-pitch links are relatively low, so they don't have to be very big— and on the Mi-28 they are not. This contrasts to the Apache; its pitch links were designed not for load-carrying ability but from a vulnerability standpoint. Ground rules for both the Apache and the Sikorsky Black Hawk dictated that a single 50-caliber round could not prevent the helicopter's continued flight. Thus many items on the Apache are redundant—such as the dampers—and others are larger than they might be otherwise.

Other comparisons

Both the Apache and the Havok have a cambered tail pylon to unload the tail rotor in forward flight (Figure 100-3). The Havoc's horizontal stabilizer, a two-position unit, appears to be in a nosedown position, which is what you would expect for high speed but not for preparation for the next takeoff.

The two conventional airspeed pitot tubes are positioned in front of the Mi-28 gunner's canopy. This was found not to be a good position on the Apache, so its pitot tubes were moved to the wing tips.

Both aircraft, however, have backup airspeed systems primarily for low speed. The Havoc has a small sensor mounted on a blade tip. Theoretically, this should be a very good system; it uses the tip speed's amplifying effect to sense the pressure difference between the advancing and retreating blades. The Apache's low-speed system is in Pacer System's whirligig mounted above the rotor head.

Figure 100-4 Tail Rotors

Surprisingly, the Russians have adopted the Apache's tail-rotor system (Figure 100-4). On both aircraft, the four-bladed rotor is actually two, two-bladed teetering rotors set about 6 inches (15 cm) apart. In each case, the two rotors are not at right angles to each other. There is no exotic reason for this; a study of the geometry will show that it simply makes it easier to join the control system with both rotors.

The Apache tail-rotor controls are external to the shaft and thus inboard of the rotors. But the Mil bureau elected to use an internal system with the pitch arms picking up the control system outboard. The two configurations are probably comparable in terms of weight and drag.

Unlike the Hind, with its nose wheel, the Mi-28 has a tail wheel, like the Apache. The main landing gear on both the Havoc and Apache is of the "trailing-arm" type (Figure 100-5). The Havoc gear appears to be shorter, thus creating less drag. But it also seems to have less oleo stroke to absorb hard-landing energy. Still, the Soviets claim the Mi-28 is designed for survivable landings of up to 49 feet per second (fps)—compared to the Apache's 42 fps.

The Soviets obviously learned from Afghanistan the dangers of a hot engine exhaust. Many Hinds were shot down with American-supplied Stinger infrared homing missiles. Both the Havoc and the Apache designers have provided ways of diluting and cooling the exhaust gasses with outside air. The Mi-28 has air inlets about halfway back on the engine nacelles, and downward-pointing exhaust stacks.

The Mil designers had an interesting tradeoff study to do here. (I wonder if the possibility of setting grass fires was one of the factors.) If

Figure 100-5 Main Landing Gear

significant jet thrust comes out of these downward-pointing nozzles, hover performance is enhanced. Conversely, these unique exhausts produce a high drag in forward flight. Soviet designers apparently opted for the hover performance, while McDonnell Douglas designers sought high speed by aiming their exhaust nozzles back and only enough to the side to block the view of the hot engine parts from a pursuing missile.

The Mi-28 carries its 30mm gun ammunition in bins on the turret. This negates the need for long flexible ammunition tracks as on the Apache (which presented big developmental problems). Also, Mi-28 ground crewmen can easily load ammunition.

On the other hand, drag is higher and the turret's inertia is increased, thus making the gun harder to aim. In addition, the Havoc can carry only 300 rounds, whereas the Apache holds 1,200 rounds for its 30mm chain gun.

Performance comparison

The Havoc is considerably larger than the Apache, and therefore it cannot hide as easily. Even though the two aircraft have nearly the same power loading, the Havoc is penalized by higher disc loading.

A simple calculation shows the Apache has 22% more power than it needs to hover; the Havoc has only a 17% margin. Thus the Apache should be more lively in maneuvers that depend on good power.

On the other hand, maneuvers depending on maximum rotor thrust give the Mi-28 the advantage. With more blade area, the Russian helicopter should pull about 4% more load factor before encountering blade stall.

The maximum speed claimed for the Mi-28 is 162 knots. This is almost exactly the maximum level-flight speed of the AH-64. The degree of drag "cleanliness" is probably about the same on both aircraft. The Havok's extra installed engine power is therefore of no advantage, and is nullified by the aircraft's higher weight and larger size.

The Mi-28, Ship 032, as exhibited at the 1989 Paris Airshow was obviously not ready for battlefield operation. The IR jammer, chaff and flare dispenser, and many antennas that would eventually be needed were not installed.

In conclusion

Although the Mi-28 Havoc shows many advances over the Mi-24 Hind and some technological features not found on the AH-64 Apache, a superficial comparison does not indicate the Havoc would have a significant advantage over the Apache on the battlefield, except for its ability to carry more rockets and missiles into combat.

101 Evolution Of Sikorsky Tails

With most helicopter manufacturers, a new model's design is only partially finished when it makes its first flight. Almost all undergo some redesign before they enter production. Even experienced companies such as Sikorsky Aircraft go through this process.

Creating a pitchup

Both the CH-53E Super Stallion and the UH-60 Black Hawk started out with low, fixed-incidence horizontal stabilizers. Sikorsky engineers had predicted that these would produce satisfactory stability in forward flight. Such a design—as shown in Figure 101-1 for the Super Stallion—is structurally sound, simple, minimizes tail shake, and prevents people from walking into the tail rotor.

However, initial flight testing indicated that such a design created "pitchup" during a low-speed flare. As shown in Figure 101-2, the main-rotor wake would suddenly strike the tail as the helicopter slowed down.

The resulting download on the surface pitched the helicopter noseup unless the pilot promptly pushed the cyclic stick forward. Sikorsky test pilots considered this would unduly increase the workload during combat flight.

And on both the Super Stallion and the Black Hawk, the problem was exaggerated by a center of gravity (CG) position aft of the main-rotor shaft. In normal flight, the canted tail rotor produced an up-force that compensated for the aft CG. But in a flare, where little or no tail-rotor thrust was being generated to overcome main-rotor torque, the tail-rotor cant offered little compensatory benefit.

The two Sikorsky design teams took different paths to solve their problem. The Super Stallion team reverted to the previous high-tail configuration used on the earlier A through D versions of the CH-53 (Figure 101-3). Because it is in "cleaner" air, the tail surface could be reduced almost by half.

Meanwhile, the Black Hawk team opted for a "stabilator" (Figure 101-4). This all-moving tail surface can be aligned with the local main-rotor down wash at low speed to minimize the download.

Figure 101-1 Prototype CH-53E With Original Low-Tail Position

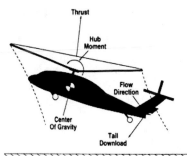

Figure 101-2 Main-Rotor Flow Field During Flare

Figure 101-3 Production CH-53E With High Tail Position

Figure 101-4   Stabilator On The Black Hawk

Other benefits

With the stabilator, flying qualities in regimes other than low-speed flight could be improved. The stabilator-incidence angle on the Black Hawk is automatically controlled by a computer whose primary input signal is airspeed. But it also takes in signals from the collective stick, a pitch-rate gyro, and a lateral accelerometer. Here's how each of these secondary signals is used.

• The collective input increases the stabilator-incidence angle in climb, and decreases it in autorotation. This minimizes the trim shift usually produced by large changes in stabilizer angle of attack when going between these two conditions.

• The input from the pitch-rate gyro increases the incidence during a noseup pitching maneuver. This produces a nosedown moment that increases pitch damping and makes the helicopter easier to fly in gusty air.

• The lateral accelerometer signal helps compensate for the pitching moment associated with changes in the canted tail rotor's thrust when wind gusts from the side produce inadvertent sideslip. With a side gust from the right, for instance, the tail-rotor thrust is decreased. Since its thrust vector is canted up 20°, the tail rotor up-load is also decreased, thus the helicopter would normally want to pitch up.

At the same time, the downwash pattern from the main rotor swings to the left, placing the stabilator in an area of strong downwash behind the rotor's advancing side. This also contributes to the noseup-pitching moment. The lateral accelerometer fastened to the airframe senses the sideward acceleration and triggers a change in the stabilizer's incidence to minimize this "pitch-with-sideslip coupling."

Except for the lateral accelerometer input, an almost direct copy of the Sikorsky stabilator scheme is used on the McDonnell Douglas AH-64 Apache for exactly the same reasons.

The S-76, too

From their experiences with the CH-53E and the UH-60A, Sikorsky designers were convinced that the S-76A would have similar problems. They therefore equipped the medium twin for initial flight-testing with a variable-incidence stabilator whose incidence could be changed from the cockpit.

There was, however, a pleasant surprise. The designers found that a fixed-incidence surface was satisfactory.

Why? The variable-incidence stabilator wasn't required for two reasons: the S-76A doesn't have a canted tail rotor, and civil-certification requirements for stability are more modest than the military's.

When the heavier S-76B came along, however, it bore a new problem. As with many modem designs, the S-76A has a cambered airfoil on the

Figure 101-5   The S-76B Horizontal Stabilizer With Symmetric Airfoil And Gurney Flan

horizontal stabilizer that is mounted inverted. This airfoil keeps the horizontal stabilizer from stalling in climbs when it is carrying a high download.

During tests of the S-76B's stability augmentation system (SAS), Sikorsky pilots found that it was important to also keep the stabilizer from stalling when carrying a high upload, as happened following simulated SAS hardovers.

The solution was to design a symmetrical airfoil for the B model, and add a double "Gurney flap" at the trailing edge (Figure 101-5). The lift characteristics "before and after" are illustrated by Figure 101-6.

Flight tests showed that, before the modification, to recover full control from a hardover of 5%, the pilot had to use half of the longitudinal control. But after the modification, he had to use only a third. Sikorsky believes eliminating tail stall will also reduce pilot workload in such tasks as the return-to-target maneuver in which high stabilizer angles of attack are encountered.

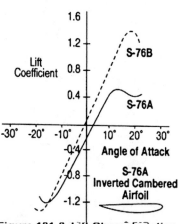

Figure 101-6 Lift Characteristics Of S-76A And S-76B Horizontal Stabilizers

Vertical stabilizer

The military requirements for the Super Stallion and the Black Hawk specified that the aircraft should be able to maintain level flight home after complete tail-rotor loss. The original design of the two ships' vertical stabilizers gave them enough area to compensate for main-rotor torque at about 80 knots while the helicopter was sideslipping no more than 20°. Not only was the area sufficient, but the surface's sideforce was biased using an offset, cambered tail on the CH-53E and a fixed rudder on the UH-60A.

The intentions were good, but there emerged a problem. Because of these large surfaces, it was impossible to fly sideward as fast as desired—or to hold position in a crosswind.

Figure 101-7 Sikorsky UH-60 Vertical Stabilizer

This begged the question: What's more important—the ability to fly back to the base after losing tail-rotor thrust or the ability to hold heading in a crosswind?

The decision was to favor the latter, and on both helicopters, most of the vertical stabilizer's trailing edge was removed (Figure 101-7 and Figure 101-8). (You can also observe results of the same tradeoff on the truncated vertical stabilizer of the McDonnell Douglas AH-64A Apache.)

Although the fly-home-without-a-tail-rotor capability was not required on the S-76A, its vertical stabilizer area, too, was reduced during the flight-test phase. In this case, the upper 15 inches (38 cm) was removed to decrease the amount of roll moment that is generated in a sideslip—the dihedral effect.

Shortening the vertical stabilizer is a well-known way of improving the lateral-directional dynamic stability with regard to a phenomenon known

Figure 101-8 Sikorsky CH-53E Vertical Stabilizer

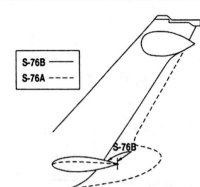

Figure 101-9 S-76B Modified Tail Pylon

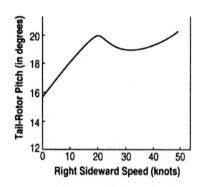

Figure 101-10 Tail-Rotor Pitch Required For Right Sideward Flight

as "Dutch Roll." With the S-76B, the area was reduced a little more (Figure 101-9) to help sideward flight.

Tail rotor

A prerequisite in tail-rotor design is the ability to compensate for main-rotor torque and still provide adequate directional control in a crosswind from the right. A 35-knot crosswind is usually taken as a design goal. But Sikorsky flight-testing on both the Black Hawk and the S-76 indicates that the tail-rotor thrust requirements may actually be higher at some lower crosswind speed.

Figure 101-10 shows the tail-rotor pitch required in right sideward flight in ground effect, and it reveals that flight at about 20 knots may require more pitch than at 35 knots.

At about 20 knots, the helicopter loses its ground effect as it overrides the ground vortex, and there is unfavorable interference as the tail rotor ingests some of the main-rotor's wake. (During Apache flight-testing, it was also found that the tail boom can develop high drag, apparently because the energy of the impinging main-rotor wake was converted to high pressure on the right side.)

The capability of the Black Hawk's original tail-rotor design turned out to sufficiently overcome this unexpected requirement. But the S-76A's tail-rotor design was not adequate for the heavier S-76B, and consequently both the blade chord and the control range were increased for the B-model.

Sikorsky's experience—having to make configuration changes between the first flight and production—is not unique. I'm familiar with no helicopter design that hasn't undergone some change—which proves we still have more to learn about these complex machines.

102

Which Way Should The Rotor Turn? And Where Should The Pilot Sit?

What could be more logical? Russian rotor blades advance to the left while American rotor blades advance to the right. Is there a good reason for this?

No. But it does make an interesting story. Igor Sikorsky was not concerned about which way the main rotor turned in the beginning. On the VS-300, it rotated clockwise when viewed from the top (Figure 102-1) but on his next design, the XR-4, it rotated counterclockwise (Figure 102-2). The decisions were strictly based on the design of the power train and the number of direction reversals convenient when reducing the engine rpm from a couple of thousand to a couple of hundred at the rotor.

Figure 102-1 The Sikorsky VS-300 With Clockwise Rotation (When Viewed From Above)

On the VS-300, this reduction was partially done with a multi-belt drive but on the XR-4, the transmission consisted entirely of gears and the direction of rotation was just how it came out with good engineering practices.

In flight, the direction of main-rotor rotation raises only one question for the pilot: "Which pedal do I push to keep the fuselage from turning as I increase power by raising the collective-pitch lever?" Figure 102-3 shows that on the VS-300 with clockwise rotation, the pilot had to push the right pedal but on the XR-4 it was the left.

The VS-300 remained on flight status while the XR-4 was going through its development flying and the same test pilot, Les Morris, flew them both during this period. He recently told me that, in going from one to the other, he was never bothered by the fact that when adding power to the VS-300 he used a different foot than on the XR-4. The reason Les didn't have a problem is because good pilots are amazingly adaptable.

Heeding yaw cues

This is borne out by David Green as he discusses his experiences in flying French helicopters: "When the collective of a U.S. helicopter is increased during hovering flight, the pilot must move the left pedal forward to compensate for an increase in main-rotor torque. Right pedal is required under similar circumstances in a French helicopter where the main rotor turns in the opposite direction.

Figure 102-2 The Sikorsky XR-4 With Counterclockwise Rotation

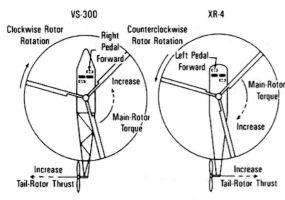

Figure 102-3 Required Pedal for Increasing Main Rotor Torque

"One might expect a pilot to have trouble switching from the U.S. to the European configuration but, generally, there are no problems when the yaw-rate cues are sufficiently strong. But some piloting errors do occur when the strength of the heading-rate cue decreases.

"In my own experience, I can report no problem associated with takeoff or hovering flight. But at high altitude or while operating in heavy haze, I have found my left foot moving forward with up collective. That is, when the visual cues were weak, my learned response (nurtured for 22 years in U.S. helicopters) took over, even in the European machine."

Despite this "no big deal" effect, all Sikorsky helicopters since the XR-4 have used the same counterclockwise rotation. I suspect it became "tradition" and has been maintained even when the other rotation might have saved a stage of gearing and despite the fact that recent Sikorsky designs have included mechanical coupling between the main-and tail-rotor collective-pitch systems. This mechanical coupling reduces the necessity of the pilot having to do anything at all with his feet as he changes collective pitch.

Bell's blade reversal

The original developers of Bell helicopters also had no prejudices on the direction of rotation and reversed it between the counterclockwise-rotating Model 47 and the clockwise-rotating Model 48 shown on Figure 102-4. This was an eight-to-10-passenger helicopter of which 13 were built for the U.S. Air Force as the H-12 in the late '40s.

Figure 102-4 The Bell H 12 with Clockwise Rotation

Apparently at least one pilot complained that this aircraft required opposite foot motion from the Model 47 he had trained on. Bell engineers must have taken this to heart since all their subsequent single-rotor helicopters have had the traditional "American" rotation.

Turning to Russia

Russian engines have always rotated in the opposite direction from American engines. Thus it would seem natural that on their early single-rotor helicopters, the rotors would also rotate in the opposite way.

This was true in the first Mil design, the Mi-1, but on its competitor, the Yak 100, the desire to make an almost exact copy of the Sikorsky S-51 resulted in the American rotation. For other reasons, I'm sure, the Yak 100 was a failure and Aleksandir Yakovlev started building tandem-rotor helicopters whereby he could build rotors turning in each direction. Mikhail Mil went on to build many more single-rotor designs: each with the advancing blade on the left, thus establishing the Russian "tradition" which, as seen in Figure 102-5 on the Mil Mi-26, they are continuing in a big way.

Figure 102-5 Mil Mi-26 (and a nice size comparison with the H500)

French rotation

How the French came to adopt the Russian rotation is a story about chance. At the end of World War II, as part of the spoils of war, the French brought home a captured German Focke-Wulf 61 with its oppositely turning side-by-side rotors.

(Historical aside: The FW-61 is often erroneously referred to as the FA-61 for Focke-Achgelis. It was actually designed and built while Focke was still associated with Wulf about a year before the formation of Focke-Achgelis. I got this clarification from the Messerschmitt-Boelkow-Blohm historians.)

On the first French post-World War II helicopter development, the design team, which was the nucleus of what later became Aerospatiale, chose to make a single-rotor helicopter using one of the Focke rotors. In choosing which one, the designers considered the direction their engine turned and the logical gear train, and decided to use the clockwise-turning rotor. This has persisted as the French "tradition" which has been followed except when building American designs under license. With few exceptions, helicopter designers in England, Germany, and Italy have chosen the American way.

The recommendation

Just as Les Morris was able to fly both the VS-300 and the XR-4 during the same day with no effort in retraining his feet, so today David Green and many other pilots can easily go from American to French helicopters. For this reason, it no longer seems necessary for designers of single-rotor helicopters to be bound by tradition if they can save a pound of transmission weight or a dollar of transmission cost by throwing tradition to the winds.

Side-by-sides

Looking at side-by-side rotor aircraft such as the Bell XV-15, designers have to decide whether the blade tips over the fuselage are to go forward or aft. This type of helicopter was pioneered in Germany and Russia and most of these aircraft had the blades over the fuselage going forward. When this was tried after World War II in America on the McDonnell XHJH-1, it was found this aircraft was easier to fly backward than forward! The lesson was taken seriously by the design team which eventually produced Bell's XV-3 tilt-rotor convertiplane; its son, the XV-15; and its grandson, the V-22-all of which have the blades over the fuselage going aft (Figure 102-6).

Where should the 'pilot' sit?

Drivers of American cars sit on the left. Pilots of American airplanes sit on the left. Pilots of a few American helicopters sit on the left-but most sit on the right.

How come?

Figure 102-6 Bell XV-15 With Blades Going Aft Over Fuselage

Also, if you design a two-man attack helicopter with tandem seating, should the pilot sit in front or in back? These are design questions that have no apparent answers.

Wrong control at right time

The left-vs.-right question arose as soon as the first two-place helicopter was developed. Les Morris describes his experience as the test pilot for Sikorsky in his book, *Pioneering the Helicopter.* After discussing the problem of manually coordinating engine power and collective pitch with the twist-grip throttle, he wrote the following comment:

"As though I hadn't enough to keep me busy, I foolishly added one more needless complication to the assignment. In the VS-300, I had always flown with the main pitch lever in my left hand. However, the XR-4 (Figure 102-7) was designed to be flown from the left side, which meant that the pitch lever between the seats was at my right.

Figure 102-7 Les Morris in The Left Seat of The Sikorsky XR-4

"As I look back on it, I wonder why I didn't follow Mr. [Igor] Sikorsky's guarded hint and sit on the [right] side where all controls would be in their accustomed places. But I didn't and, while nothing serious came of it, it was many hours before I mastered an inordinate desire to use the wrong control at the right time!"

Another of Morris' explanation for right-hand pilots' seats appeared in a letter to *Rotor & Wing International.*

"The answer is found in the statement above-that I was planted firmly in the left seat and with only 56 hours of helicopter time and 36 hours in type, I was not about to reverse my control orientation at the same time I was training the first helicopter student pilots. That would be dangerously stacking the deck against me when I was called on for instantaneous correction of a student's goof. So I remained in the left seat while they happily oriented themselves to the right seat.

"Later, it was easy and safe for a competent right-seat pilot to check out another competent right-seat pilot, while reorienting himself to the left seat with its reverse control orientation.

"Sounds confusing-and it was at that time (1942-'43) but we could ill-afford the potential penalty of confusion at the controls when there was only one precious bird. That bird might not have made the Smithsonian had the decision been otherwise!"

A pilot poll

Les Morris was not the only one to take credit for the right-seat placement. Robert Knecht, head of the U.S. Navy's rotary-wing development from 1946 to 1959, had his explanation printed in the August 1980 issue of R&WI

"Firmly planting the pilot in the right seat occurred after a poll was taken of many U.S. Navy, Marine, and Army helicopter pilots," he wrote. "The majority interviewed preferred the right seat. With only two hands to operate the early helicopters (which at most times required three), it became hazardous for the pilot to sit in the left seat and make control-panel adjustments with his right hand.

"Remember, we did not have autopilots and the collective had locks. The practice was to lock the collective, move the left hand to the cyclic, and the right hand off the cyclic to adjust panel controls.

"With rescue hooks mounted from the starboard side, it was natural to place the pilot on the same side, where he could watch the operation."

Knecht reported that the Navy's experience with the Piasecki HUP-1 Retriever "also reinforced the decision to plant pilots in right seats. These aircraft, which had the pilot sitting in the left seat, operated from a plane-guard station situated on the aft starboard quarter of an aircraft carrier. Their job was to rescue crewmen of aircraft ditched while approaching the carrier. The HUP-1 pilot would view the carrier deck as well as approaching fixed-wing aircraft making landings.

"In the event of a ditching, the helicopter was supposed to sweep down with minimum reaction time," Knecht explained. "But with the HUPs, the pilot flew in a slight 30° to 45° translation attitude to the carrier in order to reduce the power requirements of a highly underpowered helicopter. This attitude put the pilot's line of sight out through the port side of the cockpit, away from the centrally located pedestal instruments. Placing the pilot in the right seat would have allowed him to look past his instrument panel to the carrier deck operations."

When Piasecki produced the successive HUP-2, the manufacturer ignored the Navy's recommendation to change the pilot seat, Knecht noted. However, from that time on, specifications called for right-side seating for pilots as a Navy requirement.

It seems possible that the selected hoist position and the plane-guard station were results of the pilot being in the right seat rather than the causes.

Instructor left, student right

Yet another pioneer pilot offers his comments on the issue, in the American Helicopter Society's Vertiflite magazine. He is George Townson, who goes all the way back to the autogyro days.

"The early (1940 era) helicopters had one collective-pitch stick located between the seats. It had always been traditional for flight instructors to sit in the left-hand seat and for students to solo from the right.

"These students, who in many cases moved up to high ranks in the military, could only fly from the right-hand side. They eventually became the ones who procured the helicopters for the service and naturally dictated that they should be flown from the right-hand side.

There were very few exceptions to this rule, [however] certain Bell H-13s were flown from the left and the Hiller H-23 was flown from the center with a passenger on either side of the pilot."

"It was more difficult than you might think for the pilots of early helicopters to change seats. The only collective-pitch stick (called the "total pitch" in early aircraft) was between the two seats. When in the left seat, the pilot operated it with his right hand and used his left on the cyclic (formerly called the "azimuth" control). However, when the pilot switched to the right seat, he would have to swap hands on the two levers."

"The controls were directly linked to the blades, with no hydraulic assist against the in-flight loads on the blades. Therefore, the force to move the collective was significant, while the cyclic moved with comparative ease. These different loads often made flying difficult and rather erratic immediately after a pilot changed from one seat to the other."

"Changing hands on the controls was merely annoying, however. The throttle operation became a real problem."

"When the collective was held in the left hand, the twist-grip or motorcycle-type throttle was opened by rolling the hand away from the body. Conversely, in the right hand, it had to be rolled toward the body. There were some thrilling moments when early pilots changed seats and wound up chopping power just when they needed it most.

"Fixed-wing aircraft are flown from the left-hand seat and all the necessary controls are placed in view of the left-hand pilot," wrote Townson. "The reason the pilot sits on the left is so that when he is approached by another aircraft head-on he can alter his course to the right and keep other aircraft in sight as they pass."

"If the pilot was about to overtake a slower aircraft, he would alter his course to the right to keep the slower aircraft in sight from his left-hand seat as he passed. And, when two aircraft approach each other at a right angle, the pilot viewing the aircraft to his right will alter his course, passing to the rear of that aircraft. Thus he keeps the oncoming aircraft in sight at all times.

"If the pilot was sitting in the right, he wouldn't be able to see other aircraft as well while crossing, overtaking, or passing them," Townson concluded.

No real logic

In his article on cockpit design, David Green, former test pilot and now R&WI technology assessment editor, claimed that today "there is really no rational reason" for the pilot to sit in the right seat.

"The reason behind the right seat has nothing to do with any great engineering logic. It just happened to come out that way. Igor Sikorsky meant for the pilot to be in the left seat but because of early vehicle training problems, the first operational pilots learned to fly in the right seat."

Green continues by offering his views on the right-seat pilot position.

"When you consider the need to work with airplanes in left-hand traffic patterns, [sitting in the right seat] makes little sense. With the helicopter in a left bank, a right-seat pilot's line of sight is blocked by the overhead of the cockpit cabin, which normally supports circuit breakers, switches, and engine controls.

"Approaching a hover spot, the pilot must flare to stop and in the flare, the view over the nose is often inadequate. When it is, or when there is an obstruction in the overrun, the pilot will often approach with a crab angle. A sideward flare will be used, or the helicopter will be stopped short and air taxied so that the pilot can see the spot out the right side.

"When this approach is flown in U.S. helicopters, left pedal is required to sideslip to the right. More left pedal power requires more tail rotor power. If the pilot were to sit on the left, he would hold right pedal and less power would be required.

"Seems like the U.S. helicopter pilot is on the wrong side or the U.S. main rotor is turning the wrong way."

But a R&WI reader, J. B. Gilstrap, promptly responded to Green's suggestion in the R&WI Letters column. "Please don't put the pilot on the left side again–unless you are going to give him a co-pilot and an autopilot.

"Pilots prefer the right seat because they don't like to switch hands on the cyclic to change a radio frequency. It's a lot easier to use the left knee to hold the collective and throttle and the left hand to make the adjustments on controls on the panel.

"It is second nature to sense control requirements and respond with the right hand, even when you're left-handed. Also, the cyclic grip is tailored to the right hand.

"I cannot see any benefits to placing the pilot in the left seat. If a pilot shoots an approach, it will probably be in a right-hand pattern. If he joins IFR traffic at the end of an instrument approach, he is going to be monitored by radar and his instructions are to avoid fixed-wing traffic anyway, i.e. he can shoot whatever kind of approach he needs.

"Furthermore, most IFR approaches are straight in. If circling approaches are required, they are just as likely to involve a right-hand circle as a left-hand circle.

"Don't mess up a good thing. Keep the pilot on the right, so his left hand can be used for a good purpose."

And so the controversy goes on and on.

Front or back?

But what about that other situation, the tandem seating in an attack helicopter?

Obviously, the person in front has the best view. Should this be given to the pilot or to the copilot/ gunner/observer?

Apparently, each design team-including ones in Germany, Italy, and Russia-has weighed the options and, with only one exception that I know of, opted for giving the window seat to the copilot/ gunner/observer. The one exception was on the Bell YAH-63, the prototype competitor to the Hughes (now McDonnell Douglas) Apache. Its seating was reversed because of the challenging nap-of-the-earth flying envisioned for this type of helicopter.

103 One-Man Helicopters*

*Courtesy of the American Helicopter Society in whose magazine, Vertiflite, this appeared in the March/April 1982 issue.

After the helicopter concept had been proven feasible by the first generation of inventors, many designers in the 1940s and 1950s went to work to develop tiny aircraft so that you and I could fly where we wanted, when we wanted, and with a minimum of fuss. You could call these designs "motorcycles of the air." A least 30 of these aircraft got off the ground, but although some were technically satisfactory, none fulfilled the promise.

The Hoppi-Copter

The simplest helicopter design is one that you strap on your back like a pack and then rely on your legs to be the landing gear. The first of these that captured the public's attention was the Pentecost Hoppi-Copter (Figure 103-1). In 1945, Horace Pentecost built a small coaxial rotor assembly powered by a 20-hp two-cylinder air-cooled engine.

Figure 103-1 Pentecost Hoppi-Copter

One of the first things he learned was that legs do not make a good landing gear. There are several reasons for this:

• Mating the rotor system with its "fuselage" is bound to be an awkward maneuver;

• Laying the rotor assembly down in the mud after a flight is not a good idea;

• Getting away from the aircraft quickly is difficult; and

• Two size 101/2B boots just don't provide the tread and stability required for safe landing operations.

For these reasons, the second Hoppi-Copter model sprouted landing gear. This model had a 40-hp engine, and films of it in hover showed that the pilot was busier than a one-man band.

Before the test program had advanced very far, a sad thing happened to Pentecost and his company. He had given 10% of the voting stock to the lawyer who had helped with the incorporation, and later when Horace and his wife divorced, he found himself a minority stockholder with only

45% of the action. Thus when his ex-wife and the lawyer got together, he could not prevent the power play that kicked him out of his own company.

Pentecost was out, but not down. He formed Capital Helicopters in Schenectady, N.Y., and designed a pulsejet-powered, one-man helicopter with a projected cost (in 1954) of $2,500. A mockup was built but apparently no flights were ever made.

In the meantime, Hoppi-Copter was acquired by a group of investors in the Washington, D.C., area. In 1956 they tried to raise the necessary capital to certificate the aircraft by offering 300,000 $1 shares, but were not successful. The original Hoppi-Copter can now be seen hanging from the ceiling of the Smithsonian Air & Space Museum.

The Hoppi-Copter was just the first of many. The minimum helicopter appealed to both teenagers and the military, and there was no shortage of designers intent on satisfying either or both markets.

The ramjets

Following World War II, helicopter engineers all over the world became intrigued with the possibility of using the new German inventions, the ramjet and the pulsejet for power. Since these units worked best at high subsonic speeds, and since blade tips also operate at high subsonic speeds, the combination appeared to be a natural.

The first ramjet machine to fly was McDonnell's "Little Henry" (Figure 103-2). It had two ramjets of 10-pound thrust rating (about 13 hp each at full tip speed) and an empty weight of 285 pounds. It was built under an Air Force contract and designated the XH-20. The project began in 1946 and continued for about five years, taking it through an extensive but fruitless flight-test program. Little Henry is now hanging from the rafters in the Air Force Museum at Wright-Patterson AFB.

Another of the ramjets was the Hiller XHJ-1, first flown in 1950. The two 40-pound thrust engines were similar to Little Henry's because they were developed by the same engineer. Each ramjet was fed by fuel lines through a rotating seal in the hub from a tank in the fuselage. A spark plug in each unit served as an igniter. Starts could be made by hand propelling the rotor up to about 50 rpm, but normally it was started with a two-cycle gasoline motor as part of the ground equipment.

Sometimes the igniters did not work. In this case, the standard procedure was for the flight-test engineer to toss lighted matches into the engines as they whizzed by. If this procedure took too long, there would soon be a path of raw fuel on the ground which would invariably be set on fire by an ill-tossed match. When this happened, it was imperative that the engines start at once since the only escape from the resultant ring of fire was by helicopter.

Figure 103-2 McDonnell's "Little Henry"

The XHJ-1 evolved into the "Hiller Hornet" (Figure 103-3), which also had the Air Force designation of H-32 and the Navy designation of HOE-1. As a condition of the military contract, Hiller was to obtain FAA certification for both the ramjet engine and the total aircraft. The ramjet was certificated in 1954 after a 150-hour test, but the FAA objected to the very high autorotative rate of descent of the Hornet and never did certificate it.

Despite this setback, about 40 ships were delivered to the Army, Air Force, and Navy for evaluation, where it was found that the high fuel consumption of the ramjets severely limited the usable range and endurance, and that

Figure 103-3 XHJ-1 Ramjet Powered Hiller Hornet

hot weather performance was only marginal at best. These basic problems spelled the end of the project.

In the Netherlands, another ramjet-powered helicopter family began flying in 1955, resulting in the "Kolibrie" or Hummingbird. This aircraft was designed from the beginning as a farm machine and was very simple and rugged. One co-designer was Jan Drees, who later became a Bell Helicopter vice president. Three prototypes were built and an airworthiness certificate was awarded, followed by a production run of 10. Kolibries were used as agricultural aircraft in the Dutch Lowlands and in Israel for the next 10 years.

Helicopters with rotors driven at their tips do not need a tail rotor for torque compensation, but they do need some device for directional control. It has always been tempting to install a simple hinged vane, which uses the rotor downwash in hover to provide the necessary yawing moment.

The only trouble with this scheme is that in certain flight conditions, such as a landing flare, there is no rotor downwash and not enough forward speed to make the vane work. For this reason, such helicopters are vulnerable to rolling over if they land with too much sideward velocity. Almost all of the jet-powered designs which started out with a vane ended up with a small tail rotor since it works in all flight conditions.

The pulsejet

The pulsejet powerplant was used on a number of small experimental helicopters including the Marquart "Whirljet," and American Helicopter's "Top Sergeant," "Buck Private," and "Jet Jeep" or XH-26 (Figure 103-4). Five of the latter were built for the Air Force under a program similar to the Hiller Hornet—and ended up with similar results.

One problem with jet-powered rotors was that burning fuel at the tip of the rotor made noise—lots of it. However, this was during an era when technical progress was glamorous, and since only a few experimental

Figure 103-4 American Helicopter XH-26 Jet Jeep

Figure 103-5 Rotor-Craft Pinwheel

Figure 103-6 Kellett XH-15

Figure 103-7 The Djinn

machines were scattered around the world, noise was not considered much of a problem.

In fact, the designers thought the public would put up with a little noise in return for the enormous benefits these new aircraft would bring. It is no reflection on these pioneers that their crystal balls were too cloudy at the time to see the environmental sensitivity which developed over the next few decades. It now seems quite certain that none of these noisy tip-burning helicopters could ever have been put into general service.

A somewhat quieter tip-drive system was the hydrogen peroxide rocket, which powered two of the one-man helicopters. When hydrogen peroxide is squirted against a sliver-plated screen, it turns into a high-pressure steam jet; another natural for helicopters.

The Navy had used this system for powering torpedoes for years, and so it had some confidence in its ability to handle this highly corrosive material. Thus it is not surprising that both of the hydrogen-peroxide-powered helicopters were Navy projects.

The Rotor-Craft "Pinwheel" (Figure 103-5) was built in 1954 and plans for a civil version envisioned a price of about $1,000. The prototype was about to be delivered to the Navy after three years of development and 250 flights when it was severely damaged in a hard landing.

This ended the program at the time, but the designer persisted and 20 years later was awarded a new Navy contract to deliver three aircraft, now called "Mini-Copters," for evaluation. For reasons that I do not know, the contract was never fulfilled.

The Kellett XH-15 (Figure 103-6), nicknamed "Stable Mable," was primarily a variable-stability research helicopter using the same type of hydrogen-peroxide rockets as the Pinwheel. It demonstrated hands-off flying using gyros for stabilization, but was another "cul de sac" project.

The Djinn

Another relatively quiet tip-drive system used on a small helicopter was the cold pressure jet on the French "Djinn" (Figure 103-7). In this case, a turbine engine with an oversized centrifugal compressor was used. Part of the compressed air went into the combustion chamber and out through the turbine, but most of it was bled off and ducted up to the hollow blade spars of the two-bladed rotor.

This was one of the few jet-powered helicopters that was successfully developed without a tail rotor. Its directional control came from a rudder mounted in the exhaust stream of the turbine.

In this country, Republic Aviation Corp. acquired the rights to the Djinn and obtained certification in 1958. The Army bought five and turned them over to the Air Force for testing at Edwards AFB.

Like the Hiller Hornet, it was found to be underpowered, but even at altitudes above its absolute ceiling, it could be hopped across the desert by overspeeding the heavy rotor on the ground, making a jump takeoff, and flying for half a mile before having to land because of low rotor speed.

One of the most interesting minimum helicopters was the DeLackner Aerogyro. As hard as it is to believe, one of the reasons a hovering helicopter is unstable is because its center of gravity is hanging below the rotor. If you could turn it upside down, it would have better flying qualities and also be more useful as a lawnmower.

Not only would such a helicopter be more stable, but if it were small and if you were to stand on it, it could be controlled with instinctive foot and leg motions. This was demonstrated by Charles Zimmerman at the National Advisory Committee for Aeronautics (NACA) who elevated a number of people on a platform supported by a jet of compressed air and later by a small air-powered rotor. On his own, Zimmerman then built a flying device consisting of a plank with a reciprocating aircraft engine driving a fixed-pitch propeller at each end. The pilot stood in the middle between the two propellers which spun at about ankle height. Engineers who saw the device dubbed it the "Jesus Shoes."

Zimmerman sold the machine to Stanley Hiller, who after some brief flights, retired it but used the concept to develop a semi-successful line of ducted fan stand-on flying platforms.

Donald DeLackner was also intrigued by the concept, but directed his efforts toward a low disc-loading coaxial design powered with a 40-hp water-cooled engine. Hovering was no problem for either this or the Hiller devices, but forward flight was. Neither could trim out the noseup moments that were generated above about 10 knots and thus they became "Prisoners of Hover."

Benson B-9

Igor Bensen is best known for his small autogyros, but he has also built several helicopters. The B-9 (Figure 103-8) was a coaxial machine, but the B-10 was similar to the Zimmerman device except that the propeller planes were in an even more-sensitive location, and the pilot sat down and controlled by vanes in the propeller downwash. The ultimate in this line was the Bensen "Flying Carpet," in which lift was provided by 10 go-cart motors each with a six-foot rotor.

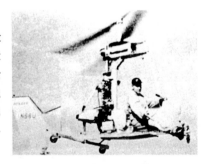

Figure 103-8 Bensen B-9

The Rotorcycle

Military interest in small helicopters led to a Marine design competition in 1954 for a one-man, foldable "Rotorcycle" which could be used for observation, liaison, messenger missions, self-rescue, escape, and small tactical operations. The program attracted many individual designers, but only two contracts were awarded: to Hiller and to Gyrodyne.

The Hiller XROE-1 (Figure 103-9) design was a more-or-less conventional shaft-driven, main-rotor/tail-rotor helicopter, except that

Figure 103-9 Hiller XROE-1

in the interests of compactness, the tail rotor was mounted on a short, down sloping boom that put it under the main rotor at about 80% radius rather than behind it.

The main rotor had a diameter of 19 feet. Servo paddles were used for control and damping as on the H-23, but on this smaller machine, it was found necessary to decrease the control sensitivity by using a 2:1 gearing ratio between the servo rotor and the main rotor. Empty weight of the aircraft was 290 pounds.

One of the competition requirements was that non-pilots could learn to fly the helicopter in four hours. This was no problem in pitch and roll, but because of the short tail-moment arm and small yaw moment of inertia, directional control was ticklish, especially in case of an unexpected engine failure. This was fixed by installing a simple yaw damper whose gyro was powered by dry cell batteries.

The Gyrodyne XRON-1 (Figure 103-10) was a coaxial helicopter with 15-foot-diameter rotors. It was the first coaxial to solve an inherent directional-control problem that had plagued previous machines of this type.

To produce a yawing moment, these aircraft had used differential collective pitch to unbalance the induced torque between the two rotors. The system worked well in powered flight, but in autorotation the effect of collective pitch on induced torque was lost or even reversed, much to the consternation of the pilot. On each blade of the XRON-1, aerodynamic tip brakes were installed; these were operated by pedal motion so that torque unbalance was effective for all flight conditions.

The helicopter started out with a 40-hp Nelson engine, but before the program was over, it had flown with both a 72-hp Porsche engine and a 62-hp Solar turbine as the rotor diameter grew from 15 feet to 17 feet and then to 20 feet.

Both Hiller and Gyrodyne delivered five of their designs to the Naval Test Center at Patuxent River, Maryland. The Marines gave them a thorough evaluation but no production contract. One of the factors that influenced this decision was a congressman's review which was sparked by a mother who complained about sending her enlisted Marine son into combat riding on such an "obviously dangerous" vehicle without flight training equivalent to that given commissioned pilots.

Good ideas die hard, however.

The Hiller design was licensed to a French company which built 25 ships to fulfill a Swiss army desire to replace horses during mountain maneuvers. The price of $25,000 turned out to be too Alpine for the frugal Swiss to buy any more.

That was the end; but John Nichols, Hiller's R&D manager at the time, recently said that if someone would drop an up-to-date powerplant in his lap at the right price, he would see that the XROE-1 project was resurrected.

The Gyrodyne design had a somewhat more extensive afterlife. With a bigger turbine engine and remote-control equipment, it became the pilot-less torpedo-carrying QH-50 DASH (Destroyer Anti-Submarine Helicopter) of which several hundred were built for the U.S. Navy.

Helicopter golf

Just to show that pilots who fly small helicopters have more fun than anyone else, I will quote from a report by Jim Ryan, the Gyrodyne test pilot, discussing an unusual application for the helicopter during the televised coverage of a golf tournament. "At one of the conferences preceding the show, I suggested that we attempt to make the helicopter demonstration more interesting by playing the last part of the 18th hole from the rotorcycle. At the time this suggestion did not meet with much enthusiasm and the idea was forgotten. On the morning of the television show, about half an hour before we were to go on, the producer rushed up, shoved a golf club in my hand and told me to start practicing, but they only gave me two golf balls.

Figure 103-10 Gyrodyne XRON-1

"The program started. The helicopter demonstration opened up with my trying to pitch to the green from the top of a hill and 130 yards up the fairway. I took a prodigious swing and tore up an immense divot. I looked down and the ball was still there. Trying to pass this off as a practice shot, I took more careful aim and tried a second time.

"The ball dribbled over the edge of the hill and was at least out of sight. Foreseeing the possibility of such an occurrence, we had planted a ball down by the edge of the green. [Quiz shows aren't the only thing that's rigged.] "I jumped in the helicopter, started it up by myself, and the engine surged to well over 4,000 rpm. The old engine drive-shaft universals were covered with a rubber boot packed with grease. One of these broke on the engine surge, throwing grease all over me and the helicopter.

"At least the flight down to the edge of the green was uneventful, but when I landed I failed to notice a slight up-slope by the edge of the green. Stopping the helicopter, I got out and was amazed to see the machine promptly drop back on its tail, with the nose sticking up in the air about five feet. The high weight of the Porsche engine installed in the old design airframe had moved the center of gravity of the machine too far aft for the upslope. Trying to appear as though this were quite normal, I took off the putter which was taped to the side of the fuselage, and then proceeded to four-putt the green. This disaster had all been my idea; I was shattered".

Enough said.

104 Convertiplanes

The Bell Boeing V-22 Osprey tiltrotor aircraft is what is known generically as a "convertiplane." That is, it is an aircraft that can convert from a helicopter to an airplane in flight to take advantage of the best characteristics of each.

The V-22 represents one more step down a very long road for the conception of a helicopter-turned-airplane. This road was started during the years following World War II, when the U.S. Air Force was charged with the responsibility of developing a helicopter for itself and the U.S. Army.

It is understandable how the people who flew P-51s and B-29s would be impatient with aircraft that poked along at less than 100 knots. They were therefore motivated to develop rotorcraft that could fly fast, hence thoughts of a convertiplane.

Just how the helicopter was to magically transform into an airplane was left to the clever designers—and they did come up with some clever designs. There were even two industry-wide Convertible Aircraft Congresses in which about a dozen more-or-less well-thought-out approaches to the problem were discussed.

Sparkplug to the Air Force's convertiplane project was the late Paul Haueter at Wright Field, Ohio. He was instrumental in getting a design competition going in 1950. Three entries—from McDonnell Corp., Sikorsky Aircraft, and Bell—won development contracts to build two prototypes each of aircraft designated the XV-1, XV-2, and XV-3 respectively.

Help from Germany

The McDonnell XV-1 (Figure 104-1) was largely designed by two German engineers, Kurt Hohenemser and Frederick Doblhoff, who came to the United States following the war. Hohenemser had been the aerodynamicist and dynamicist for the Anton Flettner organization, manufacturer of the world's first

Figure 104-1 McDonnell's XV-1

production helicopter, the Flettner Model 282 synchropter. Twenty-four were built before the Third Reich collapsed.

Hohenemser's contribution to the XV-1 project was his understanding of stability, control, and blade dynamics. (Much later as a professor at Washington University in St. Louis, Mo., he was to have a profound influence on many of today's helicopter dynamicists.) The German engineer came directly to McDonnell in 1946, primarily to work on the world's first twin-engine helicopter, the XHJD-1. A big (for its day) rotorcraft with side-by-side rotors, it started flying in early 1946 before promptly running into some serious dynamic problems.

The other key engineer, Doblhoff, had built the first pressure-jet helicopter. It was constructed in Austria under restrictive wartime conditions. For example, flight-testing was conducted using the rationed one barrel of kerosene fuel per month.

After the war, Doblhoff first went to Wright Field, where his pressure-jet-rotor experience was used for development of the Kellett/Hughes XH-17 flying crane (Chapter 38). In 1950 he joined with Hohenemser at McDonnell in time to draw up a proposal for the Air Force's convertiplane competition.

The McDonnell XV-1 was basically an airplane with a pressure-jet rotor. It was powered by a 550-hp Continental piston engine, which could drive either a fixed-pitch propeller for high-speed flight or a pair of compressors, which supplied air to the rotor for hover and low-speed flight.

A three-bladed rotor used tension-torsion packs of steel straps to carry the centrifugal loads. These packs provided high inplane stiffness, which eliminated the possibility of ground resonance, but caused high control loads. Therefore, a dual hydraulic control system was installed. Each of the three blades contained a fuel line that fed a tip burner to produce the thrust required to power the rotor.

Fighting the flap

The rotor was unique; unlike most rotors, it provided nearly neutral angle-of-attack stability. A conventional rotor is unstable. When it encounters an up-gust in forward flight, it flaps back—thus trying to pitch the helicopter more noseup. However, changing collective pitch will also make a rotor flap. Decreasing collective makes the tip-path plane flap nosedown. So, Hohenemser came up with a scheme to use decreased collective to compensate for the aft flapping due to a gust.

The rotor hub was gimbal-mounted to the rotor shaft but each blade was separately hinged to the hub so that when it coned up under a thrust load, its pitch was decreased—that is, it had pitch-cone coupling.

Thus when an up-gust increased rotor thrust, the coning also increased. But the collective pitch decreased and the rotor tried to flap nosedown to compensate for the normal tendency to flap noseup. As a result, the rotor caused only slight instability, which could easily be taken care of by a horizontal stabilizer.

Interesting byproducts of the pitch-cone coupling were an effective blade self-tracking capability and an automatic pitch reduction to go into autorotation upon engine failure. The reduction occurs as the rotor slows and the coning increases.

The XV-l's horizontal stabilizer was free-floating and controlled by a servo tab operated by the longitudinal cyclic stick. With this scheme, it tended to align itself with the rotor downflow in low-speed flight but operated as a conventional airplane control at high speed. Other airplane controls— ailerons and rudders—were attached to the cockpit controls at all times.

Figure 104-2 Fixed-Pitch Fan On XV-1 Tail Boom

Although a helicopter with a pressure-jet rotor needs no tail rotor for antitorque, it does need some device for directional control at low speeds. On the XV-1, engineers installed a small, hydraulically powered, fixed-pitch fan at the end of each tail boom (Figure 104-2). The thrust was controlled by rpm and direction of rotation as the rudder pedals modulated the amount and direction of the hydraulic-fluid flow to the fans.

From mode to mode

The XV-1 could be converted in flight through four separate rotor-control-system configurations. In the helicopter mode, the rotor gimbal was free to tilt, cyclic and collective pitch controlled the rotor, the tail fans gave directional control, and all engine power went to the compressors. As forward speed was increased, the aircraft was put into a free-hub autogyro mode and all power went to the propeller.

The next step was fixed-hub autogyro mode. Here the gimbaled hub was locked to the swashplate by dropping the collective pitch lever to its downstop. Finally, to achieve the airplane mode, the manual input to the longitudinal rotor control was replaced by the input from a rotor-speed governor.

Since the swashplate and hub were locked together, the governor used longitudinal hub tilting to keep the rotor at one-half its value in helicopter flight. In this mode, the rotor supported only about 20% of the aircraft weight, thus essentially eliminating blade stall and rotor-induced vibrations.

The combination of high forward speed and low rotor speed produced tip-speed ratios of unity or greater, which means the rotor entered flight conditions not previously investigated. For this reason, the XV-1 was the first aircraft with a rotor design to rely heavily on wind-tunnel tests. Between 1949 and 1953, it entered a wind tunnel at least 16 times.

In addition, one rotor model was mounted on a truck and tested on the Utah salt flats. Tests were frequent on the XV-l's rotor because, early in the program, blade oscillation was found to occur once every other revolution, causing possible instability at high speeds. This problem was solved by introducing pitch-lag coupling with the help of a change to blade-retention geometry.

Before actual flying, the XV-1 was placed in the full-scale wind tunnel at Moffett Field, Calif., where it was flown through its complete flight envelope. In February 1954, the first hover flight was made and about a year later a conversion to airplane flight was accomplished. McDonnell eventually reached speeds of more than 200 mph while testing the two prototypes in St. Louis, Mo. The XV-1 was then evaluated by Air Force pilots who gave it good marks for flying qualities but found it was underpowered in cruising flight.

By the end of the convertiplane development, the XV-1 rotor was switched over to a small flying crane, the McDonnell Model 120D, and was used for several years in that development program.

Sikorsky's XV-2

Of the three competing designs, the XV-2 stopped-rotor aircraft was certainly the most advanced concept. Designated as the Sikorsky S-57 (Figure 104-3), it was to have a single-bladed, counterbalanced, pressure-jet rotor that could be stopped and retracted in flight. Instead of a propeller for forward propulsion, Sikorsky chose to design around a single jet engine whose exhaust could either be ducted aft through a nozzle or into a compressor which furnished air to the rotor blade.

Figure 104-3 Sikorsky's Stopped-Rotor S-57

Two different wing planforms were designed for the S-57, a rounded delta and a more conventional straight wing. Wind tunnel models were built to test each configuration.

Sikorsky's convertiplane never left the drawing board. No suitable powerplant was available; in 1950, the choice of jet engines was limited.

Although the XV-2 project was essentially over by 1951, Sikorsky was asked to revive the program in 1954. The Air Force wanted to study the problem of starting a rotor by autorotative forces should a power failure occur in airplane flight. In addition to the one-bladed rotor, a two-bladed rotor, which would have been much lighter, was built and tested. The Air Force found that, yes, the rotor can be started but the first revolution will be traumatic to everyone on board, because the aircraft would pitch and roll as the blade started rotating.

Start of the tiltrotor

The Bell convertiplane entry was a tiltrotor aircraft, the forerunner of the Bell Boeing V-22 Osprey. With 40 years of development, this design concept represents one of the best examples of stick-to-it-iveness in the helicopter industry.

The tiltrotor's primary designer was the late Bob Lichten, who incidentally preferred his concept be called a "prop-rotor;" he thought "tilt" described something about to fall over.

Figure 104-4 Bell XV-3 With Two-Bladed Teetering Rotors

The XV-3 was powered by a single 450-hp Pratt and Whitney R-985 piston engine. It was installed in the fuselage, driving both rotors through a cross-shaft in the wing. The transmission had two speeds, normal for helicopter flight and half normal for airplane flight.

The original rotor was about as non-Bell as you could get. It had three highly twisted flapping blades with hinge offset. They were mounted on rather long shafts to ensure clearance in maneuvers and during running takeoffs with partial rotor tilt.

In the helicopter mode, the aircraft was controlled by the two rotors. Pitch control was by longitudinal cyclic, roll control by differential cyclic, and directional control by differential longitudinal cyclic.

The airplane controls operated all the time but the rotor controls were phased out during conversion to the airplane mode, which could be done in as little as 10 seconds or stretched out indefinitely. In airplane flight, the pilot used his collective stick to adjust the pitch of the propellers.

Rotors designed for hover and used as high-speed propellers present prodigious engineering challenges since the dynamic and aerodynamic environments are quite different in the two flight regimes. Any mechanism with a large, floating, rotating mass has potential dynamic problems, but these are compounded if the support structure has stiffness properties that are not well matched with the rotating element.

This became evident early in the XV-3's test program; while airborne, the first ship encountered rotor instability (commonly called "ground resonance" for articulated rotors). Under wing struts were added to stiffen the system; however, this did not solve the problem and in October 1956 a catastrophic instability occurred in flight. The aircraft was destroyed and the pilot was seriously injured. Back to the drawing board.

For the No. 2 aircraft, engineers built new rotors, which were more typically Bell. They were two-bladed teetering rotors with the under slung feathering-axis hub which had been recently developed for the Model 47 (Figure 104-4).

The Air Force suggested Bell test the XV-3 with its new rotors in NASA's full-scale wind tunnel. The thorough preflight investigation throughout the XV-3's extensive flight envelope in 1957 resulted in some improvements in the rotor's dynamics. The most significant were shortening the rotor shafts by 26 inches (66 cm) and the rotor diameter by 24 inches (60 cm).

A cautious flight-test program over the next three years led to flights up to 181 mph, full conversions, gear shifts, and recoveries from power failures in all flight regimes. Air Force pilots did much of the testing at Edwards AFB, Calif. Like the McDonnell XV-1, the pilots found the XV-3's flying qualities acceptable but performance poor due to low engine power.

Conclusions

The two flying aircraft that came out of the convertiplane program proved that a slow but maneuverable helicopter could indeed be transformed into a moderately fast airplane—but the price in extra weight and complexity was high. Also, during the convertiplane's development, conventional helicopters were being made to go faster and STOL (short takeoff and landing) aircraft were being developed to operate from smaller and smaller landing fields. Thus the relative advantage of the convertiplane had diminished and neither the XV-1 nor the XV-3 reached production.

Good ideas don't die easily, however. Scattered enthusiasts in both the military and industry kept the convertiplane spark alive. In the late 1960s, that spark flared up into a flame when the Army requested proposals for a "composite aircraft." (In this case, composite refers to the combining of a helicopter and an airplane, not to the materials that aircraft are increasingly being made of.)

Instead of asking for small test beds as it had in the past (and been criticized for), this time the Army specified an operational aircraft with considerable performance capability. It was to have 6,000 pounds (2,700 kg) useful load, a hover ceiling of 6,000 feet on a 95° day, a disc loading no higher than 15 pounds per square foot (10 desired), a lift-to-drag ratio of at least 10, and speeds of at least 300 knots (preferably 400).

After many proposals were submitted, the Army chose Bell with its tiltrotor, Hughes Helicopters with its stoppable, triangular, hot-cycle, pressure-jet rotor; and Lockheed, which had designed a rotor that could be stopped, folded, and stowed. Following a six-month preliminary-design study, Bell and Lockheed were selected to carry on with detail design and model testing for another five months. By that time, however, the Vietnam conflict was gobbling up the Army's money, so the composite-aircraft program came to a halt.

Figure 104-5 Bell's XV-15

But again the convertiplane concept didn't die. Bell scaled down the rotors and transmission of its composite-aircraft design and began fabrication and development of a new aircraft with high-powered turbine engines. In 1972 Bell received a joint Army/NASA contract for the XV-15 (Figure 104-5). Its successful demonstration over the next few years led directly to the Bell Boeing V-22 Osprey program.